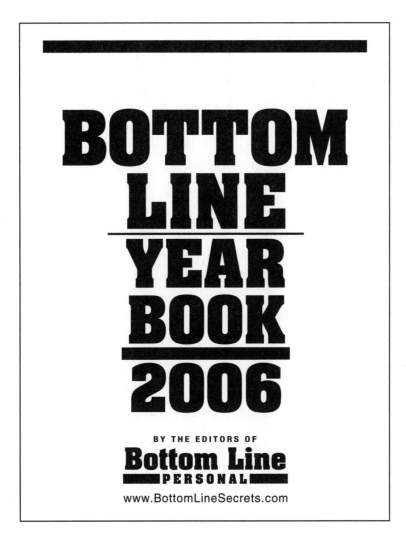

BOTTOM LINE YEAR BOOK 2006

BY THE EDITORS OF

Bottom Line
PERSONAL

www.BottomLineSecrets.com

Contents

PART TWO: YOUR MONEY

7 • MONEY SMARTS

8 • INSURANCE ANSWERS

9 • TAX GUIDE

10 • INVESTING NOW

11 • CONSUMER WATCH

PART THREE: YOUR FINANCIAL FUTURE

12 • RICHER RETIREMENT

13 • ESTATE PLANNING KNOW-HOW

PART FOUR: YOUR LEISURE

14 • THE TRAVEL REPORT

15 • JUST FOR FUN

16 • CARS AND DRIVERS

PART FIVE: YOUR LIFE

17 • HOME AND FAMILY LIFE

18 • PERSONAL POWER

19 • BUSINESS AND CAREER SUCCESS

20 • ULTIMATE SECURITY

1

Health Update

Medical Breakthroughs: Cutting-Edge Treatments For Arthritis, Cancer, Diabetes, Stroke and More

Medical science today is perpetually in motion, producing research that can fill up hundreds of medical journals every week. Although individual studies may be highly publicized, not all of them turn out to be valid. Authentic medical breakthroughs result from accumulated research and clinical experience. *The most important recent breakthroughs...*

ARTHRITIS

More than 20 million Americans suffer from osteoarthritis, a wear-and-tear joint condition that causes disabling pain. The nonsteroidal anti-inflammatory drugs or NSAIDs, such as *ibuprofen* (Advil), are frequently prescribed for osteoarthritis, but they often must be taken in high doses that can cause gastrointestinal pain and bleeding. Glucosamine, a natural supplement that stimulates cartilage production, is gentler but less effective than the NSAIDs.

Breakthrough: A Temple University study published in the *Journal of Pharmacology and Experimental Therapeutics* confirmed that taking glucosamine makes it possible to use a lower NSAID dose and achieve better pain relief with fewer side effects.

Self-defense: If you take an NSAID for osteoarthritis, also take 500 milligrams (mg) of glucosamine (with or without chondroitin) three times daily. After three weeks, half the NSAID dose may provide all the pain relief you need.

BREAST CANCER

For most breast cancer patients, removing only the tumor and a bit of surrounding tissue

Isadore Rosenfeld, MD, Rossi Distinguished Professor of Clinical Medicine at Weill Medical College of Cornell University in New York City. He is the author of numerous books, including the latest, *Dr. Isadore Rosenfeld's Breakthrough Health: Up-to-the-Minute Medical News You Need to Know* (Rodale).

(lumpectomy) results in the same survival rate as removal of the whole breast (mastectomy). This is true unless, of course, the tumor is large or aggressive—or there are multiple tumors that weren't detected.

Breakthrough: Researchers at the University of Pennsylvania in Philadelphia have found that magnetic resonance imaging (MRI) is more accurate than mammogram in detecting the full extent of the breast cancer.

Self-defense: If you're planning a lumpectomy, first have an MRI scan of both breasts. If other tumors are found, a mastectomy may be necessary.

DIABETES

Of the 18 million Americans who have diabetes, 80% will eventually develop heart disease. The other possible complications include amputation of a foot or blindness. Controlling blood sugar, eating prudently, managing body weight and exercising significantly reduce the risk for complications.

Breakthrough: A study conducted at the University of Alberta in Canada found that people with diabetes benefit from taking an angiotensin-converting enzyme (ACE) inhibitor drug, such as *ramipril* (Altace) or *enalapril* (Vasotec), which is usually given for high blood pressure. When added to a diabetic treatment regimen, including the diabetes drug *metformin* (Glucophage), the ACE inhibitor cut death rates in half, most likely because of its strengthening effect on the heart muscle. This occurred even when blood pressure was normal.

Self-defense: If you have diabetes, ask your doctor about taking an ACE inhibitor.

LEG PAIN

Fatty deposits can narrow the arteries of the leg (atherosclerosis), depriving muscles of oxygen and causing pain when you walk. This condition, known as *intermittent claudication,* affects more than 4 million Americans. Sometimes exercise and/or medication, such as the clot-buster *cilostazol* (Pletal), improves circulation enough to ease the pain.

When these approaches don't work, doctors recommend angioplasty—the same treatment that is used for blocked coronary arteries. During this procedure, a balloon is inflated in the affected artery to widen the opening. But half the time, the artery closes again (an occurrence called restenosis) within months.

Breakthrough: In a new procedure called cryo-balloon angioplasty (cryoplasty), recently approved by the FDA, the angioplasty balloon is filled with nitrous oxide, which freezes the plaque and prevents scar tissue from forming. After cryoplasty, restenosis occurs about 20% of the time, less than half as often as it does with traditional angioplasty.

Self-defense: If you have intermittent claudication that has not improved, ask your doctor about cryoplasty.

MITRAL VALVE LEAKAGE

When the mitral valve (between the chambers on the left side of the heart) doesn't close properly, blood leaks back every time the heart beats, a condition known as mitral valve regurgitation or insufficiency. Dangerous infections may result, and the heart can become enlarged and weakened, causing shortness of breath and even heart failure.

Until recently, the standard approach was to operate and replace the leaky valve *after* symptoms had appeared. This corrects the problem, but not the damage to the heart that already has occurred.

Breakthrough: Surgeons at the Mayo Clinic have shown that when the valve is repaired rather than replaced, patients do better. When the condition is diagnosed by an echocardiogram and the repair operation is performed *before* the onset of symptoms, such as shortness of breath, patients live longer (10-year survival rate was 70% compared with 50% for those who had a replacement).

Self-defense: If you have mitral valve leakage, consider early valve repair—before symptoms appear.

STOMACH CANCER

This is the second most common malignancy worldwide and the cause of 12,000 deaths in the US each year.

It's been known for years that infection with *Helicobacter pylori,* the same bacterium that causes ulcers, increases stomach cancer risk, but no one had shown that eradicating the infection reduces the cancer risk.

Breakthrough: In a seven-and-a-half-year Chinese study of 1,600 people infected with *H. pylori,* none of those who were treated with antibiotics developed stomach cancer, while six of those given a placebo did.

Self-defense: Think about screening for H. pylori (a simple breath test), particularly if you have digestive problems, such as heartburn or a family history of digestive-tract cancers. If the test is positive, talk to your doctor about taking a course of antibiotics.

STROKE

Stroke claims 120,000 American lives yearly and disables thousands more.

Breakthrough: Cholesterol-lowering statin drugs can cut stroke risk—even when cholesterol levels are normal. The British Heart Protection Study involving 20,000 people (some with high cholesterol, some without) found that one-third fewer strokes occurred among people taking a statin, compared with the placebo group.

Self-defense: If you're at increased risk for stroke, because of a family history of stroke or a related medical condition, such as diabetes, ask your doctor about taking a statin—even if your cholesterol is normal.

The Seven Common Symptoms Not to Ignore

J. Edward Hill, MD, president of the American Medical Association and an editor of the *American Medical Association Family Medical Guide* (Wiley). He is a family physician at North Mississippi Medical Center and a member of the faculty at the Family Medicine Residency Center, both in Tupelo.

A few years ago, I experienced fatigue that got worse and worse. I ignored it for a long time—and then my heart stopped. I needed emergency bypass surgery. Extreme fatigue had been the only symptom of a serious heart condition.

Symptoms we all experience occasionally, such as upset stomach or headache, rarely are cause for concern. Yet even mild symptoms may be a sign of serious underlying illness. The challenge is knowing when you can treat yourself and when you need medical attention.

Common symptoms—and when they may be dangerous...

ABDOMINAL PAIN

This is one of the most difficult symptoms to evaluate because it can be caused by hundreds of conditions.

Usual causes: Gas, stress, viral or bacterial infections (such as food poisoning).

Warning: Abdominal pain that lasts more than a day or two...causes severe cramps...or is accompanied by other symptoms, such as persistent nausea or vomiting, should be evaluated by a physician. *The problem could be...*

●**Appendicitis.** Patients will often experience fever or nausea as well as intense stomach pain. The pain typically begins around the navel and shifts to the lower-right abdomen over six to 12 hours. If the appendix is not surgically removed before it ruptures, it can cause a life-threatening infection called peritonitis.

●**Gallbladder disease, gallstones, ulcers and stomach cancer** can cause abdominal pain ranging from sharp and intermittent to dull and constant.

BACK PAIN

Back pain is a leading cause of lost work days. Even minor back injuries can cause excruciating pain.

Usual causes: Muscle pulls or spasms cause about 90% of back pain. Apply an ice pack as often as possible during the first 24 hours after pain starts...switch to heat after 24 hours...and take a non-steroidal anti-inflammatory drug, such as aspirin or ibuprofen, to control pain and swelling.

If back pain does not improve after a week, see your doctor.

Warning: Back pain that is accompanied by fever and neurological symptoms, such as tingling, numbness or shooting pains down one or both legs, is potentially serious. These symptoms may indicate a spinal infection, which is relatively rare but can cause permanent damage. See your doctor or go to an emergency room immediately.

CHEST PAIN

Any pain in the chest should be taken seriously because this is a common symptom of heart attack.

Usual causes: A musculoskeletal injury caused by overexertion. Working all day in the yard or pushing too hard at the gym can result in a muscle pull between the ribs or in the upper chest. This could cause a dull ache or shooting pains.

If pain occurs only when you move your body in a certain way, it is probably caused by a strained muscle or inflammation in the ribs (costochondritis). The pain usually subsides in a day or two.

Warning: Suspect a heart attack if the pain is accompanied by a pressing or crushing sensation, radiates out from the chest to other parts of the body (such as the breastbone, jaw, arms or neck) and/or is accompanied by heavy sweating, nausea or vomiting. Call 911 immediately. Then take an aspirin, unlock your door and wait for help to arrive.

Severe chest pain that occurs in patients who recently have had surgery or been bedridden due to illness or injury may be caused by a pulmonary embolism (a blood clot in the lung). Again, get medical assistance immediately.

CONSTIPATION

The frequency of bowel movements is highly variable—from twice a day to several times a week may be normal. Any change in your usual habits deserves attention.

Usual causes: Most constipation is due to insufficient fiber and/or water in the diet. Try to get at least 25 grams (g) of fiber daily. Start the day with a high-fiber cereal, such as oatmeal...snack on fresh fruits...and eat more beans, whole grains and vegetables. Drink two quarts of liquid daily (water is best).

Also, exercise for at least 20 minutes most days of the week. Exercise stimulates intestinal contractions that promote bowel movements.

Warning: Sudden constipation or alternating bouts of diarrhea and constipation may be

a sign of colon cancer. Call your doctor—you may need a colonoscopy to determine if cancer is present.

FATIGUE

It's normal to be exhausted after a hard day, but persistent fatigue isn't normal, especially when it suddenly worsens.

Usual causes: A combination of inadequate sleep and bad diet, such as loading up on coffee or junk food, can cause fatigue. Caffeine is a stimulant—but after the initial stimulation, people frequently experience "rebound fatigue." Junk food usually is high in carbohydrates, which can cause a surge in blood sugar followed by a drop, resulting in fatigue.

Limit your intake of caffeinated beverages to one or two servings daily. Go to bed and get up at the same times most days of the week. Eat nutritious meals, and exercise regularly—it promotes deeper sleep.

Warning: Fatigue can be a symptom of almost all acute and chronic diseases, but people who experience significantly more fatigue than usual—in the absence of any lifestyle changes—should suspect underlying heart disease and get an immediate checkup. This is especially true for women because fatigue, not chest pain, often is the first symptom.

HEADACHE

Anyone who gets headaches more than once a month or is incapacitated by a headache needs to undergo a complete medical workup immediately.

Usual causes: About 90% of headaches are tension headaches, caused by fatigue or emotional stress. Aspirin, ibuprofen and acetaminophen are all effective at relieving pain—see which works the best for you. Stress-reduction techniques, such as yoga, also can help.

Migraine headaches are more severe, but they usually can be controlled or prevented with ibuprofen or prescription drugs, such as *sumatriptan* (Imitrex).

Warning: Headaches that increase in frequency...are unusually severe...or are accompanied by other symptoms, such as nausea, slurred speech or vision changes, should be brought to a doctor's attention immediately.

These headaches could be a sign of stroke, infection in a brain blood vessel, meningitis or even a brain tumor.

Important: Call 911 if you suspect a stroke or experience an excruciating headache that comes on out of the blue. This is known as a "thunderclap" headache, and it may be the result of a potentially fatal ruptured blood vessel in the brain.

HEARTBURN

Most of us have experienced this burning sensation behind the breastbone.

Usual causes: Indigestion, often from eating fatty or spicy foods.

Warning: Gastroesophageal reflux disease (GERD) is a common cause of heartburn. Mild cases can be treated with antacids, but GERD that occurs more than once a week can cause serious damage to the esophagus. There also is a link between chronic GERD and esophageal cancer. Patients usually require acid-blocking medications, such as *omeprazole* (Prilosec) or *ranitidine* (Zantac).

Helpful: If you require antacids more than once or twice a week, see your doctor.

New Way to Combat Cancer

William Joel Meggs, MD, PhD, professor and chief of the division of toxicology at the Brody School of Medicine at East Carolina University in Greenville, NC. He is the author of *The Inflammation Cure: How to Combat the Hidden Factor Behind Heart Disease, Arthritis, Asthma, Diabetes, Alzheimer's Disease, Osteoporosis and Other Diseases of Aging* (McGraw-Hill).

Ever since the discovery of C-reactive protein (CRP), the blood-borne inflammation indicator, the association between inflammation in the body and heart disease has been firmly established.

Now: Recent research has shown that many other common health problems are also associated with inflammation, such as Alzheimer's disease, arthritis, asthma, diabetes, osteoporosis and even cancer.

According to a number of scientific studies, any long-term inflammation (lasting months to years) has the potential to cause cancer. This includes inflammation associated with arthritis, gum disease (gingivitis), even a pulled tendon (tendinitis) or inflamed elbow, hip or shoulder (bursitis).

Medical research has focused primarily on the link between inflammation and malignancies of the breast, lung, esophagus, colon and prostate.

Multiple studies conclude that inflammation damages cells and can cause them to become cancerous. This means that all cancers potentially may be affected by inflammation.

WHAT IS INFLAMMATION?

Inflammation is the body's natural response to injury, bacteria, viruses and many other foreign agents. It causes tissues to swell, blood vessels to expand and the body to release various chemicals, such as hormones, enzymes and cytokines. This process helps to kill germs and repair tissue in case of injury and, generally, rids the body of bacterial or viral threats. If the invader is cancer, however, these same inflammatory responses can fuel the disease.

THE INFLAMMATION LINK

All cancers start out as normal body cells. If those cells come under assault, they can transform into cancer cells. *This can occur during one of three stages...*

In the *initiation stage,* a healthy cell goes through a series of mutations to become precancerous. Mutations are caused by a number of different factors, such as viruses, exposure to toxic chemicals or ultraviolet radiation—and chronic irritation and inflammation. For example, too much exposure to sunlight can cause precancerous skin cells, and prolonged irritation from heartburn can promote the development of precancerous cells in the esophagus.

In the *promotion stage,* the mutated precancerous cell becomes active and begins to multiply, starting the process that creates a tumor. If inflammation is present, natural body chemicals are released that can directly activate the nondividing cells, turning these precancerous cells into growing cancers.

Finally, in the *progression stage,* cancerous cells spread. Here, too, inflammation can help cancer. Sometimes inflammatory cells that are called *macrophages* enter tumors and produce chemicals that enable the tumor to generate new blood vessels that connect to the body's blood supply. The tumor feeds like a parasite, continuing to grow and spread.

BEYOND BASIC PREVENTION

Everyone knows the basic cancer prevention strategies, such as not smoking, limiting sun exposure and eating a healthful diet. Most people don't know that other lifestyle changes also curb cancer risk by decreasing inflammation in the body.

Most effective...

●**Maintain a healthy weight.** Fat cells produce inflammatory chemicals. Research that was just conducted at the University College London Medical School in England suggests that up to 30% of the inflammation-related protein called interleukin-6 (IL-6) in blood comes from fat tissue. This means that the more fat in the body, the more inflammation there will be.

●**Get enough sleep.** The body needs seven to nine hours of sleep each night to regenerate. Young people who are sleep-deprived have the type of inflammatory and immune changes usually seen only in the aged. Trouble falling or staying asleep can be a sign of an inflammation-related disease, such as arthritis, allergies, diabetes or heart disease.

●**Eat anti-inflammatory foods.** Many people strive to eat a diet rich in fruits, vegetables and whole grains. A key benefit of these foods is that they contain anti-inflammatory substances that help reduce overall inflammation.

Best inflammation fighters: Leafy green or cruciferous vegetables (spinach, chard, brussels sprouts)...berries (blackberries, blueberries, raspberries)...legumes (black beans, chickpeas, peas)...and omega-3–rich fish (salmon, tuna, herring).

●**Avoid inflammatory foods.** Most animal products—such as meat, poultry, cheese, butter and milk—are inflammation triggers.

●**Don't ignore chronic illness.** If you have avoided seeing a doctor for heartburn, bursitis, gingivitis or any other seemingly minor problem, make an appointment today. This is espe-

cially important if you experience weeks of unexplained fatigue—a sign that inflammation could be lurking somewhere in your body.

Chronic inflammation, even in a specific site such as the hip or gums, can mean long-term inflammation throughout the body. Better to treat a small health problem today than cancer tomorrow.

Helpful: Many inflammation-related disorders end in *–itis.*

●**Consider a statin drug.** Statins, such as *atorvastatin* (Lipitor) and *pravastatin* (Pravachol), are routinely prescribed to help lower cholesterol levels and reduce inflammation in people at risk for heart disease. Recent studies have shown that statins also may help prevent colon, kidney and skin cancer.

New finding: In a retrospective analysis of 3,000 Israeli men, a University of Michigan researcher found that taking a statin decreased colon cancer risk by 46%.

Scientists believe that statins work, in part, by inhibiting an enzyme called *farnesyltransferase.* This enzyme is involved in cell proliferation, and blocking it may stop cancer progression.

Caution: Statins can cause side effects, such as muscle weakness, nausea and headache. Ask your doctor if a statin would benefit you.

●**Ask about NSAIDs.** Decades of research have now shown that taking nonsteroidal anti-inflammatory drugs (NSAIDs) can reduce the risk for certain malignancies—especially colorectal, breast, lung and ovarian cancers—by 18% to 40%. Risk for prostate and bladder cancers also may be reduced.

However, NSAIDs have many side effects, including increased risk for stomach ulcers and internal bleeding.

If you are at high risk for cancer because of family history or a chronic inflammatory disease, the benefit of taking an NSAID may outweigh its potential risks—especially if you're at low risk for heart disease. You should ask your doctor for advice.

Caution: Never take any over-the-counter medication, including aspirin or *ibuprofen,* for more than 10 consecutive days without consulting your physician.

Beat Cancer With "Smart" Drugs

Ronald M. Bukowski, MD, director of the Experimental Therapeutics Program for Taussig Cancer Center, The Cleveland Clinic, and professor of medicine at Cleveland Clinic Lerner School of Medicine.

Until just recently, surgery, chemotherapy and/or radiation were the only treatment options for cancer.

Now: A new group of targeted, molecular-based "smart" drugs, taken as daily pills, are controlling the growth of malignant cells without serious side effects.

A leading cancer specialist at the renowned Cleveland Clinic discusses these breakthrough treatments below...

HOW SMART DRUGS WORK

Cancer cells start out as normal human cells that mutate—as a result of a genetic problem or environmental assaults, such as cigarette smoke or pesticides. After several mutations, the cells start to behave much differently from normal cells, growing and multiplying out of control.

Analogy: You might think of cancer as a car alarm that has been activated. When you take a sledgehammer to the alarm, you'll silence it, but you'll also cause extensive damage to the car. That's similar to the overkill effects we see with chemotherapy and radiation—these treatments help kill cancer cells, but they also can damage healthy cells, causing serious side effects.

Finding the wiring diagram for the car would allow us to snip the appropriate wire to turn off the alarm. That's how many of the smart drugs work—by using scientists' knowledge of the inner workings of cancer cells to interrupt their "circuitry" without damaging healthy cells.

For smart drugs to work, the medication must be precisely targeted. And to do this, substances called *monoclonal antibodies* are created. Injected into the body through a vein, they track down and attach themselves to distinct proteins found on the surface of cancer cells.

Monoclonal antibodies fit the cancer proteins precisely, just like a key fits in a lock. In most smart drugs, monoclonal antibodies are paired with other cancer-fighting chemicals that attack malignancies.

Three types of smart drugs...

- **Conjugated monoclonal antibodies.** Smart drugs can act like poisoned darts when monoclonal antibodies are paired with cellular toxins. Once it is attached to the cancer cell, the smart drug delivers a radioisotope or small dose of chemotherapy directly to the cancer. This is how the leukemia drug *gemtuzumab* (Mylotarg) and the non-Hodgkin's lymphoma drugs *ibritumomab tiuxetan* (Zevalin) and *tositumomab* (Bexxar) work.

- **Unconjugated monoclonal antibodies.** Smart drugs can change or disrupt the cancer cell's biology in a way that slows its growth or causes it to die off. The most exciting of these treatments is the colorectal cancer drug *bevacizumab* (Avastin), which interrupts the cancer cell's connection to the body's blood supply. Without blood, tumors starve and die.

A first-line treatment for metastatic colon cancer, bevacizumab is being tested for lung, kidney, breast and pancreatic cancers. Test results should be known in one to two years.

Other drugs in this group—the colorectal cancer drug *cetuximab* (Erbitux) and the breast cancer drug *trastuzumab* (Herceptin)—block cancer cell growth when used in combination with chemotherapy. Small-molecule drugs—including the multiple myeloma drug *bortezomib* (Velcade), the lung cancer drug *gefitinib* (Iressa) and the leukemia and gastrointestinal cancer drug *imatinib* (Gleevec)—block cancer growth from within the cells.

- **Radioimmunoconjugates.** Smart drugs can help to label the cancer cells so that the body's own immune system can help destroy them. Because cancer cells start out as normal cells, our immune systems don't ordinarily recognize them as something dangerous.

The non-Hodgkin's lymphoma drug *rituximab* (Rituxan) and the leukemia drug *alemtuzumab* (Campath) attach to the surfaces of cancer cells and then send out signals that the body recognizes as foreign. The immune system responds, sending antibodies to kill the marked cancer cells.

LIMITATIONS OF SMART DRUGS

Targeted therapies work for some people, but not for everyone—or for every type of cancer. Today, one in five cancer patients is a candidate for smart drugs.

That's because each type of cancer has its own set of mutations, so a smart drug for breast cancer, for example, won't necessarily work for kidney malignancies. Once we know how each type of cancer cell works, drugs can be designed to interrupt their signals and either stop or slow the cancer growth.

Some cancers are much more difficult to stop than others. Instead of having just one type of growth signal to control, multiple circuits must sometimes be interrupted. That's why smart drugs may be used *in addition* to chemotherapy and radiation. As our knowledge increases, we will be able to develop specific drug cocktails that will knock out all the cancerous circuits at once.

Smart drugs, such as gefitinib, are given to all patients with a particular type of malignancy, such as resistant and recurrent non-small-cell lung cancer, but not all patients respond positively. That's because our individual genes can alter the way we are affected by treatments. We hope to one day be able to quickly customize smart drugs for each person, based on analyses of individual genetics and tumor characteristics.

WHERE TO GET SMART DRUGS

FDA-approved smart drugs are rapidly being used as therapy for the cancers they have been shown to help. Patients no longer need to go to specialized cancer centers to receive these medications. All oncologists know about them. Cancer patients who aren't candidates for the FDA-approved smart drugs should ask their oncologists about clinical trials testing new smart drugs or other medications. To learn more about clinical trials, go to the National Institutes of Health Web site at *www.clinicaltrials.gov.*

FDA-APPROVED SMART DRUGS

Blood cancers…

●**B-cell chronic lymphocytic leukemia.** *Alemtuzumab* (Campath) increased survival in 33% of those treated.

●**Chronic myelogenous leukemia.** *Imatinib* (Gleevec) normalized leukocyte and platelet counts in more than 80% of those treated.

●**Acute myeloid leukemia.** *Gemtuzumab* (Mylotarg) delayed disease progression in approximately 30% of those treated.

●**Multiple myeloma.** *Bortezomib* (Velcade) slowed disease progression in approximately 23% of those treated.

Breast cancer…

●**Metastatic breast cancer.** *Trastuzumab* (Herceptin) increased survival time when used with chemotherapy, compared with chemotherapy alone. Tumors shrank approximately 26% in women treated.

Gastrointestinal cancers…

●**Metastatic colorectal cancer.** *Bevacizumab* (Avastin) prolonged survival rates by five months when used with chemotherapy. *Cetuximab* (Erbitux) shrank tumors or delayed their growth in approximately 23% of patients.

●**Gastrointestinal tumors.** *Imatinib* (Gleevec) shrank tumors in 54% of those treated.

Lung cancer…

●**Non-small-cell lung cancer.** *Gefitinib* (Iressa) shrank tumors in approximately 10% of those treated.

Non-Hodgkin's lymphoma…

●**Follicular non-Hodgkin's lymphoma.** *Tositumomab* (Bexxar) reduced symptoms in up to 71% of those treated.

●**Low-grade or follicular B-cell non-Hodgkin's lymphoma.** *Rituximab* (Rituxan) shrank tumors in approximately 48% of those treated. When used after rituximab, *ibritumomab tiuxetan* (Zevalin) reduced symptoms in 80% of those treated.

Cancer Patients Often Don't Get Enough Chemotherapy

A recent study indicated that nearly one-half of breast cancer patients receive too small a dosage of chemotherapy or have treatments less frequently than they should. Side effects are a common reason for low doses. If you experience side effects with chemotherapy, ask your physician about alternatives to reducing the dosage or increasing the interval between treatments.

Helpful drugs: *Palonosetron* (Aloxi) and *ondansetron* (Zofran) combat nausea and vomiting. *Epoetin* (Procrit) minimizes anemia-related fatigue. *Pegfilgrastim* (Neulasta) and *filgrastim* (Neupogen) boost white blood cell count.

Gary H. Lyman, MD, MPH, director of the health services and outcomes research program, James P. Wilmot Cancer Center, University of Rochester Medical Center, NY.

Most Common Causes of Cancer

Obesity is the second-leading cause of cancer. It is responsible for an estimated 25% of cancers in developed countries.

Leading cause of cancer: Tobacco use.

Tim Key, DPhil, reader in epidemiology at University of Oxford, England, and leader of a study of diets of 500,000 people in 10 different countries, presented at a meeting of Cancer Research UK.

Dangers of Worrying

Norwegian scientists tracked 62,591 people and found that those who scored high on an anxiety test were 25% more likely to have premalignancies.

Theory: Psychological stress and anxiety depress the ability of the immune system to track and destroy precancerous cells.

American Psychiatric Association, 1000 Wilson Blvd., Arlington, VA 22209.

Where Skin Cancer Is Likely to Strike

Cancer on the skin is more likely to strike on or near scar sites.

New finding: Among 92 patients who developed *basal cell carcinoma* (cancer of the outer layers of the skin), a significant number of their lesions were located on or near scars. The scars were due to previous surgery, blunt or sharp trauma, burns or dog bites.

Theory: Scarred areas of the body are more vulnerable to ultraviolet light.

Self-defense: Before going outdoors, apply sunscreen (with a sun-protection factor of at least 15) on all sun-exposed areas. Also, consult a physician if you notice a new wound on or near a scar.

Irfan Ozyazgan, MD, assistant professor of plastic and reconstructive surgery, Erciyes University, Kayseri, Turkey.

Reliable Sources of Cancer Information

If you or someone you care about has cancer, check out these free, reliable sources of cancer information…

●**American Cancer Society** (800-227-2345, *www.cancer.org*) helps locate cancer-related resources in local areas and offers interactive help with treatment decisions.

●**Association of Cancer Online Resources** (*www.acor.org*) is an on-line network of support groups and has a searchable archive.

●**Cancer Information Service** (800-422-6237, *cis.nci.nih.gov*), a National Cancer Institute site, offers research, statistics and personal responses to questions.

●**FindCancerExperts.com** provides names and contact information for nationally recognized pathologists and tells how to get a second opinion.

New Ways to Spot Heart Attacks Before They Occur

Richard Stein, MD, associate chairman of medicine and chief of medicine, Singer Division at Beth Israel Medical Center, New York City. He is a spokesman for the American Heart Association.

While heart attacks remain the leading cause of death in the US, the death rate from heart attacks has actually declined 25% from 1987 to 1997 and continues to go down. One important reason has been the steady improvement in a doctor's ability to detect diseased coronary arteries *before* a heart attack occurs.

Why this is so important: Between one-third and one-half of all people who suffer heart attacks exhibit no outward signs of heart disease until their first attack. Of this group, one out of four end up dying—usually before reaching the hospital.

Most people get their low-density lipoprotein (LDL, or "bad") and high-density lipoprotein (HDL, or "good") cholesterol levels checked out regularly. But a number of the newer heart tests allow doctors to get an earlier and clearer sense of whether their patients are at risk for a heart attack. *The tests fall into three categories...*

●**Tests that evaluate whether there is any narrowing of the coronary arteries due to atherosclerosis (plaque buildup).** Currently, a *coronary angiogram* is the gold standard for detecting narrowing of the coronary arteries. It involves threading a catheter through an artery in the groin until the tip lies in the heart. Dye is injected through the catheter into the heart and X-rays of blood flowing through the coronary arteries are taken.

An angiogram is currently given to patients who report symptoms of coronary artery disease (CAD), and who have a high probability of having CAD—because they have had a heart attack in the past or have had angioplasty and stenting, or have tested positive on an exercise stress test.

Drawback: Angiograms are invasive procedures that carry a certain amount of risk. Serious complications—such as a heart attack or stroke caused by nicking the arterial plaque with the wire or the catheter used in the procedure—occur in approximately one of every 1,000 procedures.

However, new scanning technologies are now providing doctors with noninvasive alternatives for evaluating the coronary arteries. *These include...*

●*Coronary artery calcium scan.* This technique uses an electron beam CT-scan (EBCT, or Ultrafast CT-scan) to measure the calcium content of the coronary arteries. Because calcium is a key component of arterial plaque, a patient's calcium score is a good indication of how much plaque is in his/her arteries.

Now available in most medical centers, calcium scans take about a minute to complete. A low score (below 100) signals little or no coronary artery disease. A high score (400 or above) indicates significant plaque buildup, and should be followed up with an angiogram, a stress nuclear test and/or a stress echocardiogram.

●*MRI scan.* Research is also now being conducted on potential challengers to the Ultrafast CT-scan, including magnetic resonance imaging (MRI) scans of the coronary arteries. Already utilized to diagnose various types of heart problems (such as heart muscle function problems and the thickness of the heart's walls), MRI scans are now starting to be used to evaluate coronary artery anatomy and blood flow.

●*Helical CT-scans,* which let doctors see the coronary arteries in great detail, much as if they were looking at an angiogram.

CT and MRI techniques should come into increasing use over the next few years.

●**Tests that look for signs of inflammation.** A heart attack is caused when a piece of arterial plaque ruptures, resulting in a blood clot that blocks the coronary artery, cutting off blood flow to the heart. The more inflamed this arterial plaque is, the more likely it is to crack or fracture.

To help determine whether heart patients are at high risk of a heart attack, doctors are now beginning to identify and screen for the various markers of inflammation.

• One such screen is the high-sensitivity *C-reactive protein (CRP) test*. This test measures the blood levels of CRP, which is produced as a by-product of the inflammatory process. Less than five is considered a low score, five to 20 is intermediate and 20 or above is considered high.

The test is not definitive in itself, but when combined with other risk factors, such as cholesterol ratio, smoking, diabetes and family history of heart disease, it can help predict the 10-year heart-attack risk of patients. In particular, it is now being employed to help physicians decide how aggressively they should treat those patients who have apparently normal cholesterol levels, yet may be at increased risk of heart attack due to other risk factors, such as high blood pressure.

• Doctors are also in the early stages of evaluating several other blood tests that are more specific markers for inflammation in the artery walls. *Myeloperoxidase* (MPO) may be useful in the diagnosis of heart attacks that are in progress. A study at the Cleveland Clinic found that with patients who walk into a hospital with chest pain, assessment of MPO scores—in addition to the usual EKG and other blood tests—enabled study doctors to identify 90% of those individuals who were experiencing a heart attack.

Follow-up studies found that even among those who were not having a heart attack, high MPO scores were linked to a high risk of having an acute cardiac event (heart attack, stroke, angioplasty or coronary bypass) sometime over the next six months. Results from clinical studies on MPO tests are expected soon.

• Elevated levels of *p-selectin* and *vascular cellular adhesion molecule* (VCAM)—markers for damage to the lining of the artery walls—have also been linked to increased risk of a cardiac event, as have low levels of *glutathione peroxidase 1* (an enzyme substance that works to prevent inflammation). Research is being done in a few laboratories to develop a test for glutathione peroxidase 1.

• **Tests for blood levels of substances that contribute to arterial plaque buildup.** All annual physical exams include the measurement of LDL cholesterol, HDL cholesterol and the amino acid *homocysteine* in the blood. Elevated levels of LDL and homocysteine and low levels of HDL have all been linked to increased risk of an acute cardiac event.

Now, doctors are beginning to look more closely at the various subtypes of LDL cholesterol in the bloodstream.

Reason: LDL particles come in a variety of sizes. Research has shown that small, dense LDL particles are more likely to cause atherosclerosis than large, "fluffy" LDL particles.

By measuring the blood levels of a cholesterol component that's known as *apolipoprotein B* (apoB), doctors can further determine the risk from LDL. From this, they can then deduce how much of a patient's LDL is made up of small, dense particles—and whether more aggressive treatment is warranted.

Testing for apoB is widely available. Those who should consider it are people whose LDL is in the normal range but who may be at increased risk of CAD because of other risk factors—especially diabetes.

Bad Cholesterol Just Got Worse

Steven Nissen, MD, medical director for The Cleveland Clinic Cardiovascular Coordinating Center, Cleveland. His study of 654 adults with high LDL cholesterol levels was presented during the 2003 Annual Meeting of the American Heart Association.

Heart health for individuals at high-risk (which includes those who have coronary heart disease) can be improved more than was previously believed by lowering "bad cholesterol" in the blood to levels lower than those recommended in the current national guidelines, says a new study.

Current guidelines recommend that LDL "bad" cholesterol be reduced to a measured level of 100. But the new study indicates that aggressive use of statin drugs to reduce the level to 70 may completely stop clogging of the arteries.

Findings: Adults with LDL readings of more than 125 and symptoms of coronary disease were randomly assigned to two different drug treatments. One treatment reduced LDL to an average of 110, the other to an average of 79.

After 18 months, plaque in arteries increased by an average of 3% in the first group, but decreased by 1% in the second group.

Some doctors take these results to mean that there is no such thing as too low LDL.

Surprising Effect Of Cholesterol-Lowering Statins

In a recent study, statins helped to form new blood vessels to bypass blocked arteries.

Implication: These new vessels help supply blood to parts of the heart that aren't getting enough due to blocked vessels, thereby reducing heart attack risk.

Richard H. Karas, MD, PhD, codirector, Molecular Cardiology Research Center, Tufts–New England Medical Center, Boston, and leader of a study of 94 patients, average age 65, published in the *American Heart Journal.*

Two Powerful Drugs In One

A new anticholesterol medication packs the power of two drugs in one. Approved by the FDA, Vytorin contains *simvastatin* (Zocor), which reduces cholesterol synthesis in the liver, and *ezetimibe* (Zetia), which prevents cholesterol absorption. In studies, this drug reduced LDL "bad" cholesterol levels by 50% to 60%, more than the statins *atorvastatin* (Lipitor) or simvastatin alone.

Bonus: Since Vytorin contains a lower dose of statin medication, the risk for side effects, such as muscle pain, is reduced.

Theodore Feldman, MD, medical director, wellness and prevention, Baptist Cardiac & Vascular Institute of Miami, Coral Gables, FL.

Blood Thinner Alert

Restrict vitamin K if you take blood thinners regularly. Too much vitamin K can cause clots that could lead to heart attack or stroke. Foods high in vitamin K—including broccoli, cauliflower, cabbage, brussels sprouts—can decrease the effectiveness of blood-thinning medication.

Important: If taking blood thinners, don't make any dietary changes without checking with your doctor, since any change in diet may also affect blood coagulation.

Carisi Anne Polanczyk, MD, professor of cardiology, cardiovascular division, Hospital de Clinicas de Porto Alegre, Brazil.

Read This If You Have High Blood Pressure

Rebecca Shannonhouse, editor of *Bottom Line/Health,* 281 Tresser Blvd., Stamford, CT 06901.

Anyone who takes high blood pressure medication could be paying *at least* 10 times more for drugs than is appropriate—and facing risks of unnecessary complications, such as heart failure.

A landmark study of 33,000 patients suggested that low-cost diuretics, such as Diuril and Dyazide, may be the best choice for many patients with hypertension. Despite this compelling evidence, nearly 80% of prescriptions for blood pressure medications still are written for newer, much higher-priced drugs.

A year's supply of diuretics may cost as little as $26,* compared with $280 for the generic ACE inhibitor *lisinopril*...$680 for the calcium channel blocker Norvasc...and $652 for the beta-blocker Toprol-XL, according to the on-line pharmacy drugstore.com.

Why do so many doctors continue to ignore the evidence that is in favor of diuretics? "The older drugs aren't promoted by drug companies," says Curt D. Furberg, MD, PhD, professor

*All prices subject to change.

of public health sciences at Wake Forest University and a principal investigator of the diuretic study. *According to Dr. Furberg, you're probably a good candidate for diuretics if…*

●**You have been recently diagnosed with hypertension.**

●**You're age 65 or older.**

●**You have uncomplicated hypertension** at any age (no organ damage or other risk factors for heart disease).

There are times when the newer drugs are best. Patients with both high blood pressure and heart failure may need an ACE inhibitor. Those who have had a heart attack may do better on a beta-blocker. But for most patients, diuretics are preferable.

Beware of Aspirin Resistance

For the majority of patients, daily aspirin therapy can lessen the risk for cardiovascular attack by 25%.

New study: Stable cardiovascular patients, some of whom were found to be "aspirin resistant" by a blood test called *optical platelet aggregation,* took a daily dose of 325 milligrams (mg) of aspirin. After two years, 24% of the aspirin-resistant group had died or suffered a heart attack or stroke, compared with only 10% of the aspirin-receptive group.

If you've been prescribed aspirin therapy: Ask your doctor if an aspirin-resistance test is advised. Aspirin-resistant patients can use *clopidogrel* (Plavix) as an alternative.

Eric Topol, MD, chairman, department of cardiovascular medicine, The Cleveland Clinic, Cleveland.

Common Antibiotic Boosts Risk of Sudden Cardiac Death

Wayne A. Ray, PhD, director of pharmaco-epidemiology and professor of preventive medicine, Vanderbilt University School of Medicine, Nashville, and the leader of a study of 1,476 cases of sudden cardiac death, published in *The New England Journal of Medicine.*

In a new study, people taking *erythromycin* had twice the risk of cardiac arrest as those not on the drug. People taking erythromycin with certain other medications had a more than fivefold increase in risk.

Among the drugs that interact with erythromycin: The blood pressure drugs *diltiazem* (Cardizem, Tiazac) and *verapamil* (Calan, Isoptin, Verelan)…antifungal drugs *fluconazole* (Diflucan), *ketoconazole* (Nizoral) and *itraconazole* (Sporanox)…*ritonavir* (Norvir) and other protease inhibitors, which fight HIV…the antibiotic *clarithromycin* (Biaxin). Grapefruit juice also interacts with erythromycin.

Good news: Risk returns to normal after patients stop taking erythromycin.

Also: Patients taking *amoxicillin*—a drug used in much the same way as erythromycin—did not show increased risk.

Trans-Fat Alert

Some varieties of the same food may have unhealthful trans fats, while others don't.

Examples: General Mills's Total Raisin Bran has trans fats, but Post's and Kellogg's raisin brans don't. Regular Cheerios contains no trans fats—but Apple-Cinnamon and Multi-Grain Cheerios do.

To avoid trans fats: Read labels, and don't buy products that list hydrogenated or partially hydrogenated oils.

Tara Parker-Pope, health columnist for *The Wall Street Journal.*

The Bottom Line On Eating Fish

Eric B. Rimm, ScD, associate professor of epidemiology and nutrition at Harvard School of Public Health in Boston.

For years, doctors and dietitians have been recommending that we eat fish to help prevent coronary heart disease. But recent reports about high levels of mercury, polychlorinated biphenyls (PCBs) and other toxins in some of the most popular types of fish have caused many health-conscious individuals to rethink their diets.

Eric B. Rimm, ScD, a leading expert on the nutritional value of fish, clears up the confusion below…

●**Is fish still a healthful food choice?** Absolutely. Research going back to the 1970s has established that omega-3 fatty acids from fish are a major weapon in the fight against heart disease and sudden death from heart attack.

The anti-inflammatory effects of omega-3s are so powerful that scientists are researching their effects on a host of other diseases, including type 2 diabetes, rheumatoid arthritis and prostate cancer. There also is some evidence that omega-3s can improve cognitive function and even may help protect against Alzheimer's disease. If people stopped eating fish, all these benefits would be lost.

●**What about the mercury and other contaminants found in fish?** All fish do contain some pollution-related mercury. Larger predatory fish have higher mercury levels because they take in and store the mercury found in the smaller fish they eat. Smaller fish have the least amount of mercury.

Because mercury may affect the neurological development of children, the FDA recommends that women who are pregnant or might become pregnant…women who are breast-feeding…as well as young children should entirely avoid eating the fish with the highest mercury levels—shark, swordfish, king mackerel and tilefish. In addition, these groups should eat no more than 12 ounces (about two regular-sized portions) per week of fish that contain lower mercury levels, such as shrimp, canned chunk light tuna, pollack and catfish.

Women who are not likely to become pregnant and all adult men can choose to follow the same recommendations if they want to be as safe as possible.

●**Shouldn't we be concerned about the levels of PCBs that are now being reported in fish?** PCBs and other toxins do pose some health threat and may even contribute to cancer development, particularly such hormone-related cancers as breast cancer. But I'd like to put the risk into perspective.

First, the data, based mainly on animal studies, are limited regarding actual dangers of these toxins in fish. We don't know whether the levels of PCBs found in fish are actually dangerous to humans. However, several studies have shown that people who eat fish at least once a week have a lower risk for sudden death from heart disease and a lower risk for overall mortality.

Second, it comes as a surprise to most people to learn that we eat PCBs all the time. Of all the PCBs in our diet, one-third come from milk and cheese…one-third come from chicken, beef and pork…and one-third come from fish. Almost all food products contain PCBs, even those labeled organic. Typically, organic foods contain PCB levels that are 1/10th to 1/1,000th that of conventionally grown foods.

If you stop eating fish and start eating steak, for example, you'll be getting approximately the same amount of PCBs, but you'll be missing out on the healthful omega-3 fatty acids.

Third, the recent study that generated all the media reports about PCBs in salmon set out to discover whether there were differences in toxin levels, based on where and how they were harvested.

The researchers, based at the University at Albany in New York, learned that some farmed salmon—specifically those from Scotland—have higher levels of PCBs than wild salmon.

The reason the salmon from Scotland contained higher PCB levels was because the fish meal fed to them had more PCBs than that used in Chile or the Pacific Northwest.

Farmed salmon from Chile have nearly the same PCB levels as wild salmon. Since most salmon sold in the US comes from Chile, we have less of a concern here than do people living in Europe.

Anyone who is concerned about PCBs can choose to eat only wild salmon. When buying salmon in the grocery store, ask to see the shipping container. It is typically labeled with the country of origin and whether it is wild.

●**Could we avoid the toxins altogether by taking fish-oil capsules or flaxseed supplements?** Not necessarily. The research is still ongoing, but there is some evidence that fish-oil capsules contain, per gram of oil, the same levels of PCBs as the fish they come from. They also may contain very small amounts of mercury. Although eating fish is more beneficial, fish-oil supplements are an option if you do not like the taste of fish.

Flaxseed oil also contains the omega-3 fatty acids, but they are different forms of omega-3s, which don't act identically to those found in fish and may not be as beneficial.

●**How should people eat fish to get the most benefit with the least harm?** Vary the types of fish you eat. Limit your intake of shark, swordfish, king mackerel and tilefish to once a month to reduce your exposure to high levels of mercury.

Aim to eat fish high in omega-3 fatty acids at least once or twice per week. These include herring, mackerel, salmon, trout, tuna, shellfish and sardines.

If you eat canned tuna, choose chunk light. Albacore and solid white have an average of three times more mercury than chunk light. Flaky white fish, such as cod, are not high in omega-3s, so they offer very little benefit.

Stroke Stopper

A new FDA-approved device removes blood clots in people experiencing a stroke. The *mechanical embolus removal in cerebral ischemia* (MERCI) retriever is threaded up from the groin into the affected artery and used like a corkscrew to pluck out the clot. It can be used up to eight hours after stroke onset. The intravenous drug *tPA* can dissolve clots, but it cannot be used more than three hours after stroke onset...or in patients with bleeding disorders or who have had surgery recently.

Gary Duckwiler, MD, president of the American Society of Interventional and Therapeutic Neuroradiology (ASITN), Fairfax, VA, and professor of radiology, University of California, Los Angeles.

A New Lifesaving Strategy

Karl B. Kern, MD, professor of medicine, University of Arizona Sarver Heart Center, Tucson, and a member of the team that developed continuous chest compressions (CCC).

For more than 40 years, cardiopulmonary resuscitation (also called CPR) has been used as emergency treatment for cardiac and respiratory arrest.

Now: A new method, known as continuous chest compressions (CCC), eliminates mouth-to-mouth breathing and is believed to greatly improve survival rates.*

With traditional CPR, rescuers alternate 15 chest compressions to circulate blood with two mouth-to-mouth breaths. However, chest compressions are stopped for 16 seconds to give the breaths. Those repeated bouts of 16 seconds without circulation are deadly.

In one early study, Seattle phone dispatchers advised rescuers about how to perform CPR or CCC on cardiac-arrest victims. Survival increased by 50% in the CCC group.

To perform the CCC method on a person who has stopped breathing—and/or who has lost his/her pulse...

●**Call 911 immediately.**

●**Place the victim on his back.** Put one hand on top of the other, and position the heel of the bottom hand on the center of the chest. Lock your elbows, and use your body weight to perform forceful chest compressions (100 per minute).

*Children age 8 or younger should receive traditional CPR.

•**If a portable defibrillator is handy, use it** by following the recorded instructions.

If you have a known heart condition: Consider buying a defibrillator for home use.

Typical cost: About $2,000.

New Alzheimer's Risk

A recent study of more than 800 people has found that type 2 diabetes can increase a person's risk of developing Alzheimer's disease by up to 65%.

Theory: Diabetes causes a buildup of glucose in the brain that may damage brain cells.

Self-defense: All adults should exercise, eat healthfully, maintain a healthy weight and also check their blood pressure and cholesterol levels regularly to reduce the risk for dementia. Diabetics also should keep their blood sugar (glucose) levels under control.

Zoe Arvanitakis, MD, neurologist, Rush Alzheimer's Disease Center, Rush University Medical Center, Chicago.

Antibiotics Fight Alzheimer's Disease

In a new study, patients with mild to moderate Alzheimer's who took 200 milligrams (mg) of *doxycycline* (Doryx) and 300 mg of *rifampin* (Rifandin) daily for three months performed significantly better on a mental function test than did those taking a placebo.

Theory: The antibiotics interfere with the accumulation of amyloid plaques, protein fragments that are found in the brains of patients who have Alzheimer's.

If you're diagnosed with Alzheimer's: Ask your doctor about antibiotic therapy.

Mark B. Loeb, MD, associate professor, department of pathology and molecular medicine, McMaster University, Hamilton, Canada.

Red Meat/ Arthritis Connection

Eating red meat increases risk of rheumatoid arthritis.

Recent study: People who ate more than 88 grams (3.1 ounces) of red meat every day were twice as likely to develop the disease as those who ate less.

Self-defense: Intake of red meat and other protein should not exceed 10% to 15% of total daily calories.

Dorothy Pattison, PhD, RD, former research dietitian at the University of Manchester, United Kingdom, and now a research fellow in epidemiology and public health at University College in London. Her study of 264 men and women was published in *Arthritis and Rheumatism*.

Much Better Relief for Rheumatoid Arthritis

Rheumatoid arthritis can be alleviated with a new drug therapy.

New finding: Patients who took a combination of the arthritis drug *methotrexate* (Rheumatrex) and the psoriasis drug *alefacept* (Amevive) experienced four times as much symptom relief from joint swelling and tenderness as those taking methotrexate alone. Alefacept eases arthritis pain by controlling the cellular activity believed to cause the immune disturbance of rheumatoid arthritis.

If you have rheumatoid arthritis: Ask your doctor if this drug combination would be right for you.

Matthias Schneider, MD, professor of medicine, Heinrich-Heine University, Dusseldorf, Germany.

Common Antibiotic Can Help Knee Osteoarthritis

In a study of 431 women that took place over 30 months, patients given 100 milligrams (mg) of *doxycycline* twice daily lost 33% less cartilage than patients given placebos. They also were less likely to report increased knee pain. Doxycycline is the first drug shown to fight cartilage loss. And, treatment with this antibiotic may continue indefinitely.

Possible side effects: Sun sensitivity, gastrointestinal upset, irritation of the esophagus and, rarely, liver or kidney problems.

Kenneth Brandt, MD, professor of rheumatology and director of the Multipurpose Arthritis and Musculoskeletal Diseases Center, Indiana University School of Medicine in Indianapolis.

Better Knee-Replacement Surgery

Less-invasive knee-replacement surgery may be better than traditional knee surgery for 30% of patients. The new technique requires an incision of three inches instead of the traditional 12 inches. It also avoids cutting through both the muscle and tendon that enable the knee to flex.

Result: Less pain, recovery up to three times faster and greater flexibility of the knee.

This new operation is suitable for patients who have osteoarthritis but not rheumatoid arthritis. It is not advised for people who have had major knee surgery...are obese or have enlarged knees...or are over age 80.

Alfred J. Tria, Jr., MD, clinical professor of orthopedic surgery at Robert Wood Johnson School of Medicine, New Brunswick, NJ.

The Very Good News About Hip Replacement

David Nazarian, MD, a hip- and knee-replacement specialist with Booth, Bartolozzi, Balderston Orthopaedics, Philadelphia. For more information on joint replacement, log on to *www.3bortho.com*.

More than 200,000 hip-replacement operations are done every year in the US, and with very good reason—for those who are sidelined by a severely arthritic hip, replacing the diseased joint with an artificial hip is the only permanent way to eliminate pain and restore mobility.

With a success rate of well over 90%, hip-replacement surgery is highly effective. Prosthetic hips will typically last about 20 years and allow users to engage in a full range of pain-free physical activity. Advances in surgical techniques and materials are making this procedure even safer and the results longer lasting.

WHEN IS IT NECESSARY?

The most frequent reason for needing to have hip-replacement surgery is osteoarthritis, a disease brought on by years of impact and other physical stress, which progressively attacks the cartilage in the hip joint. The other leading reasons are rheumatoid arthritis (inflammation in the lining of the joints) and avascular necrosis, in which the blood flow to the bone endings is impaired. As arthritis worsens, cartilage becomes worn away to the point where the nerves of the joint are exposed—leading to significant pain when the bones of the exposed joint rub against each other during physical activity.

Because an arthritic hip can cause pain in a variety of places—including the groin, buttock, lower back, thigh or knee—X-rays are usually needed to diagnose the problem. The first line of treatment involves conservative therapies, such as the oral anti-inflammatory medications, injections with cortisone or steroids to reduce the swelling, and glucosamine and chondroitin supplements to slow the progression of arthritis. But while these treatments may ease symptoms slightly, the condition will only worsen over time. If your pain becomes so severe that it interferes with normal daily activities, you should discuss with your primary care doctor the option of seeing an orthopedic surgeon.

NEW SURGICAL TECHNIQUES

The hip is a ball-and-socket joint, with the head of the femur (thigh bone) fitting snugly into a socket in the pelvis. In hip-replacement surgery, the joint is resurfaced by cutting away the bone endings and attaching an artificial ball and socket to the femur and pelvis.

The standard prosthesis in use today employs a socket made of a titanium alloy, which fuses with the pelvic bone over time. This socket is lined with smooth plastic, which allows the femur head to rotate freely inside it. The standard prosthesis also employs a metal ball that is attached to the femur.

The procedure typically requires a hospital stay of one to three days, followed by four to five days in a rehab facility and several weeks of home visits by a physical therapist. There can be considerable pain at first, but patients are usually up and walking the day after surgery, and they have full mobility within just a couple of months.

When considering joint-replacement surgery, keep in mind that the biggest variable by far in this operation is the skill of the surgeon. The nature of this procedure necessitates getting it exactly right the first time, so having it performed by an experienced surgeon is essential.

Studies have shown that orthopedic surgeons who perform hundreds of joint-replacement operations each year have the best success rates, with much lower rates of such complications as bleeding, formation of dangerous blood clots and postoperative infection.

In addition, more experienced surgeons take much less time to do joint-replacement procedures. My own team, for example, which performs 1,000 joint replacements a year, can do a hip replacement in 35 minutes or less—compared with an average operating time of one-and-one-half to two hours. This means less time under anesthesia, less blood loss, less trauma to the body and a faster recuperation time.

Our center has also helped pioneer a number of new techniques that further minimize the trauma to the patient's body. *These techniques include...*

●**A minimally invasive approach,** using new instruments and guidance devices which allow hip replacement with a four-inch incision, rather than the standard eight- to 12-inch incision used by most surgeons. This allows faster healing and reduces risk of infection.

●**Use of a medication called Procrit** that will build up a patient's blood count prior to surgery, which can often negate the need for a blood transfusion.

●**Having the patient donate one unit of blood on the same day of surgery.** This will decrease the amount of blood required if a transfusion is called for, since the fresh blood can carry several times more oxygen per unit than blood that's been stored for several weeks.

NEW PROSTHETIC DEVICES

While prosthetic hips themselves last indefinitely, over many years, the bone attached to the prosthetic hip can deteriorate, causing the attachment to loosen. When this happens, the artificial hip will need to be replaced again—a process called *revision replacement*. Revision replacement is more complicated than the initial procedure, since there's less bone to work with. As a rule, the replacement prosthesis does not last as long as the initial artificial hip.

Since the metal-and-plastic prostheses currently in wide use have been shown to last 20 years or more, this problem mainly occurs in people who have hip-replacement surgery in their 40s or 50s. Not only will this group live long enough to require a second hip replacement, but they also tend to put more stress on their artificial hips in their daily lives.

In an attempt to extend the life of artificial hips, a number of new prosthetic devices recently approved by the FDA are being used in limited numbers. *These include...*

●**A metal or ceramic lining for the hip socket** instead of plastic.

●**A ceramic ball on the femur head** instead of metal.

Prosthetic hips that have either the standard metal ball with a metal lining or a ceramic ball with a ceramic lining have been discovered to have lower wear rates than the standard artificial hips in laboratory tests—but it will take at least 15 years before it's known whether they hold up longer in actual use. Since these devices are not widely available, you may have to raise these options with your surgeon.

Bone Zapper

A new, hand-held device detects osteoporosis—at a fraction of the expense of current tests—and could allow physicians to stop bone deterioration at a much earlier stage. This pistol-shaped device emits sound waves that penetrate skin and measure bone density. It may be on the market soon.

Technology Review, 1 Main St., Cambridge, MA 02142.

Look Five Years Younger: Lunchtime "Face-Lifts" For Men And Women

Nelson Lee Novick, MD, clinical professor of dermatology, Mount Sinai Medical Center, New York City. He is the author of *Super Skin: A Leading Dermatologist's Guide to the Latest Breakthroughs in Skin Care* (iUniverse.com).

A decade ago, aggressive cosmetic surgery was the primary treatment for wrinkles, sagging jowls and other signs of aging. Patients experienced significant bruising and swelling, and the full effects of the procedures weren't visible for at least six months.

Currently, cosmetic surgeons perform three times as many noninvasive cosmetic procedures as aggressive surgeries. More than half of the procedures are done in doctors' offices instead of hospitals—and some can be completed during a lunch break. In many cases, patients see the final results immediately.

Botox has gotten most of the headlines, but there are a number of other "instant" cosmetic procedures. All of the following procedures are safe for most people and cause no scarring.

VOLUME FILLING FOR WRINKLES AND LINES

Synthetic collagen-like substances are injected into the skin to plump up depressed areas, including wrinkles and worry and smile lines. Collagen itself, one of the first filling agents, rarely lasted more than three to six months and sometimes caused allergic reactions. The new synthetic fillers last longer and are hypoallergenic as well.

The patient is given a local anesthetic, then fillers are injected into the problem spots. One syringe usually can treat the entire face. It only takes a few minutes, and changes in appearance are immediately apparent.

Different fillers...

●**Restylane** is chemically similar to the gelatinous material that supports skin collagen and elastic fibers. It retains water and plumps skin. It is especially good for smile lines, lips that have gotten thinner with age and "smoker's lines" on the upper lip. One treatment usually lasts eight to 18 months.

Approximate cost: $750 per syringe.

●**Perlane** is similar to Restylane. It's used for deeper depressions and/or furrows and costs approximately the same as Restylane. It lasts about six months.

●**Radiesse** (formerly Radiance) is the newest filler. It's made of *calcium hydroxylapatite,* the same material that makes up teeth and bone. It is ideal for the deeper smile lines and sunken cheeks. One treatment might last two to five years. It is slightly more likely than other fillers to cause temporary bruising.

Approximate cost: $1,500 per syringe.

DERMASPACING FOR ACNE SCARS AND FURROWS

This new technique uses the body's natural healing mechanisms to add volume to areas that are depressed such as acne scars and furrows. It also is effective for cellulite that's on other parts of the body.

A patient is given a local anesthetic, and a needle-like cutting instrument is used to break up fibrous bands and create a hollow space beneath the skin. The area fills with body fluids, and within a few weeks, natural collagen is created that fills the pocket and plumps and smoothes the skin surface.

● **Dermaspacing,** also called subcision, may be enough by itself to restore younger-looking skin, or this method can be used in combination with fillers.

Approximate cost: $400 per treatment.

Dermaspacing causes minor bruising that can last for several weeks. Also, some patients will need more than one treatment. It takes about a month to gauge how effectively the body will repair the area. For acne and other scars, the results may be permanent. For furrows, the results may last several months.

CHEMICAL PEEL FOR LEATHERY SKIN

Skin loses luster and gets leathery with age, especially in people who spend a lot of time in the sun. Resurfacing uses concentrated acids to restore youthful luster and texture to the skin. *Main approaches…*

● **Alpha hydroxy acids,** also called *fruit washes,* are applied to the skin. Dermatologists use products with a 70% concentration—home-use chemical peels usually don't exceed 15%. These acids diminish mottling as well as fine wrinkles, in part by stimulating the production of gelatinous tissue under the skin. Patients generally require six to 12 treatments (two to four weeks apart), with occasional touch-ups.

Approximate cost: $150 for each 10-minute treatment.

● **Beta hydroxy acids** are used in the same way, but they are somewhat more effective. Most patients require two to four treatments.

Approximate cost: $500 per treatment.

THREAD LIFT FOR SAGGING JAW, BROW, CHEEKS

Also called a "feather lift" or "loop lift," this technique helps to diminish sagging—in the jaw, brows and cheeks—and without the extensive surgery performed in traditional face-lifts. The patient is given a local anesthetic. A needle is used to insert a fine thread under the skin. The thread loops under the loose tissue and then is pulled taut and anchored to fibrous tissue under the skin or within the hairline. Depending on the area, a single thread or multiple threads are used.

The results last anywhere from three to 10 years—about the same as a traditional face-lift. Any adjustments usually can be made later by tightening up the thread or adding additional threads. If the patient doesn't like the results, the thread can be removed and the face will return to its previous appearance.

When treating multiple areas, the procedure takes about 60 minutes. When doing one area, such as the brow, it takes about 30 minutes.

Approximate cost: $2,500 for the brow or lower face.

RADIOSURGERY FOR VISIBLE BLOOD VESSELS

A small wand directs high-energy radio waves through the skin to eliminate the tiny networks of blood vessels that appear on the cheeks or around the nose, mostly in people who have rosacea or those exposed to too much sun.

The patient is first given a topical anesthetic, then the radio waves penetrate deeply into the skin without damaging the surface or adjoining tissues. The treatment takes about five minutes.

Approximate cost: $300 to treat the entire face.

SCALPEL SCULPTING FOR REMOVING MOLES

In the past, moles were excised from the skin and the resulting wound was sutured. The wound could take weeks to heal, and many patients were left with small scars from the stitches.

Scalpel sculpting doesn't require stitches. A drop of local anesthetic is placed on the mole. The mole is then "sculpted"—cut flush with the face. Normal skin grows to cover the area, usually with no scarring. In 90% of cases, the mole never comes back.

Approximate cost: $300.

There may be a darkening (repigmenting) of the area, but radio waves can eliminate this in most cases.

SANDING FOR SCARS AND FINE WRINKLES

A sterilized sanding material is used to buff away scars—from acne, injuries, etc.—as well as fine wrinkles. Normal skin covers the area once the scar tissue is removed.

Approximate cost: $400.

Scar abrasion can be combined with dermaspacing or filling. One patient had a deep scar between his eyes after being hit by a crate. I did dermaspacing to fill the area, then buffed the surface. Now he has no visible mark.

Important: Scar abrasion is most effective when performed within eight to 12 weeks after an injury/surgery to prevent long-term scarring.

No Surgery Face-Lift

A face-lift, without invasive surgery, is now possible. Thermage (or Thermacool) uses a radio-frequency tool to heat deep tissue while cooling the top layer of skin, making skin look smoother and sag less. The procedure has been approved for skin above and around the eyes, and has recently been approved for full face treatment.

About 700 doctors currently do this procedure. They advise three sessions—each costing $2,000* to $4,000. These treatments should be spaced three to four months apart. This procedure is considered cosmetic surgery and is not covered by insurance. To find a doctor who performs the procedure, visit *www.thermage.com.*

Roy G. Geronemus, MD, director, Laser & Skin Surgery Center of New York.

*All prices subject to change.

Beware Staph Infections

Dangerous staph infections are striking more people—not only hospital patients. Drug-resistant Staphylococcus bacteria can cause skin infections and, less commonly, pneumonia.

Self-defense: Wash hands frequently with soap and water, or use an alcohol-based cleanser. To prevent the spread of staph bacteria, cover open wounds until they are healed. See a physician if you experience recurrent boils—they may be caused by staph.

Sara Cosgrove, MD, director of antibiotic management and associate hospital epidemiologist, The Johns Hopkins Hospital, Baltimore.

New Light Therapy Preserves Vision

Photodynamic therapy involves injecting a light-sensitive medication called *verteporfin* (Visudyne) into a vein in the arm of a patient with age-related macular degeneration (AMD). The drug circulates through the body to the eyes. When a laser is shone into the eyes, the drug is activated and destroys the abnormal blood vessels that cause the loss of central vision in AMD. The procedure now is considered the preferred treatment to slow the progression of AMD and it is covered by most insurance plans.

Sanjay Sharma, MD, associate professor of ophthalmology and department head at Queen's University, Kingston, Ontario, Canada.

A More Reliable Glaucoma Test

Glaucoma may not be detected by the old standard screening method of measuring elevated fluid pressure in the eye.

Reason: Some people with glaucoma have normal "intraocular" eye pressure.

New approach: Elderly patients and those with a family history of glaucoma should have an ophthalmoscopy in which an ophthalmologist checks the optic nerves for any signs of damage from glaucoma, even if pressure in the eye is normal.

Darrell WuDunn, MD, PhD, an associate professor of ophthalmology, Indiana University School of Medicine in Indianapolis.

New Way to Relieve Allergy Misery

Laser submucosal resection permanently relieves nasal congestion in those patients who have not been helped by drugs and/or allergy shots. The 15-minute treatment, often covered by insurance, decreases the size of turbinates, nasal structures that swell during an allergic reaction.

Result: Less congestion and allergy-related snoring and fewer sinus infections.

Information: American Academy of Otolaryngology—Head and Neck Surgery, 703-836-4444, *www.entnet.org.*

Rajiv Pandit, MD, an otolaryngologist at Methodist Dallas Medical Center and Dallas ENT & Allergy Center.

No More Headaches

Alan M. Rapoport, MD, director and cofounder of the New England Center for Headache in Stamford, CT, *www. headachenech.com.* He also is clinical professor of neurology at Columbia University College of Physicians and Surgeons in New York City and coauthor of *Headache Relief for Women: How You Can Manage and Prevent Pain* (Little, Brown).

Headaches now send more people to the doctor than any other ailment. But only half of sufferers get the right diagnosis and even fewer find relief.

If your doctor hasn't been able to relieve your headaches, don't give up. Most headaches persist because they're misdiagnosed or improperly treated.

What your neurologist or headache specialist should look for to establish a telltale pattern…*

●**Where does it hurt** (on one or both sides of your head, in the front or the back)?

●**How does it hurt** (throbbing, jabbing, steady pain, pressure, etc.)?

●**How frequent** (twice per month, daily, etc.) and how intense (mild, moderate, severe) are your headaches?

●**What triggers your headaches** (diet, poor sleep, psychological stress, etc.)?

●**What other symptoms** (dizziness, nausea, vomiting, sensitivity to light and sound, worse with exercise, visual disturbance, etc.) accompany them?

*To locate a headache specialist in your area, contact the American Council for Headache Education at 856-423-0258 or *www.achenet.org.*

●**Who else in your family gets headaches?**

Your evaluation also should include appropriate blood tests to see if a thyroid condition, Lyme disease, infection or other illness is responsible for your headaches.

More advanced tests, such as magnetic resonance imaging (MRI) and computed tomography (CT), scan the brain for tumors, bleeding or other serious problems. These tests are necessary only when the examination or symptoms suggest cause for concern.

Headaches that are not caused by illness, injury or other conditions are called "primary headache disorders." *Most common types…*

TENSION-TYPE HEADACHE

Tension-type headache (TTH) affects about 90% of people over the course of their lifetimes. It causes a tight, squeezing sensation on both sides of the head. This used to be called "tension" headache because it was thought to be caused by emotional upset or muscle tension in the scalp or neck. Doctors recently have established that the same headache can occur without psychological stress or muscle tightness. It is not known what causes TTH, but it may result from an abnormality in the brain and/or be related to migraine. TTH is usually mild to moderate.

MIGRAINE

Migraine is the second most common kind of primary headache, affecting about 28 million Americans. The condition tends to run in families, although the genes responsible haven't been completely identified. If one parent had migraines, you have a 40% chance of having them, too…if both did, the odds rise to 75%.

Migraines are generally more severe than TTH—in fact, they can be disabling—and last for four to 72 hours.

The diagnosis is made by physicians when recurrent episodes have two out of four basic characteristics (pain that is moderate to severe …throbbing…on one side of the head…worsened by activity) and one out of the three other characteristics (nausea…vomiting…sensitivity to both light and sound).

Fifteen percent to 20% of people who have migraine experience an "aura" that occurs just before or at the start of the headache itself and lasts 20 to 30 minutes. This is primarily a visual disturbance—flashing lights, multicolored spots and zigzag lines are common.

Important: Most people mistakenly believe that "sinus headaches" are common. In reality, 90% of people who believe they suffer from sinus headaches actually suffer from migraines. When your headache is the result of acute sinus infection, you'll also have other symptoms, such as fever…red-hot skin in the sinus area…and/or a yellow-green, bad-tasting nasal or throat discharge.

Weather changes trigger migraine: A new study has confirmed what many migraine sufferers have long suspected. In 77 migraineurs who tracked their headaches for two years, 51% had weather-related migraines.

Most common culprits: Changes in temperature, humidity and barometric pressure.

If you suffer from migraine: Ask your doctor about ways to prevent migraine when weather changes are predicted.

CLUSTER HEADACHE

Cluster headache, the least common kind of primary headache, now afflicts about 2 million Americans.

The pain of cluster headache is steady and severe—often excruciating—in or around one eye. Sufferers say it feels like a tremendous pressure on the eyeball.

The pain is accompanied by one or more additional symptoms, such as tearing, a drooping eyelid, a stuffed or runny nostril or sweating over the eyebrow—always on the same side as the headache.

Besides the pain itself, the pattern is distinctive. The attacks last 45 minutes to two hours, in "clusters" of one to three a day, for a period of four to eight weeks. Typically, the headaches then go away until the following year—often around the same time—when a new cluster begins.

GETTING THE RIGHT TREATMENT

Few general physicians will take the time to deploy the entire arsenal of available headache weapons. *Even a specialist may leave out some crucial steps…*

•**Elimination of triggers.** Migraines can be set off by a number of triggers, including bright sun, high altitude, skipped meals, too little or too much sleep, alcohol, specific foods (such as chocolate and aged cheeses), hormonal fluctuations and psychological stress. Keep track of your migraines to identify your personal triggers.

TTH also can be triggered by psychological stress, and cluster headaches by alcohol.

•**Behavioral medicine procedures.** Biofeedback training, which helps sufferers recognize changes in muscle tension, heart rate and/or temperature, has been found to be helpful for TTH and migraine.

Deep breathing, guided imagery and progressive muscle relaxation techniques all tone down the "fight or flight" response which can cause or worsen headaches.

•**Vitamins, minerals and herbs.** For prevention of migraine, the strongest of scientific evidence supports the use of magnesium (400 milligrams [mg] daily) and vitamin B-2 (400 mg daily). A study conducted in Switzerland and presented at the American Academy of Neurology annual meeting found that 100 mg of the dietary supplement coenzyme Q10 taken three times daily helps to prevent migraines. Consult your doctor.

MEDICATION

For TTH and mild migraine, OTC painkillers may suffice if taken at the onset of pain. These include *acetaminophen* (Tylenol) and nonsteroidal anti-inflammatory drugs (NSAIDs), like *ibuprofen* (Motrin).

If OTC painkillers don't help, you may need prescription medication. A drug that combines aspirin or acetaminophen with a prescription pain reliever, such as Fiorinal, may help if TTH or migraine is mild and the drug is taken within 30 to 60 minutes of the onset of pain.

Triptans are the most effective drugs against migraine. If taken early, they can stop an attack before it becomes severe. The side effects can include dizziness and tingling in the fingers. Triptans are available in tablets, nasal spray and injectable forms, and they include *sumatriptan* (Imitrex), *zolmitriptan* (Zomig) and *eletriptan* (Relpax).

Caution: When medications are overused, they can make headaches more frequent and more severe. Do not take analgesics or use the triptans for headache more than two days per week. Also, do not take a triptan if you have uncontrolled high blood pressure, previous stroke or serious heart problems.

Daily preventive medications will decrease the frequency, duration and intensity of headaches. They include antidepressants, such as *amitriptyline* (Elavil)…calcium channel blockers, such as *verapamil* (Calan)…beta-blockers, such as *propranolol* (Inderal)…and anti-seizure drugs, such as *topiramate* (Topamax).

Helpful: If you have daily headaches and are overusing analgesics, start on preventive medication one month before cutting down on painkillers. Then gradually reduce the amount of painkillers you use over a two-week period to avoid worsening headache symptoms and withdrawal effects, like anxiety and insomnia.

WHEN HEADACHES DON'T GET BETTER

If the headaches persist, despite your best efforts, you and your doctor may have overlooked some of the basic tools outlined above. Many doctors do prescribe appropriate preventive drugs, but even the right ones don't always work. Why? The headache sufferer may have given up too soon. It may take up to three months for preventive drugs to help. If you still have headaches and now also suffer from side effects, such as dizziness or sleepiness, you're unlikely to want to persevere *and* increase the dose. But you may need to do so for relief.

Example: A patient with migraines had been prescribed 60 mg of the beta-blocker propranolol. After three weeks, she still had severe headaches several times a week, so she stopped taking the drug.

Solution: Beta-blockers and other preventive medications may need to be taken for two to three months before they reduce headache frequency. This patient required a much higher dose than she was getting.

For a headache calendar to help track your daily symptoms and triggers, go to *www.head achenech.com* and click on "Patients."

HEADACHE RED FLAGS

In rare cases, a headache heralds a serious medical problem, such as meningitis, brain hemorrhage, stroke or a benign or malignant brain tumor.

See your doctor if you experience…

● **The first headache of your life.**

● **A headache that gets worse over the course of several weeks.**

● **A change in your headaches**—for example, they have become worse or more frequent than usual.

Seek emergency care if you experience…

● **The worst headache you've ever had.**

● **Headache with a stiff neck, vomiting and fever.**

● **Signs of neurological abnormalities,** such as double vision, trouble speaking, weakness or numbness—unless you have had these symptoms before as part of a migraine aura.

New Treatment For Acid Reflux

Relief from acid reflux now is available with a new, minimally invasive procedure called Enteryx. This involves injecting a liquid polymer—a rubbery, spongy substance—into the valve between the esophagus and the stomach. The polymer helps the valve to open and close more completely. In new studies, the treatment stopped stomach acid from splashing into the esophagus in 70% of patients.

If your acid reflux is not controlled with medication: Talk to your doctor about Enteryx.

James Aisenberg, MD, associate clinical professor of medicine, gastroenterology, Mount Sinai School of Medicine, New York City.

Hidden Causes of Depression

Robert J. Hedaya, MD, clinical professor of psychiatry at Georgetown University in Washington, DC. Dr. Hedaya is author of *The Antidepressant Survival Guide: The Clinically Proven Program to Enhance the Benefits and Beat the Side Effects of Your Medication* (Three Rivers).

Thanks to the advances in psychiatry and psychology, medication and psychotherapy are now more effective than ever in treating the millions of Americans who suffer from depression, the most common emotional disorder.

Medication and psychotherapy, however, are not effective for everyone. While one-third of depressed individuals will get completely better, another one-third still have symptoms despite using an antidepressant and/or psychotherapy. The remaining one-third don't improve at all.

One important reason—the hidden causes of depression. These are physical conditions, such as hormone imbalances and nutritional deficiencies, that standard depression treatments alone cannot touch. That's why a thorough physical examination given by your primary care doctor should be part of the evaluation for depression, especially if treatment fails or is just partially successful.

Among the factors to consider…

HORMONE IMBALANCE

At least 60% of people with psychiatric symptoms, including depression, have abnormal levels of thyroid or adrenal hormones. All of these chemical messengers play a key role in the regulation of mood. An imbalance can interfere with sleep, impair thinking and make it difficult to carry out daily activities.

If your thyroid is functioning at a low level, you may have classic symptoms of underactive thyroid, such as weight gain, muscle weakness and/or sensitivity to cold. An overactive thyroid causes irritability and anxiety.

If your adrenals are underactive, the most common symptoms are low energy and weakness under stress. If they are overactive, symptoms might include weight gain, stomach ulcers and diabetes.

Important: Standard blood tests often fail to detect subtle thyroid imbalances that affect mood. Get further testing that measures the thyroid hormones Free T3 and Free T4.

A saliva test that measures the hormones cortisol and DHEA is the most accurate screen for adrenal dysfunction.

IMMUNE DISORDERS

Anything that impacts the immune system can lower mood, cause concentration and memory problems and trigger anxiety—mimicking or exacerbating the symptoms of depression.

This can be the result of an allergy (including food allergies), asthma or any type of chronic infection, such as mononucleosis or sinusitis. Psychiatric symptoms, including depression, are particularly common with Lyme disease. Autoimmune diseases, such as rheumatoid arthritis and lupus, can have the same effect.

NUTRITION

The nutrients that we obtain from food are the building blocks of the neurotransmitters, the messenger chemicals with which the brain cells communicate. For example, the precursor of serotonin, a key neurotransmitter in maintaining positive mood, is the amino acid tryptophan, which comes from well-digested protein. Adequate levels of zinc are needed for serotonin synthesis.

Deficiencies of vitamin B-12, folate or the minerals chromium, selenium or magnesium—perhaps too minor to cause physical symptoms—are common and can lead to depression. Taking the diabetes drug *metformin* (Glucophage) or *omeprazole* (Prilosec) and possibly other acid blockers over months or years also can result in depression.

A diet that provides too many omega-6 fatty acids (found in meat, dairy and baked goods) and not enough omega-3s (found in the cold-water fish, such as salmon and mackerel) may lead to memory problems and mood swings as well as depression.

Deficiencies of vitamin D have been linked to seasonal affective disorder (SAD), which is commonly known as the "winter blues."

Blood tests can measure levels of vitamins and minerals. A blood test known as an essential fatty acid analysis examines the composition of red blood cell membranes and will show if omega-3 and omega-6 are out of balance.

SLEEP PROBLEMS

Interrupted sleep leads to depression symptoms, such as fatigue, poor concentration and low mood.

One common cause is sleep apnea, a disorder in which breathing momentarily stops, triggering repeated, but brief, awakenings. Morning headaches, heavy snoring and high blood pressure are common signs of sleep apnea.

Nocturnal myoclonus, which causes twitching of the legs during sleep, prevents sufferers from reaching the deep, restorative stages of sleep. Because you're never truly rested when you wake up, depression can easily develop.

To detect or confirm these conditions, you may need an overnight evaluation in a sleep laboratory, located at most major medical centers. Brain waves, vital signs and body movements are monitored during sleep.

MEDICATION

A number of drugs, both prescription and over the counter (OTC), may cause depression as a side effect. *Among the most common...*

● **Heart and high blood pressure medication.** The beta blockers, such as *propranolol* (Inderal), and calcium channel blockers, such as *diltiazem* (Cardizem), are common culprits.

● **Antihistamines.** *Diphenhydramine* (Benadryl) helps control cold symptoms, but it also can cause low mood.

● **Antibiotics.** They often work by changing the way the body synthesizes proteins that are necessary for normal brain function. This can lower mood.

If you start feeling depressed not long after you begin using a particular drug, chances are the medication is to blame. Your physician can probably find an alternative medication that does not trigger depression.

The Danger of Drinking Too Much Water

Drinking too much water too quickly can dilute the blood's content of salt to dangerously low levels that may cause illness or death. That's why the advice typically given to a sick person to drink plenty of fluids can backfire. If one follows this advice to the extreme and overdoes it, he/she can be harmed.

Safety: Have your doctor tell you exactly how much fluid—and which fluids—to drink, rather than "plenty."

Marvin M. Lipman, MD, chief medical adviser for *Consumer Reports on Health,* 101 Truman Ave., Yonkers, NY 10703.

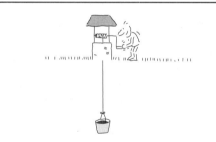

2

Inside the Health-Care System

How to Get the Same Quality Care As Your Doctor

It's a fact—doctors do receive better medical treatment. Our experience with the health-care system gives us a big advantage when it comes to finding first-rate physicians, getting the most accurate diagnoses and avoiding unnecessary risks. *You, too, can get the same superior treatment...*

HOW TO FIND THE BEST PRIMARY CARE PHYSICIANS

To find a top physician, be sure to follow these four steps...

•**Get names from other doctors**—your ophthalmologist, dentist, etc. Also, ask friends, neighbors, colleagues and nurses at your local hospital.

•**Cross-reference your list with physicians in your health insurance plan.** Doctors join and leave insurance plans all the time, so save the recommendations that you don't use for future reference.

•**Be sure the doctor you select is board certified,** licensed in your state and has no disciplinary actions against him/her.

Resource: www.docboard.org provides free background and disciplinary information, including links to state medical boards.

•**Schedule an appointment with the doctor.** He should perform certain tasks himself, such as listening to your chest with a stethoscope. Physicians who leave these routine but important procedures to a nurse or physician's assistant may have trouble making an accurate diagnosis.

The doctor should explain what he is doing and learning about you during the examination. He also should listen respectfully to what you are saying. He should not interrupt you or make you feel rushed.

Christine Dumas, DDS, and Kevin Soden, MD, medical correspondents for NBC's *Today* show. They are coauthors of *Special Treatment: How to Get the Same High-Quality Health Care Your Doctor Gets* (Berkley).

27

HOW TO GET THE BEST TREATMENT

To ensure an accurate diagnosis and effective treatment...

●**Document symptoms so you don't forget.** Note them as soon as they occur.

●**Organize your thoughts.** Rambling on with vague complaints makes it difficult for a doctor to help you in the standard 15-minute office visit. Make notes ahead of time about what concerns you.

●**Be honest about pain.** Men especially tend to downplay pain, causing the doctor to underestimate the problem.

●**Use the term *we* when talking about your health problems,** as in, *What do you think* we *should do?* The distinction is subtle, but there's a psychological impact on your doctor when you make it clear that you are a team working together.

●**Ask the golden question—***If you or someone in your family had a similar problem, which medical options/treatments/other doctors would you choose?* This will most likely prompt your doctor's honest opinion.

●**Compare treatments.** Doctors will often use *www.guidelines.gov,* compiled by the US Department of Health and Human Services and the American Medical Association. It provides guidelines for treating hundreds of conditions.

HOW TO APPROACH SURGERY

●**Select an experienced surgeon.** Look for one who often performs the procedure that you need. He is likely to have much lower patient complication and death rates.

Resource doctors use: www.healthgrades. com, which provides report card ratings on hospitals and doctors specializing in such surgeries as coronary bypass, hip or knee replacement and cosmetic.

Helpful: Your health insurance plan may limit your choice of surgeons. If your research reveals that an out-of-network surgeon is far superior, ask your primary care physician to write a letter to your insurer making a case for that surgeon.

●**Have a postoperative plan.** Surgeons often define their success as repairing the problem, but your goal is to get back to your previous state of health. Rehabilitation is particularly important after cardiac surgery and joint/orthopedic operations, such as those involving rotator cuffs, knees and wrists. Find out from your surgeon where he has sent other patients for rehab, and ask those patients for their opinions.

HOW TO HANDLE MEDICATIONS

●**Ask the doctor three questions about medications...**

●*Does my age, sex, weight or height affect the standard dosage of this medication?*

●*What are the serious side effects of this drug, and what would need to be done to counteract those side effects?*

●*Could this medication interact with any other medications I'm taking?*

Resource: *www.healthsquare.com* provides detailed information on hundreds of prescription medicines.

●**Choose one pharmacy to fill all your prescriptions.** Learn the pharmacist's name and, whenever possible, try to deal with him—not assistants—when you order a new medication. Pharmacists often are more experienced than doctors at spotting potential drug interactions and staying abreast of the latest studies and government warnings.

●**Never cut pills in half without checking with your doctor or pharmacist.** You may save money by asking for larger-dose pills and splitting them, but the medicine may not be uniformly distributed. Also, cutting pills that are coated to prevent stomach irritation or extend the release of medication can trigger adverse reactions.

THREE MEDICAL TESTS TO INSIST ON

●**C-reactive protein (CRP) test.** This test measures inflammation in the body. Men with high CRP levels have twice the risk of heart attack...women, four times the risk.

Recommended for: Anyone over age 35.

Cost: $75,* covered by some insurance plans. Ask your physician how often the test should be done.

●**Apolipoprotein (apo) test.** The amount of apo—tiny fat particles floating in your blood—is

*Prices may vary by doctor and location.

an accurate predictor of clogged arteries and of heart attack risk.

Recommended for: Anyone over age 40.

Cost: $75,* covered by some insurance plans. Ask your doctor how often you should have this test.

●**Colonoscopy.** Colorectal cancer kills more people than breast or prostate cancer. A colonoscopy—in which a fiberoptic scope is inserted in the intestine—detects most polyps.

Recommended for: People age 50 and over, every three to five years.

Cost: $1,200 to $1,500, covered by most insurance plans.

*Prices may vary by doctor and location.

Look Beyond Your Doctor's Age

John J. Connolly, EdD, former president, New York Medical College, Valhalla. He is copublisher of *America's Top Doctors* (Castle Connolly Medical Ltd., *www.castleconnolly.com*).

Whether your doctor is 30 or 70 years old, be sure that he/she has these important attributes…

●**Responsiveness.** If he is always rushed, inattentive and not responsive to your questions or concerns—or is not making a definitive diagnosis—consider finding a new doctor.

●**Hospital appointments.** Make sure your doctor is on staff at a reputable hospital. This will help ensure that all his credentials are regularly reviewed.

●**Board certification.** All doctors should be board certified. This means the doctor has completed an approved residency program in a specialty and passed the board's examination. Most doctors also must be recertified—typically every eight to 10 years—which helps to ensure that a physician of any age is up to date with all the advances in his field. Contact the American Board of Medical Specialties at 866-275-2267

or *www.abms.org* to find out if your doctor is board certified.

How to Get Your Doctor To Return Your Phone Call

Marie Savard, MD, an internist in private practice in Philadelphia and author of *How to Save Your Own Life: The Eight Steps Only You Can Take to Manage and Control Your Health Care* (Warner).

Why is it so difficult for some doctors to return patients' phone calls? Although returning calls is part of the practice of medicine, calls are a nightmare for physicians. Errors are more likely by phone than in face-to-face consultation. Doctors are rushed. They may not have the information they need to give the best advice. And few physicians are reimbursed for the time spent talking on the phone.

Advice on getting your doctor to return your phone call…*

●**Communicate your symptoms and concerns.** State your worst fear in a serious way—for example, you are worried about your sore throat because you recently were exposed to someone with strep.

Helpful: Write down what you need to say beforehand. If you are concerned about being able to express yourself adequately, consider having someone else speak on your behalf.

The most dangerous thing patients do is trivialize their own complaints. For example, saying that abdominal or chest pain may be merely indigestion. If the problem is perceived as only minor, you are less likely to be called back in a timely fashion. And don't make a tentative diagnosis or propose treatment. The more you sound like you need help, the more likely you will be called back.

*If you suspect a serious health emergency—such as heart attack or stroke—call an ambulance or go to the emergency room. Don't wait at home for a callback from your doctor.

●**Make the "gatekeeper" feel important.** The more you tell the front desk about your concerns, the better you will be served. Often a nurse will return your call instead of the doctor. If you still are concerned, explain that you have lingering questions and would like the doctor to call you back as soon as possible.

●**Be persistent—but respectful.** Ask when the physician will call you back. If the seriousness of your problem does not appear to be understood by the receptionist or nurse, repeat your concern.

Reminder: Keep the phone line open when waiting for the callback. Otherwise, it may be another hour—or even another day—before you make contact.

Patients need to talk with their doctors about phone calls before problems arise. When are calls returned? Who generally returns them? Under what circumstances would a phone consultation work as well as an appointment? Are there situations in which payment for the phone consultation would be appropriate? An agreement to pay may prompt a quicker response. And the charge may be covered by insurance (check with your provider).

Another vital topic to work out up front is how to deal with the on-call doctor when your own physician is not available.

Example: When suffering from an asthma attack on a weekend, you may be shocked to hear that the covering physician will not refill the medication that had worked for prior attacks —nor will he contact your primary physician for confirmation of the prescription.

Doctors who are not familiar with callers are less likely to prescribe over the phone. If you have a chronic condition subject to flare-ups, ask your doctor in advance what to do—including how to get the treatment you need—when he is not on call.

High-quality medical care demands an active partnership between doctor and patient—but it starts with you.

What You Should Avoid Before Medical Tests

Exercising before many routine medical tests can skew the results, possibly leading to a misdiagnosis.

Example: Moderate exercising, such as brisk walking, raises HDL "good" cholesterol …and decreases LDL "bad" cholesterol and total cholesterol levels for 30 minutes following the activity. This effect increases the possibility that existing heart disease may not be detected. Exercising 30 minutes before blood is drawn also can lead to an elevated reading on the leukocyte blood assay (a measure of the number of white blood cells), which could result in an incorrect suspicion of infection.

Self-defense: Ask your doctor if you need to refrain from exercising—and for how long— before undergoing any medical test.

Ray Sukumar, MD, a pathologist in private practice in Dover, DE.

Protect Yourself Against Superbugs

Jerome Klein, MD, professor of pediatrics and vice chairman for academic affairs in the department of pediatrics at the Boston University School of Medicine/Boston Medical Center. He is also a lecturer at Harvard Medical School, and the author of more than 450 articles on infectious diseases.

The new strains of drug-resistant bacteria, known as "superbugs," now are being documented with disturbing frequency, according to numerous studies presented to more than 2,000 US physicians who recently attended the annual meeting of the Infectious Diseases Society of America.

This is a serious problem. These bacteria are responsible for an increasing number of infections, including pneumonia, sinusitis and ear infections. In fact, bacteria that once responded to antibiotics now are resistant to one or more of these infection-fighting medications.

Example: The *Staphylococcus aureus* bacterium, known as staph, is among the most common causes of infection. About *half* of the staph found in intensive care units cannot be killed with the primary method of treatment—penicillin-like antibiotics. Drug-resistant forms of staph can cause runaway infections that can't be treated with these standard drugs.

With very few new antibiotics in the development pipeline, physicians now worry that even potent antibiotics, such as *vancomycin* (Vancocin), soon will be rendered ineffective.

Here's what you need to know to protect yourself from superbugs…

HOW RESISTANCE DEVELOPS

When a patient takes an effective antibiotic, the drug kills most of the infection-causing bacteria. A few organisms may survive because they have developed characteristics that make them resistant to the drug. Because the other bacteria have been eradicated, these organisms become the majority. When they multiply, they can create the superbug bacteria that don't respond to previously effective drugs.

These superbugs are transmitted to others in the same way that all bacteria are transmitted, through physical contact or droplets spread in the air by coughing or sneezing.

Because bacteria multiply and mutate far more quickly than scientists can develop new antibiotics, there may be fewer available treatments for common—and potentially life-threatening—infections. Patients remain sick longer, and the risk for complications rises.

Antibiotic dangers—and solutions…

Danger: Taking antibiotics for viral infections. Most people know that antibiotics treat only infections caused by bacteria and have no effect on viruses. Bacteria have more chances to develop resistance when antibiotics are used more frequently than they should be. Most doctors and patients now recognize the danger.

Example: There has been about a 25% decrease in antibiotic prescriptions for respiratory infections since 1995.

However: Doctors still write about 50 million unnecessary antibiotic prescriptions annually. Patients who insist that they be given antibiotics for an illness usually get them.

Self-defense: Only take antibiotics if your doctor is reasonably sure that the infection is caused by bacteria. The symptoms of viral and bacterial infections are difficult to distinguish, but you probably *don't* need antibiotics if you have a cold or flu.

Danger: Prescription errors. Doctors and pharmacists occasionally do make mistakes. A doctor may prescribe the wrong drug or the wrong dose. The pharmacist may misread instructions. Taking the wrong dose or the wrong antibiotic can result in a prolonged or untreated infection.

Self-defense: Ask your physician to explain what the drug does before you leave his/her office. Ask what the dose is…how often you're supposed to take it…and for how long.

Then, when you get the prescription filled, check all the information included with the drug. Make sure it corresponds with what your doctor told you.

Danger: Failing to follow instructions. Patients often fail to take antibiotics appropriately. They forget doses…or take too much or too little.

Self-defense: When you pick up a prescription, read over the label instructions before you leave the pharmacy. Ask the pharmacist to clarify information that's unclear. If the name of the drug is different from what your doctor prescribed, the pharmacist may have substituted the lower-priced generic form of the drug.

Danger: Being unaware of drug interactions. Antibiotics, just like all medications, can interact with other drugs patients may be taking. Some antibiotics are best absorbed when taken with meals. Others should be taken on an empty stomach—one hour before or two hours after meals. Herbs and supplements—calcium supplements, in particular—can inhibit absorption of some antibiotics.

Self-defense: Ask your pharmacist if the antibiotic you were prescribed will interact with any medications you are currently taking. Also ask your pharmacist whether the drug should be taken on a full or an empty stomach. Tell him about any supplements or herbs you are taking, and ask if they will interact with the antibiotic.

***Danger:* Stopping treatment early.** Most antibiotics resolve symptoms within a couple of days of treatment. However, some organisms may survive much longer. Patients who quit taking the drugs early—when their symptoms have subsided—give the hardy survivors a chance to multiply and trigger a new infection that's even harder to treat.

Self-defense: Continue taking antibiotics for the full number of days prescribed. Many antibiotics cause mild side effects, such as nausea or diarrhea. If you experience serious side effects, such as severe diarrhea or hives, call your doctor. If necessary, he can substitute a drug that's less likely to cause serious side effects.

***Danger:* Stockpiling.** Patients frequently save unused antibiotics so they can take them at some future time. Doing this can be dangerous for two reasons.

First, patients who have leftover antibiotics might not have taken the full prescription to begin with, and this makes them vulnerable to repeat infections.

Second, antibiotics that were prescribed for one condition may not work for a subsequent illness, even if the symptoms seem similar. Even if the condition is the same, taking a partial dose is unlikely to eradicate infection-causing bacteria.

Self-defense: Never save antibiotics. Take the full prescription as prescribed. If your doctor tells you to stop the antibiotic because it is not working, you are experiencing side effects or for any other reason, throw out all of the remaining pills.

***Danger:* Switching drugs unnecessarily.** Doctors treating infections sometimes prescribe a different drug if the first one doesn't seem to be working. This is appropriate in some cases, but switching to a different antibiotic may not always be useful.

Self-defense: Ask your doctor how many days it should take for the antibiotic to alleviate symptoms. If you do not experience relief in that amount of time—usually two to three days —alert your doctor.

If your doctor suggests you change antibiotics, find out why. Ask what type of organism is being treated...whether the initial diagnosis was correct...and why the new drug will be more effective than the old one.

Four Dangerous Drugs Doctors Still Prescribe

Larry Sasich, PharmD, research analyst at Public Citizen Health Research Group, a nonprofit organization that promotes research-based systemwide changes in health-care policy. The group's Web site at *www.worstpills.org* lists 182 unsafe and/or ineffective drugs. Dr. Sasich is also coauthor of the best-selling book *Worst Pills, Best Pills: A Consumer's Guide to Avoiding Drug-Induced Death or Illness* (Pocket).

The popular painkiller Vioxx made front-page headlines in the fall of 2004 when a study showed that taking it for 18 months or longer doubled the risk of heart attack and stroke. Vioxx, one of a class of drugs called COX-2 inhibitors, is estimated to have caused as many as 139,000 heart attacks and strokes in America, with 55,000 deaths. The manufacturing company finally stopped selling this drug.

In February 2005, responding to widespread criticism of the government's handling of drug-safety problems, the US Food and Drug Administration (FDA) announced that it was creating a board to warn patients about unsafe drugs.

What other drugs are dangerous? Here are four to be wary of. If you are now taking any of these, see your doctor to discuss alternatives that may be safer.

ACTOS AND AVANDIA

These drugs—prescribed to type 2 diabetics to improve blood sugar control—constitute the family of medications called *glitazones*. The first member of this family of drugs, Rezulin, was withdrawn in 2000 because it caused liver toxicity.

Studies show that Actos and Avandia may bring on heart and liver failure. Also, when patients taking other oral antidiabetic drugs are switched over to Actos or Avandia, their blood sugar levels go up—and rarely return to pre-treatment levels.

In 2001, the FDA formally warned Avandia's manufacturer after company officials made statements denying or minimizing the health risks associated with the drug.

Warning: The package inserts for Actos and Avandia state that they should not be used by anyone on medication for congestive heart failure, but doctors still are prescribing them for diabetics who have heart failure. A 2003 study in *The Journal of the American Medical Association* looked at thousands of diabetics hospitalized for heart failure and found that 16.1% had been prescribed a glitazone.

Alternative: The older class of oral antidiabetics called sulfonylureas.

CRESTOR

Approved in 2003, this is the newest in the family of cholesterol-lowering statin drugs. It has recently been shown to reverse the build-up of plaque in coronary arteries. But, it's also been reported that kidney failure or damage in people taking Crestor is 75 times higher than in those taking other statins.

Reported cases of *rhabdomyolysis,* a potentially fatal side effect that destroys muscle tissue, rivals that of Baycol, a statin that was withdrawn from the market (see "Drug Recalls" in next column).

Alternatives: There are other statin drugs that may be less dangerous. Unlike Crestor—Lipitor, Mevacor, Pravachol and Zocor have all been shown to help prevent heart attack and stroke in certain people. Crestor also is more expensive than the other statins.

MERIDIA

This widely prescribed weight-reduction drug was approved in 1997 over the objection of the FDA physician who was principal reviewer of the drug, which has similar chemical properties to amphetamines.

It has been reported that Meridia caused 124 individuals to be hospitalized and 49 deaths, all from heart problems that were associated with taking this drug.

An article in the May 2004 issue of *Archives of Internal Medicine* reviewed Meridia's effectiveness. Obese people lost an average of only 10 pounds a year, and 55% of the weight lost was regained within 18 months of stopping the drug. It did not appear to reduce illness or death caused by being overweight.

Alternative: The safest way to lose weight is by eating a little less each day and exercising a little more.

DRUG RECALLS

Here are a few high-profile drugs that have been withdrawn in the last decade…

- **Baycol.** In 2001, this four-year-old statin was withdrawn from the US market when it caused 31 deaths from rhabdomyolysis.

- **Duract.** This painkiller, first marketed in 1997, has been linked to severe liver damage and was withdrawn in 1998.

- **Propulsid.** This heartburn drug, approved in 1993, was withdrawn in 2000 after causing more than 80 deaths from heart problems.

- **Raxar.** This antibiotic, first marketed in 1997 and taken by 2.65 million Americans, was withdrawn in 1999 after it was shown to cause potentially fatal heart arrhythmias.

- **Rezulin.** This diabetes drug, approved in 1997, was withdrawn in 2000 after 21 people died from liver failure, three needed liver transplants and more than 100 were hospitalized with liver toxicity.

For a listing of drugs recalled by the FDA, call 888-463-6332 or visit *www.fda.gov.*

SAFETY RULE

For maximum safety, try not to use any drug until it has been on the market for at least seven years. A study published in *The Journal of the American Medical Association* shows that about half of new drugs are removed from the market or have significant safety warnings added to their labels within seven years.

Be on the Lookout for Drug Side Effects

Side effects from medications usually appear within 24 hours of your first dose. Common side effects include drowsiness, stomach upset, constipation and dry mouth. Some reactions, such as severe diarrhea and skin rashes, can take up to one week to develop.

Important: Call your doctor at the first sign of a problem, no matter how long you've been taking a drug. Ask if you should discontinue use.

Lisa M. Chavis, RPh, author and consumer health information expert in Tampa.

Reducing the Side Effects of Statins

Kenneth H. Cooper, MD, MPH, a leading expert on preventive medicine and the benefits of exercise and cholesterol control, and founder of the Cooper Clinic, the Cooper Aerobics Center and the Cooper Institute for Aerobics Research in Dallas. He is the author of *Controlling Cholesterol the Natural Way* (Bantam).

Statins are safe for most people, however, as many as one in 10 patients experiences some side effects, such as nausea, diarrhea and constipation. These effects usually are mild, but more serious problems occur in 1% to 2% of cases. *Here's what to watch out for...*

MUSCLE PAIN

Some patients taking statins experience muscle pain, such as aching, tenderness and/or weakness. The pain (*statin myopathy*) usually occurs in the legs, but it can occur in the arm, shoulder or other muscles.

Warning: Call your doctor immediately if you experience severe muscle pain. This may be due to *rhabdomyolysis,* a breakdown of muscle cells. It causes high blood levels of a protein that can damage the kidneys, lead to kidney failure and, rarely, death.

The risk of developing rhabdomyolysis rises when a statin is combined with another drug, such as *gemfibrozil* (Lopid), the antibiotics *erythromycin* (Erythrocin) and *clarithromycin* (Biaxin) or the antifungals *ketoconazole* (Nizoral) and *itraconazole* (Sporanox). Your doctor may advise you to discontinue the statin while taking these kinds of drugs.

Self-defense: Get a *creatine kinase* (CK) blood test to detect muscle damage, even if you don't have muscle pain. It's usually done four

to six weeks after starting statin therapy and again three to six months later. After that, it should be repeated annually or every other year if the original numbers are good.

INCREASE IN LIVER ENZYMES

This can lead to liver toxicity and permanent liver damage. The risk increases when a statin is combined with another cholesterol-lowering drug, such as Lopid or *niacin* (Niacor).

Self-defense: A blood test to check on liver function six to 12 weeks after starting statin therapy. Subsequent tests usually are given at six months, one year and every year or two thereafter. Mild increases in liver enzymes are not a problem—but more severe increases require discontinuing the drug.

TO REDUCE SIDE EFFECTS...

●**Take the lowest possible dose.** In many cases, lowering the dose eliminates side effects. Ask your doctor about combining a low-dose statin with *ezetimibe* (Zetia), a drug that inhibits cholesterol absorption in the intestine.

Example: One of my patients had muscle pain when taking 40 milligrams (mg) of *simvastatin* (Zocor). I lowered the dose to 10 mg and combined it with Zetia. This eliminated side effects and achieved the same cholesterol reduction.

●**Change drugs if necessary.** The statins with the greatest cholesterol-lowering effects, such as *atorvastatin* (Lipitor) and *rosuvastatin* (Crestor), may cause more side effects than "weaker" drugs. Switching to another statin may eliminate side effects. *Pravastatin* (Pravachol) seems to cause fewer side effects than other statins.

●**Don't drink grapefruit juice.** It increases drug concentrations in the body as well as the risk of side effects. Even waiting to take the medication for up to 24 hours after drinking grapefruit juice doesn't prevent an interaction. Avoid grapefruit products altogether while taking statins.

●**Supplement with coenzyme Q10 (co-Q10).** Statins may deplete this natural antioxidant, causing muscle pain or fatigue. I advise 50 mg of coQ10 daily when taking statins.

•**Lower cholesterol naturally with oat bran, psyllium and fruits and vegetables.** These foods will allow you to take the lowest possible dose of statins.

Faster Treatment In the ER

For faster emergency treatment, call 911 so that you arrive by ambulance or other emergency medical vehicle, rather than by car.

Recent study: Patients with chest pain who drove to emergency rooms arrived sooner than those who waited for emergency medical services (EMS). But the EMS group received initial treatment 26 minutes earlier than those using private transportation.

Reason: EMS workers start treatment as soon as they get to the patient.

Mohamud Daya, MD, associate professor of emergency medicine, Oregon Health & Science University, Portland.

On-Line Hospital Evaluations

On-line hospital evaluations can be useful, but sites collect and sort data differently, so do not rely solely on any one site. *The following sites offer free access to their rankings...*

•**US News & World Report** at *www.usnews. com* has ranked hospitals for 15 years. The rankings are based on surveys of doctors.

•**The Leapfrog Group** at *www.leapfrog group.org* gets its data from hospitals and also does its own surveys.

•**Health Grades, Inc.** at *www.healthgrades. com* uses a five-star grading system based primarily on Medicare mortality data.

•**US Department of Health & Human Services** at *www.hospitalcompare.hhs.gov/hospi tal/home2.asp* offers a Centers for Medicare & Medicaid Services program comparing hospital data in your area.

Hospitals' Best-Kept Secret

Charles B. Inlander, a health-care consultant and president of the nonprofit People's Medical Society, a consumer health advocacy group in Allentown, PA. He is the author of more than 20 books on consumer health issues, including *Take This Book to the Hospital with You: A Consumer Guide to Surviving Your Hospital Stay* (St. Martin's).

It's been said that the most dangerous place to be when you are sick is in a hospital. In recent years, reliable studies have revealed an alarming rate of surgical, medication and diagnostic errors in our nation's more than 5,000 hospitals. In fact, almost 100,000 patients die every year from hospital negligence or error, according to a study published in *The Journal of the American Medical Association*.

That figure does *not* include deaths and illnesses associated with hospital-acquired infections, known as *nosocomial infections*. Some of the more common hospital-acquired infections are due to staph infections (including a type of pneumonia)...sepsis (a bloodstream infection) ...and urinary-tract infections. More than 2 million hospitalized patients acquire a nosocomial infection each year, according to the Centers for Disease Control and Prevention (CDC). At least 90,000 of these people die from the infections. But there is no federal law that requires hospitals to disclose infection rates.

Fortunately, up to half of these infections are preventable. *Here's how to protect yourself...*

•**Insist that all staff wash their hands before touching you.** Hospital infections are spread most often through physical contact. Yet the CDC notes that more than 60% of hospital personnel do not wash their hands frequently or thoroughly enough. Hand-washing applies to all nurses who come in and out of your room, food-service personnel who touch items in your room other than your tray and clean-up crews who handle equipment that you might touch. Items that are frequently contaminated include

35

telephones, water cups and serving dishes. Do not forget doctors, who are notorious for *not* washing their hands when making routine bedside visits. For ease and convenience, many hospitals now have alcohol-based hand-sanitizer dispensers in the halls outside patients' rooms.

● **Demand fresh gloves.** Studies have found that some hospital staff wear the same gloves all day. Insist that any personnel who enter your room with gloves on change them in your presence. Also insist that they wash their hands before putting on the new gloves. This is the only way to avoid cross-contamination.

● **Monitor your catheter.** A catheter is a hollow, flexible tube that's inserted into a body cavity to allow the passage of fluids. Backed-up or dirty catheters are a common cause of hospital infections. Ask the nurse to check on your catheter to make sure that it's flowing properly each time he/she enters your room.

● **Report any problems with incisions.** Whether you had a surgical incision or a shunt inserted into your skin to receive chemotherapy, an infection can develop. Many patients feel these infections before they become visible. Let your nurse know if you detect pain or discomfort around or under the incision site. Don't be shy. It might save your life.

More from Charles Inlander...

In the Hospital? You Will Need This Type Of Doctor

Chances are you have never heard of a *hospitalist*. But if you have been in the hospital in the past five years, you may have been seen by one.

Hospitalists are primary care doctors who work strictly with hospitalized patients. They are employed by the hospital, and their job is to be your primary care doctor while you're hospitalized. They are fully trained, licensed doctors who understand and know the problems that can confront a hospitalized patient. If a new problem develops while you're in the hospital, such as an infection or an unexpected fever, the hospitalist is called in. There are 8,000 hospitalists in the US, and most hospitals now have at least one on staff. Many of the largest teaching hospitals employ more than a dozen.

The need for hospitalists emerged about a decade ago when outpatient procedures became more popular and fewer patients needed hospital care. Primary care doctors, such as family physicians, general practitioners and internists, found that they had fewer patients in the hospital at any given time. In fact, 20 years ago, the average primary care doctor spent 40% of his/her work time dropping in on hospitalized patients, compared with 10% of work time today. According to data from a recent Society of Hospital Medicine conference, most primary care physicians have fewer than two patients in the hospital at any given time. It's not efficient for these doctors to visit so few hospitalized patients, especially when they could be in their offices seeing many more patients. That's why primary care doctors like hospitalists. Hospitalists also are more readily available when problems come up. Most hospitals employing them usually have one physically present 24 hours a day, seven days a week.

Hospitalists have become increasingly popular with hospitals because of their knowledge regarding hospital-related health problems. Most nonhospital-based primary care doctors are very slow to recognize a hospital-acquired infection, a problem affecting up to 10% of all hospitalized patients. Hospitalists are better not only at identifying these infections, but also at treating them.

Hospitalists have generated some controversy. They are supposed to regularly advise family physicians on patients' status to ensure a smooth transition home, but there have been instances where this has not occurred. Cost also can be an issue. Hospitalists were expected to save insurance carriers the cost of unneeded hospital visits by patients' primary care doctors, but now there is concern that this new breed of doctor actually may be driving up some costs because he orders more tests and prescribes more therapies, such as medications. Fortunately, these practices translate into better patient care.

Because hospitals house the sickest patients, it's important to have physicians who spend 100% of their time helping them. Hospitalists are a logical solution.

Also from Charles Inlander...

A Shortage of Nurses Means More Mistakes

Not long ago, I received a letter from a man who complained that he never saw the same nurse twice during the five days he was recently hospitalized. During one of those days, the consequences were almost deadly when a nurse came into his room to give him a medicine to which he was allergic. Because he had never seen the nurse—nor was he scheduled to receive any pills—he refused to take the medication. She later returned and apologized, telling him that because of the hospital's nurse shortage, she had been assigned to work a floor that was new to her and she had entered the wrong room.

The nurse shortage in the US has become serious. The American College of Healthcare Executives recently found that 72% of hospital CEOs reported nurse shortages at their facilities. The effect of this shortage is felt most acutely in hospitals, assisted-living facilities and nursing homes. A study in *The New England Journal of Medicine* found that 53% of doctors cited the nurse shortage as a leading cause of medical errors. Even so, nursing-school enrollments are not large enough to fill the gap anytime soon. *Here's how to protect yourself...*

●**Ask about nurse-to-patient ratios.** In hospitals, there should be at least one registered nurse (RN) at all times for every six medical or surgical patients. But, in the intensive-care unit, emergency room and labor/delivery area, the ratio should be one RN for every two patients. Skilled-nursing homes should have an RN on duty at all times and at least one licensed practical nurse (LPN) for every 10 patients. Assisted-living facilities always should have at least one RN on site and an adequate number of aides to meet the medical needs that arise. Call the nurse administrator at the hospital, assisted-living facility or nursing home and ask for their ratios. If a facility exceeds the numbers listed here, consider finding an alternative.

●**Keep a log.** Because you may not see the same nurse very often, it is important for you or a family member to keep track of your care. Keep a list of the medications your doctor has ordered and the times you should receive them. When you're administered the drugs, record the times and dosage in a log. Write down the time and results when someone takes your blood pressure or temperature. Include the name of every nurse or aide who treats you and note the date, time and what he/she did. Keeping your own record lowers the chance of error.

●**When in doubt, just say *no*!** Refuse to take or do anything you're not sure about. This includes medicines and tests, especially if presented by someone you've never seen. Ask for your doctor's confirmation.

●**Call for help.** If a nurse is not responding to your call button and you need immediate help, pick up the phone and ask the operator to connect you to the nursing station on your floor. Someone *will* answer—say that you need assistance at once.

Finally from Charles Inlander...

Read This Before Having Outpatient Surgery

Very few areas in medicine have changed more radically in the last 20 years than the location where people go for surgery. More than 1,500 different surgical procedures that previously were performed only on an in-patient basis, including the removal of cataracts and colon polyps, now can be performed on outpatients who enter a facility in the morning and leave later the same day. Although outpatient surgeries are cheaper and often safer (largely because of significantly lower infection rates), a successful outcome typically depends on the type of outpatient facility you choose for your procedure.

Key points to consider...

●**Doctors' offices.** You are not paying the high overhead associated with a hospital or freestanding surgical center, so procedures performed in a doctor's office can cost up to 50% less than those in the other settings—but they come with greater risk. That's because doctors' offices are not accredited by any private or government oversight agency. In fact, under current state laws, any licensed doctor (physicians must be licensed by the state in which they practice) can perform just about any surgical procedure in his/her own office without getting any special approval. Because of this, insurance companies and Medicare may not pay for a procedure performed in a physician's office. Check to see if your insurer will pay for the procedure you need with the doctor you are considering. If not, ask the company for a list of offices that are approved for payment.

●**Freestanding surgical centers.** Often called "surgi-centers," these usually are a better choice than a doctor's office. These facilities, often independently owned by physicians or by entrepreneurs, tend to be better regulated. Most states require them to be licensed, usually by the state health department. That means they are inspected and must meet certain standards for safety, infection control and other quality-related factors. These centers also can be accredited by the Accreditation Association for Ambulatory Healthcare or the Joint Commission on the Accreditation of Healthcare Organizations. Although accreditation is voluntary for surgi-centers, it's smart to choose a facility that is accredited by one of these organizations.

●**Hospital-owned outpatient facility.** This generally is the best place to have outpatient surgery. Since it is a part of a hospital, it must meet the same regulatory standards and accreditation requirements as the rest of the hospital (even if it is not located at the hospital site). These standards and requirements are much more strict and comprehensive than for other settings. Unlike a physician's office or a surgi-center, hospital-owned outpatient facilities will collect important data, such as infection rates. Many hospitals now are making that information publicly available. Ask for the annual surgical and outpatient report. If it's not available, consider another facility.

Secrets to Successful Surgery

David Sherer, MD, physician director of risk management for the Mid-Atlantic Permanente Medical Group in Rockville, MD, and a board-certified anesthesiologist in clinical practice at Falls Church Ambulatory Surgery Center in Falls Church, VA. He is the author of *Dr. David Sherer's Hospital Survival Guide: 100+ Ways to Make Your Hospital Stay Safe and Comfortable* (Claren).

Anyone who has just set foot in a hospital knows how busy doctors and nurses are. That's why it's critical for patients to understand—and monitor—their own care.

Some commonly overlooked ways to ensure a successful surgery…

●**Supply good records.** List all of your current medications, with the dosages you take. Also list all vitamins and herbal remedies you consume, any allergies or other conditions you have and emergency contact phone numbers for both doctors and family members.*

If you have an implantable cardioverter defibrillator, list the brand, model number and when the battery was last changed. And, if you wear a pacemaker, make copies of your pacemaker card. Developed by the manufacturer of your pacemaker, it lists the make and model of your device, battery life, a telephone number for questions and other essential information.

Copy all this data, and give it to your primary care doctor, your surgeon and any other doctor who treats you. Also ask that it be stapled to the front of your chart.

Smart idea: Keep an extra copy in your wallet or purse, so it can be accessed easily if you ever wind up in an emergency room.

●**Ask for local anesthetic before getting an intravenous (IV) line or blood test.** Routine procedures, such as starting IV lines, need not be painful, but almost all hospitals fail to administer a small amount of lidocaine with a tiny needle to patients who are especially sensitive to the discomfort. Allergies to lidocaine are exceedingly rare, so it makes no sense *not* to numb the skin.

*Some drugs and herbs may need to be stopped before surgery. Check with your doctor.

During your surgical consultation, ask what the hospital policy is regarding lidocaine. Often, nurses have not been fully trained in this pain-control technique. If this occurs—or you're concerned about having a lidocaine allergy—ask for a prescription for EMLA (eutectic mixture of local anesthetic), a topical anesthetic. One hour before your operation, rub a pea-sized dab on the inside crooks of both arms and on the tops of both hands. It takes approximately one hour for EMLA to work.

Caution: Do not use EMLA on open cuts.

●**Insist on paper or plastic surgical tape to secure bandages and IV lines.** All hospitals carry paper or plastic hypoallergenic tape, which is much gentler on skin than silk tape. You usually won't get it unless you ask for it.

●**Inform your anesthesiologist if you sleep with two pillows.** *This habit could be a sign of...*

●Sleep apnea (a disorder in which breathing is temporarily interrupted during sleep). If you suffer from this condition, your tongue or the soft tissues of your throat can fall against the back of your airway and obstruct your ability to breathe during anesthesia.

In this case, your anesthesiologist might alter the method of anesthesia by performing a semi-awake intubation, in which a patient is sedated but awake so his/her swallowing and breathing reflexes are working.

●Acid reflux (a condition that allows stomach acid and enzymes to flow backward from the stomach into the esophagus). If you have acid reflux, your airway may not have the impulses needed to protect itself from stomach contents.

To prevent the stomach contents from entering the lungs, a breathing tube that delivers anesthesia and protects the airway might be preferable to an anesthesia mask.

●**Ask about having your brain waves monitored while under anesthesia.** Most people have heard horror stories about surgical patients who remain "awake" during anesthesia. Researchers estimate that this occurs once in every 1,000 people who are undergoing anesthesia.

By monitoring a system called the bispectral index (a measure of brain wave activity), doctors can provide an extra level of comfort for patients who are going in for long, difficult surgeries and may have anxiety about being aware during their operation.

●**Make sure your anesthesia team has the drug dantrolene on hand prior to your surgery.** This is especially important if you are having surgery in an outpatient center or a doctor's office. Malignant hyperthermia (dangerous increase of body temperature) occurs when a muscle relaxant is given in combination with certain inhaled anesthetics, such as succinylcholine. This condition happens only once in every 20,000 cases, but your chances of contracting it are greater if you or anyone in your family has a history of heatstroke, high fevers while under anesthesia or neuromuscular diseases, such as muscular dystrophy. If you get malignant hyperthermia, dantrolene, which interrupts the chemical reaction, is the only antidote.

●**Discuss dental work with your anesthesiologist before surgery.** Dentures, bridges and other detachable dental devices can interfere with the anesthesiologist's ability to insert a breathing tube. These dental devices also can become dislodged, swallowed and aspirated into the lung. That's why dental work should always be removed before you are wheeled into the operating room.

If you have an expensive set of veneers or crowns, ask for a plastic dental guard to protect your teeth from getting chipped by the metal laryngoscope, an instrument used to help insert breathing tubes. Every operating room has dental guards, but you often won't be given one unless you ask for it ahead of time.

New OR Trend

Some hospitals are now letting patients' families stay in the operating room during emergencies and major procedures. A growing body of evidence indicates that patients and family members benefit by staying close to one another during stressful situations.

The Wall Street Journal, 200 Liberty St., New York City 10281.

How to Choose the Right Assisted-Living Facility

Robert M. Freedman, Esq., founder and fellow of the National Academy of Elder Law Attorneys. He is a partner in the New York City elder-law firm of Freedman, Fish & Grimaldi, LLP, *www.freedmanandfish.com.*

Assisted-living facilities are the fastest-growing segment of the senior housing market, with more than 800,000 residents in approximately 35,000 facilities across the US. They offer greater independence for residents and lower prices than nursing homes, plus a degree of support not available in retirement communities.

Assisted living is popular with seniors age 80 and older who still are in relatively good health and value their independence but are no longer able to live completely on their own because they can't drive, have trouble walking, etc.

WHAT ASSISTED LIVING OFFERS

Typically, residents live in one-bedroom or studio apartments, though larger accommodations often are available. Each unit comes with a private bath and kitchenette, but many residents eat two or three meals each day in a communal dining room.

Most assisted-living facilities schedule social activities and outings. There might be a shuttle bus to the mall. There even might be a pool and tennis courts on the premises.

While these facilities don't provide the full medical support of a nursing home, most of the rooms are equipped with emergency buttons, so residents can call for help. Some facilities do check in on residents at intervals.

Assisted-living facilities usually offer access to aides for residents who require daily assistance, such as help with bathing, dressing or using the toilet.

WHAT TO LOOK FOR

In most of the states, assisted-living facilities are minimally regulated, with no governmental oversight. *To find the right facility, consider…*

●**Services.** Does the facility offer the support needed?

●**Terms of commitment.** Most facilities will permit the residents to sign up on a month-to-month basis.

●**Social atmosphere.** Talk with a few residents. Are they friendly and of a similar age and energy level?

●**Food quality.** Sample at least two meals.

●**Attractiveness of the rooms.** Is it a pleasant place to live?

●**Activities.** Do the residents seem bored or happy and active?

COST

Room, board and the basic services at an assisted-living facility cost anywhere from $1,800 to $3,500 every month. If you need help with daily living, expect to pay an hourly rate comparable to prevailing rates for home care in the region. That can add up to a few thousand dollars extra per month.

Most residents pay for assisted-living facilities out-of-pocket, but the following may help…

●**Long-term-care insurance policies written in the past five or six years** may include some coverage for assisted living. With an older policy, if the only other alternative is a nursing home and you can show that assisted living is cheaper, the insurance company might pay for the expense.

●**Medicaid might be available to seniors who have limited resources.** Check with your state's Medicaid department for details. A list of state Medicaid Web sites is available at *http://cms.hhs.gov/medicaid/stwebsites.asp.*

●**Tax deductions.** The portion of the cost of assisted living attributable to health care is tax deductible, though the part attributable to housing costs is not. Ask the assisted-living facility to provide a cost breakdown for you.

RESOURCES

●**Assisted Living Federation of America,** 703-691-8100, *www.alfa.org.*

●**National Center for Assisted Living,** 202-842-4444, *www.ncal.org.*

3

Common Health Problems, Simple Solutions

The Ultimate Cold and Flu Survival Guide

Ninety million of Americans will get a cold or the flu each year—and since most people do get more than one cold, the actual number of cases approaches 1 *billion*.

Colds and influenza are upper-respiratory infections affecting the linings of the nose, throat, sinuses and bronchial passages. Influenza may affect the lungs as well. Cold and flu symptoms are somewhat different, but in both cases, the infection will usually clear up within about one to two weeks.

There has always been a lot of confusion regarding the causes and treatments of colds and flu. *Jack Gwaltney, Jr., MD, a leading expert in infectious diseases, answers some common questions below...*

●**Is there such a thing as a "cold season"?** Yes. Colds do not disappear in the spring or summer, but they do occur more often in the cold months. We don't know exactly why.

One theory involves school schedules. Children typically have not been exposed to many viruses, and their hygiene is often not good. This makes them more susceptible to colds.

When children go back to school in the fall, the viruses get passed back and forth—and, of course, are taken home to infect others.

●**Does bundling up in cold weather protect us from getting colds?** I'm afraid not. The only way to catch a cold is from someone who's infected. If you go outside on a freezing day wearing a T-shirt, you're no more likely to get sick than someone who is bundled up for arctic weather.

●**How are colds and flu transmitted?** Most colds are spread by hand contact. The virus—

Jack M. Gwaltney, Jr., MD, professor emeritus in the department of internal medicine and former head of the division of epidemiology and virology at the University of Virginia School of Medicine in Charlottesville. He has authored more than 200 scientific studies on colds and influenza.

including rhinovirus, a family of cold viruses that's responsible for about half of cold cases—gets inside the nose, replicates and causes an increase in nasal secretions.

If you come into contact with these secretions—for example, by shaking hands with someone who has a cold who has touched his/ her nose or by touching a doorknob that he just touched and then rubbing your own nose or eyes—you'll probably become infected.

The cold virus can live on an object for up to three days, but the amount of virus declines over time. Cold and flu viruses also may cause infection in a person when they travel through the air via coughs and sneezes.

●**When is a cold most contagious?** As soon as you develop a dripping nose, sneezing and other symptoms, and continuing for about three days after that. If you still have symptoms after three days, the risk of spreading the virus is minimal because the amount of the virus in secretions will decrease significantly. It is sometimes reported that people are contagious before the symptoms even appear. That's incorrect. It's only when the virus grows in the nose and triggers the release of nasal secretions that you're able to spread it. If you're not having symptoms, you're not contagious.

●**Is hand-washing really a good defense against colds?** Washing your hands is helpful if you've been in contact with someone who has a cold. It will wash away viruses before they enter your nose or eyes.

●**Do antigerm soaps, wipes and cleansers kill cold germs?** No. They kill bacteria but are not totally effective against cold viruses. Hand-washing rinses viruses off the hands. There may be hand products in the future that kill viruses on the hands over a period of hours, but they're not available now. Iodine solutions will maintain antiviral activity on your hands for several hours, but they're impractical to use.

●**How can I tell the difference between a cold and flu?** There's a lot of variability in cold and flu symptoms. About 25% of flu cases are no more serious than a cold. In those instances, you wouldn't know which you had.

In general, flu is more severe. You'll probably have fever (above 101°F), muscle aches,

heavy coughing and severe fatigue. Typically, flu symptoms come on suddenly. With a cold, you will *not* have a fever. You'll have congestion, a runny nose and possibly a cough. The symptoms get worse over a period of days.

Flu season usually runs from late December through March and tends to infect a large number of people in a community at the same time.

●**Is it important to know whether I have a cold or the flu?** Yes. There are flu treatments—but they must be taken within 48 hours of the onset of symptoms to be effective. The antiviral prescription drugs *amantadine* (Symmetrel), *zanamivir* (Relenza) and *oseltamivir* (Tamiflu) can dramatically reduce the severity and duration of symptoms.

Smart idea: Call your doctor and describe your symptoms. If your doctor suspects the flu, ask him to phone in a prescription. If you wait for an office visit, it might be too late for the drugs to work.

●**When do I need to see the doctor for a cold or the flu?** Most colds last about one week. If your symptoms aren't improving by then, see your doctor. You may have developed sinusitis and need antibiotics.

Extended bouts of the flu can damage the lining of your bronchial tubes. This can lead to a secondary bacterial infection, such as pneumonia. Symptoms include fever and pain in the chest with cough.

●**Which over-the-counter cold remedies should I take?** There are hundreds of cold remedies to choose from. *Two best choices…*

●A first-generation antihistamine, such as *chlorpheniramine* (Chlor-Trimeton) or *clemastine* (Tavist). These will dry up nasal secretions and pass through the blood-brain barrier, affecting the sneeze center in the brain. They also may help with coughing.

The newer, nonsedating antihistamines are not as effective because they don't pass through the blood-brain barrier.

●Nonsteroidal anti-inflammatory drugs or NSAIDs, such as *ibuprofen* (Advil). They reduce headache, cough and malaise.

Start taking an antihistamine and an NSAID as soon as you think you feel a cold coming on. Keep taking them until your cold symptoms are gone.

If you need additional relief: Take a decongestant, such as *pseudoephedrine* (Sudafed). It will shrink the *turbinates,* structures in the nose that swell and cause congestion when you have a cold.

●**Why isn't there a vaccine for colds as there is for flu?** There are too many cold viruses—more than 100 rhinoviruses alone—to protect against all of them. You would have to take a really big shot to protect against all possible cold viruses.

●**Does regular exercise prevent colds?** We're not sure. In our studies at the University of Virginia over the years, we've exposed hundreds of healthy volunteers to cold viruses in the laboratory. About 95% of them become infected, including those who exercise regularly.

However, only about 75% of those who get infected with a cold virus go on to develop symptoms. It's possible that exercise makes people less likely to get sick when they've been exposed to the virus, but this hasn't been definitely proven.

●**Is there any truth to the old saying that you need to "feed a cold and starve a fever"?** No. It's just a saying with no scientific evidence to support it. You obviously don't want to starve yourself when you are sick with a cold or the flu—but you don't have to eat if you don't feel like it.

It is helpful to drink fluids when you have a cold. This helps keep mucous membranes hydrated and makes you feel more comfortable.

For more information, go to *www.common cold.org.* I am scientific editor of this Web site, which provides up-to-date information on the prevention and treatment of colds.

ARE YOU AT RISK FOR COLDS AND FLU?

If you answer *yes* to any of these questions, you may be at increased risk for colds and flu.

●**Are you a smoker?**

●**Are you in frequent contact with people who are ill?**

●**Do you work indoors in close proximity to other people?**

●**Do you forget to wash your hands with warm, soapy water** before touching your eyes or nose?

●**Do you consume more than a few alcoholic drinks on most days?**

●**Do you have a chronic illness** affecting the heart or lungs?

More from Dr. Jack Gwaltney, Jr....

Which Cold Remedies Work, Which Don't?

Some traditional cold remedies don't work at all, while others might make a difference. *A review of three popular remedies...*

●**Echinacea.** My colleagues and I examined more than 100 studies on echinacea, including nine placebo-controlled studies. In those that were performed with acceptable scientific rigor, echinacea did not appear to reduce cold symptoms or shorten the duration of colds.

Verdict: Don't bother.

●**Vitamin C.** Many people believe that taking supplemental vitamin C will prevent colds. Not true. Those who take vitamin C, even in higher doses, will get just as many colds as those who don't. However, high doses of vitamin C (about 2 grams [g] daily) can slightly dry nasal secretions when you already have a cold.

Verdict: Worth a try. Just don't count on it for cold prevention.

●**Chicken soup.** Some studies have shown that chicken soup reduces congestion and increases immune-cell activity.

Verdict: Give it a try.

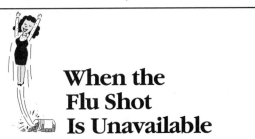

When the Flu Shot Is Unavailable

If you can't get a flu shot during the fall, antiviral supplements may be your next best option. To help ward off the flu virus, adults should ask their doctors about taking 1,200 milligrams (mg) a day of *N-acetyl cysteine,* an amino acid that has been shown to sharply reduce the incidence of symptomatic flu, and 250 to 500 mg per day of *beta glucan,* a powerful natural immune booster that works best when combined with 500 mg of vitamin C. Take these supplements for the duration of the flu season (from fall to spring).

Robert Rountree, MD, a physician in private practice in Boulder, CO. He is coauthor of *Smart Medicine for a Healthier Child* (Avery).

Natural Cold Fighters

Mark A. Stengler, ND, a naturopathic physician and founder and director of the La Jolla Whole Health Clinic, La Jolla, CA. He is also author of the newsletter *Bottom Line/ Natural Healing with Dr. Mark Stengler* and has written many books, including *The Natural Physician's Healing Therapies* (Bottom Line Books). Both of these publications are available at *www.bottomlinesecrets.com.*

Who hasn't been knocked for a loop by a cold? No matter how often we wash our hands and avoid people with colds, most of us will get sick sometime during the winter. *Below, naturopathic physician Mark Stengler, ND, author of* The Natural Physician's Healing Therapies, *tells us what we can do about it…*

•**Drink warm ginger tea**—eight ounces every two waking hours. Ginger eases congestion of the upper respiratory tract (nose and throat) and sinuses. Traditional Medicinals is a good store brand, or buy fresh ginger and boil four inches of the peeled root in six cups of water for 10 minutes. (If you can't stand the taste, warm peppermint tea is an alternative.)

•**Take lomatium root.** Available in most health-food stores, lomatium is thought to prevent viruses from replicating and stimulate the immune system. It is more potent than other popular supplements (vitamin C, zinc, echinacea) when you already have a cold. Take 30 drops of the tincture form every two to three waking hours.

•**Soak your feet each evening in warm water for 10 minutes.** Dry them, then put on cotton socks that have been placed in cold water and wrung out. Cover with dry wool or cotton socks, and leave on for 30 minutes or longer. It sounds crazy, but the contrast in hot and cold diverts blood flow away from the head and to the feet, reducing congestion. It also stimulates white blood cell activity, which improves immunity.

•**Get adequate sleep**—eight to 10 hours a night—to allow your immune system to recharge. Studies indicate that lack of sleep decreases immunity.

Rotten colds are not inevitable. Don't let the virus win!

More from Dr. Mark Stengler…

Natural Remedies That Fight Fever

Holistic treatments work with the healing properties of a fever to help fight infection or injury.* *The following remedies are available at health-food stores…*

•**Ferrum phosphoricum** is a homeopathic remedy that promotes the beneficial effects of fever. *Take two pellets of a 30C potency four times daily with* one *of these herbal remedies…*

•**Ginger** is especially helpful for those who have a sore throat and chills. Take a 500-milligram (mg) capsule or take 2 mililiters (ml) of the tincture with six ounces of water four times daily. Even better, drink a cup of fresh ginger tea four times daily.

•**Elderberry** is excellent for flu-related fever. Take 10 ml of the tincture with six ounces of water three times daily.

*Before trying a natural remedy, check with your physician if you are taking medication.

Wash Away Allergies

Allergy sufferers should take a shower after spending any time outdoors during pollen season. Pollen can collect on your skin and hair, prolonging your exposure and allergic reaction to it.

Also: Be sure to wash your hair to remove excess pollen, so it won't fall onto your pillow.

Symptoms of hay fever include sneezing… stuffy nose…and itchy eyes.

Worst offenders: Trees in the spring and grasses in the summer.

Helpful: The hours between mid- and late-afternoon (when pollen levels are lowest) are the best times for outdoor activities.

Gillian Shepherd, MD, clinical associate professor of medicine at Weill Medical College of Cornell University, New York City.

Help for Chronic Sinus Infections

Jordan S. Josephson, MD, attending physician at Manhattan Eye, Ear and Throat Hospital and a sinus specialist and functional endoscopic sinus surgeon in private practice, both in New York City.

Sinus inflammation or infection (sinusitis) typically begins with a cold or an allergy attack that impedes the normal flow of mucus. Mucus buildup creates a favorable environment for infection to set in. Patients who decrease their congestion promptly often can avoid sinusitis or at least heal it more quickly.

However: *Few people—and even some doctors—fail to recognize that other, less obvious causes can trigger sinusitis…*

FUNGUS

About 92% of patients with chronic sinusitis (lasting 12 weeks or longer) have fungus in their nasal mucus. New research suggests that the majority of patients with nonviral sinusitis have both fungal and bacterial infections. The majority of fungal infections are believed to be due to household mold or mold found in public places, such as restaurants, gyms, movie theaters, etc.

To determine the type of infection, doctors should take a history, give a physical exam and, in some cases, order a computed tomography (CT) scan and/or a sinus culture. Antibiotics and/or antifungal medications, such as *itraconazole* (Sporanox), will clear the initial infection in about two weeks in patients with acute sinusitis (lasting for less than 12 weeks). Patients who have chronic sinusitis may need to take the drugs for up to 12 weeks. Even in the absence of infection, a mold allergy can cause congestion that leads to sinusitis.

Helpful: Be vigilant about inspecting your home for mold and remove it promptly.

Also: Clean your car. The combination of heat and trapped moisture provides an ideal environment for mold growth.

NASAL POLYPS

These benign tumors in the sinus cavity can be as small as the tip of a ballpoint pen or as large as a grape. Even small polyps can obstruct sinus openings, which can allow sinusitis to develop. Polyps are diagnosed with a CT scan or endoscopy, an outpatient procedure during which a flexible, lighted tube is used to examine the nasal passages.

Most polyps are triggered by inflammation, usually due to allergies, infection or exposure to smoke or other pollutants, such as household chemicals or dust. Once polyps have formed, they can block the sinus openings and trigger more inflammation—which can lead to even more polyps.

To reduce nasal polyps, you must break the inflammatory cycle. You may need nasal steroid sprays or oral steroids, such as *prednisone,* to decrease inflammation…and antibiotics and/or oral or spray antifungal drugs, to eliminate an underlying infection. If you suffer from allergies, your physician may recommend that you take antihistamines.

Polyps that trigger sinusitis may need to be surgically removed if drugs do not help. This is an outpatient procedure that can be performed with local anesthesia. Polyps tend to recur, so medication still must be taken to control them.

DEVIATED SEPTUM

If the wall between the nostrils (the septum) is crooked because of injury or an anatomic abnormality, it can create air turbulence that irritates the sinus membranes and impedes normal drainage.

Warning signs: In addition to recurrent/persistent sinus infections, you may have difficulty breathing through your nose…snore loudly…or wake up with a dry mouth and chapped lips due to nighttime mouth breathing.

Patients with a deviated septum can try to prevent sinusitis by taking measures to reduce nasal congestion.

Helpful: Irrigate the nose with a premixed saline solution, sold in pharmacies, to reduce congestion and promote sinus drainage. Or just make your own—it's easy and cheaper. Sterilize eight ounces of distilled water by boiling it briefly on the stove, then let it cool to room temperature. Add one-quarter teaspoon of salt to the water.

Important: Be sure to measure accurately. Too much or too little salt can damage mucus-producing cells in the nose.

Once or twice daily, use a Neti pot, sold in health-food stores, to pour the fluid into one nostril until it runs out the other nostril. Repeat the procedure on the other side.

If the above strategy doesn't help, you may need surgery to repair the septum. It's an outpatient procedure performed with local anesthesia and usually takes about one hour.

NOSE BLOWING

Blowing your nose hard can force mucus, and the germs it contains, into the sinus cavities.

Helpful: Blow just one nostril at a time, by pressing one closed, then the other. This will cause less pressure than blowing both nostrils at the same time.

Also, inhale deeply so that the mucus travels into your throat, where you can swallow it or spit it out. Most people don't like to do this, but it won't hurt you and does help move mucus and prevent sinusitis.

IS IT A COLD OR SINUSITIS?

See a doctor if you suspect you have sinusitis. The symptoms are similar to those caused by colds but not exactly the same. *You may have sinusitis if...*

●**Mucus is white, yellow or green.**

●**You feel persistent pressure or pain around the nose, eyes, face and/or teeth.**

●**You breathe through your mouth and snore when you sleep.**

●**Symptoms last longer than one week.**

Natural Therapy Trio for Health Problems

John Sherman, PhD, a Monterey, CA–based registered occupational therapist for 32 years and a certified shiatsu (Japanese pressure-point therapy) practitioner for 13 years. He is also author of *Do-It-Yourself Natural Health* (New-Found Therapies).

If you're tired of taking drugs to treat common, everyday symptoms, there is a new approach that maximizes the effectiveness of well-known, time-honored alternative therapies. When used in combination, acupressure, aromatherapy and herbs* have a unique complementary effect that boosts the effectiveness of each individual therapy.

●**Acupressure**—pressure applied to meridians in the body that closely correspond to the neural pathways—triggers endorphins, enkaphalins and other pain-relieving chemicals in the brain.

To perform acupressure therapy, apply moderate pressure with the pads of your index and middle fingers or your thumbs to each of the designated areas.

●**Aromatherapy** stimulates the limbic system in the brain, the control center for our emotions. By affecting heart rate, stress levels and hormone balance, it enhances the healing effects of acupressure.

To use aromatherapy, inhale herbal essences directly from the bottle...spray into the air or onto a lightbulb...or prepare a cool compress by putting a few drops of an essence into one cup of cold water, immersing a small towel or washcloth and then wringing it out.

●**Herbs** work not only by treating a particular symptom, as conventional drugs do, but also by boosting the immune system and the body's own healing processes with fewer side effects than most drugs. Although most of the recommended herbs can be taken in tea form, we have described lesser-known ways to take them. The herbs listed in this article can be purchased at most health-food stores.

*Consult your doctor or an herbal specialist before taking herbs. Pregnant and lactating women should avoid most herbs.

CONSTIPATION

Acupressure points: Perform acupressure on the following parts of the body for up to one minute each, three times daily...

Aromatherapy: Lavender or geranium. Prepare a cool compress with two or three drops of lavender or geranium oil and leave on your face for a few minutes. Also try putting a few drops of lavender oil into the bath.

Helpful herb: Ginger. Three times daily, drink 10 to 15 drops of ginger tincture mixed in one-half cup of hot water.

EYESTRAIN

Acupressure points: Perform acupressure on these locations around the eye for up to one minute each, three times daily.

Aromatherapy: Orange blossom. Inhale directly from the bottle or spritz into the air.

Helpful herb: Mix 10 to 20 drops of lavender extract in one cup of warm water and apply to a compress. Wring out and wear over eyes for five to 10 minutes.

FATIGUE

Acupressure points: Perform acupressure on the following parts of the body for up to one minute each, three times daily...

Aromatherapy: Strawberry or peppermint. Inhale from the bottle or spritz into the air.

Helpful herb: St.-John's-wort. The extract can be taken in one 350-milligram (mg) capsule, three times a day. Or take 30 to 50 drops of liquid extract, mixed into four ounces of water, four times a day.*

*Consult your physician before combining St.-John's-wort with any prescription drug, and avoid excessive exposure to sunlight.

JOINT PAIN

Acupressure points: Perform acupressure on these body parts for up to one minute each, three times daily...

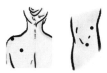

Aromatherapy: Eucalyptus or juniper. Apply the essential oils with fingertips and massage into the skin to stimulate circulation and provide a cooling effect.

Helpful herb: Cat's claw. Take one 175-mg capsule of dried cat's claw extract, twice a day, with water between meals.

Acupressure illustrations by Shawn Banner.

Vinegar Cures For Leg Cramps And More

Jamison Starbuck, ND, a naturopathic physician in family practice and a lecturer at the University of Montana, both in Missoula. She is a past president of the American Association of Naturopathic Physicians and a contributing editor to *The Alternative Advisor: The Complete Guide to Natural Therapies and Alternative Treatments* (Time Life).

For thousands of years, vinegar has held distinction as a medicinal, culinary and household aid. In 400 BC, Hippocrates recommended drinking a vinegar solution to reduce symptoms of the common cold. "Thieves' vinegar" is reputed to date from the 14th century, when thieves would wash with vinegar to protect themselves from the Plague when robbing the homes of helpless sufferers. In America, vinegar has been used since the time of the Revolutionary War to clean wounds.

More recently, vinegar is making a comeback as a medical treatment and a gourmet culinary specialty. Proponents tout vinegar as a cure for all types of ailments, including life-threatening conditions, such as cancer, high blood pressure, kidney disease and asthma. Although these claims are false, vinegar is, in fact, a very useful natural medicine. *Because it's safe, inexpensive and readily available, vinegar is worth trying for the following conditions...*

●**Arthritis.** There's no scientific evidence, but anecdotal accounts do support the use of an apple-cider vinegar solution to help relieve arthritis pain. Drink a glass of water with two teaspoons of apple-cider vinegar and two teaspoons of honey three times a day.

●**Foot odor.** To kill odor-causing bacteria, soak feet in a solution of one part vinegar (any type) and four parts hot water nightly for 15 minutes for one week. The feet should be immersed up to the ankles. Rinse with cold water at the end of the soak. Repeat this routine as it is needed.

●**Fungal infections.** Men with jock itch (a red, itching, burning rash in the groin area) will find relief by applying a mild vinegar solution one or two times daily. Make up a solution of two tablespoons of white vinegar to 12 ounces warm water...pour it over the whole groin area at the end of a shower. Do not rinse off...simply blot dry. Five days of this treatment should be adequate. For other fungal infections, such as athlete's foot or mild nail fungus, soak the affected body part in the same type of solution used for jock itch for five minutes daily until the infection is gone.

●**Leg cramps and osteoporosis.** In both women and men, these conditions generally are caused by poor dietary absorption of minerals. To help, add one teaspoon of any type of vinegar to four ounces of water and drink during each meal. As an alternative, simply eat a salad with a vinegar-based dressing whenever you can. Vinegar's acidity will help your digestive tract to draw minerals from your food and make them more available for absorption into your bloodstream.

●**Vaginitis.** Women with bacterial or yeast vaginitis respond well and quickly to treatment with vinegar. Douche with a vinegar-and-water solution two times per day for up to five days. Purchase Massengill's premixed plain vinegar douching solution in disposable bottles. Or you can douche with your own solution, using one tablespoon white vinegar per six ounces warm water.

More from Dr. Jamison Starbuck...

Natural Cures for Cold Fingers and Toes

Cold extremities are not always just about the weather. Whenever a patient of mine complains of cold hands and feet, I consider whether it could be related to poor thyroid function, anemia or Raynaud's disease (a condition in which small arteries, usually in the fingers or toes, constrict in response to exposure to cold). Cold extremities are a primary symptom of all these conditions. Cold hands and feet can also be a secondary symptom of other conditions that affect circulation. These include rheumatoid arthritis, lupus, arterial disease and high blood pressure.

If you have chronically cold hands and feet, see your doctor. Ask for a screening physical and get blood tests—a complete blood count (CBC), as well as a thyroid profile, lipid panel and C-reactive protein test—to determine if your symptoms may be caused by anemia, a thyroid disorder or heart disease.

If your physician finds no physical cause for your problem, here's my advice...

●**Bundle up!** This seems obvious, but you'd be amazed at how many of my patients who complain of cold hands and feet fail to wear proper clothing in cold weather. When you are outdoors, wear thick, lined wool mittens (not gloves), wool socks and insulated shoes or boots. Carry your dress shoes or athletic shoes and socks in a bag, and put them on only after you have arrived inside a heated building. In addition, wear a scarf and a hat.

●**Eat warm food.** In the coldest months, choose soups, stews, roasts and hot cereal over salads, sandwiches and cold cereal. Cooked food already has begun to be broken down, requiring less work than cold food to digest. This leaves your body with more energy to keep you warm.

●**Drink tea.** Although all hot beverages are temporarily warming, caffeine and other components of coffee constrict blood vessels, which promotes cold extremities. Green and black teas contain flavonoids, which promote blood vessel health and support good circulation.

●**Take supplements.** In addition to a multivitamin, be sure to get 50 milligrams (mg) of B-6 as well as 300 mg of magnesium. Vitamin B-6 promotes blood vessel health. And, magnesium helps prevent muscle spasms and encourages blood flow to hands and feet.

●**Keep moving.** Regular aerobic exercise is one of the best cures for poor circulation and cold extremities. Be sure to hydrate by drinking room temperature or warm water.

●**Use cayenne pepper.** Cayenne slightly irritates the skin, bringing blood to the area of the body it touches. To warm your feet, sprinkle one-half teaspoon of ground cayenne into each of your socks. You can experiment with the amount to see if you need more or less. If you have diabetes, do not use cayenne pepper for this purpose.

Duct Tape Really Can Cure Warts

Placing duct tape (or other tape) over warts to get rid of them is not just an old wives' tale. A recent study found that placing tape over warts is more effective at eliminating them than standard medical therapy.

The study: Participants who had warts on fingers, palms, heels or soles of the feet were divided into two groups. One group put tape on warts for six days, then soaked the warts and scraped them with emery boards, waited 12 hours and reapplied the tape, repeating the process. The other group had their warts frozen off by a doctor, which is standard therapy.

Result: After just two months, 85% of those using the tape had gotten rid of their warts, versus only 60% of those who had received the standard freezing treatment.

Dean R. Focht III, MD, fellow, division of gastroenterology, hepatology and nutrition, Cincinnati Children's Hospital Medical Center, OH.

Bunion Relief

Suzanne Levine, DPM, a podiatrist in private practice in New York City and the author of *Your Feet Don't Have to Hurt* (St. Martin's).

If a bunion (an enlargement of the joint at the base and side of the big toe) is severe, it can only be corrected by surgery. However, nonsurgical treatment can relieve painful pressure on less-prominent bunions and stave off the pain and stiffness that can develop. Wearing shoes that are wide and deep enough to accommodate the bunions is key. A podiatrist can provide footwear advice and may prescribe orthotics that will help to position your foot inside the shoe.

Physical therapy sessions in which a therapist manipulates the joint to increase the range of motion can be useful. To duplicate these simple exercises at home, sit with your feet parallel and close together but not touching. Try to bring your big toes together. Hold for 10 seconds, then release and repeat several times a day. Next, attempt to spread all of your toes apart using only your toe muscles. Hold for 10 seconds. Release and repeat several times daily.

Bunion exercise illustrations by Shawn Banner.

 **Simple Exercise For Back Pain Relief**

Ninety percent of people who complain of an aching lower back get relief with a simple exercise called a standing backward bend.

What to do: Stand with your feet shoulder-width apart and tighten your buttocks. Place your hands on your buttocks and then stretch backward as far as you comfortably can. Slowly return to an upright position. Repeat 10 times, trying to bend back a little farther each time. Perform every two hours throughout the day. Frequency can be decreased as pain subsides.

See your doctor if pain worsens, wakes you up at night or if you feel numbness in your hands or feet.

Peggy W. Brill, board-certified clinical specialist in orthopedic physical therapy with a private practice in New York City. She is also the author of Instant Relief—Tell Me Where It Hurts and I'll Tell You What to Do *(Bantam).*

New Help for Back Pain

A recent review of published studies found that chronic low-back pain sufferers who took *nortriptyline* (Aventyl) or *maprotiline* (Ludiomil) experienced less pain and needed fewer painkillers than those taking a placebo.

Theory: The analgesic properties of these antidepressants, which include inhibiting the uptake of the neurotransmitter *norepinephrine,* help relieve back pain.

If you have chronic low-back pain: Talk to your doctor about adding an antidepressant to your painkiller regimen.

Thomas O. Staiger, MD, associate professor of medicine, University of Washington, Seattle.

Common Spice Eases Knee Pain

In a recent study, participants who took two 500-milligram (mg) tablets of *gingerol,* the component that gives ginger its bite, twice a day for three months experienced the same reduction in inflammation as when they took aspirin for three months.

Caution: Ginger can thin blood, so consult your doctor before trying.

Prevention, 33 E. Minor St., Emmaus, PA 18098.

To Minimize Scars...

Scar therapy pads reduce the visibility of scars —but less expensive treatments may work just as well. Scar pads will improve the appearance of raised scars, which may be pink or white or lighter than the surrounding skin. The pads work by applying pressure to the area while holding in moisture.

Alternative: Apply a lubricant, such as petroleum jelly, to a raised scar a few times a day, then rub the scar vigorously for 10 seconds with your finger.

Important: These products and techniques are for raised scars only. They will have no effect on flat, discolored skin...or skin that is indented, such as a pockmark.

To decrease risk of scarring and speed healing, keep wounds covered continuously with an antibiotic ointment, such as Bacitracin.

Neal Schultz, MD, dermatologist in private practice at 1130 Park Ave., New York City 10128.

More from Dr. Neal Schultz...

A Quick and Safe Tan

Spray-on tans are a safe way to get attractive, even color. The spray contains *dihydroxyacetone* (DHA), which stains your skin. Full-body spray-on tans, which are done in salons for about $50, last up to four weeks. First, skin is exfoliated so that excess dead cells are removed, then lotion is sprayed on evenly.

Caution: Spray-on tans provide no sun protection, so even if you look tan, be sure to use sunscreen when outdoors.

And, do not get a spray-on tan if you have any type of skin infection or irritation, such as eczema or psoriasis.

Better Dental Care

To take better care of your teeth, use a toothbrush labeled *extra soft, ultra soft* or *sensi-*

tive. If you can't find one at a grocery store or drugstore, ask your dentist for one.

Best: Brush twice a day, and floss once a day. Limit brushing time to two minutes, and have your dentist or hygienist show you how much pressure to apply—most people brush too hard, harming teeth and gums instead of just cleaning them.

Alan Winter, DDS, a periodontist in private practice, New York City.

Amazing Five-Minute Healers

Mary Capone, a founder of the Living School of Sound, and a teacher of sound, movement and breath healing techniques in Longmont, CO, *www.marycapone.com.* She is a coauthor of *The Five Minute Healer: Self-Healing Techniques for Busy People* (Johnson).

Too, too many people believe they don't have time to learn self-healing techniques to reduce stress. However, research has shown that anyone can achieve greater fitness and well-being in just minutes a day.

Example: Daily stress and anxiety cause us to hunch our shoulders and breathe more shallowly than we should. Take a few minutes each day to sit quietly and breathe deeply. It floods the tissues with oxygen, dispels energy-draining carbon dioxide and reduces levels of "fight or flight" hormones that intensify stress and increase the risk of illness, including heart disease and cancer.

Five additional quick healing techniques for busy people…

SOOTHING SOUNDS

We're surrounded by noise—the rush of traffic, airplanes overhead, humming refrigerators, etc.—all of which can contribute to your anxiety and stress.

Five-minute healer: Listen to relaxing classical music (such as Bach, Vivaldi and Gregorian chants). Or spend a few minutes in nature. Sit by a fountain in a park…listen to the rustling of leaves…tune in to the rushing sounds of wind.

A study at a New York hospital showed that hypertensive patients obtained normal systolic blood pressure after listening to classical music or nature sounds for approximately three minutes. Other studies have shown that soothing sounds can reduce the need for pain medication by up to 30%.

LIGHT THERAPY

Sunlight helps reduce the body's production of *melatonin,* a hormone that can bring on fatigue and depression.

Five-minute healer: Take a short "sun bath." Sit outside for a few minutes each day. You'll feel refreshed and energized.

YOGA

This 6,000-year-old practice will lower blood pressure, lubricate joints and reduce fatigue.

Five-minute healer: *Modified Downward-Facing Dog* (Adho Mukha Svanasana). Stand with your legs about two feet apart facing a desk, table or chair that is a few feet in front of you. Take one deep breath, and bend at the hips, bringing your palms to the chair or table in front of you. Then, adjust your pose by walking your feet back until your arms and spine are totally extended. If your hamstrings are tight, bend at the knees slightly. Rest in this posture for several slow cleansing breaths.

AROMATHERAPY

Inhaling fragrances stimulates the limbic system, the part of the brain that governs our emotions and memory.

It takes just three seconds of smelling scents to release soothing neurotransmitters (endorphins, serotonin, etc.).

Five-minute healer: Buy essential oils, and disperse them into the air with an aroma lamp, available in health-food stores. Or add a few drops of essential oil to a simmering pot of water or to bathwater. *Popular essential oils…*

- **Basil** for mental fatigue.
- **Chamomile** for insomnia and stress.
- **Lavender** for anxiety, depression as well as insomnia.
- **Peppermint** for mental clarity and better concentration.

Yoga illustration by Shawn Banner.

Caution: Don't apply essential oils directly to skin—many are too strong and can be irritating. Instead, add one or two drops to one tablespoon of a "carrier" oil (such as jojoba or canola oil), and apply that to the skin.

PRAYER

Praying to a greater power relaxes the heart, lowers levels of stress hormones, boosts levels of soothing neurotransmitters and reduces pain.

Those being prayed for also appear to benefit. A Duke University double-blind study of cardiovascular patients showed that those who were prayed for by others had the lowest rate of complications. (The people on the receiving end of the prayers did not know they were being prayed for.)

Five-minute healer: Once or twice a day, take a few minutes to give thanks to God or whatever greater power you believe in. Bring all of your attention to the things or people who enrich your life, and let your mind quietly dwell on them.

Or sit quietly, take a few deep breaths and imagine above your head a beam of golden light that's filled with healing energies. Visualize the light surrounding your heart and body.

Sweet Treat Heals Minor Burns and Wounds

Applied topically, the combination of sugar and the antibacterial components in honey kills germs. Its thickness also creates a protective barrier over the area that's wounded, and antioxidants stop damaging inflammation. Raw honey has better antibacterial properties than processed honey.

Peter Molan, PhD, director, honey research unit, University of Waikato, New Zealand.

Great Energy Boosters

When your energy is flagging, try some of the ideas below to give yourself a lift…

● **Do something new**—join a gym, take up yoga, change your hairstyle, dress differently.

● **Figure out what you really care about,** then do something about it, either as a job or through volunteering.

● **Do something fun every day.**

● **Let go of past negative experiences**—guilt weighs you down.

● **Make decisions**—it is extremely draining to worry constantly about whether or not to do something.

Mira Kirshenbaum, PhD, psychotherapist and clinical director, Chestnut Hill Institute, Boston, and author of *The Emotional Energy Factor* (Delacorte).

Lemon Balm Boosts Memory

In one recent study, participants who took standardized word- and picture-recall tests scored significantly better several hours after taking a 1,600-milligram (mg) capsule of dried lemon balm leaf than when they were given a placebo.

Theory: The herb binds to brain chemical receptors, enhancing their ability to send and receive information.

What to do: Add three teaspoons (or three tea bags) of dried lemon balm to two cups of boiling water. Steep for five minutes and then strain. Drink daily. Or take a 1,600-mg supplement daily.

David Kennedy, PhD, professor of psychobiology and psychology at Northumbria University, Newcastle upon Tyne, England.

4

Fitness Breakthroughs

The Simplest Diet Ever

Don't be misguided by the glowing testimonials from people who have lost lots of weight with some of today's popular diets.

Fact: Nearly everyone who starts a new diet loses weight initially. Up to 95% of these dieters fail to maintain their weight loss after one year. Some people gain back even *more* pounds than they lost.

Most diets are too complex or restrictive to stick with for very long. People get frustrated counting calories or carbohydrates…shifting between confusing food phases at different weeks…or giving up the foods they love.

The basic diet that works best for my patients —one that's recommended by the prestigious Institute of Medicine—consists of 40% carbohydrates, 30% protein and 30% fat. You don't need to be exact—just checking food labels will keep you in the target zone. Over the past five years, hundreds of patients who followed my basic

diet program lost an average of one pound every one to two weeks, and a majority of these patients sustained their weight loss for a year.

My story: When I hit 210 pounds at age 46, I knew it was time to get serious about losing weight. I exercised almost fanatically at first, but managed to lose only about 10 pounds in six months, since I did not change my diet. When I started researching and implementing commonsense dietary principles, I lost 35 additional pounds.

Based on my experience, I developed three basic rules for weight loss. *I wrote these basic instructions on prescription blanks for patients who found most of the popular diet plans too complicated…*

RULE #1: EAT THREE MEALS A DAY

Approximately 70% of people who end up at weight-loss clinics have never made a habit of eating breakfast, and many skip lunch as well.

Bill Gavin, MD, cardiologist and director of the Heart Program at St. Peter Hospital in Olympia, WA. Dr. Gavin is also the author of *No White at Night: The Three-Rule Diet* (Riverhead).

Result: They're ravenous by 5 pm and often consume more calories at dinner than they would if they ate three sensible daily meals.

Sample meals…

Breakfast: Two tablespoons of natural peanut butter on half a bagel.

Lunch: Nonfat yogurt and two sticks of string cheese…chicken caesar salad…or nonfat cottage cheese and fruit or tomatoes.

Dinner: Lean meat, fish or fowl of your choice and all the salad and vegetables you like.

Snack: Stick of string cheese and an apple or a protein bar.

Dinner is the largest daily meal for most of Americans. That is the opposite of what you need for weight loss.

In laboratory studies, rats that consume most of their calories at night gain more weight than animals who are given an equal number of calories spread throughout the day.

The body secretes more insulin for the same carbohydrate intake as the day progresses. This may cause calories consumed late in the day to be stored as fat.

It is acceptable to distribute all your calories equally at each meal, but you'll lose weight more efficiently if you get most of your calories at breakfast and lunch and fewer at dinner.

Helpful: Do not eat anything within three hours of going to sleep. That is when your body's metabolism is slowest. The calories that you consume at that time are not burned for energy, so they have a greater tendency to go into storage.

RULE #2: EAT LEAN PROTEIN WITH EVERY MEAL

It curbs hunger more effectively than fat or carbohydrates.

Try this: On one morning, have a bagel for breakfast. Slather it with all the jam you want. Write down how many hours after breakfast you get hungry.

The next day, eat another bagel topped with two tablespoons of natural peanut butter. You will discover that you do not get hungry for an additional two hours because of the protein in the peanut butter.

Eat at least 10 to 15 grams (g) of protein with each meal. That's roughly the amount in three

egg whites…two tablespoons of natural peanut butter…one-half cup of nonfat cottage cheese …one-half cup of cooked soy beans…or one-and-a-half ounces of turkey. This is the minimum amount that is needed to curb hunger. The average person requires more overall— about 1 g of protein daily for every two pounds of body weight.

Self-test: If you're hungry one to two hours after eating, you probably are not consuming enough protein.

RULE #3: EAT NO WHITE AT NIGHT

This means no white rice, bread, potatoes or pasta at your evening meal. You'll also want to avoid red potatoes, brown rice, whole-wheat bread and starchy vegetables, such as corn and peas. Dinners should consist of lean meat, fish or poultry, and all the salad and nonstarchy vegetables, such as green beans, carrots and broccoli, you want.

The "white" carbohydrates tend to have a high glycemic index, a measurement of how fast blood sugar rises after eating. Foods with a high glycemic index produce a high insulin response. They can increase your blood sugar about 90% as fast as pure sugar.

The increased insulin response causes your blood sugar to decrease rapidly, which in turn causes more hunger. Eating these high-glycemic foods at night causes higher insulin levels than if the foods are eaten earlier in the day. This almost guarantees weight gain.

During the initial few months of your diet, you might want to give up white, starchy foods altogether. Once you have reached your target weight, you can reintroduce them into your diet —but never at night, and not as a substitute for fruits and vegetables.

Self-test: If your energy slumps within one to two hours after eating, you've probably had too many carbohydrates.

DR. GAVIN'S OTHER SECRETS

Nearly everyone who follows these three simple rules will lose weight. *To lose weight more quickly, do the following…*

●**Drink at least one-and-a-half to two quarts of water daily.** Water, along with oxygen, is needed to burn body fat. When you are trying to lose weight, it is important to have an adequate water intake so that your body will continue to burn fat for needed calories.

•Exercise at least 30 minutes seven days a week. Exercise, such as walking, bicycling and swimming, burns fat and builds muscle tissue. Muscle is metabolically more active than any other tissue in the body. That's why muscle burns more calories per hour, even while you are sleeping.

Helpful: When you're trying to lose weight, exercise in the morning. Your body is less efficient in the morning, which causes a higher calorie burn. Morning exercise also boosts metabolism throughout the day.

Important: Don't restrict *all* fats in your diet. The traditional advice to cut back on all fats is helpful for weight loss, but it is not optimal for cholesterol control. Restricting your intake of beneficial fats, such as olive oil, can decrease levels of HDL "good" cholesterol.

Put an End to Food Cravings

Beat food cravings by resisting them for five to 10 minutes. After that amount of time, they may go away on their own. To get through the crucial minutes, focus on the emotions you feel when you get the cravings—dealing with your feelings through deep breathing or meditation can make food cravings disappear. Have an anti-urge strategy ready so you have an alternative to eating, such as gardening, working on a scrapbook or calling a friend. Or try refocusing the craving—when you feel that you must grab something to eat, reach for a carrot instead of a doughnut.

Kelly Brownell, PhD, psychologist and director at Yale Center for Eating and Weight Disorders, New Haven, CT.

Tea Helps Weight Loss

A recent study of more than 1,100 people found that those who drank tea at least once a week for more than 10 years had 20% less total body fat and 2% less abdominal fat than those who drank none. The study took into account lifestyle factors, including age, physical activity and food intake. Results applied to black, green and oolong tea.

Theory: Tea may increase metabolic rate while lowering absorption of sugars and fat-producing molecules.

Chih-Hsing Wu, MD, associate professor at the Obesity Research Center, department of family medicine, National Chang Kung University Medical College, Tainau, Taiwan, and the leader of a study of more than 1,100 people, reported in *Obesity Research*.

Another Simple Drink Helps You Lose Weight

Drinking water increases your body's metabolic rate—causing it to burn extra calories—partly because it must heat the water to body temperature. Though modest, this effect is real.

Estimate: A person who increases his/her water consumption by 1.5 liters per day for a year would burn an extra 17,400 calories for a weight loss of about five pounds.

Also: Water has no calories, so if you drink it as a substitute for calorie-laden drinks (such as soft drinks), it will help you lose weight by reducing caloric intake.

Michael Boschmann, MD, Franz-Volhard Clinical Research Center, Berlin, Germany, reported in *WebMD*.

Artificial Sweetener Alert

Eating artificial sweeteners encourages your body to increase its calorie intake.

Best strategy: Reduce your sugar intake gradually. If you must use an artificial sweetener, the best is *sucralose* (Splenda), which is created from sugar and has no calories.

Also good: Stevia, a natural zero-calorie alternative that is sold as an herbal supplement.

Trulie Ankerberg-Nobis, RD, clinical research coordinator and staff dietitian at Physicians Committee for Responsible Medicine, Washington, DC.

Why the French Don't Get Fat: Secrets to Permanent Weight Loss

Will Clower, PhD, president and founder of the Path Healthy Eating Curriculum, an educational and consulting program based in Pittsburgh that teaches weight-control strategies in corporate and academic settings. He is also a neurophysiologist and former neuroscience historian at the University of Pittsburgh and the author of *The Fat Fallacy: The French Diet Secrets to Permanent Weight Loss* (Three Rivers). He decided to write the book after living in France for two years, where he lost weight despite eating cheese, cream, butter and chocolate, *www.pathonline.net.*

The popular diets that sweep America are almost unheard of in France. The French don't count carbs or fill up their pantries with low-fat snacks. They eat foods that make diet-conscious Americans cringe—buttery croissants, rich cheeses, fat-laden pâtés. Few belong to health clubs.

Yet the French don't get fat. In France, the obesity rate is only about 8%—while about 30% of Americans are obese. The French are three times less likely than Americans to get heart disease. And they live longer—men live an average of two years more...women live three years more. Why are the French trimmer and healthier?

Americans focus on what they should not eat. They will look at a piece of pie and say to themselves, *I shouldn't eat that—it will make me fat.* Eating becomes less about pleasure than avoiding hazards. That's the main reason why many people don't stick with a diet. A Tufts University study showed that 22% of people on low-carb or low-fat diets abandoned them after two months. After a year, the dropout rate was almost 50%.

The French have a healthier relationship with food. They don't have to diet because they're not overweight. *And they're not overweight because they...*

●**Choose quality over quantity.** A Frenchman would rather have 10 perfect pommes frites than a plateful of soggy French fries or a small dish of creme brûlée rather than a mass of store-bought cookies. Also, the stomach stretches and demands more food if you take big servings on a regular basis.

Helpful: Take a little less than you think you want. Studies show that people typically overestimate the amount of food that they need—and once it's on the plate, they tend to eat it even if they have had enough. If you're going out to eat, share an entrée or just have an appetizer as your main course.

●**Savor each bite.** It's common in France to linger for hours over meals. Eating quickly will almost guarantee that you will take in excess calories. It takes 15 to 20 minutes for the stomach and small intestine to signal the brain that you're full.

Helpful...

●Make a conscious effort to take small bites. Give yourself time to appreciate the aroma, texture and flavors.

●Set down your fork between bites. Don't pick it up until you have chewed and swallowed your food. Americans often fill their forks for the next bite before they have even finished the previous one.

●Make time for conversation...and only talk when your mouth is empty. This naturally slows down the pace of meals and reduces the calories you consume.

●**Plan on seconds.** Knowing that you can have a second helping is psychologically reassuring—you're more likely to take a smaller portion the first time around if you know that you can have more. By the time you're ready for seconds, you may not want them—or you may choose to have a small dessert instead.

●**Don't combine eating with other activities.** This means not nibbling in front of the TV or while driving. The French make eating a special occasion, and they rarely snack.

●**Forgo "faux" foods.** A lot of things we eat are little more than an accumulation of chemicals. If you look at the labels on chips, sodas and other snacks, you'll see *partially hydrogenated oils, sodium stearyl lactylate, polysorbate 60,* etc. Also because these products lack flavor, they're often loaded with corn syrup.

The French rarely eat processed foods or have soft drinks. Most of their diet consists of grains, legumes and fresh fruits and vegetables. They get fewer sugar calories…and the fiber that is in natural foods slows digestion and increases feelings of satiety.

●**Get enough healthy fat.** The French don't worry about fat. About 35% to 45% of their daily calories come from fat. Some comes from the saturated fat found in butter, cheese and red meat, though the French eat red meat only about once a month. They mainly eat fish or game meats, such as rabbit or pheasant, which are naturally low in saturated fat.

Most of the fat the French consume comes from nuts, fish and olive oil—healthy fats that cause you to feel full without elevating cholesterol or heart disease risk. (The French also drink wine regularly, and wine—in particular, red wine—has been shown to improve cardiovascular health.)

Adequate fat intake increases metabolism—by as much as 15%, compared with diets that are very low in fat and calories. Eating fat will cause you to burn up more calories…and promote the absorption of beta-carotene and other fat-soluble nutrients.

●**Get exercise every day.** Even though the French don't work out in gyms as often as the Americans, they are not sedentary. They ride bikes. They go for long walks.

I usually advise people to try dance classes, yoga or tai chi. These activities burn calories and are much more enjoyable for most people than lifting weights or running on a treadmill in a health club.

Beer Does Not Cause "Beer Bellies"

A study of 2,300 beer drinkers in the Czech Republic—the nation with the world's highest per capita consumption of beer—found little difference in the waist-to-hip ratio between beer drinkers and nondrinkers. After adjusting for factors such as physical activity and education, individuals in the highest consumption category were found to be no more likely to be overweight than people who drank less or not at all.

Martin Bobak, MD, reader, department of epidemiology and public health, University College, London.

Beware Designer Coffee Drinks

Designer coffee drinks can sabotage your diet. Coffee drinks such as Dunkin' Donuts' Coffee Coolatta with cream and Starbucks' Iced Caffe Mocha Espresso have as many as 350 calories and more than 20 grams of fat per 16-ounce serving. That is more than 17% of the recommended daily total calories and more than 30% of the recommended daily total fat.

Self-defense: Request that it be made with 2% or skim milk…and order the smallest size.

US Department of Agriculture, Washington, DC.

How After-Dinner Snacks Can Aid Weight Loss

If you are a "night snacker" or someone for whom after-dinner snacking significantly contributes to a weight problem, consuming a low-calorie snack about 90 minutes after dinner may help to curtail eating and overall daily caloric intake—and promote weight loss.

Good choice: One serving of low-calorie ready-to-eat cereal with fat-free milk.

Jillon S. Vander Wal, PhD, assistant professor, College of Nursing, Center for Health Research, Wayne State University, Detroit.

Willpower Is the Key to Weight Loss and Other Myths

James M. Rippe, MD, associate professor of medicine at Tufts University School of Medicine, Boston, and founder and director of the Rippe Lifestyle Institute, a top health research organization in Shrewsbury, MA, *www.rippehealth. com*. He also is coauthor, with the editors at Weight Watchers, of *Weight Watchers—Weight Loss That Lasts* (Wiley).

Most misconceptions about losing weight are founded on a kernel of truth, with complicated explanations that can make them sound completely true. People who don't separate the myths from the facts are almost certain to take wrong turns that interfere with losing pounds and keeping them off.

Weight-loss expert and cardiologist James M. Rippe, MD, teamed up with Weight Watchers more than 10 years ago to rigorously study the group's techniques. Along the way, he has exposed some of the most common diet myths. *Here are his latest findings…*

MYTH #1: MOST DIETS FAIL

A study in the 1950s reported that about 95% of diets fail. This, along with similar findings in 1992 from the National Institutes of Health, gives the impression that it is almost impossible to lose weight and then keep it off. This destructive myth discourages many people from even trying to lose weight.

Reality: New data from two large databases —the Weight Watchers survey and the National Weight Control Registry Program—indicate that success rates are much higher than previously thought. On average, those who make a concerted effort to lose weight manage to keep off about 75% of the pounds for two years. After five years, most have kept off at least 50%.

Success rates are higher than they used to be because of advances in weight-loss methods. We now know that there are four key components —wise food choices, regular exercise, positive lifestyle changes (such as setting short- and long-term goals) and emotional support. People who incorporate all of these elements tend to be successful at losing weight and keeping it off.

MYTH #2: WILLPOWER IS THE KEY TO WEIGHT LOSS

Many people assume that they haven't lost weight in the past because they lack the necessary mental toughness.

Reality: They often choose diets that are too difficult to maintain—no one has that kind of willpower. *Instead…*

●**Practice flexible restraint.** Put a moderate level of control on your eating. Studies have shown that people who exert high dietary restraint—counting every calorie, eating certain foods at specific times, etc.—are less successful than those who try to take a more balanced approach. The idea is to make sensible everyday changes and avoid all-or-nothing thinking.

Example: Someone who eats too much at a party might make up for it not by fasting the next day, but simply by eating a little bit less.

●**Have nutritious food available.** Dieters often fail because of poor planning. Stock your refrigerator and pantry with sensible choices. Don't keep cookies, ice cream, potato chips or other unhealthy temptations in the house.

MYTH #3: YOU CAN LOSE WEIGHT WITH EXERCISE ALONE

Regular exercise is very important for weight loss—but it is almost impossible to lose weight through exercise alone.

Reality: It takes significant exercise to burn off enough calories to lose weight. To lose one pound of fat through exercise alone, a person needs to burn an additional 3,500 calories over what he/she is currently burning. For a sedentary, 170-pound person to lose one pound a week without dietary changes, he would have to walk at least five miles a day. It takes about an hour on a treadmill to burn off the calories from one medium-sized bagel, and that's without butter or cream cheese.

The best way to lose is to combine physical activity with a reduction in calories.

Bonus: Exercise builds muscle, and muscle can burn up to 70 times more calories than fat can during normal metabolism. People who are physically active maintain a higher metabolism even during times of rest, which results in faster and easier weight loss.

People who are sedentary may have a drop in metabolism of 15% to 20% between the ages of 30 and 50. Those who stay active—particularly with muscle-building strength training—don't experience this decline and are less likely to gain weight than those who don't exercise.

MYTH #4: CALORIES DON'T MATTER

Fad diets over the years have identified particular foods or types of food as a leading cause of weight gain. In the 1990s, it was fat. Today, carbohydrates are the problem. There also have been claims over the years that grapefruit, celery and other foods cause the body to burn additional calories. What each of these concepts has in common is the assumption that calories are somehow less important than other factors in losing weight.

Reality: Cutting calories is the key to losing weight. It does not matter whether calories come from fat, protein or carbohydrates. Shave 3,500 calories weekly by giving up desserts, for example, and taking smaller portions at meals.

Popular diets such as Atkins and South Beach are appealing because they are all based on the fantastic promise that you can lose weight very quickly without much effort. But there's no evidence that restricting carbohydrates to the levels called for in these diets is any more effective than traditional dieting. It even may be counterproductive because few people are willing to stay on these diets very long.

MYTH #5: WEIGHT-LOSS SUPPLEMENTS ARE SAFE

Health-food stores sell dozens of products that purport to safely increase metabolism and speed weight loss.

Reality: Some supplements are stimulants that increase heart rate, blood pressure and metabolism and suppress appetite. They may aid in weight loss temporarily, but they can cause severe side effects, including anxiety and insomnia.

Some of these products, such as those containing *ephedra* or *phenylpropanolamine,* have been banned because of the potential dangers.

Low-Carb Diet Danger

The popular low-carbohydrate diets, which are typically high in protein and fat, often are low in fiber.

New finding: Adults who ate three servings of fiber-rich whole grains a day during an 11-year period reduced their risk for death from any cause by up to 23%.

High-fiber foods help to maintain a healthy body weight, improve cholesterol levels and lower blood pressure. The recommended daily fiber intake is 30 grams (g).

Foods rich in fiber: One pear (10 g)...one cup of raspberries (8 g)...and one cup of lentils (16 g).

Lyn M. Steffen, PhD, RD, assistant professor of epidemiology at the University of Minnesota School of Public Health, Minneapolis.

When to Eat Carbohydrates

Exercise depletes glycogen, the main source of energy for physical activity. Only carbohydrates can replace glycogen. Eat half a gram (g) of carbs per pound of body weight.

Example: A 150-pound person should eat 75 g, about the amount in one cup of cooked pasta.

Good post-exercise carb sources: Pasta, English muffins, oatmeal, whole-grain cereals, low-fat yogurt.

Cedric Bryant, PhD, chief exercise physiologist, American Council on Exercise, San Diego.

Low-Carb Is Not Low-Cal

Many dieters eat low-carbohydrate protein bars, muffins, brownies and other foods—but low-carb foods often are high in calories.

Self-defense: Read labels for calorie information. Limit between-meal snacks to 100 calories or less.

Suzanne Havala Hobbs, DrPH, RD, clinical assistant professor, School of Public Health, University of North Carolina at Chapel Hill, and author of several books, including *Vegetarian Cooking for Dummies* (Hungry Minds).

More from Suzanne Havala Hobbs...

Before You Reach for That Donut...

If you decide to treat yourself to a fattening snack and want to walk it off later, here is how far you'll have to go. *A 155-pound person would need to walk at a moderate pace for...*

●**More than two hours for a Big Mac.**

●**More than two hours for a large order of fries.**

●**Two hours for two glazed donuts.**

●**A little more than an hour for one cup of Breyers vanilla ice cream.**

●**Almost one hour for a Snickers bar.**

A smaller person would have to walk even longer at the same pace to burn the same number of calories.

Example: Someone with a weight of 125 pounds would have to walk for two hours to burn off the same number of calories that a 250-pound person would burn in one hour of walking at the same pace.

The Best 20-Minute Workout Ever

Brad Schoenfeld, a certified strength and conditioning specialist for 16 years. He is the owner and operator of the Personal Training Center for Women in Scarsdale, NY, and the author of *Look Great at Any Age: Defy Aging, Slim Down, and Optimize Health in Just 60 Minutes a Week* (Prentice Hall).

Each year, the average American over age 30 gains body fat. That's because most of us lose approximately 1% of our muscle mass annually—and the less muscle mass you have, the fewer calories you burn.

Strength training helps increase and maintain muscle mass. It promotes new bone formation, which helps men and women prevent osteoporosis. Strength training also boosts HDL "good" cholesterol and enhances mood by increasing *endorphins,* "feel good" chemicals in the brain.

The following nine exercises can be performed in your home in just 20 minutes.* All you need is one pair of dumbbells and a flat bench or a straight-backed chair.

Choose dumbbells that are heavy enough so that the last repetition of each set feels somewhat difficult. Once the last repetition starts feeling easy, then it is time to move up to a slightly heavier weight. You can purchase dumbbells in one- to 12-pound weights at a sporting-goods store for approximately $1 per pound.

Before each workout: Warm up with at least five minutes of light aerobic exercise, such as jogging in place, jumping rope or riding a stationary bicycle. A warm-up loosens the joints, helping to prevent injury.

To build maximum strength: Perform eight to 10 repetitions of each exercise.

For best results: Perform three workouts a week. The combination of exercises allows you to train your entire body in only 20 minutes. To prevent injury, always leave at least 48 hours between strength workouts so that your muscles have time to recover and repair. For cardiovascular health, incorporate 30 minutes

*Consult your doctor before beginning any exercise routine.

of aerobic exercise, such as walking or swimming, at least three days per week.

SHOULDER PRESS

Target muscles: Shoulders.

What to do: Sit upright on the edge of a bench or chair. Grasp a dumbbell in each hand, with palms facing away from your body, and bring the weights to shoulder level. Next, lift both dumbbells directly up over your head, moving them toward each other so that when your arms are extended (with the elbows slightly bent), the dumbbells are gently touching. Feel the contraction in your shoulders. Then slowly lower the dumbbells to the starting position.

ONE-ARMED DUMBBELL ROW

Target muscles: Back.

What to do: Bend over. Place your left hand on a flat bench or on a chair while keeping your feet planted firmly on the floor. Be sure to maintain this position throughout the entire exercise.

Grasp one dumbbell in your right hand and just let it hang. Keeping your elbow close to your body, pull the dumbbell up and back. Feel a contraction in the muscles of your upper back. Then slowly lower the dumbbell to the starting position. Reverse sides and repeat with left arm.

FLAT CHEST PRESS

Target muscles: Chest.

What to do: Lie face up on a bench or on a mat on the floor, with knees bent and feet flat on the ground. Grasp one dumbbell in each hand, palms facing away from your body, and bring them to shoulder level, directly above your armpits. Then lift both dumbbells directly up over your chest and move them toward each other until they gently touch. Feel a contraction in your chest muscles. Then slowly lower the dumbbells to the starting position.

SEATED BICEP CURL

Target muscles: Biceps.

What to do: Sit upright on the edge of a flat bench or chair. Grasp a dumbbell in each hand

and let them hang at your sides, palms facing away from your body. Keeping your upper arms pressed against your torso, raise up both dumbbells until your hands stop just short of your shoulders. You will feel a contraction in your biceps. Then slowly lower the dumbbells to the starting position.

OVERHEAD TRICEP PRESS

Target muscles: Triceps.

What to do: While standing, grasp one end of the dumbbell with both hands. Raise your arms up above your head, then bend your elbows and let all the weight hang down behind your head as far as comfortably possible. With both your elbows pointed toward the ceiling and your arms pressed against your ears, very gradually straighten your arms until you feel a contraction in the backs of your upper arms. Then lower the weight to the starting position.

DUMBBELL SQUAT

Target muscles: Quadriceps.

What to do: Stand with feet shoulder-width apart and toes pointed slightly outward. Grasp a dumbbell in each hand and let them hang at your sides. Very slowly lower your body until your thighs are almost parallel to the floor, or as far as comfortably possible. (When you have knee problems, even lowering a quarter of the way can be beneficial.) Your lower back should be slightly arched, and your heels flat on the floor. When you reach the "seated" position, slowly straighten your legs and return to the starting position.

STIFF-LEGGED DEADLIFT

Target muscles: Hamstrings and glutes.

What to do: Stand with feet shoulder-width apart. Grasp a dumbbell in each hand and let your arms just hang in front of you. With your two knees straight (but not locked), bend forward at the hips and permit the dumbbells to travel down along the line of your body until you feel a stretch in the backs of your legs. Contract your buttock muscles as you very slowly rise up to the starting position.

STANDING CALF RAISE

Target muscles: Calves.

What to do: Stand with feet shoulder-width apart. Grasp a dumbbell in your left hand, resting your right hand against a wall or the back of a chair for balance, if necessary. Raise both heels off the ground as high as possible, transferring your weight to the balls of your feet. Feel a contraction in your calf muscles. Then slowly return to the starting position.

ABDOMINAL CURL

Target muscles: Abdominals.

What to do: Lie face up on the floor with knees bent and arms folded across your chest. Keeping your lower back on the floor, slowly raise your shoulders up and forward toward your chest until you feel a contraction in your abdominal muscles. Then slowly return to the starting position.

20-minute workout illustrations by Shawn Banner.

If You Walk to Work Out…

Talking during your walking workout can be dangerous.

Reason: Talking causes short periods of reduced abdominal muscle activity that leaves the spine temporarily more susceptible to injury.

Theory: The same muscles are used for both breathing and control of your back. If you walk and talk at the same time—causing you to inhale rapidly and exhale slowly—the central nervous system is faced with competing demands.

Self-defense: Walk—or jog—silently.

Paul Hodges, MD, professor of physiotherapy, University of Queensland, Brisbane, Australia.

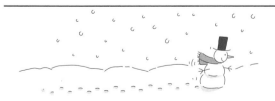

Tone Your Abdominals Without the Dreaded Crunches

Jorge Cruise, a weight-loss coach based in San Diego who has counseled more than 3 million clients through his Web site, *www.jorgecruise.com.* He is also the author of *8 Minutes in the Morning to a Flat Belly* (Rodale) and *The 3-Hour Diet* (HarperCollins).

If you believe that a flat stomach improves only your physical appearance, think again. Reducing and toning your waistline also helps to lower your risk for diabetes, heart disease, breast cancer, high blood pressure and back pain—all of which are more likely to occur in people with excess belly fat.

Stronger abdominal muscles can improve your posture as well, and help you lift, bend, twist and balance more easily.

NO MORE CRUNCHES

Many people assume that abdominal crunches are the best way to tone up the stomach. That's a misconception.

Crunches are performed by lying on your back with knees bent and hands behind your head, and contracting your abs while raising your shoulders approximately two inches off the ground.

Besides being very uncomfortable to perform, crunches work only one area of your abdomen—the area just above your navel, and the one area of the belly that's usually strongest for most people.

The four exercises described below work all four of the major abdominal muscle groups…

The *transverse abdominus* (the corset-like muscle that wraps around your pelvis and helps hold your internal organs in place)…the *upper rectus abdominus* (the upper part of the large muscle that forms the much-sought-after "six-pack" along the front of your abdomen)…the *obliques* (located along either side of your abdomen, these muscles help you to twist and bend from side to side)…and the *lower rectus abdominus* (the lower part of the "six-pack" muscle, which extends below the navel).

FLAT-BELLY PROGRAM

For the best possible results, perform the following workout, three times a week (at least 48 hours apart).*

Example: Monday, Wednesday and Friday. The full workout takes about eight minutes to perform. You should start seeing results in three to four weeks.

What you'll need: A sturdy, straight-back chair and an object weighing approximately two to five pounds, such as a small medicine ball or a hardcover dictionary. Use sufficient weight so that you feel resistance and fatigue toward the end of the one-minute set—but are able to finish in good form. Perform each exercise seated in the chair with your feet flat on the floor. Sit tall and lengthen your spine.

Move 1: **Seated vacuum.** Works the transverse abdominus.

What to do: As you exhale, suck your navel in toward your spine as far as you can.

Contract your stomach to squeeze all of the air out of your lungs. Hold for just three seconds. Next, inhale while you reverse the exercise, making your belly as round as possible. Hold for three seconds. Then slowly repeat all of these movements for about one minute.

Move 2: **Seated crossover.** Tones the upper rectus abdominus.

What to do: Bend your arms 90 degrees so that your elbows are in line with your chest and your fingers and forearms point up toward the ceiling.

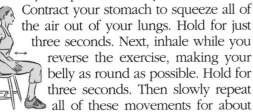
As you exhale, bring your left elbow and right knee toward each other until they are nearly touching. Next, inhale as you return your elbow and knee to the starting position. Repeat with your right elbow and left knee. Alternate right and left sides for one minute.

Move 3: **Seated torso rotation.** Focuses on the obliques.

What to do: Use both hands to grasp the two-to-five-pound object.

*Consult your doctor before beginning any exercise routine.

Hold it level in front of your chest with your arms extended. As you exhale, twist to the right. Keep your back straight and your head and neck in line with your torso, so that you are always facing the object while you turn. Next, inhale as you return to the starting position. Repeat on the left side. Then, alternate sides for one minute.

Move 4: **Captain's chair.** Firms the lower rectus abdominus.

What to do: Use your fingers to grasp the front edge of the chair on either side of your hips.

Press your palms against the chair surface for increased stability. As you exhale, slowly bring your knees toward your chest, trying not to arch your lower back. Hold this for three seconds. Slowly lower your knees as you inhale. Repeat for one minute.

When finished, return to Move 1 and repeat the entire sequence.

Abdominal exercise illustrations by Shawn Banner.

Secret to Burning More Calories

Just thirty minutes of strength training with weight machines will burn off more calories (about 240) than walking for 30 minutes (about 200). And weight lifting boosts metabolism by 25% for an hour after exercise, burning even more calories.

Helpful: Perform 30 minutes of weight training three times a week in addition to at least 30 minutes of aerobic exercise daily.

Wayne Westcott, PhD, exercise physiologist for South Shore YMCA, Quincy, MA.

Simple Way to Build Strength and Boost Energy

Lisa Holtby, a Seattle-based yoga instructor for over 10 years and the author of *Healing Yoga for People Living with Cancer* (Taylor).

Many people assume that yoga requires great strength and flexibility. Fortunately, that's just not true.

Because yoga gently stretches and works the muscles without the high impact of most aerobic exercise, even people who are in a weakened state due to illness can use it to build up strength and flexibility, boost energy and promote circulation in the muscles and joints—all beneficial to healing.

The following regimen is appropriate for most adults, even those who suffer from chronic conditions, such as arthritis, diabetes, cancer or heart disease. Just be sure to consult your doctor before starting.

The program takes about 30 minutes and can be practiced daily.

Helpful: Record the instructions, or you can have someone read them to you.

RESTING POSE

What to do: Lie on your back on a mat or large towel with your arms at your sides, palms facing up, and your chin and forehead aligned horizontally. If your chin points upward, place a neatly rolled, small towel under your head  and the back of your neck's natural curve.

Breathe slowly in and out. On your inhalations, draw air into the whole length of your lungs. The exhalations should be slightly longer than your inhalations. Maintain this same breathing pattern during the following exercises. Recline in the resting pose for five to 10 minutes. Then sit upright in a straight-backed chair to practice the following yoga poses.

Perform each pose for 10 to 20 long, slow breaths. On your inhalations, notice how your breath expands your ribcage. On your exhalations, move more deeply into the pose without straining.

SEATED MOUNTAIN

Purpose: Lengthens the spine, opens the chest and relaxes the shoulders.

What to do: Sit upright in a straight-backed chair, with feet flat and hip-width apart. Place 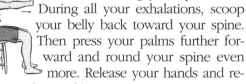 your hands at the crease where your thighs join up with your pelvis. Lean your torso forward about 12 inches. Tilt the front of your pelvis forward a bit so that your lower back arches. While keeping a slight arch in your lower back, sit upright again. Press your tailbone downward. You will feel your abdominal muscles contract.

Then, rest your hands on the front of your thighs, palms down (pictured above). Gently roll your shoulders up, then back, so that your chest is open, and press your shoulder blades toward your back. Press down through your feet and lengthen down through your tailbone. On exhalations, lengthen up through your spine.

SEATED CAT

Purpose: Stretches upper and middle back.

What to do: While sitting upright, interlace your fingers and turn your palms forward, facing away from you. Stretch your arms forward, rounding your spine. During all your exhalations, scoop your belly back toward your spine. Then press your palms further forward and round your spine even more. Release your hands and return to starting position.

SEATED TWIST

Purpose: Releases tension in the back and lengthens the spine.

What to do: While sitting upright, press both your feet into the floor and then slowly twist your upper body to the right, keeping your head directly above your pelvis. For leverage, rest your left hand against the outside of your right thigh, palm outward.

On your exhalations, slowly deepen the twist. Return to starting position. Repeat on the opposite side.

SEATED WINGS

Purpose: Strengthens the upper back and opens the chest.

What to do: Sit upright. Gently shrug your shoulders up, then back, so that your shoulder blades press toward your back. Reach out from the center of your chest and back to extend your arms out wide, all the way through your fingertips. Press your arms straight back as you lift your chest up and forward. To be sure your lower back is comfortable and safe, pull your belly back toward your spine and lengthen your tailbone down. Slowly return to starting position.

SEATED HALF MOON

Purpose: Stretches muscles on the sides of the torso.

What to do: Sit upright. Gently shrug your shoulders up, then back, so that your shoulder blades press toward your back. Then side bend to the right with your torso. Place your right hand on your waist or onto the chair seat for stability. Keep your shoulder blades pressed in toward your back, then stretch your left arm way out to the left, then up in a big arc to the right. Slowly return to starting position. Repeat on the opposite side.

SEATED COBRA

Purpose: Opens the chest and strengthens the back.

What to do: While sitting upright, very lightly shrug your shoulders up, then back, so that your shoulder blades press toward your back. Interlace your hands behind your head with your elbows wide apart. On your exhalations, lift your chest up and back into a backbend. To keep your lower back comfortable and safe, pull your belly back toward your spine and lengthen your tailbone down. Release your arms and rest your hands comfortably in your lap.

SEATED WARRIOR

Purpose: Stretches the hips and legs and lengthens the spine.

What to do: Sit sideways on the chair so that the left side of your body faces toward the chair back and your right leg is in line with the front of the chair seat. Still sitting on the chair, step your right leg back into a lunge, with your weight on the ball of your foot. Your left thigh will rest on the chair seat, with your left leg at a right angle and left foot on the floor. Rest your hands comfortably on the chair back and seat. To stabilize your pelvis, draw your left thigh back into its hip joint and your right thigh forward into its hip joint. To keep your lower back comfortable and safe, draw your belly back toward your spine and lengthen your tailbone down. Now press your right heel back and lengthen your left thigh forward. Return to starting position. Repeat on the opposite side.

SEATED TURNING WARRIOR

Purpose: Stretches hips and legs, releases back tension and lengthens the spine.

What to do: Sit sideways with your right side facing the chair back and your left leg back. To keep your lower back comfortable and safe, lengthen your tailbone down as you draw your belly back, toward your spine. Very slowly turn your torso to the right, as in the Seated Twist. With every exhalation, deepen the twist. Repeat this exercise on the opposite side.

Finally, repeat the resting pose (on page 64) for 10 minutes.

Strength exercise illustrations by Shawn Banner.

Exercise Saved My Life

Jeff Berman, New York City–based founder of FORCE, a program that has helped hundreds of cancer patients. He is author of *The FORCE Program: The Proven Way to Fight Cancer Through Physical Activity and Exercise* (Ballantine).

Fourteen years ago, at age 32, I was diagnosed with *chronic lymphocytic leukemia,* an unusual variety of cancer that typically strikes people over age 65. Doctors told me that there was no cure. The best they could do was put me through repeated rounds of chemotherapy to keep the disease in check and relieve symptoms, such as difficulty breathing, fever and fatigue. Life expectancy for patients with this cancer is five years.

FIGHTING CANCER

Before my diagnosis, exercise had always been a big part of my life. I ran, cycled and lifted weights. I competed in a triathlon. After I was diagnosed, I wondered if exercise could help me fight cancer. Although exercise hadn't prevented me from getting cancer, it had made me more physically sensitive to a small swelling in my neck, thereby resulting in earlier diagnosis and treatment.

When I asked my doctors about the role of exercise in cancer treatment, they were skeptical. Even though studies have suggested that exercise might help prevent certain cancers, no one was studying whether it could help people who already had the disease.

I resolved to stay in good shape. Though I cut back on the intensity of my workouts—no more triathlons!—I continued to exercise regularly. I developed a "chemo-friendly" workout, anticipating energy highs and lows and building workout routines around them as best I could.

Fourteen years after my diagnosis, I'm living a happy and fulfilled life. I even got married two years ago. I'm not claiming that exercise cures cancer. My cancer is not cured. Every few years, when the swelling in my head and neck gets out of control, I go through cycles of chemo. But I have beaten the odds—I'm alive.

MORE PROOF

During the past 10 years, scientific studies have shown that physical fitness does help fight cancer and contributes to a better quality of life.

Example I: A 1996 German study of 32 patients who received high-dose chemotherapy and bone marrow transplants found that those who used treadmills regularly not only had stronger muscles, they also showed improved blood counts and had more energy.

Example II: Researchers at the University of Alberta reviewed 24 studies on exercise and cancer and reported their findings in 1999. They found that exercise reduced nausea and fatigue and led to greater physical strength and emotional well-being.

Seven years ago, I founded a lifestyle education program to help cancer patients fight the disease and lead balanced lives. It's known as FORCE (Focus on Rehabilitation and Cancer Education). Even if you don't have cancer, this program may lower your chances of getting it.

Important: Talk with your physician before embarking on this program. These techniques are meant to enhance medical treatments prescribed by an oncologist, not to replace them. Your doctor may recommend modifying or postponing certain exercises.

EXERCISE GUIDELINES

•**Keep it simple.** Walking is a great overall conditioner. To avoid overexerting yourself, start with a 10-minute walk twice a week. If you are too tired to walk 10 minutes all at once, aim for a total of 10 minutes throughout the day.

Each week, increase your walking time by two minutes per session, to up to 20 minutes. Gradually add days until you are walking four or more times a week.

•**Try strength training.** Cancer, chemo and radiation can weaken the muscles. Try strength training on one or two of the days that you don't walk. (Do this after you have established a regular walking routine.) Strength training also can help minimize bone loss, which occurs in some women who undergo early menopause as a side effect of chemotherapy. *Two exercises to try…*

•Double knee hugs strengthen the abdomen and stretch the lower back. Lie on your back, and slowly bring your knees to your chest. Wrap your hands around your shins. Exhale slowly as you lift your head toward your knees. Inhale as you lower your head to the floor. Repeat five to 10 times.

•Chair squats strengthen thighs, hamstrings and buttocks. Put a chair against a wall. Slowly lower yourself as if to sit. As soon as your buttocks touch the chair, slowly raise yourself back to standing. If standing back up is difficult, use a chair with armrests. Repeat five to 10 times.

•**Always respect what your body is going through.** It's fine to feel mildly sore or fatigued after exercising, but pain or exhaustion is a signal to back off exercise immediately. If you are going through chemotherapy or radiation, it's particularly important to pace yourself. After chemotherapy treatment, I take a day or two off from exercising and resume gradually.

5
Natural Healers

Superfoods Fight Heart Disease, Cancer, Diabetes and More

Most health-conscious eaters will try to do their very best to follow the basic dietary recommendations, such as eating seven to nine daily servings of fruits and vegetables. Unfortunately, these guidelines really do not tell us which foods will provide the maximum nutritional value.

Now: Researchers have targeted a handful of specific superfoods that contain phytonutrients (disease-fighting plant-based chemicals), vitamins, minerals and healthful fatty acids. These nutrients act as powerful antioxidants (to fight heart disease, cancer, even the aging process)... anti-inflammatories (to reduce inflammation that can lead to heart disease, eye disease and cancer)...and immune system boosters (to help in warding off infection).

This is not to say that these foods are the *only* ones worth eating. Each has "healthful cousins" that are nearly as beneficial.

Example: Any vegetable in the cabbage family (brussels sprouts, cauliflower, bok choy) offers some of the same benefits as broccoli. But broccoli combines the greatest number of healthful nutrients.

THE TOP THREE

When it comes to nutritional value, three foods qualify as the best of the best...

●**Blueberries contain more antioxidants than any other fruit.** Besides plentiful quantities of vitamins C and E, blueberries contain such phytonutrients as anthocyanins (which give the fruit its distinctive color) and ellagic acid. These phytonutrients work synergistically —that is, the unique combination of nutrients maximizes the benefits of each.

Steven Pratt, MD, an assistant clinical professor of ophthalmology at the University of California, San Diego, and senior staff ophthalmologist at Scripps Memorial Hospital in La Jolla, CA. He is coauthor of *SuperFoods Rx: Fourteen Foods That Will Change Your Life* (William Morrow).

Research shows that blueberries have anti-inflammatory effects, improve mental performance and also reduce the rates of urinary-tract infection.

Healthful cousins: Red grapes, cranberries, blackberries, cherries, raspberries, boysenberries, strawberries.

Goal: One to two cups fresh or frozen daily.

●**Salmon is an excellent source for the omega-3 fatty acids,** which control inflammation and keep cell membranes healthy. It's also rich in vitamin D, selenium and protein.

Increasing your intake of the omega-3s will reduce your risk for coronary artery disease, cancer and age-related macular degeneration. Omega-3s also have been shown to lower high blood pressure and ease symptoms of arthritis and lupus.

Important: Much of the salmon available today is raised on fish farms, where it is exposed to high levels of contaminants, such as PCBs. Whether fresh, canned or frozen, buy only salmon that is specifically marked *wild Alaskan.*

Healthful cousins: Halibut, sardines, herring, sea bass and trout, which are all low in mercury. Canned albacore tuna is rich in omega-3s, but it's best to limit consumption to one can per week because of possible mercury content.

Goal: Three ounces of fish, two to four times per week.

●**Spinach is rich in the antioxidants lutein and beta-carotene…**the minerals calcium, iron, magnesium and zinc…and omega-3 fatty acids. It's also a good source of betaine, a fat-derived compound that fights elevated homocysteine, a cardiovascular risk factor. A number of studies now link spinach consumption with lower rates of colon, lung, stomach, ovarian, prostate and breast cancers. It also appears to protect against cataracts and age-related macular degeneration.

Healthful cousins: Kale, collards, Swiss chard, mustard greens, romaine lettuce.

Goal: Two cups raw or one cup steamed every day.

HIGH IN THE HIERARCHY

●**Oats are the nutritional powerhouse of whole grains.** They are a rich source of fiber, including beta-glucans, which help to protect against heart disease…and minerals, including magnesium, potassium, zinc, copper, manganese and selenium, all of which lower the risk for high blood pressure, diabetes, cancer and heart disease.

Healthful cousins: Wheat germ, flaxseed, whole wheat, barley, buckwheat, millet and amaranth.

Goal: Five to seven daily servings (one serving equals one slice…one-half cup cooked… three-quarters to one cup dry).

●**Pumpkin is rich in healthful carotenoids.** It is also the best source of the combination of alpha-carotene (twice as much as carrots) and beta-carotene—which work optimally as a team.

Carotenoid-rich foods (not the supplements) have been shown to reduce the risk for lung, colon, breast and skin cancers. Canned 100% pure pumpkin is just as nutritious as fresh.

Healthful cousins: Carrots, sweet potatoes, butternut squash.

Goal: One-half cup most days.

●**Tomatoes are a cornucopia of carotenoids**—alpha-carotene and beta-carotene, lycopene, lutein, phytoene and phytofluene.

All are beneficial, but lycopene does deserve special mention. It's been linked to reduced rates of cancer (particularly prostate malignancies). When joined with lutein, lycopene also fights age-related macular degeneration.

Important: Although uncooked tomatoes have higher levels of other carotenoids, the lycopene in cooked tomatoes is most readily absorbed by the body.

Healthful cousins: Try watermelon or pink grapefruit.

Goal: One daily serving of processed tomatoes (one-half cup sauce) or healthful cousins (one watermelon wedge…one-half pink grapefruit), and multiple servings of fresh tomatoes each week.

●**Walnuts contain omega-3 fatty acids,** vitamin E, potassium, protein, fiber and cholesterol-lowering compounds known as plant sterols.

Studies suggest that eating a handful of nuts (about one ounce) five times a week lowers the risk for heart attack by up to 50%.

Caution: Because nuts are high in calories, do not overindulge.

Healthful cousins: Almonds, pistachios, sesame seeds, pecans.

Goal: One ounce, five times a week.

OTHER SUPERFOODS

To round out the list above, try to incorporate oranges...soy...tea (black or green)...raw or cooked broccoli...yogurt (with live cultures)... skinless turkey...and/or beans (pinto, navy, lima, chickpeas) in your diet on all or most days of the week.

Live Longer and Feel Great: The Simple Strategy Of Centenarians

Bradley J. Willcox, MD, clinical assistant professor, geriatrics for the University of Hawaii as well as a physician-scientist for the Pacific Health Research Institute, which conducts research on aging and chronic disease, both in Honolulu. He is also coauthor of *The Okinawa Diet Plan: Get Leaner, Live Longer, and Never Feel Hungry* (Clarkson Potter).

It *is* possible to eat more and live longer. Just ask the Okinawans. In 2000, my brother and I (both of us researchers at Harvard Medical School at the time) pored over 50 years of research on the inhabitants of Okinawa, a chain of islands in Japan that touts the world's highest concentration of centenarians.

We discovered that their rates of killer diseases, such as cancer, heart disease and stroke, are among the lowest in the world, largely because of their diet, physical activity and close family relationships.

Now: New analysis of dietary data has uncovered additional details on the Okinawans' healthful eating habits.

CALORIC DENSITY

Foods differ in the ratio of calories to weight. The more calories per gram (g) or ounce a food contains, the more fattening it will be. This principle is known as caloric density (CD).

Here's the trick: If you consume two to three pounds of food a day, you'll probably feel satisfied. This is true whether the food contains 2,100 calories (as it will if you eat like most Americans) or 1,600 calories (as it will if you eat the low-CD Okinawan way).

That's because humans are programmed to eat a set amount of food—not just a quota of calories. Okinawans actually eat *more* than the Americans—an average of 2.5 pounds a day versus two pounds for Americans.

The traditional Okinawan diet includes some foods familiar in America (such as sweet potatoes and watermelon)...some that have made inroads into many American kitchens (such as tofu and shiitake mushrooms)...and others that might require a sense of adventure and a trip to a specialty-food store, including daikon (Japanese radish), adzuki beans and edible seaweed, such as wakame and hijiki.

GO THREE TO ONE

It isn't only what's in the Okinawan diet that counts—it's also the proportions.

Just follow this simple rule: Since animal products have higher CDs than vegetables, legumes, fruits and grains, consume at least three times more plant-based foods than meats and seafood or dairy products.

Another three-to-one rule applies to your plant-based foods: Eat about three times more "featherweight" plant-based foods than denser ones. A featherweight food contains fewer than 0.7 calories per g.

Example: Eat plenty of fresh strawberries, grapefruit, broccoli, carrot sticks and cantaloupe...and as much tofu, salsa, vegetable soup, fat-free cottage cheese and low-fat plain yogurt as you want. But have smaller portions of high-CD foods, such as bread (even if it's whole wheat) and nuts.

GET ENOUGH PROTEIN

Because protein is vital to maintaining all the cells, muscles and other tissues of the body, nature made this nutrient more satisfying than fats or sugars. Without sufficient protein—no matter how much fat and sugar you eat—you'll still be hungry. Adults should get 0.4 g of protein per pound of body weight daily.

Example: A 180-pound man needs 72 g of protein per day.

Once you adopt a low-CD diet and your calorie intake drops, you'll be eating a higher proportion of protein. Meat is a rich source, but it comes packaged with fat. Fish is less calorie-dense, and its fats are healthful omega-3s.

Helpful: Get most of your protein from plant sources, such as legumes and grains, and the rest from fish. Soy, a legume, is particularly valuable. It contains all the necessary amino acids.

KEEP FIBER IN MIND

Fiber, the nondigestible substance found in plants, adds bulk without calories to foods—so the more fiber, the lower the CD. High-fiber foods keep the edge off your appetite longer.

Bonus: Fiber aids digestion and reduces cholesterol. The phytonutrients (plant-based chemicals) found in fiber appear to lower the risks for cancer and diabetes.

The easiest way to increase your fiber intake is to start the day with a breakfast cereal that contains at least 5 g per serving.

Also: Substitute whole-wheat bread and pasta and brown rice for refined grain products. Add high-fiber beans and lentils to salads.

CHOOSE WATER-RICH FOODS

Like fiber, water adds volume without calories. Foods with high water content fill you up just as effectively as those that are loaded with fats and sugars.

To decrease the CD of your meals, water must be in the food.

To add more water to your daily diet...

● **Start your meals with soup whenever possible.**

● **Steam vegetables rather than baking or grilling them.** This will keep their water content high.

● **Eat water-rich stew as a main dish.**

EAT FREQUENT MEALS

Six small meals and snacks a day will keep your energy level up and your hunger down. You eat less, overall, when you graze rather than gorge.

Especially important: Never skip breakfast. A healthy, high-fiber morning meal that includes some protein, such as yogurt, makes it easier to resist fatty, sugary foods throughout the day.

DON'T DEPRIVE YOURSELF

Completely swearing off foods you really love won't work in the long run—sooner or later, cravings win out.

Instead: Meet yourself halfway. Eat just half a pastrami sandwich, and cut the meal's CD with vegetables. Finish with fresh fruit.

If you feel the urge for sweets, have a piece of hard candy. Drink hot cocoa to satisfy your chocolate craving—an eight-ounce serving has a low CD of about 120 calories, while a 1.5-ounce chocolate bar has about 220 calories.

Coffee as a Miracle Health Drink

Tomas de Paulis, PhD, coffee chemist and research assistant professor of psychiatry, Institute for Coffee Studies, Vanderbilt University Medical Center, Nashville.

The health benefits from drinking coffee continue to be reported—and to the extent where they almost seem too good to actually be true.

Coffee decreases diabetes risk. Drinking six cups a day slashed risk of diabetes by 54% for men and 30% for women in an 18-year Harvard study. Even drinking only one cup a day was found to reduce risk by several percent.

At least six additional studies indicate coffee drinkers reduce their risk of Parkinson's disease by up to 80%.

And other studies have reported that drinking at least two cups of coffee a day can reduce risk of colon cancer by 25%, risk of gallstones by 50% and risk of liver cirrhosis by 80%.

There's even evidence that coffee drinking offsets some of the health damage caused by smoking and excessive drinking—those who engage in such health vices but also drink coffee have been reported to suffer less heart and liver damage than those who don't.

And other studies have indicated coffee may help to control asthma, relieve headaches, lift spirits and even prevent cavities.

Coffee can also increase athletic performance and endurance—until recently, it was a controlled substance at the Olympic Games.

Moreover, coffee is even good for children. One study in Brazil indicated that children (age 12 average) who drank coffee with milk were less prone to depression and were more alert in school. No study indicates that coffee consumed in reasonable amounts is in any way harmful for children.

Supplement Information

R eliable dietary-supplement information is now available from *The Natural Pharmacy* (TNP), a database that explains the uses and safety of nearly 500 supplements. TNP is prepared by physicians and pharmacists and is available for free at the on-line supplement site, *www.iherb.com/health.html.* Other on-line resources of supplement information tend to be sketchy or biased.

David Schardt, MS, senior nutritionist, *Nutrition Action Healthletter,* 1875 Connecticut Ave. NW, Washington, DC 20009.

Five Little-Known Ways to Lower Heart Attack Risk

Michael Mogadam, MD, clinical associate professor of medicine at George Washington University School of Medicine in Washington, DC. He is also author of *Every Heart Attack Is Preventable: How to Take Control of the 20 Risk Factors and Save Your Life* (New American Library).

M ost Americans know all of the traditional heart disease risk factors—lack of physical activity, high cholesterol, high blood pressure, diabetes, obesity and smoking. Although these are important, there also are lesser-known risk factors. *Ways to avoid them...*

•**Boost your HDL level.** Though high LDL ("bad") cholesterol has long been considered the major culprit in heart attack risk, low HDL ("good") cholesterol actually is the bigger risk factor, especially in women. About 70% of women and half of all men with coronary artery disease (CAD) have low HDL cholesterol.

What to do: If you're a woman with HDL below 55 or a man with HDL below 45, take steps to boost your good cholesterol. Engaging in regular, vigorous exercise can raise HDL levels by 10% to 15%. Limiting carbohydrates to less than 45% of your daily diet and increasing monounsaturated fats (found in olive, canola and hazelnut oils) can raise HDL levels by 10%. Cholesterol-lowering statin drugs also may raise HDL levels by as much as 10%. Taking 1,500 milligrams (mg) of the B vitamin niacin under the supervision of a health-care provider can raise HDL by 25% to 30%.

Note: At high doses, niacin can cause side effects, such as flushing, liver problems and irregular heart rhythm.

Warning: Low-fat diets invariably lower HDL levels, which may actually *increase* heart attack risk. To ensure a healthy cholesterol ratio, don't simply eliminate fats from your diet. Monounsaturated and nonhydrogenated polyunsaturated fats should provide up to 30% of your daily calories.

Good sources: Olive oil, canola oil, nuts and avocados.

•**Determine your LDL size.** LDL cholesterol particles come in two sizes—large (type A) and small (type B). A predominance of type B particles increases risk of CAD by 300% to 500%, *even when LDL levels are normal* (less than 100).

Reason: Small LDL particles pass through the inner lining of coronary arteries more easily, possibly triggering a heart attack.

What to do: If you have low HDL cholesterol levels (below 45 for men and below 55 for women), particularly if any family members developed CAD before age 55, have your LDL particle size measured. This simple blood test is widely available, and many insurers now cover the cost.

The best way to decrease your type-B LDL count is to eat a healthful diet comprised of 30% fat, mostly in the form of monounsaturated fats, and limit carbohydrate intake to no more than 45% of total calories.

To boost your intake of beneficial omega-3 polyunsaturated fats, eat two to three seafood meals weekly. Choose the fattier fish, such as salmon and tuna.

Self-defense: Pregnant and lactating women should ask their doctors about limiting intake of fish due to its mercury content.

Avoid the trans-fatty acids and the omega-6 polyunsaturated fats found in margarine, fried foods, baked goods, corn and safflower oils.

●**Know your birth weight.** A low birth weight is a significant and independent risk factor for heart attack, hypertension and diabetes in adulthood. Research has shown that people who weighed less than 5.5 pounds at birth are three times more likely to develop CAD than people who weighed more than 7.5 pounds at birth.

What to do: Tell your doctor if you had a low birth weight (less than 5.5 pounds)—and show him/her this article. Many health-care providers are unaware of the increased risks associated with low birth weight.

If you were a very small baby, ask your doctor to test regularly for other coronary risk factors, such as hypertension, elevated cholesterol, diabetes and LDL particle size. These factors should be treated aggressively to offset the unalterable risk of low birth weight.

●**Choose heart-healthy beverages.** The heart-protective benefits of alcohol have been well-established. When consumed in moderation (one glass daily for women and no more than two glasses daily for men), wine, beer and mixed drinks reduce CAD by 30%.

Researchers now are discovering that water also may play a role in preventing heart attack. Physicians at Loma Linda University recently reported that drinking five or more glasses of water daily (versus two or fewer) reduces fatal heart attack risk in men by 51% and in women by 35%.

Water seems to protect against heart attacks by making blood less likely to clot. Minerals in

hard tap water, such as calcium and magnesium, also may help guard against heart disease.

What to do: Drink from six to eight 8-ounce glasses of water daily. Ask your local water utility if your water is hard (mineral rich) or soft. Even soft water from the tap may be a healthier choice than filtered bottled waters, which are generally stripped entirely of minerals.

Helpful: Consider installing a faucet-mounted home water filter that removes waterborne parasites from your water but doesn't filter out the beneficial minerals.

Good brands: Moen and Culligan.

●**Take folic acid.** This B vitamin has been shown to lower levels of homocysteine, a protein in the blood that significantly increases risk for cardiovascular disease when it is elevated. Folic acid also lowers the risk for heart attack and stroke.

In continuing research of more than 80,000 nurses, the risk for heart attack was reduced by about 6% for every additional 100 micrograms of folic acid in their diet.

What to do: Eat more folic acid–rich foods, such as spinach, asparagus, lima beans, wheat germ and fortified cereals. If your homocysteine level is greater than 9, you may need to take a folic acid supplement daily.

The Natural Way to a Healthy Heart

Allan Magaziner, DO, director of the Magaziner Center for Wellness and Anti-Aging Medicine in Cherry Hill, NJ, *www.drmagaziner.com.* Dr. Magaziner also is a clinical instructor of family practice at the University of Medicine and Dentistry of New Jersey–Robert Wood Johnson Medical School in New Brunswick, NJ. He is coauthor of *The All-Natural Cardio Cure* (Avery).

Cardiovascular disease will kill 1 million Americans this year—despite billions of dollars spent trying to stop it. Prescriptions for cholesterol-lowering drugs have skyrocketed, even though 75% of patients who start taking them discontinue use within two years because of side effects, such as muscle aches, diarrhea or nausea. We pay $10 billion a year for blood pressure drugs, yet these drugs don't work adequately for many patients.

Good news: Research proves that certain foods and supplements can help to lower your total cholesterol and blood pressure without all the side effects—and expense—of prescription pharmaceuticals.*

FOOD

By now, most people know that the omega-3 essential fatty acids (EFAs) found in cold-water fish make this one of the most heart-healthy foods. That's why I tell my patients to eat low-mercury, cold-water fish, such as wild salmon or halibut, three times a week.

My other favorite cardio-friendly foods…

●**Oat and rice bran.** All whole grains contain cholesterol-lowering soluble and insoluble fiber. But oat and rice bran contain the most soluble fiber, which has the greatest cholesterol-lowering effects.

Scientific evidence: Research suggests that a diet rich in oat bran can reduce total cholesterol levels by 10% and LDL "bad" cholesterol levels by 8%. Additional studies suggest that rice bran may have similar benefits.

Smart idea: Eat three one-half cup servings of oat or rice bran per week.

●**Sterol-enriched spreads.** Plant sterols are compounds that block the body's absorption of cholesterol.

Scientific evidence: Research indicates that consuming approximately 3 grams (g) daily of plant sterols reduces overall blood cholesterol levels by an average of 10% and LDL "bad" cholesterol levels by 14%.

Best source: Plant sterols are found in vegetable oils, nuts, whole grains, fruits and vegetables. Because it's difficult to get sufficient quantities, your best bet is to consume food products, such as sterol-enriched spreads and orange juice.

Smart idea: Get 2 to 3 g of plant sterols daily. One tablespoon of Take Control or Bene-

*col spread has 1.7 g…eight ounces of Minute Maid Heart Wise orange juice has 1 g.

●**Nuts.** In addition to plant sterols, nuts offer a healthy mix of monounsaturated fats, fiber and polyphenols, compounds that help block the oxidation of LDL cholesterol—a process that slows or prevents arterial plaque buildup.

Scientific evidence: Studies show that eating three ounces of walnuts daily for four weeks reduces total cholesterol levels by 12% and LDL cholesterol levels by 18%. Other studies have shown similar results for almonds, cashews, pecans, macadamias and pistachios.

Smart idea: Eat a handful of one or a combination of these nuts daily.

●**Potassium-rich foods.** Potassium works in combination with magnesium to balance sodium in the body and decrease blood pressure. If you're taking a diuretic for high blood pressure, you may be excreting potassium via your urine and should be extra vigilant about eating a diet that is rich in potassium.

Scientific evidence: A study published in the medical journal *Chest* confirmed that eating a potassium-rich diet enabled cardiac surgery patients taking diuretics to maintain adequate potassium levels.

Best sources: Bananas, oranges, tomatoes and dried apricots.

Smart idea: Eat at least one serving per day of a potassium-rich food.

SUPPLEMENTS

For general heart health, I tell my patients to take the following supplements daily—a good multivitamin/mineral, such as one made by Solgar or Twinlab, *plus* a 1,000-milligram (mg) vitamin C supplement…400-international unit (IU) vitamin E** supplement…a 50-mg B-complex vitamin…and an omega-3 supplement that has at least 360 mg of *eicosapentaenoic acid* (EPA) and 240 mg of *docosahexaenoic acid* (DHA).

To lower blood pressure and regulate heart rhythm, I suggest calcium (1,200 mg) and magnesium (600 mg), plus 400 IU of vitamin D in addition to the multivitamin.

*People who take medication for heart disease also can follow these recommendations to lower their dosages or stop taking the drugs altogether. Consult your physician.

**Due to the possible interactions between vitamin E and various drugs and supplements as well as other safety considerations, be sure to talk to your doctor before taking vitamin E.

If you have heart disease, ask your doctor about also trying…*

•**Arginine** (3,000 mg daily). Also called L-arginine, this amino acid triggers the production of nitric oxide, a naturally occurring substance that lowers blood pressure.

Who should consider taking it: Anyone who has hypertension, angina, peripheral artery disease, high cholesterol or systemic inflammation (a major risk factor for cardiovascular disease confirmed with a blood test for C-reactive protein).

Helpful: Do not take L-arginine two hours before or after consuming protein (meat, fish, etc.). The amino acids in the food will block absorption of the supplement. Take arginine with a carbohydrate, such as bread, pasta or fruit. If it doesn't cause gastrointestinal upset, take arginine on an empty stomach.

•**Coenzyme Q10** (100 to 300 mg every day). This fat-soluble compound is abundant in heart muscle, where it helps provide the heart with the oxygen and energy it needs to beat properly. Insufficient coQ10 can lead to congestive heart failure or arrhythmia.

Cholesterol-lowering statin drugs block the production of coQ10—which may explain the muscle aches and fatigue many patients experience while taking these medications.

Who should consider taking it: Anyone who is taking a statin…is diagnosed with hypertension, high cholesterol, angina, congestive heart failure or systemic inflammation…or is over age 60 (coQ10 levels decline with age).

*Consult your physician before starting these supplements, particularly if you are pregnant, nursing, have liver or kidney disease or are taking prescription medications.

Cinnamon… The New "Statin"?

Cinnamon may work almost as well as statin drugs to control cholesterol and triglycerides. It was found to be equally effective in a recent study of people with type 2 diabetes—

and may also work for healthy people. Cinnamon contains a substance that seems to help the body utilize insulin more efficiently. The study indicated that one-half teaspoon per day was enough—but speak with your doctor before stopping any prescribed medication.

Richard Anderson, PhD, research chemist at the USDA Beltsville Human Nutrition Research Center, MD.

More Natural "Statins"

Jay S. Cohen, MD, adjunct associate professor of family and preventive medicine and of psychiatry at the University of California, San Diego. He is the author of What You Must Know About Statin Drugs & Their Natural Alternatives *(Square One). His Web site is* www.medicationsense.com.

If you do not have cardiovascular disease (or multiple risk factors) or diabetes, check out cholesterol-lowering supplements before you commit to statins. Supplements are less likely to cause side effects. *Proven statin alternatives, all available at health-food stores…***

•**Inositol hexaniacinate,** a form of niacin, reduces LDL levels by about 20% and raises HDL levels by up to 30%. It's less likely than other forms of niacin to cause facial flushing. The typical dose is 500 milligrams (mg) two to three times daily.

•**Policosanol,** a waxy substance from sugar cane wax and beeswax, lowers LDL levels by up to 25% and raises HDL levels by up to 10%. The typical dose is 10 to 20 mg daily.

•**Red yeast rice** contains a chemical compound produced from the fermentation of rice, similar to the active ingredient in *lovastatin* (Mevacor). It can lower LDL levels by 20% to 25%. The typical dose is 1,200 mg twice daily.

Caution: Don't take red yeast rice if you're already taking a statin.

In addition to taking a statin or natural alternative, consider daily supplements, such as fish oil capsules (1,000 mg)…coenzyme Q10 (100 to 200 mg)…and magnesium (200 to 400 mg).

**Consult a health-care practitioner who is knowledgeable about the use of natural supplements.

Tomatoes Fight Heart Disease, Too

Lycopene, the phytonutrient that gives tomatoes their red color, has been shown to fight malignancies of the prostate, lungs and stomach.

New finding: Women who had the highest levels of lycopene in their blood were only half as likely to develop cardiovascular disease as those with the lowest levels.

Theory: Lycopene prevents LDL "bad" cholesterol from being oxidized and deposited in arterial plaques.

Although this study focused on women, researchers believe these findings also may hold true for men.

Helpful: Add to your diet a serving per day of lycopene-containing foods, such as one-half cup of tomato sauce, one-half pink grapefruit or one cup of watermelon.

Howard D. Sesso, ScD, assistant professor of medicine, Harvard Medical School, Boston.

Nobel Prize Winner's Breakthrough—Prevent Heart Attack and Stroke With Nitric Oxide

Louis J. Ignarro, PhD, winner of the 1998 Nobel Prize in Medicine for his research on nitric oxide. He is also a distinguished professor of pharmacology at the University of California, Los Angeles, School of Medicine, and the author of *No More Heart Disease* (St. Martin's).

One tiny molecule produced by the body may do more than any drug to prevent heart attack and stroke.

Nitric oxide, a gas that occurs naturally in the body, is critical for healthy circulation. It helps dilate blood vessels, prevent blood clots and regulate blood pressure, and it may inhibit the accumulation of arterial plaque.

HOW IT WORKS

Nitric oxide is a signaling molecule primarily produced by cells in the endothelium (inner lining) of blood vessels. A signaling molecule fits into docking sites (receptors) on cell walls and triggers biochemical reactions. *Nitric oxide helps prevent heart disease and stroke by...*

• **Expanding blood vessels.** Nitric oxide protects the blood vessels' smooth muscle tissue from harmful constriction, and this allows blood to circulate with less force. Some doctors report that elevating nitric oxide in hypertensive patients can lower blood pressure by 10 to 60 points.

• **Controlling platelet function.** Platelets, cell-like structures in blood that can clump up together, may form blood-blocking clots, the main cause of heart attack and stroke. A vascular network that is enhanced by nitric oxide sheds platelets and inhibits dangerous clots.

• **Reducing arterial plaque by 50%.** Arterial plaque, which consists of fatty deposits in the coronary arteries, is the underlying cause of heart disease. Nitric oxide is an antioxidant that inhibits the passage of monocytes, a type of immune cell, into the artery wall. This in turn reduces the underlying inflammation that promotes plaque.

• **Lowering total cholesterol by 10% to 20%.** That's a modest decrease—but there's some evidence that nitric oxide is even more effective when combined with the cholesterol-lowering statins. Nitric oxide lowers cholesterol through its antioxidant activity. The preliminary research suggests that stimulating nitric oxide production in people who have elevated cholesterol makes it possible to lower their statin doses by at least 50%.

TO BOOST NITRIC OXIDE LEVELS

It is not yet known how much nitric oxide normally is present in the body or what levels are optimal. This gas is difficult to measure because it disappears almost instantly upon exposure to air. Research scientists can measure levels with electrodes inserted in blood vessels. Simpler tests are needed before doctors can measure nitric oxide as part of standard checkups.

Beginning in early adulthood, nitric oxide levels gradually decline, probably due to damage to the endothelial cells caused by such factors as a high-fat diet and a sedentary lifestyle.

Nitric oxide can't be taken in supplement form because it's a gas. However, patients can take other supplements that increase production of nitric oxide in the blood vessels. *These supplements, all available at health-food stores, have few if any side effects...*

●**L-arginine,** an amino acid found in meats, grains and fish, passes through the intestine into the blood. From the blood, it enters endothelial cells, where it is used to make nitric oxide.

A Mayo Clinic study found that people taking L-arginine showed significant improvement in endothelial function and blood flow compared with those taking placebos. It is hard to get sufficient L-arginine from food, so supplements are recommended.

Dose: 2,000 to 3,000 milligrams (mg) taken twice daily—for a total of 4,000 to 6,000 mg.

●**L-citrulline.** Supplemental arginine doesn't enter cells readily unless it is combined with L-citrulline, another amino acid. Melons and cucumbers are rich sources of L-citrulline, but they don't provide high enough levels to significantly increase nitric oxide levels.

Dose: 400 to 600 mg daily.

●**Daily multivitamin that includes vitamin E.** Vitamin E helps reduce the assault of cell-damaging free radicals on the endothelial lining and may promote higher levels of nitric oxide. The amount of vitamin E that is in most multivitamin/mineral supplements is about 50 international units (IU), an effective dose.

Warning: Don't take the high-dose vitamin E supplements. Recent studies suggest that people who take daily doses of 400 IU or higher may be more susceptible to heart disease and other illnesses.

●**Vitamin C.** Like vitamin E, vitamin C will reduce oxidation in the blood vessels and may cause an increase in nitric oxide. People who consume high levels of vitamin C experience a reduction in arterial plaque, which is associated with higher levels of nitric oxide. You can get vitamin C from food, but I recommend supplements because they are so convenient and easy to take.

Dose: 500 mg daily.

DIET AND EXERCISE

In addition to taking supplements, it is important to maintain a healthy lifestyle by watching what you eat and being active. *Try to...*

●**Do aerobic exercise for at least 20 minutes three days a week.** It stimulates endothelial cells to continuously produce nitric oxide, even on days that you don't exercise.

●**Minimize intake of saturated fat.** Saturated fat, found in such animal products as red meat, poultry, butter and whole milk, contributes to the accumulation of arterial plaque and impairs nitric oxide production.

Better: Olive oil, fish and flaxseed. The fats found in these foods help protect the endothelium by elevating levels of beneficial HDL cholesterol and lowering the harmful LDL form.

●**Eat more fiber.** The dietary fiber in grains, fruits and vegetables lowers blood pressure and LDL cholesterol and raises HDL, thereby protecting endothelial cells.

Bonus: Many of the foods that contain fiber also are rich in antioxidants, which inhibit the cell damage that lowers nitric oxide. Eat at least 25 grams (g) of fiber daily—and drink at least eight eight-ounce glasses of water each day to make sure that the fiber moves through your system properly.

Best Ways to Cut Your Risk of Stroke

Ralph L. Sacco, MS, MD, professor of neurology and epidemiology, Columbia University Medical Center, New York City. Dr. Sacco is also the national spokesperson for the American Stroke Association, *www.strokeassociation.org.*

Every year, some 750,000 Americans suffer strokes. Although quick treatment with clot-busting drugs can sharply reduce the damage caused by a stroke, treatments have to be given within the early hours of the stroke's occurrence.

Only 1% to 2% of US stroke victims arrive at a hospital in time to get treated with anticlotting medication. This makes it even more important that people do their best to prevent strokes. They can do this by lowering or eliminating their stroke risk factors. *Here are the major risk factors that can (and can't) be changed and how to manage them effectively…*

RISK FACTORS YOU CAN'T AVOID

There's nothing you can do about some risk factors. The more you have, the more vigilant you need to be about those that you can control. *Non-modifiable factors include…*

●**Age.** The risk for stroke goes up steadily with age.

●**Gender.** Since women usually live longer than men, they suffer more disability and deaths from stroke.

●**Race and ethnicity.** African-Americans are two times more likely to both suffer a stroke and die from one than white Americans are. The stroke risk among Hispanic-Americans also appears to be nearly double that of white Americans in the same communities.

●**Genetic history.** If your father, mother or sibling has had a stroke, you may be at elevated risk as well.

RISK FACTORS YOU CAN MANAGE

Here are the major stroke risk factors that can be managed, and how to handle them…

●**High blood pressure (hypertension) is the biggest risk factor of all.** Clinical studies have proven conclusively that whenever high blood pressure is lowered, risk of stroke is also reduced.

Risk-reduction strategy: While a low-sodium diet and 30 minutes of daily exercise can help control blood pressure, most people with hypertension (defined as blood pressure of 140/90 or higher) also require medication, such as beta blockers, calcium-channel blockers or diuretics, to reach a "normal" blood pressure of 120/80.

People who have moderately elevated blood pressure (121–139/81–89) should seek treatment if they're overweight or have other stroke risk factors. There's also growing evidence that achieving a blood pressure even lower than 120/80 reduces stroke risk even more.

●**Diabetes.** Having diabetes—defined as a fasting blood sugar level of 126 milligrams per deciliter (mg/dl) or higher—increases the risk of stroke due to increased incidence of small and large blood vessel disease.

Risk-reduction strategy: Work closely with your doctor to manage your blood sugar levels through diet, exercise, regular blood-sugar testing and taking insulin, if necessary. For people with other stroke risk factors, treatment may even be warranted at prediabetic blood sugar levels (more than 110 mg/dl). Also, more aggressive control of cholesterol and blood pressure is necessary.

●**High LDL ("bad") cholesterol.** While elevated blood cholesterol has not been directly linked to increased stroke risk (as it has to coronary artery disease), evidence does suggest that people who take statins to lower their LDL cholesterol may also reduce stroke risk.

Risk-reduction strategy: Take statins, maintain a low-fat diet and exercise to boost HDL ("good") cholesterol. For people who have a low stroke risk, the LDL target is typically 160 mg/dl. With several risk factors present, the target drops to 130. For those at high risk for a stroke, the target might be 100 or even 70.

●**High triglycerides (a blood lipid).** Triglyceride levels of 150 mg/dl or higher have been shown to increase stroke risk in people with preexisting heart disease.

Risk-reduction strategy: Maintain a low-fat diet and take triglyceride-lowering medication, such as statins and fibrates (which are another group of cholesterol-lowering drugs).

●**Other heart conditions.** Atrial fibrillation (an abnormal heart rhythm in the heart's upper chambers, which allows blood to pool and clot), congestive heart failure and valvular heart disease have been linked to increased stroke risk.

Risk-reduction strategy: Prompt diagnosis and treatment. Also, possibly, the use of blood thinners such as warfarin.

●**Prior stroke or heart attack.** Someone who has had a stroke is at much greater risk of having another. Heart attack survivors are also at increased risk for stroke.

Risk-reduction strategy: Aspirin and other antiplatelet drugs significantly reduce the risk of another stroke or heart attack.

●**Cigarette smoking.** Smoking will increase stroke risk significantly, in part because smoking damages the walls of the blood vessels, making formation of stroke-causing blood clots more likely.

Risk-reduction strategy: Quit immediately.

●**Heavy use of alcohol.** Up to two alcoholic drinks a day for men and one for women may *reduce* risk of stroke. Drink more than that, however, and the pendulum begins to swing in the other direction.

For women and men, over five drinks a day raises stroke risk by increasing the blood's tendency to clot (and contributes to hypertension and heart and liver disease).

Risk-reduction strategy: Men should limit themselves to two drinks a day…women, one drink. (Be sure to seek treatment for alcoholism if necessary.)

●**Physical inactivity and obesity.** Being overweight, inactive or both increases not only stroke risk, but also your risk for high blood pressure, high cholesterol, heart disease and diabetes.

Risk-reduction strategy: A calorie-restricted diet. Thirty minutes of aerobic exercise, most or all days of the week.

●**Plaque in the carotid arteries.** Almost 20% of all strokes occur when the carotid arteries of the neck, which supply blood to the brain, are blocked by a blood clot. This is more likely to occur in people whose carotid arteries are narrowed by plaque buildup.

Risk-reduction strategy: Diagnostic tests include ultrasound scans, angiograms and magnetic resonance angiograms. Treatments include medication (anticoagulants, antiplatelets, statins or other lipid-lowering drugs) and surgical procedures (endarterectomy—surgery to clean out the carotid artery—and angioplasty or stenting).

●**Transient ischemic attacks (TIAs).** TIAs are "warning strokes" or "ministrokes." Treating a TIA promptly by getting urgent medical attention can reduce your risk of a full-blown stroke.

Risk-reduction strategy: Learn these warning signs of a TIA or stroke. Call 911 and get to a hospital immediately if you notice any of them. *They are…*

●Loss of vision in one or both eyes.

●Sudden numbness, weakness or tingling on one side of the body.

●Sudden and severe headache for no apparent reason.

●Sudden trouble walking or talking.

Natural Stroke Preventer

Getting more fruit in your diet will help you prevent stroke.

Recent finding: People who ate almost one pound of fruit a day (the equivalent of about five standard-sized apples or pears) had a 40% lower risk for ischemic stroke, which occurs when a clot blocks an artery, than those who ate one-third of a pound of fruit a day.

Theory: The antioxidants, minerals and fiber found in fruit help prevent stroke by fighting common risk factors, such as elevated blood pressure and cholesterol.

Soren Paaske Johnsen, PhD, associate professor of clinical epidemiology, Aarhus University Hospital, Denmark.

How to Protect Yourself from the Diabetes Epidemic

Christopher Saudek, MD, a professor of medicine at Johns Hopkins University and director of Johns Hopkins Diabetes Center, both in Baltimore. He is former president of the American Diabetes Association and coauthor, with Sandra Woodruff, RD, of *The Complete Diabetes Prevention Plan* (Avery).

Everyone is at risk for diabetes. It is three times more common today than it was 40 years ago—and the numbers are rising. About 18 million Americans have type 2 diabetes, the most common type, and another 16 million eventually will get it if they don't take the right steps now.

Good news: Type 2 diabetes almost always can be prevented—and even reversed—with lifestyle changes. A Harvard University study that followed more than 84,000 people for 16 years found that a healthy lifestyle—exercising, eating healthful foods, maintaining a healthful weight, etc.—lowered diabetes risk by 91%.

See the seven important diabetes-prevention strategies below…

●**Get tested.** Nearly everyone who has diabetes passes through the prediabetes stage first—when blood glucose (sugar) levels are elevated but not yet high enough to be considered diabetes. Prediabetes causes no outward symptoms but increases risk of heart attack or stroke by 50% and greatly increases risk of full-fledged diabetes.

You should ask to be screened for diabetes every three years starting at age 40. Get tested annually if you have any diabetes risk factors—you are overweight…sedentary…have a family history of diabetes…or have a waist circumference of greater than 40 inches in men or 35 inches in women.

Main tests…

●Fasting plasma glucose (FPG) test. Blood sugar is tested first thing in the morning after an overnight fast. A normal reading is 70 to 99 milligrams of glucose per deciliter (mg/dl) of blood. Anything higher means that you have prediabetes (100 to 125 mg/dl) or diabetes (126 mg/dl and over).

●Oral glucose tolerance test (OGTT). Blood sugar is tested after an overnight fast and again two hours after you drink a glucose solution. On the second test, a normal reading is below 140 mg/dl. A reading of 140 to 199 mg/dl means that you have prediabetes, and anything over 200 mg/dl indicates diabetes.

These two tests are effective in most cases. However, the FPG, which is easier and more convenient, may overlook some prediabetes patients. Your doctor can advise you on which test is best for you to take.

●**Lose 10 pounds.** The increase in diabetes is directly related to obesity. This link is so strong that doctors have coined the term *diabesity* for weight-related diabetes.

Excess fat causes cells to become resistant to insulin, the hormone that carries glucose out of the bloodstream. A large study found that an average weight loss of about 10 pounds reduces the risk of diabetes by 58%.

Weight loss is particularly important if you have excess abdominal fat. People who store fat primarily around their middles, the so-called "apple" shape, have a higher risk of diabetes and cardiovascular disease than those who store fat in their hips and thighs (the "pear" shape).

Any diet can work as long as you burn more calories than you consume. The popular low-carbohydrate diets, such as Atkins, can be very effective, but they tend to be too high in fat for long-term health and are hard to sustain.

●**Eat whole grains.** Everyone should switch from refined grains (white bread, white flour, white rice) to whole grains (brown rice, oatmeal, whole wheat, etc.). Whole grains slow the absorption of glucose in the bloodstream, thereby minimizing blood-sugar spikes that stimulate appetite and increase the risk of weight gain and diabetes.

●**Fill half your plate with produce.** Fruits and vegetables are low in calories and high in fiber. They fill you up, so you're less likely to eat other higher-calorie foods. Aim for seven or more servings daily. This isn't as hard as it may seem. A serving of fresh fruit or vegetables is one-half cup…a serving of leafy greens is one cup. One banana equals two servings…a typical wedge of watermelon is three servings.

For serving information, go to the Produce for Better Health Foundation's Web page, *www. 5aday.com/html/consumers/serving.php.*

Some people think that fresh produce is too expensive, but a US Department of Agriculture report released in 2004 showed that the seven recommended daily servings of fruits and vegetables cost $1 or less. The study showed, for example, that consumers who balk at spending 97 cents for a pound of peaches don't realize that they are getting more than four half-cup servings at roughly 24 cents each.

●**Limit fat consumption.** Fat has twice the calories of carbohydrates and protein. All fats can lead to weight gain, but saturated fat also increases cholesterol and heart disease risk.

Choose lean meats and low-fat dairy…avoid trans-fatty acids ("hydrogenated" oils)…and use canola, soybean or olive oil for cooking and salad dressing. They contain beneficial mono-unsaturated and polyunsaturated fats.

●**Avoid sugar.** The average American eats about 150 pounds of sugar annually. Sugar is digested and absorbed very quickly, promoting spikes in glucose and insulin levels that lead to diabetes and heart disease. It also contributes to obesity.

●**Get moving.** Exercise makes the body's cells more responsive to insulin and improves their ability to remove glucose from the blood. Exercise also lowers blood sugar by burning glucose for fuel and promotes weight loss—especially from the abdomen.

The landmark Diabetes Prevention Program sponsored by the government found that walking for 30 minutes a day at a moderate pace, along with weight loss and a healthful diet, reduces the risk of diabetes by more than 50%.

A combination of aerobic and strength-training exercise is optimal. About 75% of glucose disposal takes place in the muscles. Weight lifting increases muscle size and promotes more efficient glucose metabolism.

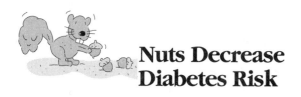

Nuts Decrease Diabetes Risk

Eating a handful of nuts or peanuts or one tablespoon of peanut butter five times a week protects against adult-onset diabetes. These foods are high in unsaturated fat, fiber and magnesium, which helps improve insulin sensitivity and glucose metabolism and lower cholesterol levels. Read food labels carefully, and use these foods as only one part of a well-balanced diet.

Rui Jiang, MD, research fellow, department of nutrition, Harvard School of Public Health, Boston, and leader of a cohort study of the Nurses' Health Study, published in The Journal of the American Medical Association.

Amazing Cancer Stoppers

Patrick Quillin, PhD, RD, clinical nutritionist located in San Diego, www.nutritioncancer.com, and previous vice president of nutrition for the Cancer Treatment Centers of America. He is the author of 15 books, including the best seller Beating Cancer with Nutrition *(Nutrition Times). He edited the textbook* Adjuvant Nutrition in Cancer Treatment *and organized three international symposiums on that topic.*

Every year, more than 1.4 million Americans are diagnosed with cancer. Nearly half of all Americans eventually will get the disease—and about 25% of them will die from it. But there is a powerful way to reduce your risk of getting cancer.

Specific nutrients and foods can help prevent or correct cellular, hormonal and other imbalances that may lead to cancer. The supplements that are mentioned here are available at health-food stores and some supermarkets.

FISH OIL

The most common nutritional deficiency in Americans is low *eicosapentaenoic acid (EPA)*. It is one of the omega-3 fatty acids found in the oil of fatty fish, such as salmon and tuna. A healthy diet will have a 1:1 ratio of omega-3 to omega-6 fatty acids (found in vegetable oils). The typical American diet has a 1:16 ratio.

EPA helps prevent cancer by improving cell membrane dynamics—the ability of each cell to receive hormones and signals from other cells while also absorbing essential nutrients and expelling waste products. EPA also increases immune function and lowers levels of hormones that contribute to breast and other cancers, such as *estradiol*.

What I recommend to my patients: One tablespoon of fish oil daily. For capsules, follow dosage recommendations on labels. Carlson Laboratories, Dr. Sears, Nordic Naturals and the Pharmax brands are reliable. Take it in the middle of a meal to avoid "fishy" belching or reflux.

CLA

Another fat that helps prevent cancer is *conjugated linoleic acid* (CLA), found in the meat and milk of grass-eating animals, such as cattle, deer, sheep and goats. CLA helps build healthy cell membranes, permitting the cells to absorb nutrients, process hormones and expel waste. It's hard to find CLA-rich foods in the markets because most livestock in America are fed grain, not grass.

What I recommend to my patients: Three grams (g) of CLA a day. You can get that from an eight-ounce serving of grass-fed beef. Look for such brands as Lasater Grasslands Beef, available at most specialty food stores. On days when you don't eat grass-fed red meat, you can take a CLA supplement—three 1-g soft-gel capsules a day.

VITAMIN D

People who live in Boston have, on average, double the risk for breast, colon and prostate cancers, compared with residents of San Diego. Why? Many scientists think it's because Bostonians, like other northerners, don't get enough vitamin D, which is produced whenever skin is exposed to sun.

Vitamin D is one of the most powerful anti-cancer nutrients. It facilitates the absorption of calcium, a mineral that not only builds strong bones but also is critical for "telegraphing" messages between cells. Poor cell-to-cell communication can contribute to cancer. Studies show that levels of vitamin D in fortified foods rarely equal the claims made on the labels. There is a debate as to whether synthetic vitamin D—the kind found in supplements—provides the same cancer protection as the naturally produced vitamin D.

What I recommend to my patients: During the summer, get 15 minutes a day of the midday sunshine with no sunscreen (without burning) on the face and bare arms. The body stockpiles vitamin D in the liver, so you're set for the rest of the year.

VITAMIN C

In a report published in the *American Journal of Clinical Nutrition,* 33 of 46 studies showed that vitamin C protects against cancer. Cancer feeds on blood sugar (glucose)—and lowering chronically high blood sugar is crucial to preventing cancer. When you get enough vitamin C, you cut in half the amount of blood sugar that enters cells.

What I recommend to my patients: 500 to 1,000 milligrams (mg) of vitamin C a day, in three divided doses, taken with meals. Cancer patients may need higher doses, which usually are given intravenously.

Other ways to normalize blood sugar levels include regular exercise, weight loss and a diet that emphasizes lean meats, beans, nuts and produce. Five daily servings of fruits and vegetables nets you 300 mg of vitamin C.

SELENIUM

During the four-year Nutritional Prevention of Cancer Trial, scientists gave 1,312 participants either 200 micrograms (mcg) of the trace mineral selenium or a placebo. The results showed that selenium lowered the risk of prostate cancer by 63%, colon cancer by 58% and lung cancer by 46%.

Selenium can strengthen the immune system, help to repair DNA damage and protect cells against toxins.

What I recommend to my patients: 200 mcg of selenium a day. Look for *selenomethionine*—selenium bound in yeast—because it is absorbed the best. A particularly good food source is Brazil nuts (just four nuts will provide 200 mcg).

Caution: More is not better. Selenium supplements in doses of 2,000 mcg or higher can be toxic.

GREEN TEA

Literally hundreds of studies have now proven that green tea and its various extracts can prevent and, in some experiments, reverse cancer. These extracts work by different mechanisms, among them *apoptosis* or "programmed cell death." In other words, green tea orders cancer cells to commit suicide.

What I recommend to my patients: Drink three eight-ounce cups of green tea a day. If you don't like the taste, take supplements of green tea extract, available in capsules. Be sure to follow the dosage recommendation that's on the label.

KILLER CONSTIPATION

Chronic constipation creates toxemia in the colon. Cancer-causing chemicals from the environment are ingested but not expelled quickly. Normally friendly food-digesting bacteria then produce toxins that end up in the bloodstream.

What I recommend to my patients: To ensure a daily bowel movement, get plenty of high-fiber foods…drink 64 ounces of filtered or bottled water a day…and exercise regularly. Prune juice and figs often relieve constipation. Or try a gentle herbal laxative, such as *psyllium* (Metamucil), following the dosage recommendation on the label.

An Orange a Day Keeps Cancer Away

Daily consumption of citrus fruits, such as oranges, reduces risk of mouth, larynx and stomach cancer by up to 50%.

Reason: Citrus fruits contain high levels of antioxidants, which strengthen the body's immune system.

Another benefit: One serving of citrus fruit as part of the recommended five daily servings of fruits and vegetables can reduce stroke risk by 19%.

Katrine Baghurst, PhD, the program manager and researcher for the Commonwealth Scientific and Industrial Research Organization in Adelaide, Australia, and leader of a study of a meta-analysis of 500 papers, published in *Horticulture Australia.*

A Slice of Prevention

Researchers who recently tracked 8,000 Italians report that those who ate pizza one or more times a week were 59% less likely to get cancer of the esophagus and 26% less likely to develop colon cancer than the participants who did not eat pizza.

Reason: Tomatoes and olive oil have been shown to reduce the risk for various cancers.

International Journal of Cancer, Heidelberg, Germany.

Rheumatoid Arthritis Is Linked to Diets Low In Vitamin C

Among study volunteers taking part in long-term research on chronic disease and diet, those who developed two or more swollen joints had the lowest vitamin C intake.

Theory: Vitamin C acts as an antioxidant, squelching the activity of free radicals. This prevents the tissue damage that can lead to joint inflammation.

Self-defense: Get at least 60 milligrams (mg) of vitamin C daily from fruits and vegetables.

Good choices: Red peppers (283 mg per cup)…strawberries (98 mg per cup)…and oranges (70 mg per orange).

Dorothy Pattison, PhD, RD, former research dietitian at the University of Manchester, United Kingdom, and now a research fellow in epidemiology and public health at University College in London.

Natural Healing For Arthritis

In a recent finding, the levels of two enzymes known to cause cartilage damage were lowered in 13 out of 15 people who took cod liver oil twice daily for 10 weeks.

Theory: The balance of omega-3 fatty acids and vitamins found in the oil may be responsible for the benefit.

Helpful: Ask your doctor about taking a 1,000-milligram (mg) capsule or one teaspoon of cod liver oil per day. Check the label to be sure the oils are free of contaminants, such as mercury and polychlorinated biphenyls (PCBs).

John L. Harwood, PhD, DSc, head, school of biosciences, Cardiff University, Cardiff, Wales.

Natural Help for Migraines

Available in pharmacies as well as in health-food stores, coenzyme Q10 (coQ10) has long been used to treat high blood pressure, heart disease, cancer and Parkinson's disease.

Recent study: Migraine sufferers who took 100 milligrams (mg) of liquid coQ10 three times a day for three months averaged 3.2 migraines per month versus 4.4 migraines per month before the study. Those who received a placebo reported no change.

Seymour Diamond, MD, founder and director, Diamond Headache Clinic, Chicago, *www.diamondheadache.com.*

The Best Mattress for a Bad Back

Firm mattresses may not be the best choice for people with chronic low back pain.

Recent study: Among patients who used a medium mattress, 82% reported improvement in pain after three months, compared with 68% of those using a firm mattress.

Francisco M. Kovacs, MD, PhD, director of the scientific department, Kovacs Foundation, Palma de Mallorca, Spain, and leader of a study of 313 people with back pain, published in *The Lancet.*

Let the Sun Shine In

Surgery patients in sunny rooms had drug costs 21% lower than those of equally ill patients in darker rooms.

Possible reason: People feel less pain when they are in a better mood, and sunlight seems to improve mood.

Bruce Rabin, MD, PhD, medical director of the Health Lifetime Program at the University of Pittsburgh, and leader of a study of 89 spinal-fusion patients, published in *Psychiatric Medicine.*

Natural Pain Relievers That Really Work

Mark A. Stengler, ND, a naturopathic physician and founder and director of the La Jolla Whole Health Clinic, La Jolla, CA. He is also author of the newsletter *BottomLine/Natural Healing with Dr. Mark Stengler* and has written many books, including *The Natural Physician's Healing Therapies* (Bottom Line Books). Both of these publications are available at *www.bottomlinesecrets.com.*

For most people, prescription and over-the-counter (OTC) pain relievers are fine for occasional use, but they carry increasing risks the longer they are taken.

Aspirin and other nonsteroidal anti-inflammatory drugs (NSAIDs), such as *ibuprofen* (Advil), *naproxen* (Aleve) and *ketoprofen* (Orudis KT), can cause digestive problems, including internal bleeding. *Acetaminophen* (Tylenol) is potentially toxic to the liver and kidneys after months of use. Prescription drugs that contain either barbiturates, such as *phenobarbital* (Solfoton), or opiates, such as *oxycodone* (OxyContin), are potentially habit-forming.

These are among the reasons why many people are turning to natural pain relievers, which include vitamins, minerals, herbs and homeopathic remedies (highly diluted natural substances made from plants, minerals and animal products).*

Natural pain relievers aren't as strong as pharmaceutical products, so they may not work as fast. But because they are less toxic, they typically are much safer over the long run, especially for treating chronic pain.

Both drugs and natural pain relievers block the body's pain signals, but natural remedies will also enhance the body's own recuperative power to repair injured tissue and fight disease. *The following are some of my favorite natural pain relievers...*

ARTHRITIS AND BACK PAIN

• **Methylsulfonylmethane (MSM).** This compound, which occurs naturally in living organisms, works as a potent anti-inflammatory. It decreases muscle spasm and slows down the

---

*Even when a natural remedy (or drug) does effectively relieve pain, it is important to discover and treat the underlying cause. Consult your physician, especially if muscle or joint pain or other symptoms worsen.

overactive nerve impulses that may cause this condition.

Because most back pain is the result of muscle spasm and inflammation, MSM often brings lasting relief and can prevent future episodes. In addition, it has been shown to ease the pain associated with fibromyalgia and osteoarthritis.

Typical dosage: For preventive purposes (for arthritis, chronic back pain, fibromyalgia, etc.), 1,000 to 2,000 milligrams (mg) daily, indefinitely. For relief of acute pain, the effective dose will depend on individual factors, such as weight and age. Start out with 3,000 mg per day and increase in increments of 1,000 mg every two to three days, until you experience relief or reach 6,000 mg daily.

Helpful: Take MSM with food to minimize digestive upset.

●**Boswellia.** This herb, which is widely used in Ayurvedic (Indian) medicine, is another anti-inflammatory that treats both rheumatoid arthritis and osteoarthritis. A review of 11 German studies found that boswellia brought substantial benefits to 260 people who had not responded to conventional medical treatment. Most were able to curb their intake of anti-inflammatory medication.

Typical dosage: 1,500 mg of a standardized preparation (containing 60% to 65% boswellic acid), three times a day for six weeks. For long-term use, decrease the dosage to 750 mg, three times a day.

●**Rhus toxicodendron.** This homeopathic remedy, derived from poison oak, is particularly helpful for rheumatoid arthritis or osteoarthritis pain that is worse in the morning and improves with motion and activity…or arthritis pain that flares up just before a storm or in very damp weather.

Typical dosage: For long-term use for pain that's chronic, take a 6C potency pellet, two to three times daily.

INJURY

●**Arnica.** When pain is the result of a bump or bruise, this homeopathic remedy can be extremely effective, sometimes within minutes. It also is very helpful for muscle soreness after overexertion.

Typical dosage: Dissolve two 30C potency pellets under your tongue every 15 minutes for a total of up to three doses per day, until the pain goes away.

Arnica is also available as a cream or tincture. Apply it directly to the painful spot.

●**Rhus toxicodendron.** This homeopathic remedy, also used for arthritis, is ideal for strains and sprains. Besides relieving pain, it also helps to speed recovery.

Typical dosage: Dissolve one 30C potency pellet under your tongue, two to three times daily for two days.

●**Bromelain.** This protein-dissolving enzyme is found in pineapple stems. It effectively reduces the swelling and bruising that cause pain for days after injury. Bromelain breaks down the blood clots that form as a result of physical trauma, restoring circulation and healing damaged tissue.

Typical dosage: 500 mg, three times daily between meals. Look for a bromelain preparation standardized to 1,600 milk-clotting units (MCU) per 500 mg.

Caution: Bromelain can have a slight blood-thinning effect. Check with your doctor before taking it if you're on blood-thinning medication, such as *warfarin* (Coumadin).

NERVE PAIN

●**Capsaicin.** A potent compound found in cayenne pepper, capsaicin apparently blocks the messenger chemical *substance P* from carrying pain signals along the nerves.

It can be highly effective against the often severe pain of shingles (*herpes zoster*). Capsaicin also relieves diabetic neuropathy, the pain that develops usually in the legs and feet of diabetics because of nerve damage.

Typical dosage: Apply a cream that contains 0.025% to 0.075% capsaicin extract to the painful area, two to four times daily.

Natural Remedies For Chronic Skin Problems

Chronic skin problems, such as eczema, psoriasis and acne, are some of the most common reasons people visit dermatologists. Conventional topical treatments (ointments and lotions) are helpful, but many people find they work only temporarily.

The majority of chronic skin problems need to be addressed internally as well as externally because they often are the result of internal problems related to digestion, detoxification and liver function.

Several natural remedies are effective, and they rarely have side effects. Allow four weeks for improvement of chronic skin problems... one to two days for acute flare-ups. For each condition, you can use all the remedies recommended. Unless otherwise noted, they prevent as well as treat the condition. All are available in drugstores and/or health-food stores.

Important: Never start a new treatment without consulting your doctor, especially if you are taking any medications or are pregnant.

ECZEMA

• **EPA (*eicosapentaenoic acid*).** This long-chain fatty acid in the omega-3 family has potent anti-inflammatory properties. The highest concentrations are found in fish and fish oils, but EPA also is prevalent in other foods, such as flaxseed and walnuts.

It is hard to get enough EPA from fish and/or walnuts, so I suggest that adults take fish oil in a dosage containing 1.8 grams (g) of EPA daily or two tablespoons of flaxseed oil daily, whichever you prefer.

• **Evening primrose oil.** This contains a different essential fatty acid known as *gamma linolenic acid (GLA),* which helps reduce skin inflammation. Take 2,000 milligrams (mg) of primrose oil daily.

• **Probiotics.** These good bacteria prevent food sensitivities that often are connected with eczema. Friendly bacteria are found in yogurt (look for products with live cultures, such as Horizon Organic and Stonyfield Farm). Good bacteria also are in sauerkraut, kefir (a cultured milk product, like yogurt), miso and cottage cheese. It's hard to get enough from food, so I suggest a supplement. Take four billion organisms (usually one to two capsules) daily between meals.

• **Sulphur.** This homeopathic remedy will soothe skin and relieve itching. It is particularly helpful if eczema is worse after bathing and in warm environments. For acute flare-ups, take two pellets of a 30C potency twice daily for one week. Then stop taking this remedy, unless the symptoms return.

• **Chamomile (*Matricaria chamomilla*).** Chamomile contains a group of phytonutrients that have strong anti-inflammatory properties. Apply a cream to the affected areas two to three times daily until symptoms disappear.

• **Oatmeal baths soothe itchy skin.** Tie up one-quarter cup of oats in cheesecloth or a leg from nylons, and let water from the tap run over it before you soak in the bath. Oatmeal also can be purchased as a powder and added to your bath. Pat, don't rub, yourself dry.

PSORIASIS

• **Fish oil.** Take 5 g twice a day. It will significantly reduce the itching, scaling and redness of psoriasis lesions.

• **Dandelion root (*Taraxacum officinale*).** This supports liver detoxification, which improves psoriasis. Take 300 mg of the capsule form three times daily with meals.

• **Aloe vera.** One study showed that a 0.5% aloe vera cream used for four weeks significantly relieved psoriasis lesions. Apply aloe vera cream twice daily.

ACNE

• **Zinc.** One double-blind study found that taking 30 mg of zinc for three months was an effective treatment for acne for almost one-third of patients. Adults should take 45 mg of zinc twice daily with meals for three months and then reduce the dosage to 30 mg daily for long-term supplementation. To maintain mineral balance, take zinc in conjunction with copper at a dose of 3 to 5 mg once a day.

●**Burdock root (*Arctium lappa*).** This herb treats many of the causes of acne, including hormonal imbalance, inefficient liver activity and skin bacteria. You can take 300 mg of the capsule form, 30 drops of tincture or one cup of tea three times daily.

●**Fish oil.** Take supplements or flaxseed oil in the dosages recommended for eczema (see EPA on page 85).

●**Tea tree oil gels or creams.** Tea tree oil is an antiseptic and an anti-inflammatory. Apply topically once daily.

WOUNDS/BURNS

●**Aloe vera.** Apply this topically twice a day until the burn or wound is healed. Look for a product that contains a high concentration (80% or higher) of aloe.

●**Calendula officinalis.** This soothing herb is an antiseptic. Apply it as a gel or cream twice a day.

●**Vitamin C.** Take 1,000 mg twice daily to promote wound healing. For quicker healing, take 400 international units (IU) of vitamin E* and 30 mg of zinc daily as well.

*Due to the possible interactions between vitamin E and various drugs and supplements as well as other safety considerations, be sure to talk to your doctor before taking vitamin E.

Supplements Can Cause Eye Problems

Chamomile, ginkgo biloba, licorice and echinacea can bring on retinal bleeding, conjunctivitis or temporary loss of vision when consumed in larger-than-recommended doses —especially when in combination with prescription drugs that have a similar effect.

Self-defense: Make sure that your doctor is aware of all the supplements you are taking, as well as all prescription and over-the-counter medicines.

Leland W. Carr III, OD, dean, professor of optometry, College of Optometry, Pacific University, Forest Grove, OR.

Natural Remedies for Hearing Loss

Michael D. Seidman, MD, director of the division of otologic/neurotologic surgery, department of otolaryngology–head and neck surgery, Henry Ford Health System in West Bloomfield, MI. He also is director of the Otolaryngology Research Laboratory, a codirector of the Tinnitus Center, medical chair of the Center for Integrative Medicine for the Henry Ford Health System and founder of Body Language Vitamin Company, *www.bodylanguagevitamin.com.*

About 28 million Americans have trouble hearing. The most common cause is the general wear and tear on the ears as you age. This is triggered by the gradual weakening and eventual death of hair cells in the inner ear or degeneration of the auditory nerve, or both. *To protect your hearing…*

BLOCK SOUND

Sound is measured in decibels (dB). A whisper is 15 dB…normal conversation, 50 to 60… a rock concert or jet engine, 120…a gunshot or firecracker, 140. If you have to raise your voice to be heard, you're listening to an 85-dB sound or higher.

Sounds above 85 dB can permanently damage ears by destroying the hair cells of the inner ear. This includes sounds you might not think are dangerous, such as a blow-dryer (85 to 90 dB) or loud music in an exercise class (110 dB).

I suggest carrying earplugs with you. They reduce sound by 18 to 22 dB. Use them when flying, on a hunting trip, mowing the lawn, riding a snowmobile and blow-drying your hair. Spongy, compressible plugs or waxlike plugs, available at most drugstores, do a good job.

TAKE NUTRITIONAL SUPPLEMENTS

These antioxidants, available at drug and/or health-food stores, may help fight hearing loss by reducing cell-damaging free radicals. As always, check with your doctor before starting any supplement.

●**N-acetylcysteine (NAC).** NAC is a biochemical precursor to *glutathione,* an antioxidant shown in numerous studies to reduce hearing loss in animals exposed to loud noise. A federally funded experiment with humans now is in progress. In the study, 600 marines at Camp Pendleton in California are undergoing rifle training—which typically reduces hearing in about 10% of trainees—while taking a supplement that contains NAC. I suggest 500 milligrams (mg) of NAC two or three times a day.

●**Alpha-lipoic acid and acetyl-L-carnitine.** Scientists studied three groups of aging rats for six weeks. Group 1 received alpha-lipoic acid. Group 2 got acetyl-L-carnitine. Group 3 didn't get any supplements. Before and after the supplementation, the rats' hearing loss was tested. Group 3 had an "expected age-associated deterioration" in hearing of three to seven dB. But Groups 1 and 2 had an "actual improvement in hearing" at varying frequencies—a great result.

I suggest taking 150 mg of alpha-lipoic acid daily and 600 mg of acetyl-L-carnitine daily.

●**Other antioxidants and supplements that are scientifically proven to help protect hearing** include vitamin C (500 to 800 mg daily), which improves hearing of low frequencies...vitamin E* (200 to 600 international units [IU] daily), which improves hearing of high frequencies...and lecithin (500 to 750 mg daily), which resulted in 75% improvement in hearing in lab animals, compared with a placebo.

IMPROVE HEALTH

Like every organ, ears need good circulation for optimal function. People who have a high total cholesterol and LDL and/or excess weight may have a reduced blood supply to the inner ear, which can cause hearing loss. *To improve your circulation...*

●**Eat a diet rich in fruits and vegetables** and low in saturated fat.

●**Exercise regularly**—at least 30 minutes of aerobic exercise four times a week.

●**Don't smoke.**

●**Maintain an appropriate weight.**

●**Drink lots of water**—eight eight-ounce glasses a day.

If these lifestyle measures are not effective, your doctor may recommend statin drugs to lower cholesterol.

*Due to the possible interactions between vitamin E and various drugs and supplements as well as other safety considerations, be sure to talk to your doctor before taking vitamin E.

A WORD ON HEARING AIDS

If you feel that you might need a hearing aid, see an audiologist. Ask your doctor for a recommendation.

An audiologist can determine the type of hearing aid that is best for your problem and properly fit it to your ear. *Also...*

●**Don't hunt for "bargains."** Good hearing aids range from $600 to $3,000, depending on the type. They usually are not covered by insurance or are partially covered at best.

●**Buy two.** If you have hearing loss in both ears, wear two aids.

●**Give your hearing aid a chance.** At first, most people don't like how a hearing aid feels. Break yours in. Wear it for two hours the first day, then three, then four, etc.

HOW'S YOUR HEARING?

If you answer *yes* to one or more of the following questions, consult an audiologist...

●**Do I frequently ask people to repeat themselves?**

●**Have I been turning up the TV?**

●**Do I know that people are speaking** but often can't tell what they're saying?

●**To hear better, do I turn an ear** in the direction of the person speaking?

●**Do I find it difficult to hear children's or women's voices?**

●**Do I have trouble hearing words that contain S, F, Sh, Ch, H or soft C sounds** (all of which have higher frequencies than other sounds)?

Natural Relief for Allergies and Asthma

Richard Firshein, DO, director of the Firshein Center for Comprehensive Medicine, which specializes in treating allergies and asthma, New York City. A sufferer of asthma himself, he's also the author of *The Nutraceutical Revolution* (Riverhead) and *Reversing Asthma* (Warner).

Millions of Americans suffer from asthma and allergies, frequently triggered by such airborne substances as mold, dust mites or pollen. The immune system identifies these normally harmless substances as dangerous and releases inflammatory chemicals that trigger sneezing, wheezing and congestion as well as other symptoms.

The drugs used for these conditions—antihistamines, inhaled steroids, etc.—curtail symptoms but frequently cause side effects such as fatigue or anxiety.

Better approach: Studies have shown that many over-the-counter supplements act as natural antihistamines/anti-inflammatories that can reduce or prevent allergy or asthma flare-ups —without side effects. My patients who use nutritional supplements often are able to stop taking asthma and allergy drugs or significantly reduce the dosages. You can take one or all of the supplements below daily, but always check with your doctor first.

QUERCETIN

Quercetin is a member of a class of nutrients known as bioflavonoids. It is a powerful anti-inflammatory that helps to prevent the lungs, nasal passages and eyes from swelling after allergen exposure. It also inhibits the release of *histamine,* a chemical that triggers allergy and asthma flare-ups.

What I recommend to my patients: 300 milligrams (mg) twice daily. If your symptoms are severe, increase the amount to 1,000 mg twice daily until symptoms abate. Then switch back to a maintenance dose of 300 mg twice daily. Quercetin works better for prevention than short-term treatment. It usually takes several weeks to become effective.

VITAMIN C

This potent antioxidant has a mild antihistamine effect.

What I recommend to my patients: 500 to 1,000 mg each day. Vitamin C may cause diarrhea in some people. Divide the daily amount into two doses to reduce the risk of this side effect. Also, patients with a history of kidney stones should talk to their doctors before taking vitamin C supplements.

NETTLES

A traditional herbal remedy for allergies, nettles inhibit the body's production of inflamma-tory prostaglandins. In one study of 69 allergy patients, 57% had significant improvement in symptoms after taking nettles. Nettles work quickly, often within hours, and can be taken during flare-ups.

What I recommend to my patients: 300 to 600 mg daily.

MAGNESIUM

This mineral is a natural bronchodilator that relaxes muscles in the airways and promotes better breathing. Supplementation with magnesium may be especially helpful if you're taking corticosteroids or other asthma drugs—they tend to decrease the amount of magnesium in the body.

What I recommend to my patients: 200 to 600 mg daily.

ALLERGY TESTS

Your doctor may recommend skin or blood tests to determine if your allergies are caused by dust mites, mold, pollen, etc. Once you know what you're allergic to, you can take steps to minimize exposure.

Example: If you're allergic to dust mites, you can buy mattress and pillow casings that are impervious to allergens…and use a vacuum that has a high-efficiency particulate air (HEPA) filter.

Beer Builds Better Bones

Dietary silicon, found in whole grains and their products (such as beer), decreases bone loss *and* promotes bone formation. Beer is an especially good source because it is readily absorbed. Other sources of silicon include oat bran, barley and rice.

Warning: More than two drinks per day for men or one for women is considered harmful.

Ravin Jugdaohsingh, PhD, senior research fellow, gastrointestinal laboratory, Rayne Institute, St. Thomas's Hospital, London.

The Oxygen Cure: Easy Steps to Boost Your Energy and Alertness

Daniel Hamner, MD, physiatrist (physical rehabilitation specialist), sports medicine physician and the owner and founder of the Peak Energy Program in New York City. He is coauthor of *Peak Energy: The High-Oxygen Program for More Energy Now* (St. Martin's).

Every cell in the body requires oxygen to function properly. The brain alone uses at least 12% of the total oxygen that people inhale.

Problem: The breathing habits of most people don't always provide all the oxygen that the brain and body need.

Oxygen deprivation is a leading cause of persistent fatigue—a condition that accounts for up to 15 million doctor visits annually, making it one of the most common health problems in the US. It also causes mental fogginess and, in some cases, depression.

My story: For years, I barely had enough energy to get through my workdays. I started reading about energy-enhancing techniques—everything from yoga to the latest research in exercise physiology. I quickly realized that all of these techniques aim to increase oxygen levels in the body.

At the age of 47, I developed—and began practicing—a high-oxygen program. Within a matter of months, my oxygen usage rose from 42.7 milliliters (ml) of oxygen per kilogram of body weight per minute to 55 ml—a big 30% increase. At the same time, my energy levels rose dramatically.

SEVEN STEPS TO BETTER OXYGENATION

Nearly everyone can increase oxygen levels and experience a significant boost in energy in as little as two weeks. *Here's how…*

●**Step 1.** Take a pro-oxygenator. The herbal supplement ginseng enhances the body's ability to utilize oxygen. A four-week study of oxygen utilization found that people taking ginseng experienced a 29% improvement in oxygen transportation to tissues and organs.

Typical dose: 400 to 600 mg once daily.

Caution: Do not take ginseng if you have high blood pressure. And, if you are taking medication, consult with your physician before trying ginseng.

●**Step 2.** Stand straight. Poor posture, rounding the shoulders, stooping forward, etc.—can inhibit oxygen intake. People who stand up straight, roll back their shoulders, push their chests out while they squeeze their shoulder blades together and keep their chin up can increase lung capacity greatly.

Helpful: To ensure proper form, practice this while looking in a full-length mirror.

●**Step 3.** Exercise. Aerobic exercise increases pathways in the body that carry oxygen to the cells. People who start an aerobic exercise program experience an immediate increase in oxygen usage and energy.

My recommendation: Walk fast, run, swim, bike, etc.—for a minimum of 60 minutes three days a week.

Resistance training will increase strength and endurance. Consult a physical trainer or other exercise professional for a strength-training regimen that works the muscles in your upper and lower body and your core (trunk).

My recommendation: Twenty to 30 minutes of strength training at least three times a week.

●**Step 4.** Eat "charge-up" foods. A diet high in complex carbohydrates—fruits (such as apples and oranges)…vegetables (such as carrots and spinach)…whole grains…legumes (such as peas and black beans)…etc.—significantly improves the blood's ability to transport oxygen to cells. A high-fat diet does the opposite—it reduces the blood's oxygen-carrying capacity.

●**Step 5.** Practice instant-energy breathing. You can reverse fatigue almost instantly with a yoga breathing technique that floods cells with oxygen and boosts energy for 15 minutes or longer. *What to do…*

●Sit up straight and take 20 to 30 quick, panting breaths. Only your belly should move, not your chest.

●Take a deep breath, filling your lungs with air…and hold for 30 seconds. This gives the blood in your lungs time to absorb as much oxygen as possible. If you can, gradually work up to holding your breath for 60 seconds.

•Exhale completely. Press your hand against your belly. This puts pressure on your lungs and forces out more of the used air.

After completing the exercise, walk briskly for 10 minutes, if possible. This will pull additional air into your lungs and increase the circulation of oxygen-rich blood cells.

•**Step 6.** Stop smoking—and avoid secondhand smoke. Smokers tend to have less energy and more depression than nonsmokers, in part because they get less blood and oxygen to the brain. Smoking—as well as exposure to secondhand smoke—increases blood levels of carbon monoxide, a waste chemical that contributes to fatigue. Smoking also causes higher levels of arterial plaque—fatty accumulations that inhibit circulation.

People who attend smoking cessation programs, such as SmokEnders, or who use stopsmoking products, such as nicotine patches, are about twice as likely to quit the habit as those who try to stop on their own.

Important: Take 1,000 milligrams (mg) of vitamin C daily when trying to quit smoking. Each cigarette inactivates 25 mg of vitamin C in the body.

•**Step 7.** See a physician if you have low energy. Fatigue is a common first symptom of hundreds of medical conditions, including iron-deficiency anemia, food allergies, heart problems and cancer. Consult your doctor if you experience mental fogginess or low physical energy for more than a few weeks.

ARE YOU GETTING ENOUGH OXYGEN?

Most people can check out their own oxygen levels with this simple test…

•**Stand in front of a step.** Relax for a moment, then check your resting heart rate.

To do this: Place the tips of your index and middle fingers on the thumb side of your wrist. Count your heartbeats for 30 seconds, then multiply by two.

•**Rapidly step onto and off of the step for one minute.** Check your heart rate again. It probably has risen quite a bit—from, say, 80 beats to 120 beats per minute.

•**Rest for one minute, then check your heart rate again.** If it returned to the resting level, your blood is carrying adequate oxygen.

If it stayed elevated above the resting level for more than one minute, your heart is trying to compensate for low blood levels of oxygen.

New Folate Benefit

The latest research suggests that the B vitamin folate may play a role in clinical depression. One recent study found that women with low folate levels in their blood are twice as likely to suffer from depression symptoms as those with higher levels.

Sources: Leafy greens, broccoli, oranges, beans, peanuts, corn, fortified grain products.

Martha S. Morris, PhD, epidemiologist, Human Nutrition Research Center on Aging, Tufts University, Boston.

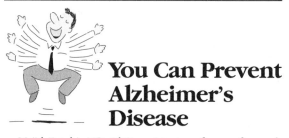

You Can Prevent Alzheimer's Disease

Majid Fotuhi, MD, PhD, assistant professor of neurology at Johns Hopkins University School of Medicine and director of the Memory Disorders Unit at Sinai Hospital, both in Baltimore. He also is clinical instructor in neurology at Harvard Medical School in Boston and the author of *The Memory Cure: How to Protect Your Brain Against Memory Loss and Alzheimer's Disease* (McGraw-Hill).

The scientists who research Alzheimer's disease (AD) have yet to discover what causes the formation of abnormal protein structures (called plaques and tangles) that destroy brain cells.

However: It's now clear that certain lifestyle practices can guard against the inexorable memory loss and personality changes associated with this dreaded disease.

Evidence: In a landmark study of 678 Midwestern nuns, autopsy reports found that the brains of one-third of the 251 nuns who died in the course of the study had the plaques and tangles of AD but did *not* show symptoms of the disease. On the other hand, some nuns who showed *fewer* plaques and tangles had experienced AD symptoms.

ASSAULTS ON THE BRAIN

AD gets the lion's share of attention, but it's just one of many enemies that menace the brain as we grow older. *Among them…*

•**Inflammation.** This is a normal defense mechanism in which the body's immune system destroys foreign molecules, such as viruses, by releasing high-energy molecules, including free radicals. With aging, a mild degree of inflammation occurs in joints, skin and the brain, causing arthritis, skin wrinkles and memory problems.

•**Ministrokes.** Each ministroke (blockage of tiny blood vessels within the brain) may kill too few cells to have noticeable impact, but if ministrokes occur hundreds—or even thousands—of times, they take their toll.

It's the *cumulative* impact that counts—the plaques and tangles of AD, plus all the other sources of damage. Anything you do to promote the overall health of your brain may delay —or even prevent—memory loss and other AD symptoms.

PROTECT YOUR BRAIN

Many of the same practices that lower your risk for heart attack and stroke also reduce the chances that you will develop AD.

•**Control your blood pressure.** High blood pressure narrows blood vessels and reduces blood flow to the brain, depriving it of oxygen and nutrients. This makes brain cells more vulnerable to AD damage and raises the risk for ministrokes.

Scientific evidence: Numerous studies have linked rising blood pressure with declining memory. A Scandinavian study of 1,449 middle-aged volunteers, reported in the *British Medical Journal,* found that those with mild hypertension—130 to 140 systolic (top number)—had twice the chance of having AD 20 years later. Those with more severe hypertension—141 to 160 systolic—had nearly three times the risk.

Self-defense: Keep your blood pressure at 120/80 or below. If it exceeds 130/90 despite efforts to bring it down—losing weight, exercising and quitting smoking—you may need

medication, such as diuretics, beta-blockers or calcium channel blockers.

•**Lower cholesterol.** High cholesterol levels cause narrowing of blood vessels, which impairs circulation in the brain and may lead to ministrokes. Some research now indicates that high cholesterol promotes the development of AD plaques.

Scientific evidence: The same Scandinavian study found that people with total cholesterol above 250 milligrams per deciliter (mg/dl) were more than twice as likely to develop AD in later life than those with normal levels.

Self-defense: Aim for total cholesterol under 150 mg/dl. A healthy diet, exercise and smoking cessation can help bring it down. If your cholesterol remains above 150, talk to your physician about medication.

Statins, such as *pravastatin* (Pravachol) and *atorvastatin* (Lipitor), are the drugs of choice for elevated cholesterol. Several studies have found that individuals taking these drugs have 60% to 80% less risk of developing AD than those not taking them.

DIET FOR A HEALTHY BRAIN

Like the rest of your body, your brain must be well fed to function optimally…

•**Eat at least five servings of fruits and vegetables daily.** They contain antioxidant vitamins and phytochemicals that protect brain cells from damage by free radicals.

Best antioxidant food sources: Blueberries, pomegranates, carrots and the green, leafy vegetables.

There is one antioxidant that deserves particular attention—vitamin E.

Scientific evidence: A Dutch study of 5,395 people, age 55 or older, published in the *Journal of the American Medical Association,* found that those consuming the most vitamin E in foods and supplements had 43% less chance of developing AD than those consuming the least.

Boost your intake of vitamin E–rich foods, such as whole grains, avocados and olive oil.*

•**Have fish twice weekly.** Cold-water fish, such as both wild salmon and mackerel, contain

---

*If you take vitamin E in supplement form, be sure to check with your doctor for the dosage that's right for you.

omega-3 fatty acids that function as antioxidants as well as counter inflammation that can damage brain cells. Fish consumption also has been linked to improved circulation.

Scientific evidence: A study of 815 people, ages 65 to 94, found that those who consumed fish once or more weekly had 60% less risk of developing AD than those who did not.

●**Drink in moderation.** Temperate consumption of alcohol—two glasses of wine, two beers or one drink containing hard liquor daily—keeps brain cell membranes more flexible, which lets them function better.

Caution: Consuming greater quantities of alcohol, especially as you grow older, has been shown to impair memory and damage brain and other tissues.

Scientific evidence: A Dutch study published in *The Lancet* found that older adults who consumed mild to moderate amounts of alcohol daily had a 42% lower risk for dementia.

ACTIVITY FOR THE BRAIN

Brain function has been shown to improve in people who are active—both mentally and physically.

●**Stay mentally active.** Mental workouts will stimulate the release of growth factors—chemicals that spur brain cells to forge a rich network of cells that can compensate if some cells are disabled by AD.

Scientific evidence: A study of 801 Catholic priests and nuns, all age 65 or older, found that participants who spent the most leisure hours in activities that demanded thinking—like reading books, playing cards, solving crossword puzzles—had half the AD risk of those who spent the least time involved in such pursuits.

Self-defense: Read books that make you think…follow political developments around the world…learn a foreign language…play games, such as chess, that require cognitive skills.

●**Get regular exercise.** Physical activity stimulates brain growth factors, improves circulation and reduces the risk for ministrokes.

Scientific evidence: A University of California at Los Angeles study that followed 6,000 women, age 65 or older, for six to eight years found that the more miles they walked daily,

the lower their risk for dementia. Other studies that included men had similar results.

Self-defense: Just a little exercise makes a lot of difference. Do something active—brisk walking, tennis or dancing—for at least 30 minutes each day.

REDUCE STRESS

Chronic stress impairs memory in the short run and can increase Alzheimer's risk. That's because stress triggers the release of *cortisol,* a hormone that damages brain cells—especially those in the memory-regulating region called the hippocampus.

Chronic stress also can lead to depression. When an individual is depressed, the brain's chemical activity declines.

Scientific evidence: In a study published in *Neurology,* people with depression were more likely to develop Alzheimer's than those who were not depressed.

Self-defense: If you're under constant stress, reevaluate your life to lighten the load as much as you can. And, if you think you could be depressed, seek an evaluation from a physician or mental health professional.

Curry May Fight Alzheimer's

The ingredient that gives curry its distinctive color, curcumin, is filled with potent antioxidants called phenols that may also have anti-inflammatory properties. Curcumin triggers the production of an enzyme that protects against the oxidative diseases—possibly including Alzheimer's. Further research is needed to determine whether curcumin will boost health in humans. For now, consider eating Indian food once a week or adding a teaspoon or two of curry to vegetables and meat dishes you make at home.

Nader G. Abraham, PhD, professor of pharmacology, New York Medical College, Valhalla, NY.

Alzheimer's Self-Defense

In a new study, people who consumed less than 14 milligrams (mg) of the B vitamin niacin per day were three times more likely to develop Alzheimer's disease.

Theory: Niacin helps maintain normal neural function.

Helpful: Strive for the recommended daily intake of 14 mg for women and 16 mg for men from niacin-rich foods, including fortified cereal (20 mg per cupful)...lean poultry (11.8 mg per each half breast)...and canned tuna (11.3 mg per three ounces).

Martha C. Morris, ScD, associate professor of medicine and preventive medicine, Rush Institute for Healthy Aging, Chicago.

 # The Healing Power of Hope Is Real

Jerome Groopman, MD, professor of medicine at Harvard Medical School, and chief of experimental medicine at the Beth Israel Deaconess Medical Center, both in Boston, *www.jeromegroopman.com.* His research focuses on the basic mechanisms of cancer and AIDS. A staff writer in medicine and biology for *The New Yorker,* Dr. Groopman is author of *The Anatomy of Hope: How People Prevail in the Face of Illness* (Crown/Random House).

For nearly three decades, I have treated patients with blood diseases, cancer, hepatitis C and AIDS. Early on, offering hope to very sick patients felt dishonest—but as medical science advanced, it became easier to help my patients sustain hope because I believed in it more myself.

A PRACTICAL EMOTION

I have seen the power of hope influence the outcome of illness by supplying the courage to undergo treatment.

Example: Harvard physician George Griffin,* age 61, demanded prolonged, painful and aggressive treatment for his advanced stomach

*Names have been changed to protect patients' privacy.

cancer. As a world-class expert on the disease, he knew his chances of success were almost nonexistent. His colleagues, concerned that such treatments would cause unnecessary suffering and he would die anyway, called his determination "madness."

Amazingly, the treatments worked. Now, having lived another 17 years, George says, "It was my right to choose what I did. I deeply wanted to live, so I had to fight."

To hope under extreme circumstances was an act of defiance that let George live life on his own terms. It's part of the human spirit to endure and give miracles a chance to happen. I no longer refuse my patients the opportunity to hope.

TAKING HOPE STEP BY STEP

What if a patient is determined not to hope? Construction worker Dan Conrad puzzled our hospital staff by stubbornly refusing treatment for non-Hodgkin's lymphoma, which is often curable. Finally, we learned the source of his negativity. He had remained at a friend's hospital bedside during lengthy disabling treatments for lung cancer and, in time, death. Although he had a different disease, Dan foresaw the same fate for himself.

I thought of George. At the core of his experience was a real sense of control over outside forces. Maybe Dan needed that sense, too. With his wife's help, I talked him into permitting the first step of treatment, with the assurance that he could stop at any time.

What turned the tide in Dan's attitude was being seated for a chemotherapy treatment next to a woman who had been free of the same disease for years. Her success gave him hope. Greatly cheered, Dan completed the treatment. A decade later, he remains well.

THE BODY'S SIGNALS

I suspect that Dan's brain subconsciously translated his first physical symptoms as prefiguring death. *Give up,* it told him. Before the advent of modern medicine, this would have been accurate. Yet within hours of beginning treatment, all Dan's vital functions—breathing, digestion, blood circulation—improved. Deep in his brain, messages of growing health replaced those of looming death.

The less hopeful we feel, the fewer endorphins and enkephalins (hormones that block pain) and the more cholecystokinin (a hormone that blocks endorphins) our bodies release. Breaking that cycle is key. The first spark of hope can do it, setting off a chain reaction.

George's and Dan's stories illustrate the two components of hope. The first is to organize knowledge and develop a clear view of what is happening, including the difficulties and obstacles that need to be faced. Once that task has revealed the possible path to a better future, we experience the second element of hope—an energizing, uplifting experience that gives us the will to prevail.

BODY/MIND CONNECTION

We often speak of the mind/body connection, recognizing that our emotions and state of mind can affect our health. Just as powerful is the body/mind connection, when our physical state leads the way.

Example: Small reductions in fatigue, a common element of illness, can have a major impact on hope. Bertha Putterman refused to accept any treatment for her chronic leukemia despite her doctors' insistence that it could help. When a specialist noticed that Bertha's anemia was worsening, he increased her dose of *erythropoietin,* a medication that stimulates the production of red blood cells, which carry oxygen around the body.

That simple improvement made Bertha feel ready to accept more treatment. Negative signals from her tissues had filled her mind, allowing no room for hope. Now they relented.

IT HAPPENED TO ME

In 1979, while training for the Boston Marathon, I ruptured a lumbar disk. Back pain led to surgery, then more surgery.

For 19 years, pain ruled my life. I couldn't walk through the neighborhood with my wife or teach my sons to play baseball. At work, I had to move carefully. As a physician, I had learned about the need for hope, yet for myself, I had abandoned it completely.

In desperation, I submitted to back massage, which led to muscle spasms that sent me to my rheumatologist. After prescribing medication and rest, he then referred me to Dr. James Rainville, a renowned rehabilitation physician whose hospital had returned NBA player Larry Bird to the basketball court after spine surgery.

Dubious, I went. Dr. Rainville convinced me that following a carefully supervised exercise regimen would retrain my muscles and dispel the pain—meanwhile producing more but temporary pain, which I should ignore.

I was frightened, but I believed him. He gave me hope, and hope saw me through it. In a little over a year, my body relearned its strengths. I could hike up hills and walk a mile.

Taking the first step to health can be the hardest part, especially when we fear pain and suffering. Hope solidified my resilience through arduous treatments.

For my patients and for me, hope has helped us over hurdles that we otherwise could not have cleared, moving us forward into a place where healing could occur.

6

Personal Health

Why Sex Is Good for Your Health

Was it good for you? Scientists now have a definitive answer to that classic post-sex query. The answer is *yes—very good for you.*

A recent review of dozens of studies shows that sexual expression is good for the heart… the immune system…and the reproductive system. Plus it helps to control pain, stress and depression.

An active sex life may even extend your life. A Welsh study of more than 900 men ages 45 to 59 showed that those who averaged two or more orgasms per week had half the risk of dying during the 10-year period of the study, compared with those who had orgasms less than once a month.

How does sexual expression work to benefit the body and mind? Doctors worldwide are searching for answers, but one biological fact stands out—sex triggers the release of many powerful chemicals.

BENEFITS

•**Longevity.** In addition to the Welsh study, a study of 252 men and women in North Carolina showed that frequency of intercourse was a significant predictor of longevity for men.

In a Swedish study of 392 older men and women, married men who stopped having sex before the age of 70 were more likely to die by age 75 than married men who continued to be sexually active (for women, there was no association between frequency of sexual intercourse and mortality).

•**Heart disease.** In the Welsh study, men who had orgasms less than once a month had

Beverly Whipple, PhD, RN, a certified sex educator, counselor, researcher and professor emerita at Rutgers University–Newark. She is a coauthor of the international best seller *The G-Spot and Other Recent Discoveries About Human Sexuality* (Dell) and *Safe Encounters: How Women Can Say Yes to Pleasure and No to Unsafe Sex* (Pocket). She was a consultant for the report "The Health Benefits of Sexual Expression" for the Planned Parenthood Federation of America, Inc.

twice the rate of fatal heart attacks, compared with men who had orgasms two or more times a week.

Possible explanation: The hormone DHEA is released with orgasm. Research on middle-aged men suggests that the lower the level of DHEA in the blood, the higher the risk of heart disease.

●**Breast cancer.** In a French study of 146 women ages 25 to 45 who had never had children, those who had sexual intercourse less than once a month had a higher risk for breast cancer than those who had sex more often.

Possible explanation: Sexual arousal and orgasm leads to increased levels of the sex hormone *oxytocin,* which may help prevent breast cancer.

●**Immunity.** Two psychology professors at Wilkes University in Pennsylvania measured levels of *immunoglobulin A* (IgA) in 112 subjects. This immune factor is essential in defeating viruses. Subjects who had sexual intercourse once or twice a week had IgA levels that were 30% higher than those who didn't have sex.

●**Reproductive system.** A woman's reproductive health is directly affected by her sex life. A study of more than 2,000 women found that sexual activity and orgasm during menstruation may protect against endometriosis. In this disease, cells of the uterine lining, or endometrium, grow in some other part of the pelvic area, such as the ovaries, cervix or bladder, and can prevent pregnancy.

Studies also show that regular intimate sexual activity with a partner enhances fertility by regulating menstrual patterns.

In addition, sex can help prevent premature births. A 2001 study of 1,853 pregnant women showed that those who had some type of sexual activity after 24 weeks of pregnancy—sexual intercourse with orgasm, sexual intercourse without orgasm and/or orgasm without sexual intercourse—were somewhat less likely to deliver prematurely.

Before this study, it was theorized that sexual activity between 29 and 36 weeks increased the risk of early delivery. (Always check with your doctor about when or if sex should be avoided during pregnancy.)

●**Pain.** Many medical reports show that sex relieves pain, including back pain, menstrual cramps, arthritis and migraine.

Example: In one study, stimulation of the female lab rats caused the pelvic nerve to release *vasoactive intestinal peptide* (VIP). When injected into animals, VIP has a pain-blocking power stronger than morphine.

●**Insomnia.** A psychologist who surveyed 1,866 US women found that 32% had masturbated in the past three months to help get to sleep more easily.

Possible explanation: The hormones released may act as a natural sedative.

●**Emotional health.** Studies show that sexual satisfaction is a strong predictor of higher quality of life.

Examples: A Canadian study of 75 men between the ages of 18 and 27 showed that men who were not sexually active had the highest risk for depression. In one American study, the women who masturbated indicated a higher level of self-esteem than women who did not.

Studies also show that sexual activity and orgasm reduce stress, which may be related to the release of oxytocin.

BETTER SEX

To improve your sex life, avoid these behaviors, which can interfere with the enjoyment of sexual expression…

●**Not communicating with your partner.** Don't expect your partner to figure out what you enjoy on his/her own. Tell or show your lover what you like. He'll enjoy it more, too.

●**Being goal-oriented.** If you are focused solely on achieving orgasm, sexual expression is like a staircase. Each step leads to the next, and you don't stop to enjoy where you are—every look and caress.

If you are pleasure-oriented, sexual expression is like a circle. Any activity on the circle—holding hands, cuddling, kissing—is an end in itself and doesn't have to lead to anything else. In pleasure-oriented sensuality and sexuality, you and your partner enjoy every moment and reap the health benefits.

Best Time for Sex

Male and female hormones peak between the hours of 5 am and 9 am, making sex more pleasurable for both partners. Early morning also is the best time to conceive—men's testosterone levels are highest then, giving sperm a fertility boost.

Men's Health, 33 E. Minor St., Emmaus, PA 18098.

Sex-Enhancing Supplement For Men And Women

The amino acid *arginine,* the "sex vitamin," can provide the benefits of its prescription drug competitors, such as Viagra and Levitra, but with fewer side effects and at lower cost. Arginine helps synthesize nitric oxide, which increases blood flow to the genitals. This increased blood flow promotes sexual arousal.

Daily dose: 1,500 to 5,000 milligrams (mg).

Caution: People who are taking medication for chronic conditions such as heart disease or diabetes should take arginine only under a doctor's supervision.

Andrew L. Rubman, ND, associate professor of clinical medicine, I.W. Lane College of Integrative Medicine, Winter Park, FL, and medical director of the Southbury Clinic for Traditional Medicines, Southbury, CT.

Foods That Worsen Menopause

Depending on your symptoms, there are specific foods to avoid when you are going through menopause.

If you suffer from hot flashes: Avoid caffeinated beverages, such as coffee, tea and cola…alcohol…spicy foods…and hot drinks.

Nausea: Avoid fatty, greasy foods, including junk foods, rich sauces and high-fat cheese.

Mood swings: Eat regularly throughout the day. Have a snack when you are hungry…and don't skip meals.

Calcium loss: Avoid diets that are high in protein and sodium. Cut back on processed foods, salty snack foods and prepared mixes.

Headaches: Stay away from red wine and beer. Also avoid coffee and chocolate, although caffeine may help alleviate a headache, depending on the individual.

Suzanne Havala Hobbs, DrPH, RD, clinical assistant professor, School of Public Health, University of North Carolina at Chapel Hill, and author of several books, including *Vegetarian Cooking for Dummies* (Hungry Minds).

So Long, Pap Smears?

Most cervical cancers are triggered by infection with *human papilloma virus* (HPV). Some researchers propose replacing routine smears with blood tests for HPV. Only women who test positive would need a follow-up Pap. More research on this method is needed. For now, be sure to get a regular Pap smear.

New Scientist, Reed Business Information Limited, 151 Wardour St., London.

Nonsurgical Uterine Fibroid Treatment

ExAblate uses magnetic resonance imaging (MRI) and ultrasound to target and destroy these noncancerous growths. Recovery time is faster than with surgery.

Risks: Slight chance of skin burns, cramps, nausea or urinary tract infection. ExAblate can't be used on fibroids that are close to the bladder or other organs. It is not intended for women who are—or hope to become—pregnant. The treatment currently is available in parts of the US and Europe.

More information: Insightec Image Guided Treatment Ltd. at 866-392-2528, *www.uterine-fibroids.org*.

Elizabeth Annella Stewart, MD, an associate professor of obstetrics, gynecology and reproductive biology, Brigham and Women's Hospital, Harvard Medical School, Boston.

Hidden Health Hazard

More than 10% of women who are of reproductive age now have *polycystic ovary syndrome* (PCOS), which may lead to diabetes and heart disease. The cause is unknown but may be linked to excess insulin.

Consult an endocrinologist if you have two or more symptoms—excess facial or body hair, acne, fertility problems, irregular periods, high blood pressure and/or insulin resistance.

Treatment options: Diet, exercise and *metformin* (Glucophage) to regulate insulin.

Resource: Polycystic Ovarian Syndrome Association, 877-775-7267, *www.pcosupport.org*.

Rhoda Cobin, MD, clinical professor of medicine at Mount Sinai School of Medicine in New York City and a former president of the American Association of Clinical Endocrinologists.

Breast Cancer Indicator

A woman's weight gain after age 18 indicates her risk of breast cancer later. Women who gained 30 to 40 pounds between the ages of 18 and 57 were 40% more likely to get breast cancer than women who gained no more than five pounds. Women who gained more than 70 pounds had twice the risk.

Possible reason: Fat cells synthesize estrogen, so heavier people have higher estrogen

levels—and high estrogen increases breast cancer risk.

Heather Spencer Feigelson, PhD, senior epidemiologist, American Cancer Society, Atlanta, and leader of a study of 1,934 breast cancer cases, reported in *Cancer Epidemiology, Biomarkers & Prevention*.

Powerful New Breast Cancer Drug

A new breast cancer drug cuts risk of recurrence in postmenopausal women. Women who took the standard five-year treatment of *anastrozole* (Arimidex) after surgery for breast cancer were 52% less likely to develop cancer in the remaining breast than women taking *tamoxifen*. Unlike tamoxifen, anastrozole is not associated with increased risk of stroke and blood clots, but it does increase bone fracture risk. Patients should be sure to get annual bone-density exams.

Anthony Howell, MD, a medical oncologist at University of Manchester, Christie Hospital NHS Trust, Manchester, England. His study of 9,366 postmenopausal women was published in *The Lancet*.

Eat Your Broccoli

Broccoli may help prevent breast cancer. Recent research shows that the biochemical *indole-3-carbinol* (I3C), found in broccoli, kills breast cancer cells. It works like chemotherapy, switching off genes that regulate cell growth—however, unlike chemo, it doesn't kill healthy cells. I3C supplements are available, but there's no evidence that they prevent cancer. For now, the best way to get I3C in your diet is to eat more cruciferous vegetables, such as broccoli, kale, cabbage and brussels sprouts.

Fazlul H. Sarkar, PhD, a professor of pathology at the Karmanos Cancer Institute of Wayne State University in Detroit, and author of many studies on I3C and cancer, including one published in *Nutrition and Cancer*.

Seaweed to the Rescue

Japanese women get less breast cancer than Americans, possibly because about 10% of their diet consists of kelp, a form of seaweed. In laboratory studies, animals given kelp had lower levels of *estradiol,* a hormone associated with breast cancer. Kelp can be purchased at specialty grocery stores. Don't take kelp supplements—they're too high in iodine.

Journal of Nutrition, 9650 Rockville Pike, Bethesda, MD 20814.

New Hope for Ovarian Cancer

Survival rates for ovarian cancer might be increased with a promising new blood test. Chemotherapy can cause changes in tumor cells —called *gene methylation*—that makes them resistant to chemotherapy. The new blood test, which identifies methylated genes, could help to determine how a relapse should be treated.

Examples: If the tumor cell genes are not methylated, further chemotherapy may work on its own. However, if methylated genes are detected, special *demethylating* drugs that now are being developed could be used to restore the patient's sensitivity to chemotherapy.

Similar approaches are now being studied to improve breast and lung cancer outcomes. The test is being used in a clinical trial in the UK.

Robert Brown, PhD, professor of cancer therapeutics, Cancer Research UK Beatson Labs at the University of Glasgow, Scotland.

Fertility Booster

In a recent finding, men who drank coffee regularly—more than one cup (eight ounces) a day—showed more active sperm, which would increase the likelihood that their partners would become pregnant.

Fabio F. Pasqualotto, MD, PhD, director of conception, Center for Human Reproduction, Caxias do Sul, Brazil, and leader of a study of sperm motility in 750 men.

Tasty Way to Reduce Risk of Prostate Cancer By Half

A recent study found that men who ate no fish or small amounts of it were at least twice as likely to develop prostate cancer as those who ate moderate or large amounts. Another study found that men who ate the most fish were the least likely to develop advanced prostate cancer. And a third study found that prostate cancer is very rare among the Inuit men living in Greenland who generally consume large amounts of fish.

UC Berkeley Wellness Letter, 2018 Shattuck Ave., Berkeley, CA 94704.

A Better Way to Predict Prostate Cancer

A new way to predict prostate cancer is up to 95% accurate and eliminates unnecessary biopsies. A *nomogram* assigns risk using age... digital rectal exam results...ultrasound...and density of prostate specific antigen (PSA), which is serum PSA divided by prostate volume.

Example: In the past, a 60-year-old man with PSA of five was believed to have a 25% chance of prostate cancer. But a *nomogram,* would find his risk less than 5%, assuming PSA density is very low and his ultrasound doesn't suggest cancer—so a biopsy might be avoided.

Mark Garzotto, MD, a urologic oncologist at Portland Veterans Administration Hospital and Oregon Health & Science University, both in Portland.

New Hope for Advanced Prostate Cancer

Zoledronic acid (Zometa), a type of bisphosphonate medication used to treat bone cancer, may help reduce complications in advanced prostate cancer that has spread to bone. It also may have antitumor properties. *Abarelix* (Plenaxis) can fight bone pain and other symptoms, such as weight loss and fatigue. Only men with very advanced cancer can use abarelix and only under carefully controlled conditions. It may be appropriate for 5% to 10% of men who have prostate cancer.

Sheldon Marks, MD, associate clinical professor of urology, University of Arizona College of Medicine, Tucson.

Cranberries Fight Prostate Cancer

In new research, disease-fighting flavonoids found in cranberries destroyed human prostate cancer cells in laboratory experiments.

Theory: Flavonoids interfere with the signals that tell cancer cells to proliferate.

More research is under way to confirm these findings. In the meantime, eat homemade cranberry sauce, snack on whole dried cranberries (sold in supermarkets) and/or drink 100% cranberry juice.

Peter J. Ferguson, PhD, research associate, London Regional Cancer Program, London, Ontario, Canada.

Is Radiation After Prostate Surgery for You?

Results from a recent study that compared prostate cancer patients who had radiation following surgery with those who didn't—or who waited until the cancer returned to have radiation therapy—may help you decide. Sixty-nine percent of the men who got early radiation remained cancer-free for five years after surgery, compared with 31% of those who decided to forgo this treatment. Men not treated with radiation within six months also were four times more likely to die during the study period.

Self-defense: Ask your doctor if you're a candidate for early postoperative radiation therapy.

Good news: Prostate cancer radiation therapy generally is well-tolerated. Only 10% of patients in this study experienced side effects, such as mild rectal irritation and fatigue.

Cesare Cozzarini, MD, department of radiochemotherapy, San Raffaele H Scientific Institute, Milan, Italy.

A Better Vasectomy

Unlike the traditional "snip and clip" procedure, the "no-scalpel" vasectomy uses a special clamp inserted through a tiny puncture in the scrotum. This procedure is less invasive, as easily reversed and just as effective as the traditional procedure.

Ice and over-the-counter pain medication, such as *acetaminophen* (Tylenol) help ease the minimal pain during the first 24 hours after this outpatient procedure.

Marc Goldstein, MD, professor of urology and reproductive medicine and surgeon-in-chief, male reproductive medicine and surgery at Weill Medical College of Cornell University, New York City.

How to Keep Colorectal Cancer at Bay

Eight ounces of milk a day cuts risk of colorectal cancer by 15%. Drinking milk *and* taking calcium supplements—up to 1,000 milligrams (mg) daily—can reduce risk by 24%.

Other ways to keep colon cancer at bay: Exercise regularly…eat lots of fruits, vegetables and whole grains…cut fat intake…have regular colon-screening tests.

Eunyoung Cho, ScD, a researcher at Channing Laboratory, Brigham and Women's Hospital/Harvard Medical School, Boston. Her analysis of calcium intake and colorectal cancer in 534,536 men and women was published in the *Journal of the National Cancer Institute.*

Natural Remedy for Irritable Bowel Syndrome

When individuals who have irritable bowel syndrome (IBS)—a disorder of the large intestine characterized by abdominal pain and changes in bowel habits and stool frequency—took up to 640 milligrams (mg) of artichoke leaf extract a day, symptoms were reduced in more than 25% of people.

Theory: Artichoke leaf extract stimulates the liver to produce bile, which helps the body to process fats and reduce bloating…acts like a natural laxative…and may promote the growth of healthful bacteria in the colon.

If you have IBS: Try one teaspoon of liquid extract mixed with a glass of water three times a day or take a 320-mg standardized extract capsule twice a day.

Caution: If you have gallstones or biliary tract disease or are allergic to artichokes, do not take artichoke leaf extract.

Rafe Bundy, PhD, research fellow, School of Food Biosciences, University of Reading, England.

Common Causes of Flatulence

Anil Minocha, MD, professor of medicine and director of digestive diseases, University of Mississippi Medical Center, Jackson, and author of *Natural Stomach Care* (Avery).

An embarrassing flatulence problem can be triggered by any of the following common causes…

•**Diseases** such as irritable bowel syndrome, Crohn's disease, ulcerative colitis and cancer can lead to excess gas and bloating.

•**Certain medications**—including calcium channel blockers, tricyclic antidepressants and narcotic-based painkillers—slow digestion and lead to excess gas.

•**Diet changes,** such as adding fiber to ease constipation, can create gas. Lactose intolerance leads to flatulence because lactose-laden foods are improperly digested.

•**Muscle tone loss** around the anal sphincter and loss of elasticity of the valve itself can weaken control.

Self-defense: Limit intake of milk products, except for yogurt with active cultures, which consume much of the lactose during fermentation. Avoid carbonated beverages and foods that are heavy in carbohydrates, such as beans, brussels sprouts, broccoli and cauliflower. Also avoid foods that contain sugars such as *fructose* (including onions, artichokes, pears and wheat) and *sorbitol* (apples, peaches and prunes). Sorbitol also is used as an artificial sweetener, as is *mannitol*—both should be avoided. Eat slowly and chew food thoroughly. Finally, consider taking Gas-X, sold over the counter.

Stop Losing Sleep Over Nighttime Urination

Jamison Starbuck, ND, a naturopathic physician in family practice and a lecturer at the University of Montana, both in Missoula. She is a past president of the American Association of Naturopathic Physicians and a contributing editor to *The Alternative Advisor: The Complete Guide to Natural Therapies and Alternative Treatments* (Time Life).

A 38-year-old female patient, Jan, came to me and said, "Doctor, I'm here because I get up eight times a night to use the bathroom. I'm exhausted and frustrated." She already had seen her family physician and two urologists. Extensive testing, including an X-ray, did not find a cause for her condition.

101

Frequent nighttime urination, known as *nocturia,* is a common but often-overlooked medical problem. For most people, a mild case—waking several times a night—is bothersome, but not a reason to see a doctor.

In my view, ignoring even mild nocturia is a mistake. Our kidneys and bladder are designed to retain urine during an eight-hour sleep. Waking to urinate more than twice a night is a medical problem. People need good sleep to lead healthy, productive lives, and we cannot sleep well if we are getting up.

If you wake up to urinate more than twice a night, consider these suggestions…

●**See a doctor.** Hypertension, diabetes, prostate problems, stroke, kidney disease and, in some cases, a tumor in the bladder can cause nocturia. Get a thorough physical, including a urinalysis, to check for a bladder infection.

●**Cut back on beverages.** Certain beverages have a diuretic effect that can lead to nighttime urination—coffee, black or green tea, alcohol, caffeinated soda and herbal teas containing dandelion, burdock, linden, nettle or parsley. Try to abstain from these beverages after 6 pm, and restrict your total fluid intake after dinner to 12 ounces of water or a nondiuretic and noncaffeinated tea, such as chamomile or peppermint.

●**Review your prescriptions.** Many commonly prescribed medicines, including diuretics used to treat hypertension, increase urinary frequency. If you have nocturia, ask your pharmacist whether any of the drugs you take may be causing the problem. If so, ask your doctor for a substitute or whether you can take the medication before 6 pm.

●**Get quercetin.** In people with allergies or certain medical conditions, which include benign prostatic hyperplasia and interstitial cystitis, inflammation is the cause of nocturia. Quercetin, a strong antioxidant, decreases inflammation and inhibits cell damage in the kidneys. Cranberries and the other dark red or purple berries, such as blueberries and raspberries, contain quercetin. Eat one cup of fresh berries daily, or take a 500-milligram (mg) quercetin supplement twice daily with meals.

●**Test for food allergies.** Food allergens act as irritants, so your body will try to eliminate them quickly through a variety of mechanisms, including urination. In Jan's case, we found that she was allergic to eggs, dairy and corn. When she avoided these foods, she woke to urinate only twice each night. To test for food allergies, consult a naturopathic physician or a nutritionally minded allergist or internist for a blood test.

Alcoholism Is Underdiagnosed

A lcohol abuse or dependence affects one-fifth of Americans at some time in their lives —but most primary care doctors fail to diagnose alcoholism and other forms of substance abuse even when patients show classic symptoms.

Reasons for underdiagnoses: The doctor might have little medical training in treating addiction…may fail to identify the symptoms…may be skeptical about treatment succeeding …may be uncomfortable discussing substance abuse…may assume that the patient will be poorly reimbursed for addiction diagnosis and treatment by his/her insurer.

If you suspect that a relative or friend has a substance abuse problem, contact an addiction medicine specialist. To find one in your area, contact the Register of Addiction Specialists at 916-987-2002 or *www.addictionspecialists.com.*

Joseph Califano Jr., chairman and president, National Center on Addiction and Substance Abuse, Columbia University, New York City, *www.casacolumbia.org.*

7

Money Smarts

Simple Ways to Cut Expenses and Save More

Now is a great time to get your financial house into good order, from expenses to investments. *Here are our three steps to help you relax and take the anxiety out of your finances...*

CUT NEEDLESS EXPENSES

People tend to forget about small purchases soon after they have made them, but these can add up fast. For example, a daily $3 cappuccino costs almost $1,100 over the course of a year. *Game plan...*

● **Jot down every purchase of more than $1 for seven days.** Exclude unavoidable costs, such as utility bills and mortgage payments. At the end of the week, tally the cost of the items you could have skipped without significantly impacting your quality of life. Most people will come up with between $50 and $100—that's

$2,600 to $5,200 every year! *Some common money wasters...*

● Purchases made while shopping just for the fun of it—not for things you need.

● ATM cash-withdrawal fees of $1.50 to $3 at machines that are unaffiliated with your bank.

● Items bought because they were on sale, even though you didn't need them.

● Late-payment fees levied by credit card companies.

● Late-return fees from video rental stores and libraries.

● **Set a savings goal based on your seven-day waste estimate.** Have a fun use in mind for the money saved.

Example: If you waste about $50 a week, resolve to save $7 a day to fund a $2,500 vacation next summer.

Bill and Mary Staton, founders of The Staton Institute, a financial education and counseling center in Charlotte, NC, *www.billstaton.com*. They are authors of *Worry-Free Family Finances* (McGraw-Hill). Mr. Staton is also publisher of the weekly investment newsletter *E-Money Digest/Guided Portfolio Service*.

Each week, put the money you would have wasted in a savings account or money market mutual fund specifically for this goal. Post a note on your refrigerator with the daily dollar amount you want to save so that you won't forget.

SHRINK BIG EXPENSES

Big expenses can't always be avoided, but they may be reduced. *Game plan...*

●**Eliminate credit card debt.** The average American family owes about $8,000 in credit card debt. Assuming a typical interest rate of 18%, that is almost $1,500 per year in interest charges alone.

Paying off credit card debt should be your top financial goal. If you can't pay it off immediately, transfer balances to the card with the lowest rate. Or apply for a new card that has attractive rates on balance transfers. To compare card offers, visit *www.bankrate.com.*

Important: Don't take out a home-equity loan to pay credit card debt. Today's low rates may be enticing, but the risk is too great. If you can't make the payments, you could lose your home. That cannot happen if your only debts are to credit card issuers.

●**Buy less car than you can afford.** Vehicles are the biggest extravagance most families have. Yet all any car really needs to do is get you from one place to the next. You can get a perfectly nice, safe and reliable new sedan or minivan for about $20,000, not the $30,000 to $40,000 many people spend.

Examples: Honda Accord (starting at approximately $20,000)*...Toyota Camry ($18,600) ...Dodge Caravan ($19,000).

Negotiating tool: Before buying a new car, look up the invoice price at *www.edmunds. com.* If you shop carefully, you can expect to pay that amount or less.

●**Be smart about big events.** The typical wedding now costs about $25,000. Parents don't like to scrimp on their child's big day, so they often borrow to finance a lavish celebration.

Better strategy: Set a limit. For example, tell your daughter that you're willing to spend up to $15,000 on her wedding. If she wants to

*All prices subject to change.

spend more, she and her fiancé can pay the difference. If she wants to spend less, she can keep the remainder. Chances are that she will happily cut costs and pocket the difference. You will save money and give the newlyweds a head start on their nest egg.

INVEST INTELLIGENTLY

The easy strategy we teach is to invest only in shares of companies that have increased their dividends per share for at least 10 years in a row. We track all these companies in our annual directory, *America's Finest Companies*®. As reported in our directory, these companies have returned an average of 16.93% annually for the 10 years through March 31, 2005, versus 10.79% for the S&P 500 Index.

You can find a stock's dividend history in the *Value Line Investment Survey,* available at numerous libraries.

Sell a stock only when the company fails to keep increasing its dividend or if another stock with a steadily rising dividend is a better bargain based on its price-to-earnings ratio (P/E).

Higher Interest Checking Accounts

Get higher interest on checking with a corporate money market account. These are offered by GE Capital (800-433-4480, *www.ge interestplus.com*)...Ford Motor Credit (800-580-4778, *www.fordcredit.com*)...and Caterpillar Financial PowerInvestment (800-504-1114, *www. cat.com/cda*). The accounts pay from over 4%** to over 5% in interest—versus an average of less than half that for bank checking accounts—and allow unlimited check writing, with charges of $10 to $25 for checks of less than $250.

Caution: Unlike bank checking accounts, the corporate money market accounts are not insured by the Federal Deposit Insurance Corporation (FDIC).

Edward F. Mrkvicka, Jr., president, Reliance Enterprises Inc., Marengo, IL, and author of *Your Bank Is Ripping You Off* (St. Martin's).

**All rates and prices subject to change.

Why Some Checking Accounts Aren't Really Free

Legally, "free" means no minimum-balance requirements and no activity or maintenance fees, such as monthly service charges.

But banks quietly impose other fees—for using your debit card…closing your account before a certain period…even calling to inquire about your balance. For some accounts, you even may be charged for talking to a teller.

Self-defense: Before you open an account, ask for a list of fees. If your bank charges for debit card purchases, use the card only for ATM services at your bank's ATMs.

Ken McEldowney, executive director, Consumer Action, a national consumer education and advocacy organization in San Francisco, *www.consumer-action.org.*

Free On-Line Bill Paying

Free on-line bill paying is available at several bank sites—and they guarantee on-time payment or they will pay the late fee. Try Bank of America (*www.bofa.com*)…Chase (*www.chase. com*)…Citibank (*www.citibank.com*)…US Bancorp (*www.usbank.com*). On-line payments also are free at HSBC Bank USA (*www.hsbc.com*) but without an on-time payment guarantee.

Several other Web sites offer free on-line payment for customers under certain circumstances. Visit BankOne (*www.bankone.com*)…Suntrust (*www.suntrust.com*)…MyCheckFree (*https://my checkfree.com*).

Money, Time-Life Bldg., Rockefeller Center, New York City 10020.

To Keep Interest Charges Low…

Your credit score determines the rate you'll be charged for a mortgage, car loan or on credit cards. *Major factors in scoring…*

●**Payment history.** Any late payments reduce your score.

●**Total debt.** A high debt load brings your score down.

●**Credit history.** The longer, the better.

●**Types of credit.** The more kinds you have, the better able to manage a loan you are considered to be.

●**New credit.** Applying for or receiving a lot of credit may reduce your score.

Jen Anthony, president, OnePay, a nonprofit debt management organization, Rockville, MD.

Use a Temporary Credit Card Number for a Risky Transaction

Leading credit card companies now provide temporary credit card numbers at no charge for use in single transactions. The number is tied to your regular account, but the party to whom you give the temporary number never sees your regular one. It is useful for making purchases when you are not sure with whom you are dealing.

Example: You want to make a purchase over the Internet from a party you aren't familiar with. The temporary number ensures that they won't have your regular number to use or give away.

Temporary numbers are now offered by Citibank, MBNA and Discover. Contact your credit card issuer for details.

Chris Hoofnagle, Esq., associate director, Electronic Privacy Information Center, Washington, DC.

Credit Card Fees Are Increasing

Credit card issuers are raising late fees and penalties by an average of 9.2%—and they expect to take in $13 billion from them this year. Grace periods also are shrinking, so more people may be hit by fees. The current grace period now averages 20.6 days, down from 27.8 days a decade ago.

Self-defense: Pay bills on time…read inserts so you know about changes in fees, grace periods, etc.

Robert Hammer, chief executive of R.K. Hammer Investment Bankers, a credit card consulting firm in Thousand Oaks, CA.

Pros and Cons of Home Loans and Margin Loans

Jerry Lerman, CPA, managing director for American Express Tax and Business Services Inc. at 1185 Avenue of the Americas, New York City 10036.

Borrowing against a home provides some handsome tax benefits. And borrowing against a securities portfolio can provide even greater tax breaks.

HOME LOANS

Under the mortgage interest rules, you can fully deduct the interest on home-acquisition loans for a first and second residence up to a total of $1 million.

To qualify as a home-acquisition loan, the money must be used to buy, build or improve your first or second home and the debt must be secured by the same residence.

Trap: Debt secured by a primary residence to buy a second home doesn't pass the second test, so the interest isn't deductible, up to the $1 million limit.

Note: If you refinance your home acquisition debt with a larger mortgage, only the amount of the original mortgage that is refinanced qualifies as home-acquisition debt.

What happens to debt secured by a home that is not home-acquisition debt? It's considered "home-equity debt."

Lower limit: You are allowed to deduct the interest on no more than $100,000 worth of home-equity debt.

Loophole: Even though less interest is deductible, you can take the deduction, no matter how the money is spent.

Example: Using a line of credit secured by your home, you borrow $150,000 to pay personal bills. Your total interest comes to $9,000 the first year.

Interest on the first $100,000 of home-equity debt ($6,000) is deductible but interest on the excess $50,000 ($3,000) is not deductible.

Loophole: You can decide to treat home-equity debt as debt not secured by your home. In some cases, this results in a larger deduction.

Example 1: If you borrow $150,000 on a home-equity line of credit and $50,000 of that is used for business-related expenses, then you can elect to treat that $50,000 as trade or business debt, which may be deductible.

Example 2: In another situation, you borrow $150,000 to purchase a second home. You can elect to have the excess $50,000 treated as investment-related debt, stating that you're holding the second home for investment.

In that case, all the interest on the excess $50,000 may be investment interest, which is deductible up to the amount of your net investment income.

Your net investment income will come from dividends and interest. You can count net capital gains, too, if that would work to your advantage, knowing that you may lose the benefit of the lower 15% long-term capital gains rate.

MARGIN LOANS

As you can see from the list below, borrowing against your home poses some problems…

1. Home-acquisition debt can be used only for buying, building or improving a home.

2. Home-equity debt is limited to the equity you have in your home.

3. Only $100,000 of home-equity debt provides deductible interest.

Strategy: Instead of borrowing against your home, borrow against your securities portfolio. Most brokerage firms extend so-called margin loans. *Ground rules...*

• **"Purpose" loans** are used for purchasing other securities (other than tax-free investments). In general, you can borrow up to 50% of the value of your collateral with purpose loans (90% for government securities such as T-bills).

Example: With $500,000 worth of stocks, bonds and funds in your portfolio, you might borrow $250,000 to buy other securities. You now hold $750,000 worth of securities, securing your $250,000 loan.

• **"Nonpurpose" loans** can be used for anything else, other than buying securities.

• **Interest rates.** You'll pay less for a margin loan than you would for credit card debt or a personal loan from a bank.

Example: For margin loans, your brokerage firm might charge one point over the prime lending rate. If the prime rate is 4%, you would pay 5% on margin loans.

Tax treatment: Purpose loans produce investment interest, which is deductible up to the amount of net investment income. Interest on loans used to buy tax-free investments like municipal bonds are not deductible.

Nonpurpose loans generally produce nondeductible personal interest. However, if the borrowed money is used in your trade or business, the interest may be deductible.

SPREADING THE RISK

Borrowing against your securities may make sense when you have a large position of one highly appreciated stock.

Let's say that you own $1 million worth of ABC Co. stock, purchased many years ago for $50,000.

Trap: If you sell the shares, you'll have a $950,000 capital gain and could owe nearly $200,000 in tax ($142,500 in federal, plus any state taxes).

If you hold the shares, though, an Enron-like disaster could wipe out a great deal of your net worth.

Strategy: Borrow against your ABC shares, and use the proceeds to invest in a diversified portfolio. The interest will be deductible, up to the amount of your net investment income, and you will reduce your exposure to a single stock.

Savvy maneuvering can cut your exposure to your large stock position and your tax bill.

For example, you borrow $1 million against your ABC shares and invest $100,000 in each of 10 different stocks. Some of your new holdings go up, others go down.

Suppose you sell the losing positions and take losses that total $150,000. You also sell enough of your ABC shares to take a $150,000 gain.

Your losses offset your gains so no taxes are due. All sales proceeds can be invested in other securities, further diversifying your portfolio.

Risk: This strategy still leaves you exposed to a steep drop in the price of ABC shares.

However, stock brokerage firms offer sophisticated techniques for limiting your losses. Often, this will involve the purchase and sale of listed stock options.

Caution: If you create too much protection for your appreciated shares, you may be subject to "constructive sale" rules that trigger gain recognition, for tax purposes. (If your options are structured in such a way as to eliminate virtually all of your risk, you have made a sale for tax purposes.)

Once you have the downside protected (limiting your risk of losses), you can then borrow against the resulting position. Your interest payments will be deductible against your net investment income.

MARGIN LOAN RISK

Margin loans pose risks. If the value of the securities used as collateral decreases, you will then face a margin call. You'll have to come up with additional cash or securities to back the loan, or some collateral will be sold.

A forced sale of appreciated collateral, in turn, will trigger a capital gains tax.

Strategy: Keep your borrowing to only 20% to 30% of the value of the collateral to reduce your exposure to margin calls. At most firms, a drop of 28% will trigger a margin call. You'll still be able to enjoy tax and investment benefits.

How to Find Real Estate Bargains

Below is some good advice on how to find values in today's overvalued real estate market…

●**Decode newspaper classifieds.** Motivated sellers use such phrases as *mortgage assumption* —you can avoid the down payment by taking over the seller's mortgage…*will finance*—you borrow from the seller…*investor liquidation* and *estate sale*—the seller needs a quick deal.

●**Ask for leads.** Leave your contact information with store owners, letter carriers, home owners who are holding garage sales, personnel professionals at local corporations, insurance agents and members of the clergy. Tell them that you buy residential real estate, and offer $100 for a lead on any property that you ultimately purchase.

●**Check on-line listings.** *My favorites…*

●The National Real Estate Investors Association has links to local networks of investors and brokers. 888-762-7342, *www.nationalreia.com.*

●Realtor.com links to properties throughout the country listed on the Multiple Listing Service (MLS), the same database real estate agents use.

Foreclosed Homes On-Line

Find foreclosed homes on-line at the Bank Homes Direct site (*www.bankhomesdirect. com*). This site, which is free to consumers, helps buyers find properties…prequalify for loans…and make purchase offers—all on-line —on bank-owned properties and ones that have gone into foreclosure.

It Pays to Negotiate Real Estate Commissions

Real estate commissions for selling a home are increasingly negotiable now. Low 4%* and 5% rates—well under the traditional 6% figure—are common these days. Even bigger bargains are available—some bare-bones discounters, such as Assist-2-Sell and ZipRealty, charge only 1% or 2%.

Best: Treat the agent's quoted rate as a starting price and haggle from there.

Money, Time-Life Bldg., Rockefeller Center, New York City 10020.

*All rates subject to change.

Mortgage Traps

Now that interest rates are on the rise, so are sneaky tricks by the mortgage industry to drum up business.

Watch out for the bait and switch—you're offered an attractive low rate, which becomes higher at closing. Or your closing is stalled deliberately so that your rate lock expires and a new, higher rate is assigned.

Self-defense: Get everything in writing from the lender—not just the mortgage broker, if you use one. Make sure that the mortgage broker explains his/her fees, which should not exceed 1% on a loan of more than $100,000 or 0.5% on a loan of more than $500,000. To avoid processing delays, gather documentation and fill out applications as quickly as possible. If you think the lender is stalling, file a complaint with your state banking department or attorney general.

Michael Moskowitz, president, Equity Now, a New York City–based direct mortgage lender licensed in six states, *www.equitynow.com.* He has addressed the state banking supervisors on ways to prevent fraud and helped develop a bill in New York's state assembly to prevent lending abuses.

Choosing the Best Real Estate Agent for Your Home

Adriane G. Berg, Lebanon, NJ–based attorney, speaker, stockbroker, host of a personal finance radio show on the Business Talk Radio Network and the author of *How Not to Go Broke at 102! Achieving Everlasting Wealth* (Wiley). For more information, go to *www.wealth102.com*.

Choose a real estate agent who specializes in selling your kind of house. Most people assume that multiple listing services, which share data about available properties, have leveled the playing field among all real estate agents.

Reality: A listing agent who understands your neighborhood can increase your selling price by thousands.

Example: A New Jersey couple in their 60s owned an 11-room Victorian home. It was architecturally stunning but lacked central air conditioning and was costly to heat. The first broker advertised the house as "Large Victorian. Needs Work." The best offer was $500,000 and only if the couple was willing to renovate it first. A second broker marketed it to buyers of historic homes.

The house sold for $680,000—no renovations required.

Little-Known Financial Aid Fact

High-tuition colleges will give students more need-based financial aid than lower-cost schools. They often have large endowments to use for aid purposes.

Result: If you qualify for need-based aid, you may end up paying less at an Ivy League or other top-rated school than at a state school, where aid is limited.

Raymond D. Loewe, CLU, ChFC, president and owner of CollegeMoney, Marlton, NJ, *www.collegemoney.com*.

A Family Can Lose Money With Tax-Favored College Savings Plans

Susan M. Dynarski, PhD, assistant professor of public policy, John F. Kennedy School of Government, Harvard University, Cambridge, MA.

College savings plans, such as Coverdell Education Savings Accounts (ESAs), 529 plans and the *Uniform Transfers to Minors Act* (UTMA) accounts, all offer tax-favored treatment for college savings. But a study released in 2004 indicates that they actually can do more harm than good.

Trap: The savings will increase a family's wealth, which in turn can reduce a student's eligibility for financial aid. This reduction, combined with the effects of the Tax Code, can cost more than 100% of the amount accumulated in the tax-favored investment account—meaning that the family loses from saving.

This is a particular risk for middle-income families who are on the margin for aid, which often include families with incomes of as much as $100,000 per year.

Analysis shows that such families with savings in an UTMA account will lose more than 100% of savings because these assets are heavily assessed by financial aid formulas as the student's own wealth that is available to pay tuition.

Savings in an UTMA account could cost as much as $1.24 for every $1 saved. Savings in 529 plans and ESAs receive a lighter assessment as parental property but still reduce available financial aid for such families, and so may return less than expected.

Better: Such families may receive the best returns on saving through an IRA or another retirement plan that is tax-favored and is not assessed at all under financial aid formulas, preserving maximum tuition assistance.

Grandparents should beware of placing investment assets in a child's name for similar reasons. They may do much better by keeping assets in their own name to preserve eligibility for tuition aid, and later making a gift to the child's family as needed.

Important: Every family's situation is different. Be sure to discuss college saving strategies with a college tuition aid expert to see how—and if—they will pay off after counting their effects on eligibility for tuition aid.

How Out-of-State Students Can Pay In-State Tuition

David Wright, senior research analyst for State Higher Education Executive Officers, a Boulder-based association of postsecondary education institutions, *www.sheeo.org.*

Typically, students who attend public colleges outside their home states will pay about four times the tuition rate that residents pay.

Good news: There is a way to go out of state and pay in-state tuition rates.

Opportunity: Most states quietly provide reduced-tuition degree programs for students from certain neighboring states. A student generally can qualify only when the program he/she wants to major in isn't available at the public college or university in his home state.

Example: He wants to specialize in marine biology, but his state's school only offers degrees in general biology.

If his state's school offers a similar program but he still prefers the out-of-state school, he may be able to shade this requirement by crafting a course of study in his chosen field that isn't quite like the one his home state offers. He should just make sure that less than half the course work overlaps what's available in his state.

The student should apply to the school first. After he is accepted, he can apply for tuition reduction.

Two types of programs provide lower tuition for out-of-state residents...

TUITION RECIPROCITY AGREEMENTS

There are four regional programs. Some also offer reciprocity at graduate, medical and professional levels. In the Southern program, out-of-staters pay the in-state rate. In New England and the Midwest, they typically pay about 150% of the in-state rate—but sometimes less, and still well below what out-of-staters normally pay.

Example: Under the New England Regional Student Program for 2005–2006, a student from Connecticut (or another New England state) could attend the University of Massachusetts at Amherst for $10,135—a savings of $8,262 over the out-of-state tuition rate and $857 more than the in-state tuition of $9,278.

The four programs...

● **New England Regional Student Program (NERSP)** covers Connecticut, Maine, Massachusetts, New Hampshire, Rhode Island and Vermont. 617-357-9620 or *www.nebhe.org/explain. html.*

● **Midwestern Higher Education Compact (MHEC)** for Kansas, Michigan, Minnesota, Missouri, Nebraska, North Dakota and Wisconsin. 612-626-8288 or *www.mhec.org/resources_stu dentexchange.html.*

● **The Southern Regional Education Board (SREB)** for Alabama, Arkansas, Delaware, Florida, Georgia, Kentucky, Louisiana, Maryland, Mississippi, North Carolina, Oklahoma, South Carolina, Tennessee, Texas, Virginia and West Virginia. 404-875-9211 or on the Web at *www.sreb. org/programs/acm/acmindex.asp.*

● **The Western Interstate Commission for Higher Education (WICHE).** Alaska, Arizona, California, Colorado, Hawaii, Idaho, Montana, Nevada, New Mexico, North Dakota (also a member of the MHEC), Oregon, South Dakota, Utah, Washington and Wyoming. 303-541-0200 or *www.wiche.edu/SEP/WUE.*

GOOD NEIGHBOR POLICIES

These bilateral agreements give students in one state reduced tuition at an adjacent state's colleges. Good neighbor policies always involve two contiguous states—and usually have some limitations.

For instance, the student may have to live within 150 miles of the adjoining state's school. In some cases, reciprocity is limited to students in just one or two counties in the adjacent state.

A recent survey of interstate good-neighbor policies showed 30 states offering such policies.

You can download this report from *www.sheeo. org/finance/t&f_web/Section%20B-7.pdf.*

Financial Help for Older People Returning to College

Nancy Dunnan, a financial adviser and author in New York City. Ms. Dunnan's latest book is titled *How to Invest $50–$5,000* (HarperCollins).

There are a variety of ways older people can obtain financing if they wish to return to or start college. *See below...*

● **Contact college admissions offices about special loans or scholarships.** Because of the growing number of nontraditional students, colleges hold evening classes, weekend courses and even offer child-care facilities and access to babysitting pools—all designed to make it easier for adults to crack the books.

● **Set up a 529 plan right away.** Your contributions and earnings grow free of federal tax. And, when you withdraw money, it, too, is federal tax free—as long as you use it for tuition, fees, books or supplies. It can be for a part-time, full-time or distance learning program. You control the account and can change the beneficiary to another family member at any time. So if you decide not to go to school, the money can be used to pay for the education of a relative—your child, spouse, siblings, cousin, niece, nephew, parent or grandparent.

Caution: If you take the money out for any non-college expenses, you must pay income tax plus a 10% penalty.

● **Check with your employer.** Many will foot some or all of the bill if the course work is related to your job. In some cases, you may be required to earn a B in the course in order to be reimbursed for your tuition.

● **Check your own state plan.** There are a number of advantages to opening a 529 plan in your state. Many allow residents to deduct a portion or all of their contributions from state

taxes. A number of states also reduce fees for residents.

For more information: The College Savings Plan Network at *www.collegesavings.org* has a wealth of information.

Do You Know When to Call a Lawyer? Take This Quiz to Find Out

Janet Portman, JD, managing editor of Nolo Press in Berkeley, CA, America's leading source of self-help legal information and publisher of plain-English law books, including *Every Landlord's Legal Guide* and *Tax Savvy for Small Business.* Go to *www.nolo.com* for more information.

Which everyday legal problems can you deal with on your own—and which ones require a lawyer? Take this quick quiz to test your legal know-how. ***Answers follow on pages 112-113.***

1. Your neighbor starts constructing a small fence, which actually is on your property. *The best action to take...*

a. See a lawyer and sue to make him/her stop building.

b. Wait for the town's zoning officials to take action against your neighbor.

c. Talk to your neighbor about his mistake. If the fence isn't taken down quickly, follow up with a letter politely but firmly insisting that it come down.

2. The dishwasher in your apartment is worn out and has stopped working. The landlord won't replace it. *You should...*

a. Replace the dishwasher and deduct the cost from your next month's rent.

b. Withhold your rent until the landlord replaces the dishwasher.

c. Sue in small-claims court.

3. You take family leave to care for your ailing mother, and then your employer fires you. *You should...*

a. Hire an attorney and file a lawsuit because it is illegal to fire someone who takes family leave.

b. Find out from your employer the reasons for the termination.

c. Do nothing. The family leave laws don't apply to caring for employees' parents.

4. A coworker frequently tells dirty jokes and stories about his sexual exploits, and it makes you uncomfortable. *You should…*

a. Ignore him and hope he gets the message that you aren't amused.

b. Tell him that he is making you uncomfortable. If that doesn't work, make a complaint within the company.

c. File a lawsuit against your employer for sexual harassment.

5. Your father is going to have a risky operation. He tells you that if things go badly, he doesn't want any medical "heroics" to prolong his life. *Before he goes into the hospital, you should do this…*

a. Have a talk with his doctor and convey his wishes.

b. Assure him that you'll convey his wishes if and when it's necessary.

c. Help him prepare a living will, and bring it with you to the hospital.

6. A police officer calls to say your son, who is away at college, has been arrested for drug possession. *You would be wise to…*

a. Do nothing, since you are sure that the charge won't stick and it will blow over quickly.

b. Call the college to see if it can intervene and persuade the police to drop the matter.

c. Have an attorney, even if it is just your family attorney, contact the police and tell them not to question your son until he has obtained legal representation.

7. Your daughter would like to convert her furniture-making hobby into a business. She has asked you to join in the venture. *Before beginning operations, you should…*

a. Go to an attorney and have the business incorporated.

b. Form a limited liability company for your daughter and yourself.

c. Keep things simple by forming a partnership, and just obtain your business license and permits.

8. You loaned your nephew several thousand dollars, but he won't repay it. You want to sue, but the lawyer with whom you've spoken wants too much money. *You should…*

a. Let the matter go.

b. Find out if your nephew will consent to mediation.

c. Sue, but act as your own lawyer.

ANSWERS TO QUIZ

1. c. You have a legal right to have the fence moved off your property—but you also want to keep relations with your neighbor as pleasant as possible. There's nothing more unpleasant than a festering dispute with someone you see every day. Calmly explain that the fence is on your property and needs to be moved. This isn't the kind of issue that zoning officials get involved in—they don't care unless the fence violates local rules about height or materials. See a lawyer only as a last resort.

2. c. In nearly every state and municipality, landlords must maintain a livable, safe rental that complies with basic safety requirements. When landlords fail to live up to that responsibility, tenants in about half the states can repair the problem and deduct the cost from the rent …or withhold the rent until the landlord takes action. These remedies are available only for serious problems (ones that make the unit unsafe or uninhabitable). Losing the use of a dishwasher doesn't make a home unlivable. Using these legal remedies for this issue risks eviction. If negotiation (including mediation) doesn't solve the problem, the safe route is a small-claims lawsuit in which you ask the judge to reduce the rent by an amount that reflects the rental's market value without a dishwasher.

3. b. The federal *Family and Medical Leave Act* (and similar state laws) do cover care for employees' parents. If you get fired shortly after taking family leave, talk to your employer and get all the facts. You can't be fired because you are taking family leave—but you can be terminated if it would have happened anyway.

For example, if your entire department was laid off because the company decided to outsource its work, your termination on that basis would be legal because it wasn't done to punish you for taking the leave—it would have happened whether you took the leave or not.

If you can reasonably conclude that you were fired because of the family leave, contact a lawyer.

4. b. Talk to your coworker and make sure he knows that you want him to stop. Many boorish employees don't even realize that their behavior offends others. Most of the time, a harasser who is confronted and asked to stop will cease his boorish behavior.

If your coworker continues to bother you, complain in writing to your employer's human resources department, a manager or someone who has a high position in the corporation. Making a complaint lets the company know there is a problem and gives management an opportunity to fix it. It's a necessary precondition for collecting damages from the employer if you later file a sexual harassment lawsuit.

5. c. The best way for anyone to ensure that they get the type of medical treatment they want (or don't want) is to prepare documents directing their own care. In a living will, you state your treatment wishes in case you are ever unable to speak for yourself.

It's also very important to prepare a durable power of attorney for health care, in which you name a trusted person to work with doctors, oversee your wishes and make decisions on matters not covered by the living will. (In this case, it sounds like your father will name you to fill that role.) These documents go by different names, depending on the state that you live in.

You can prepare one using software such as *Quicken WillMaker Plus 2006* (Nolo, $49.99).*

A patient representative at the hospital also should be able to provide you and your father with the correct documents for your state.

6. c. After an arrest, it's usually not a good idea to talk to the police without talking to a lawyer first. Talking to the police without an attorney can damage the case for your defense, and criminal defense attorneys almost univer-

*Price subject to change.

sally advise their clients to remain silent until an attorney has assessed the charges and counseled the client.

Your best response is to retain a lawyer, who will contact the police and instruct them not to interrogate your son. The lawyer should visit your son and tell him not to talk to the police until the lawyer himself has had a chance to talk to him.

7. c. Operating this business as a partnership should be sufficient, at least at first. To clarify each party's rights and responsibilities, however, make a written partnership agreement. Get started by taking care of the governmental registration and filing requirements with which all businesses must comply—obtain your federal employer identification number…register the business name…and get a business license, seller's permit and any other required licenses or permits.

Later, if the business grows, you could incorporate or form a limited liability corporation (LLC), which will shield you from personal liability for business debts and allow you to save on taxes.

8. b. Mediation is a confidential process in which parties who are having a dispute meet with a neutral third person (the mediator) to try to work out their differences.

If you come to an understanding about how to resolve the conflict—perhaps you design a repayment plan—the mediator can write up an agreement that will be binding in court.

If you aren't able to resolve the conflict, you can end the mediation and sue. Most mediations are successful, so you have a good chance of emerging with both your money and your valued family relationships.

Legal Self-Defense for Unmarried Couples

Martin Shenkman, CPA and attorney who specializes in trusts and estates in New York City and Teaneck, NJ. He is also the author of *The Complete Book of Trusts* (Wiley). His Web site, *www.laweasy.com,* offers free sample forms and documents.

If you're an unmarried senior, it's vital that you know who will be legally authorized to make all the financial, health care and legal decisions on your behalf should you become disabled. You also must know who will receive your assets when you die.

Matters become complex when you live with a partner, since that person will not become the decision maker or heir by default. Some other person may be by act of law—perhaps to the partner's detriment.

And matters become even more complex if one also has a spouse and children from a former marriage whose interests conflict with the partner's.

HOW TO PROTECT YOURSELF

There are eight documents you need to have for legal safety…

●**Power of attorney (POA).** Execute a durable POA (one that does not expire when you become incapacitated) which will authorize a trusted individual to manage your financial, tax and legal affairs if you cannot. You may wish to authorize your partner to take these actions because if you don't, he/she won't be able to. *Cautions…*

●Special POAs may be required for special purposes. For example, the IRS has its own POA form (IRS Form 2848, *Power of Attorney and Declaration of Representative*) and rules. Other institutions you deal with, such as banks and brokerage firms, may have their own POA forms and rules as well, so check that out before simply exercising a generic POA.

●A standard POA may authorize too much —for example, by letting your agent change beneficiary designations on your insurance and IRA/pension accounts. This could unravel your entire estate plan, so work with an adviser to carefully craft a POA to provide the authority you wish, and no more.

●**Health-care proxy.** This authorizes a specific individual to make health-care decisions for you should you become incapacitated.

Make sure that this individual knows your wishes. If you think conflicts may arise between this person and other family members, try to resolve them in advance—or at least make your wishes well known. (Use a living will, which is a document that can be used to spell out your health care wishes.)

If you have a partner, be sure to expressly state that he should be given all the rights of a spouse to visit you if you are ever hospitalized. Otherwise he might not get extended visiting hours and other spousal preferences.

●**Will.** The toughest emotional decisions, and potentially the greatest conflict among your loved ones, will result from how much and what you leave by bequest to whom. So specify your bequests and your wishes clearly and unambiguously in your will.

Problems: Conflicts are especially likely to arise if you leave significant amounts to a nonspousal partner instead of your family. But if you pass everything to your family (as will happen if you don't have a will), your relatives may refuse to help your partner.

Idea: To help ease conflict, consider leaving assets in trust to your partner so that on his demise, they will pass to your family members. This enables you to protect your partner while also providing for your family members.

Safety: You may want to name an independent third-party trustee, such as a bank or trust company, to control such a trust and make distributions from it under terms you specify. This will keep both your partner and your family from obtaining indirect control of it through a "friendly" trustee, and managing it to the other's detriment.

●**Beneficiary designations.** Be sure these are up to date for insurance policies and retirement accounts. It's a very common error to have obsolete beneficiaries. You may wish to change them when you enter a new relationship and after other kinds of changes in family circumstances.

Tactic: It can be better to provide for a partner by naming him beneficiary of an insurance policy or of a retirement account rather than through your will. This is because transfers to beneficiaries occur automatically at death—and you will avoid probating a will in a way that aggravates a former spouse and children.

●**Investment plans.** Protect your financial security by carefully diversifying assets across a range of investments for safety (so you can't lose too much on any one) and to meet your future income needs.

The best investment plan will vary for each individual. If you have a partner, you should consider both of your finances. Consider using the same investment planner as your partner to coordinate your planning.

Remember that if you are disabled, the person you authorize through a POA to manage your investments will need to know your plans in order to follow them. Explain your investment plan in a written document, and make it available to that person.

●**Property/liability insurance.** Be sure all assets are covered. If you have a partner and you each own assets in your own names, you might need separate insurance and umbrella (personal excess liability) policies. Each of you may need to be listed as being covered on the other's insurance.

Tip: Use the same property insurance consultant and coordinate all coverage.

●**Life insurance.** Nonmarried partners overlook the importance and uses of life insurance more often than married couples do. If one partner is still working and supporting you both, you have a clear insurable need.

Life insurance also can be used to provide for a partner while leaving other assets to family members to avoid disputes.

Consider use of life insurance in both your investment and estate planning.

●**Living-together agreement.** If you live with a partner, the two of you are not covered by the standard laws that govern the division of property in a divorce of married persons. This could place both of you at risk, to the extent that each relies on promises of the other.

Consideration: If one partner has much more wealth and/or income than the other, the poorer partner may become dependent and highly vulnerable should the relationship start to sour.

Safety: Consider drafting a legal agreement that governs what happens if the relationship ends. It may be an awkward subject to bring up—but it's much better and easier to address these issues while on good terms than when you are having a period of trouble.

Also consider: Determine whether your state has a domestic partnership law and how that will affect your planning.

Alert: Consider what may happen if the relationship suffers as the result of you becoming incapacitated while your partner retains control over all your wealth through a POA—he may walk off with your funds. Request that your attorney include safeguards against this, such as a restriction on gifts or transfers to your partner, in the agreement.

What to Do When You're Thinking of Divorce...

Margery Rubin, founder of DivorceSource, which offers nonlegal counseling on the practical problems of divorce, New York City. A fashion advertising and public relations executive, she launched the firm after her own divorce—from a New York City divorce attorney—dragged on for four years. Her e-mail address is divorcesource@aol.com.

Protect yourself if your marriage is failing and divorce is a possibility. Consult with an attorney who specializes in matrimonial law about your rights and for guidance through the first stages of divorce. Get recommendations from your family attorney, your accountant or friends who have divorced.

Go through all your household financial documents—bank statements, brokerage accounts, tax returns and mortgage papers. You need to become familiar with all the assets that will be divided in the divorce.

You also need to know how much it costs to live—so that you'll know how to structure the eventual financial settlement. Your lawyer can advise you on how to make sure your spouse isn't illegally moving assets from joint accounts.

Also, create a support system—friends can help, but you also may need a psychologist or psychiatrist. Your personal physician can help you find someone with experience in counseling patients going through a divorce.

How to Talk to Your Aging Parents About Money

Carrie Schwab-Pomerantz, president of the Charles Schwab Foundation in San Francisco, as well as founder of Schwab's Women Investing Network, an initiative to educate women investors. She is also a coauthor, with her father, Charles R. Schwab, of the book *It Pays to Talk: How to Have the Essential Conversations with Your Family About Money and Investing* (Three Rivers).

Do you know whether your parents have enough income to make ends meet… what kind of retirement savings they have…how they would foot the bill if one or both needed full-time medical care?

If you find these topics difficult to broach, you're not alone. Talking to one's parents about money can be awkward—especially since parents are used to giving advice, not taking it.

Even if your parents resist your initial approach, persevere. It's essential to discuss these subjects before there is a crisis. The more you know about your parents' finances—their retirement plans, insurance coverage and estate plan —the better prepared you will be to help them in the future.

Also, you need to realize that appearances can be deceiving.

Example: A colleague's father, who was a vice president for a wholesale food business, owned a large house, drove luxury cars and always took great vacations. It was not until after his father's death that my colleague discovered his father's only income had been from Social Security—his high lifestyle was financed by an ever-growing home-equity loan and large credit card debt.

GETTING STARTED

It is best to start gradually by asking just a few questions. Include your siblings and their spouses in the discussion so that it becomes a family initiative. If they prefer not to get involved, keep them informed to prevent future disagreements.

Respect your parents' privacy and their need for independence. Initiate the conversation in a nonthreatening way so that they will be more likely to open up to you.

Conversation starters: If your parents are not retired, ask how they envision their lives in retirement. Share what you've been thinking of for yourself. Gingerly steer the conversation toward money.

If they are retired, ask them to advise you about your own retirement planning. You then can ask, "How did you and Dad come up with a plan?"

Talking about the latest headlines can be an icebreaker—falling or rising interest rates or a change in the stock market can generate a discussion about money.

Records you will need: To help them plan, ask your parents to provide you with relevant paperwork, including all their brokerage statements, Social Security benefit reports, retirement plan statements—and bring a calculator. (For a list of all the necessary documents, see the list on pages 117 to 118.)

If your parents don't want to share all the details with you, encourage them to see a financial adviser.

KEY TOPICS

●**Living expenses.** Do your parents have enough income set aside to stay comfortable financially for the rest of their lives? In general, today's retirees live longer and lead more active lives than in the past. They travel, indulge their hobbies, even return to school and launch new careers and businesses. All this costs money.

Conversation starters: If your parents need financial help and you're in a position to pitch in, offer to pick up a particular expense. You will relieve their financial burden while preserving their dignity. You could say, "Dad, you made sacrifices for me over the years. Now I hope you'll agree that it's my turn to do something for you."

You can give gifts of $12,000 per recipient annually ($24,000 from couples) and avoid paying federal gift tax. Payments for medical care made directly to a medical service provider on behalf of a parent are exempt from gift tax.

●**Health-care needs.** In the event of serious illness, are your parents properly insured? If they are age 65 or older (or if they are disabled or otherwise unable to work), Medicare is available, including the new prescription drug benefit program, Medicare Part D. However, Medicare does not cover many preventive care costs or routine expenses, such as eyeglasses, dental care and hearing aids.

Also talk about long-term-care insurance—or other insurance that provides benefits if your parents become unable to perform certain activities of daily living, such as bathing or dressing.

Resource: Medicare, 800-MEDICARE, *www. medicare.gov/longtermcare/static/home.asp.*

Conversation starters: Use someone else's medical crisis as a springboard to a discussion. You could say, "I've been thinking about Uncle Bill's stroke. If that happened to you someday, would you be prepared financially?" Or perhaps, "I am worried that you will run out of money if you have a medical crisis. It would ease my mind if we could plan for that possibility now."

●**Estate planning.** Do your parents' wills reflect the recent changes in tax law and your family, such as a divorce? Have they discussed estate planning options? Has each parent signed a durable power of attorney for finances and one for health care so that an authorized person can manage their affairs if they are incapacitated? Have your parents recently reviewed beneficiary designations for bank and brokerage accounts, insurance policies, retirement plans and government programs?

Conversation starters: Approach your parents with an opening line such as, "Did you hear that Joe passed away? That makes me wonder whether all your affairs are in order."

Make it clear that you're not looking for details about who is being left what. Focus on the fact that you want to honor their wishes.

Keep your emotions in check. Likewise, if your parents become defensive or quiet, don't take it personally. Their feelings are probably caused by a fear of death not by a lack of love or trust.

●**Finding an attorney.** Despite the proliferation of do-it-yourself books and estate-planning software packages, this is not a task that your parents should tackle on their own. They should work with an attorney who specializes in wills, trusts and estate planning. To find one, contact American College of Trust and Estate Counsel, 3415 S. Sepulveda Blvd., Los Angeles 90034, *www.actec.org,* or National Academy of Elder Law Attorneys, 1604 N. Country Club Rd., Tucson, Arizona 85716, *www.naela.org.*

RESOURCES

●**For general advice...**

 ●*How to Care for Aging Parents,* by Virginia Morris (Workman).

 ●*Protect Your Parents and Their Financial Health: Talk with Them Before It's Too Late,* by Susan Richards (Dearborn).

●**For estate planning...**

 ●*Best Intentions: Ensuring that Your Estate Plan Delivers Both Wealth and Wisdom,* by Victoria Collins (Dearborn).

●**For health care...**

 ●Centers for Medicare & Medicaid Services, 877-267-2323, *www.cms.hhs.gov.*

DOCUMENTS TO REVIEW WITH YOUR PARENTS

You will be better able to help plan your parents' financial future if you have access to the following documents...

●**Statements for all bank and brokerage accounts,** including retirement and pension accounts.

●**Social Security statements.**

●**Real estate deeds.**

●**Titles to everything else they own,** such as cars and boats.

●**Mortgage papers for their home if they own...**or the lease if they rent.

●**Other loan documents.**

●**Credit card statements.**

●**Insurance policies** (health, life, disability, car, long-term-care, homeowner's/renter's and umbrella).

●**Tax returns for the last three years.**

●**Wills, living trusts, durable powers of attorney** for finances and health care.

●**Partnership agreements.**

●**Personal documents,** including birth certificates, prenuptial agreement, marriage certificate, divorce settlement, Medicare cards and passports.

How to Help with Interest-Free Loans

Barbara Weltman, an attorney based in Millwood, NY, *www.barbaraweltman.com.* She is author of *J.K. Lasser's 1001 Deductions and Tax Breaks* (Wiley).

If you want to help a child, grandchild or other individual buy a home, pay college bills or meet other expenses, but don't want to risk giving your money away outright in case you need it later, an interest-free loan may fit the bill…

●**There are no adverse tax consequences to such loans**—as long as they do not exceed $10,000.

●**Loans larger than $10,000 but not exceeding $100,000 may result in "imputed interest"**—i.e., be treated for tax purposes as if they carried a market rate of interest. But imputed interest will exist only to the extent the recipient of the loan has investment income of over $1,000.

So, if loan proceeds are used for a purpose such as buying a home when the recipient has no investment income over $1,000, there will be no tax consequences, even for a loan that is as large as $100,000.

With an interest-free loan, you will retain the right to be repaid later, though if it turns out you don't need the money, you can later forgive all or part of the loan as a gift.

And in the meantime, you help the loan recipient with the 0% interest financing terms.

When interest-free loans exceed $100,000, you will have imputed interest, regardless of the borrower's investment income.

Technical rules apply, so consult an expert before acting.

Pay Attention to Due Dates

Some credit card issuers specify to the minute when payments are due. If you are five minutes late, you are charged a late fee.

Self-defense: Read your credit card statement to find the exact due date and time.

Daniel Ray, editor in chief, Bankrate.com, North Palm Beach, FL.

Billions of Dollars Go Unclaimed Each Year: How to Get Your Share

Mark Tofal, a consumer advocate who specializes in unclaimed property, Palm Coast, FL. He is the author of *Unclaimed Assets: Money the Government Owes You!* (NUPA), available from the author and at various libraries. His Web site is *www.unclaimedassets.com.*

The government has more than $30 billion in cash and other assets that belong to millions of Americans—including investments and bank accounts…Social Security payments and tax refunds…insurance proceeds …and more.

Assets are deemed abandoned in the eyes of the law when contact with the owner is lost— typically due to a name change after marriage or divorce, an unreported change of address, incomplete or illegible records or clerical errors.* States and the federal government make only limited efforts to find the owners and return the

*Family members must present proof that they are entitled to a deceased relative's assets—generally a will and a death certificate or documentation provided by the estate's executor or administrator.

cash, so you'll have to find it on your own by contacting government or other sources directly. You also can use my Web site, *www.unclaimed assets.com,* to search for these assets for a fee. *Here's where to look...*

INSURANCE POLICIES

Life insurers are among the largest holders of unclaimed money. Hundreds of millions of dollars in policy benefits go unclaimed every year upon the deaths of the insured because beneficiaries aren't aware that policies exist.

In addition to policy benefits, many policyholders and heirs are entitled to an unexpected windfall. As more mutual life insurance companies have demutualized, millions of current and former policyholders have become entitled to receive stock, cash and policy credits.

Demutualization is the process of converting a *mutual* life insurance company—which is owned by its policyholders—to a *public* company that is owned by shareholders. The compensation awarded after demutualization can be substantial. And, as a stockholder, you share in the company's dividends and benefit from its increased share price. (You can sell your shares at any time without affecting your policy benefits.)

Millions don't know that they are entitled to receive compensation. The companies that have demutualized include Anthem Life, AXA Equitable Life, John Hancock Life, MetLife, Mutual of New York, Nationwide, Phoenix Life, Principal Life and Prudential Insurance Company of America. Claims can be made at any time, but it's best to act fast. Unclaimed stock may be sold by a government-appointed custodian after a relatively short period of time. After that, you are entitled only to proceeds of the sale and may be obligated to pay capital gains tax. For more on unclaimed policy and demutualization benefits, contact the individual insurance companies.

REBATE CHECKS

Manufacturers and retailers make their rebate forms time-consuming and complicated. Also, rebate applications may be rejected for any number of reasons, often without notification to the customer. Keep copies of your application. Send it "return receipt requested" so that you have proof that it was delivered. If you don't receive a check after applying for a rebate, fol-

low up with a written inquiry. Include copies of the application and the mailing receipt. If this doesn't work, contact the merchant's customer service department. If all else fails, file a complaint with your state's attorney general. Contact the National Association of Attorneys General (202-326-6000, *www.naag.org/ag/full_ag_table. php*) or the Federal Trade Commission (877-382-4357, *www.ftc.gov*) for a list.

If you receive a rebate check but fail to cash it within the specified period, call the payor and request a reissue. Often you will be asked to return the expired check before a new one will be sent. If your request for a reissue is refused, ask whether the funds have been remitted to your state office of unclaimed property, as required by law. If they have not, you can contact unclaimed-property officials and request a compliance audit. Those companies found guilty of violations have been forced to pay penalties and interest totaling millions of dollars.

OTHER SOURCES OF LOST FUNDS

State databases: Each state and the District of Columbia maintain a database of unclaimed property. All except Delaware may be searched on-line. To search by state, go to the National Association of Unclaimed Property Administrators' Web site, *www.unclaimed.org.* Check every state in which you have lived, worked or conducted business. Search using maiden names and any previous married names as well as middle names and middle initials. Also search for names of deceased relatives.

Delaware, where hundreds of businesses are incorporated, holds millions of dollars for residents of other states. Why? When the owner of an asset can't be located, the assets are transferred to the merchant's state of incorporation. If you have lost track of stock in a Delaware corporation, contact the Delaware State Escheator (800-828-0632, *www.state.de.us/revenue/infor mation/Escheat.shtml*).

Federal databases: Contact the appropriate agency. *Two common sources...*

•**Bureau of the Public Debt for US savings bonds.** The value of unredeemed US savings bonds—those that have reached "final maturity" and are earning no interest—currently exceeds $9 billion. In addition, newly issued bonds and interest payments are returned by the post office as undeliverable each year. For more information, log on to *www.treasurydirect.gov/indiv/tools/sbtdhunt.htm* or call 800-722-2678.

To replace lost, stolen or destroyed savings bonds, you will need to submit Form 1048, *Claim for Lost, Stolen or Destroyed United States Savings Bonds.* You can get it on-line at the Web site above.

●**IRS for income tax refunds.** In 2005, more than 84,000 tax refund checks worth 73 million were returned to the IRS by the post office. If you have moved since filing your last return, file IRS Form 8822, *Change of Address,* to help avoid this problem. Checks that were returned must be reissued upon request. If a request is not made, the IRS credits the amount to the return filed in the succeeding year.

If your refund check has been lost, destroyed or voided due to the passage of time, contact the IRS and request a reissue. (Treasury checks generally are negotiable for up to one year after date of issue.)

If you don't file a tax return for any period during which you are due a refund, you lose the right to the refund after three years. This is particularly important to heirs of deceased taxpayers, who may be owed refunds as a result of overpayments made during the year of death.

The Automatic Millionaire's Get-Rich Secret

David Bach, founder and CEO of FinishRich, Inc., financial advisers and educators in New York City. He is also the best-selling author of *Smart Couples Finish Rich... Smart Women Finish Rich...*and *The Automatic Millionaire* (all from Broadway).

Sticking to a budget means depriving yourself today for the sake of your future well-being. Few of us have the discipline that this requires—we dine at expensive restaurants ...buy new cars every two or three years...and spend $3.50 for a cup of coffee. Result? Even people who have decent incomes live from paycheck to paycheck.

To save steadily, most people need to override human nature. How? By putting savings on autopilot. Arrange for a certain percentage of each paycheck to be tucked away. Doing so takes little discipline or effort. Many employers have automatic payroll-deduction plans for retirement accounts. You also can arrange for your bank or mutual fund firm to take money out of your bank account every month.

HOW MUCH TO SET ASIDE

Start out small. Save 1% of your salary. Soon, you can bump that up to 3%. Your goal should be to save at least 10%. Those with grander objectives should save 15% to 20%. You will be amazed by how little sacrifice is involved.

Say you now buy lunch at the office every day. By brown-bagging it (at a cost of $1 per day instead of $8), you can save $35 a week, or about $150 a month. If you earn a 7% annual return, that savings would increase to $73,791 in 20 years.

The best way to save is with a 401(k) or another tax-advantaged plan. If you save after-tax dollars, the federal government by itself takes about $3 of every $10 you earn. When you put $10 into a retirement plan, the entire sum goes to work and won't be taxed until withdrawal.

PAY DOWN YOUR MORTGAGE

Making regular mortgage payments is a form of forced savings.

To accelerate the process, see if your bank will allow you to pay off your mortgage early, perhaps by making one payment every two weeks instead of one a month. By following this system, you will make 26 half payments, or the equivalent of 13 monthly payments each year. You could pay off a 30-year mortgage in about 23 years.

Consider that a $250,000 30-year mortgage that has an interest rate of 8% will cost you $410,388 in interest. By paying biweekly, you will pay $119,000 less.

8

Insurance Answers

When Your Health Insurer Says No— How to Fight Back

A recent US Supreme Court decision against two participants in separate managed care plans in Texas underscores how difficult it has become to sue HMOs, PPOs and other health insurance companies. Therefore, it has become even more important to be a strong advocate for your own care.

PREVENTING PROBLEMS

Here is what to do to see that your insurer covers the treatments you need...

●**Get your doctor 100% behind you.** Your physician can be your strongest ally. In cases where treatment is not clear-cut, the insurer ultimately may defer to his/her recommendation. *If your doctor refuses to recommend a treatment that you think you need...*

●Ask him why, but be diplomatic. Tell him, "I want to take responsibility for my condition. Can you tell me what information you relied on to determine that I don't need this treatment?"

●Learn enough about your condition to ask intelligent questions. You might say, "Are you familiar with X (a reliable source that you trust), which recommends this protocol?"

Sources worth checking...

☐ Health Web, a compendium of health sciences libraries at *www.healthweb.org.*

☐ Medline Plus, from National Institutes of Health and US National Library of Medicine at *www. medlineplus.gov.*

☐ University of Iowa School of Medicine at *www.lib.uiowa.edu/hardin/md.*

☐ The Health Resource at 800-949-0090. For a fee, you can get medical research tailored to your specific problem.

Rhonda D. Orin, Esq., managing partner in the Washington, DC, offices of the law firm of Anderson Kill & Olick LLP. She specializes in representing policyholders in insurance coverage disputes across the country. She is author of *Making Them Pay: How to Get the Most from Health Insurance and Managed Care* (St. Martin's).

If your doctor still isn't convinced, present him with a second doctor's opinion that supports the treatment. You may have to pay for the second opinion, depending on your insurance policy's rules.

●**Get a copy of your company's health plan from your employer.** Compare it to the shortened version that you received when you became eligible for coverage. If there are any discrepancies that pertain to your condition, notify your employer.

●**Check your state's mandatory benefits laws.** These regulations, which are not well-publicized, require health plans to cover specific illnesses and conditions. Call your state's department of insurance to see if your condition must be covered under state law. Contact information for state commissioners is available from the National Association of Insurance Commissioners (816-842-3600 or *www.naic.org/state_web_map.htm*).

Examples: Many states, including New York and California, require insurers to cover certain forms of infertility treatment. Maryland and some other states require coverage of gastric bypass surgery for morbidly obese patients.

If your insurer denies coverage even after you have reminded the representative of your state's mandate, forward the denial letter to your state insurance commissioner and ask for help.

Exception: Mandatory benefits laws may not apply to health plans that are fully funded, with claims paid by an insurance company, and do not apply to the government-run insurance programs, such as Medicare.

WINNING AN APPEAL

Most insurers require a written appeal within a certain number of days of the denial of treatment, and they in turn promise a decision within a certain number of days.

Caution: Don't drop your plan while negotiating—you have greater leverage if you are still a member. *To further boost your odds...*

●**Keep detailed records of the facts regarding your case**—not just insurance company correspondence and test results. Insurers often win because they maintain more detailed records than consumers do.

Also, keep notes of telephone conversations with insurance representatives. Include their names, titles, office locations and phone extensions. After every important conversation, send the person with whom you spoke a letter summarizing key discussion points. (If you can't get the representative's name, ask for his identification number.) In the letter, request that he write back if you misstated anything he said. If he doesn't object to doing this, it will strengthen your case.

●**Keep your cool.** Fighting an insurer can be extremely frustrating, but don't ever swear or use foul language on the phone or in a letter. That just allows the insurer to portray you as difficult and unreasonable.

●**Stick to the facts.** Insurers don't care how much you have suffered. They only want to know if their decision was correct based on an analysis of your medical records, other medical evidence and their internal policies.

Example: You're 48 years old and your doctor recommends a colonoscopy, but your HMO refuses to cover it, stating that the test is only for people over age 50. To get approval, you will need documentation—(a) a letter from your doctor telling why you need to have a colonoscopy (there is a family history of colon cancer)...(b) recent data from the American Cancer Society that directly supports his opinion...(c) a statement from another physician saying that a colonoscopy is recommended.

●**Ask that your employer get involved.** Your company may have some leverage with the insurer, especially in disability insurance cases in which a condition affects your day-to-day abilities.

●**Follow the appeals procedure exactly.** Otherwise, an insurer may reject your appeal based on procedural grounds.

Most common: Failure to file required paperwork by deadlines.

●**Use as much of the insurer's own language as possible,** including terms from your plan documents. Always refer to the section number and the page where you found the citation.

Helpful: View samples of appeal letters at the Center for Health Care Rights Web site at *www.healthcarerights.org/letters/samletintro.html*.

• **If you lose your appeal, consider filing an external grievance.** All states will give you the legal right to be heard by an independent panel if your internal appeals are rejected. Call your state's department of insurance for details.

Alternatives: The state's department of insurance may investigate complaints. Send them the same material that you used for your appeal to your insurer. The agency will investigate within six months and order corrective action if necessary, including requiring the insurer to pay for all valid claims.

Your state attorney general also may be willing to open an investigation. You can obtain the contact information for your state attorneys general from the National Association of Attorneys General (202-326-6000, *www.naag.org/ag/full_ag_table.php*).

How to Buy Health Insurance on Your Own

Karin Grablin, CPA, CFP, financial planner for Mott & Associates, 415 32 St. W., Bradenton, FL 34205. Licensed in both health and life insurance, she writes frequently for the *Bradenton Herald* on personal finance topics.

If you need to line up your own health insurance, where can you look and how affordable will it be? *The main options…*

SPOUSAL COVERAGE

If you're married and your spouse is insured through an employer, family coverage may be available.

Cost: Be prepared to pay a significant amount to add your coverage to your spouse's plan. Nevertheless, you'll be paying for group health insurance, which probably will be cost-effective.

COBRA

If you've recently retired or severed employment and are unable to get spousal health coverage, the federal *Consolidated Omnibus Budget Reconciliation Act of 1986* (COBRA) may provide temporary relief.

How it works: After you leave a company that has been providing health insurance, you can maintain that coverage for up to 18 months, in most cases.

Exception: If you worked for a company with fewer than 20 employees, COBRA will not be applicable.

Saver: Several states have their own COBRA laws covering small companies.

Cost: You'll pay both the employer's and the employee's share. This can be quite a bit more expensive than just the employee's share, if any, you had been paying.

Example: Say you had been paying $150 per month for family coverage under Company ABC's health plan. When you take early retirement, you might find yourself paying several times that much per month for the same coverage under COBRA.

Even at the higher price, COBRA may be less expensive than the other alternatives.

Key: COBRA may be particularly attractive if you suffer from a serious medical condition that would make the expense of your own coverage even higher.

ASSOCIATION COVERAGE

If you can't get coverage from an employer, join a group. Many associations and organizations offer group health insurance as a member benefit.

Some college alumni associations offer health insurance. The same goes for some local chambers of commerce. AAA offers health insurance to members.

Advantage: If you join a long-established organization that provides a wide variety of member benefits, you might benefit from group insurance.

Disadvantage: Some "organizations" serve little purpose other than as the providers of health insurance. Therefore, they tend to attract a large number of people who are in poor health and unable to get affordable coverage.

Result: Such plans may start out with teaser rates for health insurance, then stick policyholders with steep rate increases.

Look before leaping into an association plan. Find out how much coverage will be included —beware of low limits—and whether there are protections against rate increases.

MANAGED CARE

Many employers provide medical insurance that involves health maintenance organizations (HMOs) or other forms of managed care. You may find that membership in such a plan is an affordable option.

How they work: You'll pay a set fee, generally per month. This will entitle you to a wide variety of health-care services, maybe at a nominal per-visit cost.

Advantage: In many geographic locations, managed care plans are less expensive than other options for individual health insurance. They tend to be particularly cost-effective for checkups and other preventive care not covered by traditional health insurance.

Disadvantage: You'll lose freedom of choice with managed care. Typically, you will have to go through one physician (the "gatekeeper"), who'll decide whether to refer you to a specialist. If you do go outside the approved network, you may have to pay some or all of the cost.

INDEMNITY POLICIES

These policies offer traditional health insurance. Indemnity policies may be available in your area from organizations such as a local Blue Cross/Blue Shield affiliate or from a private insurance company.

Problem: They're expensive.

How they work: You can pick any doctor or hospital you want. The insurance will help pay for the treatment you receive.

Costs: Besides the premiums, you'll also be responsible for deductibles and co-payments.

Example: You might have a policy with a $1,000 deductible, which means you pay for the first $1,000 worth of medical treatments each year. Subsequently, you might pay 20% while the insurer picks up the other 80%.

There may be a stop-loss amount for your out-of-pocket expenses, after which the insurer pays 100% of medical and hospital costs.

Trade-off: The higher the deductible, the lower your annual premiums. Increasing your deductible from, say, $1,000 to $2,500 should cut your premiums dramatically.

With a high-deductible policy, you agree to pay relatively modest medical bills and have protection against a catastrophic loss.

HEALTH SAVINGS ACCOUNTS

Introduced in 2004, health savings accounts (HSAs) combine health insurance with tax-free savings for health costs. They are similar to the Archer medical savings accounts which have been around for a few years.

How HSAs work: You buy qualified high-deductible health insurance (an indemnity policy, as described above). Once that is done, you can make tax-deductible contributions to an HSA.

Some insurers offer you the insurance policy and the HSA, along with savings options. You also may find a bank or other trustee to open your HSA. According to *www.hsainsider.com,* a nonprofit organization that promotes health-care reform, the two largest HSA trustees are HSA Bank (*www.hsabank.com*) and First HSA (*www.firstmsa.com*).

Requirements: The policy must have a deductible of at least $1,050 for individual coverage, and $2,100 for families. You won't have to pay anything further once you have spent no more than $10,000 (less with some policies) in any one year.

Limit: Your contribution to the HSA in any given year can be as large as the deductible on your health insurance. So, with a $1,050 deductible, you can put as much as $1,050 per year into an HSA.

The maximum HSA contribution for 2006 is $2,700 for individuals, or $5,450 for those with families—even when your deductible is higher. These numbers will increase with inflation in future years.

Key: The HSA contribution is an above-the-line tax deduction. You can write it off even if you don't itemize your medical and other personal expenses.

Payoff: HSA withdrawals that are used to pay qualified medical bills, including expenses for over-the-counter medications, are tax free. There are no restrictions on your choice of doctors or hospitals.

Money you don't spend right away can stay in the HSA, enjoying tax-deferred growth. You may build up a fund you can use for future health-care needs. At age 65, the balance in the HSA account also may be used to supplement retirement income (subject to income taxes).

Looking ahead: The premiums on a high-deductible policy are relatively low, so they might not increase as much each year as do traditional health insurance costs. Therefore, an HSA may help you to control cost increases in future years.

Most People Really Do Need Long-Term-Care Insurance...How to Choose the Best Policy

Les Abromovitz, a lawyer who has offices in Pittsburgh and Boca Raton. He is author of *Protecting and Rebuilding Your Retirement* (Amacom) and *Long-Term Care Insurance Made Simple* (Practice Management Information).

Sixty percent of Americans over age 65 will need long-term care at some point in their lives. The typical nursing home stay now costs about $70,000 per year—and much more in some cities. Few people can afford to pay such amounts for an extended period. Yet only about 7% of Americans have long-term-care (LTC) insurance policies, which cover nursing home, assisted-living and at-home care.

Contrary to what many Americans believe, health insurance, including Medicare and Medicare supplemental (Medigap) policies, usually doesn't pay for LTC expenses. If you don't have LTC insurance, you must pay for these costs out of pocket, unless you qualify for Medicaid—and Medicaid only kicks in after your assets have been depleted.

Having coverage increases your chance of getting care at home or in an assisted-living facility, rather than having to go into a nursing home. It is an especially wise purchase for those who have a family history of dementia or another condition or disease that could require extended care.

Even if you have substantial assets, you might want to buy a no-frills LTC policy and use your own money to pay for noncovered expenses.

WHEN TO BUY LTC INSURANCE

Since you never know when you might need long-term care, start shopping when you're in your 50s. Consider buying a policy before age 50 if your health or family history suggests an increased chance of needing long-term care. A physical usually isn't required, but you must complete an application with medical questions. Rates are the same for men and women, but they vary based on your health.

Sample cost: For $1,390* per year, a healthy 50-year-old man could buy an LTC policy from one major insurance company with coverage of $200 per day for up to four years and a rider to protect benefits against inflation. By age 85, he will have paid $48,650 for the policy.

A 65-year-old man would pay $2,941 per year for a comparable policy. At that rate, by age 85, he would have spent $58,820 for the policy—$10,170 more than if he had purchased it at age 50, even though he was insured for 15 fewer years. (These figures assume no rate increases or changes in health status.)

SHOPPING FOR COVERAGE

Choose carefully. Once you purchase a policy, you effectively are stuck with it. Switching would only mean paying higher rates based on your more advanced age and perhaps declining health.

●**If your employer offers LTC insurance, that may be your best bet.** Group policies tend to cost less than individual ones...contract language often is more straightforward...and you may even be able to purchase coverage for your parents through your employer. Policies are portable if you change jobs, so you won't have to requalify for insurance, at potentially higher rates.

●**If you buy individually through an agent, find one who specializes in long-term care.** Policies are complex—an insurance generalist could make a mistake that is costly to you.

*All rates subject to change.

125

Example: Some policies make it difficult to collect on benefits. For instance, a company may use a different criterion for in-home coverage than for other long-term care, something nonspecialists have been known to overlook.

Ask your state's insurance bureau for a list of LTC agents in good standing in your region. Links to state insurance departments can be found at *www.naic.org* (click on "NAIC States & Jurisdictions"). Obtain quotes from at least three insurers.

INSURER CREDENTIALS

Make sure the insurer…

● **Has claims-paying ability rated at least A+ by A.M. Best.** Your agent should have these ratings. *A.M. Best Top-Rated LTC Carriers…*

 ● Allianz Life Insurance Company of America.
 ● AEGON Life Investors Insurance Company of America.
 ● Lincoln Benefit Life Company.
 ● Massachusetts Mutual Life (available since 2000).
 ● MetLife.
 ● New York Life.
 ● Prudential Insurance Company of America.
 ● State Farm.
 ● Thrivent Financial for Lutherans.

Note: These insurers have been offering LTC insurance for at least five years, unless otherwise noted.

● **Is committed to the business.** If a carrier decides to sell its business, you still will be covered, but there is no guarantee that the new insurer will have the same claims-paying ability. Look for companies that have been offering LTC policies for at least five years.

Don't be lured by a big name. Some quality companies have now given up on long-term care and have sold these divisions to less credit-worthy insurers.

● **Has not increased premiums significantly.** So-called "fixed" premiums are subject to change. While insurers can't target individual policyholders for an increase, they can, with regulatory approval, raise rates for everyone in a rate classification. In recent years, some policyholders have been hit with increases of 15% to 50%. Ask your state's insurance department which firms have raised rates, and avoid those companies. Also, budget for rate increases—as much as 50% over the life of the policy.

New wrinkle: "Partnership policies," which combine private insurance and Medicaid, are offered by four states—California, Connecticut, Indiana and New York. When LTC needs extend beyond the period covered by private insurance and Medicaid kicks in, the policyholder may not have to use up his/her assets.

Example: If you buy an LTC policy under the New York State Partnership for Long-Term Care program and use three years of nursing home care, six years of in-home care or some combination, you may apply for state Medicaid benefits and retain your assets. You will, however, have to contribute any income you have, such as Social Security, to your care costs.

POLICY CHECKLIST

Seven features and options that are really worth the money…

● **Adequate daily benefit.** Look for a benefit of at least $200 per day. Anything less will not fully cover nursing home care. Also look at the cost of long-term care in your area. Someone in New York City might need a daily benefit of $300.

● **Inflation protection.** If you think nursing homes are expensive now, just wait. Average expenses are expected to quadruple by 2030, according to the American Council of Life Insurers. Look for inflation protection of 5% per year. "Bargain" policies often don't have this. You might pay twice as much as you would for a policy without this feature.

● **Flexible coverage.** *In addition to a nursing home, it should cover…*

 ● In-home care for medical and nonmedical services. Without coverage for nonmedical services, you may not be able to stay at home even if your policy does cover in-home care. Your policy should cover the cost of hiring someone to perform household chores, though certain chores are unlikely to be covered, such as lawn care or snow removal. Look for in-home-care coverage equal to 75% to 100% of your policy's daily benefit. *Note:* Policies differ as to whether they'll pay a relative to provide in-home care.

• Alternative plan of care, such as home modifications for wheelchair use.

• Assisted-living facilities.

• Adult day care.

• Respite care—services provided by a substitute caregiver.

• 90-day elimination period. Most LTC policies require payment out of pocket for a short time before benefits kick in. If this "elimination period" is shorter than 90 days, your premiums could be prohibitively expensive. If it's longer, you could incur thousands of dollars in costs before coverage begins.

• Benefit period of at least three years. The average nursing home stay is two and a half years. State insurance regulators determine the shortest benefit period that may be sold in a state. A lifetime benefit may be unaffordable.

• Tax qualification. Most LTC policies are "tax-qualified," meaning policyholders don't pay state or federal income tax on benefits. Group policies also can be tax-qualified.

Helpful: You can deduct LTC insurance premiums within limits and other medical expenses if they exceed 7.5% of your adjusted gross income and you itemize. Also check for state tax breaks. LTC insurers have been pushing for more favorable tax treatment of premiums.

• Easy eligibility. Pay attention to the policy trigger, which is described in the policy and the outline of coverage. It determines if and when benefits are paid out. Look for a section entitled "Eligibility for Benefits." Make sure the trigger is no more restrictive than suffering a cognitive impairment or an inability to perform at least two of six activities of daily living (ADLs), such as dressing and using the toilet.

Helpful: Some companies offer couple discounts and/or allow couples to share benefits in their policies.

FEATURES TO AVOID

• Nonforfeiture of benefits rider promises some continued coverage even if you become unable to pay premiums. Given the cost, it typically is better to decline this option and put the money you save in an emergency fund.

• Return of premium rider ensures that your heirs will receive some cash if the policy is never used. You're better off skipping this rider and investing the savings on your own.

Mastering Medicaid Nursing Home Rules

Martin S. Finn, Esq., CPA, partner in the law firm of Lavelle & Finn LLP, Latham, NY. Mr. Finn is coauthor of *The Complete Trust Guide* and *Estate Planning Techniques for Mid-Sized Estates* (both from Professional Education Systems Institute).

If you or your parents reach a point where 24-hour custodial care is necessary, be prepared for sticker shock. The average cost of a shared room in a nursing home is reaching $62,000 a year, while a private room costs about $70,000 a year. In some parts of the US, especially the Northeast, annual nursing home costs can run into six figures.

HELP FROM THE PUBLIC PURSE

Those figures aren't very daunting if you are wealthy or bought a generous long-term-care insurance policy. But people who don't have money or insurance may be able to count on Medicaid, the federal-state assistance program.

To qualify, you must have few assets and little income. Medicaid will then pay for your stay in a nursing home. *Financial limits…*

• You can own a house and a car. However, Medicaid likely will put a lien on your house and seek reimbursement of its nursing home payments from a future sale.

• You generally can have no more than a few thousand dollars in assets (known as "resources" in some states).

• Income limits vary by state but they're usually no more than about $50 per month for someone living in a nursing home—about $600 for someone living in his/her own home.

When one married individual needs to go on Medicaid but the other doesn't, the spouse who isn't applying for Medicaid also faces limits.

Spousal rules vary by state, but the national maximum amounts for the non-Medicaid spouse are around $95,000 for assets and $2,400 per month of total family income.

Don't confuse Medicaid with Medicare in regard to nursing home expenses. Medicare pays about 10% of nursing home costs, mainly for skilled nursing care and services involving medical attention. (Most care provided in nursing homes is unskilled custodial care.)

PLAYING THE GIVEAWAY GAME

You might think that you can give all your assets to your children and then immediately qualify for Medicaid. However, the rules don't permit it.

When you apply for Medicaid, you'll have to present all of your financial records, including those from your bank and brokerage accounts. Transfers or below-market sales to friends or relatives will be revealed. And a formula may delay your eligibility for Medicaid.

How it works: Medicaid keeps records of average monthly nursing home costs in your area. The value of transfers you have made, divided by that average cost, is the formula for determining your waiting period.

Example: The average monthly cost of nursing home care in your area is $5,000. (This number can be obtained from your state's Medicaid office.) If you transfer $100,000 to your children, you'll have a 20-month wait before you can qualify for Medicaid ($100,000 divided by $5,000). If you transfer $50,000, you'll have to wait for 10 months ($50,000 divided by $5,000).

Limit: When you apply for Medicaid, only your transfers for the previous 36 months count. (If a check of your financial records reveals any transfers to a trust, the "look-back" period will be extended to 60 months.)

Tactic: If making a large outright transfer, wait at least 36 months before applying for Medicaid. The rules state that all property transfers will count toward establishing a waiting period.

How it works: When you apply, all transfers within 36 or 60 months must be reported. If that includes a huge transfer, that number will be used to set the waiting period, as above, and the waiting period might be 10 years, or longer. If you wait until 36 or 60 months after you have made any transfers, the previous transfers won't count and you can become eligible for Medic-

aid right away, providing you meet the income/assets tests.

Example: You would like to preserve your $500,000 worth of assets for your children, yet you also want to qualify for Medicaid. In your area, the average monthly cost of nursing home care is $5,000.

On April 30, 2006, you give $500,000 to your children. This money is an outright gift, not in trust.

In May 2009, you can apply for Medicaid. The 36-month look-back period won't include your April 2006 transfer. Thus, you can qualify for Medicaid right away. Medicaid will pay any nursing home costs.

Huge trap: If you apply early—before the 36-month period lapses (even by a single day), your transfer will be counted. You'll have to wait a total of 100 months ($500,000 divided by $5,000) from the date of the transfer before you can qualify for Medicaid.

SPENDING IT DOWN

Don't give away all of your assets if you think you'll need nursing home care some day.

Reality: Residents who can pay their own way will have a wider choice of nursing homes because some facilities (often, the most desirable ones) will not accept Medicaid enrollees. Some homes accept a limited number of Medicaid enrollees. And in homes where Medicaid participants are accepted, "private-pay" residents may get better treatment.

Strategy: Give away some assets but keep some, too. (Giving in advance gets them into relatives' hands and out of the nursing home's reach.) You can then enter the nursing home of your choice as a paying customer. Once you've spent down your assets to the Medicaid limits, you can apply for public assistance.

Benefit: If you've chosen a nursing home that accepts Medicaid enrollees, you can stay in that home. The staff is not likely to know of your changed status so you will continue to receive first-class treatment.

Example: You have $100,000 in assets. You give $50,000 to your children but keep $50,000. You then go into a nursing home that charges $5,000 per month. During the next 10 months, you spend down your $50,000 on nursing home payments.

After the 10 months are up, you can apply for Medicaid, which will pay your ongoing nursing home bills. The nursing home is not likely to evict you, and your family will have preserved the $50,000 in assets that you've transferred.

Key: This "half-a-loaf" strategy is better than losing all of your assets to nursing home costs.

Trap: If you start out as a private-pay resident in a nursing home that does not take Medicaid enrollees, you later will have to move to another nursing home that participates in Medicaid, at a time when you might have little or no choice of facilities. It's vital to make a savvy initial choice.

WHEN TRUSTS HELP

Although the outright transfers have a shorter look-back period, there may be some situations in which it would be advantageous for you to incur the legal fees and the potentially longer wait for Medicaid eligibility that results from making transfers to a trust.

For example, a trust might work better if the intended recipient of your assets is…

● **A spendthrift,** likely to squander your gift.

● **In a troubled marriage,** so your assets may be subject to a property settlement.

● **Disabled,** so you desire to provide long-term security for him/her.

Loophole: Gifts to a disabled child or to a trust created for that child's benefit don't count as transfers for the purpose of determining Medicaid eligibility. You can make such a transfer of any amount today and then apply for Medicaid tomorrow.

For more on Medicaid and nursing home costs, see *www.elderlawanswers.com,* a site put together by a network of elder law attorneys… AARP's site, *www.aarp.org*…and *www.cms.hhs. gov/medicaid,* an Internet site sponsored by the federal government.

Life Insurance Loopholes

Edward Mendlowitz, CPA, shareholder in the CPA firm WithumSmith+Brown, 120 Albany St., New Brunswick, NJ 08901. He is also the author of *Introducing Tax Clients to Additional Services* (American Institute of CPAs).

Smart insurance buyers can save a bundle in taxes, both in life and in the execution of their estates, if they look into the following strategies…

***Loophole:* Life insurance proceeds are income tax free.** This is true even if only a few premium payments were made. However, life insurance premiums are not tax deductible.

● **Life insurance proceeds are partly or totally estate tax free** if the policy (or part of it) is owned by the beneficiary, not the insured.

Better: Use an irrevocable life insurance trust (ILIT) as the policy owner. If children or other individuals own the policy, it becomes available to an ex-spouse or unintended strangers in the event of divorce or a lawsuit against the child. The proceeds are estate tax free if you have no control over the policy.

Caution: Making your estate the beneficiary subjects the proceeds to tax.

● **Do not let your spouse own the policy.** A policy that's owned by the decedent or his/ her spouse is taxed in the estate if both die simultaneously. Instead, use an ILIT as owner of the life insurance policy.

● **Do not name a former spouse as beneficiary.** If you do, the proceeds will be included in your estate because the policy will have been owned by the decedent.

Better: Set up an ILIT as owner in accordance with your divorce agreement.

***Loophole:* So-called "Crummey letters" make annual gifts to a trust to pay for the life insurance premiums eligible for the $12,000 annual gift tax exclusion.** (A Crummey letter notifies trust beneficiaries of their right to withdraw the amounts given to the trust.) If the beneficiaries do not waive their rights to their portion of the gift via a Crummey letter, the gift is subject to gift tax.

Loophole: Policies purchased by an irrevocable life insurance trust are not subject to a "waiting period." When existing policies are transferred to a trust, there is a three-year waiting period before proceeds are tax exempt.

Strategy: When policies are transferred to new trusts, the clock starts ticking. If the insured dies within three years, the proceeds are subject to estate taxes. Buy an inexpensive three-year term policy to cover estate taxes.

Loophole: Use income from life insurance proceeds to pay an "allowance" to children's guardians if both parents die. Establish the allowance provisions in the will or trust.

Loophole: Avoid "transfer for value" taxation that applies when an owner sells the policy to the insured... a partner of the insured...a partnership in which the insured is a partner...or a corporation in which the insured is an officer or shareholder.

Trap: When the policy is sold to any of the buyers listed, the excess of the proceeds over the premiums paid is taxable income to the recipient of the death benefit.

Loophole: Write an "apportionment" clause into your will. This designates that estate taxes attributable to inadvertently owned life insurance proceeds will be paid by the recipient, not the estate.

Loophole: Employer-paid group term insurance premiums are tax free up to $50,000 of life insurance. Premiums paid for policies over that are taxable at reduced rates determined by IRS tables.

Loophole: Whole life insurance creates a tax-free buildup of cash value that offsets premiums in later years. When paid as part of the life insurance proceeds, it is not taxed ...nor when borrowed from the policy...when withdrawn, it is tax free to the extent of total premiums paid.

Loophole: Match insurance to your coverage needs using the tax deferral features of life insurance. Universal life insurance provides flexibility to modify the face amount or premium when personal circumstances change.

Variable life combines life insurance with a tax-deferred or sheltered investment fund.

Benefits: The insured "owns" the investment part of the policy, including the investment risk. When the insured dies, the proceeds are income tax free. Also, the insured can borrow against the cash value.

Outright distributions are subject to income tax to the extent that they exceed total premiums paid. They are not subject to penalty for distributions made before age 59½—variable annuity distributions are.

Loophole: Payments made under a life insurance policy to a terminally ill insured are income tax free, like a "death" benefit.

Loophole: Fund shareholder and partnership buy-sell agreements with life insurance. When the death benefits are received, the recipient pays no income tax. The proceeds are then used to purchase the deceased owner's shares tax free. Be aware that you cannot deduct premium payments, and C corporations may be liable for alternative minimum tax.

Loophole: Fund cross-purchase agreements with life insurance. When a buy-sell agreement is funded with life insurance, the entity uses the proceeds to acquire shares. With a cross-purchase arrangement, the remaining owners receive the death benefits and then use them to buy the shares. This way, they get a tax-favored stepped-up basis for the shares.

Slash Car Insurance Costs

For some quick ways to cut your auto insurance costs, take a look below...

●**Take the highest deductible you can afford.** A $1,000 deductible may reduce the cost of collision and comprehensive insurance by as much as 40%.

●**Drop collision and comprehensive coverage** when the value of a car is less than 10 times the premium.

●**Take every discount available.** Various insurers will provide discounts for low-mileage driving; for having an antitheft device, air bags, antilock brakes, daytime running lights; for having "good student" (sometimes defined as a B+ or better average) and college student away-from-home drivers and for carrying auto and homeowner's insurance with the same company.

Jeanne Salvatore, vice president, consumer affairs, Insurance Information Institute, New York City, *www.iii.org.*

Home Insurance Smarts

Sharon Emek, a partner in CBS Coverage Group, Inc., an insurance agency in New York City which now represents more than three dozen insurance companies, *www. cbsinsurance.com.* A licensed insurance broker, she has 25 years of experience in the business.

The expense of homeowner's insurance is increasing again. *How to save 25% on home insurance costs…*

MAKE YOURSELF LESS OF A RISK

Your homeowner's premium depends on which "tier" your insurer puts you in. Your tier depends primarily on your claims history and credit score. Top-tier home owners can pay significantly less than those in the bottom tier.

Keep score: Few people know what their scores are or whether they are accurate. *To find out, order a copy of your credit report from each of the three national credit rating agencies…*

- **Equifax,** 800-685-1111, *www.equifax.com.*
- **Experian,** 888-397-3742, *www.experian. com.*
- **TransUnion,** 800-916-8800, *www.tuc.com.*

Under the *Fair and Accurate Credit Transactions Act of 2003* (FACT), you can receive one free credit report per year from each of the reporting agencies. Check each report for accuracy. You might find loans and/or credit cards listed for someone with a similar name.

To improve your credit score…

- **Pay off debt you don't need to carry.**
- **Close credit card accounts that you do not need.**
- **Correct errors,** such as a credit card you canceled or a bill that isn't yours.

Once you have improved your score, you or your agent can ask the insurer to reconsider your "credit insurance score"—derived from all your risk factors—and put you in a better tier.

To cut your premiums…

Since the primary purpose of insurance is to protect you from major losses, not to pay for relatively minor expenses, raise your deductible. Switching from a $250 deductible to a $1,000 deductible could save you as much as 25% on premiums. Then, if you suffer a loss anywhere near $1,000—even up to $1,500—cover it yourself instead of filing a claim.

The more claims you file and the bigger they are, the higher your premium. People with low credit scores tend to file more claims than those with high scores. File too many claims—more than one in any two-year period—and your insurer may not renew your coverage.

LOSS-PROOF YOUR HOUSE

Avoid common claims by maintaining your house properly…

- **Fix even minor roof leaks promptly,** and keep rain gutters clean.
- **Trim dead branches,** and remove dying trees before they fall and cause damage.
- **Install windstorm shutters** if you're in a high-wind area.
- **Improve drainage around the house,** and/or install an automatic sump pump if your basement tends to flood.
- **Check heating, electrical and plumbing systems, and the roof every few years.** It's best if a professional does this so problems are caught. Keep your chimney clean and unobstructed. The older your house is, the more important such maintenance becomes.

SHOP AROUND

Sticking with one insurer for the long haul might earn you a renewal discount of 5% or so on your premium. It also could get you more personal attention when you have a claim.

Still, don't just automatically renew year after year. Comparison shop among insurers at least every three years. The Internet makes it easy to get quotes from dozens of companies. Even if you normally buy your policy directly from an insurer, get several comparison quotes on exactly the same coverage from an independent agent.

You can buy homeowner's insurance on-line, but I don't advise this. There are so many variables that you probably need expert advice to get the right coverage.

Strategy: Use on-line quotes to get an idea of the price, but buy from an agent.

LOOK FOR TRUE REPLACEMENT COST

Buy a policy that pays the true replacement cost of any loss. Avoid the cash-value policies, which cost less but only pay the depreciated value of your loss. Insure only what might be damaged or destroyed. Don't insure land since it doesn't burn and can't be stolen.

Every insurance company will provide a cost-estimator worksheet to help you determine replacement cost. Some companies will send a representative to do a free on-site appraisal.

Don't overinsure by buying a market-value policy. Market value is what a buyer would pay for your home. In a hot market, that amount could exceed the cost of rebuilding the home. The opposite advice applies if you're in a fading neighborhood, where replacement cost might exceed market value.

STICK WITH QUALITY

A low premium won't be a bargain if the company is gone when you file a claim. Buy from a company with a rating of at least A minus from A.M. Best Co., *www.ambest.com.*

LOOK FOR DISCOUNTS

There's no haggling with insurers. Rates are set for groups who share attributes, not on a case-by-case basis. *But discounts are available...*

●**Alarm discount.** Up to 15% off if the home is protected by a comprehensive system (heat, smoke and burglar) linked to a central monitoring station. The insurer may insist on a system linked to the house wiring with a battery back-up rather than one that uses only batteries.

●**High-value item discount.** You can save on the cost of coverage for "scheduled" items, such as high-end jewelry, if they are kept in a safe-deposit box at a bank rather than in a drawer at home. (A home safe is not likely to get you the discount.)

●**Multipolicy discount.** Many insurers discount if you buy multiple coverage from them, like auto, liability and homeowner's.

●**Other potential discounts.** *Nonsmoker,* when no members of a household smoke... *mature home owner,* for seniors or retirees... *renovation discount,* for upgrading old electrical, plumbing, heating or other systems.

KEEP YOUR POLICY UP TO DATE

Do an annual review to keep your coverage up to date. Add any costly new acquisitions—jewelry, paintings—to your policy, and inform your insurer about any significant remodeling.

Remember to reduce or eliminate coverage on items that aren't worth what they used to be. The costly projection TV you bought just a few years ago is worth far less today.

GAPS IN COVERAGE

Generally, homeowner's policies cover most common types of damage, including damage caused by fire, smoke, rain, lightning, wind, hail, snow, ice, theft, explosions, vehicles and the malfunction of electrical systems, plumbing, heating, air conditioning or appliances.

Damage from earthquakes or floods is not covered in standard policies. You need separate policies if you're in an area prone to flooding or earthquakes. For hurricanes, you may be covered for high winds, but not for flood.

Trap: Thinking coverage for rain damage will automatically reimburse you, say, if your deck collapses, after a few days of downpours. The insurers might say this type of damage is the result of flood, not the rain itself.

Even if you don't live in a flood-prone area, consider flood insurance. Contact the Federal Emergency Management Agency (800-480-2520 and 202-566-1600, *www.fema.gov/nfip*). Premiums vary widely, from a few hundred to a few thousand dollars a year, depending on the location of a house, its age and type of construction.

Finally, you need at least $1 million in personal liability coverage to protect assets from lawsuits. An "umbrella" policy will take over where liability coverage on your homeowner's and auto policies leaves off. The cost is about $150 a year per $1 million in coverage.

9

Tax Guide

The Best Strategies for Joint Ownership of Assets

Holding assets—such as bank accounts, securities, or real estate—jointly is very common, especially among married couples.

Joint ownership also may be used by cohabitants and elderly individuals who want a younger person to be able to pay bills, handle investments, etc.

There probably will be income, gift and estate tax consequences of joint ownership. *Here are the rules...*

INCOME TAX

If income-producing property is held jointly by a married couple filing a joint tax return, the income tax consequences are straightforward—the couple owes tax on the income.

But what if the married couple files separate returns? Or if the co-owners aren't married and thus can't file a joint return?

Typically, the income will be taxed 50-50 between the joint owners.

If the funds in a joint account belong to one person, that person's name will be listed first on the account, along with his/her Social Security number. If the joint account has combined funds, each person's share of any income from the property is determined by state law.

Example: Sam Miner has put his niece Sarah's name as joint owner with right of survivorship on his bank and brokerage accounts so that she can help manage his affairs if it should become necessary.

Sam and Sarah should make sure that Sam's Social Security number is the one on the account, so that each annual Form 1099 reports income taxable to Sam, not to Sarah.

GIFT TAX

Putting a spouse's name on property as joint owner won't trigger gift tax because spousal gifts

Sanford J. Schlesinger, Esq., a founding partner and head of the wills and estates department of the law firm Schlesinger Gannon & Lazetera LLP, 499 Park Ave., New York City 10022.

are untaxed. The situation is different for non-spouses and non-US-citizen spouses, though.

In general, putting someone's name on an account won't trigger a gift if assets aren't withdrawn by the noncontributing joint tenant. (There may be exceptions under some state laws.)

Adding a joint tenant to real estate becomes a taxable gift if the new joint tenant has the right under state law to sever his interest in the joint tenancy and receive half of the property.

Example: Sam puts Sarah's name on his accounts. As long as Sarah leaves those accounts alone, no gift is incurred.

Trap: Say that Sarah takes $20,000 from Sam's bank account. A gift tax return may have to be filed and gift tax might be owed.

Strategy: Sarah should keep careful track of her use of Sam's assets. If she writes a $20,000 check to an assisted-living facility, for example, to provide care for Sam, no gift will have occurred.

On the other hand, if Sarah writes out that $20,000 check to buy a car for herself, that will be a gift from Sam unless she can show that the car was used solely for Sam's care.

Caution: Joint accounts owned by unmarried couples are potentially troublesome. Suppose, Bill Smith and Carol Jones are unmarried but living together. Bill earns all the income, which goes into a joint account.

Trap: Every check that Carol writes might be considered a gift if she uses the funds to pay for her personal expenses. That's the case even if Bill writes checks to pay for personal items Carol has charged on a credit card.

This problem isn't easy to resolve if Carol spends more than $12,000 from the account on herself—that's the annual gift tax exclusion for 2006.

Strategy: Maintain careful records of all expenses from joint accounts. Money that is used for common expenses generally won't be considered a taxable gift.

ESTATE TAXES

Property held as "joint tenants with right of survivorship" (JTWROS) must go to the survivor. This might create estate tax problems.

Example: Dan and Ellen Collins are married and have $4 million in assets. Everything is owned as JTWROS. They are also the beneficiaries of each other's retirement accounts.

If Dan dies in 2006, everything will pass to Ellen, who will now have a $4 million estate.

Trap: This arrangement prohibits them from leaving anything to other heirs, including their children, upon Dan's death. Thus, they won't be able to use the federal estate tax exemption, set at $2 million for 2006 to 2008.

Suppose, in our example, Ellen dies in 2007 with the $4 million estate. That would be $2 million over the exemption amount, taxed at 45%, so the federal estate tax bill would be $900,000.

That tax could have been avoided with a $2 million bequest at Dan's death in 2006. That bequest might have gone to their children, for example, or to a trust that's structured to benefit Ellen but be out of her estate.

Strategy: Families with estate tax concerns should modify their use of joint ownership between spouses. Each spouse should have some assets in his own name that can be left to other parties or to a trust at the first death, sheltered by the estate tax exemption.

CAPITAL GAINS TAX

When assets pass from a decedent to heirs, estate tax is not the only concern. Under current law, appreciated assets get a step-up in basis as of the date of death. (An alternative valuation date, six months later, also may be used for all estate assets, if this produces a lower estate tax.)

This step-up can eliminate capital gains tax.

Example: Ed Russell owns $1 million in stocks and stock funds, held outside of his retirement plans. His basis in those securities is $200,000.

A sale during Ed's life would result in an $800,000 capital gain and a $120,000 tax bill, assuming all the securities qualify for the 15% rate on long-term gains.

Assuming no predeath sale, if Ed owns those securities by himself and leaves them to his wife, Phyllis, she'll have a stepped-up basis of $1 million. She could sell them after his death for $1 million and owe no capital gains tax.

Trap: If Ed holds these stocks as JTWROS with Phyllis, they will all pass to her at death but only half (Ed's half of the joint account) will get a basis step-up, giving her a $600,000 basis ($500,000 in his half and $100,000, or half the original cost basis, in her half).

As a result, a sale for $1 million would produce a $400,000 capital gain ($1 million minus her new $600,000 basis) and a $60,000 tax bill, at 15%.

Strategy: Highly appreciated assets might be held in sole name rather than jointly, to get a full basis step-up.

The rules are a bit different in the states with community property laws (Arizona, California, Idaho, Louisiana, Nevada, New Mexico, Texas, Washington and Wisconsin). Here a spouse can leave his half of community property to a nonspouse. But, if community property is left to a spouse, the spouse who inherits might be able to get a full basis step-up.

In the above example, if they live in a community property state, Phyllis may get a $1 million basis on the securities she holds, after inheriting Ed's half.

If so, she can sell the shares after Ed's death for $1 million and owe no capital gains tax. Check with a professional adviser to see if specific actions (such as putting community property in writing) are necessary in your state to qualify for a full basis step-up.

Moneysaving Tax Moves: Get Started Now

Bob D. Scharin, Esq., editor of Warren, Gorham & Lamont/RIA's *Practical Tax Strategies,* a monthly journal for tax professionals in New York City. He has edited leading tax publications for more than 20 years.

Do not wait until year-end to start planning your taxes. *By taking all these steps, you can cut your tax bill for 2006 and future years...*

●**Max out your retirement plan.** Contribute the maximum to your 401(k) plan or other employer-sponsored retirement plan this year. You can defer tax on up to $15,000 in contributions to a 401(k), 403(b), 457 or similar defined-contribution plan. If you'll be at least 50 years

old by year-end, you can contribute another $5,000. Over a period of 10 years, that extra $5,000 could grow, tax free, to $9,830, assuming an annual return of 7%. Contributions to 401(k)s must be made by the end of the year for a 2006 tax benefit.

●**Create a Savings Incentive Match Plan for Employees (SIMPLE) account** if you're self-employed or run a sideline business. You can make SIMPLE as well as 401(k) contributions. SIMPLE plans are desirable if you'll have a small amount of self-employment income this year. You can contribute (and deduct) up to 100% to a maximum of $10,000. People of age 50 or older can contribute an additional $2,500. Other small-business retirement plans usually permit no more than a 25% contribution. To get SIMPLE write-offs for 2006, you must set up a plan by September 30. They can be established at most financial institutions.

●**Evaluate estimated tax payments.** If you file estimated taxes, your third payment is due September 15. By then, you should know your total 2006 income.

Safe harbor: If your payments through the third quarter are at least 100% of your 2005 tax liability, you are protected from a penalty by a "safe harbor" rule, even if you end up owing more tax because your income increases. If your adjusted gross income (AGI) was more than $150,000 in 2005, the requirement rises to 110%.

Example: Filing jointly, you and your spouse had a total AGI of $180,000 in 2005 and owed $30,000 in taxes. To reach the safe harbor, your estimated tax payments through the third quarter must be at least $33,000—110% of $30,000.

If you don't have enough withheld from your paychecks, you must send the balance to the IRS in quarterly estimated payments to qualify for the safe harbor.

Trap: If you make larger tax payments during the year's last two quarters, you could owe a penalty for underpayments in earlier quarters. To avoid this, have more tax withheld from paychecks near year-end. Income tax withholding is treated as if it were paid evenly throughout the year.

Loophole: If taxes owed for 2006 will be lower than they were in 2005, you can pay less withholding and estimated tax this year and avoid a penalty if total payments are at least 90% of your 2006 obligation.

●**Profit from losses.** Stocks are struggling, and with interest rates rising, bonds sold before maturity may have lost their value. If you have losses, consider selling securities or funds to take tax deductions.

Loophole: You can deduct up to $3,000 of capital losses in excess of capital gains from your wages, pension, interest and other higher-taxed income. Additional losses then can be carried forward to future years.

Example: You end the year with $20,000 in losses in excess of capital gains (not paper losses). You can take a $3,000 deduction in 2006 and carry forward the other $17,000. The excess losses can offset future gains—up to $3,000 per year—effectively making those gains tax free.

Trap: If you sell a security and buy it back within 30 days, the loss won't count. This is known as the "wash-sale rule." To avoid it, wait at least 31 days to buy back the same security. *If you want to remain invested throughout the whole process...*

●Purchase a similar but not identical security. For example, take a loss on one large-cap growth fund, and immediately buy another large-cap growth fund.

●Buy new shares of the stock you wish to sell. Then wait more than 30 days, and sell the original lot. To use this strategy this year, you must purchase the duplicate lot before November 30.

●**Be smart about school bills.** If you plan to sell appreciated securities to pay a child's college tuition, give the securities to the student, who then can make the sale.

Advantage: Your child will have to report the capital gain, but he/she will be in a low bracket and owe tax at a 5% rate, not your 15% rate. This year, a married couple can give up to $24,000 in assets to each of any number of recipients, without owing gift tax.

●**Fund an Education Savings Account (ESA).** While 529 savings plans are worthwhile for funding higher education, unless your state happens to provide a tax deduction, it is better to first fund a Coverdell Education Savings Account (ESA). The limit is $2,000 per year per student. There are income limits for ESAs. Married couples with incomes over $190,000 can't make a full contribution.

If you're over the limit, you can give money to children, grandchildren, etc., who can contribute to their own ESAs.

Benefits: Like 529s, ESAs permit income to accumulate tax free. Withdrawals are tax free if the money is used for certain education-related expenses. *But ESAs have advantages over 529s...*

●Withdrawals may be used for a range of education expenses, such as tuition, room and board, uniforms and computer equipment, beginning in kindergarten. 529s must be used for college costs.

●You have complete control over how the money is invested. 529 investment options are selected by their sponsors.

●There is no time limit for tax-free withdrawals. Tax-free withdrawals from 529 plans are scheduled to expire after 2010, though Congress may extend them.

●**Pay a parent's expenses.** If you support a parent—even though he/she lives elsewhere—you might be able to claim him/her as a dependent. In 2006, you can deduct $3,300 for each dependent, whether or not you itemize. In the 25% federal tax bracket ($61,300 to $123,700 in taxable income on a joint return), a $3,300 deduction saves you $825. There may be big state tax savings as well.

To claim a dependency exemption for a parent, several tests must be met but these are the two toughest...

You must provide more than half of your parent's support, and...

Your parent's gross income must be less than $3,300. Gross income does not include untaxed Social Security benefits or the interest on tax-exempt investments.

Strategy: Track all your parent's expenses carefully—food, medical care, etc.—and make sure that you pay more than 50% of them during the year. If your parent lives in your home, put a value on the housing you supply.

•Ward off the AMT.* Increasingly, middle-income taxpayers are encountering the alternative minimum tax (AMT). If you are subject to the AMT this year, you will lose federal deductions on state and local taxes as well as miscellaneous itemized deductions.

Strategy: Postpone AMT income. For example, defer the exercise of certain types of stock options or don't make early payments of real estate and state income tax around year-end, since they are not deductible for AMT purposes. AMT planning is complex. So, arrange a mid-year meeting with your tax preparer to discuss strategies that will work for you.

*AMT is a tax that an increasing number of Americans must pay instead of regular tax. You must calculate your tax with and without AMT and pay the higher amount. Especially vulnerable are people with many dependents, high state income tax or high miscellaneous deductions.

Out-of-State Sales Tax Trap

Mark A. Plostock, a CPA who lectures for the New York State Society of CPAs on state and local tax issues. He maintains a practice in Syosset, NY.

Don't make the mistake of believing you can escape owing local sales taxes by making purchases from outside of your home state via mail-order, phone or Internet.

Reality: Every state that imposes a sales tax on sales made in-state also imposes "use tax" on purchases made from out-of-state sellers.

The difference is that while sales tax is collected by sellers, use tax is legally owed by purchasers and must be self-reported if not collected by the seller.

The self-reporting requirement applies because a state cannot require an out-of-state seller to collect use tax if the seller has no operations in the state—but the tax is still owed by the purchaser.

What's changing: The states have long considered it almost impossible to collect use tax from individuals, and in the past usually didn't try—but this is beginning to change.

Now 18 states have a line on their personal income tax return where taxpayers are told to self-report use tax, and many states are increasing enforcement efforts to collect unpaid use taxes and the lost revenue they represent.

Example: States are identifying interstate sales (and purchasers) by exchanging information obtained in audits of in-state retailers about their out-of-state sales.

Therefore, if you buy "big ticket" items from out of state or items from abroad, your state is increasingly likely to find out about it. (The Customs Bureau informs state revenue departments about items brought to the US from overseas.)

Business alert: Use taxes have become the top audit target of many state tax agencies. This is because businesses make large interstate purchases and have records that document them—making use taxes an easy target for the auditor.

Danger: If you own a business that isn't paying use tax on out-of-state purchases, it could be piling up big liabilities in back taxes, penalties and interest. Even worse, if it is required to file a state tax return to report use taxes and has not done so, no statute of limitations will apply to the back taxes—letting the state collect back taxes for any number of past years, instead of being limited to the usual three.

Consult a local state tax expert.

Boost Income, Save on Taxes and Help a Charity With a Gift Annuity

Irving L. Blackman, CPA, founding partner, Blackman Kallick Bartelstein, LLP at 10 S. Riverside Plaza, Chicago 60606, *www.taxsecretsofthewealthy.com.*

With interest rates near historic lows, it is difficult for many people to safely secure enough investment income to meet their living needs.

But there's a way to do it—while saving taxes and helping a charity.

How: Invest in a "charitable gift annuity" (CGA) sponsored by a nationally recognized charity, such as The Salvation Army or UJA-Federation of New York.

With a CGA, you donate an asset to charity and in exchange receive an annuity for life. At the end of the CGA's term, the charity retains the value of the asset. *Four advantages…*

●**You avoid ever paying capital gains tax** on the asset you donate to charity.

●**You'll receive more income than from a CD or a bond.**

●**A portion of the income will be tax free.**

●**You get an income tax deduction up-front** for the present value of the interest the charity will get at the end of the CGA's term.

Example: One individual who is age 66 and in the 33% tax bracket owns stock now worth $100,000 for which he paid $50,000. He wishes to exchange the stock shares for a safe, income-producing investment.

Selling the stock to reinvest the proceeds will result in $7,500 of capital gains tax ($100,000 –$50,000 x 15%) leaving $92,500 to invest. If re-invested in 10-year US bonds, the interest rate will be only about 4%—paying less than $4,000 annually. Riskier high-grade corporate bonds yield only about 5%, to provide less than $5,000 annually, all of which will be taxable.

However, by donating the stock to a CGA, the individual will first save the $7,500 capital gains tax.

Then, using numbers from the CGA calculator provided by the American Heart Association, the annual payout would be…

●$6,100 cash, or 6.1%, and

●$1,732 of this would be tax free, making the payout equivalent to 8.4% taxable, plus

●A one-time tax deduction of $35,204 in the year you gift to the CGA.

Unlike with a bond, principal is not returned. But if you are expecting to consume all these funds during your retirement years anyway, that doesn't matter.

Options: A CGA can last the length of both lives of a married couple, and deferred CGAs can be purchased when you are young, say in your 30s or 40s, to provide income later in life —while you obtain an up-front tax deduction.

Details of the amount and tax treatment of annuities vary with the facts of each case.

To find out how a CGA might work in your situation, use the calculator provided by the American Heart Association and Gift Legacy. Go to *www.americanheart.org* and in the search box enter "planned giving," then click on "For Planned Giving Donors," then "Planned Giving Calculator."

CGAs are offered by many other leading charities, so investigate their terms as well.

Vacation-Home Tax Loopholes

Bob Trinz, senior tax analyst at Thomson/RIA, which provides tax information and software to tax professionals. He edits several RIA publications, including *Federal Taxes Weekly Alert.*

There's no place like home under the tax code. If you own a home—even a vacation home—and rent it out each year, you can claim all kinds of tax breaks. *Here's a rundown…*

●**If you rent out your home for 14 days or fewer per year,** the income is tax free. This might be especially lucrative if your home is near the site of a major sporting event or in a resort area. If you go over the 14-day mark, all the rental income must be reported.

Caution: You won't be able to claim rental-related tax deductions, such as cleaning and advertising.

If you own a business or professional practice, those 14 tax-free days can include days your vacation home is rented to your company for an executive meeting or employee picnic. This won't work for sole proprietors.

As long as you charge a fair rental price, your company can take a deduction while you enjoy the tax-free income. Be sure to consult your company's tax adviser before employing this strategy.

If you rent out your vacation home for more than 14 days a year, it may be taxed in one of two ways...

•**As rental property.** Your second home is considered rental property if you personally use it for no more than 14 days and rent it out for more than 14 days...or you use it for more than 14 days but this use represents no more than 10% of the number of rental days.

Example: You use your vacation home for 30 days a year and rent it out for 335 days. Your personal use is less than 10% of your rental days, so your vacation home is considered rental property.

Drawback: If your vacation home is treated as rental property, you might lose some mortgage interest deductions.

If you have a loss on the rental, you might be able to deduct it right away. Losses of up to $25,000 can be deducted each year if your adjusted gross income (AGI) is $100,000 or below. For AGIs above $100,000, the maximum deductible loss gradually declines. It disappears when AGI reaches $150,000.

If these losses can't be deducted right away, they can be deducted when you sell your vacation home. Rules are complex, so consult your tax adviser.

•**As a residence.** In the above example, if you had rented the home for only 329 days, your personal use would have accounted for more than 10% of the rental period, so the home would be taxed as a residence. This means that you probably would be able to deduct your mortgage interest and property taxes.

Drawbacks: You will be taxed on rental income, although expenses such as utilities and insurance can be used to offset it. No rental losses can be deducted, even when you sell your home.

Shrewd Ways to Use Your Home as a Tax Shelter

Diane Kennedy, CPA, a tax strategist for more than 20 years, and founder of D. Kennedy & Associates located in Phoenix. She is also coauthor of several books, including *Real Estate Loopholes: Secrets of Successful Real Estate Investing* (Warner Business) and the author of *Loopholes of the Rich* (Wiley). Her Web site is *www.legaltaxloopholes.com.*

From a tax perspective, there's never been a better time to own a home. *Below are four loopholes to take advantage of...*

SHORT-TERM OWNERSHIP

The home-sale exclusion is one of the most generous tax breaks in the Internal Revenue Code. Married couples can avoid tax on up to $500,000 in capital gains ($250,000 for a single person). This break can be used over and over.

To get it, you have to have owned the home and used it as your principal residence for at least two of the five years before the sale. Most people, however, don't realize how easy it is to use the exclusion even if you do not meet this two-year test.

Loophole: If you needed to move out of a house before the two years were up because of an "unforeseen circumstance," you still can get a partial tax break. Unforeseen circumstances are defined very liberally. They include, for example, natural disasters, a change in your employment or becoming self-employed, divorce or legal separation and multiple births from the same pregnancy.

How it works: Say you are promoted—or even demoted—at work. This is considered a change in employment, so you can sell your house and take a partial tax break even if you don't satisfy the two-year test. The same is true if you start, change or discontinue a business.

Example: You would like to move from the appreciated property in which you have lived for less than two years. Before selling, you start a simple home-based business. Assuming that you sell the house after living in it for one year, you would get half of the maximum tax break because one year is half of two. You and your spouse could exclude up to $250,000 (half of $500,000) of any gain on the sale. And, a single filer could exclude up to $125,000 (half of $250,000).

HOME-OFFICE DEDUCTION

Some people don't deduct depreciation for a home office because they think it will cause them to owe tax on the gain allocated to the office when they sell the home. But, this is not the case.

Loophole: As long as the home office is part of your house—and not a separate structure—you will get the full principal-residence capital gains exclusion.

How it works: If you have taken a depreciation deduction for the office portion of your residence, you need to "recapture" the depreciation when you sell the home.

Example: If you have taken $10,000 of depreciation and are in the 25% bracket, you would owe $2,500 in tax—25% of $10,000—when you sell the home. You can keep whatever is left of the $500,000 or $250,000 exclusion on gains.

Paying less tax now (by depreciating) is worth more than the cost of recapturing depreciation later. For rules on depreciation, see IRS Publication 946, *How to Depreciate Property,* available by contacting 800-829-3676, *www.irs.gov.*

ASSET PROTECTION

In these litigious times, it's very easy to imagine someone tripping on your driveway and suing you, putting your home and other assets then at risk.

Strategy: To protect your home from creditors, transfer it to a single-member limited liability company (LLC). This isn't necessary if you live in states with "unlimited homestead protection"—where equity is protected—such as Texas and Florida, and you've lived there for more than two years.

Loophole: Under new regulations, home owners who make such transfers still will be entitled to the mortgage interest deduction and capital gains exclusion. There can be only one owner, perhaps you and your spouse holding the title as joint tenants. You don't need to file an additional business tax return for the LLC.

DIVIDE AND CONQUER

You may be able to sell part of your property at a profit and still get the benefit of the capital gains exclusion.

For example, your home sits on 40 acres. A developer buys 39 acres, from which you make a $300,000 profit. Then, a year later, you sell the house and the remaining acre for an additional $150,000 profit.

Loophole: According to the Treasury Department, you are allowed to take the full $500,000 or $250,000 capital gains exclusion on the combined gain if you complete the "split sale" within two years.

In the example above, the total $450,000 gain ($300,000 plus $150,000) would be tax free, provided the house was sold within two years of the prior sale of the land and all other conditions were met.

More from Diane Kennedy, CPA...

Tax Filing Smarts for Unmarried Couples

Unmarried couples can reduce taxes and increase write-offs. One partner should take the standard deduction while the other should itemize and take all deductible costs the two incur together, such as mortgage interest and property tax deductions. They will get more of a deduction and be in lower tax brackets than if they were married and filing jointly. This tax benefit is not available to married couples.

Let Uncle Sam Pay for Your New Motor Home Or Boat

Robert C. Hoye, TC Memo 1990-57.

A recreational vehicle (RV) or trailer that has sleeping, cooking and toilet facilities qualifies as a residence under the Tax Code. *Tax breaks...*

•**Interest paid on a loan used to acquire an RV may be deductible** as home mortgage interest under normal "second home" rules.

•**If you drive it to away-from-home work locations and stay in the RV instead of a hotel,** ownership costs become deductible as a business expense. The percentage of total costs that qualifies for a deduction equals the amount of business use divided by total use. This can include costs for widening a driveway to accommodate it, building a shed to house it, and depreciation on the RV.

Note: You can rent the home to others to receive tax-free income. If you rent it out for no more than 14 days a year, the rental income is tax free. If you exceed that limit, the normal rules for vacation home rentals apply.

If it has living quarters as described above, a boat can qualify as a residence, too. Therefore, interest paid on a loan used to buy it can qualify for the mortgage interest deduction.

These deductions combined with today's low interest rates create a great opportunity to buy a boat or RV on favorable financing terms.

When Support Is Deductible

Edward Mendlowitz, CPA, shareholder in the CPA firm, WithumSmith+Brown, 120 Albany St., New Brunswick, NJ 08901. He is also the author of *Introducing Tax Clients to Additional Services* (American Institute of CPAs).

When you pay more than 50% of the support for an individual, tax benefits can result…

•**When the individual's income doesn't exceed $3,200 in 2005 or $3,300 in 2006** (excluding tax-exempt income, such as from municipal bonds and the tax-free portion of Social Security), you may be able to claim him/her as a dependent to obtain a tax exemption of $3,200 in 2005 and $3,300 in 2006.

•**Even if the individual has income exceeding the limit,** you may be able to deduct medical expenses you pay on his behalf if the individual is a relative. (A "relative" is a parent, grandparent, sibling, child, grandchild, aunt, uncle, niece, nephew or in-law.)

Mistake: Many people fail to claim these tax breaks because they provide less than half of the individual's income—and so mistakenly assume that they provide less than half of the individual's support.

Key: "Support" includes only amounts that are actually spent on items of support, such as housing, food, clothing and medical care. It does not include income that is saved.

Example: A retired parent has a pension and Social Security income, while you pay medical bills for him. By having the parent save enough income in the bank (by putting money in the bank, he isn't using the money to pay for support) so that you pay more than 50% of his support in the form of medical payments and other items, you can obtain a deduction for the medical bills.

Tactic: When several people together provide most of an individual's support with no one person paying more than 50%, they can file a multiple support agreement, IRS Form 2120, *Multiple Support Declaration,* to obtain a dependency exemption and assign it to one member of the group (which can change from year to year), provided he pays more than 10% of support. This also enables that person to deduct medical bills paid on the dependent's behalf.

Tax Time Tax Savers

Sidney Kess, attorney and CPA at 10 Rockefeller Plaza, New York City 10020. Mr. Kess is the coauthor/consulting editor of *Financial and Estate Planning* and coauthor of *1040 Preparation and Planning Guide 2006* (both from CCH). Over the years, he has taught tax law to more than 710,000 tax professionals.

When you prepare your 2006 tax return, due April 16, 2007, don't overlook all these last-minute tax-saving ideas. And remember to use what you discover when preparing your 2006 return to plan tax-saving strategies for 2007.

STATE SALES TAX DEDUCTION

You can deduct either the state sales tax or the state income tax you paid during the year if you itemize deductions. This new law is primarily meant to give a state tax deduction to persons who live in states that have no income tax.

If you live in a state with an income tax, check the numbers both ways—you may be better off deducting sales tax. This is especially true if you made a big-ticket purchase during the year of a car, boat, aircraft or prefabricated home. If this is the case, you can add the sales tax paid on it to the amount shown on the IRS state sales tax deduction table to increase your deduction.

INVESTMENT RESULTS

Take care when reporting investment gains and losses...

●**Double-check the 1099s you received.** Don't just assume these are correct—erroneous 1099 rates of as much as 10% have been reported in the investment industry. If you rely on an incorrect 1099, you will either overpay your taxes...or underpay them, and possibly incur a penalty.

●**Include reinvested dividends in the cost of shares sold.** One of the most common mistakes investors make is not including reinvested dividends in the cost basis of mutual funds and stock shares—erroneously increasing taxable gain when they are sold.

●**Check eligibility for tax-favored dividends.** Not all dividends qualify for the 15% tax-favored maximum rate.

Examples: The distributions on preferred stock, dividends paid by real estate investment trusts (in most cases), distributions from credit unions and mutual savings banks that are called dividends but which are actually interest.

Planning for 2007: Use your investment results from 2006 to decrease taxes in 2007. For instance, if you carry over a net capital loss from 2006, you can utilize the losses from 2006 to offset 2007 capital gains.

Use IRS Publication 550, *Investment Income and Expenses,* to see that all of your investments qualify for the lowest possible tax rates under the recent law changes.

●**Maximize use of IRAs.** Contributions to these legal tax shelters for 2006 can be made as late as April 16, 2007. The maximum contribution for 2006 is $4,000—plus another $1,000 if you are age 50 or older.

Even if you participate in an employer's qualified retirement plan, you can deduct the full $4,000 IRA contribution if your adjusted gross income (AGI) is $50,000 or less on a single tax return or $75,000 or less on a joint return. (The deduction phases out as income rises to $60,000 on a single tax return or $85,000 on a joint tax return.)

Full contributions to Roth IRAs, which provide totally tax-free returns, can be made when modified AGI doesn't exceed $95,000 on a single return or $150,000 on a joint return (phasing out when income increases to $105,000 and $160,000, respectively).

Spousal IRAs: All IRA contributions must be made from earned income. But the income earned by one spouse can be used to fund an IRA contribution for the other. So when one spouse has at least $8,000 of earned income and the other has none, both can make a full $4,000 IRA contribution.

Correcting mistakes: Say that you made your IRA contribution early in the year and then later events rendered you ineligible—perhaps your income unexpectedly rose above the eligibility limit—you should withdraw the excess contribution by the due date of your tax return (including any extensions) to avoid having to pay a penalty.

2007 contributions: In 2007, the IRA contribution limit for those age 50 or older is again $5,000. The earlier in the year you make your 2007 contribution to your IRA, the more tax-favored investment returns you are likely to receive, so be sure to contribute early.

CHARITY DEDUCTIONS

Deductions for legitimate gifts to charity can be lost if documentation for them doesn't meet IRS requirements.

For all contributions of $250 or more, you must obtain an acknowledgment letter from the charity by the time you file your tax return. An appraisal is needed, too, if the gift is an item or a group of similar items valued at more than $5,000—$10,000 for nonpublicly traded stock.

Warning: Donations of vehicles to charity have become "audit flag" items, says the IRS. If you deduct one, be sure the car you donated is not overvalued on your return—and have the documentation to prove it.

OTHER LAW CHANGES

Several other recent tax law changes could affect tax bills for military families, lawsuit plaintiffs, those who donate patents and intellectual property to charity, owners of small businesses and others.

Find the tax law changes explained in IRS Publication 553, *Highlights of 2006 Tax Changes,* at *www.irs.gov,* or call 800-829-3676.

BREAKS FOR PAST YEARS

When you prepare your 2006 tax return, you may find a tax-saving idea that you could have used in past years too, but overlooked. If so, you can still claim such tax breaks for up to three years back and obtain refunds. File IRS Form 1040X, *Amended US Individual Income Tax Return.*

Deadline: If you filed your 2003 return on or before April 15, 2004, then April 16, 2007, is the deadline for amending it. Don't let a possible refund expire.

EXTENSIONS

If you need more time to pull together your records and fully document items such as charitable contributions, you can get an automatic six-month filing extension simply by filing IRS Form 4868.

But this extension does *not* extend the time to pay tax due for 2006. If you think you'll owe, estimate the amount and enclose this payment with the extension to avoid the interest and penalty charges.

Great Tax Savers For Seniors

Laurence I. Foster, CPA/PFS, consultant and former partner at Eisner LLP, 750 Third Ave., New York City 10017. Mr. Foster was chairman of The Personal Financial Specialist Credential Committee at the American Institute of CPAs.

Plan your tax-saving moves before the end of the year. You'll face a steeper tax bill if you wait until after December 31 to take action. *Tax savers to consider now...*

PERSONAL TAX-SAVING TACTICS

•**Use "catch-up" wage withholding to avoid underpayment of penalties.** Check whether your taxes to date are underpaid for the year—this is most likely to be the case if you had nonwage income (such as from your investments) on which you have not paid estimated tax.

If so, make up the shortfall by increasing tax withheld from your last paychecks before year-end comes around.

Why: Withheld taxes are treated by the IRS as having been paid evenly over the year. By increasing withholding near year-end, you can retroactively avoid an underpayment penalty for an earlier estimated tax quarter that you would incur if you paid the same tax with a catch-up estimated tax payment.

•**Double up on deductions subject to AGI "floors."** Some items are deductible only to the extent that they exceed a percentage of adjusted gross income (AGI).

Examples: Medical expenses to the extent that they exceed 7.5% of AGI...miscellaneous expenses (including employee business expenses, investment and legal expenses, etc.) to the extent that they exceed 2% of AGI.

Strategy: If expenses for these items are large enough to take the deductions this year, accelerate additional expenses into this year by scheduling and paying for last-minute medical and dental appointments, subscribing to business publications, etc., before year-end. If they are not, postpone paying for such items until after December 31 to help get you over the limit next year.

●**Prepay state and local taxes.** Final state and local income tax payments for 2006 may not be due until April 16, 2007—but if you pay them by year-end, they are deductible on your 2006 federal tax return. The same rule applies to state and local property taxes.

Caution: If you are subject to the alternative minimum tax (AMT), you may not want to pre-pay state and local taxes and you also may not want to double up on deductions as described previously.

●**Make contributions to a charity.** To be deductible this year, the charitable gift must be made by year-end. You will need to obtain an acknowledgment letter from the charity for any gift worth $250 or more—a canceled check is no longer sufficient proof of a gift.

Strategy: If you own appreciated stocks or mutual fund shares that you have held for more than a year, donate them instead of cash. You'll get a full deduction for your contribution and avoid ever having to pay capital gains tax on the donated securities.

●**Use credit cards to pay deductible expenses.** Charges are deductible when made even if not paid off until a later year.

Note: The card must be a general-use one, such as Visa or American Express, not a store charge card.

●**Convert a traditional IRA to a Roth if your AGI isn't more than $100,000.** Roths can pay tax-free income, while payments from traditional IRAs are taxed at top rates as ordinary income. Roths are not subject to minimum annual distribution requirements beyond age 70½, making them more flexible for saving and funding tax-favored bequests.

Catch: Whenever a conversion is made, the value of the traditional IRA (minus any nonde-ductible contributions to it) is included in tax-able income.

Opportunity: Making a conversion by year-end is a "can't lose" move. If the stock market goes up the next year so that the IRA's value increases, a conversion now will be less costly tax wise than one made later. If, after making a

conversion this year, the market goes down and the IRA's value decreases, you can undo the conversion as late as October 16, 2006, to make another conversion later on better terms. If you don't make a conversion this year, you may never again have the chance to do so at such low tax cost.

●**Go on a gambling holiday if you have winnings to date.** If you have net gambling winnings and will file an itemized return, additional gambling until year-end will be subsidized by the IRS—since any losses you incur will be deductible up to the amount of your winnings. So, if you gamble more and win, you'll win, while if you lose, you'll get a deduction.

●**Use your annual gift tax exclusion.** This enables you to make gifts of up to $12,000 each to as many recipients as desired, free of gift tax. The limit is $24,000 when gifts are made jointly by a married couple. Such gifts can reduce fu-ture estate taxes, as well as future income taxes when used to shift income-generating assets to a person in a lower tax bracket.

If a gift is made by check, be sure it's early enough so the check clears the bank—complet-ing the gift—by year-end. Check with your tax adviser to find the best course of action for your particular situation.

LAST-MINUTE MOVES FOR INVESTORS

●**Take tax-saving losses.** If you've realized net capital gains to date this year, but you have losses in your portfolio, realizing some losses by year-end can save tax dollars at no economic cost other than, possibly, trading commissions.

Best: End with a net capital loss of $3,000, the most that can be deducted against ordinary income. *How...*

●Make "bond swaps," selling a bond that has declined in value and buying another differ-ent but similar one.

●Sell the shares of a mutual fund that have declined in value, then buy back shares of a dif-ferent but similar fund—or wait 31 days and buy back the same ones.

●**Protect tax-favored dividends.** New law makes "qualified dividends" subject to a top tax rate of only 15%. But to be "qualified," divi-dends must be paid on stock that you have held for more than 60 days. So always beware of making year-end sales of stock too soon and forfeiting the lower rate on the dividends.

●**Defer interest into next year.** If you are receiving taxable interest on savings, invest it in a CD that will mature after year-end. You will defer the tax due on the interest from this year into next year.

More from Laurence Foster, CPA/PFS...

Don't Get Caught by the Nanny Tax: Rules for Household Employers

In recent years, nominees for the Director of Homeland Security, Secretary of Labor and Attorney General were not appointed due to their failure to pay the "nanny tax" for workers they employed in their homes.

Do not let the rules snare you. Here's what you need to know to pay the taxes you owe—and avoid incurring the tax needlessly...

LEGAL REQUIREMENTS

Persons you employ to work in your household are treated in general just like other employees—meaning that employment taxes are due on the wages paid to them.

Examples: Nannies, babysitters, drivers, maids, housekeepers, health aides, private nurses, caretakers, yard workers and similar domestic workers.

Two taxes are owed on their wages—FICA taxes (for Social Security and Medicare) and FUTA taxes (for unemployment insurance).

If you pay a household employee...

●**$1,400 or more in cash wages in 2005 ($1,500 or more in 2006),** you must pay FICA taxes on the employee's wages at a total tax rate of 7.65%. You must also withhold and remit the same amount (another 7.65%) from the employee's wages.

●**Less than the amount above, you do not have to report and pay FICA tax.**

●**$1,000 or more in any calendar quarter to all household employees combined,** you must pay FUTA taxes on the first $7,000 of each employee's wages—generally at a 0.8% rate. (The tax is 6.2%, but a 5.4% credit usually applies if state unemployment tax is paid on time.)

Note: You are not required to withhold federal or state income tax from the wages of household employees, but may agree to do so voluntarily.

WHO QUALIFIES

The fact that you hire a person to do work for you doesn't automatically mean that he/she is your employee.

If you direct and supervise how the work is done, the worker will be an employee.

But if the worker does a job without being subject to your supervision, can set his own work schedule, provides all his own tools and equipment, and is free to subcontract the work to others, he probably is not an employee.

No single one of these facts is determinative, but the more that exist, the more likely it is that the worker will qualify as an independent contractor, for whom you do not owe employment taxes, instead of as an employee.

For more information, see IRS Publication 15-A, *Employer's Supplemental Tax Guide.*

Also, if a worker is supplied to you by an agency or firm that takes responsibility for the work being done, such as a landscaping firm or babysitting service, the worker probably will be an employee of the agency or firm rather than you. *Moreover, you do not owe...*

●**FICA and FUTA taxes on wages paid to a spouse,** your own child under age 21 or a parent (in most cases).

●**FICA tax on the wages of an individual who is under age 18 at any time during 2005 or 2006** unless the person's principal occupation is providing household services.

TAX STRATEGIES

Employment taxes are owed only on the cash wages of household workers. And, they are not owed on noncash compensation provided to workers, such as the value of food, lodging, clothing and other noncash items.

Household employees can also be provided with tax-free benefits, as other employees can.

Examples: Reimbursement of up to $105 per month for the cost of commuting on public transportation to work...reimbursement of up to $205 per month for parking near your home when the employee drives to work.

By converting part of an employee's wages to such tax-free compensation, you can reduce the employment tax bill.

Some strategies for managing the employment tax bill...

●**Paying the employee's half of the tax.** Often, a household employee will want to receive a set amount of wages in cash, and not have withheld tax reduce that amount. In that case, it may be simplest to pay the tax for the employee.

Example: The employee wants to receive a set $100 per week. A wage of $100 per week would result in payment of $92.35 after the 7.65% FICA tax is withheld. But you can pay the FICA tax for the employee, letting him receive the full $100. The extra $7.65 you pay is not counted as "wages" for FICA purposes and so itself not subject to employment tax.

And, the extra $7.65 you pay on behalf of the employee is included in his taxable income —so for income tax purposes, the employee's weekly income increases to $107.65.

●**Hitting the FICA tax wage threshold.** If you don't expect a worker to earn the threshold amount from you, you need not withhold FICA tax from wages. But when wages exceed that amount, you'll owe back taxes. *Options...*

●Withhold tax on wages from the first dollar, then pay them back to the worker if wages don't reach $1,400 in 2005 or $1,500 in 2006.

●Don't withhold tax from the beginning— but warn the worker that extra "catch-up" withholding will be taken from pay if wages reach the threshold amount.

●Don't withhold tax from the beginning— and if wages reach the threshold, pay the FICA tax for the employee yourself, so the worker's after-tax pay isn't reduced.

Note: FUTA tax is not withheld from employee pay—as the employer, you always have to pay it yourself.

FILING REQUIREMENTS

How to file and pay employment taxes on household workers...

●**Obtain an Employer Identification Number (EIN).** This is required to report employment taxes.

How: Just file IRS Form SS-4, which you can obtain from the IRS Web site, *www.irs.gov,* or by calling 800-829-3676. Or request one electronically through the IRS Web site by going to the site map and first clicking on "Small Business/Self-Employed" and then on "Employer ID Numbers (EINs)."

●**Send a copy of each of your employee's W-2s to the Social Security Administration (SSA).** The SSA will send the information to the IRS. Employees must receive their W-2s by January 31 after year-end. The SSA must receive the copy by February 28.

●**File Form 1040 Schedule H with your tax return.** The employment taxes that you owe for household employees are reported on your personal income tax return Schedule H (Form 1040).

Pay employment taxes on household employees' wages as you would other personal income taxes you owe—by increasing your wage withholding or quarterly estimated tax payments to cover them.

Information: IRS Publication 926, *Household Employer's Tax Guide for Wages Paid,* gives the details of the federal tax rules covering employment taxes for household employees.

Alert: The above describes only the federal tax rules for household employees. Also, check your state's tax rules for unemployment and income taxes. Publication 926 lists contact information for all the state employment agencies at *www.irs.gov/pub/irs-pdf/p926.pdf.*

Also from Laurence Foster, CPA/PFS...

  ## How to Get New Tax Savings from Old Tax Returns

You may be able to reduce your taxes for prior years by filing IRS Form 1040X, *Amended Tax Return.*

You can do this not only to correct errors but to get tax refunds for past years by changing filing strategies, claiming overlooked deductions and using retroactive tax breaks created by Congress and the IRS.

BASIC RULES

Amending a tax return is easy. You simply file the short 1040X form and state the change you are making on it. You do not have to refile your entire return, though you may need to attach a copy of the page or schedule you are changing.

You can amend a return up to three years after you originally filed it. *Tax-saving reasons for amending returns...*

●**Incorrect 1099s.** Upon examining all your 1099 information returns after you file, you may find that one or more overstated your income.

Alert: A survey found that almost 10% of all information returns filed by investment houses for 2003 contained mistakes—so double-check yours for this year and past years.

●**Changing filing status.** A single filer may not realize until after filing that he/she qualifies for tax-saving head of household status.

Also, married couples who file separately may save taxes by switching to joint status.

Common: Spouses who separate on hostile terms often file separately to protect themselves from each other's potential liabilities. But separate filing almost always increases their combined tax bill in such cases. If they can agree to work together, they can later file an amended return to claim joint status, get a refund and split the tax savings.

Note: It's not possible to switch from joint to separate status on an amended return.

●**Multiple support agreements.** When a number of family members contribute to pay most of the support of a retired parent or other relative but no one person pays more than half the support, they might qualify as a group to claim a dependency exemption for the relative and assign it to one person among them.

How: File IRS Form 2120, *Multiple Support Declaration.*

If this tactic is overlooked, amended returns can be used to file multiple support agreements for up to three years back, claiming dependency exemptions to get refunds.

●**Worthless securities and bad debts.** These are deductible only in the year they become worthless—but that often is not known until a later year, especially when litigation is involved.

Note: These items can be deducted up to seven years back on an amended return, instead of the normal three years.

Review your portfolio and if you find any securities or debts that went bad in the past seven years, deduct them now for a refund.

●**State tax refunds.** It's a common error to report these in income when they should be tax free or partially tax free.

A state tax refund is included in federal taxable income only if, and to the extent that, the original state tax payment was deducted on a previous year's federal return.

If you switched from claiming the standard deduction to itemizing deductions in the past three years, check to be sure you didn't pay tax on a refunded state payment that you didn't originally deduct.

Snag: The alternative minimum tax may eliminate the deduction for state taxes even if you filed an itemized return. Also, high-income individuals have their itemized deduction phased out as income rises. If you were in either situation and later received a state refund you paid tax on, double-check its taxability.

●**Casualty losses.** When a casualty loss occurs in a presidentially declared disaster, a deduction can be claimed either on that year's tax return or the prior year's return.

Filing an amended return for the prior year often results in a quicker refund—and maybe a larger one, too, depending on your tax bracket and other items on the return that impact the deduction.

●**Errors and omissions.** If you do discover that you made an error on a past year's return, or failed to report an item of income, filing an amended return to correct the mistake will minimize taxes by stopping interest from running on the liability, and increasing the chance that the IRS will waive any penalties it can apply.

AUDIT RISK

Filing an amended return will probably not result in extra audit risk.

Amending a tax return does not extend the statute of limitations for the original tax return to give the IRS any more time to audit it. And in the typical case, the IRS looks only at the particular item being amended on the return.

An amended return will draw an extra look from the IRS only if the item being amended is unusual or has a big effect on the tax bill—and even then, if the amendment and the rest of the return are proper, file it to assure you pay no more tax than you owe.

Don't Throw Tax Records Out Prematurely

Many people needlessly increase their taxes by discarding their tax documentation before they should.

All credit card and bank statements can be tossed after three years, when audit risk normally ends. But brokerage and mutual fund statements should be kept because they show the cost of investments. Without them, you can't document reinvested dividends, and so may needlessly increase gains tax on future sales of shares. Keep records documenting the cost of anything you invest in for as long as you own it plus three years.

Jean Chatzky, the financial editor for *Today* on NBC and editor-at-large for *Money* magazine. She is also the author of *Pay It Down!* (Portfolio). Her Internet site is *www.jean chatzky.com.*

The IRS May Owe You Some Money

Check to see if the IRS owes you money at the National Taxpayers Union (NTU) Web site, *www.ntu.org*. Click on "Find Out if the IRS Owes You Money," then enter your name and state to find out if you are owed any federal tax refunds.

Very Valuable Tax Deductions Even If You Don't Itemize

Mary Wilson, CPA, JD, senior tax manager, Rothstein Kass, an international accounting and consulting firm in Roseland, NJ, *www.rkco.com.*

Many taxpayers don't take the common tax deductions—for mortgage interest, charitable donations and medical expenses. The reason? They do not "itemize" by claiming these or any other expenses on Schedule A of Form 1040.

It is easy to see why. For many people, the standard deduction—in 2005, $10,000 (joint); $5,000 (single) and for 2006, $10,300 (joint); $5,150 (single)—is higher than the total of their itemized deductions, so they're better off taking the standard deduction.

There are several smart ways to really boost your tax savings even if you don't itemize and instead take the standard deduction. A number of so-called *above-the-line* write-offs are available. *Common examples...*

INDIVIDUAL RETIREMENT ACCOUNTS (IRAs)

In 2005 and 2006, you can contribute up to $4,000 to an IRA ($4,500 in 2005 and $5,000 in 2006 for taxpayers age 50 and older). Roth IRA contributions are never tax-deductible. *But there are situations in which you can deduct contributions to a traditional IRA...*

•**If you are not covered by an employer-sponsored retirement plan.**

•**If your income is under certain thresholds,** even if you are covered by an employer-sponsored retirement plan. All single filers must have incomes of less than $50,000 to be eligible for a full IRA write-off. For joint filers, the limits are $70,000 in 2005 and $75,000 in 2006.

Lesser deductions are available for those with incomes up to $60,000. For joint filers, the limits are $80,000 in 2005 and $85,000 in 2006.

•**If your joint income is under $150,000 and only one spouse works.** The nonworking spouse can take this deduction even if the working spouse is covered by an employer-sponsored retirement plan.

HEALTH SAVINGS ACCOUNTS (HSAs)

HSAs, created under the 2003 Medicare drug law, became effective in 2004, and are now growing in popularity.

How HSAs work: They are IRA-like accounts that can be used to pay health-care expenses.

Contributions: In order to deduct your contributions to an HSA, you must be covered by a high-deductible health plan and not covered by Medicare. For 2006, the annual deductible on health insurance needs to be at least $1,050 ($2,100 for joint filers).

You can contribute as much as the amount of your policy's deductible, to a maximum set by the IRS.

For example, with a $1,050 deductible, you can put as much as $1,050 per year into an HSA.

If you will be age 55 or older by year-end, you can contribute $700 more than the policy deductible. The maximum HSA contribution for 2006 is $2,700...or $5,450 for those with family coverage. If you have an HSA, you still can contribute to an IRA, a 401(k) and a flexible spending account at work.

Withdrawals: Withdrawals can be made tax free from the HSA to pay medical bills. Unused HSA money can be carried over to subsequent years to grow tax deferred through investments in mutual funds, stocks, bonds, etc.—potentially for decades. Money withdrawn before age 65 that is not used for health-related purposes is subject to income tax and a 10% penalty. After age 65, you pay only income tax.

STUDENT-LOAN INTEREST

You can deduct up to $2,500 worth of interest paid on student loans this year, regardless of how many students there are in the family and regardless of whether the loan financed higher education for you, your spouse and/or a dependent.

ALIMONY

Alimony is 100% deductible for the payer and is considered taxable income for the recipient. If you're the payer, you'll have to provide your former spouse's Social Security number on your return so that the IRS can check on the resulting tax collection.

MOVING EXPENSES

If you need to move due to a new job or for other business reasons, certain expenses are deductible—costs to transport household goods and personal effects as well as your travel to the new residence. This includes lodging but not meals. Your new workplace must be more than 50 miles farther from your old home than your former workplace was from your old home.

EARLY WITHDRAWAL PENALTIES

If you cash in a bank CD, any resulting penalty can be deducted.

SPECIAL WRITE-OFFS FOR THE SELF-EMPLOYED

• **Self-employment retirement plans.** If you have self-employment income, even from a sideline business, several types of retirement plans are available, among them SEP, SIMPLE, individual 401(k) and Keogh plans. Contributions to these plans are deductible regardless of whether you itemize. For the rules on deducting these contributions, check IRS Publication 560, *Retirement Plans for Small Business,* available by calling 800-TAX-FORM or visiting *www.irs.gov.*

• **Self-employment tax.** The bad news is that self-employed individuals must pay both the employer's and the employee's share of Medicare and Social Security taxes. The good news is that you can deduct half of those payments even if you don't itemize.

• **Self-employment health insurance.** You can deduct 100% of health insurance premiums that you pay for yourself, your spouse and your dependents. The amount you deduct can't exceed your self-employment income.

Energy Act Tax Breaks

The 2005 *Energy Act* gives individual taxpayers only a few tax breaks...

• **A tax credit for the purchase of hybrid or clean-fuel vehicles** ranging from $400 to $2,400, depending on fuel economy and vehicle size. The tax credit phases out when total energy-efficient car sales of the manufacturer exceed 60,000 vehicles.

●**A $2,000 credit for installing solar hot-water heating,** solar-generated electricity, or fuel cells.

●**A $500 credit for energy-saving home improvements** such as insulation (maximum $200 for energy-efficient windows).

These tax credits generally apply only in 2006 and 2007.

Barbara Weltman, an attorney based in Millwood, NY, *www.barbaraweltman.com*. She is author of *J. K. Lasser's 1001 Deductions and Tax Breaks* (Wiley).

Little Mistakes That Can Cause You Big Trouble With the IRS

Martin S. Kaplan, CPA, 11 Penn Plaza in New York City, *www.irsmaven.com*. He is a frequent speaker at insurance, banking and financial planning seminars and is the author of *What the IRS Doesn't Want You to Know* (Wiley).

Simple tax paperwork mistakes can cause big problems. Fixing them can cost time, aggravation and advisers' fees—and maybe extra tax as well. *Simple mistakes to avoid...*

●**Check-writing snags.** Any check sent to the IRS that doesn't state on its face exactly for what and for whom it is written may be lost or misapplied.

Important: On every IRS check, write your Social Security number (and, if married, that of your spouse), the number of the tax form that the check accompanies and the tax period for which the payment is made (such as "Form 1040-ES, 2nd quarter" for a personal estimated payment). If it is a business payment, write the Employer Identification Number.

Trap: If a payment isn't designated to a specific tax and period, the IRS can apply it any way it chooses. If you owe more than one tax liability—perhaps because you have an ongoing tax dispute or run a business that pays several different types of tax—the IRS may apply the payment in a way that maximizes your liability.

●**Proof of filing not established.** For every time-sensitive form, keep proof of timely filing, such as a certified mail receipt. Do this not just for tax returns but for all important filings.

Example: One self-employed individual filed for a second extension, using regular mail, by dropping off the form in a post office on the deadline date of August 15, 2003—just before the Northeast blackout hit. Due to the blackout, the extension wasn't postmarked on that date and it was received by the IRS late. The IRS rejected the extension, added late-filing penalties and said the individual's retirement plan contributions made after August 15 for the prior year were improper.

The individual finally got the extension accepted by going to IRS Appeals, but the process took months with potential big penalties looming—all of which he could have avoided by simply obtaining a certified mail receipt from the post office.

●**Form 1099s don't match the tax return.** If you receive a Form 1099 reporting that an amount of income was paid to you, the IRS will expect to find that income on your tax return.

Snag: Sometimes such an amount is not income to you—the 1099 may be erroneous, or it may report a check sent to you at year-end that you did not receive until after the start of the following year.

Mistake: If you don't report the income, IRS computers will flag your return and the IRS will contact you to find out why you didn't.

Better: Ask the income payer to issue a corrected version of any erroneous 1099. Otherwise, report the 1099 amount on your tax return so that the IRS sees it, then subtract a correcting amount, adding a note of explanation. Keep records of what you did so you can explain it to the IRS with minimum trouble if it contacts you.

●**Not filing Form 1099-R to document withholding from retirement plan distributions.** If you take a distribution from a retirement plan, tax normally will be withheld from it at a 20% rate. For pension distributions and Social Security benefits, you can elect to have tax withheld from payments.

Snag: Normally 1099s don't have to be filed with your tax return, but a Form 1099-R issued by a retirement plan that reports withholding must be filed with your return (as a W-2 is)—

the IRS will want to see it before giving credit for the withheld tax. If it isn't filed, your return will be flagged.

Important: Examine the 1099-Rs issued by retirement plans. Otherwise, you may not remember the withholding, or it may occur by mistake—and if you aren't aware of it, you may fail to take credit for it. If you overpay your taxes, the IRS is a lot less likely to contact you than if you underpay.

●**Inadequate charitable contribution documentation.** People commonly forget documentation rules for noncash charitable contributions. When such a contribution exceeds $500, Form 8283, *Noncash Charitable Contributions,* must be filed with the return. If a contribution exceeds $5,000, there must be an appraisal, too.

In addition, gifts of all kinds (including by cash and check) of $250 or more must be documented by an acknowledgment letter from the charity. The letter need not be filed with the tax return but must be obtained by the time the return is filed. Otherwise the deduction can be disallowed on audit—even for a donation that was perfectly legitimate.

●**Name change upon marriage or divorce not matching Social Security number.** A name change upon a marriage or a divorce can cause the name to no longer match the individual's Social Security number, with the result that tax payments get miscredited.

Safety: Promptly report a name change to the Social Security Administration (SSA) by filing Form SS-5, *Social Security Administration Application for a Social Security Card,* at its local office, or call 800-772-1213 for instructions on how to report a name change by mail. The SSA will inform the IRS. Since that can take time, include maiden and marital name on the first post-marriage or postdivorce tax return filed.

Example: If Ms. Jane Jones marries Mr. Smith, she can then file her first tax return as Jane Jones Smith.

●**Omitting Social Security and taxpayer ID numbers.** *To claim...*

●A dependency exemption for an individual, you must report that person's Social Security number. This rule includes newborn children.

●An alimony deduction, you must report the Social Security number of the person receiving the alimony payments.

●A dependent care credit, you must report the Social Security number of the person, or the taxpayer ID number of the entity, paid to provide the care.

Omitting these numbers will cause the disallowance of the items until you provide them.

●**Multiple filings in the same envelope.** If you need to make two or more separate filings with the IRS, don't mail them in the same envelope. If you do, there's a good chance that whoever opens it at the IRS will process only one of the filings while thinking that the other is just some sort of unnecessary supporting material, ignoring it.

Send each filing in its own envelope with its own separate certified mail receipt if proof of filing may be necessary.

There Are Three Ways to File Electronically— Which Is Best for You?

Barbara Weltman, an attorney based in Millwood, NY, *www.barbaraweltman.com.* She is author of *J.K. Lasser's 1001 Deductions and Tax Breaks* (Wiley).

Almost 66 million Americans filed their personal tax returns electronically during last tax season. More will do so this year —and you may want to join them if you haven't already. E-filing saves time, money and effort in managing your tax return—and for most taxpayers, it's free.

ADVANTAGES

An e-filed tax return is sent to the IRS electronically rather than on paper. *Advantages of e-filing...*

●**Faster refunds.** An e-filed tax return gets a refund in about half the time of a paper return, usually about three weeks instead of six. You can get your refund in only 10 days if you combine e-filing with electronic direct deposit of your refund into your bank account.

●**Easier proof of filing.** To have proof of filing of a paper tax return, you must send it to the IRS by certified or registered mail, or IRS-approved express delivery service, and keep the receipt. This is expensive and slow, and you may have to wait in line at the post office. Many people don't bother and just send their returns via regular mail—and sometimes those returns get lost.

But every e-filed tax return receives an electronic acknowledgment from the IRS within just two days—and it's free.

●**Fewer mistakes.** E-filed returns are automatically checked for the most common mistakes that delay the processing of paper returns, such as missing information, omitted tax forms, math errors, missing signatures, etc. (Your e-file signature is a confidential personal identification number.)

If there is such a mistake on your e-filed tax return, it will be caught immediately and you can fix it right away—preventing return and refund processing delays.

●**Attractive payment options.** If a payment is due with your return, you can pay by credit card and get frequent-flier miles or other credit card bonuses. Or you can arrange for an electronic transfer from your bank account as late as April 15 even if you file earlier—allowing you to use the money until then.

●**State e-filing.** This year, 37 states and the District of Columbia allow you to e-file returns at the same time as the federal return.

More uses: In addition to e-filing your Form 1040, you can obtain an automatic four-month filing extension on-line. Quarterly estimated tax filings also can be e-filed, and electronic payments can be made with both filing extensions and estimated tax filings.

HOW TO E-FILE

There are three methods of electronic filing…

●**IRS Free File.** This free filing service, organized jointly by the IRS and tax-preparation firms, was created several years ago to provide filing services for qualified taxpayers. For more on Free File, see the next column.

●**Through a tax professional.** Numerous tax professionals today e-file their clients' tax returns. This is the most common method of e-filing, with 46 million returns filed in 2005. The fee for such e-filing is negotiated with your professional or may be included in the return preparation fee.

●**Using your personal computer.** Leading tax software packages (such as *TurboTax* and *TaxCut*) that are used to prepare tax returns on home computers now have e-file options. This year, 16.7 million returns were e-filed from home computers.

IRS FREE FILE

The Free File program is useful for the majority of taxpayers, although many do not know about it. Services are offered by more than a dozen return preparation firms.

Key: Every tax return preparation firm determines for itself who qualifies for its free service. For 2005 returns Free File was restricted to those with adjusted gross income of about $50,000.

How Free File works: At *www.irs.gov*, click on "IRS E-File," then "Free File," and read the Frequently Asked Questions (FAQ) list to learn more about the program. *Then…*

●**Look for free services for which you may be eligible.** Do this by simply scrolling through the list of offerings. Click on "Start Now!" to access the list.

●**Link to the free service you've chosen.** When you find the service that you want to use, click on the provider's link and you will be taken from the IRS Web site to the provider's Web site.

●**Prepare and file your return.** You can then prepare your return using the provider's proprietary software over its Web site, and file the return with the IRS—all for free.

The service providers in the Free File program are commercial businesses, so they may try to sell you other products or services, but you do not have to buy anything else to use Free File.

Also, many of the commercial service providers do not reveal on their own regular Web sites or in their promotional literature that they participate in IRS Free File—because they don't want to give away for free what a lot of customers will pay for.

Therefore, in many cases, the only way you'll learn about the provider's free filing service is by going through the IRS Web site to the Free File section.

FOR MORE INFORMATION

For a great deal more information about IRS e-filing services, click on the e-file logo at *www.irs.gov*. There you'll learn how to arrange direct deposit of tax refunds and electronic payments, gain more details about the services mentioned here and learn about a wide range of other new e-file options—such as those for self-employed persons and small businesses.

Tax Filing Help from the IRS Web Site

James Glass, a tax attorney based in New York City and contributing writer to *Tax Hotline.*

The IRS Web site, *www.irs.gov,* is a valuable resource that can help you minimize your tax bill and make it easier to file your return. *Ways you can use the site…*

TAX LAWS AND IRS RULES

Congress tends to enact new tax laws every year, and the last two years have seen more law changes than most. These changes can affect your tax bill—and even give you opportunities to file amended tax returns for prior years to claim tax refunds. The IRS is always changing and updating its own rules as well, and these can affect your tax filings, too.

The IRS Web site can inform you about important law changes and rule changes you will not want to miss.

How: At the IRS site, click on "Individuals," then on "1040 Central." That will take you to an information page including "Tax Law Changes" that detail the new laws that affect personal returns …"News Releases" about IRS rules and operations…and "Fact Sheets" about key recent developments at the IRS that are important to many taxpayers.

AUDIT-PROOF YOUR RETURN

The IRS Web site can help you file a return that will stand up to an IRS auditor, should one ever call. *Resources to use…*

● **IRS audit guides.** These can be invaluable to owners of small businesses. They are the same audit guides that IRS agents use when conducting audits. So, by obtaining one that fits your situation, you can learn in advance what an IRS auditor would be looking for if your return were examined—and use that knowledge to shore up your return and make it audit-proof.

Audit guides are available free for nearly 50 different kinds of businesses, ranging from auto-body repair to veterinary medicine.

Audit guides also exist for individuals who are subject to the alternative minimum tax (AMT), those who have received lawsuit awards and settlements and those who make investments that generate passive losses.

To find the audit guides, go to *www.irs.gov,* click on "Businesses" and then on "Audit Techniques Guides" as well as on "Market Segment Understandings."

● **Publications.** The IRS has free publications explaining the tax rules for almost every item that may affect your tax return.

To find the publication you want, at *www.irs.gov* enter its subject in the search box, or click on "Forms and Publications" for a complete list.

● **Frequently asked questions.** To find the IRS's answers to the most frequently asked tax questions on a wide range of subjects, log on to *www.irs.gov/faqs.*

FILING FORMS AND INSTRUCTIONS

If you file a paper return, you can download forms and instructions you need from the IRS Web site. It's much easier and faster than ordering forms and waiting for them to arrive by mail. You can also file on-line with the IRS's new Free File electronic filing program (see previous article for details).

FILING ALERTS

If any last-minute problems arise during the filing season—such as mistakes discovered in IRS forms or publications, or problems at IRS Service Centers—you can learn about them at the IRS Web site. Go to *www.irs.gov,* click on "Newsroom" and then on "Problem Alerts."

FREE HELP WITH YOUR RETURN

If you find you still have problems preparing your return, the IRS Web site can direct you to free assistance…

● **The Volunteer Income Tax Assistance Program (VITA)** helps those with incomes of $37,000 and below.

● **Tax Counseling for the Elderly (TCE)** provides free tax help to those age 60 and older.

Learn more about these programs by going to *www.irs.gov,* clicking on "Individuals," and then "Free Tax Return Preparation for You by Volunteers."

In addition, the IRS site can tell you whether free walk-in assistance is available to you at your local IRS office.

From *www.irs.gov,* click on "Contact IRS" and then "Contact My Local Office." There you will find both a map and a state-by-state listing of local IRS offices, including addresses, hours when help is available and phone numbers to call for further information or to make an appointment if necessary.

FOLLOW-THROUGH

After you file your tax return, you can track the status of your refund on the IRS Web site. At *www.irs.gov,* click on "Where's My Refund?"

Then, going forward, you can stay informed about tax law changes and IRS news as they happen in the coming year by subscribing to free IRS electronic newsletters. From *www.irs. gov,* click on "The Newsroom," and then on "e-News Subscriptions."

There you may find a number of electronic newsletters that can help you, from the *Digital Dispatch,* which reports on general tax news nationwide, to newsletters on special topics, such as self-employment tax issues and managing qualified retirement plans.

With these e-letters keeping you informed, you will be able to make good use of the IRS Web site year-round.

Beware of Fraudulent Tax Return Preparers

IRS Fact Sheet FS-2005-8.

The IRS warns that you are responsible for what is reported on your tax return even if your tax return preparer commits fraud on it without your knowledge to reduce your tax bill.

To avoid a fraudulent preparer…

● **Avoid a preparer who claims that he/she can obtain larger refunds** or a much lower tax bill than other preparers…bases his fee on the amount of your refund…or who makes any promises that just seem too good to be true.

● **Make sure that the preparer signs your tax return** as its preparer and provides you with a copy for your records.

● **Consider whether the preparer or the preparer's firm will be around to answer questions** about your tax return for at least three years after it is filed.

● **Ask the preparer questions about anything that you don't understand** on your return before signing it.

● **Learn the preparer's credentials.** Is he an accredited tax preparer, enrolled agent (EA), certified public accountant (CPA), licensed public accountant or tax attorney?

Only attorneys, CPAs and EAs can represent taxpayers before the IRS in all matters, including audits, collection and appeals. Other return preparers are permitted to represent taxpayers only for audits.

● **Ask around.** Do you know anyone who has used the tax professional? Was he satisfied with the service that he received? Were there any problems?

If you suspect tax fraud or know of a fraudulent preparer, report this to the IRS by calling 800-829-0433.

Is Your Tax Return Being Prepared in India?

Some tax practitioners, including CPA firms, are outsourcing the preparation of income tax returns to countries offering cheap labor. India is often used. When returns are done this way, the tax practitioner signing your return still has primary responsibility for the accuracy of the return.

Risk: Your private financial information is being transmitted to a developing country where the risk of identity theft is increased.

Best bet: Ask your tax adviser where your tax return will be prepared this year and act accordingly.

Ms. X, Esq., a former agent with the IRS who is still well connected.

More from Ms. X, Esq....

Using the Freedom of Information Act

After an audit, a formal request made to the IRS for copies of agents' workpapers in your file will generally be honored.

Exception: The IRS will generally claim that a report written by a special agent that is used as the basis for a decision to prosecute a taxpayer is exempt from disclosure.

Reason: The IRS may claim that the release of a special agent's report would adversely affect law enforcement activities by prejudicing the government's case.

If the IRS refuses to disclose a document you want, you can bring the IRS to federal court and let a judge make the determination.

Also from Ms. X, Esq....

Martha Stewart's Mistake and the IRS

A valuable lesson to be learned from Martha Stewart's conviction for lying during a federal investigation is that any taxpayer contacted by the IRS should never speak to the IRS. The tendency of most taxpayers questioned by the IRS is to misrepresent or lie about a fact that they think will cause them to owe more tax. This is illegal, and Martha was convicted of it.

Better approach: Have all representations made by your attorney. A knowledgeable attorney knows what to say and what not to say to the IRS. So avoid handling the matter yourself and thinking that the IRS agent will never figure out the truth.

Watch Out! IRS Audit Rates Are Going Up

Frederick W. Daily, Esq., a tax attorney based in Incline Village, NV, and author of Stand Up to the IRS *and* Tax Savvy for Small Business *(both from Nolo.com).*

IRS audit rates are rising again after falling to all-time lows. Commissioner Mark Everson says enforcement now is a top priority of the IRS, and it is just ramping up.

Yet, though rising, audit rates remain far below what they were several years ago. *All about IRS audit risk now...*

FACTS AND FIGURES

In recent years, IRS audit rates plunged to record lows as the IRS underwent a widespread reorganization.

In 2004, the number of IRS revenue agents had declined by 24% from 1995—to 12,255 from 16,078—as the number of personal tax returns filed rose about 13%.*

Many IRS personnel were "between jobs" during the reorganization, others were shifted from enforcement tasks to improving "customer service" and the IRS's total level of employment fell about 17% since 1995 as more funds were spent on modernizing computers and other systems. The reorganization is almost over now, and the IRS is dedicating new resources to reverse the decline in enforcement.

Audit numbers: During 2004, the audit rate for all individual tax returns rose 18% from 2003. Moreover, the audit rate for high-income

*All data from the IRS and the Transactional Records Access Clearinghouse, Syracuse University, *http://trac.syr.edu.*

taxpayers—those with incomes over $100,000 —rose by 42% from 2003. So it is clear that the audit rate has bottomed out and is rising again.

While these increases may seem impressive in percentage terms and do indicate that a corner has been turned, actual audit rates remain very low by historical standards. Even after the increase, the audit rate for all individual tax returns in 2004 was only 0.77%—only one in 129 returns was audited. This was down 54% from 1996, when the audit rate was 1.67%.

Moreover, far fewer taxpayers actually face an auditor in person than the audit rate indicates, because the IRS includes mail inquiries about tax returns in its audit figures as "correspondence audits." Subtracting these, the face-to-face audit rate remained at an all-time low 0.15% in 2004, about the same as in 2002 and 2003— only one taxpayer in 625 was called to actually meet with an IRS auditor.

Even for high-income taxpayers, the audit rate was just above 1% in 2004—only 1.39% of their returns were audited. This was down by 51% since 1996, when 2.85% were audited, and down by more than 74% from 1992, when about 5.28% were audited.

The rate of face-to-face IRS audits for high-income taxpayers was 0.35% in 2004—only one in 250 faced an auditor in person. That was down slightly from 2003 but down by more than three-fourths from 1996 when 1.7% faced in-person audits—and by more than seven-eighths from 1992, when 2.9% did.

AUDITING SMARTER

IRS audit rates may never climb back up to mid-1990s levels, but this does not mean that audit risk is not increasing for many.

Key: The IRS is trying to audit "smarter" than in the past. Its reorganization in large part involved installing new information systems to enable it to enforce the tax laws more efficiently. And it recently concluded a "national research program" of audits designed to learn more about taxpayer behavior so that it can select audit targets more effectively. *The IRS is now taking a closer look at…*

●**K-1 matching for pass-through entities.** More than $1 trillion each year is reported on Schedule K-1s filed by partnerships, S corporations and trusts that pay income to individuals. But, unlike Form 1099s and W-2s, the IRS historically never matched these to individual tax returns—which it believes contributed to significant underreporting of such income.

The IRS has been testing out a new computer matching program for K-1s that checks them against individual tax returns. The IRS says such matching is now a high priority. Therefore, the owners of pass-through entities can expect to receive more "computerized" scrutiny in the future than they have in the past.

●**High-income individuals.** While the rate of all personal audits remains low by historical standards, the IRS is shifting resources to target high-income individuals—as evidenced by the 85% increase in the audit rate of persons who have income of more than $100,000 during the last few years.

In fact, the IRS says it is emphasizing audits of individuals who have income of more than $250,000, although it has not released specific audit-rate data for such individuals.

●**Executive compensation.** The IRS says that test examinations conducted last year of the returns of top executives of 24 businesses in a wide range of industries found numerous problems—ranging from misreporting of benefits to outright nonfiling. As a result, it says it is initiating a new examination program directed at executive compensation packages.

Targets: Deferred compensation, fringe benefits, stock-based compensation, golden parachutes, asset-protection arrangements and other compensation package elements.

An IRS official said that the agency intends to double the number of executive audits.

●**Offshore transactions.** The IRS is aggressively pursuing those who utilize foreign bank accounts as well as other foreign entities to escape taxes.

Example: It is examining retailer credit card records to identify the individuals who use foreign-issue credit cards to tap foreign bank accounts that have not been reported on US tax returns. Once it finds such a person, it is often able to get that individual to name the "promoter" who arranged the setup. And when it identifies the promoter, it often is able to get the promoter's list of all its other "clients" who have such foreign accounts.

●**Tax shelters.** The IRS is putting more effort into fighting abusive tax shelters, which have been aggressively promoted over the Internet.

Example: It has started an information-sharing program with 45 states in which it now shares "leads" with state tax agencies to avoid any duplication of effort in order to be able to examine a larger number of shelter cases. The IRS has announced that more than 20,000 leads have already been shared under the program.

SCOPE OF RISK

While IRS enforcement has not picked up dramatically yet, it is clear that it has moved off its lows and is on the way back up.

Unlike the mid-1990s, when Congress cracked down on the IRS for *its* "abuses," Congressional leaders are now demanding that the IRS crack down on tax evaders. And with surging national deficits, the government has proposed a budget increase for the IRS that includes funds to add 5,000 new personnel—reversing the previous decline of the IRS workforce.

In short, the pendulum has now swung back from customer service to enforcement and can be expected to stay there in coming years.

Although some of the IRS's new programs—such as K-1 matching—may not be felt by many taxpayers yet, they can be expected to become more efficient and affect more in the future.

With tax returns generally being audited a year or two after they have been filed, taxpayers should manage their tax planning now for the growing audit risk they face in the future.

 **IRS Audit Triggers**

Sandy Botkin, Esq., CPA, former IRS attorney and now president of the Tax Reduction Institute in Germantown, MD, *www.taxreductioninstitute.com*. He is author of *Lower Your Taxes—Big-Time* (McGraw-Hill).

There are a variety of known audit triggers. *You might be contacted by the Internal Revenue Service if...*

●**The income reported on your tax return doesn't match** the amounts that are reported on 1099 and W-2 forms.

●**You fail to report income,** such as interest or dividends.

●**You fail to sign your return,** or you use the wrong Social Security number.

●**You move money offshore but don't declare it.** You must report offshore accounts if assets exceed $10,000. Account holders may access these accounts through debit or credit cards—the IRS receives lists of such account-holders from credit card issuers and audits of offshore account offers.

●**You set up "family estate trusts,"** otherwise known as "pure trusts," which assign property and other assets to an independent trustee and pay your living expenses. These trusts don't pass muster with the IRS.

●**You claim your personal expenses as deductible business expenses.** You can convert only certain personal expenses to business expenses. Even then, you must have a legitimate business with an honest expectation of profit.

IRS "Dirty Dozen" Tax Scams Update

IRS News Release IR-2005-19.

The IRS has updated its "dirty dozen" list of most common tax scams, some with taxpayers as victim, and others with taxpayers as perpetrator.

●**Misuse of trusts.** Promoters make money selling trust arrangements while promising all kinds of tax benefits that trusts don't deliver.

●**"Claim of right" doctrine.** People deduct amounts equal to their wages as a "necessary expense" of obtaining income.

●**"Corporation sole."** A provision religious leaders use to separate themselves from personal ownership of church assets is twisted by tax evaders to try to avoid liability for taxes as well as debts.

●**Offshore transactions.** Use of foreign-issue credit cards, foreign bank accounts or foreign trusts to hide transactions and income from the IRS.

●**Employment tax evasion.** Schemes that claim taxes do not have to be withheld from employees' wages.

●**Return preparer fraud.** Tax return preparers promise larger refunds than anyone else, divert tax refunds, overcharge or commit other wrongdoing.

●**Credit counseling agencies.** The agencies make claims that they can fix credit ratings while charging high fees or monthly service charges. They have become the primary focus of the IRS Tax Exempt and Government Entities Division.

●**"No gain" deduction.** Similar to "claim of right," tax filers attempt to eliminate all of their adjusted gross income by deducting this amount as a miscellaneous itemized deduction on IRS Schedule A.

●**Abuse of charitable organizations and deductions.** Using tax-exempt organizations to shield income (e.g., moving income from a taxable account to a charity but retaining control over the funds).

●**Zero return.** Promoters tell you to enter all "zeros" for income and withholding and to enter "nunc pro tunc" (Latin for "now and then").

●**Frivolous arguments.** A variety of claims that the income tax is voluntary or that income tax is unconstitutional.

●**Identity theft.** Scammers send out phony notices, apparently from a bank or the IRS, requesting that confidential information be sent to them right away.

Danger: The IRS warns that even honest taxpayers who are duped by these scams may end up owing "staggering" amounts in back taxes, interest and penalties. To find out more about these and other tax scams, go to *www.irs.gov,* click on "Newsroom" and on "Tax Scams/Consumer Alerts."

To report suspected wrongdoing to the IRS, call the IRS's Tax Fraud Hotline, 800-829-0433.

IRS Tracks Foreign Account Schemers

IRS News Release IR-2004-19.

In 2003, the IRS began seeking out unreported foreign bank accounts through records of credit cards used to tap them, while offering owners of these accounts decreased penalties if they came forward, reported them voluntarily and informed the IRS about the sponsors and promoters of such accounts.

Result: More than 1,300 taxpayers came forward. So far, the IRS has collected more than $170 million in taxes, interest and penalties. But, most important, the IRS has obtained the names of nearly 500 scheme and scam promoters, approximately half of whom were previously unknown to it.

Key: The IRS says that it is now obtaining each promoter's "participant list," which names all the other people for whom the promoter set up such accounts who haven't turned themselves in. With these names and the knowledge the IRS has obtained from the promoters about how offshore accounts are set up, the IRS expects to catch many more owners of unreported foreign accounts.

"The likelihood of [these tax evaders] hearing from us is increasing daily," says the IRS.

10

Investing Now

Top Financial Planner Tells How to Invest Now For Safety and Growth

Bonds, particularly long-term bonds, will not be as attractive going forward because as interest rates rise, bond prices fall.

Investors should currently focus attention on short-term cash equivalents, such as Treasury bills, money market funds, bank accounts and CDs, whose yields will become more attractive as rates go up.

SITUATION OVERVIEW

Interest rates are going to rise, but probably not as much as many people expect—unless there's a big run-up in inflation.

In terms of asset allocation, I still believe that the traditional 60% stocks and 40% fixed income is a good place for most investors to start. It creates a solid foundation to see you through all kinds of markets.

For instance, during the crazy period from March of 2000 through March 2003, the S&P 500 stock index fell by 45%, but my model portfolio of 60% stocks and 40% bonds lost only 6%. Diversification pays!

You can adjust the 60/40 ratio based on your age, financial situation and risk tolerance—but I strongly urge clients, no matter how old they are, to keep at least 40% in stocks.

GO FOR GROWTH

In uncertain times, growth of capital becomes just as important as income. To get that growth, you'll need stocks—both growth and value stocks. And, don't forget how the tax laws relating to capital gains and dividends have made stocks more competitive from an income standpoint.

Most dividends are taxed at only 15%, and the maximum rate on long-term capital gains (for stocks held more than one year) has fallen from 20% to 15% as well. I see a continuing trend for

Jonathan Pond, president, Financial Planning Information Inc. at 1 Gateway Center, Newton, MA 02458 and author of *Your Money Matters* (Putnam). For more information, visit *http://yourfinancialroadmap.com*.

159

companies to raise their dividends or initiate dividends if they haven't paid them in the past.

Bonus: Investors who fear a downturn in the stock market should pay special attention to dividend-paying stocks because they tend to be offered by financially strong companies with very solid balance sheets. Such companies can tolerate economic declines better than most and tend to hold their value better in a declining market. Favor companies that have a long history of raising dividends regularly.

One caution: There's an old saying that a 3% for-sure dividend is better than a 6% maybe dividend. Watch out for those companies whose dividends just seem too good in relation to their stock prices. It may be a warning sign that the dividend is unsustainable.

When choosing your no-load large-cap stock funds, allocate 60% to growth and 40% to value.

SMALL- AND MID-CAP STOCKS

In my experience, the single biggest mistake investors make is not having enough money in small- and mid-cap stocks. That is particularly true of older, more conservative investors who only want to hold large-caps. This risk aversion became much worse after the market rout of 2001–2002.

Fact: Over one-, three-, five-, 10- and 15-year periods, small-cap (S&P 600) and mid-cap (S&P 400) stocks have outperformed large-cap (S&P 500) stocks in annualized total return. Over the year ending on December 31, 2004, large-cap stocks grew by 11%, mid-cap by 16% and small-cap by 23%.

I fully expect that 10 years from now, small- and mid-cap stocks will again have outperformed the large-caps. Therefore, I recommend putting 25% of your total stock portfolio into a well-diversified selection of both small- and mid-cap stocks.

THINK INTERNATIONAL

I also believe that all investors should have some foreign stocks. They didn't do much for many years, but currently they are performing well—in many cases better than US stocks— and they provide valuable diversification. I suggest putting 15% of your stock portfolio into international mutual funds.

BEWARE OF REAL ESTATE

Real estate stocks and real estate investment trusts (REITs) have had quite a run in recent years, but they are likely to suffer as interest rates rise. Also, their dividends do not qualify for the favorable 15% tax treatment. They still provide good income, though, so I would not sell those you currently hold—but I don't advocate making a commitment to new purchases right now.

BONDS

Instead of including a long listing of possible bonds and bond funds—many of which are good choices—I refer readers to the three fund companies that I think offer the best selection of bond funds at the most reasonable cost…

- **Fidelity,** 800-343-3548.
- **PIMCO,** 800-223-2413.
- **Vanguard,** 800-523-1154.

Guidance on what to choose…

- **Short- and intermediate-term funds** for now since interest rates are moving up.

- **Ultrashort (one year or less maturity) funds** for cash you will need soon.

- **Treasuries and (depending on your tax bracket) tax-free municipals** for your taxable accounts.

- **Corporate bond funds** are appropriate for retirement accounts.

- **Also consider Treasury inflation-protected securities (TIPS)** for up to one-quarter of your bond allocation (held in tax-deferred accounts).

Long-Term-Investing Basics

The legendary Sir John Templeton gives his advice on long-term investing…

- **Focus on your maximum total return after taxes.**

- **Realize that you can do better than most investors only if you do something different** than what the majority does.

• **Buy at times when everyone is pessimistic...**and sell when everyone is optimistic.

• **Bear markets are only temporary**—in the long run, earnings per share trend upward and so do market indexes.

• **Look worldwide for stocks**—you will find better values and have better diversification.

• **Sell an asset when you have found a much better bargain to replace it.**

Sir John Templeton, renowned international investor, in *The Book of Investing Wisdom,* edited by Peter Krass (Wiley).

Your Money: Wise Ways to Boost Profit And Cut Risk

Harold Evensky, CFP, chairman of Evensky & Katz, fee-only investment consultants at 2333 Ponce de Leon Blvd., Coral Gables, FL 33134. He lectures on investments and retirement planning internationally.

An average investor buying and selling individual stocks makes about as much sense as a novice golfer trying to beat Tiger Woods.

Problem: It's easier for average investors to determine what is a good company than what is a good stock. Think of how much money investment institutions spend on researching stocks to buy—talking with companies' customers, competitors, trade experts, etc.—and they still don't make their money on trading stocks. They make most of it charging you for investment advice.

Smartest approach for individuals: Indexing—buying the same stocks that make up a particular market index, such as the S&P 500. Low-cost index funds, which require no active stock selection or market-timing management, outperform most active managers over time.

Why indexing pays: Indexing isn't foolproof, because when the whole stock market, or the part of it that your index is following, goes down, you'll go down, too. But over a full market cycle, index funds will usually produce above-average returns because their trading expenses are much lower than those of actively managed funds and they remain fully invested at all times.

Some people resist indexing because they want to get better than "average" results. Well, think of it instead as "par" investing (what would be normal for an *expert*). It's guaranteed to be better than average because expenses are lower. If you put together a portfolio of par-performing funds, you'll do pretty well in a market in which very few active managers actually beat par.

MARKET OUTLOOK

We believe that in the next five to 10 years, returns from stocks are going to be only modest—substantially lower than in the last 20 years and even lower than the long-term historical average of about 10% per year. We expect the S&P 500 returns to be in the 8% or 9% range and intermediate-term domestic bonds to be in the 6% range, which is historically average.

Because of these lower projected returns, we believe that index funds offer the best way to improve results by at least controlling management and trading expenses as well as taxes. If you're earning only 8% to begin with, after subtracting for expenses, taxes and inflation, you would earn only about 2.5% net in real return. That doesn't leave much wiggle room to take a chance on picking the best-performing funds.

We also like exchange-traded funds (ETFs)—baskets of securities mimicking an index—that trade all day like stocks (mutual funds can only be bought at close of market each day). ETFs are often less expensive to buy and maintain than mutual funds, but they do entail a broker's commission, so they are suitable mainly for big, one-time investments. Mutual funds are more appropriate for those who invest monthly.

ASSET ALLOCATION

Long-term performance mainly depends on how your money is allocated among a variety of stocks (large-cap, small-cap, growth, value, international, etc.), bonds and cash.

That decision is unique to an individual. It shouldn't be simply a function of your age or of how much money you have. It should also take into consideration other personal factors, such as risk tolerance.

We often advise clients to start out with the conservative allocation of 40% fixed income (bonds, etc.) and 60% stocks. If they need more income and can live with the day-to-day volatility of stocks, then they can increase the stock allocation. If they have enough of a financial cushion that they don't need so many stocks to protect against inflation and they want to decrease volatility, they can then increase fixed-income investments.

CORE VS. SATELLITE INVESTMENTS

For their stock portfolios, we recommend that clients think in terms of 80% core investments, such as conservative index funds and ETFs… and 20% satellite investments, which can be almost anything—commodities funds, utilities, emerging markets—that will hopefully do at least two percentage points better than the market each year.

Core candidates: Put 50% of your stock portfolio into one or a combination of broad market index funds.

Consider putting 10% *each* into mid-cap and small-cap value funds for stronger representation in those sectors.

Finally, for the last 10%, consider diversifying with an international fund.

Satellite holdings: These should be 20% of your stock portfolio.

BOND FUNDS

For the typical 40% bond portfolio, we like several funds that concentrate on Treasury inflation-protected securities (TIPS). For high-income investors, we like tax-free municipal bond funds of various maturities. We also include a taxable international bond fund that could offer protection against a falling dollar.

A Simple System for Picking Moneymaking Stocks

Pat Dorsey, CFA, director of stock analysis for Morningstar, Inc., an independent stock and mutual fund analysis company in Chicago, *www.morningstar.com.* He is also the author of *The Five Rules for Successful Stock Investing* (Wiley).

With about 6,000 major publicly traded companies in the US alone, you can't possibly research all the stocks—but you can use these simple guidelines to quickly weed out ones that don't merit further examination, saving time and money.

You can find the data you'll need on company financial statements or at free financial Web sites, like *www.morningstar.com* or *http://finance.yahoo.com. Here's what to look for…*

●**Operating income.** Many firms have exciting ideas—but if they have never achieved operating income, they have not turned those ideas into profits.

Where to find it: Income statement.

Example: Sticking with profitable companies might have helped investors steer clear of the Internet bubble. Very few dot-com stocks posted positive operating income in the late 1990s. One of the few exceptions was eBay (NASDAQ:EBAY), which has had an operating profit every year but one since its 1998 initial public offering. Not coincidentally, eBay has been one of the few dot-coms to prosper since the sector's shakeout.

●**Cash flow from operations.** Companies can exaggerate profit numbers, but if cash flow from operations—the amount of cash a business is generating—is positive, you can rest assured that the firm truly is making money. At the least, this figure should have been positive for two out of the past three years.

Where to find it: Cash flow statement.

●**Free cash flow.** This is the money that a company generates beyond what it requires to operate. Free cash flow is equal to cash flow from operations minus capital expenditures (the cost of upgrading buildings and equipment).

Rule out any company that is not generating free cash flow. Divide free cash flow by sales to compare companies of different sizes—a small operation won't generate the same free cash flow as a conglomerate.

Exception: You might want to buy stock of a company that isn't generating free cash flow because it is pouring its money into profitable research or expansion—as The Home Depot (NYSE:HD) did until 2002. There's no guarantee that such efforts will be profitable—but if the company has quality ideas, this would be a productive use of its cash.

Where to find it: Cash flow statement.

●**Return on equity (ROE) of 10% or more.** ROE is calculated by dividing net income by shareholders' equity. If a company has not generated at least 10% ROE for four out of the past five years, it's not worth your trouble.

Where to find it: Net income is listed on the income statement. Shareholders' equity appears on the balance sheet.

Caution: In the financial sector, look for at least 12% ROE. Most financials have heavy debt, which can inflate ROE.

●**Consistent earnings growth.** Some variation from year to year is to be expected—but if earnings growth is huge one year and negative or nonexistent the next, it means one of two things...

●The stock is in a cyclical industry, such as semiconductors or agricultural machinery. Cyclicals are not appropriate for buy-and-hold investors.

●The stock carries big risks. The company might be locked in a fight with formidable competitors or dependent on just one or two products for too much of its revenue. Neither is an appealing prospect for an investor.

Where to find it: Income statement.

●**Low debt.** Be wary of any company that has a debt-to-equity ratio above 1.

Where to find it: Balance sheet, which lists liabilities and shareholders' equity.

Exception: Contemplate investing in such a stock only if it is in the financial sector, where higher debt is typical, or if both of the following are true...

●It is a proven firm in a stable industry.

●Its debt is decreasing as a percentage of assets. If a company is heading out of debt, it might not be a problem.

Example: Food company General Mills (NYSE:GIS) has a debt-to-equity ratio of about 1.4—but it also has a long-term record of success in an industry that's known for stability. If General Mills made computer chips instead of breakfast cereal, its debt would be a red flag.

WHAT TO AVOID

●**Tiny, untested companies with market capitalizations below $100 million.** Do not buy any stock that doesn't trade on the New York Stock Exchange (NYSE), American Stock Exchange (AMEX) or NASDAQ. Shares traded on smaller exchanges are more likely to be disappointments than opportunities. Look for firms that have been public companies for at least five years. Avoid initial public offerings—they're too speculative for most portfolios.

●**Foreign companies that do not have shares traded in the US.** You will be better off sticking with American depositary receipts (ADRs)—receipts for shares of foreign corporations that trade on US stock exchanges. These companies are subject to US reporting requirements. JP Morgan provides information on ADRs—call 866-576-2377 or visit *www.adr.com.*

●**Frequent "other" charges in the financial statements.** These usually reflect one-time expenses, such as the cost of a restructuring effort. Practically every firm has the occasional "other" expense, but stay away if there are big negative numbers listed for successive years. The company might be trying to disguise an ongoing problem as a one-shot cost.

Where to find it: A line labeled "Other" on the income statement.

●**Rising number of outstanding shares.** If this number is increasing by more than 2% a year, the company is making significant acquisitions or employees are being given lots of stock options. Since so many acquisitions fail, it's generally best to avoid acquisitive companies. Excessive options also dilute the value of existing shares—bad news for investors.

Where to find it: Balance sheet.

Helpful: It's a plus if the number of outstanding shares is shrinking—for instance, through buybacks. Buybacks signal that management is optimistic about the company's future—plus a reduction in outstanding shares boosts share price by increasing per-share earnings.

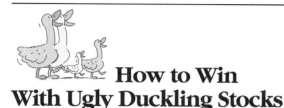

How to Win With Ugly Duckling Stocks

Robert A. Olstein, manager of the Olstein Financial Alert Fund in Purchase, NY, 800-799-2113, *www.olstein funds.com.*

During a stock market rally few stocks are attractively valued. To find real bargains, you must look at "ugly duckling" stocks —issues that investors have scorned because of a scandal or due to some other devastating business setback. *Here's how to find ugly duckling stocks…*

FOLLOW THE HEADLINES

You can discover ugly ducklings simply by reading newspaper headlines. The worse the news, the lower the stock price will sink.

Don't wait to invest until the company has faded from the spotlight. Think about buying as soon as the company has made it into the headlines and the stock price is plummeting. You're likely to find the best value in the stock—meaning that you can continue purchasing shares— as long as it stays in the headlines.

Example: We bought stock in Tyco when its problems first appeared in the news, long before the trial of its now deposed CEO Dennis Kozlowski. The stock was $13 a share. At press time it is $25.74, but that's still down from a peak of nearly $60 at the start of 2002.

FOLLOW THE MONEY

An ugly duckling stock won't become beautiful again until it generates cash. The companies whose businesses generate plenty of cash can overcome almost any type of obstacle. We concentrate on what is called free cash flow,* which

*Net income plus depreciation, minus capital expenditures plus/minus changes in working capital.

measures what is left after the big bills have been paid. That money can be used to get the company back on track.

Where to look: The Consolidated Statement of Cash Flows, which generally can be found toward the back of the company's annual report. Look at total cash in the cash flow statement and how fast (or slowly) it is growing from year to year. When free cash flow exceeds net income, income is likely to grow faster in the future, even if it is depressed now. That's because the more cash the company has at its disposal, the more it can afford to finance the sort of future growth that generates profits.

Any well-researched story about the company in the financial press also will discuss its free cash flow.

LOOK FOR ENCOURAGING SIGNS

When we invest in an ugly duckling stock, we like to see new management. Why would we want to invest in the management that sunk the company? *We also look for as many of the following attributes as we can find…*

●**Higher profit margins in the past.** Go back to before the company's troubles began, and look for any margins that are substantially higher than they are currently. A company that once had higher profit margins should be able to restore them.

●**Sale of two to five valuable assets** that are no longer useful in the business. You'll find reports of such asset sales in the news and in quarterly company reports.

●**A net operating loss carryforward** that can shield taxes in the future. You'll find it in the notes to the company's Consolidated Financial Statement.

●**"Hidden assets,"** such as ownership of a high-performing subsidiary or an equity interest in another public company. That, too, will be in notes to the financial statement.

●**A dividend.** We will not buy a stock just because it pays a dividend, but it is a big plus. It means that we get paid for holding on until the price recovers.

RECOGNIZE MISTAKES

Keep up with corporate developments by reading both general and industry news and company reports. A situation may prove worse than expected. Take your loss and move on.

Example: We estimated that an operator of hospitals hit hard by government allegations of improper Medicare billing and unnecessary surgery could eventually earn a profit margin as high as 8%. But when the company sold hospitals producing revenue of $2.6 billion for a paltry sum, there was little hope. The inability of the company to realize any value from its assets prompted us to sell the stock. Shares at press time sell for $7.24, which is significantly less than what they sold for at the start of 2004.

Don't expect to own only ugly ducklings—you might find just two or three a year.

Broker Checkup

Is your brokerage paying high enough interest on your cash? For many investors, the answer is *no*. At the end of each trading day, "sweep accounts" receive the proceeds from customer trades or cash deposits that aren't yet invested. More firms—especially those with their own banks—now pay savings deposit rates instead of the higher money market rates on these accounts. Some have made this change without the customer's consent.

Self-defense: Ask your stockbroker which accounts are available and about the long-term interest rate—not just the introductory rate.

Grace Vogel, executive vice president of member-firm regulation, New York Stock Exchange, New York City.

From America's Most Successful Investor

Warren E. Buffett's popular annual letters to his shareholders contain the insights about investing and markets that have made him America's most successful investor. Letters all the way back to 1977 are now available free on his company's Web site at *www.berkshire hathaway.com.*

Dividend Powerhouses: Stocks That Pay in Any Market

Joseph Lisanti, editor in chief of *The Outlook,* Standard & Poor's weekly investment advisory newsletter at *www.spoutlookonline.com.* Its risk-adjusted performance ranks seventh among all of the financial newsletters tracked by *The Hulbert Financial Digest* since June 1980. He is coauthor of *The Dividend Rich Investor* (McGraw-Hill).

When the stock market is struggling, investors should pay special attention to dividend-paying stocks, which provide income in any market environment.

Bonus: In downturns, dividend-paying stocks are resilient. Income-oriented investors are reluctant to dump a stock as long as the dividend checks keep coming.

HELP FROM UNCLE SAM

In the past, taxes on dividend income were higher than on capital gains. Rather than provide shareholders with rising dividends, many companies chose to boost their stock prices by investing cash in the business or buying back their stock.

A buyback increases earnings per share—and also raises a company's share price—by lowering the number of outstanding shares.

Dividend income now is taxed at the same rate as capital gains. In 2003, the top tax rate on most dividend income was slashed to just 15%, down from an ordinary income tax rate of as high as 38.6%. That makes dividends more valuable to shareholders.

FINDING DIVIDEND DYNAMOS

More companies are using their cash to increase dividends. Look for the companies that have increased their dividends every year for the past decade. Unlike quarterly earnings, dividends can't be fudged. Companies that consistently pay generous dividends must have solid businesses.

If a company has a long record of raising dividends, it is going to do everything in its power not to break that habit. Investors would view any cut in a stock's dividend as a sign of serious trouble.

Lessons from a Scaredy-Cat Investor

Jean-Marie Eveillard, retired copresident and portfolio manager of First Eagle Funds, New York City, *www.first eaglefunds.com.*

After 35 years as a successful investing professional, Jean-Marie Eveillard received the Fund Manager Lifetime Achievement Award from Morningstar, Inc. It recognized his outstanding performance, constant commitment to shareholders and courage to go against what the crowd is doing.

In the fall of 2001, Mr. Eveillard was celebrated on the pages of *Bottom Line/Personal* as a "scaredy-cat" fund manager who successfully protected his global stock portfolio from the bear market. Financial talk-show host Louis Rukeyser called Mr. Eveillard "one of the best companions a cautious American investor can have on financial voyages abroad."

Here Mr. Eveillard shares his value-investing secrets…

● **You have worked in this business for decades. How has the investment game changed?** The game has really changed for the worse, as recent scandals have demonstrated. When I started in the mutual fund business in 1979, the industry was smaller and marketing people didn't run the show. Today, the industry latches on to the latest fad…and most of the mutual fund firms are more interested in gathering assets than in improving returns.

Since the late 1990s, almost all growth fund managers have become "index huggers." To match the return of the S&P 500, all they want to own are "New Economy" stocks, such as Cisco, Intel and Oracle, which are vastly overvalued. This investment style wins temporarily —but not over the long haul.

On the other hand, value managers may look like idiots for a while, but their shareholders come out winners if they stay the course.

● **What does the term "value investing" mean to you?** Warren Buffett always said that he would rather buy a good business at a fair price than a fair business at a good price. I, on the other hand, purchase what I perceive to be good businesses at fair prices as well as fair businesses at good prices.

I am more sensitive to price than to market outlook. I also watch economic and cultural trends. For example, there are cheap stocks in Japan, but I have limited my allocation there because the government hasn't been able to enact the political and financial reforms that are necessary to revive the economy.

I don't jump into a sector with such systemic risk, no matter how inexpensive its stocks are. At the same time, generally speaking, valuations are so high in the US that we have to look elsewhere.

● **How do you find all of these values?** I search for stocks that trade below the companies' intrinsic values—the amount a knowledgeable buyer would pay in cash for the entire business. I only investigate businesses that I understand. I would rather look at a plumbing business than a biotech company.

My guiding principle is to avoid the loss of money rather than to make money as quickly as possible. [*Editor's note:* Mr. Eveillard's global fund has had only two losing years during the 25 that he has been running the fund. It was down by a mere 0.26% in 1998 and down by 1.27% in 1990.]

● **What kinds of holdings are in your portfolio?** I always have focused on the small companies that fall under the radar of most institutional investors…organizations that have hidden earnings potential that is masked by conservative accounting…stocks with valuable hidden or peripheral assets, such as real estate or excess cash…and companies that have long profit-loss cycles that make them unattractive to short-term investors—temporary employment agencies and newspaper publishers, to name a few.

●**What was your gutsiest investment bet?** I don't make gutsy investments. I try to figure out the odds and play the percentages. In 2002, I bought Lucent Technologies "junk" bonds with a 13.25% coupon at 65 cents on the dollar. These bonds then traded back to par—100 cents on the dollar. Outsiders might think that buying such risky bonds took guts, but my thinking was to balance the reward of the coupon against the risk that the company would end up bankrupt, which in my opinion was low.

Lucent was losing tons of money at the time, but our analyst pointed out that the company had enough cash to survive for another two years or so, by which time the company might well be stabilized.

●**What should the average investor be doing now?** Americans should now have 25% to 35% of their portfolios in overseas funds, preferably in a diversified international fund. I don't understand the reluctance of Americans to invest overseas. One would think that all the accounting scandals of the last few years would make them more wary of domestic investments and less fearful of foreign stocks.

They also should have 5% in gold—stocks, coins or bullion—to serve as an insurance policy against a stock market collapse or global catastrophe.

●**Are there any investments that you regret making or opportunities that you missed?** Of course, but if you regret every stock you didn't buy that went up and every stock you did buy that went down, you probably shouldn't be an investment manager.

●**What has been your biggest career challenge?** The low point was during the late 1990s tech-stock bubble, when my fund lagged the market averages. Even though the fund was up by nearly 20% in 1999, more than half of Global Fund shareholders had sold out by 2000.

Sticking to my guns proved to be the right decision. It's better to lose half of your shareholders than to lose half of your portfolio value, which is what happened to numerous funds when the bubble burst. First Eagle Global's assets now are at $15.2 billion. The fund has been up every year since 2000, so my shareholders have asked, "What bear market?"

Listen In on Conference Calls

L isten to management conference calls for free over the Internet at the same time that institutional investors do. The Web sites such as *www.bestcalls.com* and *www.vcall.com* list times when conference calls are made—or check out a firm's own Web site. Listen especially closely when expert analysts repeatedly question management regarding a specific issue, such as a planned acquisition. This means the issue could affect the stock price.

John E. Deysher, CFA, portfolio manager, Pinnacle Value Fund, New York City, *www.pinnaclevaluefund.com.*

The Longevity Portfolio: How to Profit From the Aging Of America

Elizabeth K. Miller, CFA, CIC, managing director for Trevor Stewart Burton & Jacobsen Inc. in New York City. The firm manages approximately $750 million in private client and institutional assets. Its approach to investments focuses on economic trends to capture fixed-income and equity returns while providing capital protection.

P eople age 65 and older numbered an estimated 36.3 million in 2004, representing about one in eight Americans.

By 2030, that number will nearly double, representing approximately 20% of the population, according to US Census Bureau projections.

There are numerous theories about how the financial markets will react as the baby boomers access their retirement savings to finance their later years. Most baby boomers will work much longer than the previous generations, delaying their savings withdrawals as long as possible. Additionally, in coming years, many boomers are set to inherit substantial wealth from their parents. These assets probably will help finance their retirement living.

Finally, a large question mark will be the saving and investing practices of the Echo Boom—the children of baby boomers. This generation is purchasing homes and contributing to Social Security just as the baby boomers are preparing to retire.

Here are high-quality stocks that I think will benefit from the aging of America….

TRAVEL

Seniors love to travel, and increasingly they will be healthy enough to do so for many years. This will boost stocks in the leisure industry.

The all-inclusive pricing of cruises appeals to many seniors, and the fundamental outlook for the industry remains strong. You also might want to try a hotel chain with popular destinations.

HEALTH CARE

Pharmaceutical organizations are confronting near-term challenges as their blockbuster drugs of the 1990s now face patent expirations, unsafe drugs are withdrawn from the market and new drug pipelines are drying up. However, much of this bad news already is reflected in the stock prices for this industry.

The ongoing trend of developing new drugs for chronic conditions ultimately will make the pharmaceutical companies wonderful long-term investments. In the meantime, the aging population's demand for medical devices continues to grow strongly.

LIFE INSURANCE

As people reach their 50s, they then begin to purchase more annuities, which can provide tax-deferred savings and steady income during retirement. Older people also purchase whole-life insurance policies to facilitate retirement income and estate planning.

Even though New York State Attorney General Eliot Spitzer has focused attention on unfair business and sales practices in the insurance industry, these companies are fundamentally strong and can afford to make whatever regulatory changes will be required.

RESTAURANTS

With much more leisure time and disposable income than when they were raising their families, older people tend to dine out frequently.

Investment Winners And Losers in the Energy Crunch

Charles T. Maxwell, senior energy analyst with the investment firm of Weeden & Co., Greenwich, CT.

The new energy economy will help some stocks and hurt others. *Here's what to expect, by sector…*

●**Winning sectors.** *Those related to energy and conservation will prosper with breaks from market corrections…*

●Energy. The upturn in oil, natural gas and other energy stocks will continue. In 1982, energy stocks accounted for 28% of the value of the New York Stock Exchange. Energy's share now is about 7%—and is likely to reach 15% within 10 years.

●Nuclear revival. Faced with soaring costs for alternative energy, Americans will become less concerned about the safety of nuclear power. This shift will benefit companies that provide uranium …builders of turbines for nuclear power plants… and companies dealing in plant safety and disposal of spent fuel.

●Energy conservation. Expect to see more efficient electric motors and new technologies for wind utilization, hydrogen-powered vehicles, compressed natural gas for buses and photovoltaics for turning solar power into energy.

The biggest story now is energy conservation. What tech stocks were to the 1990s, energy conservation stocks will be to the 2010s and 2020s.

●**Losing sectors.** Those that rely on hydrocarbons (oil derivatives) for fuel and raw materials will suffer higher relative costs.

Examples: High hydrocarbon-consuming industries include makers of petrochemicals, cement, glass, tires and rubber. Aluminum will be needed to produce the lighter vehicles the new world energy economy will require, but the high oil and gas prices probably will depress some aluminum companies' profits.

Industries that rely on low oil prices also will suffer—automakers, builders of trucks and trucking companies, airplane builders and airlines, hotel, motel and resort operators, land developers and builders of vacation homes.

The World's Best Stock Bargains from A Top Global Stock Picker

Bernard R. Horn, Jr., president and portfolio manager of Polaris Capital Management, Inc., an investment firm located in Boston. He is portfolio manager of Polaris Global Value Fund (PGVFX), a no-load fund that invests in US and foreign stocks. 888-263-5594, *www.polariscapital.com.*

Bernard Horn, Jr., has built a reputation for finding bargain stocks from around the world. *He thinks the real values are to be found abroad...*

FAVORITE MARKETS

Based on where we see the best values, our favorite markets are the United Kingdom and Japan. Other Asian economies and South Africa are close behind.

Price check: Our ideal company today has free cash flow that is growing at about its country's growth rate for gross domestic product (GDP). It sells at a price-to-free-cash-flow ratio of less than the world average of 9.

STOCKS WE LIKE

Here are the best global values today...

- **Automotive suppliers.** We are concerned about weaker car manufacturers because there is so much global overcapacity. We do like the auto suppliers.

- **British home builders.*** The housing market still is strong in Great Britain.

- **Japanese utilities.** Utilities are inexpensive and should benefit from the country's economic recovery.

- **Korean electronics.** Korea's growing industrial base and its location in the heart of Asia should help it produce faster economic growth than either the US or Europe.

US VALUE

You can still find some pockets of value in the US...

*These stocks do not trade as American depositary receipts (ADRs) but can be bought in the local market.

- **Health-care providers.** Since most health-care spending can't be postponed, this industry can raise prices without much resistance.

- **Banks.** Banks typically do well as interest rates rise—rates charged on loans go up faster than the bank's own borrowing costs. We are interested in small regionals that could become takeover targets.

- **Utilities.** Utilities now have strong enough growth prospects to offset increased borrowing costs from higher rates.

- **Oil.** Oil prices are at historic highs, and new oil supplies are not keeping up with demand. I don't expect a sharp decline any time soon. Oil also is a hedge against political uncertainty. We find value in large integrated global companies.

- **Natural resources.** Stronger economies will increase demand for raw materials.

Best Way to Buy Foreign Stocks Now

Vivian Lewis, editor of *Global Investing,* New York City, *www.global-investing.com.*

There hasn't been a single year since 1970 in which the US was the best performer among the world's 23 largest stock markets. In 2005, the US ranked seventeenth.** Many investors know that foreign stocks provide valuable diversification. Yet so few of us keep 20% to 25% of our long-term stock portfolios in foreign stocks, as many advisers recommend.

One reason: Costs. Commissions for foreign stocks can be hefty. Also, before purchasing them, you must convert dollars into the foreign currency and pay an exchange transaction fee.

Another hurdle: The typical minimum purchase amount is $20,000 per foreign stock.

There is a cheaper, easier way for investors who want to own individual stocks to purchase foreign shares—American depositary receipts (ADRs). These US securities represent a fixed number of foreign shares. Brokers create ADRs

**According to financial adviser Robert Kreitler, using data from MSCI.

by buying foreign shares and depositing them in American banks. ADRs of more than 2,000 foreign companies trade on US exchanges. Such companies must meet US accounting standards.

Buying an ADR is as easy as purchasing a US stock. You pay standard commissions, and there is no need to exchange currency. Dividends are paid in dollars. Foreign taxes withheld from dividends can be recovered each year via the foreign tax credit on your income tax return.

GETTING DIVERSIFIED

Many multinationals offer ADRs, but you will get little diversification from the best-known names. For example, Nestlé is a Swiss company with an ADR, but it derives most of its sales from the US. Not surprisingly, its shares often track major US stock indexes.

To get better diversification, include ADRs of some smaller companies.

Insider Trading Alert

Beware of insider trading if you work for—or have access to any information on—a public company. To avoid this illegal act, ask anyone who gives you a stock tip where he/she got the information. Make sure the information is either publicly available or that it is the result of independent research and that there is no agreement to keep the information confidential. Never give inside information to anyone, even your spouse. And, don't encourage family members to buy or sell stock in your company—the transactions may look suspicious even if they are innocent. Also, learn your company's trading policies when you buy or sell shares.

Dan Brecher, Esq., a New York City attorney specializing in claims against brokerage firms.

Protect Your Stock's Value With Options

If a stock is priced at $100/share for example, buy *put options* that give you the right to sell the stock at $90/share within 12 or 24 months. Then sell *call options,* which let someone else have the right to buy your stock at $120/share over the same period. This structure is called a *collar.* The cost of the put and the proceeds from the call should be equal to restrict your downside and ensure that you get at least $90/share. If the stock price falls below $90, you still can sell it for $90. If it rises above $120, you can sell it or buy back the call option.

Caution: Options trading is very complex— consult a knowledgeable financial adviser.

Christopher Cordaro, CFA and CFP, Regent Atlantic Capital LLC, Chatham, NJ.

Investing in Exchange-Traded Funds: A Shrewd Idea with Big Tax Benefits

David W. Cowles, CPA, CFP, director of investments, Boone Financial Advisors, 433 California St., San Francisco 94104. He has served on the board of directors of the Financial Planning Association's San Francisco chapter.

The use of exchange-traded funds (ETFs) is now soaring. Just five years ago, there were only about 35 ETFs. Today, there are more than 300, representing many types of securities, so investors can put together a diversified portfolio of ETFs. Or, ETFs may be used to fill out a portfolio that includes other, more traditional investments.

While there are several reasons for their increasing popularity, such as low expense ratios, tax benefits are among the advantages of ETFs that are most prized by investors.

ETFs hold a number of different securities, providing diversification. Unlike mutual funds, though, ETFs trade on exchanges like stocks. An ETF will have an initial public offering of shares and perhaps some secondary offerings. Subsequently, those shares trade among investors through brokers, rather than with the fund company.

Each ETF is designed to track a particular index. It might be a stock market index, such as the S&P 500, or a less familiar index tracking intermediate-term bonds, or an assortment of real estate securities, for example.

TAMING TURNOVER

Like index funds, ETFs are tax efficient.

Key: An ETF generally holds the stocks or the bonds that make up a particular index. The components of indexes seldom change. Thus, ETFs seldom sell securities. They're true buy-and-hold vehicles.

Advantage: Unlike mutual funds, ETFs usually do not have trading gains. In some years, trading gains have created huge tax headaches for mutual fund investors, but ETF holders have not had this problem.

For example, say you invest in a successful mutual fund. Then a month later, the manager decides to take profits on oil stocks and move into utilities.

"Your share" of the oil-stock profits will be passed through to you, even though you were not a shareholder while those oil profits were made. Some of these profits may be short-term gains, taxed at steep ordinary income rates.

Moreover, you will owe tax currently even if you reinvest the capital gains distribution as most investors do.

Trap: This unpleasant scenario can be especially hard to take when the stock market turns down. In a bad market, mutual fund investors often redeem shares, forcing managers to liquidate appreciated holdings to raise cash.

Example: Janus Fund lost nearly 15% in 2000, the year the tech-stock bubble burst. Yet investors had to pay tax on nearly $4 per share in capital gains distributions at a time when the fund's share price was around $35.

This experience was by no means unique. Many funds had larger losses and made larger distributions of taxable gains.

Bottom line: When you invest in a low-turnover, index-tracking ETF, you avoid this type of tax trouble.

SPECIAL TREATMENT

Certain mutual funds offer low turnover and tax efficiency, as well. Indeed, there are many index mutual funds from which to choose.

But, even when compared with index mutual funds, ETFs offer tax advantages.

Key: When they alter their portfolios due to a change in the underlying index, ETFs do not sell the securities they hold. Instead, they make "in-kind redemptions." These transactions involve large blocks of shares transferred among arbitragers, specialists and market makers.

Loophole: Under the Internal Revenue Code, in-kind redemptions do not generate taxable gains to a fund. That's true even when the securities transferred by the fund have appreciated in value.

ANOTHER BENEFIT

Similarly, a rash of sales won't affect investors in an ETF as much as redemptions might hurt those in an index mutual fund.

For instance, Vanguard REIT Index Fund (a real estate investment trust mutual fund) currently has unrealized capital gains equal to 30% of its value. If investor interest in real estate stocks suddenly plummets and there are massive shareholder redemptions, this fund would have to sell stocks, realizing taxable gains.

These gains would then be distributed to all remaining shareholders, even those who didn't sell shares.

The difference: If, instead of a mutual fund, you held an ETF that invests in REITs, such as the streetTRACKS's Wilshire REIT Index Fund (AMEX:RWR), any shareholder selling would not cause capital gains distributions because there would be no change to the underlying stocks held in the portfolio.

Only the selling shareholders might incur capital gains. The continuing shareholders of this ETF would not owe taxes because of other shareholders' transactions.

Bottom line: Many ETFs have been on the market for years without ever having to make a distribution of taxable capital gains to their shareholders.

CLEANING UP

The tax advantages of ETFs can go well beyond the avoidance of unwanted capital gains distributions.

One popular strategy among savvy investors is "loss harvesting." When a stock or fund decreases in value, a capital loss can be taken.

Advantage: Realized capital losses can offset capital gains, present or future, essentially making gains tax free.

Trap: Once a loss has been taken, the same security can't be repurchased during the next 30 days.

That's where an ETF can be used. An ETF can serve as a replacement for the security that you have sold, long or short term.

For example, you hold shares in a leading pharmaceutical company, but a highly publicized study raises doubts about one of its drugs, sending the stock price down.

Now you have a large paper loss on that stock—but you have not lost faith in the stock or the drug sector as a good holding.

Strategy: Sell the drug stock to realize a capital loss for tax purposes. You can't buy back the stock immediately, but you can buy an ETF such as Pharmaceutical HOLDRS (AMEX:PPH), which owns major drug companies.

Such a sale and purchase does not violate the wash-sale rules and won't jeopardize your tax loss.

Outcome: If you wish, after 30 days you can repurchase the drug stock you've sold. By then, the wash-sale rules don't apply.

If the stock has rebounded during your 30-day "time-out," you will pick up at least some of the gain through holding the ETF.

Related strategy: You could buy an ETF immediately after taking a loss on a similar mutual fund, without triggering a wash sale.

In addition, you can take a loss on one ETF and buy another right away, even if the replacement is in the same asset class.

Let's say that large-cap stocks lose ground this year, so your holding of iShares S&P 500 Index (AMEX:IVV), one large-cap ETF, is underwater. You can take a tax loss and immediately purchase iShares Russell 1000 Index (AMEX:IWB).

Although these two ETFs are highly correlated, they track different indexes so they're not identical. Selling one and buying the other the same day won't annul your tax loss.

Key: Such tactics are practical because ETFs do not impose redemption fees on investors who buy and sell soon afterward. Such fees are increasingly common among mutual funds.

Caution: While ETF investors avoid redemption fees, they must pay transaction costs on each trade, just as they do when trading stocks. Therefore, you'll probably do best by buying and selling ETFs through an ultra-low-cost discount broker.

THE RIGHT ACCOUNT

To take advantage of the tax benefits, ETFs should be held in a taxable account. If you hold ETFs in a tax-deferred retirement account, you will enjoy other ETF advantages, such as low expenses and easy tradability, but all their tax advantages will be wasted. For more information about ETFs, log on to *www.etfconnect.com,* sponsored by Nuveen Investments, and *www. morningstar.com.*

Additional Tax-Sheltered Alternatives to Mutual Funds

Marilyn Gunther, CFP, president, Center for Financial Planning, 26211 Central Park Blvd., Southfield, MI 48073. A past president of the Michigan International Association for Financial Planning, she has been named one of the nation's top financial advisers by *Worth* and *Medical Economics* magazines.

Several major mutual fund families have been implicated in highly publicized scandals. All these families permitted selected investors to engage in improper trading and pocket no-risk, short-term profits. Such in-and-out moves may have diluted the earnings of long-term shareholders while increasing expenses that all must bear.

Going forward: There is no way to know whether more fund families will be named. However, you may want to seek other ways to invest besides (or in addition to) mutual funds.

Bonus: Some alternatives to mutual funds offer tax advantages to investors.

INDIVIDUAL SECURITIES

By buying individual stocks and bonds, you can control your own tax position. Buying and holding winners, for example, can defer taxable gains. If you take gains, you can take offsetting losses to avoid owing tax.

What's more, you can determine your own investment strategy.

Example: You can emphasize funds with dividend-paying stocks to take advantage of the 15% tax rate on dividends.

SEPARATE ACCOUNTS

Also known as managed or "wrap" accounts, these programs are offered by numerous financial advisers.

How they work: After going over all your goals, risk tolerance, etc., the adviser will suggest a lineup of money managers. Each money manager will pick the securities that you'll own in a given category.

Examples: One manager might focus on large-cap domestic growth stocks, another on stocks from developed foreign markets, etc.

Such an approach provides you with a number of advantages…

● **Diversification.** You'll own many different securities in multiple asset classes.

● **Professional portfolio management.** Your stocks and bonds will be chosen by people who have solid performance records.

● **Access to elite managers.** By investing through these programs, investors with moderate-sized portfolios may have access to money managers who usually are available only to the very wealthy.

● **Congruence of interests.** Typically, investors in these programs pay an asset-based fee rather than commissions. Your adviser is motivated to enlarge your account, not churn it.

● **Less chance of trading improprieties.** What about exposure to the improper trading practices of some mutual funds? With a separate accounts program, you own your own securities. If another investor takes quick profits, it won't affect yours.

● **Tax efficiency.** Participating managers promise to customize trading to take investors' tax situations into account. They can hold on to the winners, take losses and refrain from selling until securities qualify for long-term gains, etc.

VARIABLE ANNUITIES

These investments offer buyers the chance to choose among subaccounts, many of which resemble stock or bond funds. Your contract value will grow or shrink, depending on how these subaccounts perform.

Caution: Many variable annuity subaccounts are managed by the same companies that run mutual funds. Check to see if you're comfortable with the people who'll be responsible for your investments.

Although mutual fund families do manage money in variable annuities, improper trading practices are less likely due to higher fees and the lack of easy liquidity.

If you invest within a variable annuity, you can enjoy several tax benefits…

● **Tax-free buildup.** Investment earnings will not be taxed as long as they are held within the annuity.

● **Tax-free switches.** You can move money from one equity subaccount to another without paying any tax.

Outside of an annuity, on the other hand, switching among mutual funds is considered a taxable event. That's true even within the same fund family.

● **Tax-free exchanges.** You can replace one annuity contract with another without owing tax, under Section 1035 of the Tax Code.

● **No capital gains distributions.** As a mutual fund investor, you owe taxes on the fund's realized net gains, even if you didn't sell your fund shares. Annuities don't pay out such gains.

● **Tax-sheltered income.** If you choose to annuitize a variable annuity and receive lifelong income, part of your payment stream will be a tax-free return of capital.

Trap: Variable annuities have tax disadvantages, as well. Investment earnings are taxed at ordinary income rates when withdrawn. You don't enjoy the low tax on capital gains.

Strategy: If you keep money in a variable annuity for 10 years or longer, the value of tax deferral may outweigh the loss of the capital gains tax break. A long holding period also will reduce your exposure to surrender charges for liquidating the annuity before a certain minimum holding period.

Be sure to avoid withdrawals before age 59½. Such distributions are usually subject to a 10% penalty tax, in addition to income tax.

Other advantages: Some variable annuities now offer "living benefits" by offering you the chance to gradually withdraw the amount you have put in, even if your chosen subaccounts lose money.

Other variable annuities promise to increase your account value by at least 5% per year. In order to cash in on this guarantee, you must annuitize the contract with the same insurance company.

Such guarantees enable you to invest in stock market subaccounts without worrying about the loss of money.

These guarantees come at a price. You'll pay higher expenses each year, so weigh the costs before buying.

VARIABLE LIFE INSURANCE

If you have a need for life insurance, consider investing inside a variable life insurance policy. In some ways, these resemble variable annuities. You invest via mutual fund look-alikes. Current income taxes are avoided, and the chances of trading improprieties are reduced by higher fees.

The tax benefits of variable life insurance are even more substantial than they are for variable annuities…

●**Death benefits.** At your death, your beneficiaries will receive insurance proceeds that exceed the policy's cash value. Typically, these proceeds will be free of income tax.

●**Living benefits.** You can take policy loans and withdrawals, and if handled carefully, these distributions can provide an ongoing stream of tax-free cash flow.

Trap: If you withdraw or borrow too heavily, the policy will lapse and deferred income tax will be due.

Again, you'll have to hold on to a variable life policy for a period of years before the tax benefits offset the up-front costs. But, if you have a real need for life insurance, these vehicles can enable you to avoid mutual fund pitfalls and gain access to tax-free investment income.

Finding Funds You Can Trust

To find a mutual fund you can trust, look for a high-quality firm that leads the way in corporate governance.

Key measures we look at: How investors have done with the firm's funds…whether the firm launches new funds responsibly…the experience, skill and integrity of management… clarity of communication with shareholders… internal regulatory compliance and risk controls.

Among the large firms that meet these criteria now: American Funds, Fidelity Investments, T. Rowe Price Group and The Vanguard Group.

Smaller firms include: Davis Selected Advisers, Dodge & Cox and Longleaf Partners.

This is by no means an exhaustive list of the firms with the highest standards.

For more information, you can research funds on the Morningstar database at many public libraries or at *www.morningstar.com.*

Russel Kinnel, director of mutual fund research, Morningstar, Inc., Chicago. He edits *Morningstar FundInvestor.*

Smarter Mutual Fund Buying

Owning shares in too many mutual funds can hurt returns. If you have more than 10 mutual funds, your paperwork, including tax record-keeping, becomes onerous…fees may be higher than necessary because some fund families charge fees for transfers among funds and tax-preparation fees increase with each holding…and fund holdings may overlap, reducing diversification.

Best: Choose one fund in each of these categories—large-cap stock, mid-cap stock, small-cap stock (a growth and value for each) as well as international stock, natural resources stock, bonds and real estate investment trusts (REITs).

Avoid narrowly focused funds, such as single-industry or single-region funds. If you have too many funds, sell ones with similar objectives—even if you have to pay capital gains tax.

Ric Edelman, chairman of Edelman Financial Services Inc., Fairfax, VA, which manages $2.4 billion in assets for clients throughout the country. He is author of *Discover the Wealth Within You* (HarperCollins).

About Corporate Bonds

The inflation-linked corporate bonds provide higher yields than Treasury inflation-protected securities (TIPS) but are not federally guaranteed. With TIPS, the principal is adjusted twice a year to reflect changes in the Consumer Price Index, but you receive these adjustments when the bond matures, and coupon payments are semiannual. With the corporate bonds, you will receive interest and principal adjustments monthly. Buy bonds rated A or better.

Marilyn Cohen, president of Envision Capital Management, Inc., Los Angeles, *www.envisioncap.com.* She is also author of *The Bond Bible* (Prentice Hall).

Pros and Cons of Zero-Coupon Bonds

No investment is 100% safe, however zero-coupon bonds are high on the list. If you require money for a family member's college tuition, retirement or to meet other long-term financial goals, they are a good solution.

Zeros, unlike regular bonds, pay no interest until maturity, hence the name "zero coupon." (In bond jargon, the word "coupon" means "interest.") They are sold at a deep discount, well below the $1,000 standard bond price. The interest then builds up and is paid to the bond owner in a lump sum upon maturity.

There are two types—US Treasury zeros and municipal zeros. (There are also a handful of corporate zeros, but they are very rare.)

Three disadvantages: (1) Yields are lower than for ordinary bonds—often one-half to one percentage point lower. (2) The IRS insists that taxes be paid annually on zeros, even though the owner is not receiving interest payments. (3) Their prices in the secondary market are quite volatile—you could conceivably lose money if you had to sell before maturity.

You Don't Need A Lot of Money To Make It Big in Real Estate

Real estate entrepreneur Carleton Sheets, author of *Real Estate: The World's Greatest Wealth Builder* (Bonus) and creator of the training program "How to Buy Your First Home or Investment Property with No Down Payment." For more information, go to *www.carletonsheets.com.*

The days of small-time investors making a killing in real estate are now over. Home prices in such hot markets as Boston and San Francisco have nearly tripled since 1999. Going forward, rising inflation and a strengthening economy will cause the mortgage rates to climb, eroding profits on real estate investments until rents have a chance to catch up. The Federal Reserve predicts that US housing prices during the next two years will grow at the slowest pace in more than three decades.

Despite these trends, one real estate strategy will excel—buying and renting out single-family homes. You don't have to be wealthy to be a successful landlord. You can use the equity in your existing home to get started, and you may qualify for generous tax breaks.

Owning one or two rental properties takes less time—and is less risky—than managing a stock portfolio, and there's always an up-and-coming real estate market that is waiting to be discovered.

Reality check: Owning rental property is a classic get-rich-*slow* strategy. Rental income covers the mortgage payments and operating expenses while providing you with a small positive cash flow.

However, you can increase the rent to keep up with or outpace inflation over the long term. You also can expect a profit when you sell—historically, home values have appreciated by about 5% a year, which is above and beyond the rental income.

How to start making money in single-family properties…

THE RIGHT KIND OF HOUSE

●**Look within a 20-mile radius of where you live.** You'll be better able to figure out the value of real estate in a familiar area. Unless you live in a hot market, you should be able to find affordable properties in your town.

If you can't afford property in your town, expand your radius to 50 miles. Look for mid-income neighborhoods, since homes in these neighborhoods stand the best chance of appreciating in price.

●**Buy sought-after properties.** Single-family homes with three bedrooms and two bathrooms appeal to a range of tenants. Avoid houses with only one or two bedrooms—they may be less expensive, but they are harder to rent or sell.

Also avoid condominiums and co-ops—you lack control. The building association may reserve the right to approve tenants. For instance, applicants might be turned down if they are pet owners.

●**Look for the popular features.** Choose a house that has at least one of the features that renters desire—fenced-in yard…garage…fireplace…central air-conditioning…finished basement…or proximity to the best schools, public transportation and supermarkets and shopping districts.

THE RIGHT DEAL

●**To ensure that the price is right, look up sales of comparable properties.** *My favorite resources for valuing property…*

●The recorder's office at your county courthouse has records of a home's past and current owners and sale prices.

●The tax assessor's office has information on a property's assessed value, its square footage, improvements, etc.

You also may find this information on-line—*www.statelocalgov.net* has links to municipal sites for all states.

●DataQuick.com (888-604-3282) provides reports on comparable sales, local crime rates, neighborhood demographics and real estate market trends. *Cost:* $5* to $10 per report.

●**Make sure that you will profit from the investment.** Any rental property should generate monthly income of at least 1% of the purchase price.

Example: I was interested in a house in an area where the rents were about $900 per month. Therefore, I knew that I could pay up to $90,000 for the house ($900 is 1% of $90,000). Even after I subtracted all of my projected expenses, including mortgage payments, maintenance costs, property taxes and insurance, I was left with cash flow of $100 a month.

TURNAROUND OPPORTUNITIES

●**Consider deeply discounted properties as you become more experienced.** *They are likely to need work and may entail complex legal issues…*

●Real estate owned (REO) properties. Banks and institutional lenders are anxious to sell these foreclosed properties. Ask to see the REO lists at local banks. Try my site, *www.bankforeclosurelist.com,* to view more than 40,000 REO properties around the country.

●Government-auctioned property. Contact Housing and Urban Development (202-708-1112, *www.hud.gov*)…or Department of the Treasury (202-622-2000, *www.treas.gov/auctions*) for information on auctions of federally owned properties.

FINANCING OPTIONS

●**Try to get financing from the seller.** You'll be able to make a lower down payment

*All prices subject to change.

than if you finance through a bank. In today's rental market, I find that as much as 15% of sellers are willing and able to finance purchases.

The seller acts just like a bank, allowing you to use the property as collateral. You issue the seller a note with an agreed-upon interest rate (similar to the prevailing bank rate), then make mortgage payments directly to him/her.

If you default on your payments, the seller can foreclose on the property. As with any real estate deal, you should use an attorney or title company to assist with the closing.

Many sellers want extra assurances that you will make your mortgage payments. *Here's what you can offer…*

●**Earmark part of the rent you collect toward your principal.**

Example: When a student from my real estate seminar wanted to buy a residential property in Florida, the seller was willing to finance the $180,000 purchase but wanted 10% up front. The student only had $10,000. To close the deal, he gave the seller preference on the property's cash flow—the first $500 in rent each month—until the additional $8,000 was collected.

●**Put up more collateral than the property is worth**—a "blanket mortgage."

Example: Another student found a rental house that was selling for $480,000. The student already owned other property, and he had no cash for a down payment. Therefore, he offered additional collateral—a property he owned in Vermont that was worth $60,000 and his personal residence in which he had $40,000 worth of equity. In lieu of a down payment, he put up $580,000 in collateral for the $480,000 house.

Important: Use a blanket mortgage only if you are absolutely confident that you can make your mortgage payments.

MANAGING THE PROPERTY

●**Hire a management company** if you do not want to maintain the property yourself.

Typical cost: Half of one month's rent for finding and screening the tenants…10% of the gross monthly rent for managing the property. Factor this in when you assess the net income of a prospective purchase. Ask for referrals from landlords in the area.

●**Run a credit and criminal check on any prospective tenants.** Ask for references from employers and past landlords. Companies such as Intelius (*www.intelius.com*) can run background checks for a fee.

●**Reward renters for prompt payments.** I charge rent that is 5% to 10% higher than the going rate, then offer that amount as a rental discount if the tenant pays on time.

●**Charge more than the monthly rent for the security deposit.** Otherwise, tenants may skip the last month's rent and tell you to use the deposit instead.

●**Keep two months' rental income in reserve** to protect against vacancies.

●**Make sure you have adequate property and liability coverage.** Consult an agent who has insured rental properties.

Helpful resources…

●Landlord.com (408-374-9400) provides free forms, such as lease agreements, as well as online calculators.

●National Association of Independent Landlords (800-352-3395, *www.nail-usa.com*) has links to state laws.

Gigantic Tax Breaks Just For Real Estate Investors

William G. Brennan, CPA/PFS, CFP, Capital Management Group, LLC, 1730 Rhode Island Ave. NW, Washington, DC 20036. Mr. Brennan is a frequently quoted expert who has written extensively on the topics of income tax and investment planning.

Today's low interest rates and recent property appreciation may entice you to buy investment real estate. If you take such a step, focus first on the deal's profit possibilities.

But also factor in the following tax breaks, which can make a successful real estate venture even more rewarding.

TAX-FREE CASH FLOW

Real estate investors may claim some of the noncash deductions, such as depreciation. So, if you receive net positive cash flow from your property, some or all of that cash may avoid immediate income taxation.

For example, you buy a small office building. This year, your net cash flow from rents, after paying all of your expenses, puts $10,000 in your pocket. For tax purposes, though, you wind up with an $8,000 loss, after taking depreciation tax deductions. Therefore, you owe no tax on the $10,000 you put in your pocket.

Trap: The depreciation deductions will lower your basis in the property. A lower basis, in turn, will increase your capital gains tax on an eventual sale.

Loophole: Under the current law, the tax on prior depreciation deductions is capped at 25%. Thus, you may defer income tax normally owed at rates up to 35% and pay those taxes years later at a 25% rate.

The ultimate loophole: Under current law, certain assets (including real estate) left to heirs get a basis step-up to market value. Thus, if you hold on to your investment property until death, the tax-free cash flow you receive during your lifetime will remain untaxed.

LOSS DEDUCTIONS

In the above example, you wound up with an $8,000 paper loss, after depreciation. Can you deduct such a loss? Perhaps.

Your ability to deduct such losses depends on several factors, especially your adjusted gross income (AGI).

Basic rule: Losses from rental properties are known as passive losses. For many taxpayers, such losses are deductible, up to $25,000 per year.

Required: For you to take the full $25,000 deduction, your modified AGI (MAGI) must be no more than $100,000. Over $100,000, this deduction is phased out, $1 for every $2 over the threshold.

Thus, you can take no deduction when your MAGI is $150,000 or greater.

Let's say you own a rental property that turns in tax losses every year. This year, your MAGI is $95,000. You can deduct losses up to $25,000.

Next year, your MAGI goes up to $130,000. You're $30,000 over the threshold, so your maximum loss is cut by $15,000 ($30,000 ÷ 2).

You can deduct up to $10,000 worth of losses from this rental property.

Say your MAGI reaches $160,000 the following year. Now you can deduct no losses, in most cases.

In our example, with an $8,000 paper loss, you can have MAGI up to $134,000 ($150,000 − $16,000) and take a full deduction right away. With a MAGI of $136,000, for instance, only $7,000 can be deducted currently.

Loophole: Any passive losses that you cannot deduct right away may be carried over to future years, where they can offset any income from rental properties.

Eventually, when the property is sold, any unused losses will be deductible against your ordinary income in the year of sale. The sale proceeds, meanwhile, will be taxed at favorable capital gains rates.

Loophole: The laws are more favorable if you spend so much time as a landlord that you get to be treated as a real estate professional.

Required: If you spend more than half of your working time on real estate and at least 750 hours a year, you're entitled to deduct any losses right away, regardless of your AGI.

LEARNING TO LOVE LEVERAGE

You'll probably want to buy real estate with as small a down payment (and as much borrowed money) as possible, as long as you can borrow at an attractive fixed rate.

Strategy: When you borrow money to buy investment property, ask for the debt to be "qualified nonrecourse." This means that only the property (not your other assets) secures the debt. Your downside is limited if things don't work out.

Currently interest rates on real estate loans are relatively low, by historical standards. And, that only makes the use of leverage even more appealing. Leverage, in turn, will magnify any gains on investment property.

For example, you buy investment property for $400,000, making an $80,000 (20%) down payment. A few years later, your property has grown in value to $500,000.

That's a $100,000 profit on an $80,000 outlay —a 125% gain on a 25% increase in the property's value.

Tax break: The interest you pay on this loan will be tax deductible against your income from the property.

And, refinancing an appreciated property can allow you to pull out tax-free cash.

For instance, as above, you buy a property for $400,000, putting $80,000 down, and see it appreciate in value to $500,000.

Strategy: Instead of selling, triggering a tax, you refinance the property. With property valued at $500,000, you might be able to borrow $400,000 (an 80% loan-to-value ratio).

Result: You can use your new loan to pay off what's left of the original $320,000 loan and keep the excess $80,000 tax free. Borrowing money won't create a tax obligation.

Drawback: Now you're paying interest (perhaps at a higher rate) on a $400,000 loan, not a $320,000 loan, so your payments will be higher. However, the fact that your property has appreciated in value may indicate your rental income has gone up or could go up, so you'll be able to cover the higher debt service.

ENDGAMES

As mentioned, rather than sell your property, triggering a tax bill, you can hold on until death. Your heirs may avoid paying income tax because of a basis step-up.

Note: Estate tax might still apply.

Alternative: Enter into a *like-kind exchange* —generally referred to as a "Section 1031" exchange after a section of the Tax Code—for a different investment property. Such a maneuver may defer any taxable gains.

Let's say you are ready to retire and move to Florida. You no longer wish to manage the big office building you own up north, especially now that you would be a long-distance landlord.

Strategy: Sell your office building, and have the proceeds held by an unrelated intermediary. Then find a low-maintenance property, such as a self-storage center, selling for approximately the same price near your new home in Florida.

Instruct the intermediary to use the proceeds from the original sale to buy the replacement property on your behalf.

Caution: There are various deadlines you have to adhere to guarantee that such an exchange will be tax free. Working with an experienced professional, either an attorney or accountant, is recommended.

Alternatively, you can do an Internet search under "1031 exchanges" to locate companies specializing in these transactions. And consult someone you trust in the real estate business for a referral.

As long as you enjoy neither cash from the transaction nor debt reduction, you can exchange properties in this manner tax free.

Caution: A tax-free exchange reduces the depreciable basis of the replacement property.

Variation: You can exchange commercial property for a home that you rent to tenants. If the rules are followed, no tax will be due.

Bonus: In the future, you can move into the house yourself without triggering any tax. After living in the house for two or more years, you can sell it and claim the $250,000 capital gains exclusion on the sale of a primary residence, or $500,000 if you're married.

Year-End Tax Moves for Investors

Glenn Frank, CPA, PFS, CFP, senior vice president at Wachovia Wealth Management, Inc. in Waltham, MA. He is listed among the nation's top 100 wealth advisers by *Worth*.

Investors may have significant gains as well as losses for this seesaw year. This will generate opportunities as well as pitfalls.

Key: The moves you make between now and year-end can pay off, when you file this year's tax return. Some of the moves are basic, others sophisticated.

THE $3,000 QUESTION

Try to wind up the year with a net capital loss of at least $3,000.

Loophole: A net capital loss up to $3,000 can be deducted from your ordinary income. In a 35% federal tax bracket, for example, you can save $1,050 (35% of $3,000). Your total tax savings may be even greater, counting state and local income tax.

Trap: If you fail to offset all of your capital gains, you may wind up with short-term gains on positions sold after you've held them a year or less. Such gains will be taxed as ordinary income, at rates of up to 35% on your federal tax return.

Excess losses: What if your net capital loss is greater than $3,000? Any excess loss can be carried forward to future years to offset future capital gains. If you have no gains to offset in a future year, loss carry forwards may be deducted, up to $3,000 per year.

Strategy: Tally up realized gains and losses before year-end. Make trades that will give you a $3,000 net loss.

Example: Counting all your trades so far this year, you have a $10,000 net capital gain. You can sell securities by year-end, realizing $13,000 worth of losses, for a $3,000 net loss.

Key: Don't be reluctant to take additional capital losses. If you wind up the year with a net capital loss that's over $3,000, the overage is "banked" for use in the future.

WASH-SALE RULES

After you sell securities at a loss, you must be careful how you reinvest.

Trap: If you buy back the same securities right away, your loss won't be recognized, for tax purposes. *To lock in the tax loss...*

●**Wait 31 days.** After that, you can buy back the same stock or bond you sold. But, if you're out of the market for that long, you might miss a quick run-up in the price of that security.

●**Double up.** Yet another way to avert the wash-sale trap is to *first* buy a similar position to the one you already own and want to sell for a loss. Wait for 31 days, then sell your original lot.

Example: You plan to take a tax loss on 500 shares of Mattel but you think the company's stock may bounce back shortly. So you buy another 500 shares of Mattel.

After waiting 31 days, you sell the first lot at a loss. You've maintained your position (from the second lot you purchased) yet you still have a deductible tax loss.

Caution: This strategy eliminates the risk that a stock will run up while you're not holding it, but creates the risk that the stock collapses while you're holding an enlarged position.

Key: A double-up strategy must be in place by late November in order to create a tax loss for the year.

●**Reinvest in something similar.** As long as the replacement security is not substantially identical to the one you sold at a loss, that loss will be allowed on an immediate sale (including one made before 31 days are up).

Example: If you sold Pfizer at a loss, you can reinvest the proceeds in Merck right away. The two drug stocks may move in sync with their industry, but the results won't be exactly the same.

Bond strategy: Rising interest rates have depressed bond prices. You could enter into a "bond swap" that's arranged by your broker, in which you take a tax loss on bonds you hold while replacing them with bonds that are similar but from a different issuer or with a different maturity.

FUND FACTS

When you calculate your gains and losses for the year, don't forget to include capital gains distributions from mutual funds.

Trap: Mutual funds are required to distribute net realized gains to shareholders. If you hold a fund in a taxable account, such distributions are taxable income, even if you choose to reinvest them in the fund.

Hedge funds also may make taxable distributions of capital gains to investors.

Above, it was assumed that you had $10,000 worth of net realized capital gains from trading for the year. If you also receive $2,000 worth of capital gains distributions from funds, your net gain for the year goes up to $12,000.

Thus, you need to realize $15,000 worth of losses to wind up the year with a $3,000 net capital loss.

Strategy: Include capital gains distributions when you make your year-end calculations. Call your fund companies to find out if such distributions are planned for December.

Trap: Some fund distributions are short term. Again, net short-term gains are heavily taxed, at rates up to 35%, so you should try for offsetting capital losses.

Caution: Don't invest in a mutual fund just before a scheduled capital gains distribution. You'll get some of your own money back right away…and owe tax on that payout! Instead, check with the fund before investing around year-end. Wait to buy until after the record date of the distribution.

TAX-FREE GAINS

What if, instead of net gains for the year, you are sitting with a large realized loss instead?

Loophole: In this situation, you may be able to take capital gains, tax free.

For example, say you have $10,000 worth of net capital losses so far this year. You can take $7,000 worth of capital gains by year-end (including fund distributions).

Result: You'll still wind up with a $3,000 net loss, which you can deduct. The proceeds from your year-end gains won't be taxed.

Loophole: If you wish, you can take gains and immediately reinvest in the same security that you sold. The wash-sale rules do not apply to gains.

Why would you do this? The sale and repurchase increases your basis (price paid) in that security. A higher basis, in turn, probably will reduce the tax you'll owe on a future sale.

Key: Selling and immediately repurchasing the same security means that you'd rather have a higher basis on the appreciated holding than a capital loss you can carry forward. Also, keep any transaction costs in mind.

LOST CAUSES

Did you buy stock in a business that failed? If so, you can take a capital loss in the year that your holding becomes worthless.

Key: To be considered worthless, a security you own must have absolutely no value. If it has scant value, you can't claim a capital loss.

Trap: Demonstrating worthlessness, for tax purposes, may be difficult.

Strategy: Realize your capital loss by selling your interest in the business to an unrelated party for a nominal amount.

Example: You can sell a worthless security to your neighbor or the brokerage firm for

$1. As long as you make the sale by December 31, you can claim a capital loss for 2006.

AMT Warning: The Seven Worst Traps For Investors

Sidney Kess, attorney and CPA at 10 Rockefeller Plaza, New York City 10020. Mr. Kess is the coauthor/consulting editor of *Financial and Estate Planning* and coauthor of *1040 Preparation and Planning Guide 2006* (both from CCH). Over the years, he has taught tax law to more than 710,000 tax professionals.

The alternative minimum tax (AMT) creates traps for unwary investors that may cost them deductions and increase the tax due on normally tax-favored income.

Make it your goal to maximize investment returns after tax—not to avoid AMT. In some cases, AMT may be avoided. While in others, it should be willingly incurred but managed to avoid costly mistakes.

HOW THE AMT WORKS

The AMT is a tax computation every taxpayer must consider. It increases the tax owed by a growing number of people every year. Under AMT, many deductions and other tax breaks available under normal rules are disallowed.

Examples: Personal exemptions; the federal deduction for state and local taxes.

The AMT then applies to the resulting "AMT income" at a rate of 26% or 28%. The final tax bill owed is the greater of that computed under regular tax or AMT rules.

In 2005, the amount of income exempt from AMT was only $50,800 on a joint tax return or $40,250 on a single return—so even those with moderate incomes may have been subject to it. (The 2006 exemption figures were not yet available at press time.)

TRAPS FOR INVESTORS

●**Long-term gains and qualifying dividends.** These are taxed under regular tax rules at a top rate of only 15%. This top rate applies under AMT rules, too. But long-term gains and dividends can still trigger the AMT. *Two ways...*

●Higher state taxes. If you live in a high-tax state—such as New York or California, which tax long-term gains and dividends at normal rates—gains and dividends will increase the state tax bill. And a large deduction for state and local taxes is a primary cause of AMT liability.

●Increased AMT income. Capital gains and qualified dividends are counted in AMT income for purposes of determining whether AMT applies and can push it up over the exempt amount. In addition, when AMT income exceeds $150,000 on a joint return or $112,500 on a single return, the exempt amount is reduced by 25% of the excess.

Example: Taking $4,000 of capital gains can *reduce* the amount of income that's exempt from·AMT by $1,000 (25% of $4,000). *Impact:* AMT will become due at its normal rate (26% or 28%) on an additional $1,000 of income.

●**The tax-exempt bonds.** Some tax-exempt bonds are taxable under AMT rules. Interest from private activity bonds issued by state and local government after August 7, 1986 increases AMT income.

Example: Bonds to construct a new sports stadium.

Trap: These bonds usually pay more interest than the fully tax-exempt bonds, so some tax-exempt bond funds hold them to boost returns. A person lured into investing in such a fund while subject to AMT may end up owing unexpected tax.

New: Leading mutual fund families now offer "AMT free" bond funds.

Examples: Fidelity Spartan Tax-Free Bond Fund (FTABX)...Oppenheimer AMT-Free Municipal Fund (OPTAX).

For more on AMT and munis, visit The Bond Market Association Web site at *www.investingin bonds.com.*

●**Incentive stock options (ISOs).** A stock option lets one buy shares of stock for less than market value.

If the option is an ISO, then under normal tax rules, the discount is tax free when the option is exercised, and any gain on the shares isn't taxed until they are later sold.

Trap: Under AMT rules, the discount is taxable at the time the option is exercised—even though exercising the option provides no cash with which to pay the tax.

Danger: If the value of shares acquired with ISOs falls before tax is paid on them, one can end up owing more tax than the gain on the shares—or even more than the entire value of the shares.

This occurred in several notable cases when the technology stock bubble burst. People who had used ISOs to buy shares thinking their exercise was tax free—without knowing about AMT—wound up owing tax bills larger than the value of their shares after share prices collapsed.

Example: An individual uses ISOs to pay $5 to buy shares worth $30. The $25 discount is subject to AMT, creating a tax bill of about $7 per share. The shares then fall in price to less than $7. The individual now owes more tax on each share than the value of the share itself.

Safest: When exercising ISOs, consult with your adviser about whether it creates AMT liability and, if so, how to best pay the taxes due *then.* If the stock later falls, whatever value it retains will at least be tax free.

●**Real estate and property taxes.** When people think of high-tax states, they usually think of states with high income taxes. But some states that have low income taxes have high property taxes, such as New Hampshire and Maine.

Snag: Real estate investments made in these states can result in high property tax payments—which can create AMT liability the same way state income taxes can.

●**Home-equity interest.** Under normal rules, interest on up to $100,000 of home-equity borrowing is deductible as mortgage interest no matter how one uses the borrowed funds.

But under AMT rules, interest is deductible on a home-equity loan only if the loan funds are used to acquire or improve one's residence. Also, under AMT rules, mortgage interest is not deductible on a loan used to acquire a motor home or boat as a second residence.

Saver: If a home-equity loan is used to fund investments, then interest may be deductible as investment interest under AMT rules. But you must be able to document the use of the funds from the loan for the investment to secure the deduction.

• **Investment expenses.** These normally are deductible among miscellaneous itemized deductions, which can be written off to the extent their total exceeds 2% of adjusted gross income (AGI).

Snag: This deduction is not permitted under AMT rules.

• **Pass-through entities.** If you own an interest in a business that is organized as a pass-through entity—an S corporation, partnership or limited liability company—items on its return that can create AMT liability will pass through to your personal tax return.

Trap: If you are a passive investor in the business, you might not even consider your AMT exposure—until you find yourself with an unexpected AMT bill when you prepare your tax return.

SELF-DEFENSE

The first step to avoiding AMT investment traps is projecting the potential AMT liability in advance—if you don't learn that you are subject to AMT until you prepare your tax return, it will be too late to do anything about it. AMT rules are very complex, so make the projection with the help of an expert.

If you find that you will owe AMT, then review all of your investment strategies to manage it effectively.

The best strategies will differ in each case and as circumstances change, so stay in touch with your adviser.

Tax-Advantaged Dividends

Dividends on preferred stock do not necessarily qualify for favorable tax treatment. The top rate on qualified dividends now is 15%. Preferred shares usually are structured as debt by the companies that issue them or are issued by REITs—so they are taxed at ordinary income tax rates, not the special 15% rate. Find out which preferred stocks are eligible for the tax-advantaged rate at *www.quantumonline.com.*

Are Emotions Driving Your Investments? Traps to Avoid

Richard Geist, EdD, a clinical instructor in psychology, department of psychiatry at Harvard Medical School in Boston, and founding member of the Massachusetts Institute for Psychoanalysis, where he is on the faculty. He is also president of the Institute of Psychology and Investing, Inc., a consulting firm in Newton, MA, and the author of *Investor Therapy* (Crown Business).

Most of us recognize that many investors base decisions on emotion rather than logic. The trouble is that few of us believe we're among them.

To find out how much emotion influences your investments, look back over your stock and mutual fund trades for the past year, and note the reason for each purchase and sale. If trades were motivated by the headlines of the day or your eagerness to make a quick profit, chances are emotion played a key role.

Good news: Once you recognize that emotions are guiding your decisions, you can take steps to separate them from investments. Alternatively, you can choose the stocks and funds suited to your particular psychological bias.

How to deal with psychological traps…

HERD MENTALITY

It is only human to follow the winners. In investing, those are the people who have made money. Unfortunately, by the time an investment sector posts strong returns, there's often little advantage left to plowing money in.

Today, there is a herd mentality concerning short-term investing. Our qualitative research shows that fear of terrorism, anxiety over developments in Iraq and the memory of the recent bear market have made investors more likely to sell for a quick profit—typically, in less than a year—no matter what sector they are in.

Solution: When an investor herd goes in one direction, look for opportunities in stocks and funds that are left behind. Today, these include companies that recently have had problems but have solid fundamentals—good management, a healthy market share, low debt and a history of earnings growth over the last decade.

IMPATIENCE

It's impossible to predict the ideal time to sell a stock, but impatient investors are notorious for selling just before a stock takes off.

Test your own patience: Are you reluctant to start reading long books? In conversations, are you annoyed when people don't get to the point? If you answered *yes* to either question, there is a good chance that you are an impatient investor.

When you look back over your trading record for the past 12 months, check the price of each position you sold three to six months after you sold it. (If you can't find past transaction statements, ask your financial institution for copies or download them from its Web site.) If you regularly sold shares that continued to rise in price, impatience may have played a role.

Solution: Add up the profits you could have made by holding on longer. Merely seeing the total may be enough to cure you.

If you simply can't break the habit of selling shares prematurely, consider buying stocks that *should* be sold for a quick profit.

These frequently are in companies that take advantage of new trends—especially technology stocks. If shares in cutting-edge companies rise, the increase is likely to be fast. Holding these risky stocks long after their initial rise can be a mistake if the fundamentals don't support the gain, though there certainly are exceptions to this rule.

FEAR OF LETTING GO

This is the opposite of impatience. It means hanging on to shares long after you should have sold them.

When you look at your trades of the past year, check the price of stocks three and six months before you sold them. Look also at the stocks you own now, and compare current prices with prices three and six months ago.

If you find that you consistently hang on to shares after they rise and then fall, it is likely that you're afraid of selling. Why might this be?

One possibility: If your costliest mistakes always seem to occur at certain times of the year—for instance, around the anniversary of a painful event, such as the loss of a loved one—the memory could be subconsciously influencing your investment behavior.

Solution: Continue to keep records of your trades, and periodically note profits that you missed because you hung on too long.

If this doesn't stop you from keeping losing stocks, stick with stock funds that have performed well in both up and down markets. By following this strategy, you won't be hurt by your fear of letting go.

Helpful: Free fund-screening tools are available at *www.morningstar.com*. If you do not have a computer, research funds at a public library computer.

OVERREACTING TO NEWS

Don't let the headlines determine your stock trades. Individual investors are seldom knowledgeable or dispassionate enough to profit from the news.

Example: Airline stocks suffered after the September 11 disaster as many investors worried about a drop in tourism. Yet very few individual investors got out of the stocks quickly enough to contain their losses.

Professional investors interpret and react to the news more quickly than most individual investors do. As a result, stock prices are affected by news before most individuals have time to respond. In fact, several fund managers did buy airline stocks right after September 11, 2001, and then sold them when they rebounded.

Solution: Before buying or selling a stock, ask yourself whether the decision is influenced by a news event. If it is, review the company's fundamentals—management, competitive position and outlook for its industry sector. Go ahead only if the fundamentals justify the trade.

Think twice before buying or selling shares purely on the basis of trends you see on financial news sites in a day's first hour of trading.

11

Consumer Watch

Over 50? Get Big Discounts, Great Deals, Free Money!

If you are worried about meeting expenses as you age, here's some good news. You can get free vision care, college courses and even discounted stock commissions when you are 65 or older. And, special deals on travel, movies, health clubs and more are available to people as young as age 50.

Some of my favorite moneysavers specifically for the golden years…

TRAVEL/LEISURE

•**Fly for less.** Turmoil in the industry has eliminated most, but not all, of the airfare deals for seniors…

•United Air Lines' Silver Wings Plus offers significant savings for all travelers age 55 and older. You get travel credits, double bonus miles and zone fares.* Members also receive discounts

*Prices and offers throughout are subject to change.

and privileges from United Airlines' well-known travel partners. The cost of membership is $24/month or $264/year. 800-720-1765, *www.silver wingsplus.com.*

•Southwest Airlines offers people age 65 and older 20% to 70% off regular fares. Tickets are fully refundable, but they cannot be transferred to younger travel companions. 800-435-9792, *www.southwest.com/travel_center/seniors.html.*

•America West Airlines provides a senior discount to travelers 65 years old and over on some itineraries. 800-235-9292, *www.americawest.com.*

•**Hunting and fishing licenses.** Many states do not require residents age 65 and older to carry fishing or hunting licenses, or they offer them for free. Many other states offer seniors 50% off the cost of licenses. To find the licensing bureau in your state, go to *www.background checkgateway.com/huntfish.html.*

Matthew Lesko, a Kensington, MD–based best-selling author of more than 100 books on how to get free services and products, including *Bottom Line's Big Fat Book of Free Money for Everyone* (Bottom Line Books, *www. bottomlinesecrets.com*).

PRODUCT DISCOUNTS

More than 125,000 unadvertised discounts are available at *www.seniordiscounts.com.* Type in your zip code and a category (retail, restaurants, entertainment, etc.). The site will generate a list of discounts, locations in your area and phone numbers. *Examples...*

●**AMC theaters** give moviegoers age 55 and older $2 off ticket prices.

●**Bally's Health Clubs and the YMCA** offer discounts to seniors. Discounts and age requirements vary by location.

●**Jiffy Lube and Midas** offer discounts to seniors. Discounts and age requirements vary by location.

●**Kohl's Department Stores** offers customers age 62 and older 10% to 15% off of purchases made on selected Wednesdays.

AARP DISCOUNTS

AARP offers dozens of significant discounts for members age 50 and older.

Annual membership fee: $12.50. *Some of my favorites...*

●**20% off all Reebok and Rockport outlet store purchases.**

●**5% to 30% off at major rental-car companies,** such as Avis, Hertz and National.

●**10% off of AOL's standard unlimited monthly Internet plan.**

●**10% off installation of an ADT home-security system.**

Information: 888-OUR-AARP (888-687-2277) or *www.aarp.org/benefits.*

EDUCATION

●**Older Adult Service and Information System (OASIS),** a not-for-profit program that's sponsored by Federated Department Stores, May Department Stores Company Foundation and BJC Health Care, offers free noncredit classes in the humanities, health and computers for people who are age 50 and over. OASIS's 26 cities include Chicago, Houston, Denver, Indianapolis, Los Angeles, San Antonio and Washington, DC.

Information: 314-862-2933, *www.oasisnet. org.*

Many universities offer free classes for seniors. Contact your local university.

HEALTH CARE

●**Rock-bottom drug prices.** Go to *www. needymeds.com* and select the medication you need. The site provides a link to the manufacturer's Web site for details about its discount drug programs.

For lists of specific discounts at drugstores in your state, log on to *www.suddenlysenior.com/ cheapdrugs.html.*

●**Free eye care.** EyeCare America, sponsored by the Public Service Foundation of the American Academy of Ophthalmology, puts callers in touch with local ophthalmologists who provide free eye care to senior citizens. Care can include treatment of cataracts, glaucoma and macular degeneration.

Requirements: The program is for people age 65 and over who have not seen an ophthalmologist in the last three years and who do not belong to an HMO or the Veterans Benefits Administration.

Information: 800-222-3937, *http://eyecare america.org/eyecare/public.*

FINANCIAL SERVICES

●**Track down forgotten pension money.** Did you work someplace 20 years ago that is no longer in business? Don't give up on collecting the money that you're owed.

You can search for money by your name... company name...or state where the company was headquartered. Since the Pension Search Program began in 1996, the Pension Benefit Guaranty Corp. (PBGC) has helped more than 19,000 people recover more than $75 million.

Average benefit: $3,675. There is $75 million waiting to be claimed.

Information: At *www.pbgc.gov* click on "Workers & Retirees," then "Pension Search," or call 800-400-7242.

●**Ask your bank/brokerage firm about perks for seniors.** To attract older customers, many banks and brokerage firms offer senior services packages to their customers who are as young as age 50.

Package features: No monthly service fees or per-check charges…commission discounts…discount eyewear and pharmacy services…accidental death insurance…higher interest rates on savings accounts and on certificates of deposit (CDs) than younger customers get.

Examples: UMB Bank's Preferred Status account gives seniors age 50 and over a discounted safe-deposit box…free checks, money orders, traveler's checks and notary services (800-821-2171, *www.umb.com*). Bank of America's Advantage for Seniors program offers preferred rates on money market accounts, CDs and IRAs…free cashier's and traveler's checks (800-900-9000, *www.bankofamerica.com*).

Surprising AAA Discounts

In addition to cheaper rates on most major hotels and discounts on vacation attractions, American Automobile Association (AAA) members can obtain discounts that average 35% on generic drugs and 15% on brand-name drugs at eight out of 10 pharmacies.

Other discounts: 10% off from Payless Shoe Source…30% off glasses at LensCrafters…10% off most Gateway computers.

On-line-only discounts: 5% off books at Barnes & Noble (*www.aaa.com/barnesandnoble*)…20% off of flowers through *www.ftd.com/aaa*.

Find additional discounts, including those tailored to your own local area, by logging on to *www.aaa.com/save*.

Average annual AAA membership fee: $60.

Gail Acebes, director of partnership programs at AAA, Heathrow, FL.

Little Tricks That Save Big Money

Sue Goldstein, the author of more than 70 books in the *Underground Shopper Bargain Shopping* series, including *Underground Shopper/Online* (SBI). She also hosts a radio program in Flower Mound, TX. Her Internet site is *www.undergroundshopper.com*.

Deborah Taylor-Hough, the author of *Frugal Living for Dummies* (Wiley) and *A Simple Choice: A Practical Guide to Saving Your Time, Money and Sanity* (Champion). She publishes the free e-newsletter *Simple Times* from Olympia, WA. Her site on the Web is *http://members.aol.com/dsimple/times.html*.

Donna Watkins and her husband, Randal, who live in Palmyra, VA, and run the free on-line newsletter *The Frugal Life*, available at *www.thefrugallife.com*. Their moneysaving ideas were contributed by visitors to their Web site.

Economists insist that inflation is low, but you would never know it from looking at most people's energy bills or their children's college costs. *To find out how to save on these and other expenses, see below…*

SUE GOLDSTEIN
Underground Shopper

●**Shop at Internet liquidators and consignment stores.** *I have found many bargains at discount stores, but prices often are even lower at their on-line counterparts…*

●Overstock.com (800-843-2446) and SmartBargains.com (866-692-2742) are best for items like fine jewelry, electronics, designer accessories and more.

●Bluefly.com (877-258-3359) offers high-end designer clothes for men and women. *One recent example:* Marc Jacobs red denim pants, $94.99—73% off the retail price of $355.

●Playitagainsports.com (800-433-2540) buys, sells and trades new and used sports gear and equipment, including treadmills, exercise bikes and elliptical machines.

●Dgse.com is a jewelry discounter that specializes in preowned Rolex watches that are substantially less than retail prices. Other pieces of jewelry are discounted by up to 50%.

●**Get the feel of a $1,500 mattress for less than $300.** Beddingtoppers.com (800-834-2473) offers durable foam mattress toppers that fit over your current mattress. They are made with the same memory foam used in higher-priced mattresses to hug the contours of your body.

Cost: Full size, up to $209…queen, as much as $259…king, up to $289. Shipping is free.

Extra-deep-pocket sheets are needed, but it should help your current mattress last longer.

●**Replace hardware on doors, furniture and cabinets.** It's a fast and cheap way to give your home a new look. Home stores have only limited selections.

Better: Goknobs.com (888-465-6627) offers more than a half million choices at great prices.

●**Pamper yourself for less at the beauty schools.** A student hairdresser will cut your hair under their teacher's supervision for much less than salons charge. Facials, massages and spa pedicures are low-cost indulgences. Look in the Yellow Pages under "Beauty Schools."

●**Get low-cost blood tests at mobile clinics.** Offered through local health fairs, these mobile clinics have very low overhead, so the blood tests are inexpensive. They're great for people who don't have insurance or whose deductibles are higher than the cost of the test. Check your local newspaper listings.

●**Investigate discount drug programs.** Pharmaceutical firms will provide free drugs to anybody who qualifies, but there are more than 2,000 companies and each has a different program, criteria for acceptance and paperwork.

Prescription Assistance Services for Seniors or PASS (800-727-7479 or *www.pass4rx.com*) handles the paperwork and communication among you, your doctor and the pharmaceutical companies. Despite the name, you don't have to be a senior citizen to participate. After paying an enrollment charge of $25, you at first pay $30 per prescription. After 90 days, you pay only $15 per prescription for a 30-day supply. Some programs have an income ceiling of $18,000 for singles…$24,000 for couples. Others will waive the limit if a catastrophic illness has created a financial burden.

DEBORAH TAYLOR-HOUGH
Simple Times

●**Double and triple your shopping discounts.** Print out coupons from these Web sites, and use them at your favorite on-line and traditional retail stores.

Favorites: *www.slickdeals.net* and *www.flamingoworld.com.*

Alternative: Visit rebate sites, such as *www.ebates.com* and *www.mypoints.com.* Click on their links to popular on-line retailers, such as Barnes & Noble, Nordstrom's and Target.

●**Encourage your college grad to work off student-loan debt.** Congress passed legislation that enables some federal agencies to repay as much as $6,000 in government student loans (up to $40,000 per employee) for each year a graduate is employed by the US federal government. Congressional employees and those in military service often are eligible, as are some college graduates who teach full-time in schools that serve low-income students and those who specialize in subjects that lack qualified teachers.

Information: 800-433-3243 or *www.finaid. org/loans/forgiveness.phtml.*

●**Slash food bills.** Textured Vegetable Protein (TVP) costs much less per serving than meat, is low in fat and has no cholesterol. TVP works best in spicy dishes—spaghetti sauce, soups, etc. It comes in dry form and must be reconstituted in boiling water. For more information on TVP and additional soy products, see *www.thesoydaily.com.* Available at health-food stores or at *www.healthyharvest.com.*

Helpful: Find recipes at *www.fatfree.com/ recipes/meat-analogues.*

DONNA WATKINS
The Frugal Life

●**Use half the amount of nuts that baking recipes require.** Some nuts sell for $8 or more a pound. If you toast them before adding them to recipes, the flavor intensifies, so it won't taste like you used less.

●**Make your old refrigerator much more energy efficient.** Spread a thin layer of petroleum jelly on the rubber gasket seals along the inside of the door. This prevents mildew and keeps in cold air. Avoid frequently opening and closing the refrigerator door, especially when the weather is warm.

●**Chop the cost of firewood.** Ask a local orchard if you can buy its pruned branches. They should dry by winter. For example, apple wood costs less than store-bought firewood and burns very well.

Negotiating Trick

Don't seem too happy when negotiating. You will probably not get as good a deal. People who scowl or seem about to get angry usually do better in negotiations because they are thought to be at or near their limit. Someone who is smiling is thought to be willing to be pushed a little more. So, do not hesitate to act indignant, for instance, when negotiating to buy a car. But avoid actually getting angry.

Donald Moine, PhD, business psychologist, Rolling Hills Estates, CA, author of Ultimate Selling Power: How to Create and Enjoy a Multi-Million Dollar Sales Career *(Career Press).*

How to Save Even More Money at Warehouse Clubs

Phil Lempert, supermarket guru and food trends editor for NBC's *Today* show. He is also host of the syndicated *Shopping Smart* show on the WOR radio network and the author of four books, including *Being the Shopper* (Wiley). His Web site is *www.supermarketguru.com.*

Warehouse clubs such as BJ's Wholesale, Sam's Club and Costco Wholesale can really help you save a lot of money. In the past, they sold mainly bulk food and household goods in a no-frills environment. Recently, they have started offering everything from eyeglasses to insurance.

Be careful, though. Many items purchased at warehouse clubs cost more than those purchased at traditional stores. *Here, the best and worst deals...*

BIG SAVINGS

Your savings on these great club buys will more than cover the annual cost of membership —$40 at BJ's, $45 at Costco, $35 at Sam's...

•**Eyeglasses.** Many warehouse club locations now have on-site optical departments that turn out well-made eyeglasses for about 50% less than your local optician—a savings of $60 or more per pair. Some locations even offer eye exams. Contact lenses may be available as well.

Prices are comparable to those at discount Web sites, but you don't pay for shipping.

•**Small, disposable nonfood items.** These products are perfect as bulk purchases because they don't go bad or take up much storage space. Expect to save up to 50% off of supermarket prices—sometimes more.

Among the best buys: Toothbrushes, razor blades, dental floss, soap, deodorant, garbage bags, sandwich bags, printer toner cartridges, contact lens supplies and batteries.

Example: One name-brand toothbrush might cost $3 in a supermarket. In a discount club, you'll pay perhaps $5 for a six-pack of the same brush, an annual savings of $13 per family member if you change toothbrushes every two months, as recommended by most dentists.

Caution: Batteries and contact lens supplies eventually go bad, so avoid buying more than you can use before their expiration dates. Do not store extra toothpaste and deodorant in the bathroom—they'll last longer if kept in a cool, dry place.

•**Alcoholic beverages.** Wine, beer and liquor at the warehouse clubs sell for 20% to 25% below prices in supermarkets and liquor stores. However, you might have to buy bigger bottles. You will find top brands as well as warehouse club brands.

Note: The selling of alcohol by warehouse clubs is prohibited in some states. Generally speaking, if the supermarkets in your state are allowed to sell alcohol, then warehouse clubs can as well.

•**Gasoline.** Many of the warehouse clubs now have their own on-site gas stations—with prices that typically are 10 to 20 cents per gallon lower than other stations in the region. If you drive 10,000 miles a year in a vehicle that gets 25 miles to the gallon, that 10- to 20-cent discount translates into $40 to $80 a year—as long as you don't have to go too far out of your way to get to the warehouse club.

•**Prepaid phone cards.** Warehouse clubs sell domestic long-distance phone cards for as little as three cents a minute. That is a better rate than you're likely to find on prepaid calling anywhere else.

Important: No matter where you purchase them, prepaid phone cards are a good deal only if you actually use them. Roughly 20% of all minutes purchased on prepaid phone cards are never used because the cards are lost or forgotten.

SHOP WITH CAUTION

Savings are possible at warehouse clubs on the following items, but shop carefully—you might find better prices elsewhere…

●**Consumer electronics.** Warehouse club prices on consumer electronics likely are below the regular prices at other major retailers. Warehouse clubs, however, may not stock a good selection of leading brand names…and special offers are common on consumer electronics elsewhere. You might find an even better deal during a sale at a national chain or on-line at such sites as Overstock.com and Buy.com.

●**Canned and frozen foods.** Even in a can, food doesn't stay fresh forever. Buying canned foods in bulk makes sense—but only if you'll consume it within a year. Bulk purchases of frozen foods are smart only if you have the freezer space—for example, if you have a second freezer in the basement.

●**Insurance.** Some warehouse clubs now offer auto and homeowner's insurance—but their prices may or may not beat quotes you can get elsewhere, so don't buy until you have shopped around. To compare insurance rates, check out these Web sites, *www.insure.com* or *www.insweb.com.*

●**Diet beverages.** These drinks start to lose their sweetness after three or four months. Don't buy in bulk unless you will drink it all before then.

Caution: If your warehouse club (or any store) keeps carbonated beverages outside in the summer, don't purchase these bottles or cans. Prolonged exposure to heat can rob soda of both sweetness and flavor. Similarly, don't store soda in a hot garage.

BAD DEALS

Not everything for sale at a warehouse club is a moneysaver…

●**Bulk perishable foods.** Warehouse club prices for perishable foods typically are no better than supermarket prices. Supermarket profit margins on food are so thin that it's tough for the warehouse clubs to do much better—and if food you purchase in bulk goes uneaten, you will lose money.

Examples: Spices aren't a wise bulk purchase—they start to lose their flavor in as little as two months, and many attract insects. The five-liter tins of olive oil that are sold at warehouse clubs are a good deal only if you can get through that much olive oil in a year. After that, it will begin to go rancid.

●**Premier memberships.** Some warehouse clubs try to sell special high-end memberships. For an extra charge each year, you can get additional savings and exclusive offers. These premier memberships don't make sense unless you're buying in quantity for a restaurant, business or large family.

SMART SHOPPING STRATEGIES

Other ways you can make warehouse shopping more advantageous…

●**Avoid the dolly.** All the warehouse clubs offer customers large dollies to wheel through the aisles. The size of these dollies makes even large purchases look small—until you get to the register. Stick to a shopping cart to keep purchases in perspective.

●**Use coupons selectively.** Some warehouse clubs accept coupons, but because so many food items are packaged in unusual sizes and quantities—and since warehouse clubs offer limited brands—you're better off using coupons at the supermarket for items that you buy regularly. Besides, unlike many supermarkets, warehouse clubs do not offer you double and triple coupon days.

Cut Your Grocery Bill By 75%

Susan Samtur, the author of *Cashing In at the Checkout* (Back in the Bronx Press) and editor of *Refundle Bundle,* a newsletter that reports on coupons and refunds, Box 140, Yonkers, NY 10710, *www.refundlebundle.com.*

If you clip coupons from the Sunday newspaper, your average savings per coupon is 81 cents. That's not bad—but if you look beyond the obvious places, your savings can be extraordinary. I use coupons to reduce my weekly spending for food and household items from $100 to less than $25. I often get staples such as toilet paper, spaghetti sauce and razor blades for free. *My best savings now...*

ON-LINE DISCOUNTS

On-line coupons have a greater average face value (97 cents per coupon) than store coupons and a longer average time until expiration (4.8 months versus three months). There are many discount resources, so it's very easy to be overwhelmed. Some require you to provide your name and e-mail address. To save time, bookmark a few Web sites that you'll use regularly.

●**Coupon clearinghouses.** These provide coupons from many manufacturers. Print and use them when you shop. When you have the time, visit several sites—one may offer bigger discounts than another for the same product. *Best sites...*

- *www.coolsavings.com*
- *www.homebasics.com*
- *www.refundsweepers.com*
- *www.smartsource.com*

●**Retail savings sites.** *Some of these sites feature savings at Old Navy, Eddie Bauer and Payless ShoeSource, among other stores...*

- *www.keycode.com*
- *www.bluefly.com*
- *www.couponparadise.com*
- *www.eversave.com*

●**Manufacturers' Web sites.** Look on the packages of favorite products for the manufacturer's Web sites. See if the sites offer promotions, coupons and/or rebates. *A few that are particularly generous...*

- *www.chickenofthesea.com*
- *www.clairol.com/brand/blonding/offers/trymefree.jsp. Example:* Full purchase price refund of up to $10.99 on any product from the Clairol Perfect Highlighting and Blonding Collection.
- *www.colgate.com*
- *www.cottonelle.com. Example:* $1.50 off the price of any two packages of Cottonelle Fresh Folded Wipes.

●**Discount codes for on-line shopping.** Stores depend on weekly sales, coupons and shopper's clubs to attract buyers. On-line merchants provide discounts using promotional codes. You type in the code when you go to the checkout page.

Recent example: www.barnesandnoble. com gave $5 off any purchase of $50 or more, plus free shipping on two or more items after I registered for its on-line newsletter. Since the purpose of a discount code is to attract buyers to on-line stores, you may find them on Web sites other than the ones where the coupons will be used.

Some sites with generous coupon codes and promotions...

- *www.couponmountain.com*
- *www.currentcodes.com*
- *www.dealcatcher.com*

●**Manufacturers' rebates.** Some retailers have taken all the hassle out of getting manufacturers' rebates. Simply register at their Web sites—for example, log on to *www.riteaid.com ...www.walgreens.com...www.truevalue.com...* and *www.officemax.com.* When you make an eligible purchase at one of these stores, enter the transaction number listed on your receipt. The manufacturer will mail you a check in four to six weeks. These rebates can total more than $100 a month, so check back frequently.

●**Free products.** Check manufacturers' Web sites for free products. You'll also find lots of free products at *www.freebiemaniac.com.*

DOUBLE AND TRIPLE YOUR SAVINGS

I try to combine discounts from different sources. I'm able to get many products for free or close to it because I create "triple plays," combining savings from store sales, newspaper coupons and Web sites.

Example I: A 12-pack of Pepsi was advertised at my local supermarket for $2. A rebate sticker on the cans offered $10 back if I mailed in proofs of purchase for three 12-packs and three bags of Lay's potato chips. I purchased the three bags on sale for $5, less 75 cents off because I used three 25-cent coupons that I found on the Frito-Lay Web site. *Final cost for the soda and chips:* 25 cents—$10.25 minus the $10 rebate.

I love "double coupons." If I had made my purchases using double coupons at the supermarket, the soda and chips would have cost me nothing.

Example II: I could get two 96-tablet economy packages of Sudafed nasal decongestant at my neighborhood Eckerd drugstore for $7. I went to *www.eckerd.com* to get an additional $1 rebate. I also had a newspaper coupon for $1 off each package. *Final total:* $4—a saving of more than 40% off the sale price.

Wine for Less

Many wine stores offer discounts of 10% to 20% when you buy 12 bottles—and the bottles don't all have to be the same type or brand of wine.

SmartMoney, 250 W. 55 St., New York City 10019.

Consider Preowned Electronics

Purchasing preowned computers or electronics often makes sense. Major companies, such as Dell and The Sharper Image, have outlet stores on their Web sites where refurbished items can sell for as much as 50% less than retail prices.

Money, Time-Life Bldg., Rockefeller Center, New York City 10020.

Get Deep Discounts On Merchandise

The Unclaimed Baggage Center purchases luggage and packages that are left on airlines. Items are then sold at deep discounts online at *www.unclaimedbaggage.com* and at the store in Scottsboro, Alabama. The merchandise can include cameras, clothing, electronics, jewelry and sporting goods.

The Only Shopping Web Sites You May Ever Need

Joseph T. Sinclair, Vallejo, CA–based author of several books about the Internet, including *eBay the Smart Way* (Amacom).

You can save a lot by buying second-hand items on-line, but not everyone wants to go through the hassle of bidding at auction sites such as eBay. *Here are two moneysaving options for buying used and new items on-line...*

FROOGLE

The leading search engine Google now offers a shopping site called Froogle (*www.froogle.com*). Froogle does have paid ads, but they are posted only on the right side of the search results page. Item listings are free and submitted by individual merchants.

How it works: Type "digital copier" into Google, and it will produce a list of more than 200,000 Web sites, some selling copiers, most not. Type the same entry into Froogle, and you will see only links to digital copiers for sale by on-line merchants. Each listing displays price, make, model number and other important details. Most also include photos.

If you're looking for a specific model, type in the model number or name. Then you can click to sort the results by price. In seconds, you'll know the best deals available on-line. Most of the items listed on Froogle are new. Items are shipped by the merchants.

To search only for secondhand products, include the keywords "used"..."condition"... "refurbished"...or "preowned" to filter out the majority of the new goods.

Note: Froogle includes some sellers from eBay and Amazon.com.

For used items from Amazon.com, the shipping costs can be a few dollars more than the standard Amazon shipping costs. On eBay, the merchants determine shipping costs.

CRAIG'S LIST

At most shopping Web sites, the heavier the item, the less likely you will save money after shipping costs. Craig's List (*www.craigslist.org*) solves this problem by connecting buyers with sellers in their own region.

Best for: Secondhand furniture, appliances, exercise equipment, sporting goods, bikes and other large, heavy items.

Examples: Recently on Craig's List, you could find a $100 treadmill in Boston...a $60 solid teak desk in the San Francisco Bay area ...and a $150 leather recliner and ottoman in New York City.

The service is available in over 75 US cities and many international locations.

Another plus: The sellers are local, so you can see the items before you buy.

Craig's List's regional focus makes it a lot like newspaper classifieds, with one important twist—sellers don't pay for postings. With no classified ad expense, sellers generally offer attractive prices.

The Web site also is great for last-minute concert and sporting-event tickets. Sellers will offer steep discounts when a change in their plans prevents them from attending. This Web site also features help-wanted and personal ads as well as real estate listings.

Internet Shopping for Retail Discounts

You can save money when shopping by going to a retailer's Web site through a portal instead of going to the site directly.

Retailers pay fees to Internet portals that direct customers to them. The portals pass part of these fees on to customers through discounts.

The typical discount is around 4%, and you can combine it with coupons and other bargain offers available to you. Portals work with many major retailers, including Lands End, the Gap and Barnes & Noble.

Leading portals: Butterflymall.com, Ebates. com, FatWallet.com, RebateShare.com.

Many more bargains: For a listing of more than 200 Web sites offering coupons and discounts on various products, visit the Yahoo! Shopping Directory at *www.yahoo.com.* Click on "Business," then click on "Shopping and Services," then on "Coupons, Sales and Discounts."

Shrewder On-Line Shopping

Hillary Mendelsohn, founder of thepurplebook, LLC in Beverly Hills, CA, *www.thepurplebook.com.* She is also the author of *thepurplebook: the definitive guide to exceptional on-line shopping* (Random House), which lists more than 1,700 on-line shopping sites in 19 different categories.

Shopping on-line takes you outside of the old, familiar stores and malls and brings a global bazaar right to your door. The variety of goods available on-line is breathtaking— with many items you will never see at the mall —and prices are often lower than you would pay elsewhere.

And yet, on-line shopping can be filled with many perils. You may be shopping with merchants you've never dealt with before (some of them half a world away), you don't get to see items before buying them and identity thieves could steal your most personal information.

Here's how you can be a savvy and safe on-line shopper…

FINDING WHAT'S BEST ON-LINE

While virtually every mass-market retailer sells on-line today, the beauty of the Internet is being able to find off-beat merchants selling hard-to-find treasures. Whatever you are into, from gourmet foods to sports memorabilia, it's available on-line. *Here's how to find it…*

●**Know how to search.** I love Google, but my favorite search engine for finding goods on-line is Dogpile (*www.dogpile.com*). Once you enter what you're looking for, Dogpile offers invaluable tips to help you refine your search. It also provides fewer results to wade through than most search engines. Once you decide to buy an item, such as a specific brand and style of shoes, go to BizRate.com (*www.bizrate.com*) to see which on-line merchant offers the best price. Take into account shipping prices when doing your comparison.

●**Look for contact information.** The hardest thing to find on-line is a telephone number that will let you make personal contact with the merchant—to ask questions and resolve disputes. I won't list a site in my book that doesn't have a listed phone number.

Hint: If a site doesn't have a listed phone number, sometimes you can find it by searching *www.yahooyellowpages.com.*

●**Demand quick and easy shopping.** You should be able to complete the on-line transaction without a lot of wasted time and keystrokes. Avoid any site that requires you to enter tons of information (name, address, e-mail address, etc.) just to find out if an item is in stock.

●**Go with your gut.** If the site seems flimsy —without all the information you need to make your selection—skip it.

HOW TO HAGGLE

You will often pay less for an item on-line, since many sites don't charge sales tax and may offer free shipping. Mass-market retailers are doing more to encourage on-line shopping—including offering discounts. If you register with them, you can receive e-mail on their special offers, advance notification of sales plus coupons and discounts.

Even if a store doesn't specifically mention discounts to on-line shoppers, it may be possible to negotiate a better deal for yourself.

Most sites include a comments box on the order form. Use that box to ask for a lower price, or free shipping or gift wrapping.

Don't expect a biggie like Wal-Mart or L.L. Bean to bargain with you on-line. However, a smaller retailer may be willing to deal…especially if the item is one of a kind, such as a piece of handmade jewelry.

HOW TO SHOP SAFELY

While most identity theft does not take place on the Internet, you still want to exercise caution. *Here's how…*

●**Patronize sites that use a secure server.** This means that any information you enter on-line is encrypted before being transmitted. The standard for security is 128-bit encryption, and sites that offer it will usually display that information prominently.

Favor sites that display the VeriSign Secured Seal to indicate they use a secure server. The seal is in red, with a black checkmark.

●**Pay with your credit card—rather than with a debit card.** Your bank card number and often your PIN must be transmitted with a debit card transaction, making you vulnerable to hackers. Also, if there is a problem with the merchandise or the billing, or if the order was never shipped, you can withhold payment for the purchase from the credit card issuer. When you use a debit card, the money comes out of your bank account the instant you complete the transaction.

HOW TO TOUCH THE MERCHANDISE

The biggest problem with on-line shopping is that you can't hold the item in your hand and examine it for color, size, quality, etc.

Solution: Use sites that do the best job of illustrating and describing what you're buying.

If color is a factor, for example, you'll want to be shown all the colors in which the item is offered. With clothing, you'll want a chart of sizes, an explanation of how the items are sized and a guide to help you pick the size you'll need.

Important: Since there is always a certain amount of guesswork involved when shopping on-line, the merchant's return and exchange policies are critical. You must be able to return the item within a reasonable amount of time—at least 30 days—and get a full refund rather than just store credit against another purchase.

FOREIGN SHOPPING

You're not limited to the US when shopping on-line. You can purchase from merchants anywhere in the world. However, I do set a much higher standard for the international sites that I list in my book.

The site must be in English. It must offer a currency converter, showing the price of the item in both dollars and in the local currency. The site must also offer size conversion charts so you understand the difference between US sizes and European or British sizes.

Important: The cost of shipping must be reasonable, even if the item is coming from far away. If you're not careful, the cost of shipping can exceed the value of the item. The best international sites keep their shipping costs close to what it would cost to have the item shipped from a domestic supplier.

HOW TO RESOLVE COMPLAINTS

Most of the time, your on-line shopping will go without a hitch. Merchants have been selling on-line long enough to have ironed out the issues that made for trouble at the beginning.

Still, things can go wrong. Anticipate trouble by collecting all the documents you might need in case something does.

Save all records of your on-line order, including any e-mail the company sends you to confirm your purchase. Print the order page before you press the submit button. That will give you a copy of the order page just as you prepared it, with the color, size and shipping method that you selected.

If there's a complaint that can't be resolved with the merchant, or you think you've been a victim of fraud, complain to the Federal Trade Commission (FTC). This agency of the government polices on-line shopping.

Visit the FTC Web site at *www.ftc.gov* to see what your rights are, and for instructions on filing a complaint. "E-consumer.gov" is a special area of the FTC site that handles cross-border on-line shopping complaints.

More from Hillary Mendelsohn...

Some of My Favorite Sites

The following shopping Internet sites are both useful and user-friendly. *Give them a try...*

● **Accessories.** Hats in the Belfry (*www.hatsinthebelfry.com*). Every hat you can imagine is here, from dignified headwear to a purple Mad Hatter's top hat.

● **Entertainment.** Audible.com (*www.audible.com*) offers a huge selection of audio books.

● **Epicurean.** Pop's Wine and Spirits (*www.popswine.com*) has a great selection. Petrossian Paris (*www.petrossian.com*) sells caviar, pâté and other gourmet delicacies.

● **Gadgets/electronics.** B&H (*www.bhphotovideo.com*) bills itself as the world's leading retailer of imaging equipment at discount prices.

● **Health/beauty.** Sephora at *www.sephora.com* puts thousands of high-quality beauty products at your fingertips.

● **Home/garden.** Cooking.com (*www.cooking.com*). Everything on this site is so well laid out that even a novice cook will have no trouble navigating it.

● **Pets.** Doctors Foster & Smith (*www.drsfostersmith.com*). All your pet needs plus the expert advice of veterinarians.

● **Sports/outdoors.** Tourline Golf at *www.tourlinegolf.com* has great deals on used golf clubs and more.

● **Stationery/gifts.** Star Treatment at *www.startreatment.com* has wonderful gift baskets.

● **Travel.** Magellan's (*www.magellans.com*). This Web site has appliances and accessories for every travel need.

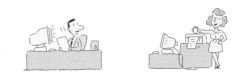

Better Shopping On-Line

Before you shop on-line, search for promotional discounts for clothing, appliances, shoes, electronics, music and more. These discounts are applied during checkout if you include the proper code. Retailers put these codes on other sites as advertisements to lure you to their sites.

Best sources for promotional codes: *www.currentcodes.com...www.dealcatcher.com ...www.dealhunting.com.*

Mary Hunt, editor of *Debt-Proof Living,* Box 2135, Paramount, CA 90723, *www.debtproofliving.com.*

More from Mary Hunt...

Pay Less for the Internet

You don't have to shell out the standard $24 a month for AOL. Instead, get unlimited Internet access through Wal-Mart for just $6.95 a month. Go to *www.walmart.com* and click on "Internet Access."

Alternative: *www.cyberhotline.com* offers unlimited ad-free access for $13.95/month.

Moneysaving Phone Service Options

Here are two ways that you can lower your phone bill...

● **Get rid of old, wired home phones and replace with cell phones.**

Advantages: Lower cost, especially for long-distance charges which often are much lower for cellular service—and greater convenience, since phones can be carried from room to room or when traveling.

● **When you have a high-speed Internet connection,** such as by cable or DSL, phone service often is available through it at much lower than standard rates. Some companies, such as Verizon, provide free filters that keep the signal clear and offer a 30-day money-back trial period.

Bob Carlson, editor of *Bob Carlson's Retirement Watch,* 3700 Annandale Rd., Annandale, VA 22003.

Wise Ways to Beat Skyrocketing Utility Bills

Harvey Sachs, director of buildings programs, American Council for an Energy-Efficient Economy, a nonprofit organization that promotes energy efficiency and provides consumer information, 1001 Connecticut Ave. NW, Washington, DC 20036, *www.aceee.org.*

With utility rates increasing in so many parts of the country, it's time to consider all the ways to save on home energy expenses.

WATER HEATERS

Heating water is one of the largest fuel expenditures for the typical household. *Two new options can make a big dent in the bill...*

● **Electric heat-pump water heaters.** Developed with help from the Department of Energy, these heaters are more efficient than conventional electric water heaters because their technology makes use of the heat in the air that surrounds them. They are sold under the EMI (800-228-9364, *www.enviromaster.com*), Utica (315-797-1310, *www.uticaboilers.com*) and Dunkirk (716-366-5500, *www.dunkirk.com*) brands. Another manufacturer to check out is Nyle Special Products (207-942-2865, *www.nyle therm.com/waterheating_comm.htm*).

Disadvantage: The initial cost. A 50-gallon heat-pump water heater typically costs $1,200 versus about $300 for a comparable conventional model (without installation). In most US climates, however, the additional cost can be recouped in three or four years unless there's an unexpected drop in fuel prices. Historically, natural gas water heaters have been cheaper than electric heaters.

It also pays to contact your utility company to see if it offers rebates on this and other energy-saving devices.

• **Tankless gas water heaters.** These devices have been used elsewhere in the world for many decades and are now gaining popularity in the US. When you turn on the hot water, a flame immediately heats the water as you use it, eliminating the need to keep water hot 24 hours a day.

Manufacturers include Bosch (800-503-5028, *www.bosch.us*), Eemax (800-543-6163, *www.eemaxinc.com*) and Rheem (800-432-8373, *www.rheem.com*). A natural gas unit that supplies about two gallons of water a minute at 120°F to 130°F typically costs at least $1,000 installed.

You can recoup the initial cost in about three or four years.

Caution: Before buying an instant gas water heater, ask your utility company whether the connection to your house can supply enough gas for the device in addition to all your other appliances. Some connections won't, and the cost of increasing the capacity is rarely worth the expense.

WINDOWS

Replacement windows are popular remodeling measures. If you are replacing your windows anyhow, the extra expense of purchasing energy-efficient windows is generally small, and will be repaid quickly.

On the other hand, the energy savings from efficient windows won't cover the whole price of window replacements.

Reason: An energy-efficient three-by-five-foot window typically costs $400 installed. But, even in the coldest regions of the country, it won't cut fuel bills by more than about $2 a year per square foot of glazing compared with most older windows. In this case, that's $30—a cost that would take nearly 13 years to recover.

Choose only energy-efficient windows that are rated by the National Fenestration Rating Council and listed by the Energy Star program of the Environmental Protection Agency. *The most efficient have a low...*

• **U factor.** On a scale of 0.20 to 1.20, the rating indicates how well windows prevent heat from escaping.

• **Solar heat gain coefficient.** On a scale of zero to one, this rating measures how efficiently windows keep out heat during the summer. Energy Star recommendations vary by region.

Information: 888-782-7937 and *www.energystar.gov*.

Once obsolete windows have been replaced, the next heating and cooling system you buy will not have to be as powerful as the current one—a further savings.

FURNACES

New furnaces are much more fuel efficient than the systems built 15 years ago. The best of these are condensing furnaces that squeeze out the last bit of heat by capturing energy from the steam made in the combustion process.

If your furnace is more than 15 years old, replacing it with a new condensing furnace will typically save 20% on fuel costs, especially in colder regions. *For the biggest fuel savings...*

• **Look for a condensing furnace that has at least a 90% annual fuel utilization efficiency (AFUE) rating,** which is the federal government's measure of overall performance.

• **Hire a contractor who understands systems, not just equipment.** To find one, ask several contractors to look at your house and recommend a furnace. Eliminate from consideration any contractors who don't examine the heating system and house construction, including the insulation. Many good contractors will begin by asking this question—*Are any areas of the house often uncomfortable?*

These energy-aware contractors may suggest adding insulation or upgrading the duct system to enable you to purchase a smaller and less-expensive furnace. A contractor who does this is likely to be reliable to work with.

LIGHTBULBS

Switch over to compact fluorescent lightbulbs anywhere the light is used for more than about two hours per day. They use far less electricity and last longer than conventional incandescent bulbs—10,000 to 20,000 hours versus 750 to 1,000 hours. (Today, there are fluorescent bulbs that work with dimmers, a feature they once did not have.)

Doing the math: A 100-watt incandescent bulb costs about 75 cents, compared with $11 for a 23-watt compact fluorescent that puts out a similar amount of light. The compact fluorescent uses only $8.06 of electricity over three years, assuming that it stays on for four hours every day and electricity costs 8 cents a kilowatt-hour.

During the same three years, you would require six incandescent bulbs that would use $35.04 of electricity. When all costs are considered, the net savings with the fluorescent is $20.48—and the fluorescent would still have nearly four more years of life.

When replacing conventional bulbs, begin with the ones you use most often because that is where the payback is fastest.

Note: Don't buy halogen bulbs unless you need to for decorative purposes and understand their drawbacks, such as high energy usage and temperatures that are so high that the bulbs can be a fire hazard. Halogen torchères *are* fire hazards—throw them out.

AIR CONDITIONERS

The end of the summer is an ideal time to find bargain prices on central air-conditioning systems. But don't be tempted into buying one that's more powerful than you need. Ask contractors for the smallest unit that will effectively cool your house.

Reason: While an overly powerful AC system never runs all the time, at less than full-time operation it can't remove as much water from the air—a prime function.

Result: A clammy environment that will promote mold, particularly risky in humid parts of the country.

When replacing an air-conditioning system, buy one with a seasonal energy efficiency ratio (SEER) rating from the Department of Energy of 13. The SEER 13 rating becomes standard in 2006, but these air-conditioning systems are already widely available.

Advantage: Systems with this rating use approximately 23% less energy than those with the current standard of SEER 10.

How to Recycle Warm Water to Cut Energy Bills

Stephen Elder, home inspector and home-repair specialist, Pittsboro, NC.

Money spent on heating water literally goes down the drain after the water has been used.

New: A heat exchanger can be installed in place of a shower drainpipe to transfer heat from waste water to supply water coming from the water heater. Incoming supply water can be preheated by as much as 30°F, reducing the energy required for heating water and lowering your overall energy bill.

Result: The cost of taking a shower can be halved, and the effective capacity of an electric water heater can be tripled.

For more information on drain water heat recovery, visit the GFX heat-recovery system Internet site at *www.gfxtechnology.com,* or you can contact the distributor, WaterFilm Energy, Inc., at 631-758-6271.

Best savings: Installation costs, such as those for plumbing, wall repair, painting, etc., must be added to the cost of the heat-recovery unit. Savings are considerably greater when the unit is installed during new construction or during a remodeling project.

Read Service Contracts Carefully

Some companies, including nanny-placement agencies and debt-settlement companies, are now incorporating indemnity clauses that shield them from liability and put you at greater risk. If a dispute erupts—or if you suffer some loss or an injury caused by the company's negligence—after you have signed a contract that includes such language, you won't be able to sue for restitution.

Best: Cross out this language in any contract before signing. If the company refuses to accept this, look for another company.

Michael Greenfield, Walter D. Coles Professor of Law, Washington University, St. Louis.

How to Avoid Getting Ripped Off By Repairpeople

Tim Carter, a master licensed plumber and former contractor in Cincinnati, who writes "Ask the Builder," a nationally syndicated newspaper column on home-improvement projects. His Web site is *www.askthebuilder.com.*

Allan Gallant, a master electrician and owner of Gallant Electric in Bedford, MA. During the past eight years, he has appeared regularly as a guest expert on the PBS TV show *This Old House.* Mr. Gallant also appears regularly on *Ask This Old House.*

Leonard Geffner, founder and president of Abbey Locksmiths, a leading provider of locks and burglar-alarm systems to homes and office buildings in New York City for more than 50 years.

When you hire plumbers, electricians and locksmiths, always get a written estimate before any work begins and a final bill after completion. Also ask for a written warranty for any repairs. *Other ways to avoid costly rip-offs...*

PLUMBING
Tim Carter, "Ask the Builder"

Finding a reputable plumber...

•**Ask for a referral from neighbors or a real estate agent.** Realtors know plumbers— nothing derails a home sale faster than watermarks on the ceiling.

•**Ask to see the plumber's license from the state** and a certificate of workers' compensation insurance. Generally, a professional will offer you copies of these documents when the bid is presented. If he/she does not, find one who will.

Avoiding problems...

•**Find a plumber before an emergency.** You will pay top dollar for last-minute service from someone you find in the Yellow Pages. For example, some plumbers triple their prices on weekends.

Best: Find a plumber who charges flat rates for specified services. It's almost always cheaper than paying by the hour.

•**Don't buy parts yourself.** Your plumber knows which brands he prefers and can purchase them at a professional discount of up to 35%. Besides, if you buy the parts yourself, the plumber may not warranty his work. To compare products, try these sites, *www.keidel.com... www.ferguson.com...*and *www.faucet.com.*

•**Check the plumber's work before he leaves your home.** Look for leaks...turn new valves on and off to see if they work...check for adequate water flow volume and pressure. Also check for damage to household surfaces —countertops and floors. Hold him responsible if his tools scratched or tore the wallpaper.

ELECTRICITY
Allan Gallant, *This Old House*

Finding a reputable electrician...

•**Ask for a recommendation from a general contractor** who has done work around your house. He sees the electricians' work before it is hidden by walls.

Ask a candidate these questions...

Have you done a job that is somewhat similar to mine? If the answer is *yes,* call at least one reference. Ask if the job was completed on time, within budget and neatly, with minimal disruption in the home. If the answer is *no,* try to locate an electrician who has done similar work.

Will you be driving a truck stocked with tools and materials? Electricians who do save you time and money.

Also: Ask for the electrician's license number and how long he has been licensed—you want one who has been licensed for at least two years.

Avoiding problems...

•**Use an electrician only when it is absolutely necessary.** Learn how to reset a circuit breaker or change a blown fuse. Always check that a tripped circuit breaker or blown fuse is not the cause of your electricity loss, especially in summer, when air conditioners are running. It takes less than five minutes and can save you a $100 service call.

For instructions on simple electrical projects: *Wiring 1-2-3: Install, Upgrade, Repair, and Maintain Your Home's Electrical System* by The Home Depot (Meredith)...and *http://home repair.about.com/od/electrical.*

●**Don't pay an inflated permit fee.** When your electrical work requires new circuitry, the electrician is required to obtain a permit from your municipality. The expense of the permit is based on the estimated cost of the job—generally about $25 per $1,000 of work. Some electricians might charge an hour or so of labor for the time it takes to get the permit. Anything more is unreasonable.

●**Make sure repairs are itemized in the estimate.**

Examples: The cost of cutting holes in walls or digging trenches for outdoor lighting. You might save money by having a handyman do such work. It's usually your responsibility to replace drywall, repaint or relandscape.

●**Make sure the electrician labels circuit breakers** or fuses and electrical panels before he leaves. It will save you time and money in the future.

Note: To report poor workmanship or fraud, call your local city hall and ask for the local and/or state wire inspector. Inspectors have the power to fine or withhold permits from electricians who rip off consumers.

LOCKS
Leonard Geffner, Abbey Locksmiths

Finding a reputable locksmith...

●**Ask your local police department to recommend a locksmith** and/or alarm specialist. Many locksmiths today also are in the alarm business.

●**If you find a locksmith in the Yellow Pages, make sure that he has a physical location** at the address listed.

●**Be sure the alarm system qualifies for discounts** on your homeowner's insurance. Installing a monitored system should reduce your annual premium by 15% to 20%. Adding deadbolt locks should trim another 2%.

Avoiding problems with locks...

Common scam: You lock yourself out and call a locksmith, who quotes you $50 for a service call. He should be able to pick open the standard mortise lock without damaging it. Instead, he damages your lock on purpose and then charges $400 for a replacement.

To prevent a locksmith from ruining your lock, get an estimate before he starts his work. Ask him if he can avoid damaging your lock and exactly what it will cost if damage occurs.

Avoiding alarm-system problems...

●**Beware of offers of alarm systems installed for "free" or "$99."** These offers are not free or low cost because there are likely to be add-on charges and you're typically required to sign a five-year contract to use the company's central monitoring service.

Cost: About $1,500.

Better: Only hire a qualified locksmith, or shop among several alarm companies. Request that the professional use only Ademco and/or Napco products, the best in the industry. Also, insist on instruction in using the system, and keep your notes handy.

●**Contract with a central monitoring service on a flexible basis,** preferably month to month.

How to Slash The High Cost of Chronic Health Conditions

David Nganele, PhD, the president of DMN Healthcare Solutions, a health-education organization located in New York City. He is the author of several books, including *The Best Healthcare for Less* (Wiley), and founder of Harmony Health Communications, where he created award-winning disease-management programs in cooperation with doctors, drug companies and community groups. His Web site is *www.thebesthealthcareforless.com.*

A chronic disease can be financially devastating even for someone who has health insurance. Benefit limits often are reached before the condition is under control.

People without insurance may be forced to borrow money or sell assets when faced with such conditions as recurring cancers, heart disease, depression and diabetes.

Making lifestyle changes—quitting smoking, improving your diet and exercising—can reduce the need for medication for many conditions. In addition, sufferers can eliminate some expenses entirely by understanding how hospitals, drug companies and doctors do business. *Most effective cost-saving strategies...*

AT-HOME CARE

•**Become an expert.** Learning all you can about your illness may help you to discover lower-cost treatments and aspects of the condition that even your physician may not know about. You'll also benefit psychologically from putting yourself in charge instead of relying solely on your doctor.

•**Contact associations that specialize in your condition.** They can help you to locate low-cost treatment centers and suggest ways to prevent your condition from worsening.

Example: Including supplemental chromium, magnesium and vanadium in your diet may help with diabetes.

Associations for several common illnesses...

•American Cancer Society at 800-227-2345, *www.cancer.org.*

•American Diabetes Association at 800-342-2383, *www.diabetes.org.*

•American Heart Association at 800-242-8721, *www.americanheart.org.*

•American Kidney Fund at 800-638-8299, *www.kidneyfund.org.*

•Depression and Bipolar Support Alliance at 800-826-3632, *www.dbsalliance.org.*

If you're unsure of the appropriate organization, contact the American Medical Association (800-621-8335, *www.ama-assn.org*).

•**Investigate alternative treatments,** such as acupuncture and biofeedback. Many now are covered by insurance. Even if they're not, they may cost less and be more effective than conventional treatments. For information, contact the federal government's National Center for Complementary and Alternative Medicine at 888-644-6226 or *www.nccam.nih.gov.*

•**Buy drugs in large quantities to save on copayments.** Most insurers charge a copayment for each prescription drug, regardless of the drug's cost. Copayments today can be as high as $50.

Ask your doctor to write you 90-day prescriptions, instead of 30-day. You will decrease your copayment by two-thirds.

Example: If you take eight prescription medicines—not so unusual for someone with a chronic condition—and have a $30 copayment, your cost will fall by $1,920, or two-thirds—from $2,880 (8 x $30 x 12) to $960 (8 x $30 x 4).

If your insurance company won't allow more than a 30-day supply of a drug from a local pharmacy, ask your health insurer if it uses a mail-order drug service. They typically supply 90-day quantities. Most insurers prefer that you order by mail because it holds down their costs.

•**Ask your physicians for free samples.** Pharmaceutical companies give away billions of dollars worth of samples for doctors to pass on to patients. Don't be embarrassed to ask. If your doctor doesn't have samples, ask him/her to prescribe generic drugs. For all but a very small percentage of patients, generics are just as effective as brand-name drugs. If you do have insurance, you may have a smaller copayment with generic drugs.

Example: A patient who suffers from depression and does not have drug coverage typically pays about $687 for 90 tablets of Prozac in 40-milligram (mg) strength. The generic equivalent represents a savings of 30% or more.

•**Take part in a clinical trial.** Each year, thousands of people who have chronic ailments receive free treatment by taking part in trials designed to assess new drugs and procedures. The drug industry or the National Institutes of Health (800-411-1222, *www.clinicaltrials.gov*) coordinates most of these trials.

Important: Participants are given a consent form explaining the trial. Read it, and ask questions before signing.

Some trials are *open*—all the participants are given the medicine being tested and are given the results of the trial at each stage.

Other trials are *double-blind*—some of the participants are given the treatment while others just receive a placebo. This prevents test results from being skewed by psychological factors. Patients—and often the doctors who administer the drug—are not told who has received the drug and who has received the placebo.

Despite the risk that you won't receive any treatment, don't rule out a double-blind trial. If you take part in one, you have about a 50-50 chance of receiving cutting-edge medication.

Even if you get the placebo, doctors typically take you out of the trial if your condition worsens, so you can resume treatment on your own.

HOSPITAL-BASED CARE

●**When you are hospitalized, put your primary-care physician in charge.** Doctors unfamiliar with your health history might recommend costly, unnecessary procedures.

Primary physicians, as a rule, will recommend fewer procedures than other doctors at a hospital. Your primary doctor already is familiar with your condition and may have tried a variety of treatments for you in the past.

You even might ask your primary physician to help check your hospital bill for inaccuracies. As a patient with a chronic illness, you need to be vigilant about not reaching insurance policy limits sooner than necessary.

●**Consider getting treatment at a teaching or government-run hospital or clinic.** These institutions usually charge patients according to their ability to pay. They can make sense for people with limited incomes, especially those who lack insurance or have passed their insurance limit.

Information: Health Resources and Services Administration, 800-400-2742, *www.hrsa.gov.*

●**Negotiate with the hospital and other providers.** Pay what you can now, and work out a payment plan for the rest. Or ask for a fee reduction. A hospital or doctor nearly always will compromise because reducing the bill may be cheaper than paying a collection agency or not collecting at all.

●**Get the opinion of more than one doctor before any procedure.** Second opinions increase your chance of finding less expensive —and perhaps more effective—treatment.

Example: Cancer treatments vary greatly in cost and in outcome. Since few doctors are experts in all procedures, it's best to weigh the options with different specialists.

Many chronic disease sufferers do not seek more than one opinion because they think that their insurance won't pay for a second one. In fact, most policies pay for two or three consultations as long as the doctors are in the insurer's network of approved physicians.

The Best On-Line Pharmacies

Nancy Dunnan, a financial adviser and author in New York City. Ms. Dunnan's latest book is titled *How to Invest $50–$5,000* (HarperCollins).

To find out if a Web-based pharmacy is legitimate, begin by asking your health insurer who it has made arrangements with. Many major insurance companies have set up discount plans with the on-line or mail-order pharmacies.

If you do not receive prescription benefits, check the on-line pharmacies with the National Association of Boards of Pharmacy (*www.na bp.net*) to find out if the site is a licensed one. On the home page, go to the "Internet Pharmacy" button. And, take time to read the helpful consumer tips in this section.

Name recognition is another factor. Large companies, such as Costco (*www.costco.com*), Drugstore.com (*www.drugstore.com*) and Walgreens (*www.walgreens.com*), are not only legitimate, they often provide some of the lowest prices within the US.

Finally, don't overlook your neighborhood drugstore. Due to the intense pressure from on-line and mail-order competitors, some have not only reduced their prices but will also deliver for free.

12

Richer Retirement

Best Ways to Live Off of Your Retirement Savings

As people live longer, their retirement can last 30, 40, even 50 years. *Two main requirements for a secure retirement…*

• **Your retirement fund must be tapped regularly** to support a comfortable lifestyle.

• **If you withdraw too much too soon, you and/or your spouse might run low** on spending money.

How to withdraw from your retirement fund each year without running out of money one day in the future…

FINDING THE MAGIC NUMBER

Withdraw a reasonable amount the first year of retirement. Then increase your withdrawal each year to keep pace with inflation.

Example: You take $50,000 from your IRA the first full year of retirement. If inflation is 4% that year, you increase your withdrawal by 4% the next year, to $52,000, and so on, each year. This will maintain your purchasing power. The challenge is to arrive at a "reasonable amount" for the Year One withdrawal. If too large, your retirement fund will be depleted quickly.

Much research has gone into determining a prudent Year One withdrawal.

Bottom line: Drawing down your retirement fund by about 5% in Year One is a feasible plan for many retirees.

You'll be on safer ground with a 4% withdrawal. Beware—starting out at the 6% level will just increase the risk that you will outlive your money.

If you have other retirement resources (such as a pension or a second home that you can sell), you might consider taking on more risk, within the range of 4% to 6%, with a higher initial payout.

Ted Saneholtz, CPA/PFS, CFP, ChFC, president, Summit Financial Strategies, 110 Northwoods Blvd., Columbus, OH 43235. He has been listed among America's top financial advisers by *Medical Economics, Bloomberg Wealth Manager* and *Worth* magazines.

PICKING THE RIGHT POCKET

Deciding how much to withdraw is only the first step.

Next: Decide which account to tap.

Example: Should your $50,000 per year come from a tax-deferred plan, such as an IRA, or from money held in a taxable account?

Often, drawing down the taxable account first —until it's depleted—makes sense.

Reason: Keeping money in your IRA permits a longer period of tax deferral. Also, you'll pay a 10% penalty if you take money from your IRA before age 59½. There are some exceptions to this penalty, such as disability. Check with your tax professional.

The situation changes after you reach age 70½. Then you're *required* to take minimum distributions from your IRA. You'll face a penalty of 50% of the money you should have taken out, but didn't.

Calculating the minimum withdrawal can be complicated, so be sure to work with a knowledgeable adviser.

Strategy: At age 70½, plan your withdrawals around your required distributions.

Example: At age 72, you need to tap your retirement funds for $60,000. Your required IRA distribution for the year is $35,000. You might take $35,000 from your IRA, as required, and the other $25,000 from a taxable account.

Be aware that money coming from your IRA will be reduced by income tax, and adjust your spending plans accordingly.

Strategy: If you find yourself in a low tax bracket in any given year, convert a portion of your regular IRA to a Roth IRA. A Roth IRA can grow tax free during your lifetime and continue tax-free accumulation for your beneficiaries.

Trap: Delaying all IRA withdrawals until after age 70½ will increase your balance and your required distributions. This can push you into a higher tax bracket.

INCOME OR GAINS?

Another concern about converting a retirement fund to cash flow is working out the mechanics of tapping your portfolio.

With savings yields and stock dividends at low levels today, it's unlikely you can meet your cash flow needs from interest and dividends alone. You'll probably have to liquidate some securities or bank deposits. A "bucket to bucket" approach can provide discipline, helping to keep your cash flowing.

How it works: Maintain 12 to 18 months' worth of spending money in a cash reserve, such as a money market fund.

Example: You'd like to spend $60,000 over the next 12 months, in addition to what you will get from Social Security. Thus, keep $60,000 to $90,000 in a money market fund for ready access.

For bill paying, money can be transferred from this cash "bucket" to a checking account. Alternatively, you can arrange for regular transfers, simulating a paycheck deposit into your checking account.

Having an ample amount in a money market fund will enable you to respond to emergencies. You won't have to make hurried portfolio decisions during times of stress.

Next step: Gradually, your cash bucket will be drained. Each quarter, you must decide how to replenish it. *Options…*

● **Use current income.** Even in today's low-yield environment, you're bound to have some investment income from interest and dividends. If you want to withdraw, say, 5% of your portfolio this year, get halfway there by pulling out 2.5% worth of current yield.

Key: The investment income in your taxable account will be taxed anyway, so it might as well be moved to the cash bucket.

If you're withdrawing money from your IRA, it may make sense to tap its income, too. This will allow the stocks and bonds in your IRA to stay in place longer.

● **Rebalance your portfolio.** Cash in what's up rather than what's down.

Example: At this point in your life, you might want an asset allocation that's equally divided between stocks and bonds. Suppose, though, that recent market strength has pushed stocks up toward 60% of your portfolio. In this scenario, you would sell some stocks to raise cash and then head back toward your desired stock-bond split. On the other hand, if bonds have pulled ahead of stocks, you might sell bond fund shares or use the cash from maturing bonds.

Caution: Recognizing significant capital gains might lead to the taxation of additional Social Security benefits.

Strategy: Take gains every other year, thus subjecting Social Security benefits to taxation only in alternating years.

Example: If your modified adjusted gross income (MAGI) is normally less than $32,000 (or $25,000 for singles) except for the capital gains income you recognize each tax year as you create cash from your portfolio, then you would be better off recognizing your capital gains in *every other tax year. Result:* 85% of your Social Security benefits will be taxed in Year One and 0% in Year Two.

Recognizing half the gains in Year One and again in Year Two will cause 85% of your Social Security benefits to be taxed in *both* years!

●**Sell the losers.** If your portfolio doesn't need rebalancing, sell the securities on which you have paper losses in a taxable account. This provides immediate tax losses while deferring taxable gains.

●**Sell the bonds.** If neither rebalancing your portfolio nor harvesting tax losses is enough to refill your cash bucket, lighten up on the bonds. Hold on to stocks, which can be expected to do best over the long term.

No matter what, though, your investment portfolio should be managed to balance stocks, which can provide good returns, and bonds, which can lower your risk. Cash requirements are important but they should not push you into imprudent investment moves.

Retirement Savings Rule of Thumb

Expect to need a total of 10 times your final salary during retirement. Calculate what your salary will be at retirement…multiply that by 10 …and make that your savings goal.

Breakdown: About seven times your projected final salary should be enough to pay for a lifetime annuity. When added to Social Security, the annuity will give you at least 100% of your final pay after you retire. The remaining three times your final salary can be used for investments and as a financial reserve for emergencies that come up.

David L. Wray, president, Profit Sharing/401(k) Council of America, Chicago, and the author of *Take Control with Your 401(k)* (Dearborn).

Keys to a Debt-Free Retirement

Jean Chatzky, the financial editor for *Today* on NBC and editor-at-large for *Money* magazine. She is also the author of *Pay It Down!* (Portfolio). Her Internet site is *www.jean chatzky.com.*

It's very easy for seniors to accumulate debt, but it's especially difficult for seniors to pay debt off.

Income usually falls in later years while pre-retirement spending habits linger. There are gifts to children and grandchildren. Grandparents may be asked to help with school bills or finance a child's new home or business—and it's hard to say *no.* Medical bills increase with age— unforeseen medical expenses are the leading cause of personal bankruptcies.

Even refinancing a mortgage at a lower rate, if you borrowed additional cash in the process, adds to your debt and risk.

But you can reduce debt…even eliminate it altogether. *How…*

●**Tally what you owe.** Sit down with your spouse or partner and look at how much you owe…and how much that debt is costing you.

It's easy to measure the cost of your debt when you're talking about a home or car loan. Payments and interest charges don't change from month to month.

It's harder to calculate credit card debt. For one thing, the outstanding balance and interest charges will fluctuate from month to month.

Because you're only required to make a modest minimum payment each month, your credit card debt can seem less of a burden than it really is. Focus on the outstanding balance, not that minimum monthly payment.

You'll stay in debt for a very long time if you keep using credit cards and make only the minimum monthly payments. Set a goal to pay off all the debt within three years and make your monthly payments large enough to meet that goal. Every payment should cover that month's interest and enough principal to make a noticeable dent in your outstanding balance.

Important goal: Get your debt low enough so that your monthly payments are far less than your total monthly income. The more you have left after paying off debt, the more you have to invest so that you will be able to live better in later years.

●**Reduce debt by $10 a day.** Freeing up $10 a day to pay off debts is an attainable and effective goal—this will allow a family owing $8,000 (the average credit card debt) to get out of debt in three years.

Start by cutting the amount of your monthly payment that is wasted on interest. Lay all your credit cards on the table and list the annual percentage rate (APR) for each.

Gather all the preapproved offers for credit cards with lower interest rates that you have received recently. Then call your current card issuers and use those offers to bargain for lower rates. Card issuers reduce the interest rate more than half the time.

Next, look at all your spending to see where else you can trim.

Helpful: Create a "money map"—a list of everything you spend your money on. Track spending by writing these items down in a pocket notebook for a month or so. You can use software such as *Quicken* to track spending (*www.quicken.com*). My book also offers a guide to help you total up spending.

Realizing how much you spend on gourmet coffee, meals out and other everyday expenses can help you cut back.

Challenge: *There are two areas where most people spend quite a bit more than they need to…*

●Gifts. You'll be amazed at all the birthday, holiday and just-for-fun gifts you give children, grandchildren and other family members in a year's time. Your family would gladly settle for fewer and less costly gifts today if that minimizes the risk that they'll have to support you someday.

●Technology. High-speed Internet connections can cost twice as much as regular dial-up service. *Also:* Do you really need 200 cable channels and 2,000 minutes a month on your cell phone plan? Calculate how much you're paying for technology each month—and how much you would save with a slower Internet connection and cheaper TV and cell phone service.

●**Sell what you don't use—and apply the money to paying down debt.** You can sell anything from jewelry to books to extra china to old LP records, maybe even some nice furniture in the attic or basement, at a garage sale, consignment shop or on-line through eBay. If you don't know how to use eBay, do an Internet search under "eBay sales tools" to find products that will help you. Or there are specialists who will sell your things in return for a percentage of the proceeds—generally about 30%. You'll find them by doing a search for "eBay sales consultants."

Also: You may have really needed a second car when you were working and children still were living at home—but now, you might do fine with one car.

The hardest choice—but the one with the biggest savings potential—involves selling your home and using part of the proceeds to pay down debt. Parents rarely hang on to the old family home for themselves—they may keep it because they think that their kids will want it someday. In fact, kids almost never want to move back to Mom and Dad's house.

●**Institute safeguards.** *Put some safeguards in place to keep from piling up more debt…*

●Get rid of all but one low-rate credit card. Also, think about reducing the credit line.

●Use that card sparingly. When possible, use a debit card rather than the credit card. Each use of a debit card immediately reduces your bank balance. That limits spending to what you have in your account rather than the full amount of your credit limit.

•Get a debt buddy—a friend that you can call to consult with if you're on the verge of making a major purchase. Enlist other friends to help, too. If your inner circle knows what you are up to, they're less likely to invite you along for a day of shopping.

•**Get help when you're falling short.** See a credit counselor to set up a repayment plan. You'll be required to make a monthly payment to the counselor, who then will use the money to pay off your creditors. A debt-management program from a credit counselor can take four to five years to complete.

Don't file for bankruptcy unless an expert in the field concludes that it is the only way out for you, as it will affect your credit rating for years to come, and you could be forced to sell assets for whatever they'll bring to satisfy your creditors.

A good credit counselor will review all your finances and then determine if debt management will work for you. Only in the most dire of circumstances is he/she likely to recommend bankruptcy as the best solution to your debt problems.

Warning: Not every credit counselor is on the up-and-up. You want to work with an organization that is not-for-profit and is also a member of the Better Business Bureau (703-276-0100, *www. bbb.com*) as well as the National Foundation for Credit Counseling (800-388-2227, *www.nfcc.org*).

It May Not Pay to Work Past Age 65

The tax rate on working increases at older ages, approaching 50% for some people by age 70. Also, by age 65, people typically can receive nearly as much income and benefits in retirement as by working.

Barbara A. Butrica, PhD, senior research associate at Urban Institute, Washington, DC, and coauthor of a working paper on older workers for the Center for Retirement Research at Boston College, *www.bc.edu/centers/crr.*

The Wisest Ways to Make Withdrawals from Your Retirement Accounts

Ed Slott, CPA, editor, *Ed Slott's IRA Advisor,* 100 Merrick Rd., Rockville Centre, NY 11570. Mr. Slott is a nationally recognized expert on IRA distributions. His Web site is *www. irahelp.com.*

If you participate in a 401(k) or another type of employer-sponsored retirement plan, you will have to decide what to do with your account when you leave the company. Many people roll the balance into an IRA.

Benefits: If this is done properly, not only do you maintain tax deferral, but you also control how your money will be invested.

However, an IRA rollover is not your only choice. *Other options…*

•**Take the cash.** If you do this, you'll owe income tax on the full amount right away.

•**Keep the money in your former employer's plan.** Many companies will permit you to do this.

•**Transfer money to a new employer's plan.** Even if you're not immediately eligible to participate, you can hold cash in the new plan until you can make other investments.

•**Crack your nest egg.** You can withdraw *some* of your retirement funds, pay tax on the withdrawal and then roll the balance into a tax-deferred IRA.

WHEN NOT TO ROLL OVER

Why choose one of these alternatives rather than a rollover into an IRA? *Possible reasons…*

•**You're in a cash crunch.** If you need to spend some or all of the money in your plan, you might as well withdraw it from the plan right away. That's especially true if you were born before 1936.

Loophole: People in that age group qualify for a special tax benefit. They can utilize tax-favored 10-year averaging if they take all of their money out of the plan. This could cut their taxes to a relatively low rate. (See instructions for IRS Form 4972, *Tax on Lump-Sum Distributions.*)

Trap: You don't get this tax break if you do an IRA rollover.

Key: Even if you can't utilize 10-year averaging, the current low income tax rates may make withdrawals appealing.

●You need a helping hand. If you don't want to manage your own retirement fund, you may prefer to leave the money with your former employer or transfer it to a new one. Inside an employer's plan, professionals may manage the investment options.

●You want to extend tax-free growth. Under the Tax Code, you can put off taking the required withdrawals from your company plan, even after you reach age 70½, as long as you're still working. With an IRA, you must start taking distributions after you reach age 70½.

Caveat: To postpone withdrawals beyond age 70½, you can't own more than 5% of the company that you still work for.

●You need to keep creditors at bay. Money in an employer-sponsored retirement plan is generally protected from creditors, judgments, divorce settlements, etc., under federal law.

Trap: Under the new bankruptcy law that is effective on October 17, 2005, assets in qualified retirement plans and rollover IRAs are fully protected, but assets in traditional and Roth IRAs enjoy protection only up to $1 million.

●You want to keep a borrowing option. Many of the employer-sponsored plans, including 401(k)s, permit you to borrow half of your account balance, up to $50,000, even after you leave the company. This depends on your company's plan.

Plan loans may be easier to get than bank loans, with less paperwork. Also, repayments (plus interest) go to your retirement account rather than to a bank.

Problems with an IRA rollover: You can't borrow from an IRA. Furthermore, any outstanding 401(k) loans must be repaid before a rollover, reducing the amount you will have in your IRA.

Therefore, if you have outstanding loans, or think you might want to borrow in the future, keeping money in an employer's plan may be the best choice.

●You hold appreciated employer stock in your plan. An IRA rollover can cost you a substantial tax break.

Example: Your retirement plan account now includes $50,000 of your employer's stock, which was worth $10,000 when it was contributed to your account. If you roll over your entire account, that $50,000 eventually will be taxed at ordinary income rates, now as high as 35%, upon withdrawal.

A good strategy is to withdraw the employer shares while rolling your plan balance into an IRA. You will owe tax, but only on the value of the shares when contributed to the plan, not on their current value.

In this example, you will immediately be taxed on $10,000, but the $40,000 in net unrealized appreciation remains untaxed until your shares are sold. When you sell those shares, you will owe tax at a 15% capital gains rate, assuming current law remains in effect.

THE PENALTY BOX

Between ages 55 and 59½, you're better off keeping your money in the company plan, if you expect to take distributions. If you need to tap your retirement plan, withdrawing money from an IRA before age 59½ may expose you to a 10% penalty.

Loophole: You can take money from your employer-sponsored plan, penalty free, if you were at least age 55 in the year you left your job.

LIFE INSURANCE

If your account in an employer-sponsored plan includes life insurance, you might want to keep your money in that plan to keep the policy in force.

Key: You may find it costly to continue your life insurance after you have left the company plan. If you are in poor health, you might not be able to buy needed coverage at a reasonable price.

WHEN IRAs ARE IDEAL

If none of the above reasons apply to you, you're probably better off with a rollover IRA. In some situations, IRAs are especially appealing.

Example: You're interested in a Roth IRA conversion. After five years and age 59½, all withdrawals from a Roth may be tax free.

Required: Only traditional IRAs may be converted to a Roth IRA. Therefore, you must first roll over a company plan distribution to an IRA, then convert the account into a Roth IRA.

Keep in mind that Roth IRA conversions are permitted only if your adjusted gross income in the year of the conversion is not more than $100,000. You'll owe tax on all the deferred income built up in the IRA when you convert an IRA to a Roth IRA.

Key: No matter what your reason, always ask for a "trustee-to-trustee transfer" when you execute an IRA rollover. Keep your hands off the money being rolled over.

Trap: If you handle the funds, you'll face mandatory 20% withholding on the rollover. You will have to make up the difference from your own pocket to avoid owing income tax.

Hot News Regarding Roth IRA Conversions

Barry C. Picker, CPA/PFS, CFP, Picker & Weinberg, CPAs, PC, 1908 Avenue O, Brooklyn 11230. He is chair of the New York State Society of CPAs' Employee Benefits Committee, a member of that society's Estate Planning Committee and technical editor of *Ed Slott's IRA Advisor,* 100 Merrick Rd., Rockville Centre, NY 11570. Mr. Picker is also the author of *Barry Picker's Guide to Retirement Distribution Planning,* available at 800-809-0015.

Roth IRAs offer the potential for substantial tax savings. However, income limits restrict the use of Roth IRAs by upper-income taxpayers.

New law: In 2005, a provision of a 1998 tax law took effect. Now, more taxpayers can get below the $100,000 adjusted gross income (AGI) limit for Roth IRA conversions.

ROTH IRA REWARDS

A Roth IRA is similar to a traditional IRA because investment income can build up within the account untaxed.

Distributions from a traditional IRA will be subject to income tax if contributions have been made with pretax dollars, which usually

is the case. Even if an IRA is funded with after-tax dollars, the growth in the account will be taxed upon withdrawal.

Roth IRAs, on the other hand, are always funded with after-tax dollars. Subsequently, they offer the chance for tax-free distributions.

Required: Once an individual has a Roth IRA for more than five years and is older than age 59½, withdrawals will be tax free. The five years are counted from the first day of the year that the first Roth IRA is opened.

CONVERSION FACTORS

The largest Roth IRAs—and the greatest opportunities for untaxed distribution—will result from converting a traditional IRA to a Roth IRA rather than from annual contributions.

For example, Jane King retires with $1 million in her employer-sponsored retirement plan. She rolls that $1 million to a traditional IRA, which she converts to a $1 million Roth IRA. After she has met the five-year, age-59½ requirements, all withdrawals from her Roth IRA will be tax free.

Problem: Roth IRA conversions are not permitted for taxpayers whose AGIs are in excess of $100,000 without regard to the income from conversion. This limit is the same for single taxpayers and for couples filing jointly.

However, the minimum required distributions (MRDs) from a traditional IRA starting at age 70½ do not count toward the $100,000 income limit.

If Jane King is over age 70½, she is required to take MRDs from her rollover IRA. Each year, her other income is around $90,000 while her MRD runs about $40,000.

In 2004, her $40,000 MRD and $90,000 of other income put her over the $100,000 ceiling, so she could not convert her IRA to a Roth IRA.

New era: Starting in 2005, Jane's MRD does not count in this calculation. So, as long as Jane (who files as a single taxpayer) keeps her other income below $100,000, she can convert all or part of her traditional IRA to a Roth IRA. Eventually, she can take tax-free withdrawals.

CLEARING THE HURDLES

If you are interested in a Roth IRA conversion, keep these points in mind...

● **The amount of the MRD can't be converted to a Roth IRA.** If Jane has a $1 million traditional IRA and is required to withdraw at least $40,000 this year, she can convert no more than $960,000 to a Roth IRA.

● **Amounts you withdraw from your traditional IRA,** including MRDs, will be taxable income. What is more, converting a traditional IRA to a Roth IRA triggers taxable income.

As above, Jane King takes an MRD of $40,000 and converts a $960,000 IRA to a Roth IRA. She will pick up $1 million of income, taxable at steep ordinary income rates.

Strategy: The tax on a Roth IRA conversion should be paid with non-IRA funds. Tapping the IRA to pay this tax will reduce the amount available for tax-free buildup.

Problem: Converting a large traditional IRA at one time may generate a huge income tax bill. You may not have sufficient liquid assets, outside of your IRA.

Solution: Convert a part of your traditional IRA to a Roth IRA each year, spreading out the tax bill. This approach also will cause the income to be taxed in lower brackets each year.

Loophole: A series of partial conversions won't extend the five-year waiting period for tax-free withdrawals. As mentioned, this clock starts when the first Roth IRA is established.

For example, Jane King converted $100,000 of her traditional IRA to a Roth IRA on June 20, 2005. This makes January 1, 2005, her official starting date.

Each year, she converts another $100,000. By January 1, 2010, when she reaches the five-year mark, Jane has a total of $600,000 in her Roth IRA, counting investment income.

Outcome: She can withdraw as much or as little as she wishes, tax free, even though some of the funds have been in the account less than five years.

LOOKING AHEAD

Another benefit of converting a traditional IRA to a Roth IRA is the opportunity to avoid MRDs.

Inside story: As mentioned, MRDs must be taken from a traditional IRA after age 70½. Any shortfall will be subject to a 50% penalty.

The Roth IRAs, by contrast, have no lifetime MRD rules. You can keep as much as you want inside your Roth IRA and maintain the tax-free buildup.

After converting her traditional IRA to a Roth IRA, Jane King finds that she does not need to tap this account to cover her living expenses. She leaves the account intact so it can continue to grow.

If Jane needs expensive custodial care late in life (or if she decides to spend her money on something like taking her family on a luxury cruise around the world), she can pull tax-free cash from her Roth IRA.

Endgame: If Jane never wants or needs the cash from her Roth IRA, she can bequeath the account to her children, grandchildren or other beneficiaries. Those beneficiaries, in turn, must take MRDs from the inherited Roth IRA, stretching tax-free income over their life expectancies.

UNDER THE CEILING

The benefits of a Roth IRA may be so appealing that you'll want to take specific measures to bring your income down below $100,000.

Loophole: You can convert a traditional IRA to a Roth IRA in any year that your income falls beneath $100,000. No matter how much you earn in future years, your Roth IRA conversion won't be rescinded.

Income-reduction tactics include…

● **Taking time off from work.** If you take early retirement or semiretirement, reducing your income one year, there's no reason that you can't go back to work full-time the following year.

● **Paring your investment income.** You can avoid taking capital gains or offset any gains with losses. In addition, you can put money into deferred annuities and municipal bonds, which don't produce taxable income and so do not increase AGI, rather than into bank accounts or taxable bonds.

● **Entering into a deferred-compensation agreement with your employer.** Agree in advance (in writing) to defer some earnings into a future year.

Reducing your AGI below $100,000, even if only for one year, can pay off in decades of tax-free income.

Good Gift for a Child: A Roth IRA

Seymour Goldberg, Esq., CPA, Goldberg & Goldberg, PC at 1 Huntington Quadrangle, Melville, NY 11747, *www. goldbergira.com*. Mr. Goldberg is one of the nation's leading authorities on IRA distributions.

The best gift you can make to a child or grandchild may be the funds to finance annual contributions to a Roth IRA.

Many minors earn income from summer jobs, after-school work, work done for a family business, etc. These children are eligible to make Roth IRA contributions of up to 100% of their earned income, subject to the limits outlined below. If they don't have the money to do so, you can give it to them.

Big payoff: Distributions from Roth IRAs can be totally tax free, unlike those from traditional IRAs and other kinds of retirement plans. And due to the power of compound earnings over the many future years of a young child's life, the final tax-free payout may be huge.

Example: Roth IRA contribution limits are $4,000 from 2005 to 2007, and $5,000 for later years. Starting this year, a child age 15 makes these maximum contributions for seven years, through age 21. If the average return in the IRA is 7%—the long-term average after inflation for stocks—then at age 21, the child will have approximately $42,000 in the IRA.

Without investing another dollar, the IRA will grow to more than $750,000 by the time the child reaches age 65—all tax free, making it worth much more than the same amount of money in any other kind of retirement account.

At age 21, the child will have accumulated some future retirement security without having to save any more for retirement during his/her working life.

Even better: Roth contributions can be withdrawn any time tax free. Earnings withdrawals are subject to other restrictions. So during the child's life, he will have access to the funds you provided, tax free.

Taxpayer Victory: Bigger Medical Deductions for Retirement Community Residents

Thomas Pflanz, CPA, CFP, tax partner, McGowen, Hurst, Clark & Smith, PC at 1601 Westlakes Pkwy., West Des Moines, IA 50266. He is past president of the Mid-Iowa Estate and Financial Planners Club and the Financial Planning Association of Iowa.

Maybe you (or your parents) have started to think about moving into a retirement community.

Bonus: Some of these communities offer tax-favored medical services.

Strategy: Tax benefits may reduce the net cost of living in such a retirement community. A 2004 Tax Court decision [*Delbert L. Baker,* 122 TC 143] illustrates how to justify substantial medical deductions.

IRS loses: In this case, the court ruled that taxpayers could deduct a substantial portion of the fees paid to a retirement community. The allowable deductions, treated as medical expenses, were greater than the IRS was willing to permit.

BACKGROUND

In 1989, the Bakers moved to a continuing-care community that provides four levels of living accommodations and services that range from independent living through skilled nursing care.

In exchange for an entrance fee of $130,000 and ongoing monthly fees, the Bakers were guaranteed several medical amenities.

Examples: Nursing services, if needed, and the guarantee of a bed in the skilled nursing facility, if required.

Key: The Bakers moved into an independent living unit, which provided the lowest level of care in the community. There is no indication that they needed nursing care or any unusual medical services.

Nevertheless, they deducted nearly $35,000 (more than 26%) of their $130,000 entrance fee as a medical deduction.

Off the docket: The case decided in 2004 did not involve the 1989 payment and deduction. There is no indication that this deduction was challenged.

Strategy: If you (or your parents) move into a retirement community offering medical services and pay an up-front fee, deduct a portion as a current medical expense. (See below for information on how to come up with a justifiable percentage.)

Advantage: This up-front deduction may be quite sizable. If so, you probably will exceed the 7.5%-of-adjusted-gross-income threshold necessary for deducting medical expenses.

THE 2004 CASE

The 2004 case decided by the Tax Court involved monthly payments made to the retirement community by the Bakers in 1997 and 1998. They deducted a portion of those monthly fees as medical expenses.

How they calculated this deduction: First, a representative of the community looked at its annual expenses for medical care and determined that they came to less than 20% of total expenditures.

Then, a committee of residents (including Mr. Baker) went over the community's financial records and came up with their own calculations. They added some expenses to the "medical" category.

Example: Expenses involved in an emergency pull-cord system in each residential unit.

Result: The residents' committee concluded that about 40% of the monthly fees were attributable to medical care.

Backed by this study, when they filed their 1997 and 1998 tax returns, the Bakers claimed that approximately 40% of the fees they paid each month were medical expenses, deductible on Schedule A of Form 1040.

In addition, the Bakers deducted a portion of the monthly fees they paid to the community for the use of the pool, spa and exercise facility, asserting that these were medical expenses.

THE IRS POSITION

The Bakers' tax return was subsequently audited and the deductions were questioned.

Halfway measure: On audit, the IRS was willing to permit medical deductions for nearly 20% of the Bakers' monthly fees, which was in line with the community's calculations.

However, it was less than half of the 40% deduction claimed by the Bakers. Also, the pool/spa/exercise deductions were completely disallowed by the IRS.

Changing course: The dispute eventually came to trial, with the IRS trying a new tactic.

Rather than allowing the Bakers to deduct 20% of their monthly fees, which had been the IRS's original position in court, the IRS asserted that the deductible portion of their monthly fees had to be based on actuarial calculations, taking into consideration health-care utilization and longevity.

But, the Tax Court disagreed, concluding that such an actuarial method is "so complex as to defy full explanation."

Finding: The "percentage method" can be used. That is, a percentage of the monthly fees paid to such a retirement community may be considered a medical expense.

Key: Again, there was no indication that the Bakers had used any medical services offered by the community. It was sufficient that a portion of the fees they paid were used by the community to pay for medical expenses.

Crunching the numbers: According to this Tax Court decision, the deductible percentage was based on the number of community residents and the weighted average monthly service fees.

Example: Say that you live in a retirement community with 1,000 residents. The community's total expenses are $10 million per year while medical expenses are $2 million. The deductible percentage under the Tax Court's method would be 20% per resident—$2 million/$10 million. *Result:* If the facility has 1,000 residents, each one is entitled to $2,000 worth of deductions this year—$2 million divided among 1,000 residents, regardless of individual use.

MAXIMIZING THE METHOD

In the Baker situation, the Tax Court went through the various numbers and determined that medical expenses were actually around 16% per resident.

Because the Bakers filed a joint return, two residents were involved. Therefore, they were permitted to deduct around 32% (or two times 16%) of their monthly fees paid over the two years at issue as medical deductions.

Key: The Baker method will obviously favor couples filing joint tax returns because the deduction is calculated per resident. The situation would be different, though, for single filers.

Just suppose that, in the above example, the 1,000 residents occupy 800 units—600 singles as well as 200 married couples. Assuming equal monthly charges that just cover expenses, each unit would pay $12,500 per year—$10 million divided by 800 units.

If Jane Jones lives alone, her 20% deduction under the per-unit method would be $2,500 (20% of the $12,500 that she actually pays). It would not be the $2,000 that results from the per-resident calculation.

Loophole: Residents of retirement communities that provide medical services can use either percentage method—the per-resident method as suggested by the Tax Court or the traditional IRS percentage method, similar to that used in the above Jane Jones example.

In the Baker decision, the Tax Court noted that the IRS has been using its own percentage method in rulings that go back to 1967. Thus, whichever method will provide the greater tax benefit may be used by retirement community residents, relying upon either prior IRS rulings or this Tax Court decision.

LACK OF EVIDENCE

In the Baker decision, the Tax Court denied the medical expense deductions for use of the pool, spa and exercise facility. These amenities were available to all community residents at no extra charge.

Tactic: If a community charges extra for use of a pool, spa or exercise facility, any fees paid for such purposes might be considered a medical expense if a physician has prescribed these activities to treat a specific medical condition.

Retiring Abroad Is Worth Considering

Rosanne Knorr, author of *The Grown-Up's Guide to Retiring Abroad* (Ten Speed). An advertising copywriter and writer of travel books during her working days, Ms. Knorr recently moved back to the US after spending her initial retirement years in the Loire Valley of France. She currently lives on Florida's Gulf coast.

You can immerse yourself in something brand-new and stretch your nest egg by spending at least part of your retirement outside the US.

If you don't want anything too exotic, there are US "colonies" in Mexico offering relaxation and such familiar shopping names as Wal-Mart. Or go where the people and the culture are very different from what you've known at home —and find great excitement and stimulation.

My husband and I retired to the Loire Valley in France, where American residents are rare. We made French friends, learned French cooking, shopped at the local market and learned how to make homemade vinegar. Our immersion in French life and our travels near and far created memories more thrilling than any we dreamed of when we first bought our retirement house.

WEIGHING YOUR OPTIONS

The sinking dollar has narrowed the cost advantage of retiring abroad. The dollar is the lowest in 12 years against the British pound and at an all-time low against the euro.

But there still are some bargain locales in Europe—Portugal, for instance. Closer to home, retirement living remains fairly inexpensive in Mexico and Costa Rica.

Saving money isn't the only reason for spending your retirement years in another country. The pace of life is usually slower when you move abroad and crime rates are often lower than in the US—assuming you choose your location wisely. Medicare will not cover you overseas, but medical costs are typically low enough in other countries that you can still get the health care you need.

New lifestyle: Most important is how living in another country, with another culture, can enliven and energize your senior years. Instead of doing the same old things back home, you're learning a new language or adding foreign words and phrases to your vocabulary, picking up new customs and a new way of life.

Important: One thing retiring abroad won't do is permit you to avoid paying US income taxes. You will be liable for all US taxes as long as you remain a citizen. Since most Americans won't have a local source of income abroad, they won't face local income taxes. Americans living abroad will have to pay local consumption taxes, such as the value-added tax (VAT) common in Europe. For more information, consult a tax professional knowledgeable in international tax.

WHERE TO GO

Mexico is probably the most popular choice of American retirees right now. The dollar has actually appreciated by 16% against the Mexican peso over the past five years. A couple can live in most parts of Mexico for about $20,000 a year—maybe one-third of what a comparable lifestyle would cost in the states. That covers renting a two-bedroom house, food and clothing, medical bills and entertainment. It wouldn't cover dues at the local golf club but you would have a comfortable way of life.

So many Americans have settled in Mexico that they've created an infrastructure for other Americans. You'll hear English spoken, shop at familiar stores, see American movies. Mexico is far from crime-free, but there's less street crime and burglary in the communities where Americans tend to settle than in most of the US.

The colonial cities of San Miguel de Allende (founded in 1542) and Guanajuato (founded in 1554) are both popular retirement destinations for Americans. They are just north of Mexico City, and both date back to the earliest days of Mexico, when it was a colony of Spain. Other locales with heavy concentrations of Americans

include Guadalajara and Lake Chapala, northwest of Mexico City, and Puerto Vallarta on the Pacific Coast.

Costa Rica is also popular with American retirees. Popular areas include communities around the capital city of San José.

LOOKING AT EUROPE

Assume that you'll be able to rent a two-bedroom apartment outside of popular tourist areas for roughly $1,000 per month. Spend a vacation or two in the area that interests you, so you can meet local real estate agents and shop the rental market. Once you've rented for a time, you can think about buying.

Here are some specifics…

Great Britain: London is among the world's most expensive cities and out of reach for most retirees. You would pay at least $3,000 a month to rent a one-bedroom apartment in a better part of town and at least $250,000 to buy it.

Better bets these days would include the county of Cornwall on the southwest tip of England, with charming villages on a rugged coast (places such as Falmouth and Penzance).

Also consider: Scotland. A one-bedroom apartment in Edinburgh will run about $1,000 a month—prices are lower in the countryside.

France: Expatriates from the US and the Continent are concentrated in Paris…Provence in the southeast…Dordogne in southwestern France…and the French Riviera. Prices are high in all these areas.

You'll find housing more reasonable in Normandy and Brittany in the north. Winters are chillier than in Provence but still mild compared with most of the northern US. My husband and I chose the Loire Valley in west-central France, southwest of Paris, because it isn't crowded with British and American transplants.

We paid $80,000 for our house in 1997 and sold it two years ago for $130,000. It was a four-level house with an up-to-date heating system and bathrooms. Given the current value of the euro, you would probably pay more than $130,000 to buy anything comparable today.

Italy: Tuscany (think Florence and environs) and Umbria (around Assisi and Perugia) draw lots of retirees from Britain and the US. Bargains are hard to find, but prices in both places are far less than you would pay to live in Rome or in Florence itself. The movie *Under the Tuscan Sun* has triggered a new inflow of foreign visitors to Tuscany—and for good reason. This part of Italy offers lovely scenery, villages that date back to Roman times and some of the world's best wines. Even so, you still should be able to find a rental for around $1,000 a month.

Spain: The south coast of Spain—the Costa del Sol—still draws retirees. But the seacoast villages that once charmed visitors have been replaced by wall-to-wall high-rises. You'll pay less and find more to your liking along Spain's Mediterranean coast south of Barcelona. The villages are still charming and the high-rise vacation condominiums that abound along the Costa del Sol are fewer and farther between.

EUROPEAN WILD CARD

Best European bargains these days are in a country that hasn't attracted many Americans...

Portugal: I personally love the country for its beauty, great food and friendly people. Even though Portugal uses the euro, prices still are at least 20% less than in France or Italy. Lisbon is a major cosmopolitan city but I prefer the Algarve, a region that covers about two square miles along the country's southern coast, with a warm climate and beautiful beaches, and the adjacent hill country. The Algarve is pricey by Portuguese standards, but cheaper than anything comparable in the coastal resort areas of France, Italy or Spain. You'll do best if you look inland rather than right on the water.

GETTING STARTED

Moving abroad is a big step, so give yourself time to make the right choice. There are plenty of books available, including mine. The Internet lets you do in-depth research about different locations without leaving home. Use search engines to check countries and regions that interest you.

Don't just pick up and move when you find a promising locale. Spend some vacation time there first. See if you like the culture, the food and the lifestyle. I love to visit Spain, but I'm not sure how well I would do long-term in a country that doesn't eat dinner until 10 or 11 pm.

Even when you've made your choice, give yourself an out by renting for a year before you

consider buying. Many retirees don't buy at all, but just keep renting.

More from Rosanne Knorr...

Helpful Resources on Retiring Abroad

If you're thinking of retiring abroad, be sure to consult these resources...

● **American Citizens Abroad** (*www.aca.ch*). This nongovernment organization, based in Geneva, Switzerland, is aimed at helping Americans who live abroad.

● **The Association of Americans Resident Overseas** (*www.aaro.org*). This volunteer organization represents the interests of American expatriates.

● **EscapeArtist.com** (*www.escapeartist.com*). This Web site stresses overseas real estate but offers other services to Americans living abroad.

How to Avoid the Six Major Retirement Mistakes

Jeri Sedlar, cofounder of Sedlar & Miners, a New York City–based executive search and transition coaching firm. With husband and business partner Rick Miners, she coauthored *Don't Retire, REWIRE!* (Alpha). Her site on the Web is *www.dontretirerewire.com*.

Most Americans think of retirement as just a financial target. Once they have enough saved, they assume that they are ready to retire. For many people, however, that's not the case. The psychological transition from working to not working can be so much harder than anticipated.

We interviewed more than 300 retirees and preretirees to learn what makes some retirements more satisfying than others. *Among the most common mistakes that can sabotage a retirement...*

● **Not realizing what you are giving up.** Careers provide us with more than just income.

They can be a source of companionship and provide a sense of achievement and self-worth.

Example: Dr. Hill, a small-town physician, retired at age 75 because of the increasing paperwork involved in running a medical practice. Only then did he realize how much he missed being "Doc," the trusted friend on whom the community relied for medical care.

Give some thought as to what makes your workday gratifying. You might not enjoy your retirement if you can't find a new source for that gratification.

●**Full-time travel and leisure.** Many assume that retirement will be one long vacation or never-ending golf game—but that can lose its allure in as little as two years.

Be honest about how much relaxation you can handle. You might want to work part-time or seasonally.

Example: Andy, age 59, soon to retire from a successful career in sales, is looking forward to indulging his passion for fly-fishing. He's aware that it might not sustain him for the rest of his life, so he also plans to start a fly-fishing camp for kids.

●**Retiring for the wrong reason.** Hating a particular job is not the same as being ready for retirement. Nor is it necessarily time to stop working simply because someone else's schedule says so. Do not retire just because you are offered an early retirement package or because your spouse wants to retire.

If you're not certain that you're ready to retire, don't. Look for a new job—you always can retire at a later date.

Example: Renee retired at age 60 from a career in education administration because she didn't like her new boss. Until the change in leadership, she had loved her job. Years later, she realized her dissatisfaction would have been better solved by finding a different employer.

●**Falling out of the loop.** A retired executive I spoke with said that the hardest thing about retiring was not getting any phone calls. No one seemed to want or need his opinion anymore. He felt totally disconnected from his old life.

Five years prior to retiring, take steps to ease the transition—mentor young executives so that they have a reason to come to you with future problems…look into becoming a consultant…join organizations or associations with an eye toward future leadership positions.

Example: When Jerry saw retirement on the horizon, he then persuaded his company to name him its representative to the industry association. When he left his job five years later, he had enough friends in the association to win a term as president. The nonpaying position did not demand much time, but it kept him connected to his old life.

●**Expecting to spend all your time with your spouse.** With many couples, the wife manages the social calendar. The husband then expects his wife to keep him occupied after he retires. But millions of women continue to work after their husbands retire. Even when a woman does stop working, she shouldn't be expected to plan her husband's day.

Example: One wife said of her husband's upcoming retirement, "I don't want twice the husband for half the pay." She had her friends and activities and wanted her husband to have his own friends and activities.

Before you retire, develop activities separate from your spouse, that will interest you after you leave work.

●**Ill-considered relocations.** People often move when they retire. The result can be loneliness and boredom.

Example: Dan, a former attorney, and his wife, Arlene, a former accountant, moved from New York City to a villa in France. They were back within a year. The couple missed their friends, clubs, grandkids and even racquetball.

Before you sell your current home, rent in the region you're considering for several full seasons. You may love Florida in the winter, when the weather's mild and your friends are down for the season, but not in the summer when it's hot and no one is around.

13

Estate Planning Know-How

How to Keep Your Family from Fighting Over Your Money

The more money you hope to pass along to loved ones, the greater the chance that your children will fight over it. Even close-knit families aren't immune to these problems.

Contesting a will can hold up the distribution of assets for many years. Even worse, it never resolves the emotional issues that underlie most inheritance fights, such as which of the children was loved most.

To reduce the likelihood of bitter legal disputes in your family after you are gone...

•**Treat each heir equally.** Many parents leave the largest share of their estate to the child who makes the least money. Or they put the inheritance of a free-spending child in a trust with stipulations but leave assets to his/her siblings free and clear.

Problem: Grown children often equate their inheritances with the depth of their parents' love. Children who feel they were shortchanged might sue because they believe that their siblings must have manipulated the parent.

Exception: Wills that involve family businesses. It's difficult to treat children equally if they don't all have an active interest in operating the company. If you have a family business, meet with your accountant and estate attorney to discuss business succession planning as well as distribution of nonbusiness assets among your family members. If the business is the only family asset, look into life insurance trusts or the sale of the business to provide for nonparticipating family members.

•**Reveal any big surprises before you put them in your will.** Discussions about inheritances are taboo in most families. While it's not

Adam R. Gaslowitz, Esq., a nationally recognized expert in estate litigation, and a partner in the law firm Adam R. Gaslowitz & Associates, LLC in Atlanta. He is also the chairman of the estate planning section of the Atlanta Bar Association. His cases have been featured on CNN and in *The New York Times*.

necessary to tell your children exactly what you're planning to leave to them, make them aware of out-of-the-ordinary decisions, such as unexpected large gifts to charity or to one child.

If you don't disclose the gifts in advance, it is easier for one of your children to contest the will. Courts often agree to hear a will contest if one child appears to be unusually favored over another. In addition, explain your motivation in the will itself.

You might write—*Son, I have left your sister the summer house because she will use it more. This may seem unfair, but it doesn't mean that I love you any less. It gives me great pleasure to know that she and the children will get to enjoy it. Since you and Helen work such long hours, you would hardly spend any time there anyway. I appreciate your understanding of my wishes.*

Don't go into extensive detail. You risk slandering one of your heirs, which can give him an excuse to challenge your will.

Helpful: A well-drafted "no-contest" clause in your will—which will automatically disinherit any recipient who challenges the document—is worth including, but it is no panacea. Beneficiaries might contest the will anyway, and many probate courts will refuse to honor no-contest clauses.

●**Give away sentimental objects now.** I tried a case in which a woman wanted her $30 million estate split up equally between her son and daughter. The brother and sister wound up litigating this case for years over a single piece of jewelry—a ring that was worth only a few thousand dollars that had been passed down in their family for generations.

You can sidestep such controversy by giving your beloved personal items to family members while you are alive, especially heirlooms that you do not use or wear regularly. (Discuss tax ramifications with an adviser if you think beneficiaries will sell these items down the road.)

To avoid unhappy surprises, let each of your heirs know what you are giving the others.

●**Don't unintentionally disinherit a child.**

Common scenario: Your will divides your estate equally among your children. When you fall ill and need help with such daily chores as cooking, shopping and paying bills, you rely on the child who lives closest to you. For convenience, you put the caregiver child's name jointly on your bank accounts. By law, these joint assets automatically pass to the caregiver child when you die, overriding your will—and your other children are then shortchanged.

Better: Establish power-of-attorney accounts with banks and brokerage firms so that individuals you designate—your child, a trusted friend, an accountant—can write checks and make decisions about your money on your behalf without being a joint owner of your assets.

Also remember to change your will or include flexible language that allows for tragic occurrences such as the death of a child.

SPECIAL SITUATION: SECOND MARRIAGE

A second marriage can create inheritance-planning challenges. *Smart strategies…*

●**Provide directly for children from your first marriage.** Often, a father leaves everything to his second wife with the understanding that the second wife will provide for his children from his first marriage—but taking this shortcut almost guarantees a will contest.

Better: Use marital trusts, such as a qualified terminal interest property (QTIP) trust, to earmark assets for your children upon your second spouse's death.

●**Choose a nonbiased executor.** Men often try to promote family harmony by making a second wife and one of the children from the first marriage coexecutors of their estates or cotrustees of marital trusts. This just pits the second wife against the child over such issues as how to invest assets or manage the estate.

Better: Use a bank as executor or trustee, if the will has trust provisions. Most of the large regional banks offer this service to customers.

Cost: About 1% to 2% of the estate's value on a sliding scale, based on the size of the estate.

More from Adam Gaslowitz, Esq.…

Protect Your Inheritance from Good Samaritans

Elderly people may rely on their neighbors, friends and health-care workers, but some caregivers manipulate these vulnerable individuals into putting them in their wills.

Self-defense: Look for any signs of undue influence. Do these caregivers speak poorly of family members or play on your parent's fears? Or, has your parent told you that he/she has changed his will to include gifts to religious institutions or charities? If so, consult an estate planning attorney about establishing a guardianship or irrevocable trust.

Generally, you can contest the will only after your parent has died. Then hire an attorney who specializes in inheritance litigation. Ask your estate planning attorney for a recommendation.

When—If Ever—to Write Your Own Will

David S. Rhine, CPA, regional director for family wealth planning at Sagemark Consulting, a division of Lincoln Financial Advisors Corp., Rochelle Park, NJ, *www.sagemark metro.com.*

It's tempting to try to save several hundred dollars by writing your own will—and it's easier than ever with the proliferation of books and kits that guide you through this process. But writing your own will rarely is a good idea. The procedure is far trickier than it seems, and without an attorney, it is easy to make serious errors. *Examples...*

● **You leave your estate to your spouse but fail to consider assets that your relatives may will to you.** If you're in a second marriage, assets and family heirlooms could wind up in your spouse's family rather than with your children from a prior marriage.

● **When you gather witnesses to sign the will,** one of them walks out of the room for a moment. Even that brief absence may invalidate the will because the law requires all witnesses to be present while each of them affixes his/her signature.

Will-writing kits and books usually have checklists designed to prevent mishaps, but no one is looking over your shoulder to make sure that you follow the checklist. Attorneys, on the other hand, are trained to follow the rules and are responsible for doing so.

Despite their limitations, will-writing kits and books can be helpful if you...

● **Can't afford to pay an attorney.** Books and kits usually cost less than $25, compared with the much higher fees that most attorneys charge for a simple will.

● **Want a quick education in wills before you hire an attorney.** Learning about wills, especially the legal terms, may make it easier to deal with your estate attorney—and could even save you money.

If you do decide to use a will-writing kit or book, be sure to look for one that was written by a licensed attorney and published by a company that publishes other legal materials as well.

Also, it's a good idea to read *The American Bar Association Guide to Wills and Estates* (Random House). While it's not a do-it-yourself manual, the book explains many of the complicated issues in deciding who will get your assets when you die.

Wills and estate planning are two areas that many people avoid. In fact, according to a survey by Lawyers.com, 58% of adult Americans lack a basic will. That can be a costly mistake for your heirs.

Can You Avoid Estate Tax by Relocating?

Sanford J. Schlesinger, Esq., a founding partner and head of the wills and estates department at the law firm Schlesinger Gannon & Lazetera LLP, 499 Park Ave., New York City 10022.

Some observers are speculating that the federal estate tax will be permanently repealed or greatly scaled back. That may come to pass, but planning to reduce postmortem taxation is still vital because of the 2001 tax law. This legislation reduced revenues for individual states, many of which are taking actions to raise their own estate taxes.

TOUGH TRANSITION

Before the 2001 tax act went into effect, federal law included a credit for state estate taxes based on a formula.

Upper limits: This tax credit went up to 16% while the highest federal estate tax rate was as much as 55%.

How it worked: When a decedent's estate was in the 55% tax bracket, the executor would pay the state an amount equal to the 16% credit and the other 39% would go to the federal government. Similar splits were made for estates in lower federal estate tax brackets.

As of 2005, this credit has been eliminated. The old system is scheduled to come back in 2011, but that may not happen if another tax law is passed in the interim, as many people anticipate.

Bottom line: The loss of this credit has cost many states significant amounts of money.

STATES STRIKE BACK

Some states have responded to this revenue shortfall by "decoupling" from the federal government's estate tax system. Rules differ greatly from state to state, however.

Favorite strategy: In several states, new laws call for the collection of the amount a state would have received if the old credit had remained in place.

For example, Alan Johnson lives in a state which has passed such a law. He dies in 2006 with a large estate.

Suppose, under pre-2002 law, Alan's estate would have paid $2 million to his state. The new law, passed by his state, calls for the same $2 million tax payment.

Trap: While Alan's estate pays the same $2 million to his state as it would have paid in 2001, there is no federal tax credit to reduce the federal estate tax obligation. Alan's estate winds up paying more, counting both federal and state estate taxes.

Loophole: Beginning in 2005, an estate can claim a federal estate tax deduction for state taxes paid. This deduction is scheduled to remain in effect through 2009.

Trap: A deduction from federal estate tax saves no more than 46 cents on the dollar in 2006. That's much less of a benefit than the old tax credit, which provided full shelter at 100 cents on the dollar.

Even after this deduction, the net state tax cost can be quite high. If the federal government picks up 46%, which is the top estate tax rate in 2006, a large estate would pay 54% (100 minus 46).

Result: The net cost could be as high as 8.64% (54% of 16%), from a 16% tax rate (the top estate tax rate in many states).

SQUEEZE PLAY

Some states set another tax trap. They have lower estate tax exemptions than the federal government.

Examples: In 2006, the federal estate tax exemption is $2 million. But, Massachusetts has a $1 million exemption, while in New Jersey, assets more than $675,000 are subject to estate tax.

Result: Some estates will end up owing tax to their states even when they owe no federal estate tax.

Examples: Suppose Marjorie Russell dies in New Jersey in 2006 with a $2 million estate. Her estate would owe no federal estate tax but it would owe New Jersey estate tax of $99,600.

This example assumes that Marjorie was unmarried, left nothing to charity and had not made taxable gifts during her lifetime.

TRIMMING THE TAX

What kind of planning might ease this state tax bite?

●**Gifting.** Giving away assets has long been a way to reduce federal estate tax, and this tactic might be especially valuable when dealing with state taxes. In some states, the taxable estate is not adjusted for lifetime gifts, as is the case under federal law.

Example: If John Green has given away $1 million and dies with $4 million, he is treated as having a $5 million estate by the IRS. Some states, though, do not follow the same add-back procedure, so John's estate is taxed for state and estate tax purposes on a smaller amount.

Key: Only four states currently have a gift tax—Connecticut (which might repeal its law), Louisiana, North Carolina and Tennessee.

Tactic: Execute a durable power of attorney to allow someone to make such gifts if you're no longer capable. Even deathbed gifts might produce tax savings.

While you are still capable, consider making estate-reduction gifts with borrowed money secured by your assets.

Don't give away the low-basis assets, which could provide a tax advantage if inherited at your death. Moreover, giving away appreciated assets is undesirable because the recipient will owe capital gains tax on all the appreciation if those assets are sold.

●**Balancing.** Regardless of whether you give lifetime gifts, some basic tax planning may be necessary.

Classic strategy: The first spouse to die leaves some assets to the spouse and other assets to their children. Often, these bequests are made in trust.

Given the concern over state taxes, the children's bequest might be the largest amount that won't create a federal or state estate tax—$675,000 in New Jersey, for example. The balance of the estate can be left to the surviving spouse, tax free, outright or in trust.

●**Disclaiming.** In the above scenario, you might provide for your surviving spouse to be able to "disclaim" (waive) most or all of the inheritance. The survivor can then weigh his/her health, other assets, the current tax law, etc., and decide if it makes sense to disclaim some assets to the children.

Even if that means paying some state estate tax at the first death, the federal tax savings might make a disclaimer worthwhile.

●**Moving.** Rather than going to the time and expense of extensive estate tax planning, it may be simpler to move to another state. Florida, for example, does not impose estate tax and is unlikely to do so in the future.

Relocating is particularly appealing if you already have two homes, including one in a state where estate tax is not a major concern.

Trap: Changing your "domicile" may require more than simply living in Florida for seven months a year.

Strategy: You might consider filing a declaration of domicile in your new state, registering to vote there, relocating your brokerage and bank accounts, changing your driver's license, getting new plates for your car and so on. You also might sell your house in your old state and replace it with a smaller home or apartment.

In other words, make a real move. Such a change of scenery can lead to a substantial tax savings for your loved ones.

Keep Life Insurance Out of Your Estate

Irving L. Blackman, CPA, founding partner, Blackman Kallick Bartelstein, LLP at 10 S. Riverside Plaza, Chicago 60606, *www.taxsecretsofthewealthy.com*.

You may need to use life insurance to protect assets that are substantial—such as a family's business or investments—from estate tax.

Trap: If you own the insurance policy personally, the proceeds will be included in your taxable estate. Up to half of it could go to the IRS as estate tax.

Much better: Have an irrevocable life insurance trust own the insurance policy. Insurance proceeds paid to the trust will escape both estate tax and income tax and be available for use as the trust directs.

You could finance the policy's premiums by making tax-free gifts to the trust (up to $12,000 annually, $24,000 if married, for each trust beneficiary) and/or by advancing loans to the trust that will be repaid to your estate from the life insurance proceeds.

Caution: You must not retain any "incidents of ownership" in the insurance policy once it is in the trust or the IRS can tax the policy's proceeds back into your estate. Incidents of ownership include such powers as the authority to change the policy beneficiary, cancel the policy, pledge the policy as security for a loan or borrow against it.

However, the IRS has ruled that retaining the right to be repaid from the policy proceeds for loans advanced to the trust to pay the policy premiums is not considered an incident of ownership (IRS Letter Ruling 9809032).

Technical rules apply, so consult an expert.

Estate Planning Tip

O wning assets jointly with a spouse can create estate planning pitfalls. Such property passes automatically to the surviving spouse outside the will. But, because provisions made in a will to distribute property or reduce estate taxes are bypassed, intended bequests may be invalid and tax bills increased, as the directions in a will fail to take effect.

Important: When drafting a will and estate plan, ask your attorney about the effect of *all* your jointly owned property. You may wish to change ownership to another form.

Bob Carlson, editor of *Bob Carlson's Retirement Watch,* 3700 Annandale Rd., Annandale, VA 22003.

Use an IRA to Be Charitable...and Still Leave More To Your Heirs

Jere Doyle, senior director of estate planning at Mellon Private Wealth Management, one of the nation's leading private wealth managers, One Boston Place, Boston 02108.

A little-known way to include charitable intentions in your estate planning is to make bequests from your IRA or another tax-deferred retirement account. For tax purposes, this technique will probably yield the best overall result.

Payoff: Deferred income tax can be entirely avoided. Moreover, you may be able to pass appreciated assets to other heirs, who will inherit with a tax-saving step-up in basis.

SPLIT SHIFT

Suppose, for example, that Joan Wilson is a widow with a total estate of $4 million, half in an IRA and half in highly appreciated securities and real estate. Joan wants to leave $2 million to her children and $2 million to various charities. If the appreciated assets are left to charity while the IRA goes to the children, no federal estate tax will be due, under current law.

Trap: With this plan, the children eventually will have to pay income tax on the IRA money as it is withdrawn. At a 35% rate, the ultimate federal income tax charge could be more than $700,000.

Better approach: Bequeath the IRA to charity and the appreciated assets to your children. Again, there will be no estate tax, but the children will inherit the appreciated assets with a step-up in basis, under current law.

The children would never owe any capital gains tax on the appreciation that occurred during Joan's lifetime.

Bottom line: The latter approach passes on the estate completely tax free, saving hundreds of thousands of dollars in taxes.

Caution: Planning for charitable bequests is the opposite of planning for lifetime donations. While you are alive, it generally makes a lot of sense to give away appreciated assets and let your tax-deferred retirement plans continue to compound.

SOONER OR LATER

There are four methods you can use to make charitable bequests from your retirement plan...

● **Leave your IRA directly to charity.**

● **Leave your IRA to your spouse, who will leave it to charity** at his/her death.

● **Leave your IRA to a marital trust** with all distributions going to your surviving spouse. At his death, whatever remains goes to charity.

● **Leave your IRA to a charitable remainder trust (CRT),** which can pay income to any individual you want to name, with the charity as the recipient of the remainder interest. (Ask the charity or your tax adviser to explain how a CRT works.)

Outright bequests are most suitable if you are not married or if the bequest is relatively small in relation to your entire estate. If you're married, your spouse may not want to give up the IRA to charity.

What about the other methods? If you are confident that your spouse always will be able to handle the IRA wisely and make the appropriate charitable bequest, simply leave the IRA to your spouse.

Reality check: In many situations, you'll be better off using a trust, which can provide control and protection.

TRUST TACTICS

The Tax Code permits you to create a trust where the surviving spouse gets all the income while the first spouse to die gets to name the ultimate beneficiary, which can be a charity.

Benefits: No federal estate tax will be due at the first death. In case of need, the trustee can distribute more funds to the surviving spouse.

At the survivor's death, whatever remains in the IRA goes to the charity that you've named, tax free.

Alternative: If you want to limit the survivor's income to provide more to charity, a CRT may be appropriate. With a CRT, the spouse's income will be a fixed amount or a fixed percentage of CRT assets.

If you want to name children or grandchildren to also receive income from the trust, a CRT would be more suitable.

Caution: A present value will be placed on the projected future income to younger generations, and that amount may be subject to estate taxation.

Trap: A CRT also may result in speedier distributions from an inherited IRA, so some tax deferral may be lost.

Work with a knowledgeable tax pro who can crunch the numbers and suggest the type of trust most suitable for your family and charitable goals. This is especially important whenever an IRA is left to a trust and the trust ultimately goes to charity.

Reason: It becomes more complicated to obtain an income tax deduction and extend tax deferral.

DIVIDE AND CONQUER

The above strategies may make sense if you have $2 million in an IRA and want to leave $2 million to charity. But what if you want to leave only $100,000 to charity? Or $50,000?

You can make a specific charitable bequest from an IRA or qualified plan, but the tax treatment is unclear.

Danger: If you specify, say, an $80,000 bequest, the IRS might treat that as an $80,000 withdrawal from the IRA and assess income tax on the amount. *Strategies...*

● **Name co-beneficiaries.**

Example: You might say that 4% of the IRA goes to charity while 96% goes to a family member. With a $2 million IRA, that would mean an $80,000 charitable bequest.

Note: Satisfying a fractional bequest with the right to receive an IRA is not a taxable event.

● **Split your IRA.** Break off a smaller IRA, as destined for charity.

Example: From an IRA of $2 million, you could roll over $80,000 to a new IRA tax free. The charity could be named as beneficiary of the new IRA while a family member remains beneficiary of the old IRA, which is now worth $1,922,000.

Subsequent withdrawals from the new IRA could keep the balance at $80,000, if that's the amount you intend to bequeath to charity.

Tactic: When minimum required distributions (MRD) begin after age 70½, take some of the amount from your charitable IRA, leaving more in your family IRA.

Example: You split your IRA, as above. After some years of growth, you have $2.1 million in your family IRA (going to your spouse) and $90,000 in the IRA that will go to charity.

Say your MRD for the year is $85,000. Distributions need not be pro rata, thus you can take $10,000 from the charitable IRA.

This reduces the charitable IRA to $80,000, the amount you intend to donate. Only $75,000 (the $85,000 MRD minus the $10,000 withdrawn from the charitable IRA) need be taken from your family IRA, increasing the amount that can compound, tax deferred, for yourself and your beneficiary. The same process can continue, year after year.

By remaining vigilant, you can fulfill philanthropic goals while providing for your loved ones, too.

Have a Contingency Plan

Name contingent beneficiaries for your IRAs and other retirement plans in the event that the primary beneficiary predeceases you. Otherwise, the IRA will probably be included in your estate and then may have to be withdrawn over a maximum of five years. A contingent beneficiary, under current retirement plan rules, can stretch out withdrawals over his/her life expectancy, resulting in higher tax-deferred accumulations and potentially much lower income taxes on withdrawals made over many years.

Jonathan Pond, president, Financial Planning Information Inc., 1 Gateway Center, Newton, MA 02458.

The Overlooked Trillion Dollar+ Income Tax Deduction

Seymour Goldberg, Esq., CPA, Goldberg & Goldberg, PC at 1 Huntington Quadrangle, Melville, NY 11747, www. goldbergira.com. One of the nation's leading authorities on IRA distributions, Mr. Goldberg is also author of Practical Application of the Retirement Distribution Rules *(IRG Publications, www.goldbergreports.com).*

The least understood and most complicated of income tax deductions is also the one that is most often missed—even though it could be worth a trillion dollars or more to taxpayers who are failing to claim it.

If you have deferred-income–type assets in your taxable estate—or inherit them from one —you must learn about this. *Here's the story…*

DOUBLE DANGER

When deferred-income–type assets are in your taxable estate, they can be subject to taxation at near confiscatory rates—80% or more. *Assets that face this danger include…*

- **Balances in IRAs,** 401(k)s and other tax-deferred retirement accounts.
- **Pension payments** owed to designated beneficiaries.
- **Survivor annuities** issued by insurance companies.
- **Proceeds due on installment sales.**
- **Royalty rights.**
- **Untaxed deferred interest on Series E, EE and I savings bonds.**
- **Deferred compensation coming from employers.**
- **Damage awards from lawsuits.**
- **Other income-producing items.**

The income from such items, when later paid to heirs, is called income in respect of a decedent (IRD).

Trap if you don't know the rules: The income-producing item's value is first subject to estate tax at rates up to 46% in 2006. Then the income later paid by the item—the IRD—is subject to income tax at rates up to 35%. The total tax due from adding these tax rates can be as much as 82%—leaving as little as 18% for heirs!

Example: An individual leaves $1 million in an IRA that is subject to 44% federal estate tax (this article does not consider state estate tax). The IRA's beneficiary is in the 35% tax bracket. The estate must first pay $440,000 tax on the IRA (his estate provides funds to pay this tax). Then the beneficiary must pay $350,000 of income tax payable on the distribution of the IRA balance—if he/she doesn't know the IRD rules. The total tax bill comes to $790,000 for the IRS.

TAX RELIEF FROM CONGRESS

Congress believed this full double taxation to be unfair. As a remedy, it created partial relief in the form of an income tax deduction for federal estate tax (but not for state estate tax) previously paid on an asset that creates IRD. This is often called the "deduction for IRD." It can be claimed as the IRD is paid out.

For example, an individual dies leaving $1 million in an IRA subject to 44% federal estate tax. The tax of $440,000 is paid as in the example above. The IRA's beneficiary is in the 35% tax bracket. *If he...*

•**Takes a full distribution of the $1 million,** the deduction for IRD lets him deduct $440,000 against it. As a result, he pays income tax on only $560,000—and the deduction for IRD saves him $154,000—plus state income tax savings on the deduction.

•**Takes distributions from the IRA over time,** the deduction for IRD is taken proportionately. If the IRA is distributed at a rate of $100,000 per year, the deduction for IRD is $44,000 per year until the entire $440,000 is consumed. This saves $15,400 of income tax per year plus state income tax savings on the $44,000 deduction. Any additional distributions from the IRA in excess of $1 million (due to investment returns) would be fully taxed.

OVERLOOKED DEDUCTION

The biggest mistake made with the deduction for IRD is that many people—perhaps most—*do not claim it at all*. It is the most overlooked of all income tax deductions. *Reasons why...*

•**Most individual taxpayers do not even know it exists.**

•**Professionals who deal with an estate often don't talk to each other about it,** so it falls through the cracks.

Example: Neither the executor nor the adviser who prepares an estate's tax return has responsibility for the personal tax returns of heirs who would claim the IRD deduction, and doesn't even think about it—unless there is a formal agreement stipulating that he *will* take responsibility. At the same time, the tax advisers of those heirs do not know if any estate tax was paid. Or the heirs prepare their own tax returns and are ignorant of the whole issue. So the deduction is simply missed.

•**There is no "information reporting" for the tax deduction.** No form, such as a W-2, 1099 or K-1, is filed by anyone to report the deductible amount to a taxpayer who doesn't know about it.

•**Records for past years are lost.** The IRD deduction may be spread out over numerous years—in the case of an IRA distributed over the beneficiary's life expectancy, 20 years or more. And a balance of the available deduction must be carried forward from year to year—if past records weren't prepared or were lost, the deduction is lost.

•**It's very hard to learn about the deduction.** There is no single IRS publication dedicated to explaining its application in detail—information about it is spread around different IRS publications and rulings.

Result: The deduction is routinely missed by taxpayers, often for year after year.

TRILLION-DOLLAR ERROR

The dollar volume of overlooked deductions for IRD already missed as well as what might be missed in the future stands to be huge—perhaps a trillion dollars or more.

Government data show tax-deferred retirement accounts that can produce IRD now hold $11 trillion dollars. Of this, $3 trillion is owned by persons in the highest tax brackets who are expected to owe estate tax—and both of these numbers are growing rapidly.

These retirement accounts are just one of several kinds of assets that produce IRD.

Not all of these assets will be subject to estate tax. But, if out of this more than $11 trillion, only a little more than $2 trillion eventually becomes subject to estate tax, the total deduction for IRD will be $1 trillion. As of now, most of these deductions are probably being missed!

WHAT TO DO

To save the deduction for IRD, it's essential that the tax professional responsible for an estate's tax return works together with the tax advisers of the heirs of the estate and beneficiaries of assets included in the estate, such as IRAs and pensions.

The estate's tax professional should inform each heir in writing of the amount of estate tax that was paid on each item of IRD and should spell out how the rules work. Then each heir's tax adviser must use this information to create a schedule of available deductions that may be claimed against IRD in the future.

Important: The information and schedule may have to be used for many years, long after the professionals who prepared it are gone from the scene. So it must be completely self-explanatory to be able to survive a future IRS audit and be safely stored with other vital "permanent" documents.

●**If your estate is large enough to be subject to estate tax,** discuss planning for IRD with your advisers now.

●**If you inherit an IRA or other item of IRD,** contact the executor of the deceased to learn if any estate tax was paid and obtain needed information to manage the deduction for IRD.

The technical rules for deductions for IRD are complex, so be sure you are advised by a tax professional who is very experienced in dealing with them.

More from Seymour Goldberg, Esq., CPA...

Estate Tax Trap

Don't assume that you are safe from estate tax because the amount exempt from federal estate tax—$2 million in 2006, rising to $3.5 million in 2009—is more than you own.

Trap: You may owe state-level estate tax. Some states now have a lesser exempt amount than the federal amount, such as $675,000 in New Jersey and $1 million in Massachusetts and New York. Moreover, state estate tax used to be credited against the federal tax and so didn't really cost anything extra. But this credit on the federal return was eliminated in 2005, so the state tax now is truly an extra tax. However, the state death tax *is* deductible on the *federal* estate tax return. At this time, it is not clear if the state estate tax is deductible on the state estate tax return.

Safety: Check your state's estate tax rules to see if your estate might owe a surprise tax. If your estate is large enough to owe tax at both levels, but state rules differ from federal rules, you may need to adopt separate strategies to minimize both taxes.

Vital Documents To Have and Keep

Lisa S. Hunter, Esq., partner, Certilman, Balin, Adler & Hyman, LLP, attorneys, East Meadow, NY.

Sudden disability or death of the head of a family can leave relatives scrambling to find vital documents.

Trap: If your documents are kept in a safe-deposit box, they may be impossible to obtain when needed.

Safety: Keep vital documents—such as your will, power of attorney and health-care proxy—in a safe but accessible location, such as your lawyer's office. Keep copies in your files at home—and include passwords that might be needed.

Other documents to have...

●**Contact list.** For all professionals involved with your assets—attorney, accountant, insurance agent, broker, banker and so on.

●**List of assets and investment accounts.** Insurance policies, bank and stock brokerage accounts, etc.—with account numbers.

●**List of outstanding debts and obligations.** Loans, credit card accounts, etc.

●**Titles and deeds.** To real estate, vehicles, a burial plot and other properties—all collected together at a safe location.

●**Copies of beneficiary designations.** For all IRAs, pension accounts and insurance policies, in case originals at a financial institution are misplaced.

●**Safe-deposit box records.** Location and the keys to it so it can be opened.

Useful: If these lists aren't in one location, keep a master list that tells where they can be found along with your vital documents.

Helpful Advice on Living Wills and Health-Care Proxies…You Really Must Have Both

Martin Shenkman, CPA and attorney who specializes in trusts and estates in New York City and Teaneck, NJ. He is author of numerous books, including *Living Wills & Health Care Proxies: Assuring That Your End-of-Life Decisions Are Respected* (Law Made Easy Press). His Web site, *www.law easy.com,* offers free sample forms and documents.

Whenever a television news program broadcasts stories of terminally ill patients on life support, with families feuding over whether to continue treatment, many people say, "I hope something like that never happens to me. I would rather be dead."

Life-or-death decisions ought to be very well thought over—and not made alone. Everyone needs to take steps to ensure that his/her own end-of-life decisions are respected as well as to avert misunderstandings and quarrels among family members.

VITAL STEPS

First, discuss the issue with family members and loved ones, a spiritual adviser or clergyperson, a physician and a lawyer. If that sounds like a lot of people, it is. But each has important insights to contribute. Take the steps now to be sure that, should you be in a life-threatening situation and unable to speak for yourself, the decisions made for you will be the ones you would want. These discussions also help the loved ones who will be charged with making a decision understand your feelings.

When the discussions are finished, ask your lawyer to prepare a health-care proxy and living will for you. It is essential that you have both documents.

●**Health-care proxy.** Obtain a health-care proxy or health-care power of attorney—terminology varies from state to state—designating an "agent" (a person who will act on your behalf) to make medical decisions if you cannot do so. It should specify whether the agent has the authority to sign a "do not resuscitate" order to the hospital. In addition, name a successor

agent to serve if the first agent cannot. They should not be a team. One person must be responsible. The proxy should include the right to move you to another hospital—even to one in another state, if differing state laws make the move necessary to carry out your wishes.

●**Living will.** Sign a personalized statement detailing your health-care wishes. Do you want life support continued if you are in a persistent vegetative state? Should religious restrictions prevail? What type of funeral do you want?

These two documents should be prepared to ensure that your personal preferences are followed. Living will and proxy forms are available on the Internet, and many people assume that filling one out will take care of the matter. In fact, very serious problems can ensue because Internet documents may not address such concerns as nutrition, hydration, funeral arrangements and religious observances.

TOUGH DECISIONS

A health-care proxy is the medical counterpart of a power of attorney. If you are responsible for your own or your family's finances, you also need a "durable" power of attorney, one that would become effective should you be incapacitated. But do not automatically ask the person who serves as your financial agent to hold your health-care proxy as well. If you name different people in the two documents, direct that health-care decisions be made by the health-care agent and that the person holding the power of attorney provide the funding to pay for those decisions.

Unlike those tragic situations that make the nightly newscasts, most cases are not clear-cut from a medical standpoint.

Two examples: Let's consider two elderly people who are hospitalized with pneumonia. One has always been strong and healthy, perhaps even recently ran in a marathon. If put on a respirator, he may well make a full recovery.

The other patient was suffering from congestive heart failure, end-stage cervical cancer, osteoporosis and chronic obstructive pulmonary disease before being stricken with pneumonia. Her prognosis is not good. But neither is it certain that she has no chance of recovering from the pneumonia. Unless she has signed a living will and health-care proxy making clear she does not want heroic measures under these circumstances, health-care providers are bound to do all they can to save her. Pneumonia, after all, is reversible.

If you hold her health-care proxy, her physicians can give you their best judgment and advise you, but there is no certainty of what lies ahead for her.

Will a life of pain simply be prolonged—possibly even made worse—if the patient is kept alive via a respirator or by inserting a feeding tube, or even by calling in a resuscitation team should her heart fail in the hospital? Does she want to live as long as possible, despite the pain and suffering? Some people do. Suppose she recovers from pneumonia but cannot live at home any longer. Would she want to go to a nursing home, if necessary, or does she prefer a quiet death at home or in a hospice? Does it make sense to try so-called heroic measures for a period to see if the patient improves and discontinue them if the patient makes no progress? Medical caretakers must try, unless the person holding the health-care proxy says no heroic measures are to be used.

The person holding the health-care proxy has the legal right to make such decisions. Nevertheless, other family members often disagree strongly. Maybe they feel guilty and want to keep Mom alive as long as possible without knowing what Mom herself wants. Or having seen news broadcasts about year-long family battles, they shudder and say, "Pull the plug."

FAMILY SQUABBLES

The Terry Schiavo case in Florida is an extreme example. Mrs. Schiavo was kept alive in a persistent vegetative state for 14 years. Her husband insisted she would not want to live that way. In an interview, he said she had made such a remark when seeing a broadcast about a similar case. Her parents insisted she be kept alive. The Florida legislature and Governor Jeb Bush sided with the parents.

It is impossible to know what Mrs. Schiavo's own views would have been. But if she would have had a health-care proxy and living will, the tragic quarrel could probably have been prevented.

The Schiavo case also illustrates why your health-care proxy should specifically authorize the person who is your agent to make decisions on your health care, including the use of a feeding tube. Again, as I said above, consider authorizing your agent to move you to another state, if necessary. The state laws vary significantly on this subject, so it is important to consult with an attorney in your own state who specializes in estate planning.

Families often quarrel over funeral arrangements, even though they may share a religion. One member interprets religious beliefs liberally, while another has a strict letter-of-the-law perspective. Or one wants to have an elaborate funeral with an expensive coffin, flowers and music, while another insists on a quiet, dignified service. A living will that specifically spells out what you want can avert such divisions among your survivors.

More from Martin Shenkman, Esq., CPA...

Make Loans to Heirs, Not Gifts

Seniors with wealth often make gifts to children and grandchildren. But the ups and downs of the stock market show that wealth can be lost unexpectedly. If such a thing happens after giving away too much, a generous family head may be left with too little to meet his/her own needs.

Safety: Help the younger generation by making loans to them, instead of gifts, to finance investments such as a new home, new business or higher education.

If the funds are wisely invested, the recipient will be able to repay the loan later, after profiting from it. So, if you should ever unexpectedly need the funds, you will be able to get them back, after having helped the recipient.

And if you don't need the funds in the future, you can make a gift of them at a future date.

Important: To satisfy the IRS that a loan to a family member is genuine, follow all the formalities—have a written note, set a market interest rate, have a payment schedule and see that payments actually are made on time. The note also may protect the money if the heir divorces.

Better Gifting

There's no need for most people to restrict tax-free gifts to only $12,000. Many people who learn that the annual gift tax exclusion is $12,000 per recipient ($24,000 for gifts made jointly by a married couple) needlessly restrict gifts to that amount when they could make much larger gifts tax free.

Important: In addition to annual "exclusion amount" gifts, you can make a further $1 million of lifetime gifts free of gift tax.

These additional gifts reduce the amount of your estate that will be exempt from estate tax —but with that now at $2 million and gradually rising to $3.5 million by 2009, most gift makers will not be affected anyway. Moreover, gifts of appreciating property may reduce the future estate tax by removing appreciation from an estate.

Randy Bruce Blaustein, Esq., senior tax partner at R. B. Blaustein & Co., 155 E. 31 St., New York City 10016.

Preserve Your Family's History

A personal historian can help preserve your life story, and your family's history, for further generations. If not recorded, family history can easily be lost to the young.

Helpful: Saving family histories has become a growth industry. The Association of Personal Historians (APH), founded in 1995, today has over 400 members, compared to the 15 they started out with. These include not only writers who can record your family's story, but also researchers, media firms (for making audio and video histories) and more. To find services close to you, visit the APH Web site at *www.personal historians.org*.

How to Keep More of Your Inheritance

Edward Mendlowitz, CPA, shareholder in the CPA firm WithumSmith+Brown, 120 Albany St., New Brunswick, NJ 08901. He is also the author of *Introducing Tax Clients to Additional Services* (American Institute of CPAs).

With some tax planning, recipients of an inheritance can keep more money for themselves, not give it to the IRS. *Consider these strategies...*

Loophole: **No capital gains tax on inherited assets.** Most beneficiaries pay little or no capital gains tax when they sell inherited assets because of a tax break known as stepped-up basis. The recipient's tax cost (basis) for figuring capital gains is the value on the estate tax return, not the property's cost to the decedent.

Example: You inherit a house that cost the decedent $20,000 and is now worth $150,000. You pay no tax when you receive the house and, if you immediately sell it for $150,000, you pay no capital gains tax. *Reason:* Your basis is equal to the property's value at the date of death (or six months later if the estate chose that date). Since the house was sold for the same price at which you inherited it, you pay no capital gains tax. If you sell the house for more than $150,000, the excess is taxable gain.

Loophole: **Deduct capital losses on inherited assets.** If you sell inherited property at a loss, you can deduct the loss. If you sell the house in the above example for $120,000, your tax deductible loss is $30,000, subject to annual deduction limits. Capital losses are deductible dollar for dollar against capital gains and up to $3,000 of ordinary income each year. Excess losses can be carried forward into subsequent tax years.

Loophole: **Pay executors' fees to sole beneficiaries.** Consider paying executors' fees to beneficiaries, depending on their tax picture. Estates can deduct executors' commissions. So when the executor is also the sole beneficiary, it makes sense to pay the fees if the estate is in the 50% tax bracket (including state taxes) and the executor in the 40% tax bracket (including state taxes).

Loophole: **Disclaim inheritances.** In some situations, a great deal of estate tax can be saved when a beneficiary disclaims (gives up) an inheritance.

Example: A wife leaves $500,000 to her husband, who has a $5 million estate. No estate tax is due on the wife's death because of the unlimited marital deduction. But on the husband's death, the extra $500,000 would be taxed to his estate at the top rate (about 50% including state taxes). The tax would be $250,000.

That tax could be saved if, on the wife's death, the husband disclaims the $500,000 inheritance and lets it pass to the couple's children or other beneficiaries. The gift would not be taxed in the wife's estate because of her exemption amount—her right to bequeath up to $2 million estate tax free to beneficiaries other than her husband.

Smart move: Use disclaimers with designated beneficiaries of IRAs or pension accounts. When a surviving spouse disclaims an IRA in favor of children and grandchildren as contingent beneficiaries, post-death planning can create dynasty-type extended withdrawals over the life expectancies of the children and/or grandchildren.

Caution: To be valid, disclaimers must be made within nine months of the death and meet other strict criteria—check with an estate tax adviser.

Loophole: **Redeem business stock.** If the decedent owned stock in a C corporation with high retained earnings, the stock can then be redeemed income tax free by the estate. The redemption is treated as a capital gain. There would be no income tax payable because the value of the stock is stepped up to its value on the date of the decedent's death.

Loophole: **Don't overlook the income tax deduction for estate tax paid.** Federal estate tax paid on income in respect of a decedent is deductible as an itemized deduction on your personal tax return when you report the income. Generally, when you inherit assets, your tax cost is stepped up to the asset's date-of-death value. However, this does not apply to income earned by the decedent but paid after death, including distributions from pension, 401(k), 403(b) and IRA funds.

Note: Post-death income may be subject to both estate tax and income tax. The income tax deduction mitigates some of this double tax.

Caution: The deduction is only for the federal estate tax and not state estate or inheritance tax.

Opportunity: A surviving spouse can elect to roll over a pension distribution into an IRA and defer the payment of income tax.

Loophole: **Delay the payment of the estate tax.** Estate tax can be paid in installments, with interest, over 14 years. The decision to pay estate tax on the due date or to elect installment payments is made after the death, although it is usually considered and planned for—or against—during the estate planning process.

Caution: When you elect installment payments, the IRS files a lien on the estate's assets.

14

The Travel Report

How to Be Your Own Tour Guide

There is a good compromise between traveling on your own and going on a group tour with a bunch of total strangers—think about giving self-guided touring a try.

Long popular in Europe, you'll save a bundle of money and get a customized trip. You choose your own travel dates, itinerary, level of lodging and companions.

You move along at your own pace, by yourself or with friends or family, stopping wherever you please and getting a taste of the local culture. You follow a carefully planned route with advice on what to see and do along the way and the assurance of emergency support ready to help you out if you need it.

Nightly accommodations and, often, meals, are prearranged, so you don't have to be concerned about logistics. And—a major plus—on land trips, your luggage is transported to your next lodgings, getting there before you do. *Some of the best self-guided tours…*

WALKING COASTAL NORMANDY

Averaging eight to 10 miles of walking a day, this seven-night self-guided tour along the coast of Normandy starts out at Caen, the historic town that is home to the World War II Peace Memorial and a chateau that was built by William the Conqueror.

You make your way on foot along the coast, retracing the movements of troops during the invasion of Normandy and visiting all the key beachheads, batteries, bunkers and memorials, lodging in charming country inns or family-run hotels. Among other overnight stops in this rural region, you spend one night in Bayeux, the first French town liberated in 1944.

Your luggage goes on ahead. Daily breakfast and dinner are included, along with transfers, maps and a guidebook. Most of the terrain you

---

Joan Rattner Heilman, an award-winning travel writer based in New York State. She is the author of *Unbelievably Good Deals and Great Adventures That You Absolutely Can't Get Unless You're Over 50* (McGraw-Hill).

231

cover is flat with a few short climbs. You can choose any departure date from May through September.

Cost: About $1,299* per person, double occupancy, not including airfare.

Information: Discover France, 800-960-2221, *www.discoverfrance.com.*

BIKING INN TO INN IN VERMONT

Spin your wheels at a leisurely pace around southern Vermont's rolling hills, charming villages, streams and lakes, arriving at a quaint country inn at the end of each day to spend the night, dinner and breakfast included.

You may customize the trip to suit yourself, choosing inns according to the distance you want to cover each day. One six-night itinerary with about 25 miles per day of easy to moderate biking begins in the arty village of Brandon and takes you around Lake Dunmore and into Middlebury.

Then, you explore the countryside as you ride into Vergennes, Vermont's smallest city, go south along Lake Champlain, pass through apple country and take the ferry from Larabee's Point for a visit to Fort Ticonderoga, then back to Brandon. Detailed route maps show you the way.

Cost: Varies according to room and season.

Information: Country Inns Along the Trail, 800-838-3301, *www.inntoinn.com.*

SAILING ON THE CHESAPEAKE BAY

Pick up your own 34-foot power catamaran in Annapolis, Maryland, and skipper it yourself —even if you are only a rookie boater—for a week on Chesapeake Bay's peaceful waters. You will get an introductory briefing, waterway guides with navigation maps and a captain's manual. Twenty-four-hour emergency assistance is just a phone call away.

Then, you're on your own to motor wherever you like along the Chesapeake's many miles of shoreline, harbors, rivers and coves. Stop at historic towns, eat meals aboard or in the local restaurants. You sleep on your boat, which will feature two double cabins, with a shared bath and shower, a living area and a fully equipped galley for cooking.

*All prices subject to change.

Cost: About $3,200* per week per boat plus fuel.

Information: Crown Blue Line, 888-350-3568, *www.sunsail.com.*

HIKING IN IRELAND

Enjoy this self-guided hike on Ireland's famous Dingle Way. A walking route follows old tracks, mountain trails and green roads, passing through villages and farmlands. You trek about 10 to 15 miles a day, following detailed route descriptions and maps.

Guesthouses along the way are already booked for you, your luggage is transferred and all you have to do is walk and enjoy the views. Your tour starts and finishes at the village of Camp on the north side of the Dingle Peninsula and takes you along minor country roads, assisted by yellow markers and road signs. If the weather is bad or you don't want to walk so many miles on a given day, you can take a van to your next inn for an additional charge.

Cost: Seven nights, $590; 10 nights, $700.

Information: Hidden Trails, 888-987-2457, *www.hiddentrails.com.*

CYCLING IN CALIFORNIA'S WINE COUNTRY

On this adventure, you pedal through towering redwoods, along winding rivers and past geysers, vineyards and wine chateaus in the famous Napa and Sonoma Valleys north of San Francisco.

Included are your accommodations, breakfasts, one dinner, luggage transfers, your bicycle and a ride back to your starting point at the trendy town of St. Helena. You cover an average of 30 miles (four to five hours) a day, with options for more mileage or rest days. Overnights include St. Helena…Calistoga, known for its thermal spas and mud baths…and Healdsburg, surrounded by vineyards.

Cost: About $1,700 for six days/five nights, depending on the level of accommodations and day of departure.

Information: Randonnée Tours, 800-465-6488, *www.randonneetours.com.*

BARGING ON THE ERIE CANAL

Navigate your own traditional European-style canal boat (with two to six passengers) through

*All prices subject to change.

dozens of locks on upstate New York's historic Erie Canal. You get a quick course on skippering and needn't be an experienced boatperson, especially since you can't go any faster than about six mph.

Pass through the newly restored waterway, stopping anywhere you please along the route for the night, a meal, a bike ride, a hike or a visit to an historic town.

Each boat has sleeping cabins, a kitchen and bathrooms, plus a small outside deck. Choose from two departure locations, one near Syracuse and the other near Rochester. You're on your own for all meals, which can be cooked aboard or taken on shore.

Cost: $1,995* to $2,495 per week, depending on size of the boat. The price includes fuel and tolls.

Information: Mid-Lakes Navigation Co., 800-545-4318, *www.midlakesnav.com*.

DRIVING THROUGH
THE CANADIAN ROCKIES

Hop into your rental car for a six-night driving tour that starts in Vancouver, British Columbia, and winds up in Calgary, Alberta. This self-guided tour will take you through some of the most breathtaking sights of western Canada and the Rocky Mountains.

After your first night on the waterfront in downtown Vancouver, you drive to the Lac le Jeune resort in Kamloops, stopping at Minter Gardens in Chilliwack. Ride the Hell's Gate airtram in the Fraser Canyon.

Then it's on to Jasper in the Rockies, where you get a Snocoach ride on the Columbia ice fields, followed by Lake Louise and Banff before driving to Calgary.

You may customize your trip yourself, choosing your own route, your own level of accommodations and the length of time on the road, with the costs adjusted accordingly.

Cost: About $1,650 per person, but prices vary depending on the level of accommodations you choose.

Information: Canadian Mountain Experience, 888-867-5448, *www.canadianmountain.com*.

*All prices subject to change.

More from Joan Rattner Heilman...

Great Train Trips Not Far from Home

Take an upscale train trip and you can travel in style through the most spectacular scenery in North America. Lounging in a comfortable seat or eating a good meal in the dining car while watching the world go by is undoubtedly the most relaxing way to travel. *Here are some of the best train trips on this continent today...*

ROCKY MOUNTAINEER

The Rocky Mountaineer's famous two-day, all-daylight sightseeing rail journey takes you through the Canadian Rockies, providing stunning views of snow-covered mountain peaks, dense forests, canyons and glaciers. Its luxury GoldLeaf Service features a bilevel dome coach with an observation platform on the upper level and a dining lounge below. The less expensive RedLeaf Service carries passengers in coaches with huge picture windows.

With onboard commentary along the way, the train leaves from beautiful, cosmopolitan Vancouver on Canada's west coast and ends in Banff or Calgary in Alberta, stopping overnight at a hotel in Kamloops, British Columbia. A second route ends in Jasper, Alberta.

Your meals are included in the price. You eat breakfast and lunch onboard and dinner on land. The trip can be extended into multi-day vacations with land stays and sightseeing in Victoria, Lake Louise and Jasper.

Cost: For the core two-day trip—$869* to $1,174 per person, double occupancy, depending on the season, for GoldLeaf service. For RedLeaf service it is $429 to $694 per person, double occupancy, depending on season and level of overnight accommodations. Operates April through October, with the peak season in the warmer months.

Information: 877-460-3200, *www.rocky mountaineer.com*.

*All prices subject to change.

COPPER CANYON, MEXICO

Located in Mexico's Sierra Madre Mountains, Copper Canyon is four times the size of the Grand Canyon and is one of North America's most thrilling sights. An excellent way to see it in all its glory is on this eight-day all-inclusive roundtrip adventure by Caravan Tours. You'll spend your nights in hotels along the way.

After one night in El Paso, Texas, you then go by motorcoach into Mexico to travel through rangeland, desert and apple country and stay the next night in the small lumber town Creel, the highest stop of the tour.

Here you board a private first-class railroad coach that winds past waterfalls, cliffs and tropical farmlands on your way to the colonial town of El Fuerte. There, you'll stay for two nights and go on a river float trip and a walking tour. The train continues its journey, passing through 86 tunnels, crossing 38 bridges and climbing almost 8,000 feet before reaching the village of Barrancas in the heart of Copper Canyon and where you'll check in to a picturesque lodge for the night.

The next day, you will travel back along the same route through the canyon, with a stop in Chihuahua before returning to El Paso.

Cost: $995* to $1,195 per person, double occupancy. Trips are scheduled year-round.

Information: 800-227-2826, *www.caravan tours.com.*

THE SKEENA

Perhaps the least known of the great North American rail trips is aboard Via Rail Canada's Skeena. The 725-mile, two-day daylight journey in the Canadian Northwest starts out at Jasper, Alberta, climbs the Rocky Mountains, rolls along the Skeena River valley and finally winds down to the Pacific, ending at Prince Rupert, British Columbia, a small city located on a deep fjord on the Inside Passage.

Totem Deluxe Class passengers have exclusive use of a vista-dome observation lounge car and meals (included in the cost) served at their seats. The economy class passengers can watch the beautiful scenery through panoramic windows and purchase their meals on-board to eat at their seats.

*All prices subject to change.

The Skeena stops overnight in Prince George, where passengers lodge in accommodations of their choice (price not included, and you must make your own reservations), then set forth in the morning for Prince Rupert, an historic fishing and cannery town. The Skeena runs four times a week from May through October and may be taken in either direction.

Cost: Approximately $665* (US) per person in Totem Deluxe…from $293 (US) in Economy.

Information: 888-842-7245, *www.viarail.ca.*

ANTEBELLUM SOUTH

Probably the most luxurious rail trips in North America are offered by American Orient Express. One favorite rail trip is the Antebellum South journey, a six-night, Civil War–themed tour in vintage train cars through the South. Meals, lectures and guided tours are included.

The tours travel from Washington, DC, to Savannah, Georgia (and vice versa) in March and April. Stops include Fredericksburg and Charlottesville, Virginia…Charleston, South Carolina…and Jackson and Vicksburg, Mississippi. Sleeping onboard and eating meals in the posh dining car, you visit these cities by day and explore the sites of epic conflicts between the North and the South, all explained by trained Civil War guides.

Cost: $2,990 to $5,490 per person, double occupancy, depending on the level of accommodations, which range from small Pullman cabins with berths to grand suites that offer twin beds.

Information: 800-320-4206, *www.american orientexpress.com.*

QUEBEC TO NOVA SCOTIA

Via Rail Canada's Ocean Service travels overnight in either direction between Montreal and Halifax, some 800 miles to the east, stopping at Moncton along the way. The line made its inaugural run in 1904 and has been operating ever since then.

Departing from Montreal (or vice versa from Halifax), the train follows the south shore of the St. Lawrence River, crossing the province of New Brunswick. Halifax is the cosmopolitan capital city of Nova Scotia.

*All prices subject to change.

Dubbed "a rolling bed & breakfast," Easterly Class on the Ocean features double bedrooms, private washrooms, continental breakfast and big picture windows to watch the towns and rolling countryside go by. Lounge cars are available for cocktails and socializing, while the dining cars serve the traditional Canadian cuisine. Those who are planning a stay in Nova Scotia in June through October can connect with Via Rail's day-touring train between Sydney, located on Cape Breton Island, and Halifax.

Cost: For the basic overnight journey in peak season, June through October, from approximately $292* (US) per person, double occupancy. November through May, $161 (US).

Information: 888-842-7245, *www.viarail.ca*.

COASTAL CULINARY TOUR

This six-night upscale journey aboard American Orient Express's old-fashioned rail cars runs along the Pacific coast from Los Angeles to Seattle (or vice versa), stopping along the way to see the sights. You sleep on board and eat most of your meals in the sumptuous dining car.

From Los Angeles, the train travels northward along the sandy beaches and windswept cliffs, through tunnels and over trestles, making its first stop at San Simeon to explore Hearst Castle, a 165-room mansion built by newspaper tycoon William Randolph Hearst.

In San Francisco, you take a guided tour of major sights of the city and sleep overnight at a luxury hotel. The next day, you board a bus to explore the Napa Valley and visit a couple of wineries along the way.

Then the train rolls on to Portland, Oregon, for a guided tour of the city that includes the Chinese Gardens and some microbreweries, plus a tour of the 650-foot Multnomah Falls. Back on board, the final day features views of Mount Saint Helens and Mount Rainier.

All meals, lectures and guided excursions are included. Tour dates from Los Angeles to Seattle are scheduled in May and November...and tour dates from Seattle to Los Angeles are in May.

Cost: From $2,990 up to $5,490 per person, double occupancy, depending on the level of accommodations.

*All prices subject to change.

Information: 800-320-4206, *www.american orientexpress.com*.

Also from Joan Rattner Heilman...

The Best Travel Companies for Grown-Ups

Many travel companies cater to the fast-growing 50-plus crowd, travelers who gravitate toward tours with people their own age who have similar likes and cultural interests. They also desire comfortable quarters and unhurried itineraries.

Among the top companies that make it their business to give older travelers what they're looking for...

•**Elderhostel.** For people age 55 or older and their travel mates of any age. Elderhostel's affordable one- to four-week programs—which number in the thousands—are hosted by educational and cultural institutions in all 50 states and 90 countries. 877-426-8056, *www.elderhos tel.org*.

Examples: Exploring desert culture in and around Palm Springs, California...or a cruise around Australia's Great Barrier Reef to Sydney and Melbourne.

•**50plus Expeditions** specializes in adventure travel all over the world, from visiting Ecuador's rain forests to cycling alongside the Danube in Austria. Small-group tours are escorted by local guides. 866-318-5050, *www.50 plusexpeditions.com*.

•**Grand Circle Travel's international vacations** are exclusively for people age 50 or over. They include classic escorted tours...extended stays in such destinations as Costa del Sol and Sicily...European river cruises...and a variety of ocean cruises with land-based stays in ports of call. 800-959-0405, *www.gct.com*.

•**Interhostel.** For people age 50 or older and their travel companions age 40 and over, Interhostel provides all-inclusive educational travel programs—from five days exploring New Orleans to 15 days touring in Ireland. The trips are hosted by universities or other educational institutions whose faculty and local experts lead the activities. 800-733-9753, *www.learn.unh. edu/interhostel*.

●**Overseas Adventure Travel** combines creature comforts and unique accommodations with unusual destinations that include Peru, Morocco and Botswana. These trips are rated from "easy" to "demanding." Groups are limited to 16 participants over age 50. 800-493-6824, *www.oattravel.com.*

●**Senior Tours Canada.** This is Canada's largest operator of fully escorted tours. It takes tourists age 50 and older on leisurely, "worry-free" vacations worldwide. The trips range from traditional tours to resort vacations and cruises. Destinations include Scotland and Northern California as well as a cruise through the Panama Canal. 800-268-3492, *www.seniortours.ca.*

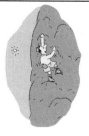

Escape to Nature Without Roughing It

Tim Jarrell, an intrepid traveler located in New York City, who often ventures into the great outdoors. He is the publisher of *Fodor's Escape to Nature Without Roughing It* (Random).

Getting away from it all and communing with nature doesn't necessarily mean roughing it. *These trips let you breathe in fresh air and feast your eyes on America's bounty without sacrificing creature comforts…*

NORTHWEST

●**Alaska.** Chena Hot Springs Resort, Chena Hot Springs. About 60 miles northeast of Fairbanks, this 440-acre resort is road-accessible and open year-round—rare among Alaska hostelries. You can stay in a contemporary hotel that has modern amenities or in more rustic accommodations, such as a trapper's log cabin. In the winter, a glassed-in, heated "aurorarium" lets you watch the northern lights (Aurora Borealis) in comfort.

Activities: Hiking, fishing, canoeing in summer…and dog-mushing, snowmobiling, sleigh rides, cross-country skiing in winter. Natural hot springs fill the resort's indoor pool, rock-lined outdoor pool, outdoor hot tub and two indoor whirlpools. 800-478-4681, *www.chenahotsprings. com.* $65.*

●**California.** The Post Ranch Inn in Big Sur. Located on the spectacular Big Sur coast, 28 miles south of Carmel, Post Ranch is one of the world's finest small hotels. Each of the rustically elegant rooms has a fireplace, wet bar and oversized slate-lined spa tub. The Sierra Mar restaurant, with its dramatic Pacific views, provides contemporary cuisine.

Activities: Yoga, nature walks. Nearby Pebble Beach has some of the best golf courses in the world. 800-527-2200, *www.postranchinn. com.* $525.

●**Colorado.** Dunton Hot Springs, Dolores. This resort complex was created on the site of an old Western town. Log cabins are decorated with Western antiques and Indian and African decorative objects. Contemporary Western fare is served at a communal table in the town's former saloon.

Activities: Hot springs fill a soaking pool in a tepee and a small, rock-lined outdoor pool. Nearby Telluride offers lots of shops and restaurants. 970-882-4800, *www.duntonhotsprings. com.* $550, including all meals.

●**Utah.** Boulder Mountain Lodge, Boulder. The main lodge has a sandstone fireplace, art gallery and outdoor hot tub overlooking a pond and bird sanctuary. The restaurant has excellent food inspired by Native American and Mormon pioneer recipes.

Activities: The drivable Burr Trail leads you to a landscape of otherworldly geological formations, with breathtaking views of brilliantly colored cliffs, canyons, plateaus and mountains. 800-556-3446, *www.boulder-utah.com.* $69.

SOUTHWEST

●**New Mexico.** Casitas De Gila, Gila. Twenty-six miles north of Silver City, this getaway offers 70 acres of hiking trails and adjoins the Gila National Forest, with 1,500 miles of trails. You'll see bighorn sheep and mule deer. Five adobe-style guesthouses have rustic ceiling beams, a kiva fireplace and a kitchen where you can cook for yourself.

*All prices quoted are for the least expensive room available, double occupancy, per night, and are subject to change.

Activities: Outdoor hot tub, stargazing (the owners provide telescopes), astronomy talks, hiking. 877-923-4827, *www.casitasdegila.com.* $95.*

●**Texas.** BlissWood, Cat Spring. Part of the Lehmann Legacy Ranch, with centuries-old oak trees, this getaway offers lodging in various houses and cabins that are furnished with rustic antiques. You can enjoy a continental breakfast in your room or in Carol's Cat Spring Restaurant. On the grounds, you can see llamas, donkeys, bison and deer.

Activities: Fishing in the catch-and-release pond, horseback riding. 800-753-3376, *www. blisswood.net.* $139.

HAWAII

●**Kalani Oceanside Retreat, Pahoa.** This resort, with its simple cottages, is situated on 19 acres on the quiet southeastern coast of the Big Island. The on-site restaurant serves mostly vegetarian cuisine made from the local organic produce. Nearby are thermal springs at Lava Tree State Park and Hawaii Volcanoes National Park.

Activities: Massage, tai chi, yoga, outdoor hot tub. 800-800-6886, *www.kalani.com.* $110.

MIDWEST

●**Michigan.** The Keweenaw Mountain Lodge, Copper Harbor. Constructed in the 1930s, these log cabins are reminiscent of cottages that have been "in the family" for years. The lodge restaurant has an old fieldstone fireplace, 30-foot log beams and delicious nightly dinner specials, including Lake Superior trout.

Activities: Hiking, golf, fishing, kayaking and other water sports. 888-685-6343, *www.at thelodge.com.* $90.

●**Iowa.** Country Homestead Bed & Breakfast, Turin. The front of this B&B faces corn and soybean fields and the Missouri River Valley…the back overlooks the Loess Hills. The mid-19th–century farmstead is decorated with photos of the owner's forebears. Breakfast often includes whole-wheat and banana waffles.

Activities: Biking, bird-watching, hiking. 712-353-6772, *www.country-homestead.com.* $75.

*All prices quoted are for the least expensive room available, double occupancy, per night, and are subject to change.

NORTHEAST

●**Vermont.** Roaring Branch, Arlington. This log cabin resort has 15 rustic cabins, some dating back to 1912 and other more modern ones with dishwashers and TVs. All have kitchens.

Activities: Tennis, ping-pong, fishing. Open from the end of May to mid-October. 802-375-6401, *www.roaringbranch.com.* $120.*

●**Massachusetts.** Cuttyhunk Fishing Club B&B Inn, Cuttyhunk. Located in the Elizabeth Islands, this inn is the former Cuttyhunk Bass Club, a refuge for 19th-century tycoons. It is modestly decorated with floral coverlets and original furniture from the 1800s.

Activities: Hiking, bird-watching, biking, fishing. Open mid-May to mid-October. 508-992-5585, *www.cuttyhunkfishingclub.com.* $135.

●**Rhode Island.** Samuel Slater Canal Boat, Central Falls. You can rent this 40-foot British canal boat, which is tied up alongside the banks of the Blackstone River. It has two cabins that sleep up to four, a fully equipped galley and a bathroom with shower. The staff brings you breakfast. This area is part of the Blackstone River Valley National Historic Corridor.

Activities: Biking, in-line skating. Open April through October. 800-454-2882, *www.tourblack stone.com/canal.htm.* $179.

●**Connecticut.** The Boulders Inn, New Preston. Forty-five miles north of Hartford, this 1890 Dutch Colonial mansion sits on Lake Waramaug, Connecticut's second-largest natural lake. Stay in the main lodge, a cottage or a carriage house. Rooms have a refined country elegance —most have a deck or patio and a wood stove or fireplace. The restaurant offers fine dining, with dishes such as olive-crusted rack of lamb, as well as a 400-bottle wine list.

Activities: Hiking, biking, canoeing, kayaking, lake swimming. 800-455-1565, *www.boul dersinn.com.* $350.

SOUTHEAST

●**Georgia.** Barnsley Gardens Resort, Adairsville. Thirty-three cottages are located on 1,300 acres surrounding the moss-and-vine-tangled ruins of an 1840s' mansion. The estate was built

*All prices quoted are for the least expensive room available, double occupancy, per night, and are subject to change.

by a British expatriate for his southern bride. The beautifully furnished suites have king-sized sleigh and poster beds, fireplaces that work, claw-foot bathtubs and 12-foot ceilings. Stroll their gardens full of Carolina yellow jasmine, honeysuckle and magnolias.

Activities: Biking, horseback riding, golf, tennis, spa. 877-773-2447, *www.barnsleyresort. com.* $285.*

• **South Carolina.** The Rice Hope Plantation, Moncks Corner. This B&B is located on a former rice plantation, dating back to 1696. It has a genteel shabbiness, with its oriental rugs and motley furnishings. Located on 285 acres on the Cooper River, it is near Francis Marion National Forest.

Activities: Hiking, bird-watching, kayaking, biking, tennis, excursions to the nearby Mepkin Abbey Monastery. 800-569-4038, *www.ricehope. com.* $85.

*All prices quoted are for the least expensive room available, double occupancy, per night, and are subject to change.

Top Scenic Drives in North America

Hit the open road on your next vacation and take in some of the best scenery in North America…

• **I-5** between Seattle, Washington and Vancouver, Canada.

• **Columbia River Gorge Scenic Drive** in Oregon and Washington.

• **Provo Canyon Scenic Byway** in Utah.

• **San Diego to rural Julian,** California.

• **Talimena Scenic Byway,** between Talihina, Oklahoma, and Mena, Arkansas.

• **The Indiana Dunes National Lakeshore,** along Lake Michigan.

• **Along Route 10 (or Ten Rod Road)** in Exeter, Rhode Island.

• **Overseas Highway** between Miami and Key West, Florida.

The Hertz Corporation, Park Ridge, NJ.

How to Pick a Reliable Tour Company

Nancy Dunnan, editor and publisher of *TravelSmart* at *www.travelsmartnewsletter.com.*

No matter where you choose to go, there are three steps you can take to safeguard your travel dollars…

• **You get protection against a travel company's failure if the company is a member of the US Tour Operators Association.** These firms must post a $1 million bond to be used solely for reimbursing consumers in case of loss due to bankruptcy or failure to refund deposits within 120 days of a trip cancellation. For a members list, call 212-599-6599 or visit *www. ustoa.com.* (The Association also has several free brochures on travel planning and safety.)

• **Check with a travel agent.** Agents who have been in business for a number of years are familiar with the reliable and not-so-reliable tour operators. Keep in mind, however, that not all tour companies work with agents.

• **Don't book your trip on-line** unless the company has an old-fashioned postal address, will send written literature that you can study and evaluate, and informs you in writing of its refund policy.

More from Nancy Dunnan…

Savvy Rental-Car Strategies

Use *www.travelocity.com* to determine the "going rate" for a rental car in the area to which you will be traveling. Check the total price, including taxes and fees, and the gas tank policy. If traveling within the next week, check *www.lastminutetravel.com.* You might be able to get a larger car at the price you would pay for a compact. Using the prices you found on the previous sites, bid a lower price for a rental car at *www.priceline.com.* If your rental-car bid is accepted, your credit card will be charged immediately.

If you still can't find the deal you want, check *www.rentalcars.com,* which tracks deals on rental-car company Web sites. And, don't overlook individual rental agency Web sites. Most post last-minute specials that toll-free operators may not know about. Many rental-car companies also offer additional discounts to members of such groups as AAA or AARP as well as teachers, government employees and military personnel.

Helpful Travel Sites

For great travel bargains and helpful information, check out these Web sites...

• **www.seatguru.com** maps the best and worst seats, by type of jet, on 27 US and international air carriers.

• **www.icruise.com** offers low cruise prices and live Webcams on ships to show you what facilities look like.

• **www.farealert.net** will track down pricing errors, including mistyped flight or hotel rates, and e-mail them to subscribers.

• **www.travelzoo.com** posts deeply discounted resort and spa stays in the "Lodging Specials" section. Discounts change regularly and are for stays within the next few weeks.

• **www.luxurylink.com** sells discount resort vacations.

The Lowest Travel Rates On-Line

Jens Jurgen, editor and publisher of *Travel Companion Exchange, www.travelcompanions.com.*

The travel Web site that offers the lowest fares on a particular route varies from day to day—sometimes from hour to hour.

To get the best deal: Check prices at the major sites—*www.expedia.com, www.orbitz.com* and *www.travelocity.com*—and the sites of individual airlines, especially low-fare carriers, such as JetBlue or Southwest or, for intra-Europe

flights only, Ryanair.com. PC users can access SideStep (*www.sidestep.com*), a free software-based search engine that gathers information about low airfares and hotel and car-rental rates from hundreds of Web sites.

Other options: Bid for tickets, hotel rooms and car rentals at *www.priceline.com...*search for low fares at *www.botwire.com.* These sites provide exact itineraries or hotel names only after your price is accepted, and travelers don't earn frequent-flier mileage.

Important: Always compare total prices—including taxes and all fees. Most independent travel sites also charge a $5 to $6 booking fee.

Newest site: Travelaxe.com, which is similar to Sidestep.com. It searches multiple hotel-booking sites simultaneously.

Little-Known Way to Get a Great Deal on a Vacation

Booking your vacation through a wholesale club such as Costco or BJ's can cost less than buying it on-line or through a travel agent. Selection is limited, so don't join a membership club just to book a trip. If you already belong, consider booking through the club. Some hotel packages were 50% less expensive at wholesale clubs than on-line.

National Geographic Traveler, 1145 17 St. NW, Washington, DC 20036.

Favorite Moneysaving Travel Web Sites

Pauline Frommer, executive editor on-line for *Arthur Frommer's Budget Travel,* New York City. Her column titled "The Savings Sleuth" has appeared on the MSNBC Web site at *www.msnbc.msn.com.*

Use these helpful search engines to scour the Internet for the best travel bargains available...

• **Mobissimo Travel Search.** This new service looks beyond US Web sites and searches the world for great deals. *www.mobissimo.com.*

• **Cheapflights.** Compare flight schedules and prices. *www.cheapflights.com.*

• **Kayak.com.** This easy-to-use site is from the cofounders of Orbitz, Travelocity and Expedia. It searches more than 60 travel sites for great deals.

For cruise seekers: Dealing with a cruise discounter rather than a cruise line directly can get you 25% to 50% off the price. Offerings vary, so check with several discounters. *Favorites…*

• **CruiseComplete,** 800-764-4410 or *www.cruisecomplete.com.*

• **CruisesOnly,** 800-278-4737 or *www.cruisesonly.com.*

• **Cruise Value Center,** 800-231-7447 or *www.cruisevalue.com.*

• **GalaxSea Cruises of San Diego,** 800-923-7245 or *www.galaxsea.com.*

Ten Secrets That Hotels Don't Want You to Know

Peter Greenberg, travel editor for NBC's *Today* show as well as chief correspondent with the Discovery network's Travel Channel. He is also author of *Hotel Secrets from the Travel Detective* (Villard) and editor of the newsletter titled *Travel News Today, www.travelnewstoday.com.*

Y ou want a hotel to be your home away from home, but many aspects of hotel pricing and policy are really anything but homey. *Here's what you need to know…*

GETTING A ROOM

• **You can get the best rate by calling the hotel's local number,** not the 800 number, which usually links callers to an off-site centralized call center. Instead of asking for the reservations desk, ask to speak with the manager on duty, the general manager or the director of sales. These people have the authority to negotiate room rates.

It's often possible to beat a hotel's best advertised price by 20%, particularly if you call just a few days before your visit. First, shop around for the best deal on a third-party Internet travel site, such as Expedia.com or Hotels.com. Don't take the deal—just jot it down.

Then call the hotel and explain to a manager or director that you know these Web sites mark up room prices by 20% to 40%. Tell the manager you would like to split the difference—say you'll pay 20% below the price you found online. Unless the hotel is filled to capacity, the manager is likely to take you up on your offer.

• **Everything is negotiable.** Think parking is overpriced? If the lot looks half empty, offer less than the daily rate. Planning to make a lot of phone calls? Some hotels offer a per-day flat fee for long-distance in the US and local calling —usually about $9.95—but you must ask for it.

• **Rooms are available even when a hotel has no vacancies.** In any large hotel, a few rooms usually are listed as "out of order" at any given time. The problem might be something as simple as a stain on the carpet or a chair that has been sent out for repairs. If you're desperate for a last-minute room in a hotel that claims to have none available, tell the manager you are willing to take an out-of-order room that has only a minor problem. You might even be able to negotiate a better rate, since the room would otherwise sit empty.

• **"Guaranteed" rooms really aren't guaranteed.** When you make a hotel reservation, you often are asked to "guarantee" your room with a credit card—but there's still a chance that the hotel will give away your room if you arrive late. Providing a credit card number improves the odds that your room will be held—but it still pays to call to confirm that you're coming if you won't arrive until after 9 pm.

SAFEGUARDING VALUABLES

• **A thief takes one credit card, not your entire wallet.** It's no secret that crime is common in hotels. The new twist is that some hotel thieves now take just one credit card when they find an unguarded wallet in a room—and leave everything else untouched. Frequently, a victim doesn't notice the card is missing until the credit line is maxed out.

Travel only with the credit cards that you really need, and check your wallet carefully if you accidentally leave it unattended.

● **Your bags aren't safe with the bellhop.** Even in elite hotels, luggage can be stolen right off the luggage carts in the lobby. Though these bags theoretically are in the possession of the bellhop, the hotel assumes no legal responsibility for the loss.

If your bag is going to sit for more than a few minutes, ask that it be placed in a secure room. Keep valuable items in the hotel safe.

Helpful: High-end luggage might impress fellow travelers, but it also impresses thieves. The cheaper or uglier your luggage looks, the greater the odds that a thief will target someone else.

● **It pays to tip the housekeeper every day.** Exchange a few pleasant words with the housekeeper if you see him/her—and leave a $2 or $3 tip each day. You'll receive better service—housekeepers are the most overworked, underpaid and underappreciated people in the hotel, so any gesture will be appreciated.

Knowing the housekeeper also reduces the chances that your room will be burglarized. Dishonest housekeepers are less likely to target guests they have met. If a burglar enters your room while it is being cleaned and pretends to be you—a common ruse—the housekeeper will be able to spot the impostor.

MORE INSIDER SECRETS

● **Hotel rooms are infested with germs.** Certain items in hotel rooms never get cleaned. The biggest trouble spots include the TV remote control, telephone and clock/radio. Travel with a package of antibacterial wipes, and be sure to clean these items when you arrive.

Also, while reputable hotels provide fresh linens, bedspreads might be cleaned only once every few months. Remove them from the beds as soon as you check in. Ask for clean blankets as soon as you arrive.

● **Lost-and-found is a great resource for cell-phone users.** If you have a cell phone, odds are that someday you'll forget to bring your recharging cord or lose it in transit. If you're staying at a hotel, there's no need to buy a replacement. Recharging cords are the number-one item left behind in hotel rooms. Most hotels are willing to lend cords from their lost-and-found—but guests rarely ask.

● **Not all concierges are really concierges.** A true concierge is the most connected person around town. He can obtain tickets to sold-out events…reservations to popular restaurants…prescriptions filled in the middle of the night…even a new heel on a shoe by 8 am. (A tip of $10 to $20 usually is appropriate—more if the concierge really worked miracles.) But not all hotels that advertise "concierge service" truly provide it. Many simply assign a regular hotel employee the role each shift.

An elite concierge wears a gold key on his lapel. It's the symbol of Les Clefs d'Or—French for "Keys of Gold"—a prestigious international concierge organization.

More from Peter Greenberg…

Best Time to Call for Lower Hotel Rates

For the best hotel rates, phone the hotel after 4 pm on Sundays.

Reason: The yield/revenue managers—the people who dictate the sliding rates for hotel rooms—are off on Sundays, so you have a better chance of getting someone at the front desk who is anxious to fill unsold rooms.

Best-Rate Guarantee From Hotels

Hotel chains are offering best-rate guarantees when you reserve rooms on their Web sites. If you find the same room for a better rate on another site within 24 hours, the chain may offer you an additional 10% off the lowest rate or even a free night's stay. Rules vary by hotel chain, and are subject to change.

Participating hotels: Clarion, Comfort Inn, Courtyard, Crowne Plaza, Days Inn, Doubletree, Econo Lodge, Fairfield Inn, Hilton, Holiday Inn,

Hyatt, Marriott, Ramada, Sheraton, Super 8 Motels, Westin and Wyndham.

USA Today, 7950 Jones Branch Dr., McClean, VA 22108.

For a More Comfortable Hotel Stay...

When registering for a hotel room, ask for something specific, such as a room with a view or one closer to the elevator, etc. This eliminates the chance that you will get stuck with an undesirable room. If you have stayed at the hotel previously, mention that when you check in. Also, never settle for an unacceptable room—instead, call the front desk and ask for a reassignment.

If you are planning to stay a week or more, write to the hotel manager personally at least one week ahead of time and ask for a "space-available" upgrade, a price break or extras, such as restaurant credits, free shoe shines or free high-speed Internet access. And, at check-in, ask to meet the manager to say hello.

Chris McGinnis, travel correspondent for CNN Headline News in Atlanta, and the author of *The Unofficial Business Traveler's Pocket Guide* (McGraw-Hill).

Tall Travelers Get Respect At These Hotels

The Hotel Monaco group—which has hotels in Chicago, Denver, New Orleans, Salt Lake City, San Francisco, Seattle and Washington, DC —offers rooms with longer beds, raised shower-heads and extra-high ceilings. The Palms Casino in Las Vegas has 22 "NBA Suites," which feature eight-foot door frames, eight-foot-long beds and furniture built specially for tall people. Accommodations do not cost more than regular rooms, but reservations are encouraged.

Everard Strong, publisher, *TALL Magazine,* Oakland, *www.tallmagazine.com.*

Hotels That Welcome Your Pet

Some hotel chains, including Loews, Sheraton and Westin, welcome guests traveling with their pets. Some chains charge a fee. Others accept only dogs and may enforce a size or a weight restriction. Check hotel requirements when booking a room.

More information: Pets on the Go (*www. petsonthego.com*) offers reviews of 30,000 pet-friendly lodgings, an assortment of pet travel suggestions, recreation ideas and pet products.

Safer Hotel Stays

The safest floors to stay on in a hotel are the third through sixth. Burglars most often target rooms on the first and second floors due to ease of entry and exit (through windows, doors to patios and pools, etc.). You are also better off on these floors in case of fire. Above the sixth floor you'll have a long walk down and firefighting equipment may have a hard time getting up.

John Fannin, founder, SafePlace Corp., 2106 Silverside Rd., Wilmington, DE 19810, *www.safeplace.com.*

What Every Air Traveler Must Know Now

Terry Trippler, a leading expert on airline rules of operation who is based in Minneapolis, *www.cheapseats.com.*

With airlines trying to conserve every dime, the "friendly skies" aren't as friendly anymore. But if you know your rights, you can save money, avoid headaches and get more out of traveling. *Here is what you need to know...*

• **When you are involuntarily bumped from a flight,** federal law requires the airline to compensate you if your new flight is delayed an hour or more.

If it is scheduled to arrive one to two hours past your original arrival time (or between one and four hours for an international flight), you are entitled to receive a refund on your ticket price and a maximum cash payment of $200, as determined by US Department of Transportation guidelines.

If you are scheduled to arrive more than two hours late (or more than four hours late for an international flight) or if the airline is unable to find you another flight, you are entitled to a refund plus an additional $400 in cash.

Helpful: The airline might encourage you to accept a voucher toward a future flight instead of cash. Voucher values must equal the amounts listed above, but they typically exceed them.

If you're interested in a voucher, negotiate for a better deal with the agent at the gate. If you're entitled to $400, try to get $1,000. Whether or not you get a greater amount generally will depend on the mood of the gate agent.

• **When you volunteer to be bumped from a flight,** the airline is free to offer any deal it wants. Once again, you have lots of leverage—airline personnel don't want to kick passengers off flights.

Example: My friends had tickets for an overbooked flight from Minneapolis to Anchorage. Since it was the last flight of the day, Northwest offered each of my friends $500 in cash, a $500 airline voucher, accommodations, ground transportation and seats on the first flight out the next day.

Helpful: Before you accept a voucher, scrutinize all the terms—expiration date, blackout dates and whether it can be transferred. The fewer restrictions, the better, but these generally can't be negotiated.

• **If your flight is delayed until the next day,** your rights depend on the cause…

• If the airline was at fault—in the case of mechanical problems or late connecting flights—you have a good chance of getting the airline to pay for a hotel room nearby. The airline is under no obligation to do so, but it's good for public relations. The airline will provide a voucher to pay for the room and generally a meal.

• If the delay was caused by weather, terrorism, a fuel shortage or a labor dispute, you are not entitled to compensation.

• **If the flight is canceled,** the airline will find another flight for you. If the flight is the next day, the airline may pay for your accommodations for the night, but it is under no obligation to do so.

• **If an airline loses your luggage,** the maximum reimbursement is $2,500 per passenger. The airlines will rarely pay the highest amount unless you can present receipts totaling that amount. You probably will have to file a claim under your homeowner's or renter's insurance to recoup the balance of the loss if it exceeds your deductible.

Self-defense: If you need to transport something valuable or very important, ship it.

Most missing bags are recovered within 48 hours. While you're waiting for your luggage, ask the airline for cash to buy necessities. If you're lucky, you might get $150, but $50 to $100 is more common. What you receive typically depends on the mood of the airline employee. You aren't entitled to anything if you have flown into your hometown.

For more helpful information on traveling: *http://airconsumer.ost.dot.gov,* click on "Travel Tips & Publications," then "Fly Rights."

Insider Tricks for Hassle-Free Air Travel

Marjory Abrams, publisher, newsletters, Boardroom, Inc., 281 Tresser Blvd., Stamford, CT 06901.

A ir travelers have not had it easy. Long security lines, extensive weather delays, lost baggage, canceled flights and other woes have turned dream trips into nightmares.

Rudy Maxa, known as public radio's *Savvy Traveler* (*www.rudymaxa.com*), is the ultimate frequent flier. I caught him en route from Los Angeles to the Caribbean—just a small fraction of the 100,000 miles or so that he flies every year. Rudy is not shy about getting his needs met when he encounters problems at the airport or in the air. *His secret strategies...*

●**If the security line is so long that you might miss your flight,** go to the front of the line, politely explain your situation to a security agent and ask him/her to move you right through the line.

●**If you need to get to a gate fast, flag down a motorized cart**—airport personnel use them to quickly navigate the facility—and hitch a free ride.

●**If you don't like your seat once you are on the plane,** look for a better seat. Move only after the doors are closed. You don't have to ask permission to change seats—but you must stay within the same class of service.

Rudy has great hassle-prevention strategies, too—beyond choosing nonstop flights...

●**Skip the check-in lines by getting your boarding pass at home.** Most airlines allow you to print them from their Web sites within 24 hours of your flight.

●**If it is clear that you will be stranded overnight,** book a hotel room right away. Airport hotels fill up fast during bad weather.

I also checked with Randy Petersen, publisher of *InsideFlyer* at *www.insideflyer.com.* "Despite all the publicity about enhanced security, people still don't get it," he says. "Passengers still are trying to go through security with knives, firecrackers, baseball bats and other prohibited objects. They hold up the line for everyone."

Randy advises travelers to check out the latest regulations of the Transportation Security Administration, on the Web at *www.tsa.gov* or call 866-289-9673.

New no-no: You are not allowed to carry a cigarette lighter or matches onto a plane.

Randy has his own trick for resolving flight-related problems quickly. On the way to the gate area, pay attention to the location of the customer service desk. If your flight is cancelled—or has a lengthy delay—go there to figure out alternatives. Don't wait at the departure gate with everyone else.

Finally, attitude matters. Yes, delays can be annoying...but they are better than flying in unsafe conditions.

The Best Mileage Cards

Mileage cards are *not* good deals if they aren't affiliated with specific airlines. Most unaffiliated cards—such as American Express Membership Rewards, Discover Miles, Bank of America Visa Travel Card and MBNA World-Points—award miles in such a way that their cash value is less than the cash value of miles given on airline-affiliated cards. Because airfares currently are so low, holders of unaffiliated cards are probably better off using cash to buy inexpensive airline seats and using their accumulated awards points for other expenditures, such as car rentals or hotel rooms.

Randy Petersen, publisher, *InsideFlyer,* 1930 Frequent Flyer Point, Colorado Springs 80915, *www.insideflyer.com.*

Easy Way to Check Airline Flight Status

Flightarrivals.com provides free flight status information while planes are in the air, including expected arrival time, updated every four minutes. The site also gives information about weather, schedule changes and airport conditions, covering airports nationwide. The site is searchable by flight number, airline and city/airport.

Send Luggage Ahead

Several services will ship luggage ahead to make travel easier—Luggage Express (866-744-7224, *www.usxpluggageexpress.com*)...Sky-Cap International (877-775-9227, *www.skycap international.com*)...Sports Express (800-357-4174, *www.sportsexpress.com*)...Virtual Bellhop (877-235-5467, *www.virtualbellhop.com*). Expect to pay $65* to $75 to ship a piece of luggage weighing about 32 pounds.

Susan Foster, packing expert, Portland, OR, and author of *Smart Packing for Today's Traveler* (Smart Travel).

*All prices subject to change.

More from Susan Foster...

Smart Travel Preparation

Before going on a trip, prepare medical histories for yourself and everyone traveling with you. Keep one copy with your passport and other valuable documents...one in your suitcase ...and one at home in a place where it can be easily located. Include doctors' names and their contact information...health insurance information, including policy numbers and the 24-hour contact numbers...type of blood...any chronic health conditions...all known allergies to foods and medicines...eyeglass prescriptions...and the name of a family member or close friend to contact in an emergency.

The Anti-Jet-Lag Diet

A diet that helps to prevent jet lag has been developed by the Argonne National Laboratory. Studies of military personnel found that those using the diet flying east were 7.5 times less likely to experience jet lag, those flying west, 16.2 times less likely. The diet is based on what cues the body to slow down or speed up—specific foods, when to eat them and how much to eat.

More information: Visit *www.antijetlagdiet. com*. You can receive a diet plan tailored for your individual travel plans through this helpful Web site.

Cost: $10.95 one-way, $16.95 round-trip (all prices subject to change).

What Never to Drink On a Plane

The tap water on more than 17% of planes recently tested contained disease-causing bacteria, including *E. coli*. Twelve airlines in the US now have agreed to new voluntary testing standards—they will test the water systems on each of their planes annually, give the results to the Environmental Protection Agency, flush on-board water systems four times a year and post signs to stop use of aircraft tap water if high levels of bacteria are found.

Best: Bring your own bottled water.

More information: *www.epa.gov/airline water.*

Environmental Protection Agency, Washington, DC.

Don't Fly When Congested

Flying in an airplane when you have a head cold or sinus congestion can cause serious damage to your eardrums.

Problem: During descent, air has to reenter your middle ear through the eustachian tube. If the tube is congested and blocked, the resulting pressure could rupture your eardrum.

Self-defense: Use a nasal decongestant, such as Afrin, one hour prior to takeoff. Chewing gum or sucking on hard candies before descent also helps. Over-the-counter earplugs, such as earPlanes, will help slow the rate of air pressure changes on the eardrum. They are available at many airport shops and pharmacies.

Stuart Rose, MD, president of Travel Medicine, Inc., Northampton, MA.

Postsurgical Air Travel Warning

Postsurgical air travel increases the risk of life-threatening blood clots. Clotting is more likely in people who have had more than 30 minutes of surgery under heavy sedation. Dry cabin air and long periods of immobility can raise risk.

Best: Don't fly for a month after surgery.

If you need to fly: Wear loose clothing... drink at least eight ounces of water every hour ...perform in-seat exercises...don't cross your legs...take a walk every hour...avoid dehydrating agents, such as caffeine and alcohol.

Important: Discuss travel plans with your physician.

Alan Matarasso, MD, a plastic surgeon in private practice, New York City.

New Passport Rules For Children

Parents seeking passports for kids age 14 and younger now have to bring the child with them to apply. Both parents must appear together...or one parent may appear and provide a signed statement of consent from the other parent.

Reason: To help prevent international child abductions and trafficking. Children's passports are valid for five years.

Information: 877-487-2778, *www.travel. state.gov.*

Kelly Shannon, press officer for the Bureau of Consular Affairs, US Department of State, Washington, DC.

Get Paid While Traveling

Cruise ship lines hire numerous seniors and retirees as photographers, casino staff, doctors, nurses, counselors, exercise trainers and more. Accommodations are austere compared with those of paying passengers—but you get paid to travel and meet people from all around the world.

Useful: To learn more and/or file a job application on-line, visit *www.cruiseshipjob.com,* the Web site of the New World Cruise Ship Employment Agency.

Unique Travel Information

Firsthand travel accounts are now available in travelers' on-line journals—or travel "blogs."

Examples: IgoUgo.com for first-person accounts of hotels, restaurants and attractions... TravelPod.com for enthusiastic postings about the joys of travel.

Beautiful Public Gardens

Public gardens are lovely and can give you ideas for your own garden. Visit Filoli Center, Woodside, CA, south of San Francisco (650-364-8300, *www.filoli.org*)...Stonecrop Gardens, Cold Spring, NY (845-265-2000, *www.stonecrop. org*)...Lady Bird Johnson Wildflower Center, Austin, TX (512-292-4100, *www.wildflower.org*) ...Garden in the Woods, North Framingham, MA (508-877-7630, *www.newfs.org/garden.htm*) ...Longwood Gardens, Kennett Square, PA (610-388-1000, *www.longwoodgardens.com*)...Dumbarton Oaks, Washington, DC (202-339-6410, *www.doaks.org/gardens.html*).

Ruth Rogers Clausen, horticulture editor, *Country Living Gardener,* 224 W. 57 St., New York City 10019.

15

Just for Fun

Have More Fun at Casinos—for Less Money

Fast-paced games, mysterious rules and big crowds make a casino intimidating. However, if you play your cards right, casinos can be great places to find excitement, see new sights and socialize. With a bit of luck, you might actually win some money. With just a little research, you can plan a fun-filled trip at a big savings.

FIND THE BEST

Large casinos are generally the most accommodating for first-time visitors and casual gamblers, frequently called "recreational players" in casino jargon. Big casinos are more likely to have the services that recreational players like, including free game instructions, first-class entertainment and gourmet dining.

Many also have sports facilities, and some—such as Borgata in Atlantic City and Mohegan Sun in Connecticut—provide health spas. Non-smoking sections, once unheard of, are now common in many US casinos.

For casual casino visitors, it's wise to go during peak hours—afternoons and evenings.

Tables are crowded and games are usually slower. That means there are more opportunities to socialize with other players and fewer chances to lose money. Off-peak hours are usually favored by serious, high-stake gamblers who may dislike amateurs at the table.

Ask the host at casinos you are considering visiting how much money you have to spend to receive complimentary meals, entertainment or a hotel room.

Note: Nearly all gambling resorts ban cameras from the casino itself, and most of them frown on cell phones.

Jerry Patterson, a gambling instructor and author of several books on gaming, including *Casino Gambling: A Winner's Guide to Blackjack, Craps, Roulette, Baccarat, and Casino Poker* (Perigee). His Internet site is *www.casinogamblingedge.com*. To get the free report "The 10 Casino Gambling Decisions That Lead to Winning Sessions," e-mail Jerry Patterson at *jpe21@aol.com* or send in a self-addressed, stamped, business-sized envelope to Jerry Patterson Enterprises, Inc., Box 236, Gardnerville, NV 89410.

To find casinos, ask a travel agent, look in the *Yellow Pages* or search an Internet casino directory. States Casinos at *www.statescasinos.com* is a good place to start.

Before visiting, call the casino or visit its Web site to check for specials on bus fares, entertainment, rooms and meals. Rooms are usually in the $175 to $300/night range, but specials can cut rates in half.

Example: The classy New York-New York Hotel & Casino in Las Vegas recently had a $69-a-night special. More economical rates can be found at the smaller hotel casinos.

Nightclubs are pricey, often more than $200 a person for dinner and a floor show. But entertainment can be lavish. Do you remember Steve Lawrence and Eydie Gorme? They still appear at casinos, including a recent engagement at the Silver Legacy Resort Casino in Reno, Nevada.

To save money, ask a casino employee or taxi driver where to find less expensive nightclubs. Many cities with casinos are also near historic or natural landmarks, such as Hoover Dam which is near Las Vegas and the boardwalk in Atlantic City.

GO FOR COMPS

A few decades ago, only high rollers could expect casinos to give them free rooms and meals. Today, thanks to competition among casinos, anyone who spends a couple hundred dollars is likely to get a complimentary buffet meal. If your gambling bankroll is $1,000 to $2,000, you may be eligible for a free room or nightclub show.

Look for the counters where the players are signing up for comp cards, or the casino hosts' area or offices to find out where to sign up for a player's card. This looks like a credit card and keeps track of your play.

Each time you play, ask the employee in charge of the game to "mark" your card. At slot machines, you insert the card in a special slot where it's marked electronically.

LEARN FIRST, THEN PLAY

Many large casinos offer free lessons in the popular games, especially craps and blackjack.

Even if you've played these games before, it pays to take lessons, which typically last about an hour. Instruction is helpful because rules are complex and game etiquette even trickier.

Examples: There are specific signals to tell the dealer how you want to play a blackjack hand…although not necessary, it's customary to tip the dealer 2% to 5% of your winnings. If you lose, there's no obligation to tip.

GAIN AN EDGE

Watching a game before you play is a good way to see whether the table is running hot or cold. It's best to choose a table with winning players. To get an idea of whether they are winning or losing, note the players' chips on the table and whether they seem happy or sad.

Also important to know: At blackjack, no shuffle is completely random, meaning that it can favor either the house or knowledgeable players.

At roulette, croupiers often operate the wheel in a way that favors some numbers over others.

Noticing these anomalies is only one way that players can gain an advantage. By studying blackjack, craps or roulette, you also can gain an edge over the casino. It's best to avoid those bets heavily weighted in favor of the house—such as the bets in the center of the layout at the craps table, the insurance bet at blackjack and betting on the inside numbers at roulette. Play the "even money" outside bets, such as red or black, instead.

While learning the basics of blackjack or craps may take less than an hour, learning the finer points can require many months.

One of the most effective ways to learn is through up-to-date books on blackjack, craps and other casino games.

For more information about casinos, gambling books and gambling tips, I recommend the *American Casino Guide, 2006* (Casino Vacations), by Steve Bourie. This guide contains a wealth of information, such as listings of all US casinos by state, and $1,000 in valuable casino coupons, including discounts on rooms, food, rental cars and lots of freebees. The book also has articles and tips by noted gambling authors.

LIMIT YOUR LOSSES

Unless you spend time studying and then become a disciplined player, expect to lose a little at a casino. *To keep losses low…*

- **Avoid the new games that casinos are touting.** The odds are very long against winning. Examples include Spanish 21, Three Card Poker and Let It Ride.

- **Set spending limits.** Most people can have fun with $100 a day. If you can't keep to a limit, don't raise it. Ask a friend to hold your ATM and credit cards. If you still can't resist breaking your budget, don't go to casinos.

- **Check the minimum bets before you start playing.** At blackjack, for instance, minimums can vary between $5 and $100. By betting at low-minimum tables, you can stretch out your budget.

- **If you have a friend with you who is good at playing, ask him/her to critique your play.** If you are interested in additional ideas and instruction on how to beat the casinos, you can start by reading my five-page report "The 10 Casino Gambling Decisions That Lead to Winning Sessions." See the source information on page 247 for instructions on how to receive a free copy.

More from Jerry Patterson...

Casinos for Fun Seekers

I recommend all the following resorts for first-time casino goers and recreational players...

- **Borgata Hotel Casino & Spa,** Atlantic City, NJ, 866-692-6742.

- **Caesars Atlantic City,** Atlantic City, NJ, 888-241-8545.

- **Trump Taj Mahal,** Atlantic City, NJ, 800-825-8888.

- **Mohegan Sun,** Uncasville, CT, 888-226-7711.

- **New York-New York Hotel & Casino,** Las Vegas, NV, 888-696-9887.

- **Paris Las Vegas Hotel Casino,** Las Vegas, NV, 877-796-2096.

- **Silver Legacy Resort Casino,** Reno, NV, 800-687-8733.

Don't Let the Casino Have The Edge

Casinos have a 3% to 7% edge over blackjack players who don't follow the basic blackjack strategy.

Best defense: Buy a basic strategy card at the casino gift shop for about $2, and use it at the blackjack table. The house has almost no advantage over players who use this card.

Helpful tips: Always split aces and eights... never split fives or 10s...never take "insurance" or "even money"...always play at a full table.

Thomas B. Gallagher, president of Thomas Casino Systems, Santa Barbara, CA.

Poker Whiz Andy Bellin's Rules for Winning

Andy Bellin, who left graduate school—where he was an astronomy and physics student—10 years ago to become a semiprofessional poker player. A contributing editor at the *Paris Review,* he lives in Los Angeles. He is also author of *Poker Nation* (HarperCollins).

Most people are terrible poker players because they are really not at the table to win, but to socialize. To become a better player, you've got to follow a few rules, which you can do without spoiling your fun *or* alienating your friends. *Here's how...*

- **Stay focused.** Be as sociable as you want at the table—but only *between* hands. As soon as the cards are dealt and until you fold, avoid conversation.

Keep your eyes on the action around you. What cards do you have in your hand? What are the odds of turning it into a winning hand? What clues can you pick up from other players' body language?

Don't drink too much alcohol, either. The more attention you pay to the game, the more often you'll win.

●**Play fewer hands.** The easiest way to make money in poker is to avoid losing money on bad hands. To achieve that, you must be willing to fold your hands early and often.

Most players think it's rude to fold early in a hand, so they will bet at least once no matter what cards they're holding. I've seen poor players raise four times on nothing hands just because they didn't want to appear timid or tight with money.

My advice: Don't bet at all unless you think you have a potentially winning hand. Instead, fold and let others make the bad bets. If other players tease you and say, "Hey, it's only a dollar," ignore them.

Don't bet wildly even if you think you do have a winning hand. The worst hand in poker is the second-best hand in the game. You'll keep feeding money into the pot, which eventually will go to the player whose hand trumps yours.

Strategy: Analyze the betting. If someone who is normally cautious keeps raising, he/she may have a better hand than you. If visible cards in your hand show strength and another player isn't frightened, fold. Save your money for the next hand.

●**Expect to lose some hands.** Bad poker players obsess over every hand. They know, to the penny, how much they're up or down for the night. They'll say, "I'm down 20 bucks and I have to get even."

If you put yourself under that kind of pressure, you will push too hard and make dumb bets. You'll finish the evening down a lot more than $20.

Right mind-set: Expect to lose some hands. Sometimes you will lose even great hands—because someone else had even better cards. Do not beat yourself up if you fold and find out later that you would have won the pot. It's OK to get bluffed. Dropping out when it looks like you won't win means that you are a discerning player—you're taking all of the factors of the game into account, not just calling every bet. That's a good thing. If you win every hand you have the cards to win, you're probably losing even more on games where you should have folded but didn't.

View poker with a long-term perspective. Accept your losses for the night, without punishing yourself. You'll be the winner another night.

●**Don't overestimate your skills.** You may not want to admit that you are a poor poker player, but the surest way to lose money is by thinking that you are better than you really are.

Example: Poor players think the way to win at poker is by bluffing. In fact, few hands in a low-stakes game are won by bluffing out another player.

Just play your hand, and don't try anything fancy. If you have a great hand, bet it hard. If you don't, fold quickly.

●**Play games where you have an edge.** When you're the dealer and can choose the game, pick one in which your position has an advantage.

Example: In games where cards are visible, such as "seven-card stud," the betting usually begins with the high card. As dealer, you could be the first to bet, the last or somewhere in between. In "draw or hold 'em," however, where all cards are face down, betting starts to the left of the dealer and then goes around the table. That offers you, as dealer, a tremendous advantage because you will get to see everyone else bet before you do.

If you have a strong hand and there have been few, if any, raises, you can think about calling and playing a little longer. The more that other players have raised, the more you should fold with anything but a very strong hand.

●**Know the odds of drawing to a hand.** Billions of poker games have been played over hundreds of years. Over that time, it has been established to a mathematical certainty the odds of drawing to a given hand. *Here are the odds…*

Your Hand	Odds Against Drawing
No pair	1 to 1
One pair	1.25 to 1
Two pair	20 to 1
Three of a kind	46 to 1
Straight	254 to 1
Flush	508 to 1
Full house	693 to 1
Four of a kind	4,164 to 1
Straight flush	64,973 to 1
Royal straight flush	649,739 to 1

Knowing the odds of drawing to a given hand is an essential part of becoming a winning poker player. Say there's $10 in the pot and you must bet $1 to stay in the game. Based on your study of other players, you believe you need three jacks to win. But the odds against finishing with three jacks are 46 to 1, while the most you can win if you take the pot is $10. Common sense tells you to fold the hand.

Important: Just knowing the odds is not enough. You must use the knowledge to keep from making bad bets. If you're the kind of player who says, "I know I'm going to lose this hand but I'm going to take a chance anyway," knowing the odds won't do you a bit of good.

●**Beware of games with wild cards.** Home poker games are filled with gimmicks, such as wild cards. Avoid them, unless you are a truly sophisticated player.

Reason: All those odds of drawing to a given hand are based on basic, straight poker. Whenever you add wild cards into the mix, the math changes. Unless you're confident you can recalculate the odds when there are four or eight wild cards in the game, stick to meat-and-potatoes poker. Let other players throw their money away on gimmicks.

Better Ways to Win a Sweepstakes

Steve Ledoux, who has won hundreds of sweepstakes prizes. He is author of *How to Win Lotteries, Sweepstakes, and Contests in the 21st Century* (Santa Monica). He is a freelance television graphic artist and writer living in Studio City, CA.

Boost your odds of winning a sweepstakes by following this very smart advice from a proven sweepstakes winner…

●**Enter local sweepstakes.** Local drawings are much easier to win than well-promoted national contests because they attract fewer entrants. Prizes include gift certificates, merchandise, dinners for two, etc. Look for entry boxes in area stores and ads in regional newspapers.

●**Opt for short-term sweeps.** The longer a sweepstakes runs, the more entries it will attract and the lower your chances become. Your odds are best in sweepstakes that last less than a month. These tend to be tied to promotional campaigns for new products, movie releases or special events.

Example: Albertson's supermarket chain held a sweepstakes that was open for just two weeks. The grand prize included two tickets to the Emmy Awards.

●**Stagger your entries.** All winners might be pulled out of the same mailbag. If your entries arrive all at the same time, they could wind up together in the wrong bag, leaving you with no shot at a prize.

If you can enter only once, do so toward the end of the entry period. This increases the chance that your entry will be near the top of the pile. You may be able to enter for friends and relatives, but make sure that you receive their permission first and an agreement to share the prize.

●**Make your entry stand out.** For in-store drawings, fold your slip of paper into an accordion or tent shape so that it will be easier for a judge to grab on to. For mail-in local sweeps, use brightly colored oversized envelopes.

●**Enter on-line sweeps.** It's easy, and you can save on postage. Read the rules carefully. You may find that you also can mail in entries, increasing your odds.

Favorite resources: Sweepstakes Advantage at *www.sweeps.ws* and Sweep the Net at *www.sweepthenet.com* list the current on-line sweepstakes.

Caution: Only enter sweepstakes that are sponsored by companies you know. Avoid the sweepstakes that require you to purchase anything, pay a fee or give personal information beyond your name, address, phone number and age.

Read Newspapers from All Around the World

Thousands of newspapers now offer free Internet editions. Leading Internet newspaper portals include *www.newslink.org, www. onlinenewspapers.com* and *www.refdesk.com/ paper.html*. These portals will link you to newspapers, large and small, across the US. You can also access the English editions of foreign language newspapers. You can read foreign papers to become familiar with a distant location before you visit or simply to learn about people in other lands, their lives and opinions.

Newsgroups: The Most Overlooked Resource On the Internet

Patricia Robison, president, Computing Independence, Box 2031, New York City 10011. She is a technology security specialist and gives seminars on business continuity and disaster recovery.

Internet newsgroups provide two-way conversations with people around the world on nearly every subject that you can imagine—investments, science, vacation spots, consumer products, hobbies, sports, politics and more.

You can use newsgroups to make lots of new friends who share your interests, to research just about any subject you can think of or simply read them for fun.

Newsgroups were created many years before there was a World Wide Web, but many Web users don't even know they exist.

HOW THEY WORK

Each newsgroup acts as a discussion group on a particular subject. There are more than 20,000 newsgroups.

People post messages and others post replies. Anyone can participate or simply observe. Many people include their e-mail addresses in their messages so that they can be reached privately.

The simplest introduction to newsgroups is through the Google Web-based newsreader. Go to *www.google.com* and click on "Groups." On the page that comes up, you will see a directory of newsgroups. You can look through it to find a group that may be of interest to you, or enter a subject in the search box to have Google find related newsgroups.

To learn how to participate, click on "Groups Help" for the simple instructions.

Bonus: Google also has an archive of past newsgroup postings dating back to 1981—so that you can locate everything anyone has ever posted on a subject of interest to you, among more than 800 million messages.

TYPES OF NEWSGROUPS

Most groups are open, so anyone can post anything in them. Some are "moderated," so that any off-topic or offensive messages are blocked or deleted.

Examples: The newsgroup *misc.taxes* is open and the scene of much vociferous debate about tax politics. The newsgroup *misc.taxes. moderated* accepts only questions about the tax law that are discussed by tax professionals—although anyone can submit a question.

Other newsgroups to try...

● **alt.folklore.urban**—for discussion of urban legends.

● **rec.boats.cruising**—for advice on boating.

● **rec.gardens**—for gardeners.

● **sci.military.moderated**—for discussion of current military affairs.

● **soc.retirement**—for talk regarding retiree issues.

● **talk.politics.misc**—for unrestrained political discussion.

Remember, in unmoderated groups, anyone can say anything. Therefore, if the group follows a controversial subject—such as politics—comments may get heated. Also, information may be unreliable.

But most newsgroups have a cadre of regular, expert members who are well informed. By "lurking"—watching the group for a while—you can learn more about who they are and whose opinion to value.

Listen to Radio Stations On-Line

Thousands of radio stations worldwide transmit programs on-line—and there are many "Internet only" stations as well. Listen to anything from Antarctica's ANET playing the blues, at *www.anetstation.com,* to the morning news from the Vatican at *www.vatican.va* (just enter "radio" in the search box). Leading radio portals such as *www.radio-locator.com* search through thousands of stations to find what you're looking for by location, broadcast format or station name.

Global Positioning Now Available for Hikers and Bikers

A global positioning system receiver, known as eTrex GPS, stores up to 500 locations. Use it with a compass to get to your destination. The *TracBack* feature lets you reverse course to your starting point.

Cost: $106.*

Information: Garmin, 800-800-1020, *www. garmin.com.*

*Price subject to change.

If You're in The Market For a Boat...

Nancy Dunnan, a financial adviser and author in New York City. Ms. Dunnan's latest book is titled *How to Invest $50–$5,000* (HarperCollins).

Just as with cars, a used boat is much cheaper—from 20% to 50% less than new. Also keep in mind that prices are lower in the cold weather, so try to buy before May.

Generally, but by no means always, the larger used boats are sold through yacht brokers (check with your local marina for names), while smaller boats are sold through the classifieds and "for sale" notices posted in marinas and marine supply shops.

Compare all the prices you are quoted with those listed in the boating industry's two reliable guides, *BUC's Used Boat Price Guide* and *NADA's Marine Appraisal Guide.* Check your public library or local marina for copies or go to *www.buc.com* and *www.nadaguides.com.* NADA's site gives both the lowest retail price currently available and the average retail price …BUC's site lists some 15,000 boats for sale and provides the asking price but not the average retail price. So spend time browsing both.

Simple Secrets for a Successful Dinner Party

Dinner parties need not be complicated. Follow these simple strategies for an evening your guests will remember…

• **Have interesting music playing when guests arrive,** such as *Café Atlantico* by Cesaria Evora or *Avalon* by Roxy Music.

• **Collect everything needed for drinks, and set it out** on a table in the living room, so that everyone can help themselves.

• **Make sure your menu is simple enough so that you can enjoy the party yourself.**

• **Serve dinner in the kitchen** to make guests feel like family.

• **Let guests help out if they want to**—it makes them feel like part of a team.

Ina Garten, Southport, CT–based cookbook author and host of the *Barefoot Contessa* TV series on the Food Network. Her most recent book is *Barefoot Contessa Family Style* (Clarkson Potter).

Great Cookbooks You May Not Have Heard Of

Nach Waxman, owner of Kitchen Arts & Letters, 1425 Lexington Ave., New York City 10128, *kalstaff@rcn.com*. It is the country's oldest and largest bookstore specializing in new and used books on food.

Each one of these cookbooks offers something special that can improve the skills of even experienced home chefs.

● **The Cuisine of California** by Diane Worthington. This book emphasizes healthful ingredients. It has been in print for more than 20 years and is one of the finest works on California cooking. The recipes include fennel, polenta and leek soup…barbecued duck with red wine and black currants…baby red potatoes with caviar. Chronicle, $15.95.*

● **Fish: The Basics** by Shirley King. Relish fish, but find the range of options daunting? This book will help you match any type of fish with all the appropriate preparation techniques and match any recipe with the varieties of fish best suited to it. Recipes range from elegant fish filets with spinach and ginger to sturdy, down-at-the-docks stews. Houghton Mifflin, $22.

● **French Provincial Cooking** by Elizabeth David. This book features good, hearty peasant food, rather than the elevated cuisine of Paris. Simple recipes encourage the cook to buy the best the market has to offer and to experiment and take risks—as the best cooks everywhere do. Try bouillabaisse…a cassoulet of Toulouse …sole stewed in cider…and an inspired selection of salades niçoise. Penguin, $16.

● **The Frog/Commissary Cookbook** by Stephen Poses et al. The Frog and the Commissary are two alas now-vanished Philadelphia restaurants that featured bold, contemporary menus. Their creative energy survives in this lively book. Try turkey scallops with lemon-caper butter…coffee-walnut muffins…sweet potato fritters. Order from the publisher, Camino, 215-413-1917, *www.caminobooks.com*. $19.95.

● **Good Things** by Jane Grigson. Rooted in English tradition in the best sense of the term, Ms. Grigson offers up such delicious dishes as

*All prices subject to change.

Cheshire pork and apple pie…roast parsnips with beef…and lemon rice pudding. It is out of print, but used copies may be gotten through bookstores that sell used books.

● **Kitchen Essays** by Agnes Jekyll. A compilation of Ms. Jekyll's essays on food that first ran in *The Times* of London in the early 1920s. Her chatty and amusing pieces deal in a light but always practical way with several marvelous period subjects like "A Little Supper after the Play," "Luncheon for a Motor Excursion in Winter" and "In the Cook's Absence." Available in the US at our store or from the publisher at *www.persephonebooks.co.uk.* $26.*

● **Parisian Home Cooking** by Michael Roberts. Mr. Roberts, a longtime chef, introduces us to the kind of easy recipes that the food-savvy French turn to after a long day at work. Their market-inspired cooking includes such pleasures as lamb chops with leeks…stewed mussels West Indian–style…asparagus on toasted brioche. Morrow, $28.

● **Taste of Country Cooking** by Edna Lewis. Although Ms. Lewis first became known as a chef at an upscale New York City restaurant, this distinguished woman's enduring reputation is based on the scrumptious old-fashioned foods of her Southern childhood, including ham biscuits…ring mold with chicken…new cabbage with scallions…and crushed peaches. Exuberant, glowing food that brings comfort to every table. Knopf, $19.95.

*All prices subject to change.

Great Opera Recordings

Barry Henry, artistic director of the Pacific Opera Company, a training ground for young opera singers in Australia and the US, based in Sydney, Australia, *www.pacific opera.com*. From the 1950s through the 1970s, Mr. Henry was a leading opera and pop singer in Europe and Australia under the stage name Henry King.

Would you like to enjoy opera more or learn more about it? These 10 wonderful recordings can form the backbone of any opera collection, whether you are new to the art or a devotee. The works are classics, and the singers outstanding.

● **Bizet's *Carmen*** performed by Rise Stevens and Jan Peerce with the RCA Victor Symphony Orchestra. Ms. Stevens brings a new personality to *Carmen,* making the opera even more exciting and dynamic.

● **Donizetti's *Lucia di Lammermoor*** performed by Angelo Bada, Giuseppe DeLuca, Amelita Galli-Curci, Beniamino Gigli, Louise Homer and Ezio Pinza with the Metropolitan Opera Orchestra. The performers' diction is perfect and the singing superb.

● **Giordano's *Andrea Chénier*** performed by Maria Caniglia and Beniamino Gigli along with the La Scala Theater Orchestra and Chorus. A spirited rendition—close your eyes and you'll think you're at the show.

● **Mascagni's *L'Amico Fritz*** performed by Tito Schipa and Mafalda Favero with the La Scala Theater Orchestra and Chorus. Provides romantic magic.

● **Puccini's *La Bohème*** performed by Licia Albanese and Beniamino Gigli with the La Scala Theater Orchestra and Chorus. It's a powerful recording of this popular classic.

● **Puccini's *Madame Butterfly*** performed by Renata Tebaldi and Giuseppe Campora with the Saint Cecilia Academy Orchestra & Chorus. An exquisite performance by Ms. Tebaldi during the peak of her career.

● **Puccini's *Tosca*** performed by Maria Caniglia and Beniamino Gigli along with Rome's Royal Opera Theatre Orchestra and Chorus. Mr. Gigli's forceful performance has all the fire that Tosca demands.

● **Verdi's *Rigoletto*** performed by Giuseppe DeLuca, Amelita Galli-Curci, Beniamino Gigli and Louise Homer along with the Metropolitan Opera Orchestra. A totally convincing performance from a masterful cast.

● **Wagner's *Parsifal*** performed by Alexander Kipnis and Fritz Wolff with the Bayreuth Festival Orchestra and Chorus. The singers do exactly what Wagner wanted—they have a conversation with the orchestra.

● **Wagner's *Tristan und Isolde*** performed by Kirsten Flagstad and Lauritz Melchior with the London Philharmonic Orchestra. Mr. Melchior and Ms. Flagstad are great Wagnerian singers.

WHERE TO BUY

Though decades old, these recordings have now been rereleased on compact disc. Many are available through Amazon.com under the *Classical Music* heading. Use the name of the opera and the performers as keywords. If some prove difficult to find, consult a music store specializing in classical music.

Unlike pop albums, many classic opera performances have been released by a number of record labels—not all of which provide satisfactory sound quality. Cetra, EMI, Naxos, Nimbus and Telefunken generally can be trusted.

Helpful: If you would like to find out more about opera, The Teaching Company provides a great course on audio or video titled *How to Listen to and Understand Opera* (32 lectures, 45 minutes per lecture). Available at some libraries and for sale at 800-832-2412, *www.teach12.com* (eight DVDs, $519.95*...32 CDs, $359.95...16 audiotapes, $249.95).

*All prices subject to change.

Gift-Giving Dos and Don'ts from Etiquette Expert Peggy Post

Peggy Post, great-granddaughter-in-law of etiquette pioneer Emily Post. She is a director and spokesperson for the Emily Post Institute in Burlington, VT, and author of *Emily Post's Etiquette, 17th Edition* (HarperCollins). Her Web site is *www.emilypost.com.*

Every holiday season, we receive hundreds of letters at the Emily Post Institute asking about the etiquette of gift-giving. *Here are the questions we get most often...*

● **Is it OK to "regift"?** *Sometimes—but proceed cautiously and follow these guidelines...*

● The item must be brand new and in its original package.

• The gift should be something the recipient would love.

• It should not be something the original giver took great care to select or make for you.

• Regifting a nice bottle of wine to a wine lover is fine. Regifting the crystal vase that your mother gave you is not. If in doubt, don't do it.

• **Someone with whom I wasn't planning to exchange gifts gave me one. Do I have to reciprocate?** No. Just thank the gift giver sincerely and leave it at that. Otherwise, you may start a new gift-giving tradition that can be very difficult to break. Of course, if that's what you would like to do, reciprocate!

• **My parents gave me a very expensive television—but it is not the one I wanted. Can I ask them if I can exchange it for a different one?** Just be honest, especially since the gift was extravagant and your parents will expect to see you use it.

First, thank them enthusiastically for the very generous gift. Try to point out something specific that requires you to return it. For example, if it's missing a feature that you were hoping for, gently suggest an exchange. Say something like, "Mom, Dad, this is an amazing gift—but this model doesn't include the surround-sound feature that I think we would especially enjoy. Would you mind terribly if I exchanged it?"

• **I've been invited to a holiday party. Should I bring a gift for the host?** Yes, but don't bring anything that distracts the host— food or flowers that need to be taken care of immediately are not the best choices.

Keep the gift simple and under $20—a bottle of wine…a small potted plant…an arrangement of flowers already in a vase…a box of holiday cookies or chocolates.

There is one exception. An open house is an informal way to celebrate and doesn't require a gift for the host, though you can certainly bring one if you choose.

• **I mail my grandchildren their holiday presents, but they never send me thank-you notes. This really bothers me. Should I talk to my son?** Start by calling and asking your son or daughter-in-law—or even better, ask your grandchildren directly—whether all their gifts arrived safely. If the answer is *yes,* drop a hint with, "Well, I'm glad to hear that. Since I didn't hear from you, I was starting to wonder if the packages made it there. Did you like the gifts?"

If you don't think that you got your message across, you will have to be more direct. Talk frankly to your son—or if the grandkids are age eight or older, speak to them. Tell them politely that it's important to you that they express appreciation when you give them a gift.

If this doesn't work, you may choose to stop sending gifts. That should get their attention— and teach your grandchildren that thank-you notes mean a lot.

• **Should I give my boss a holiday gift? What about the people who report to me and other coworkers?** Generally, you should not give a gift to the boss. It could be seen as an attempt to win favor. However, an inexpensive gift that isn't too personal from you and other employees is fine. If you and your boss have worked closely together for years, it's OK to give a small gift.

When you're the boss, it's up to you whether or not to give gifts to your staff. It's certainly a nice gesture and a great way to acknowledge those who work for you.

If you do decide to give gifts, give across the board—don't give to only one department head but not to the other two.

Good gift ideas include a nice bottle of wine, gift certificates, CDs and food items.

As for coworkers, a Secret Santa (in which each employee draws a name and gives a gift to that person) or a holiday grab bag are two of the easier ways to handle gift giving.

Food gifts also are a good idea—bring in a batch of homemade cookies or a box of chocolates to share with colleagues.

16

Cars and Drivers

How Not to Be Scammed When Buying a Car

Car scams are increasing, not just with sales of used vehicles but also new vehicles. While it may be possible to sue if you're the victim of a scam, lawsuits are expensive and lengthy. *It's much wiser to avoid scams at the outset...*

THE YO-YO SCAM

Typical scenario: The dealer asks the buyer of a new or used car for, say, a $1,500 or $2,000 down payment and mentions that interest will be 5%.

The salesperson spreads a handful of documents on a desk and asks the buyer to sign in several places. Among these papers is a document that says the buyer's purchase isn't final until all financing is confirmed by the lending company with which the dealer does business.

Often, the buyer is so eager to close the deal that he/she doesn't read each form carefully.

Moreover, unscrupulous dealers try to rush customers and handle documents with what they call a "five-finger fold" to cover up the contents.

The buyer drives off the car lot with his purchase, but then a week or two later, the dealer telephones to say that the financing didn't go through. The car dealer asks for an additional $2,000 on the down payment and says the interest rate will now be 9%.

If the buyer objects, the dealer points out that he signed an agreement saying that the purchase wasn't final until financing was confirmed. Car dealers may also apply pressure by saying the buyer's trade-in has already been sold (which is usually untrue). The buyer sees little choice and then reluctantly agrees to the new terms.

Protection: After you tell a salesperson that you will purchase a car at the offered price, refuse to sign an agreement that makes the sale

Bernard Brown, a Kansas City, MO, attorney as well as cofounder of the National Association of Consumer Advocates, located at 1730 Rhode Island Ave. NW, Washington, DC 20036.

contingent on financing, and insist that the car dealer arrange for the financing while you wait. Never sign over your title until the financing is confirmed.

Most dealers will agree to these terms. Stay away from any that won't. But even if a dealer agrees, study everything you sign to make sure that there is no language that makes the sale contingent on financing.

Yo-yo scams exist because auto dealers make a large part of their profit by selling loan agreements to large, nationwide finance companies.

Example: An auto dealer may get a 5% loan approved by a finance company but then charge the customer 9%. The dealer pockets the difference.

Such transactions themselves *may* be legal, but few customers are aware of this practice. Yo-yo scams, however, are illegal because they involve deceiving customers.

DISGUISED PROBLEMS

Many unscrupulous car dealers are experts at covering up evidence that a car has been in a wreck. A vehicle that was structurally damaged can be unsafe, and cars involved in collisions may not last as long as others.

Similarly, unethical dealers often try to hide high mileage by rolling back the odometer. Or they conceal flood damage or a vehicle's use as a delivery vehicle by sprucing up the car.

Protection: Ask the dealer to let you take a used car to a body shop, which can spot signs of a wreck, and to a mechanic who can check out the vehicle for other problems.

Many body shops and mechanics will not charge for inspecting the car because they hope to get your business later. Even if they do charge, the fee is usually less than $50.

Don't conduct business with any automobile dealer that won't let you have a used car inspected. Insist on inspection even at large national chains or if the vehicle is still under the manufacturer's warranty.

It's been my experience that most auto information services, such as on-line search services, are often not reliable for checking on whether a car has been wrecked, which is why it's especially important to have a car checked by a body shop and a mechanic before you buy it.

Reasons: You may be dealing with an honest salesperson at an unethical dealership, and evidence of a wreck can invalidate a manufacturer's warranty.

If you discover evidence that the car has suffered minor damage, negotiate the price down if the repair shop believes it's safe to drive. Otherwise, take your business to another dealer.

When shopping for a late-model used car, it's nearly always best to buy a vehicle with only one previous owner whom you can ask about any wrecks or problems that may have occurred. However, less-than-straightforward dealers often conceal a car's ownership history.

Protection: Refuse to buy a car unless the dealer lets you speak with the previous owner. That might seem like an excessive precaution, but it really isn't. If the dealer refuses to let you contact the previous owner, there is a good chance he's trying to cover up a problem.

Some dealers claim that privacy laws prevent them from disclosing owners' names, but this is untrue. In fact, after you buy a car, you'll see the previous owner's name on the title.

OVERPRICED FINANCING

While not engaging in anything illegal, many dealers charge high interest rates, often taking advantage of a buyer's eagerness to drive off the lot with a newly acquired vehicle.

To find cheaper financing: Check with your bank or credit union for the going rate on automobile loans. If the auto dealer charges more, tell him that you'll buy the car but only at whatever you discover to be the going rate. Most dealers will quickly agree for fear of losing the sale. Alternatively, tell the dealer that you'll handle the financing through your bank or other lending institution.

Smart negotiation tactics: When you first speak with a salesperson, never say that you intend to pay cash or finance the vehicle yourself. If you do, the dealership may quote a high sticker price to make up for its lost profit on financing.

It's also wise to stay away from any service contract that a dealer might offer. Evidence shows that the cost of these contracts is usually greater than the amount that will likely be paid out to the owners.

If you're concerned about future repair bills, shop for a car that's still under the manufacturer's warranty.

PHONY ADS

Today, a growing number of unethical dealers disguise their identities by placing classified ads in newspapers and local magazines.

This practice, known as "curbstoning," is often used to sell cars that have been in accidents or that have other problems. Curbstoners rely on unwary buyers who are more trusting of individuals than of dealerships.

Protection: Insist on seeing the title, which will tell you whether an individual or dealership owns the car. Don't do business with a dealership that disguises itself as an individual. The car may well have problems.

Five Reasons to Splurge on a New Car

Eric Peters, Washington, DC–based automotive columnist and author of *Automotive Atrocities: The Cars We Love to Hate* (MotorBooks International).

From a strictly financial standpoint, it pays for most people to buy used cars. *But five engineering improvements might make it worthwhile for you to consider a new model...*

- **Safer brakes.** Today, even many economy cars have four-wheel disc brakes, and antilock brake systems are becoming common. *Brake Assist*—a new feature that further reduces stopping distances during emergency braking—also is being featured in family vehicles from Toyota, Volvo and others. Brake Assist automatically applies full pressure to the system during an emergency stop if the driver fails to depress the brake pedal fully. This slows the car more quickly.

- **Intelligent navigation systems.** The latest in-car satellite navigation systems can direct you around traffic jams and help you find the best route to your destination. Real-time data about traffic conditions is uploaded into the system automatically every few minutes via the car's onboard satellite radio hookup. That data is compared against your planned route in the global positioning satellite (GPS) navigation computer. If there's a bottleneck ahead, an alternate route is displayed. Cadillac CTS and Acura RL offer this technology on some models. Intelligent GPS should filter down to less expensive models soon.

- **Bodies that don't rust—and paint jobs that last.** Today's vehicles are so well-protected against rust by multiple coats of protective undercoating and chip-resistant primers that body rot is becoming a rare sight.

- **Engines that don't pollute.** At least 95% of the combustion by-products of any 2006 model-year car is just harmless water vapor and carbon dioxide. And, several models from Ford, General Motors, Honda, Toyota and Volvo qualify as ultra-low emissions vehicles (ULEVs), with virtually no harmful emissions.

- **Improved gas mileage.** Even the worst-offender two-ton V8 sport-utility vehicle can get mileage per gallon (mpg) in the middle-teens when on the highway. And American drivers no longer have to squeeze themselves into micro-sized subcompacts to get 30 mpg.

Vastly improved fuel economy with little difference in size, power or performance can be credited to electronic fuel injection and the widespread use of overdrive transmissions. Both reduce engine operating speeds (and thus fuel consumption) once a vehicle has reached road speed. Seven-speed automatics (BMW and Mercedes-Benz) and continuously variable transmissions (CVTs) hold the promise of even bigger mileage improvements. CVTs deliver the fuel economy of a manual transmission with all the ease of an automatic.

More from Eric Peters...

The Best Preowned Vehicles

The best preowned vehicles are those certified by the manufacturer—not a used-car dealer, which can define "certified" any way it wants. Manufacturers certify only the best used vehicles and often provide an extended two-year warranty. Vehicles that do not meet the manufacturers' standards are sold to used-car wholesalers.

Before buying a certified vehicle: Check the window sticker to make sure that the certification is from the manufacturer.

Manufacturers that offer the best certification programs: Honda/Acura...Toyota/Lexus...Volvo...VW.

Also from Eric Peters...

Before You Take That Car Trip...

A pilot never takes off without running through a checklist. A road trip should be approached the same way. Even if your car is relatively new, it always is a good idea to make a quick check of vital systems before you leave for an extended trip.

●**Check that all four tires are properly inflated and in good shape.** The recommended tire pressure can be located in the owner's manual or on a sticker on the vehicle. Replace any tire that has bulges (which indicate a weakness in the tire wall that could lead to a blowout), visible cracks in the tread or sidewall, or a tread depth that is close to the wear indicators—the small bands that appear across the tread when the tire becomes worn.

●**Make sure you have all the equipment to change a tire.** This includes a properly inflated spare and all the parts of the jack. Toss an old blanket (at least 6' x 8') into the trunk along with a pair of heavy-duty gloves and an old shirt. Make sure you include a strong flashlight with fresh batteries and at least four flares so you can illuminate the vehicle if it becomes disabled.

●**Create an emergency kit.** You never know when you will have to patch a leaking hose or tie down a trunk that is too full. Round up a few basic hand tools—flat- and Phillips-head screwdrivers and an adjustable wrench—as well as duct tape and a few feet of rope. These things can get you out of a jam—or at least, to the next gas station.

●**Check that all routine maintenance has been performed.** That includes changing the oil and filter and checking the air filter, battery, brakes and cooling system. Check the belts that drive vital engine accessories for wear or cracks. Also check the condition of rubber radiator and heater hoses. These should be replaced every four years even if there are no obvious signs of wear. Install fresh wiper blades if yours are more than six months old. Top off the windshield washer fluid. Make sure headlights, turn signals and brake lights are working.

●**If you plan to pull a trailer or boat and the car has an automatic transmission,** consider having the transmission fluid and filter changed and an accessory transmission oil cooler installed if the vehicle does not already have one. The added heat created by pulling a trailer can dramatically reduce the service life of an automatic transmission and even lead to a failure on the road. The cost—about $150 to $200 installed—is far less than the $2,000 for a new transmission.

Defensive Driving: Smart Ways to Improve Your Safety on the Road

John H. Kennedy, executive director of defensive driving courses, National Safety Council, 1121 Spring Lake Dr., Itasca, IL 60143, *www.nsc.org.*

More than 2.5 million people are killed or seriously injured in road accidents each year in the US. But there's good news—with only a little bit of effort, you can improve your driving skills enough to lower your chances of being among the victims. In the process, you may also lower your insurance premiums.

Learning to drive defensively is particularly important if you're over 50 because—like it or not—vision, motor skills and other abilities diminish with age.

EARLY WARNINGS

Unfortunately, problems with one's driving are often hard to spot because abilities diminish gradually. *Be especially concerned if...*

•**Cars often honk at you.** Other drivers may be trying to get your attention because you may be driving erratically. You might not be as alert as you once were. Medication can be one of the reasons, and not everyone realizes that it's against the law to drive when ability is impaired by medication.

Apart from making you vulnerable to accidents, violations can result in hefty fines, possible loss of your license and higher insurance premiums.

Essential: Whenever a physician prescribes medication, be sure to ask if it will impair your driving ability.

•**You squint to read road signs,** or oncoming headlights look blurry. Either of these can be symptoms of eye problems, many of which can be corrected.

Essential: Have an ophthalmologist examine your eyes yearly.

•**You are often startled by a car behind you,** especially when you change lanes.

It usually happens because you are distracted or have not adequately scanned your driving environment. It's recommended that you check your mirrors every three to five seconds.

People over age 50 often become less agile, which makes it harder to turn to check the blind spots. Also avoid driving in another person's blind spot. If you cannot see the other driver's rearview mirror through his/her back window, you are probably in his blind spot. Adjust your speed to move out of this position.

Solutions: Limit lane changes, slow down—and consider a physical exercise program to improve flexibility (check with your doctor).

Also: Park your car, and ask a friend to walk around behind it. Then look in your mirrors, and, when you can no longer see the other person in each mirror, turn in your seat and note where the blind spots are. Adjust the mirrors to the best position.

DEFENSIVE DRIVING

Defensive driving courses are available in every state. Most courses include four to eight hours of classroom instruction and cost less than $65.

Statistics show that drivers who have taken courses have fewer serious accidents, and in most states, they're eligible for a reduction in insurance premiums, usually about 10%. Completing some courses may also let you remove points from your driving record.

Even in states where a premium reduction is not automatic, individual insurance companies will often cut their rates if customers offer proof that they've taken a defensive driving course.

To find a course, ask your state motor vehicle bureau. *Some of the most popular courses...*

•**The National Safety Council's "Defensive Driving Courses" and "Defensive Driving for the Mature Driver."** The National Safety Council also provides an on-line driving course (630-285-1121, *www.nsc.org*).

•**AARP's "Driver Safety Program"** (888-227-7669, *www.aarp.org/driver_safety*).

•**AAA's Driver Improvement Program course, "Safe Driving for Mature Operators."** Information on courses is available from local AAA branches, which are listed in your phone book.

EXPERT SAFETY TACTICS

To reduce the chance of a serious accident...

•**Beware of intersections,** where a high percentage of accidents occur. Defensive drivers not only slow down but also scan ahead to anticipate problems as they approach an intersection. They also keep their left foot over the brake so they can stop quickly if necessary.

Another strategy is to avoid a busy intersection altogether by taking another route.

•**Keep to a three-second following distance.** Determine that distance by counting the time it takes your car to reach a light pole or other stationary object after the car ahead has reached it.

Add a second to the distance if it's dark, and another second if it's raining. Add yet another second if the road is icy.

•**When you are caught in the glare of oncoming headlights, do not turn your head.** Instead, avoid the glare by focusing on the road itself.

•**If another driver shows any signs of anger, get out of his way.** Trying to win an argument is often a route to a serious accident. Similarly, good defensive drivers slow down to let tailgaters pass.

• **Keep your hands on the wheel at the 9 o'clock and 3 o'clock positions,** to have maximum control over the car.

• **Fasten your safety belt.** If you need an incentive for using your seat belt, imagine your body crumpled against the dashboard after a crash. It's also illegal to drive without a safety belt fastened, and convictions could increase your insurance premiums.

• **Know your braking system.** Today's antilock brakes operate very differently from older systems. If you're unsure about how to use antilock brakes, review your owner's manual. Or you can experiment using them in an empty parking lot.

Most important: In an emergency, do not "pump" antilock brakes. Instead, apply steady pressure to the pedal until you stop. For more information, visit *www.nsc.org.*

• **Familiarize yourself with the dashboard controls.** Ironically, many otherwise excellent drivers do not know what each control does. That knowledge is important because it lets you manage lights, door locks and systems that can be vital in emergencies.

• **Don't use distracting devices while driving.** Using a cell phone, even a hands-free model, is dangerous because taking your mind off the road can result in an accident. Other distractions include eating, drinking, putting tapes or CDs into a player, even adjusting the heat. If you need to make a call or do anything else that might be a distraction, pull over to the side of the road and stop.

Smart move: With so many safety steps to remember, it's wise to ask for help from anyone who frequently rides with you. Tell these friends how you're trying to drive more safely, and ask them to remind you whenever you forget.

You can increase safety even more by driving shorter distances, avoiding trips at night and taking less congested routes, particularly at rush hours.

When these steps just aren't possible, ask a friend to drive or take a taxi. With today's high cost of operating a car, taxis make more and more sense, especially when two or more people can share the fare.

Insist That Others Wear Seat Belts for Their Safety And Yours

In a car crash, unbelted passengers can become human projectiles and are a danger to other passengers—including those who are wearing seat belts.

Recent study: Belted passengers are 20% more likely to be killed in a crash when there is an unbelted person in the car.

Peter Cummings, MD, MPH, professor of epidemiology, University of Washington, Seattle.

Are Your Tires Older Than You Think?

Tire age is a new safety concern. Tire life can be affected by exposure to sunlight, ozone, ambient heat and nearness to engine exhaust compounds. Tire compounds contain antiaging chemicals that are active only when the tire is in use—lack of use actually speeds up aging.

Caution: Tire dates, which appear on or inside the sidewall, are difficult to decode. Tire dealers may sell unsuspecting consumers tires that are at the end of their life spans. Ask the tire dealer to decode the expiration date. Avoid tires that are more than a few years old, especially for an infrequently used vehicle, recreational vehicle, trailer or spare.

C.J. Tolson, editor, *MotorWatch,* Box 123, Butler, MD 21023, *www.motorwatch.com.*

Automotive Rip-Offs

David Solomon, a certified master auto technician and chairman of MotorWatch, a consumer automotive membership organization, Box 123, Butler, MD 21023, *www.motor watch.com.*

Car owners constantly need to be on the lookout for rip-offs—from an auto repair shop selling unnecessary services to the cheap knockoffs passed off as quality products. *Here are today's most common traps...*

●**Air-conditioning (A/C) system sealers** temporarily plug up leaks but ultimately create clogs, leading to compressor failure. Once a do-it-yourself sealer is used, all the A/C parts must be replaced. If you suspect a leak, have your mechanic check your A/C system.

●**Cheap A/C refrigerants** can be found for about one-tenth the price of proper refrigerants, but they can cause serious damage to hoses, seals and O-rings. Once the damage is done from a do-it-yourself kit, you will have to pay for repairs as well as the removal and disposal of the cheap refrigerant. When your mechanic is changing your refrigerant, ask what type is being used—vehicles manufactured in the last decade require R-134a—and beware of any deal that seems too good to be true.

●**Engine oil system flushing** supposedly gets rid of contaminated oil. In fact, it's unnecessary because flushing doesn't even reach the dirty parts. It also can leave behind solvents that will accelerate engine wear. Just have your oil drained and replaced according to your car's maintenance manual.

●**Fake air bags** leave you and your passengers without air bag protection. Some fakes are sophisticated enough to activate the dashboard air bag light, giving the appearance that bags are functional even if none are present. When air bags are replaced, ask for documentation showing the source of the air bag module and components. They all should come from the car's manufacturer, not a third party.

●**Odometer fraud** has reached epic proportions. Before purchasing a used car, always run a car background check to make sure that the odometer was not tampered with. Go to *www. autocheck.com* or *www.carfax.com.*

Cost: $19.99.* Or ask a reputable dealer to run a check for you.

*Price subject to change.

More from David Solomon...

Get More for Your Used Car

You can get $1,000 more for your used car if you improve its condition. Clean it inside and out, including the engine. If there are dents, contact a local body shop and ask about paintless dent repair, an inexpensive way to remove dents. Use touch-up paint to cover small chips and scratches. Also, make sure that the oil is clean, and show maintenance records if possible. And, consider getting a vehicle background check. See above for details.

Also from David Solomon...

Gas-Buying Tip

A sudden drop in gas mileage could be due to alcohol in the gas you buy. Automotive technicians are reporting that even brand-name gas can contain up to 20% alcohol. Alcohol content, which isn't posted on the pump, will cause a 10% to 15% reduction in gas mileage.

Self-defense: Try different brands. Calculate miles per gallon (mpg), and use the brand that gives the highest mpg.

Eleven Ways to Save at the Pump

Nancy Dunnan, editor and publisher of *TravelSmart* at *www.travelsmartnewsletter.com.* She also is a financial adviser and the author of numerous books, including *How to Invest $50–$5,000* (HarperCollins).

High gasoline prices make it more important than ever to save on fuel. Most people do know to avoid higher octane fuel than their cars require and to keep their cars tuned up and tires inflated. *Other moneysaving ideas that you might not have thought of...*

●**Check the gauge.** Be aware of the amount of gas in your tank. When the tank is half full, start looking for a gas station. This gives you time to comparison shop. Avoid interstate and highway gas stations—gas on a busy highway costs 10 to 15 cents more per gallon than the same brand and grade in less-trafficked areas. Buying self-service gas saves 10 cents or more per gallon. Compare prices on-line at *www.gas pricewatch.com* and *www.gasbuddy.com.*

●**Buy big-box gas.** Some wholesale clubs sell discounted gas at member-only pumps. Their gas averages about 12 cents a gallon less than gas at regular stations. Try BJ's (*www.bjs. com*).

●**Get a gas card.** Major gas companies offer a 1%* to 6% discount if you use their Master-Card or Visa when buying their brand of gas. Sunoco and ExxonMobil both have cards and rebate programs. The BP Visa Card, for example, has no annual fee and gives an introductory 6% rebate on gasoline for the first two months, 3% thereafter (*www.bp.com,* 800-278-4721).

The Visa card cosponsored by AAA gives 5% back on all purchases at the pump, regardless of brand (no annual fee, 800-551-0839, *www. aaa.com*). Pay your bill in full each month so interest costs don't wipe out the savings.

●**Don't let your car idle.** If you're going to be at a standstill for more than a minute, turn off the engine. Idling consumes up to one gallon of gas per hour. It also wastes more gas than restarting the engine.

●**Map unfamiliar routes in advance,** so you won't get lost and waste gas.

●**Drive strategically.** Combine errands to avoid shorter trips. Use cruise control—it cuts down on gas as well as speeding tickets. Avoid roads that have a long string of traffic lights. Don't slam on the brakes or accelerate rapidly —this lowers gas mileage by 33% at highway speeds and by 5% around town.

●**Buy gas early in the morning or late in the evening** when it is cool outside to reduce the amount of evaporation.

●**Take alternative forms of transportation.** Use public transportation, or even walk or

*All prices/offers subject to change.

bike. Get a scooter—Vespas and other scooters get 40 miles per gallon (mpg) to 60 mpg. Consider a diesel-powered car—they have 20% to 40% better fuel economy than gas cars. Look into a gas-electric hybrid.

●**Park in a shady spot in hot weather** so you don't need to blast the air-conditioning as soon as you get back in your car. Air-conditioning reduces fuel economy dramatically.

●**Keep the windows closed.** When traveling on highways on long trips, open windows can create air drag and reduce your mileage by as much as 10%.

●**When renting a car, choose the model that gets the best gas mileage.** Most Hondas, Toyotas and Hyundais as well as the Pontiac Vibe and Dodge Neon get 29 mpg or more in highway traffic.

To compare fuel economy among cars: www.fueleconomy.gov.

Simple Way to Save on Gas

To save money at the gas pump, just drive slower. Driving at 65 mph rather than 55 mph increases fuel consumption 20%—and driving 75 mph increases it by another 25%, according to the Federal Trade Commission.

Result: You'll travel the same distance consuming $2 of gasoline at 75 mph, or $1.60 of gasoline at 65 mph, or only $1.33 of gasoline at 55 mph.

Also: Keep your tires inflated at the recommended pressure, and keep your engine properly maintained (regular tune-ups) to get the best mileage. And don't waste money paying for premium gasoline unless your car's owner's manual specifically recommends it.

Jean Chatzky, the financial editor for *Today* on NBC and editor-at-large for *Money* magazine. She is also the author of *Pay It Down!* (Portfolio). Her Internet site is *www.jean chatzky.com.*

17

Home and Family Life

Best Ways to Accident-Proof Your Home

If you need motivation for making your house a safer place to live, take just a moment now to read over the surprising facts that are outlined below…

● **Home accidents cause about seven million injuries a year.** According to recent statistics from the American College of Emergency Physicians, about 28,000 of those accidents result in death.

● **Falls are by far the most common of home accidents.** The cost of treating a hip fracture can exceed $30,000.

Additional incentive: Making your house safer can cut homeowner's insurance premiums and will almost certainly boost the value of the house if you decide to sell it. Safer homes also reduce the chance of guests having accidents (and subsequently suing).

Many home owners, however, are so accustomed to their houses that they overlook the areas where accidents are most likely to occur. Though eyesight deteriorates with age, for instance, we often don't fix safety problems at home because we get used to the layout and to obstacles being in familiar places.

To make your house safer, take a look at four key areas…

LIGHTING

The big problem with home lighting is that it's not always available when you need it.

Example: Entering the house at night.

Solution: A remote light switch that lets you turn on an inside light from your car or as you approach your house on foot. Or when you're in one room of the house, remote switches can turn on lights in another room.

Ella Chadwell, president of Life@Home, Inc., a home-safety consultancy based in Brentwood, TN, that provides information on home accident prevention and also markets products for home safety, particularly for the senior market (800-653-1923, *www.lifehome.com*).

Remotes work at a maximum distance of approximately 50 feet and operate much like a TV channel changer.

Remote light switches are available at most large hardware and home-appliance stores.

Typical price: $30 to $50. They're not difficult to install, but if you need assistance, hire an electrician.

Other areas where lights are often not available when you need them...

●**Bedrooms.** There may be a strong overhead light and a table lamp with a bright bulb. But the lights are useless if one of them can't be turned on easily when you get up in the middle of the night.

Solution: Install a low-wattage night-light that will stay on throughout the night. These typically cost about $3 to $10 and plug directly into wall sockets.

Alternatives: Install a remote switch, and keep the transmitter within reach. Or install a touch sensor on the table lamp. Touch sensors are devices placed between the lightbulb and socket, making it possible to turn on the lamp by touching any part of it. They usually cost less than $25.

The advantage is that you can turn on the lamp without the risk of knocking it over by fumbling for the switch.

In case of power failures, also keep a flashlight within reach of the bed, and check the batteries at least once every six months.

●**Halls, stairs and large rooms.** Be sure to have light switches at both ends of stairs and hallways. In rooms with multiple entries, install switches close to each door.

Typical price: About $125 each, installed, depending on the type of light switch and the rate that electricians charge in the area where you live.

●**Porches.** Install motion-sensor lights that automatically go on when they detect motion within about 30 feet. They reduce the chance of tripping over porch steps and have the added advantage of deterring intruders.

Typical price: Approximately $50, plus cost of installation.

In addition to lights, make sure that handrails are in good repair on porches and stairs. (Strangers, such as the mailman or delivery people, who come to your door might sue if a faulty handrail causes an injury.)

BATHROOMS

You can cut the risk of accidents by spending thousands of dollars on a relatively new type of bathtub and shower designed so that you enter through a low door instead of climbing into it.

But unless you can't step over the side of the tub, there are simpler and much less expensive solutions...

●**Install one or two "grab bars" to hold on to when stepping into the tub.** Also install one near the toilet area, because it is easy to slip as you sit down. A stainless steel grab bar 1.25 inches in diameter typically costs $125 to $150 installed.

Today, grab bars are becoming popular in homes with children. That means if you sell your house, these devices may make it more attractive not just to seniors but to younger buyers as well.

●**Put a nonskid surface strip in the tub and/or shower area.** Nonskid strips usually cost less than $25 and last at least two years.

●**If you replace an old bathtub,** get a new one with a slip-resistant surface.

FLOOR COVERING

Loose rugs and carpets are especially dangerous because they're easy to grow accustomed to. If you've tripped harmlessly over a loose section of carpet, for instance, you are likely to be on guard against doing it again—until, perhaps, you're groggy from medication or distracted by a noise.

Myth: Carpeting is safer than wood flooring because, if you fall on a carpet, the injury won't be as severe.

Reality: Any fall from a standing position can be severe, particularly for older people.

As a general rule, natural wood creates the safest floor as long as it's not coated with a slippery finish. Low-pile carpeting is also generally safe except when there are bulges caused by improper installation. High-pile carpeting might look luxurious, but it often causes people to trip or lose their balance.

If you want an area rug instead of carpeting, put a slip-resistant mat under it. Secure both the rug and mat to the floor with carpet tacks. Slip-resistant mats usually cost about $3 to $4 a square yard.

Double-sided adhesive tape can also secure rugs to a floor, but frequent wear and temperature changes often cause it to come loose after a year or so.

WALKWAYS

When you clean house, get in the habit of moving electrical cords from lamps, computers, etc., far away from any area where people walk. If a cord is in an area with frequent traffic, tack it down out of the way.

Other items in pathways are often more difficult to spot because, as with poor lighting, home owners often get accustomed to them.

Examples: A pile of magazines on the floor in the den, an oversized coffee table in the living room, the dog's feeding bowl in the middle of the kitchen.

Smart move: Ask a friend or relative to walk through your house once or twice a year to spot obstacles that might be a hazard—especially at night or to guests who are unfamiliar with the house.

You might try teaming up with one or more neighbors so you can spot-check each other's houses, not just for cluttered walkways but for other hazards.

Safeguard Your Home Against Hidden Health Hazards

Alfred Moffit, senior project manager, Environmental Waste Management Associates, LLC, a full-service environmental consulting company that tests soil, air and water quality, Parsippany, NJ.

B uy a home that has hidden health hazards, and you could lose your life savings to a massively expensive cleanup.

Ignore the problem, and you might be the target of a lawsuit by a neighbor or the home's next owner. Also, as time passes and environmental regulations tighten, problems may become even more expensive to fix.

Here are five major environmental risks and what to do about them...

UNDERGROUND OIL TANKS

Buried fuel tanks often leak as they disintegrate. Tank removal can cost $1,200 to $2,000, depending on the size and where the tank is located. Fixing a significant leak that impacts soil and ground water can cost you $50,000 or more. If neighbors test their well water and discover that it is contaminated because of your leak or there are oil vapors in their home, you can be sued.

The only clue that a tank is leaking is a dramatic, unexplained increase in your heating bills or a heating failure due to water entering the system.

Helpful: Some homeowner's insurance policies cover cleanup costs. Some insurers and tank-installation companies sell tank insurance. Or check with your state's department of environmental protection—it might have programs that help pay for cleanups.

Example: New Jersey has a "Petroleum Underground Storage Tank (UST) Remediation, Upgrade and Closure Fund."

• **Home sellers.** To expedite a sale, present contractor certification from your town which proves your tank has passed a pressure test to detect leaks...or the permit documentation that a former owner removed or properly buried a tank and filled it with sand.

• **Home buyers.** The purchase should be contingent on removal of a buried oil tank or passing of a pressure test.

Cost of a pressure test: About $400 to $500.

ASBESTOS

Homes built before 1980 may have asbestos fibers in floor tiles, pipe insulation, roof material, sheetrock—even caulking. Asbestos can cause potentially lethal lung diseases, including asbestosis, mesothelioma and lung cancer. Professional removal costs up to several thousand dollars, depending on the amount of asbestos that's present.

You might not need to act. As long as the asbestos-containing tile or insulation is intact, there's no immediate health risk. If items containing asbestos begin to deteriorate and must be removed, hire a licensed asbestos abatement contractor.

●**Home sellers.** Disclose to potential buyers that you have removed asbestos and whether any asbestos remains.

●**Home buyers.** If the home was built before 1980, make the deal contingent on an asbestos test.

Cost: About $750.

LEAD PAINT

Homes built before 1978 usually have lead paint on walls, doors, trim and window frames. Lead in paint chips or dust can cause developmental problems in children. And, in adults, it can cause anemia, kidney damage, sterility and damage to the central nervous system.

If lead paint is in good condition, it usually is sufficient to paint over it.

Caution: Repainting is less effective on the edges of doors and windows. It might be necessary to remove lead paint from these high-wear areas. Sanding kicks up a huge amount of lead dust, so it's best to hire licensed lead abatement professionals if the paint is flaking throughout the home.

Cost: Up to several thousand dollars, depending on the extent of contamination.

●**Home sellers.** You must disclose the presence of lead-based paint in a home that was built before 1978.

●**Home buyers.** If a seller claims not to know about the existence of lead-based paint, be sure to make the deal contingent on a lead paint inspection.

Cost: About $400 to $700, depending on the home's size and age.

UNDRINKABLE WATER

Nonpotable well water can dramatically affect quality of life—not to mention a home's resale value. Many water-quality problems can be corrected with a contaminant filter, which costs from a few hundred to several thousand dollars,

plus monthly maintenance fees. Culligan (800-285-5442 or *www.culligan.com*) is one popular filter company. If the problem cannot be corrected, it might be necessary to drink only bottled water.

●**Home sellers.** Few states require sellers to test well water, but if you know of a problem, you should inform buyers.

●**Home buyers.** Make the purchase contingent on a water-quality test by an environmental firm.

Cost: About $350 to $500.

RADON

This naturally occurring radioactive gas is linked to increased risk of lung cancer. Homes sometimes have dangerous levels of this colorless and odorless gas in the basement or on the first floor when there is no basement. The problem can be alleviated with a venting system, but retrofitting one into an existing home can cost up to $10,000, depending on the size of the house and the concentration of radon.

●**Home sellers.** You can present proof that your home has a safe level of radon. However, the buyer probably will perform his/her own inspection. Most mortgage lenders require that this test be done.

●**Home buyers.** A home inspector can test for radon for as little as $50. Do-it-yourself tests are available in home stores, but follow instructions to make sure that the house is "sealed" properly. A reading of more than 4 picocuries per liter of air means that action is required.

Carbon Monoxide Protection

To protect against carbon monoxide leaks—have your heating system inspected now. Carbon monoxide is odorless but can bring on flu-like symptoms—such as headache, fatigue, nausea—and it may even be fatal. The most important steps in averting carbon monoxide poisoning are to check the heating system for cracks and other leaks and the chimney for blockages before turning on the furnace in the fall. Also recommended is installing a carbon monoxide alarm, which works like a smoke alarm. A combined carbon monoxide-smoke alarm is available, to have one device protect against both.

Very important: Check batteries monthly and replace every six months.

Ken Giles, spokesperson for the US Consumer Product Safety Commission, Bethesda, MD, *www.cpsc.gov.*

Drowning in Stuff? Smart Ways to Get Rid of It

Julie Morgenstern, founder of Julie Morgenstern's Professional Organizers, whose clients include the New York City mayor's office, Time Warner and the Miami Heat basketball team, *www.juliemorgenstern.com.* She is author of *Organizing from the Inside Out* (Owl).

The next time you're about to put off the task of tossing out old possessions, consider the advantages of…

●**More space to enjoy your home.** An uncluttered house or apartment is easier to keep clean and easier to entertain in and just more pleasant to be in.

●**Better organization.** Hunting for objects takes time and causes anxiety, especially when the object is important, such as a document or treasured gift. Organizing and finding items are easier when you have fewer of them.

●**Bringing joy to friends and relatives and even strangers in need.** More people than you realize may want the possessions you no longer need.

●**Lower taxes.** By giving unwanted objects to a charity, you may be eligible for an income tax deduction.

●**Profits.** When you sort through your possessions, you occasionally find items that are surprisingly valuable.

OVERCOMING HURDLES

Despite the big benefits of throwing out your unneeded possessions, many of us shrink from the task.

The biggest obstacle is the guilt that many people feel when they discard objects that came from a beloved relative. Guilt can also be strong in individuals who inherited a depression-era mentality of saving every item that might possibly be of use in the future.

Guilt can nearly always be overcome by giving unneeded items to other family members who will treasure them or to people who can genuinely use them. An old picture frame, for example, may be useless to you but treasured by a relative who knew that it came from a great-grandparent.

Don't think just of your relatives but also of friends and children of friends. A neighbor's child, for instance, could be in college, where he/she might be able to use the old couch that's been taking up space in your basement.

Fear is the other big hurdle that often prevents people from throwing out unneeded possessions. Fear typically affects those who feel more secure when they're surrounded by a trove of familiar objects.

Overcome fear by concentrating on what the effort will allow you to do—all the benefits mentioned above.

Many families hesitate to throw away objects for fear that they might be valuable. If that's the case in your home, settle the issue by getting them appraised. Once you find out what the actual value is, you can make an informed decision about keeping the item or selling it.

Professional appraisers usually charge $100 to $350 per hour and can evaluate about 10 items in an hour. To locate an appraiser, check your bank, attorney or insurance agent.

GETTING THE JOB DONE

●**Step 1.** Go through your house room by room. Examine each possession.

Ask yourself: Do I use this object? Do I love it? If you don't answer *yes* to either question, it's time to discard the item.

●**Step 2.** Put a tag on each item you want to discard. Use tags of different colors to indicate the specific way you intend to dispose of the object in question.

Example: A red tag for items to be thrown away, green for charities, blue for gifts, etc.

●**Step 3.** Begin disposing of items. Cart them to the trash, contact people you want to give them to or ask charities to take the items away.

If the job looks too daunting—or if you get bogged down once you start—ask for help from a friend or relative, or hire someone to assist. Many high school students, for example, would be eager for the $5 an hour you might pay them.

Caution: Before disposing of any object, examine it thoroughly. You may occasionally find money, jewelry or other valuables that have long been forgotten in pockets of clothing, drawers of furniture and even pages of books.

For charitable donations, IRS rules are tricky, so give to a well-known organization or consult with your accountant or tax preparer to make sure a charity is qualified, as well as for rules about receipts and other documentation.

OFF-SITE STORAGE

For most people, renting a long-term storage unit is rarely worth the $100 a month that even a small space is likely to cost. But there are exceptions.

Example: Individuals with small apartments who inherit a houseful of items for which they have no room.

People in doubt about throwing away a large number of possessions are another exception. For them, it can make sense to put the objects in a storage facility for a limited time, such as three months.

If they don't need any of the items during that time, it will then be much easier to get rid of them.

KEEP CLUTTER AWAY

To prevent yourself from accumulating unwanted possessions in the future...

●**As mentioned earlier, periodically look at items in your house and then ask yourself the two basic questions,** *Do I use this object? Do I love it?* Unless you answer *yes* to either one, dispose of the object immediately.

●**Each time you make a purchase, look for an item to throw away.** All too often, when we buy a new jacket, blouse or pair of shoes, we miss the opportunity to dispose of an old one we haven't worn for years.

There's an even greater opportunity to get rid of household furnishings, such as table lamps, whenever we buy a new one.

More from Julie Morgenstern...

Where to Send Your Stuff

Lighten the task of getting rid of clutter by contacting...

●**A charity that picks up donated goods.** Check out Goodwill Industries (800-741-0186, *www.goodwill.org*) or check the Salvation Army (*www.salvationarmyusa.org,* look in your local directory for a telephone number).

●**An organization that finds nonprofit organizations in your area** that are looking for the specific goods you want to donate. In most instances, the nonprofit will then collect the items.

Two of the best known: Excess Access (415-242-6041, *www.excessaccess.com*) and Inkindex (*www.inkindex.com*).

●**A removal service such as 1-800-GOT-JUNK?** (800-468-5865, *www.1800gotjunk.com*). The company's rates are generally low, but vary from area to area.

Better Cleaning

Try these helpful cleaning tips from a housekeeping expert...

●**Use a fabric softener sheet** to clean TV and CRT computer screens.

●**Set a hair dryer on cool,** and use it to blow dust off of lampshades and plants.

●**Damp-mop wood floors coated with polyurethane**—don't wax or use ammonia.

●**Put a drop of cologne on a lightbulb** when the light is off. When you turn the light on, it will scent the room.

●**A weak solution of white vinegar and water** cleans food preparation areas.

Tom McNulty, a writer based in Eden Prairie, MN, and author of *Clean Like a Man: Housekeeping for Men (and the Women Who Love Them)* (Three Rivers).

Longer-Lasting Bouquets

To make cut flowers last longer, cut their stems at a 45-degree angle. For poppies, also singe ends of stems over a candle flame. When roses get saggy, recut stems and lay the flowers in warm water for an hour. Fill the hollow stalks of dahlias and delphiniums with water, then close the ends with cotton and put the blooms in a water-filled vase.

Homemade flower preserver: Add one teaspoon of sugar, one teaspoon household bleach and two teaspoons lime or lemon juice to a quart of water.

Family Circle, 110 Fifth Ave., New York City 10011.

Versatile Houseplants

Keep aloe vera growing in the kitchen—just break off a leaf and rub the gel onto minor burns and abrasions to soothe the area and help it heal. Rosemary, red and yellow hibiscus, and pineapple guava can be grown in pots and used to flavor or decorate foods. Lemon verbena, lavender and scented geraniums create a pleasant odor in any room where they are grown.

Sheila Buff, author of several books on gardening, including *The Great Tomato Book* (Burford). Ms. Buff lives in Milan, NY.

Home Improvements That Pay Off

Home improvements that recoup the most when you sell…

A complete kitchen makeover returns 80%, while a more moderate updating can recover 75%…changing an attic into a bedroom suite returns 93%…turning a basement into a room for socializing brings back 79%…adding a full bathroom returns 84%.

Statistics from a Cost vs. Value Report from *Remodeling,* a renovation trade publication, Washington, DC.

Peace and Quiet

There are a variety of things you can do to make your home quieter…

•**Install insulated glass windows,** and be sure all of the air leaks between the windows and house are sealed with durable caulk, gaskets or foam sealants.

•**If your windows are single-pane,** install the highest-quality storm windows you can find.

•**Cover up walls with padded fabric or tapestry-like hangings** to help capture sound waves. Plants, carpeting and heavy draperies will also absorb sound.

•**Install solid-core doors.**

•**Caulk where the walls meet floors** and around all electrical and switch outlets.

Tim Carter, a master licensed plumber and former contractor in Cincinnati, who writes "Ask the Builder," a nationally syndicated newspaper column on home-improvement projects. His Web site is *www.askthebuilder.com.*

How to Plan a Fabulous Family Reunion

Edith Wagner, founder and editor of *Reunions Magazine* at Box 11727, Milwaukee 53211, *www.reunionsmag.com.* She is also author of *The Family Reunion Sourcebook* (McGraw-Hill).

Many families get together only when someone dies. Relatives drive or fly in for the funeral and go back home the next day, pausing only to say, "We have to get together under happier circumstances." These families may never meet under happier circumstances unless someone takes the initiative to plan a family reunion.

271

Organizing a big family reunion is extremely time-consuming. Dozens or even hundreds of relatives must be housed, fed and entertained. Yet every year, an estimated 10 million Americans attend family reunions, and close to half of all reunions are so successful that families decide to make them annual events.

GETTING STARTED

Start planning your reunion about a year in advance. Begin by enlisting the support of family members. The more relatives that are pulling for a reunion, the more likely that it will happen, and the more ways the work can be divided.

Determine how wide to cast your net. You could define your family as your grandparents with all of their descendants. Or you could broaden the list to include everyone descended from an ancestor who arrived in the US two centuries ago.

WHEN TO HAVE IT

Numerous reunions run from Friday through Sunday. One-day reunions usually aren't worth the trouble for those traveling great distances. Reunions that last longer than three days generally become tiresome.

If you ask 20 family members which weekend works for them, you will get 20 different answers. Instead, offer a choice of two or three possible weekends, and settle on the one that gets the best response.

Some reunions are held in conjunction with a milestone, such as the matriarch's birthday or the grandparents' anniversary.

July Fourth and Thanksgiving are popular reunion dates—but not recommended. Travel can be difficult and expensive over holidays…hotels are crowded…and half of the family is likely to attend their spouses' family gatherings instead.

As soon as the days are selected, send a "save the date" note to each household. As details are worked out, send e-mails, flyers, etc.

WHERE TO HAVE IT

Some families will hold their reunions in the grandparents' town. And others rotate annual reunions among the hometowns of the various branches of the family. Visiting family members stay in a hotel.

Helpful: Rent a room at the hotel even if you are organizing the reunion in your own hometown. If you stay at home, you'll miss half the fun.

Cruise ships, resorts and guest ranches can serve as the site for your reunion. You don't have to cook or arrange catering.

Budget-conscious or outdoorsy families may decide to hold their reunions at a campground. But some of the family members may not like to camp, so make sure there is a hotel nearby.

MONEY MATTERS

According to our surveys, it typically costs between $200 and $400 per person to attend a three-day family reunion, including travel, room and meals.

Organizers should not make the reunion too expensive for the family members, even if that means selecting a hotel that seems a bit downscale to some.

If there are significant differences in income levels between branches of the family, it might be possible to arrange fund-raising activities that allow wealthier relatives to pay more without any hurt feelings.

Example: One large family holds a cake auction during their annual reunion. The homemade cakes are auctioned off, and these proceeds are used to help defray the expense of the reunion. Those family members who are more well-off intentionally overpay in order to make the reunion affordable for everyone—the cakes can go for more than $100.

Most reunion organizers request a deposit in advance from every family member who plans to attend. This money is used to cover deposits for caterers, group activities, hotel rooms and restaurants.

Insisting on a check in advance also helps to ensure that family members won't back out at the last minute.

Keep careful track of the money received and the expenses. Then if you sense any grumbling over the finances, you can invite interested family members to an informal "business meeting" at the reunion so that those with questions can see how the funds were spent.

LET THE FUN BEGIN!

The most common events at family reunions are picnics, banquets, dancing and children's talent shows. And, approximately 20% of family reunions include scheduled golf outings. Some families charter buses to go shopping or to an amusement park, zoo or casino. But planned outings are not essential. Some families are content to sit around talking and eating for three days.

Other families hold sewing circles at their reunions. A square of cloth is mailed out to interested attendees months in advance. Family members can decorate these squares before the reunion, often in ways that celebrate the family. At the reunion, the squares are stitched together into a quilt, which is raffled off. (If family members want to participate but aren't big on needlework, let them know that a good copy store can easily transfer a photo onto a cloth square.)

One way to make a family reunion special is to emphasize the family's history. If a relative has researched the family's genealogy, arrange a presentation. Videotape older family members reminiscing, and play the tape at the next reunion. Tour the places where ancestors lived and worked—and the cemeteries where they are buried.

Or compile old family recipes into a cookbook for every family attending, and ask family members who live in the area to prepare the dishes your ancestors enjoyed.

Strategies for a Better Marriage From a Leading Divorce Lawyer

Robert Stephan Cohen, Esq., founding partner of the law firm of Cohen Lans LLP in New York City. His clients have included New York City Mayor Michael R. Bloomberg, supermodel Christie Brinkley and Donald Trump's former wives Ivana Trump and Marla Maples. He is author of *Reconcilable Differences: 7 Keys to Remaining Together from a Top Matrimonial Lawyer* (Simon & Schuster).

I n my 30 years as a matrimonial lawyer, I have listened to countless men and women tell me why their marriages have failed. Disagreements over money and lifestyle, and, of course, infidelity lead all kinds of couples to divorce court. Divorce is so common nowadays —expected, even—that couples start thinking about it at the first sign of trouble.

I have seen enough divorce battles up close to have a good handle on the marital mistakes couples make. Many issues can be worked out —if there's a real desire on both sides. *Here are the most common problems that endanger marriages and strategies to deal with them...*

•**Parallel lives.** A couple might live in the same house and share the same bed, but their communication may be perfunctory. They could go for days without really talking.

Both spouses are so busy with their "own" lives that they more or less forget they're married. Whether because of busy careers, child-rearing or even time-consuming hobbies, they never make time for each other.

Strategy: Carve out time for each other by picking one night a week to go on a "date." That means time together—no phone calls or kids. Also, don't let a day go by without having a conversation, even if it is by phone.

I recall one professional couple who had little free time for each other. They decided to share part of every day by walking their dog together. This simple change helped get their marriage back on track.

•**Infidelity.** Cheating spouses who want to save their marriages need to stop cheating and —assuming that they haven't been discovered —keep their mouths shut.

Strategy: That's right—don't tell. Telling a spouse about a one-night stand or an affair that has ended may make you feel less burdened and more virtuous, but you'll have created an enormous obstacle that the marriage may never overcome. Marriages fail not because of an affair, but because of the aftermath.

Warning: If the cat is out of the bag, don't try to fix things alone. Couples who successfully get past a known affair almost always do so with the help of a neutral party, such as a member of the clergy or a therapist.

•**Sexual incompatibility.** Most people who have been married for a while have sex less frequently than they once did. Some people are fine with that. For others, a lack of sex colors their view of the entire marriage.

How powerful is the sexual aspect of a marriage? In three decades, I have never had anyone come into my office wanting a divorce even though sex at home was great.

Strategy: Couples must discuss their sexual needs and wants. The increasing popularity of sexual topics in mainstream media may make it easier to broach the subject. One spouse could refer the other to a relevant article, for example, or they could go to a therapist together.

●**Problem children.** I have seen a number of marriages collapse over differences in how to deal with troublesome children. In the cases that I have dealt with, the children were heavy drug users or had serious mental illness, but even minor problems with children can damage a marital relationship.

If spouses already are leading parallel lives, they begin to line up in separate camps with their children. For instance, one spouse might hide a child's misconduct from the other. Then when the misconduct becomes impossible to ignore, the parents take opposite positions. In my experience, mothers frequently think that love and affection will alter their children's behavior, while fathers are more apt to take a tough stance. The fierce arguments that follow can destroy a marriage.

Stepparents have a particularly tough time. The children often try to undermine the new marriage because they see it as a threat to their own relationships with their parents, and they still hold on to the hope that their parents will get back together.

Strategy: Enlist the help of a neutral authoritative third party. When doctors or therapists take over much of the decision-making in terms of the child's treatment, the husband and wife can address marital issues and comfort each other, which often brings them closer together.

●**Money matters.** Financial disagreements can cause serious trouble for any couple, no matter how well-off they are. Historically, wives often have been in the dark about a couple's finances—and this is true even today.

Whether the husband insists on handling the money alone or the wife is willfully ignorant, the result often is heated arguments about finances that spiral into personal attacks on each other's

values, common sense and honesty. It can undermine a marriage when, for instance, one spouse simply tells the other that the couple can't afford a trip this year.

Strategy: For the best chance of marital success, both spouses should be familiar with the household's finances and have a say in spending and investing. Then the couple's expectations will be similar and, in many cases, more realistic.

Some people think a prenuptial agreement is unromantic, but I'm a big fan of them—and the lessons I've learned through using prenups can be applied at any time during a marriage.

I recommend that engaged, newlywed or even long-married couples talk to an accountant, financial planner or even a divorce lawyer to get a sense of how the economics of the marriage can work. Then they should continue talking about money so that things stay out in the open at home.

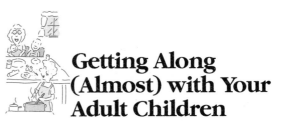

Getting Along (Almost) with Your Adult Children

Lois Leiderman Davitz, PhD, and Joel Davitz, PhD, psychologists based in Somers, NY and the authors of many books and articles on family relationships, the latest being *Getting Along (Almost) with Your Adult Kids: A Decade-by-Decade Guide* (Sorin). The couple has been married for 58 years and have two sons, ages 44 and 48.

Having a child turn 21 provides parents with a lovely feeling of accomplishment. But, as they quickly find out, parenting never ends. It doesn't really matter that the kids are in their 20s, 30s, 40s or even older, they are still the kids, and wise parents recognize that they had better hang on to those parenting skills that have served them for so long.

The purpose now, though, isn't to rear your children and instill values in them. After all, you can no longer tell your child what to do. Nor should you try. Your task is to foster and reinforce a loving relationship between you. Wrong turns, at this point, have bigger stakes attached—they can result in bad feelings that carry over for years. *How to be sure this doesn't happen in your family...*

DEALING WITH 20-SOMETHINGS

Twenty-somethings aren't really selfish. It's just that they are busy trying to figure out who they are, and they aren't terribly interested in what's up with you. The major task they face in this decade is to establish a strong identity in the world of adults. Their idea of being an adult, though, doesn't jibe much with yours—responsibility and a forward career track are not what they are cultivating, thank you, even though they may worry about it. Don't take it personally that they don't want to be like you. It simply reflects their need to declare their own identity—and it isn't going to be conservative and stodgy like yours.

What you need: Patience...lots of it. One day your son informs you that he plans to get his PhD in philosophy, a few months later he's going to be a rock singer. Count on a number of turnarounds before your 20-something finds what he really wants to do.

Helpful: Understand that you don't take up much room in your 20-something's life. While he/she might be willing to spend a little time with you occasionally, don't expect to be pals as you might have been before. Your kids will give you snippets of information, seldom the full story. And they don't want your advice unless they specifically ask.

Don't get sucked into fearing that your child's far-out ideas will become lifelong paths. You don't want to overreact—the worst thing you can do with your kids now. Be empathetic and give praise whenever you have the chance—these are hard years for your kids. Keep any criticism and opinions to yourself as your kids struggle to find their way.

TURNING 30—NOW WHAT?

At last, your children are settling down, have good jobs and are probably married with children. Enjoy the happy change, but be careful—these years are also full of traps. Your children's allegiances are changing now, broadening out to include their own family as well as that of their in-laws.

The 30s are a highly intense, highly active decade—couples have so many responsibilities that it can be exhausting to watch. They put much value on their parents now, especially if you're nearby and can help out. Whether it's watching the baby when the sitter doesn't show, picking up the kids from school or even the dry cleaning, whatever you can do to assist your busy 30-somethings is greatly appreciated. They may forget to say thank-you, but chalk it up to their pressured lives, not their lack of gratitude.

More you can do: Consider the help you offer a gift, but if the requests start to pile up, say something. You won't ruffle feelings if you explain your limits diplomatically, and negotiate the situation adult to adult.

As to what you really think about how your kids are conducting their lives, remember that just as with your 20-somethings, silence continues to be your friend. Kids in their 30s think that the way they are raising their kids is the right way—and probably miles above whatever you learned from your child-rearing years.

Unless it's something life threatening, don't say a word, even if your kids are giving their kids ice cream for breakfast. It's their choice and their family, as they will be very quick to remind you should you make the big mistake of speaking your mind.

Suggestion: Kids are happy to communicate more often with parents, but to guarantee it, be sure you have e-mail. Even if it's just a one-line message, e-mail will keep you in the same loop—invaluable for all.

40 AND ON—HOW DID THIS HAPPEN?

When in their 40s, your children might be stepping back to reevaluate decisions and make changes, whether in their jobs or their marriages. This is a time for questioning and, for many, of resetting directions. Again, don't offer advice or opinions, although your children will appreciate having someone to talk to who can understand what is confronting them—even if you actually don't!

What you can do: Your role as grandparent is especially important now. Your children are likely struggling with their teenage children, and this is a chance for you, when invited, to step in with a good sense of humor as the nonbiased onlooker. Grandkids will be happy to talk to someone who "gets them" and your kids will be relieved that you are willing to be there, which gives them a breather.

At this point, you may realize that you are becoming somewhat dependent on your children, whether for financial advice or help with your computer. Enjoy what they can do for you, but don't let them overstep.

They are no doubt starting to worry about their aging parents—be honest about when you need help and when you don't. And show them with your attitude that aging isn't something to fear but to accept. Show them that you're still pursuing the excitement of living.

Secrets to Caring for a Loved One with Dementia

Joanne Koenig Coste, president of Alzheimer Consulting Associates, a Framingham, MA–based organization that designs specialized advanced dementia programs for hospitals and nursing homes as well as for assisted-living and other community-based facilities. Previously the president of the Massachusetts Alzheimer's Association, Ms. Koenig Coste is the author of two training manuals for caregivers and one book that's titled, *Learning to Speak Alzheimer's: A Groundbreaking Approach for Everyone Dealing with the Disease* (Houghton Mifflin).

In 1972, Charles Koenig, a 44-year-old advertising executive, showed the signs of early-onset dementia. Until he died four years later, Mr. Koenig was cared for at home by his wife, Joanne Koenig Coste. Since that time, Ms. Koenig Coste, who has a master's degree in counseling and psychology, has devoted herself to better understanding the behavior of Alzheimer's and other dementia patients as well as improving their care.

Dementia is not an inevitable part of aging. More than half of people over age 100 do *not* have it. Unlike the occasional memory lapses that are a normal part of aging, dementia affects not only memory, but also thinking, judgment and the ability to learn. With dementia, mental functioning typically deteriorates over a period of two to 10 years.

Ms. Koenig Coste's principles help make life easier for caregivers, as well as people who suffer from any advanced form of dementia.

Her advice for five challenges…

●**Bathing.** A refusal to take a bath sets in early during some types of dementia because dementia sufferers feel a loss of control and no longer have the ability to "recognize" water. *To overcome that fear…*

●Choose a time at which your loved one is accustomed to bathing—not when it is most convenient for you.

●Remove or cover up highly reflective surfaces, such as mirrors, which can lead a perceptually impaired person to think that another person is in the room.

●Dye bathwater blue. This can help alleviate panic caused by a lack of depth perception resulting from the destruction of brain cells responsible for interpreting sensory material.

Do *not* use food coloring, which will stain your tub—and the person bathing. Bathwater salts that add scent and color to the water work well. These products can be purchased in drugstores.

●Always approach your loved one from the front to avoid startling him/her. Wash from the feet up, using a handheld shower head.

Sponge baths also are a good idea for dementia sufferers who are afraid of bathwater. Showers tend to be more frightening.

●Install "no-slip" strips on the bottom of the bathtub and grab bars to help prevent falls.

If bathing is a perpetual battleground, re-evaluate your own notions of cleanliness. What is best for your loved one?

●**Toilet accidents.** People with dementia often lose bladder and bowel control. *To help overcome related problems…*

●Hang a picture of a toilet (found in a newspaper ad or in a plumbing-supply catalog) on the bathroom door to remind the patient where the door leads.

●Paint the wall behind the toilet a bright, contrasting color, such as red or blue, to help the patient find and see the toilet. Many people with dementia also have glaucoma or other vision problems.

●Make sure that the patient's clothes are easy to put on and take off. Whenever possible, choose

Velcro or elastic instead of buttons or zippers. To get a catalog that carries this type of clothing check out Buck & Buck (800-458-0600 or *www. buckandbuck.com*)...and Silvert's (800-387-7088 or *www.silverts.com*).

• To reduce nighttime accidents, keep a light on in the bathroom and place a path of glow-in-the-dark tape from the patient's bed straight to the toilet.

• **"Sundowning."** Many people with dementia become agitated in the late afternoon. The diminishing light decreases their ability to see, and they wonder what they're supposed to be doing. Their powerful long-term memories tell them that they should be heading home from work, getting ready for the kids to come home from school or cooking supper. But their difficulty with short-term memory leaves them feeling very confused.

To counteract the effects of sundowning...

• Install a dimmer and replace regular bulbs with full-spectrum bulbs, such as Vita-Lites, that imitate the spectrum of natural sunlight (available at hardware stores). Turn the lights up high when the sun starts to set.

• Listen to music or play a game. Choose your loved one's favorite music. Restful, classical or new age music works better than more stimulating music, such as Big Band tunes.

Some individuals with dementia enjoy sorting playing cards by suit, but you can customize the activity to their interests and abilities.

Low-key activity helps preserve a patient's dignity and has a calming effect. Feather dusters can keep a person busy, because there's a house full of furniture to dust.

My late husband loved to garden. Although he lost the ability to choose and plant flowers, he still could dig for quite some time. He dug hole after hole and destroyed the yard, but I decided that it was more important for him to feel as if he had "gardened" than to have an attractive yard.

• **Repeated questions.** The relentless questions asked by individuals with dementia often reflect their fears and vulnerabilities. "What time is it?" really means "What am I supposed to be doing now?" It helps if you have an answer: "It's time to have a cup of coffee!"

• **Mishaps during outings.** Don't tell the patient about outings in advance, and always have a contingency plan. You may not be able to take the person, or you may have to interrupt the trip to take your loved one home. Don't buy nonrefundable tickets if you can help it.

Help for Caregivers

Jim Miller, editor of "Savvy Senior," a syndicated newspaper question-and-answer column for seniors, Norman, OK. He is also the author of *The Savvy Senior: The Ultimate Guide to Health, Family, and Finances for Senior Citizens* (Hyperion) and a contributor to NBC's *Today* show. His Internet site is *www.savvysenior.org*.

For the 44.4 million Americans who act as caregivers for sick or elderly family members, help is on hand...

• **National Family Caregiver Support Program (NFCSP)** helps out family members who care for seniors age 60 or older and grandparents or relative caregivers age 60 or older who care for children. *Services include...*

• Information about adult day care, transportation, home meals, etc.

• Counseling and support groups.

• Respite care for caregivers.

• Help with home modifications.

• **States earmark funds for caregiving families.** Contact your state's department of the aging or Eldercare Locator (800-677-1116, *www. eldercare.gov*), to get the local phone number.

• **Medicaid might cover home-care services,** special equipment, supplies, adult day care, etc. for those eligible. Contact your state Medicaid office.

Choose the Best Dog for Your Family

Labradors and golden retrievers, now the most popular breeds of dogs for families, usually are even-tempered and gentle but need plenty of exercise and attention. German shepherds, the third most popular breed, are highly intelligent. They require regular walks and, if possible, lots of mental exercise. Beagles, fourth most popular, need only moderate exercise and have low-maintenance coats, but must be leashed when in high-traffic areas because they will follow a scent intensely.

Patricia B. McConnell, PhD, adjunct associate professor in zoology, University of Wisconsin, Madison, and author of *The Other End of the Leash* (Ballantine).

Caring for an Elderly Cat

When your cat is 10 years old, schedule an exam that includes blood tests and urinalysis—these results will provide a baseline for future tests. Record your cat's weight weekly—if your cat loses more than a few ounces, take it to the veterinarian. If the cat isn't eating, spark its appetite by warming food in the microwave or adding low-salt chicken broth. Clean litter boxes daily and replace litter weekly—older cats urinate more frequently than younger ones. Also, look for changes in appearance—a cat that doesn't feel well will neglect its grooming.

Catnip, Box 420070, Palm Coast, FL 32142.

Minimize Spam

Here are some smart things that you can do to keep spam to a minimum...

●**Give your personal e-mail address only to family and friends.**

●**Use multiple addresses when shopping on-line**—cancel those that get lots of spam.

●**Create addresses using letters and numbers** mixed in odd ways.

●**Don't fill out on-line forms** unless you're sure how your e-mail address will be used.

●**Use filters and blocking software.**

Helpful: Anti-spam tutorials at GetNetWise. org (*http://spam.getnetwise.org/tools/othertools*).

Megan Kinnaird, project manager, GetNetWise.org, a project of the Internet Education Foundation in Washington, DC.

Do You Know What Google Can Do?

Lesser-known uses for Google (*www.google. com*), the Internet search engine...

●**Track packages**—simply enter a FedEx or UPS tracking number.

●**Do calculations**—type in an equation. Convert units of measurement—for instance, "teaspoons in a gallon."

●**Check on stocks**—search a stock symbol to get the company's share price, plus graphs and financial news. Track airline flights—type in a flight number for a link to a map of the flight's progress.

Dana Blankenhorn, Internet consultant for a-clue.com, Atlanta.

18

Personal Power

Seven Principles of Success and Happiness

Motivational speaker and author Jack Canfield has made the study of success in one's personal and professional lives his own life's work. He has interviewed hundreds of successful people, studied more than 3,000 books on success and given thousands of lectures on the subject. Now, Mr. Canfield has boiled down everything that he has learned about success in his recent book, *The Success Principles*. Some of those principles, such as the importance of goal setting, are very well-known. Others are just as important but not commonly understood.

Here, Mr. Canfield reveals the principles of success that are most often overlooked.

●**Develop four new good habits each year.** Most of everything we do is based on ritual. We eat at certain restaurants…wear certain clothes…brush our teeth in a certain way…and watch certain TV shows simply because that is what we have always done. These are habits, and we perform them without really thinking too much.

The trouble with habits is that they preserve the status quo, making dramatic improvement unlikely. If we want more out of life, we must be willing to evaluate and replace some of our rituals with more productive ones.

Example: Instead of spending the hour after dinner watching TV, go for a brisk walk …study a second language…read a book…or make the extra sales calls that you need to advance your career.

It takes a minimum of 25 days for the brain to build the neural links required to make a new behavior a habit. I advocate practicing a

Jack Canfield, a motivational speaker and cocreator of the *Chicken Soup for the Soul*® series, which has now sold more than 80 million books. He is CEO of Chicken Soup for the Soul Enterprises, a publishing and training company based in Santa Barbara, CA, *www.jackcanfield.com*. One of his most recent books is *The Success Principles: How to Get from Where You Are to Where You Want to Be* (Harper).

new habit for three months to ensure that it sinks in. Once it becomes second nature, add another new habit. At three months per habit, there's time to add four every year. In five years, you will have 20 new habits that will help fuel your success.

●**Practice appreciation.** The studies of employee motivation inevitably find that feeling appreciated is the single greatest motivator in the workplace, even ahead of higher wages. And yet many people fail to put the power of appreciation to full use in their business and personal lives.

When you show people that you appreciate them, you not only make them feel better, you make yourself more successful. People are more likely to help you achieve your goals if they believe that you appreciate their efforts. There's no downside—appreciation costs nothing, and no one has ever complained about being overappreciated.

Helpful: I used to carry in my pocket an index card with 10 circles on it. Every time I let someone know that I appreciated him/her, I filled in one of the circles. If at the end of the day I hadn't filled in all 10, I sent out appreciative e-mails. After just a few months, showing appreciation became second nature for me, and I no longer had to carry the cards. I haven't had anyone leave my nine-employee company in more than five years. I attribute a big part of that loyalty to everyone feeling appreciated.

●**Solicit and respect feedback.** Rather than guess how you're doing, ask. Periodically ask employees, employers, customers and loved ones to rate your performance on a scale of one to 10. If the answer is anything less than 10, ask, "What would it take to make it a 10?"

If you follow this strategy, you're encouraging people to help you become great. The main reason that people don't solicit feedback is because they're afraid of what they might hear—but the information we can obtain is worth facing such fears.

Not all feedback is accurate, but watch for patterns and never get angry at the source, even if you disagree.

●**Keep all of your agreements.** When you break an agreement, the person you let down loses faith in you and is less likely to want to work with you in the future. Even more important, you lose some faith in yourself. It's all but impossible to become a success if you don't have faith in yourself.

To avoid breaking agreements, teach yourself to say *no* to things that you would rather not do. Then you won't have to back out later. Write down everything that you agree to do on your calendar just as soon as a commitment is made—you would be surprised by how many people don't do this.

If you must break an agreement, let the other parties involved know as soon as possible, and do everything in your power to fix any problems that the broken agreement creates for them.

●**Exceed expectations.** Don't ask yourself, *How can I get a little more out of this situation?* Instead, ask, *How can I give a little more to those around me?* Sacrificing usually isn't a sacrifice—it's a path to success. If you consistently go the extra mile for clients, colleagues, employers, family and friends, you'll earn their loyalty and respect for life.

Example: When UPS went out on strike, David Morris, the owner of Dillanos, a small, Seattle-based coffee roasting company, rented a truck and drove 2,320 miles to deliver an order to a small client in Southern California. That client, It's a Grind Coffee House, is now a large franchise with 50 stores and an additional 100 planned. It is Dillanos's largest customer and has remained loyal to Dillanos because of the extra effort Morris put in years ago.

●**Reject rejection.** Rejection does not prevent success—but *fear* of rejection does. What stops a man from asking an attractive woman out on a date? What stops an inexperienced salesman from asking the most successful salesman at his firm for advice? They're afraid of rejection—afraid that if they ask, the answer might be *no*. But there's absolutely no rational reason to fear rejection.

Example: You ask a successful person to give you career advice, and he says *no*. You didn't have his advice before you asked, and you do not have his advice after. You are no worse off than when you began, so why be afraid of asking?

If you want to be a success, you must treat rejection as an illusion—a negative response conjured up by your mind that really doesn't exist at all.

●**Eliminate small obstacles.** Make a list of the problems that you would like to remove from your life—include even minor things, such as a lamp that doesn't work right. Schedule a day or two to fix as many of these problems as you can, starting with the easiest to solve.

In this way, you'll get into the habit of thinking, *I know what I want, I know how to get it.* Once you're in this mindset, you'll stop resigning yourself to your current situation and start making larger positive changes as well.

How to Maximize Appreciation

It is easy to minimize what is going right and focus on what is going wrong. But your life will become richer if you try to minimize fault-focusing and maximize appreciation.

Make an effort to see beauty where others see ugliness…value where others see uselessness…purpose where others see chaos. This is the ability to appreciate—which helps balance the tendency to be critical.

David Brandt, PhD, nationally recognized psychologist and keynote speaker based in San Francisco, and author of *Is That All There Is?* (Impact).

Easy Way to Boost Your Mood

Lift your own mood by giving someone a compliment. Compliments tend to be passed on—people who receive them are more likely to give them to others. Aim for five positive encounters for every negative one…look for things people do right…support your friends… and give real recognition with a sincere smile.

Tom Rath, global practice leader, Clifton Strengths-Finder, Gallup, Inc., Princeton, NJ, and the late Donald O. Clifton, PhD, inventor of the Clifton StrengthsFinder, an analysis tool. They are the coauthors of *How Full Is Your Bucket?* (Gallup).

The Power of Coincidence

Deepak Chopra, MD, one of the world's leaders in mind-body medicine. He is founder of the Chopra Center for Well Being, Carlsbad, CA, *www.chopra.com,* and author of more than 40 books, including *The Spontaneous Fulfillment of Desire: Harnessing the Infinite Power of Coincidence* (Harmony).

Have you ever thought about a friend you have not talked to in a long time and then received a phone call from that friend on the same day? We all experience coincidences like this. Many people dismiss them as random events, but I believe they are profoundly meaningful.

These are examples of *synchronicity*—the interconnection and interdependence of everything in the universe. I decided to explore synchronicity in everyday life because becoming attuned to synchronicity can help us fulfill our deepest desires.

Example: During my medical training, I worked in the laboratory of a famous endocrinologist. Though I had been eager to get the position, I was miserable once I started. The lab technicians were treated poorly, and the duties were mechanical. Every morning, when I would scan the newspaper, I would see an ad for a job in a hospital emergency room. I ignored it because my real dream had been to work at this world-renowned lab.

Then one day, after this endocrinologist said something especially cruel, I spotted the newspaper open to the page with the help-wanted ad. Startled by the coincidence, I finally admitted to myself that I was in the wrong job. I quit that day, applied for the emergency room position and got it. I found that I liked helping patients. Noticing a coincidence enabled me to change my destiny.

THE COINCIDENCES AROUND US

Our existence is a marvel of coincidence. Physicists point out that after the "Big Bang," the ratio of particles to anti-particles was precisely what was necessary to create the material world. The composition of the first hydrogen atoms…development of carbon and oxygen—all the factors for the creation of biological organisms required coincidences.

Nature is filled with synchronous behavior—from a group of fireflies flashing at exactly the same time to schools of fish swimming in perfect unison without apparent communication.

The more we pay attention to nature, the more we learn that synchronicity is the organizing principle of the universe. The more you appreciate this principle, the more synchronicity you will notice and experience in your life.

NURTURING COINCIDENCE

To nurture synchronicity in your life…

●**Learn to be still.** Spend some time every day enjoying a state of deep quiet. Meditation helps you shift habitual patterns of thinking so that you can recognize and act on surprising connections in your life.

To meditate: Sit in a comfortable position, close your eyes and observe your breathing. Focus on the inflow and outflow of your breath without trying to regulate it. If your breathing gets faster or slower, deeper or shallower, notice those changes without fighting them. Whenever your attention drifts away from your breath—to a noise, physical sensation or thought—gently return your awareness to your breathing. Try to do this for 15 minutes, twice a day. Set a timer so that you don't have to watch the clock.

●**Train your senses.** At least once a day, focus on one of your five senses.

Example: While focusing on your sense of touch, you might ask yourself, *What parts of my body are in contact with the chair I am sitting in? What is the temperature of the room? Does my skin detect any movement in the air?*

The more sensitive you are to stimuli and events around you, the more receptive you will be to coincidences.

Example: While at a shopping mall one day, I was captivated by the taste of strawberry ice cream, the sight of a painting of a sunset and the piped-in theme song from the movie *Goldfinger.*

A year later, I was visiting Jamaica. On a drive through the countryside, I saw a sunset that reminded me of that painting. It turned out that the place was called Strawberry Hill and the movie *Goldfinger* had been filmed there. Intrigued by these coincidences, I visited the hotel on Strawberry Hill. The hotel's spa director had wanted to meet me to learn about mind-body therapies, and we discussed the possibility of collaborating. The owner of the hotel became a close friend, and we've helped each other on several projects.

●**Explore coincidences.** When something unusual or synchronous happens in your life, ask yourself, *What is the significance?* Do not struggle or worry about the answer—it might come out later as an insight or during another encounter.

●**Keep a coincidence journal.** Write down the coincidences you observe. Whenever you notice other connections to that event, write them on the same page. As you do this, you'll discover more synchronicity in your life.

●**Be open to new experiences.** Many of us go through life avoiding risk. Instead, look for opportunities. When you take your seat on an airplane, your first instinct may be to pull out a book. Try striking up a conversation with your seatmate instead. By engaging others, you may wind up with a new business contact, friendship or insight. At the least, you will add richness to your life as well as to someone else's.

●**Set clear intentions.** When you focus on your deepest desires, you put forces into play that will bring about the fulfillment of those deep desires.

Sit quietly and write down your desires for all the different areas of your life—relationship needs, career and financial goals, spiritual aims. Look at the list each day, and create a vivid mental image of what your life would be like if all those desires were satisfied.

As you focus on your intentions, be open to the possibility that fulfillment may come in surprising ways—and that sometimes the universe has different plans for you than you have for yourself.

•**Be grateful.** Every day, spend a few minutes thinking about all the things and people in your life for which you are grateful. If a complaint or grievance comes to mind during that time, say to yourself, *Every decision I make is a choice between a grievance and a miracle. I let go of grievances and choose miracles.*

The more you do this, the more you will feel harmony between your desires and the events in your life.

How to Develop Charisma

Ruth Sherman, president of Ruth Sherman Associates, LLC, an executive consulting and training firm in Old Greenwich, CT, *www.ruthsherman.com.* She is author of *Get Them to See It Your Way, Right Away* (McGraw-Hill).

Charisma isn't something people are born with. It is a set of skills that most of us can master. *Here's how...*

DISPLAY CONFIDENCE

A charismatic person can walk into a group of strangers and quickly make friends. An uncharismatic person will hang uncomfortably on the fringe of the crowd, unable to make a connection. *If you're not naturally outgoing, mingling might be uncomfortable for you, but you can do it successfully if you follow these rules...*

•**Walk purposefully.** At a party or business function, don't wander around aimlessly. Set goals before the get-together.

Example: Resolve to meet three new people at a party or plan to give out 10 business cards at a meeting.

•**Offer intriguing introductions.** Do not simply state your name during introductions. Say something about yourself that will draw a question and lead to a conversation.

Example: Don't say, "Hi, I'm Bob Jones," say, "I'm Bob Jones. I am an attorney specializing in copyright and patent law."

•**Ensure that at least one person isn't a total stranger.** If you're anxious about entering a room full of strangers, find out who will be going and call one person ahead of time to introduce yourself.

Example: If you're attending an organization's annual meeting, call the president. Ask a question or two about the event, and then ask if he/she would be willing to introduce you around when you arrive. You'll meet plenty of people, and they'll think of you as a friend of the most important person in the group.

FOCUS ON WHAT YOU WANT

Charismatic people are passionate about the things they believe in. Those perceived as lacking charisma typically have no passion...or consider it pushy or egotistical to state their opinion or talk about successes. Be aware that for every person who finds persistence and passion overbearing, many more will find it persuasive.

Example: You send an e-mail to 20 contacts concerning a project you believe in. Two of the 20 ask to be taken off your list for future messages. How do you respond? A charismatic person wouldn't be shaken by the two who asked to be taken off the list. Instead, he would be encouraged by the 18 that didn't.

BE A GOOD LISTENER

When people believe that you value their opinions, they're predisposed to value yours. Conversely, if you appear disinterested, you can expect others to be unreceptive when you are speaking. *Strategies...*

•**Make eye contact.** Don't let your attention drift even if you are at a crowded party and your inclination is to say hello to friends who pass by.

•**Ask follow-up questions** that show you're paying attention but don't excessively challenge the speaker.

•**Put yourself in the shoes of the person speaking.** If someone is telling a story, imagine that it happened to you. When you do, your facial responses will show sincere interest.

•**Make short comments that validate the speaker's emotions.** If the story is about fighting against a bureaucracy, say, "You must have felt so powerless."

APOLOGIZE

When a charismatic person makes a mistake, he doesn't get defensive or point fingers. That alienates others and makes him appear small and petty. Strong and self-assured people accept blame and apologize, which makes others view them with respect.

How to Live Happily with Someone Who Is "Clueless"

John Hoover, PhD, personal coach, organizational behavior consultant and former marriage counselor based in Nashville. He is author of many books, including *How to Live with an Idiot: Clueless Creatures and the People Who Love Them* and *Unleashing Leadership* (both from Career Press). His latest books are *The Art of Constructive Confrontation* and *How to Sell to an Idiot* (both from Wiley).

Would you like to live more contentedly with the significant idiot in your life—spouse, partner, child, relative, roommate or best friend? You really can. But you will have to get in touch with your own inner idiot first.

I chose a strong word just to make a point. Idiots aren't stupid or deliberately mean. They are simply clueless about the powerful effects of their words and behavior on others. This cluelessness can lead to misfired communication, deepening resentment and a deteriorating relationship.

I'm a recovering idiot myself. My weakness was thinking that I could solve other people's problems by throwing around my advice. But instead of helping, I was driving many people —including my wife—away.

IDIOCY REDUCTION

Helping someone alter idiotic behavior is seldom very easy, but it is not impossible. *Some suggestions...*

●**Avoid empty expectations.** People often expect their significant idiots to change simply because they want them to. Yet without strong motivation, people do not change.

Example: Edith wished Harry would cook more, be nicer to her aunt and watch less TV. For decades, she believed that Harry would read her mind and behave in ways that were contrary to his nature. Finally, she gave up and closed herself off emotionally.

Although Edith had mentioned all of these things, Harry remained blissfully unaware of their importance to her.

Keeping it real: In a study of couples who had stayed together happily for up to 50 years, one consistent trait was the absence of unrealistic expectations about each other.

●**Remember the good parts.** If your significant idiot is your spouse or partner, start with the assumption that you got together for a reason. Excavate layers of calloused resentment until you have unearthed the attraction, affection and respect underneath.

●**Pay attention.** Be alert for your significant idiot's readiness to hear your request. Try to train yourself to become an observant and skilled listener.

●**Let it go.** The next time your significant idiot says or does something—yet again—that makes you crazy, just think of the song *Let It Snow* and sing to yourself, *Let it go, let it go, let it go.*

Some people will go to their graves trying to prove that they are right. Accept that you can both be right in your own way. Developing a more tolerant and forgiving atmosphere relaxes tension immeasurably.

●**Take inventory.** You're part of this relationship, too. Identify aspects of your personality that are tough to live with. Enlist a friend's assistance. Naming your faults might be easier for someone else.

Then decide: Do you care enough about the significant idiot in your life to change?

THE SEVEN RELATIONAL SINS

To defuse idiotic behavior, avoid committing the seven relational sins...

●**Anger.** It's a natural emotion and can be dealt with.

Mistakes: To deny that you are angry...to choose anger over healthier alternatives.

You already know what makes you angry, so use anticipation as an antidote. Give yourself the option to think, *I was aware that this might happen. It's not the end of the world.* Or, *I knew this was possible. On to Plan B.*

•**Blaming.** Blaming usually takes place in the heat of the argument and will only make things worse.

Solution: Disengage from battle. Announce that you're taking a time-out because the conversation is not working, but you'll be back after sorting out your thoughts.

Disappear, write down some solutions and come back. Keep the conversation going. Time can heal many things if you let it.

•**Criticizing.** Most people have been conditioned to respond to negativity with more negativity. Criticism breeds criticism.

If you're about to say something negative when feeling disappointed in your significant idiot, think of something positive and pay a compliment instead. Bingo!—you have just de-escalated the hostility in the air.

Bonus: Someone who is being complimented can't deflect criticism back onto you.

•**Denial.** Failing to acknowledge the truth is like holding beach balls under water. They will keep popping back up.

The energy that's required to hold the truth beneath the surface is better spent in accepting what it represents—the reality of who you and your closest relations really are—and working from there.

•**Judging.** Looking down on your significant idiot only widens the gap between you.

Disarming: Forgiving the offender. To forgive is to let something go and let it float away …to start things moving again.

•**Resentment.** Idiotic behavior breeds resentment, which is entirely unproductive. You may have heard the saying that harboring resentment is like drinking a cup of poison and waiting for the other person to die.

Unless friction in a long relationship is discussed openly and honestly, the resulting hostility won't go away. But when people work at it, the results can be phenomenal.

My recommendation: Be lovingly relentless in expressing your (reasonable) wishes.

Example: Sue says, "You never take me dancing." Stan replies, "It thrills me to take you dancing. I thought it embarrassed you to be with such a bad dancer." Sue says, "I thought

you were embarrassed. I love dancing with you. Let's go!" Misunderstandings kept them captive for too long.

The risk of expressing what you want is that the person won't change. But if you don't try, you're inviting defeat.

•**Shaming.** A step beyond criticizing behavior, shame is an assault on a person's character—a guilt trip, hardly a loving (or effective) way to change behavior.

Example: With a sigh, Dinah tells Oscar, "Shirley's husband takes out the garbage without being asked."

Instead of belittling Oscar by implication, Dinah might praise him for doing other household tasks independently…and then state how pleased she would be if that applied to the garbage, too.

BE PATIENT

Whatever is causing cluelessness in your significant idiot—and in yourself—did not happen overnight. The attitudinal adaptations required to live a happier, more fulfilling life will take time, too. Identify and pursue them—together.

How to Resolve Conflict: Eight Steps to Transform Your Relationships

Marc Gopin, PhD, James H. Laue Professor of World Religions, Diplomacy and Conflict Resolution at the Institute of Conflict Analysis and Resolution, George Mason University, Arlington, VA. He is the author of *Healing the Heart of Conflict: 8 Crucial Steps to Making Peace with Yourself and Others* (Rodale).

Conflict is inevitable in life. Partners and friends compete for the same thing—or want different things. Feelings are hurt. Pride is damaged. Anger erupts.

Most disagreements will blow over or can be resolved with just a little extra goodwill, some problem solving and a willingness to compromise. But sometimes the hurt rankles, positions harden and a cycle of resentment and revenge takes over.

In our personal lives, any destructive conflict can wreak serious damage. Family members may be estranged, friendships chilled. The human warmth that should nourish us gives way to chronic stress.

Entrenched and destructive conflicts cannot be merely patched up—they must be healed at the deep level of feelings. It takes sincere effort and a bit of wisdom to make it work. *To get there, follow these eight steps…*

BE

The ancient wisdom of "know thyself" is vital here. Even when it feels as though conflict is being forced upon you, considering what role you play in perpetuating a difficult situation can change your attitude toward others and start the healing process.

Self-examination should be a regular part of your life—develop the habit of looking objectively at your actions and the thoughts and feelings that lie behind them as if you were reading a book.

Example: A woman's relationship with her grown son was often marred by his anger. He accused her of manipulating him and intruding into his life.

At first, she couldn't imagine why he felt that way. But, with lengthy introspection, she realized that, like so many parents, she never broke a pattern established long ago—getting her children to do what she considered best, sometimes by indirect means. What may have been necessary when they were children caused irritation and anger now.

FEEL

At the heart of conflict is a mix of powerful emotions, positive and negative. Identifying and working with them represents a deeper stage of self-exploration.

This may seem painful and unnecessary—you already know what you're feeling. It's not very pleasant and you see no need to explore further. But if you do, you might find insights that suggest new ways of coping.

Example: Roger's boss assigned a project Roger enjoyed to a younger colleague. Roger's response—humiliation and anger. But through an honest exploration of his feelings (Did he really believe he was the best man for the job?

Why was the assignment so important to him?), Roger recognized that he had never felt entirely comfortable with the project and the computer skills it required, and that he resented his coworker's age because he hadn't made peace with growing older. These insights freed Roger from feeling that he had been treated unfairly and allowed him to enjoy work once more.

UNDERSTAND

There's nothing new under the sun. Although each conflict is unique to the individuals involved, in another sense it simply plays out an age-old script. The wisdom that we desire to gather with advancing years represents all that we have learned, through experience and introspection, about the world and human nature.

Such understanding can provide fertile soil for empathy, our precious ability to feel what another person is feeling.

Example: In many families, there is one child who needs extra help. He/she has had personal problems or finds it difficult to earn a living. Jack was such a son, and his parents, Paul and Sarah, would help him out financially. They were shocked and disappointed when their other children complained of "favoritism." Why couldn't they be proud that they didn't need help—and generous with their brother?

Paul and Sarah needed to understand how easily money is equated with caring. Their other children felt that their parents loved them less …until Paul and Sarah found words and gestures to make their affection clear.

HEAR

To enter into the world of those around you, including those with whom you are in conflict, you need to listen skillfully—not just to the words that people use, but to the feeling behind the words.

And not just to what they are saying to you. When you listen to what your "adversary" says to others, you're likely to see patterns that turn him into a human being with whom you can sympathize. It's difficult to remain locked in a cycle of hurt and resentment once you've truly heard the pain and vulnerability in the voice of another person.

Example: George hated it when Howard, in the next cubicle, called him "Flash"—an ironic reference to his slow, deliberate manner. It seemed too trivial to mention, but rankled him so much that he started hating Howard. Then he noticed that Howard gave everyone nicknames—a clumsy attempt by a lonely man to reach out. "Flash" didn't seem to bother him so much anymore.

SEE

Very often, the true feelings behind a conflict aren't spoken, but revealed by subtle cues like glances and averted eyes. If you can read body language as well as facial expressions, you will know when someone is hurt or offended and be able to address a troublesome situation before it deepens into destructive conflict.

Observe people who seem to get along well with others to learn about gestures—eye contact, touch and sympathetic smiles that send signals of friendship and build bridges.

Example: If things have grown awkward with a neighbor, watch his reactions when you meet. Does he seem to hold his breath when he speaks to you or avert his eyes? Is he warm at first and then cold and callous? Does the shift occur when certain subjects come up or certain kinds of remarks are made?

IMAGINE

Step back from a conflict and imagine ways that the situation can be transformed into one of harmony.

Also know that imagination can promote conflict. When we envision how much better a situation would be if certain individuals would only act a certain way, we're likely to become frustrated when they fail to get with our program. Imagining the bad things that can happen leads to fear and suspicion, which drives people apart.

Use imagination skillfully by envisioning the outcome you desire and creatively exploring the paths that might get you there. Let a vigorous determination to realize your ideals nourish your spirit.

DO

The understanding and sense of possibility that you have gained from introspection, observation and imagination come to fruition in deeds. Take action based on what you have learned about yourself and others. Even small, timely acts can forestall the deepening of disagreement into destructive conflict or provide the vital first steps toward healing a conflict that has already developed.

The most powerful actions are often symbolic—their meaning extends far beyond their practical impact. They carry messages in the language of the heart.

Example: Pat and Larry were old friends, although they never saw eye to eye politically. But during the last presidential election, feelings ran so high that "unforgivable" insults were exchanged. Now they're civil but chilly with each other. Pat misses the friendship and is sure that Larry does, too.

To start the healing action, Pat invited Larry out to dinner at a restaurant they both considered special. It was his way of saying, "Your friendship is important to me."

SPEAK

Words can speak just as loudly as actions when they're sincere and well chosen. To heal destructive conflict with words, choose words that will mean a lot to your adversary as well as to yourself.

Example: "We can shoulder this burden together" builds a warmer connection than "a joint assumption of liabilities may be called for."

Anticipate how you'll respond when words are spoken back to you…whether they are kind or cruel.

Speak honestly and out of compassion, self-knowledge and understanding. Insincerity turns honeyed words to vinegar.

Be patient, and do not be discouraged by someone's harsh words. The time may not be right for healing.

Don't be afraid to repeat words of acknowledgment or apology.

How to Best Handle Stress

Robert Barry Brooks, PhD, assistant clinical professor of psychology, department of psychiatry at Harvard Medical School in Boston, and consultant in psychology at McLean Hospital in Belmont, MA. He is coauthor of *The Power of Resilience* (Contemporary). For more information, log on to *www.drrobertbrooks.com.*

Why do some people handle pressure with ease while others feel anxious? The big secret is resilience. That's the ability to bounce back when stress strikes. Resilient adults experience just as much stress as everyone else, but they cope more successfully because they have developed the right skills.

Here are some ways to harness the power of resilience…

●**Make changes.** Do you repeat the same kind of behavior even though that behavior consistently gets negative results?

Examples: Nagging your spouse to do something he/she refuses to do…losing your temper with your children…complaining about your job.

The next time you're angry or stressed, ask yourself whether your behavior is contributing to the problem. Don't wait for other people to change. Instead, look for ways that you can change your behavior.

Example: One of my clients was unhappy because she felt that everyone at her work was unfriendly. I asked her how she might be contributing to the situation. She realized that she rarely smiled and looked away when people walked by. She then started smiling and saying hello to everyone. They looked surprised at first but smiled back. This one change greatly improved her work relationships.

Resilient people also recognize what is *not* under their control. You might worry about terrorism, but you'll be less stressed if you focus on things that you can change. Rather than dwelling on the big picture, develop an emergency plan at home.

●**See problems as challenges.** The Chinese word for *crisis* means "opportunity with danger." Don't dwell on the downside when life is difficult. Look for opportunities that are presented by the situation.

Example: Whenever a project at work is unsuccessful, some people give in to feelings of defeat and question their own competence. A stress-hardy individual asks himself, *What can I learn from this project that will help me with the next ones?*

●**Cultivate empathy.** The ability to see the world through other people's eyes is a key component of resilience. It helps you anticipate the problems that can lead to conflict and stress.

Example: One of my clients often said to his employees, "Is that the best you can do?" His intention was to motivate, but the employees heard criticism.

Eventually, he asked himself how he would feel if his employees spoke to him that way. This prompted him to change his approach and start acknowledging their effort, commenting on the positive and saying, "Let's see what we can do to improve these other areas."

●**Listen.** Poor communication creates tension and stress. Good communication means active listening—really understanding what other people are telling you.

Example: Suppose that your teenage son keeps saying that he is stupid. Your instinct as a parent might be to say, "No you're not. You're very smart." This approach almost guarantees an angry response because you're not hearing what your son is saying.

A better way to handle this would be to validate his concerns. You might say, "I'm glad that you told me how you feel. Now let's find a good solution." Validating does not mean that you agree. It just shows that you're listening and understanding what is being said.

●**Embrace your strengths.** It's easy to judge yourself harshly when you don't measure up to some external definition of success, but dwelling on weaknesses creates tremendous stress.

Instead, focus on your "islands of competence," the areas in which you are skilled. For example, you might be a caring spouse and a good coach of your kids' soccer team.

You will also be more resilient when you remind yourself of all the good things in your life—such as your spouse…children…friends… health…home…a job you enjoy…a hobby that is satisfying, etc.

●**Accept mistakes.** Many people who aren't resilient view every mistake as a personal failure. As a result, they avoid challenges—and one day wake up realizing that they're not enjoying their lives.

Those who experience the least stress tend to try different things. They're not afraid of failure because they believe that they'll recover and learn something from the experience.

Example: Suppose that you have always wanted to be comfortable speaking in front of large groups but were afraid to try. Start small. Tell a story in front of a few people at work or a party. You won't be perfect at first, but you will learn what works and what does not. Don't berate yourself if you fall short. Give yourself credit for taking the first step.

●**Help others.** The act of helping others—through volunteer work, for instance—can add meaning to your life and, in the process, reduce stress. This is true for people of all ages.

Example: When I supervised an in-patient unit for troubled youth, their hostile behavior decreased dramatically when I started saying things like, "I need your help." People want to feel that they are making a positive difference in this world. When they do, their anger and stress decrease.

Secrets to Getting Things Done

Robert Ringer, an Annapolis, MD–based motivational speaker and author of several best-selling books, including *Looking Out for #1.* His most recent book is *Action! Nothing Happens Until Something Moves* (both from M. Evans).

A lbert Einstein once said, "Nothing happens until something moves." He was speaking of science, but he might just as well have been referring to our lives. Most people are imprisoned by inertia. The only way to break free is to do something. *Here's how to take action the smart way...*

●**Put the law of averages to work for you.** I believe there are 10 rules for getting what you want. Rule number one is to *Ask.* Rules two through 10 are *Ask again.* The more times you ask for something, the better the odds that someone will say *yes*—and one *yes* can cancel out 100 *no's.* Ask different people. Ask in different ways. Ask at different times.

Example: When a phone service representative tells you that he can't do something for you, hang up, redial and speak to another rep. If that rep can't help, ask to speak to a supervisor. If that supervisor can't help, call the next day to speak to another supervisor, and so on.

●**Let motivation follow action.** A leading excuse for inaction is not feeling motivated. If you don't feel motivated to take action on an uninspiring task now, the chances are good that you won't feel motivated to do so later. The task isn't going to get any less tedious. If you force yourself to start, motivation—or at least momentum—is likely to follow.

Example: Many people have trouble sticking to an exercise program. The trouble usually isn't that they get bored while exercising and stop mid-session—it's that on most days they can't convince themselves to start at all. Once they force themselves to hit the road for a jog or get to an exercise class, their blood starts pumping and they see it through.

●**Gather information.** People often put off taking action because they don't know what to do first. A good first step is to solicit ideas and information. *Suggestions...*

●Call someone who is familiar with the subject in question or who tends to have good ideas. Be sure to ask him/her to suggest other people you should call.

●Go on-line to research information on the subject.

●Contact a relevant organization. Find out whether you can speak to its officers or members or attend a meeting.

●**Don't be afraid to be wrong.** Sometimes people are stymied because they're afraid that they're going to make a mistake. But a wrong action can let us look at a situation in positive, new ways—and form new plans.

Example: When I self-published my first book in the 1970s, I knew nothing about selling it. The only way to learn was to act. I took out an ad in a midsized newspaper and gauged the response. It was poor—my sales were not even sufficient to cover the cost of the ad—so I selected another newspaper and tried a different approach. Soon I found an ad that worked, and my book eventually became a best-seller.

●**Find people who have the power to assist you.** When you realize that someone isn't interested in helping you, don't waste any time and energy arguing. Look for someone else to work with.

Example: The woman behind the front desk at a computer repair shop returned my printer to me without its paper tray. She insisted that it hadn't had a tray when I dropped it off. I asked for the manager, but he too insisted that I must have left the tray at home. With the manager, I had an advantage—he was anxious to get back to work. When I told him I wasn't leaving until I got a paper tray, he pulled one out of a different printer for me. I had aligned our interests—we both wanted me to be on my way.

How to Make Better Decisions in Less Time

Barry Schwartz, PhD, Dorwin Cartwright Professor of Social Theory and Social Action, department of psychology, Swarthmore College, Swarthmore, PA. He is author of *The Paradox of Choice: Why More is Less* (Ecco).

At work and home, we make hundreds of decisions every day, some are trivial, some important—which soap to buy, which political candidate to vote for, how to plan for retirement. These days, high-tech communications only add to the difficulty. We need to make decisions even more quickly when we respond to e-mail or answer our cell phones.

The result? We choose haphazardly or, worse, we become paralyzed by information overload and end up making no decision.

Example: Employees complain that their 401(k) plans offer too few investment options, but research indicates that the more mutual funds an employer makes available, the less likely employees are to participate in the plan at all, even if it means passing up thousands of dollars in employer-matching contributions.

Here are strategies I have learned from my own and other social scientists' studies on decision making…

●**Learn to accept "good enough."** We all sometimes misuse our time and energy by trying to make the best choice. For instance, we might devote an hour or more to relatively frivolous decisions, such as choosing a restaurant, but spend just a few minutes picking a lawyer or doctor, often depending on just one friend's recommendation.

Better: Ask yourself how significantly one choice will affect your life. The more minor and short-term the impact, the less time you should spend making the decision.

The concept of "good enough" is difficult to embrace because it feels like you're settling for mediocrity—but "settling" often increases overall satisfaction.

Examples: You decide to write a heartfelt letter to your spouse on your anniversary. You want to choose just the right words—but after several drafts, you give up in frustration and just buy a card at a store. Yet even an imperfect letter would have been much more meaningful to your spouse.

Or you find a movie that you're interested in at the video store. Instead of taking it home and just enjoying it, you think there must be another that would better suit your mood. You spend 45 minutes scouring the aisles without success. By the time you leave—with your original selection in hand—you have wasted a good chunk of your precious leisure time.

●**Deliberately reduce the options when a decision is not critical.** Base your decision criteria on your past experience.

Examples: You have to hire a summer intern at work. If you have been able to find someone suitable in previous years by interviewing four candidates, set that as your limit.

You can apply the same technique to choosing a hairdresser, dog groomer or dry cleaner.

Spend enough time to find someone who is adequate, then get on with your life.

•**Spend a lot of time and energy on a decision only if the extra effort can yield significantly better results.** Say that you have a choice of three long-distance phone-service providers, any of which will meet your needs. You're tempted to figure out which company's plan gives you a slight advantage, but the time-consuming and confusing process will save you no more than a few dollars a month.

You shouldn't choose blindly, but give yourself only a specific amount of time to review the plans or a deadline to make a choice.

Even spending enormous amounts of time on critical decisions, such as buying a home or helping your child choose a college, may not be worth the effort. Decisions such as these often involve more uncertainty than you ever can resolve in advance.

•**Don't let marketers play you.** Companies today are brilliant at seeding dissatisfaction in consumers to get them to buy more expensive products. This applies to everything from laundry detergent to such big-ticket items as cars. Computer software makers are notorious for this, pushing Acme Software version 7 or 8 when version 6 still is adequate for your needs. Most "enhancements" are minimal or tangential to a product's main purpose.

Smart: Stick with an older product or service until you experience shortcomings that really compromise your satisfaction. You'll save money and gain time.

•**Don't keep researching products and services after you have made a decision.** Have you ever bought a new car or computer, then scanned the newspapers each week to check the current price? This behavior just creates postpurchase misgivings.

If the car's price drops below what you paid, you will feel as if you were ripped off. If the car's price increases, you will wonder what was wrong with your particular vehicle that allowed you to get such a good deal.

People derive only modest pleasure from confirming that they got a good deal and substantial dissatisfaction from finding out that they could have done better.

•**Make most decisions irreversible.** It makes sense to want to know about a return policy when you make a purchase, but being allowed to change your mind only increases the chance that you will.

On the other hand, when a decision is final, you engage in a variety of powerful psychological processes that enhance your satisfaction about your choice relative to the alternatives.

Example: Today's proliferation of no-fault divorces and prenuptial agreements has influenced many people to stop treating their selection of a partner for life as a sacred decision. During the course of a marriage, you are likely to encounter many people who might seem better looking, smarter or more understanding than your spouse.

Always wondering whether you could have done better is a prescription for misery. You're better off thinking, *I've made my decision, so this other person's qualities have nothing to do with me. I'm not in the market.*

Get What You Want: Secrets from a Former White House Negotiator

Martin E. Latz, founder and president of Latz Negotiation Institute, a training company in Scottsdale, AZ, whose clients include Eli Lilly & Co., Honeywell Aerospace and many of the nation's largest law firms. During the Clinton administration, Mr. Latz worked as a member of the White House advance negotiating team. He is author of *Gain the Edge: Negotiating to Get What You Want* (St. Martin's).

Everything is negotiable—from division of household chores to the price of a car. Many people believe that they are good negotiators because they have a comprehensive knowledge of the subject at hand and know what they want to achieve—but they often fail to gain an edge because they haven't thought about the process itself. They apply pressure or make compromises when it feels right on a gut level, rather than use battle-tested strategies that can sway the other party.

Here are the common mistakes that prevent good negotiators from being great…

***Mistake 1:* Not being aggressive enough.** You fail to negotiate aggressively because a particular situation or environment is awkward or even intimidating.

Examples: Buying a car…asking for a severance package.

It's hard to think clearly and strategize when you are up against an expert who has greater knowledge or experience…or if the issue has much greater bearing on your emotional well-being and future than on your counterpart's. *What to do instead…*

●**Gather facts that can help your cause.** Facts and statistics empower you and help to level the playing field.

Example: Joe was laid off from his law firm. He asked for two months' severance because he figured it would take him that long to get a new job.

Instead, don't ask for what you would like or need. Ask for what you *deserve*. Had Joe talked to former employees, he would have learned that the company's severance packages ranged from four to six months' pay. Knowing there was wiggle room, he could have bolstered his demands—for example, with statistics on how much revenue he had brought into the organization.

●**Let someone negotiate for you.** There's nothing wrong with admitting that certain situations rattle you.

Example: Mary is a business owner and an excellent negotiator. When her father died, she had to go to the funeral home to purchase a coffin. She knew she would overpay because she was too upset and preoccupied to do the proper research. So, she asked another family member who had experience in funeral planning to step in.

***Mistake 2:* Not negotiating with the ultimate decision maker.** You spend 30 minutes haggling with an electronics salesman over the price of a top-of-the-line home-entertainment system. After you agree on the price, the salesman reveals that he needs approval from the store manager. Inevitably, the word comes from the manager that you need to make some minor price concessions. *What to do instead…*

●**Get your counterpart to disclose the full extent of his/her authority early on.** If he is not in a position to make the decision, ask to speak to someone who has sufficient authority. Stress the importance of integrity—if you can't trust his word, it's a deal breaker. Don't accept the explanation that the underling is in charge of the deal and the manager's approval is just perfunctory.

Also, ask your counterpart several times if all issues are on the table.

Reason: The decision maker often requests concessions on issues that were not brought up during the negotiations.

Example: Many car dealerships impose a "document-preparation fee" or similarly named charge that really is just more profit for them. It magically shows up after a deal has already been struck.

●**Turn the tables.** Tell a salesperson that you need to run the store manager's last minute requests by your spouse for his final approval. You then can come back and demand additional concessions. Turning the tables this way will encourage the salesperson to stop playing games and reach a quick deal.

***Mistake 3:* Offering to split the difference.** Almost everyone has used this closing technique when a negotiation drags on. Both parties compromise and give an equal amount—but if you make the initial offer, you will tend to lose more in the end.

Example: Steve had set the price for his used BMW at $12,000. The buyer was offering $10,000. Steve said they were close enough that he would accept $11,000 to be fair. In fact, what he did was make an oral commitment to accept $11,000 without the buyer having to concede anything. The buyer called back later and said, "I still prefer to pay $10,000, but I'm willing to split the difference and offer you $10,500." Of course, Steve insisted on splitting the difference again. The car sold for $10,750—$250 less than the "fair" compromise that he initially offered.

Instead, play it cool…rather than pushing for a quick deal, wait for your counterpart to offer to split the difference.

Mistake 4: **Talking too much.** The person in charge of the discussion is the one doing all the talking, right? Actually, you lose leverage if you monopolize the conversation. You give yourself a false sense of control and wind up revealing more information than you want. Conversely, quiet negotiators present information only at the most strategic times. *What to do...*

●**Aim to ask twice as many questions as your counterpart**—exploring his needs, interests and goals and establishing a rapport—and spend twice as much time listening as speaking.

●**Use information-blocking techniques.** These let you withhold sensitive information without lying or acting so evasive that your counterpart loses trust in you.

Example: Allison was interviewing for a position as a marketing manager. During her third interview, the CEO asked her outright, "Are you seriously considering a position with any other firm right now?" The truth was that she wasn't. She didn't want to lie, however, she knew that admitting this information would weaken her leverage in the salary negotiations. *Her alternatives...*

●Answer a different question. *Response:* "I've interviewed with many companies over the past few months, and yours is my favorite." You are addressing the issue, but in an indirect fashion.

●Discount the question's relevance and ask for clarification. *Response:* "I am not sure I understand how that makes a difference to your interest in me. If we're a good fit, this will work. That's more important than anything, right?"

●Apologize for not being able to answer due to integrity, legal issues, etc. *Response:* "I'd like to tell you, but it wouldn't be fair to the other companies with which I've talked. Naturally, I would never reveal the discussions that you and I have had to your competitors."

Six Ways to Spot a Liar: Secrets from a Trainer For the FBI

Paul Ekman, PhD, professor of psychology with the University of California, San Francisco, and author of *Emotions Revealed* (Times) and *Telling Lies* (Norton). He has taught FBI and other security agents and has developed two CDs that teach lie-detecting skills through games and tests. His Web site is *www.emotionsrevealed.com.*

No matter how hard they try, liars nearly always give themselves away with words or expressions. New research—used by the Department of Homeland Security and the FBI—can help you spot these signs of deceit.

MICRO-EXPRESSIONS

These are flashes of true feelings that escape when people lie. Watch for brief expressions that run counter to a person's dominant facial gestures. They last less than a second and can occur during any part of a conversation.

Examples: When a colleague explains why he is too busy to help you on a project, look for a flash of discomfort. Or when a guest compliments the host on a lousy roast beef, watch for the brief grimace that doesn't belong on the face of a delighted diner.

GIVEAWAY EYELIDS

You can see through a disingenuous smile by watching the area between the upper eyelid and the eyebrow, known as the *eye cover fold.* When someone is enjoying himself/herself, it is slightly tightened and pulled down. It's nearly impossible for someone to lower the eye cover fold if he is not experiencing true enjoyment.

EXAGGERATED GESTURES

Whenever people fake emotion, they often go overboard. Keep an eye out for exaggerated gestures or emotions to spot a cover-up.

Example: You ask your teenage son what happened to the $10 on the table. He gets very angry—an over-the-top response that suggests he is lying.

HESITATIONS IN SPEECH

Hesitations and stammering often indicate a lie—but only if the person does it more than usual on a familiar topic.

Example: If a lawyer talks about astrophysics, he might hesitate because he is unfamiliar with the topic. If you're shopping for a computer and ask a salesperson if he has any for less than $1,200, he should have a speedy answer. Be suspicious if he hesitates. He might be thinking of selling you something that is more expensive once you pay for add-ons.

OTHER BODY LANGUAGE

The probability of a lie also increases when gestures don't match a person's words. Suspect a lie if someone…

…says he's interested in your ideas but does not make steady eye contact.

…says he agrees with you and then presses his lips together, a gesture that can indicate discomfort or anger.

…moves away from you while professing his friendship.

…says he's glad to see you but gives you an abbreviated handshake.

PRACTICED PHRASES

When people lie, they often memorize one or two pat phrases but rarely prepare for follow-up questions. Questioning someone closely is the most effective way to get the truth.

Example: Your real estate agent says he has a "great house" that's a "real steal." *What to do:* Pin him down by asking questions. You'll gain important information if he hesitates when he describes the house or flashes a phony smile when he says it is perfect for you. The more he talks, the better. When faced with really having to discuss a matter, most people resort to telling the truth.

Mixed Signals Provoke Stress

People experience less stress with the people they dislike than with those who trigger conflicting feelings—a fun-loving, yet very undependable friend, for example. Studies show that blood pressure rises when we meet people

for who we have mixed feelings, probably because we don't know what to expect.

Psychology Today, 115 E. 23 St., New York City 10010.

Everyday Etiquette

Peggy Post, great-granddaughter-in-law of etiquette pioneer Emily Post. She is a director and spokesperson for the Emily Post Institute in Burlington, VT, and author of *Emily Post's Etiquette, 17th Edition* (HarperCollins). Her Web site is *www.emilypost.com.*

Do you ever find yourself in a sticky situation and don't know what to do or say? *Here, renowned etiquette expert Peggy Post gives advice on how to handle rude kids, nosy coworkers and much more…*

CELL PHONE BLABBERMOUTH

• **When I'm near a person who is speaking loudly on a cell phone, what's the best way to ask him/her to be quiet?** It's hard to enjoy a meal, a train ride or any other activity in public when your ears are held hostage by a cell phone blabbermouth. Sometimes, simply a pointed look at the talker will get your message across. Speaking directly to the offender usually is not a good idea—it could lead to a very unpleasant confrontation.

Your best bet is to seek help from an authority—a restaurant manager, for example. He might ask the caller to move to the lobby or restroom area. If the cell phone user is on a train, speak to the conductor.

FORGETTING A NAME

• **What should you do if you're about to introduce someone and suddenly can't remember his name?** We've all been there—that awkward moment when we're starting to make an introduction but cannot remember a name. Just say, "I'm very embarrassed. I have completely forgotten your name."

If you suspect someone has forgotten your name, one of the kindest gestures that you can make is to simply extend your hand to them and say, "Hello, I'm Jane Smith. It's so wonderful to meet you."

E-MAIL RULES

• **What's the most polite way to ask someone to stop e-mailing jokes, cards or other frivolous messages?** Individuals who are inundated by e-mails often feel bothered, not flattered, by pass-along e-mails. If you're a victim of "friend spam," speak up politely and honestly, asking the friend to stop. Say, "John, I love hearing from you, but please stop sending me jokes via e-mail. I'm so busy at work that I don't have time to keep up with my personal e-mail."

• **Is it OK to e-mail a condolence note? What about a wedding or birthday party invitation?** Any invitation that you would extend over the phone can be done with e-mail, assuming that the person you are inviting looks at e-mail regularly.

E-mail also is great for confirming invitations that you've already made over the phone. *Sue, we're looking forward to having you and Dan join us at the cookout at our house on Saturday at 6 pm.*

For condolences, it's acceptable to send an e-mail first, but it always should be followed by a handwritten note. Think of the e-mail as replacing the phone call, not the handwritten note.

Very informal or last-minute baby or bridal shower invitations can be extended via e-mail, but it is better to issue traditional invitations through the mail. Ditto for wedding invitations. Only if you're getting married at the last minute in a small, informal ceremony can you send an e-mail. For any other type of wedding, a mailed invitation is appropriate.

PERSONAL HYGIENE PROBLEM

• **An acquaintance has awful body odor. What, if anything, can I do?** Since you are just an acquaintance, it would be best not to say anything to him about his problem. Speaking up directly could embarrass him greatly.

The only way that you could try to help is to mention the problem discreetly to someone who knows him well. You could suggest to the good friend that he say something like, "Matt, I've noticed that you have the same problem I do with perspiration. I didn't know what to do until I tried this product. It worked for me, and it might work for you, too." Even if Matt is embarrassed initially, he probably will appreciate his friend's concern.

If the acquaintance is a coworker and his problem is hindering his ability to interact with others, you might say something in confidence to his supervisor, who in turn could speak to him discreetly.

DINNER PARTY DILEMMA

• **I'm a vegetarian. When invited to a dinner party, should I let the host know this ahead of time? What about my husband, who is allergic to particular foods?** Upon accepting the invitation, mention any allergy that could cause a serious reaction. Explain to your hostess, "We'd love to come for dinner, but I must tell you that Bob is deathly allergic to shellfish."

Dietary preferences, such as vegetarianism, should be handled on a more individual basis, depending upon the event.

If it is a large party or a buffet, the guest should try to "make do" since a variety of foods will be served.

If the gathering is small, the dinner is in your honor or you're going to be an overnight houseguest, you should mention your restrictions to the host and offer to bring a dish to share. Say, "Thanks so much for the invitation, Joan. I should let you know that I am a vegetarian. I'd love to bring a zucchini casserole if that's OK with you."

This way, your host won't work hard only to make something you can't eat, and you'll be providing a solution to your restriction.

RUDE KIDS

• **What should I do if a child is rude and his parents are not present?** It depends on what type of behavior you have witnessed. A simple correction or explanation from a well-meaning adult whom the child knows well usually is fine—as long as the comment is made in a way that doesn't embarrass the child or criticize his parents.

For example, it would be fine to say, "Jack, in our house, we don't use language like that." Or when it's just you and your grandchild sharing a meal, you might say, "It's so much nicer when you chew with your mouth closed, Maryanne."

You needn't discuss the behavior with the child's parent unless it's particularly disruptive or outlandish. If the child's parents are there and do or say nothing, generally you will have to bite your tongue.

If you feel you must respond to the behavior, do so genially. If the child talks back, you could say something like, "I really don't appreciate the way you are speaking to me. Could you use a nicer tone?" You want to say it in a friendly way that expresses your sincere concern for how the conversation is going.

NOSY COWORKERS

●**What is the best way to keep the nosy coworkers who drop by my cubicle from reading confidential papers on my desk or e-mails on my computer?** Tell them to get lost—in a polite way, of course. While cubicle-style offices may encourage some coworkers to participate in this kind of space invasion, it is unprofessional and intrusive. Simply say, "Frank, I'll have to ask you to step back from my desk. I'm working on a confidential project. I'm sure you understand. Thanks."

Handling Put-Downs

If someone attacks you verbally, acknowledge his/her feelings but question the way they are expressed. Make a brief comment to end the encounter, such as, "I think we understand each other. Let's move on." If a put-down is indirect—"Good work for a woman"—ask the person just what he means. You may have heard incorrectly…and you are giving him a chance to apologize. For nonverbal put-downs, such as nasty looks, ask the person to translate the glance into a comment. Be sure to speak in a nonconfrontational way.

Robert E. Alberti, PhD, psychologist and marriage and family therapist in Atascadero, CA, coauthor of *Your Perfect Right: Assertiveness and Equality in Your Life and Relationships* (Impact).

How to Keep Your Mind Sharp

A change of pace is as good as a nap for keeping the mind sharp. Overdoing a task can lead to reduced performance—but a simple change of pace can restore it.

Example: A group of people was asked to do a challenging mental task in four sessions throughout the day, from 9 am to 7 pm. By day's end, their performance had declined by as much as 50%. When allowed an hour's nap in the afternoon, their higher performance levels were restored.

Next, rather than a nap, the subjects were given a different challenging mental task to do at the final session—with the result that their performance was as good as it had been when they performed the original task at the first session in the morning.

Lesson: Give yourself some kind of break during the day.

Sara C. Mednick, PhD, research associate, systems neurology laboratory, The Salk Institute for Biological Studies, La Jolla, CA, *www.salk.edu*.

Chew More, Think Better

In a new finding, people who chewed cinnamon gum—or sniffed a cinnamon scent—performed better on memory tests than people who chewed other flavored gum or sniffed other scents. Researchers have yet to determine why cinnamon confers this benefit.

Wheeling Jesuit University at 316 Washington Ave., Wheeling, WV 26003.

19

Business and Career Success

Today's Top Franchises— The Shrewd Way to Start Your Own Business

Even with the economy gaining strength, starting a business is tricky. But, franchising decreases this risk by giving you experienced partners to lead the way. Choose carefully though. Of the 2,500 franchises available in the US, only about 500 are proven growth-oriented investments.

If you want to blaze your own trail, franchising may not be for you. You have to play by the home office's rules. Franchisors may inspect your operation to ensure that you are following their procedures. A Whopper in Boston should taste the same as one in San Diego.

Here's how to get started—and the hottest opportunities now...

FINDING A FRANCHISE

Less than 20% of franchises supply earnings statements to prospective buyers. To narrow your search and reduce risk, choose a business with at least 35 operating units. *Also focus on...*

●**Price range.** Janitorial services start at less than $15,000.* Motels can cost about $2 million or more. In the mid-range are the food-service franchises, which will require an investment of between $100,000 and $1 million. McDonald's franchises cost between $466,000 and $955,500, and availability is limited. *Other costs...*

●Franchise fee. The purchase price may or may not include a onetime franchise fee. In exchange for this fee—which ranges from $15,000 to $50,000—the franchisor generally is obligated to train you, help you select a location, negotiate a lease, obtain financing and, in some cases, build and equip the site. Ask about follow-up training.

●Supplies. You might have to buy supplies from the franchisor.

●Royalties. These range from 4% to 8% of gross sales per month.

*All prices subject to change.

Robert Bond, a franchising consultant in Oakland, CA, and the author of *Bond's Franchise Guide* and *How Much Can I Make?* (both from Source Books).

- Advertising. You might have to pay fees for national or regional advertising.

- **Industry.** There are more than 600 franchises devoted to food service, 126 companies in cleaning/maintenance and 153 in automotive products/services. There are opportunities in pet products, athletic wear, lawn care, art, photography and printing. My free Web site, *www. worldfranchising.com,* lists more than 1,000 of the largest franchises. Contact these companies for their marketing materials.

DOING YOUR HOMEWORK

Before you sign a contract, research the business by talking with...

- **Franchisees.** Ask owners how much they earn, about their experiences with the franchisor and whether they would make the same investment decision today.

- **An experienced attorney who belongs to the Forum on Franchising of the American Bar Association (ABA).** You can locate one through the ABA's referral service (*www. abanet.org*) or contact your state bar association. Ask the attorney to review the offering circular. *He/she should pay attention to...*

- Policy on franchise terminations.

- Litigation against the franchisor.

- Your territory. Appropriate size varies by local population, type of franchise and a variety of other factors.

BEST OPPORTUNITIES NOW

My favorite firms offer exceptional products and treat franchisees fairly...

- **Cleaning services**

- Jani-King International. Commercial cleaning. *Total investment:* $11,000 to $34,000.* 800-526-4546, *www.janiking.com.*

- Merry Maids. Home cleaning service. *Total investment:* $23,350 to $54,450. 800-798-8000, *www.merrymaids.com.*

- ServiceMaster Clean. Both commercial and residential cleanup. *Total investment:* $28,200 to $99,900. 800-255-9687, *www.ownafranchise.com.*

- **Food**

- Blimpie Subs & Salads. Quick sandwiches. *Total investment:* $72,800 to $338,200. 800-447-6256, *www.blimpie.com.*

*All prices subject to change.

- Burger King. Fast-food chain. *Average investment:* $400,000.* 305-378-7579, *www.burger king.com.*

- Carvel Corporation. Ice cream shops. *Average investment:* $300,000. 800-227-8353, *www. carvel.com.*

- Wing Zone. Takeout/delivery chicken wings. *Total investment:* $179,500 to $229,500. 877-333-9464, *www.wingzone.com.*

- **Lodging**

- Accor North America. Motel chains, including Motel 6 and Red Roof Inns. *Total investment:* Varies by each chain. *Examples:* Red Roof Inns, $2.6 million to $2.9 million...Motel 6, $1.9 million to $2.3 million. *www.accor-na.com.*

- **Other services**

- Express Personnel Services. Placement of personnel. *Total investment:* $130,000 to $160,000. 877-652-6400, *www.expressfranchising.com.*

- Money Mailer. Direct-mail advertising services. *Average investment:* $55,000. 888-446-4648, *www.moneymailer.net.*

UP-AND-COMING FRANCHISES

Franchisors are becoming much more niche-oriented. *Specialties worth watching...*

- **Animal care**

Pet owners need a variety of services. *Promising franchises...*

- Aussie Pet Mobile. Grooming service. 949-234-0680, *www.aussiepetmobile.com.*

- Banfield—The Pet Hospital. 800-838-6929, *www.banfield.net.*

- Bark Busters. Home dog training. 877-500-2275, *www.barkbusters.com.*

- **Auction consignment**

Many people want to sell items on eBay but prefer someone else to do all the legwork. Customers keep about 40% of net proceeds. *Promising franchises now....*

- I Sold It. 626-584-0440, *www.i-soldit.com.*

- Snappy Auctions. 888-490-1820, *www.snap pyauctions.com.*

- **Bad backs/feet**

Aging baby boomers want fast pain relief. *Promising franchises...*

- Relax the Back. 800-290-2225, ext. 7955, *www.relaxtheback.com.*

*All prices subject to change.

•Foot Solutions. 866-338-2597 or *www.foot solutions.com.*

How to Get Rich

The best way to get rich is to own your own business. The median net worth of business owners is about $250,000—almost three times that of other workers.

Statistics from Market Audit, an annual survey of business ownership conducted by Claritas, marketing information firm, San Diego.

Better Working From Home

Working from home poses its own set of challenges. *Here are some tips on how to make it work…*

●**Set up your office in a place where you can close the door for privacy,** be it in a spare bedroom, garage or sunroom.

●**Hold meetings and meet with clients somewhere other than your home.**

Examples: A restaurant or the seldom-used conference room of a nearby business.

●**Plan brainstorming sessions** by bringing together a number of interesting or experienced people who are willing to toss around ideas with you.

●**Take regular breaks** which will help to re-charge your batteries.

Examples: 10-minute breaks to read… lunch away from home…or a late afternoon workout at the gym.

Robert Spiegel, Albuquerque, NM–based author of the syndicated column *eBiz* and *The Shoestring Entrepreneur's Guide to the Best Home-Based Businesses* (Truman Talley).

Better Ways to Boost Business

To increase business, don't automatically cut prices. Many business owners are tempted to boost sales by reducing the price of products or services.

Problem: Slashing your prices will significantly reduce profit margin and may encourage your competition to start a price war.

Alternatives: Rather than decreasing your price, offer your customers something extra, such as a "free" initial period in exchange for a longer-term agreement. Or extend the time that the customer has to pay.

Paul Lemberg, director, Stratamax Research Institute, a business consulting firm, Rancho Sante Fe, CA. His Web site is *www.lemberg.com.*

Increase Your Market Share

To grow market share in tough times, try these helpful strategies…

●**Add resources to marketing**—don't take them away.

●**In down markets, more qualified people are available, so hire them** to replace the underperformers. Increase employee training.

●**Put more information-technology and management staff** in the field selling.

●**Show customers how you can cut their costs** by reducing waste or saving time.

●**Go into partnership with customers** to develop and launch new products.

●**Target the customers of your weaker competitors.**

Jeffrey Fox, a marketing consultant in Chester, CT, and author of *How to Become a Marketing Superstar* (Hyperion). His Web site is *www.foxandcompany.com.*

Business Networking On the Web

LinkedIn (*www.linkedin.com*) helps professionals, entrepreneurs and small businesses link up with potential customers, investors, business partners, job candidates, employers, etc. This free service has nearly two million subscribers who are able to use one another's contacts for referrals and networking. LinkedIn's referral-only approach protects members' privacy and existing relationships through a gatekeeping system. This type of service is attractive to senior professionals who are interested in networking while limiting access to themselves as well as their contacts.

Protect Your Business From Thieves, Corporate Spies, More

Jason Paroff, Esq., director of computer forensics, Kroll Inc., a premier security firm, New York City.

Too many business owners view protecting their assets as a cost that has no revenue-producing benefit. In fact, taking the right preventive steps can save your company big money. *What to do...*

●**Develop a corporate security policy.** Make it clear that employees don't have the right to privacy with respect to what they store on your systems—all equipment and data are company property. Employees can be restricted from going to certain Internet sites or disseminating information outside the company.

●**Get employees to read and sign off on company policy** at least once a year.

SOFTWARE SECURITY

In addition to installing firewalls, which act as Internet security guards that monitor traffic between your company's internal network and the outside world...

●**Implement controls with passwords.** Any employee who does not possess a company-approved password is denied access to all or part of a computer network.

Example: Only you and your human resources personnel would have access to any salary and benefits information.

●**Prohibit downloading of sensitive information.** Software can automatically flag or disable downloads of confidential information by employees.

PROTECT PHYSICAL ASSETS

Depending on the size and location of your business, you will require different physical security systems...

●**Small companies in relatively secure areas** may do fine with just an office safe and an alarm system.

●**Larger companies with many entrances,** or firms that are located in high-crime areas, may require security guards and/or video cameras as well.

Many technology-related thefts involve small, expensive equipment that is easy to conceal, such as laptop computers. *Preventive steps...*

●**Install tracking software and motion alarms in laptop computers.** Software products such as Computrace (800-220-0733, *www.absolute.com*) cost less than $200* and will alert the police to the laptop's location as soon as the thief logs onto the Internet. Motion alarms, such as the Kensington SonicLock, cost about $15 and are available at most computer and electronics stores. When an equipped machine is moved, an alarm will sound.

●**Chain down equipment** that isn't frequently moved.

●**Make a trusted employee responsible for tracking** the firm's portable equipment and supplies.

*Price subject to change.

Protect Your Business From Legal Woes

Andrew Josephson, area copresident of the insurance brokerage Arthur J. Gallagher & Company, Glendale, CA, *www.ajg.com.*

One lawsuit can wipe out your business. And, doctors aren't the only professionals who are targeted. Architects, consultants and even travel agents may be sued by angry customers.

To safeguard your firm when apologies aren't enough...

GET PROPER LIABILITY INSURANCE

The cost depends on...

- **Your state.** California, Florida, New York and Texas have the highest rates.

- **Previous claims.** If you have faced liability lawsuits in the past, coverage will be more expensive.

- **Your industry.** Jury awards are higher in some fields. Real estate agents require more coverage than travel agents.

- **The company's assets and revenues.** The higher they are, the more insurance coverage you will need.

- **Experience.** The more experience you possess, the lower your premium.

CUT COSTS

To get the best insurance rates...

- **Ask industry organizations if they offer a group rate.**

- **Ask your peers to provide independent agent referrals.**

- **Increase your deductible.**

- **Practice prudent business management.** Have contracts reviewed by a lawyer and provide a written set of policies for employees.

Best Retirement Plans for Small-Business Owners

Roger W. Lusby III, CPA, CMA, AEP, tax partner, Frazier & Deeter, LLC, 600 Peachtree St. NE, Atlanta 30308. Mr. Lusby works with closely held businesses and writes extensively on estate and tax matters.

Tax-deferred retirement plans are among the tax shelters for small-business owners with the explicit blessing of the federal government. Moreover, such plans offer you a prime opportunity to build wealth for the days when you're no longer working.

Challenge: There are many attractive plans from which to choose. *The following seem to be the cream of the crop...*

SOLO 401(K) PLANS

These plans may make sense if you are the only full-time employee of your business. Your spouse can be on the payroll, too.

Simplicity: Participants in solo 401(k) plans merely have to file IRS Form 5500-EZ, *Annual Return of One-Participant (Owners and Their Spouses) Retirement Plan,* and then only after assets in the plan top $100,000. Administrative costs tend to be modest.

Borrowing power: You can borrow from a solo 401(k) plan that has been properly created. But, that's not the case with some of the small-business plans described below.

Upper limits: In many situations, solo 401(k) plans permit larger tax-deferred contributions than other retirement plans suitable for one person or one couple. That is because you make contributions as an employer as well as deferring income as an employee.

In 2006, each participant's account may be able to receive as much as $44,000 altogether. If you're 50 or older, you can add $5,000 this year as a "catch-up" contribution, for a maximum of $49,000.

Trap: These plans are for owners only. They won't work if you have any full-time employees. Then you'll have to have a regular 401(k) plan, which might be subject to antidiscrimination tests and may require contributions to employees' accounts.

SIMPLE IRAs

Savings incentive match plans for employees (SIMPLEs) come in two varieties—SIMPLE IRAs and SIMPLE 401(k)s. SIMPLE 401(k)s are actually not that simple. Most companies prefer the SIMPLE IRAs, where participants direct their own investments and the plans require very little maintenance.

Required: Your company can have no more than 100 employees.

The 100% solution: You can contribute 100% of your income, up to $10,000 in 2006.

Example: With a 3%-of-compensation employer match, the maximum amount that can go into your account this year is $18,000.

Catch-up: Participants age 50 and older can defer an additional $2,500 worth of income in 2006. Starting in 2007, the basic and catch-up contribution limits for SIMPLEs will be adjusted for inflation.

When they work best: Because you can contribute 100% of pay, SIMPLE IRAs may be ideal if your income is relatively low, yet you want to make a sizable contribution to your retirement plan.

SIMPLE IRAs must be offered to all employees but there are no antidiscrimination tests. You as well as employed relatives can make maximum contributions to SIMPLE IRAs, if the matching contribution formula is used—even if none of your other employees contributes, in which case no further company match of funds is required.

SEPs

If you're self-employed, a simplified employee pension (SEP) plan may be a good choice.

Easiest: You merely fill out a simple form when you set up the plan. There are no further reports and no annual tax filings.

Flexibility: You can reduce or even skip SEP contributions in a year when your cash flow is meager.

Look-back deductions: Contributions to a SEP can be made any time until the due date of your tax return, including extensions.

If you want to make a tax-deductible contribution for the prior year and you have not already established a retirement plan, a SEP is your only choice.

Contribution limits: The maximum you can contribute to a SEP for 2005 is $42,000 ($44,000 for 2006). For the self-employed, about 20% of income can be contributed, so you will need income of $210,000 in 2005 to reach the maximum ($220,000 in 2006).

Trap: SEPs are usually not appropriate for companies with more than a few employees. If your company contributes to your own account, it has to contribute the same percentage of pay for your eligible employees, too.

401(k) PROFIT-SHARING PLANS

Offering a 401(k) plan may be necessary in order for you to attract and retain exceptional employees. Often, workers will expect a 401(k) plan as a perk.

Contributions: In 2006, employees may contribute up to $15,000 worth of income to their 401(k) accounts. Those 50 or older may defer an extra $5,000.

Match: You may want to offer a company match to encourage the lower-paid workers to participate. If participation among the rank-and-file is scant, prized executives (including yourself) may find their contributions limited.

Trap: If your company sponsors a 401(k), contributions to your own retirement account will be limited to $15,000 or $20,000 in 2006, depending on your age.

Strategy: Adopt a profit-sharing plan that includes a 401(k). Profit-sharing plans are flexible. Your company can make a contribution for its employees if it has the required cash.

Payoff: You and the other top executives may receive contributions that total $44,000 or $49,000 in 2006 from the 401(k)/profit-sharing combination plan.

AGE-WEIGHTED PROFIT-SHARING PLANS

Whether or not they include a 401(k) plan, profit-sharing plans can be expensive.

Trap: If your company makes a contribution of, say, 15% of pay to your own account, it will have to contribute 15% of pay for all eligible employees.

Strategy: If you are older than most of your employees, adopt a profit-sharing plan that is age-weighted.

Rationale: Older employees will have fewer years to build up a retirement fund, so larger contributions may be justified.

Example: You are in your 50s so your company might contribute 15% of pay to your profit-sharing account, however, your assistant who is 20-something receives 5% of pay.

Key: Some very sophisticated plan designs may enable your company to skew most of its profit-sharing contributions to you and other older principals. Such plans can be expensive to create and administer but the savings in employee contributions might be worthwhile. Vesting schedules also can apply, making such plans more cost-effective.

Bottom line: If you're age 50 or older, with a much younger workforce, contact a CPA or an employee benefits professional to find out if your company can have a plan that stacks tax-deductible retirement contributions in your favor.

Smart Compensation Planning

Joel Gensler, CPA, partner in charge of business services at Eisner LLP, 750 Third Ave., New York City 10017. Mr. Gensler specializes in providing services to growing businesses and start-ups. He offers advice on day-to-day issues, structuring partnership agreements, retirement and life insurance options and other management issues.

The beginning of the year is the time for small-business owners to figure out the best ways to take compensation from their businesses year-round. *Smart strategies…*

SALARIES

When a business is organized as a regular (C) corporation or S corporation, owner/employees must set their own salaries as employees.

Salaries must be "reasonable"—that is, they must be in line with what other firms in the market pay for similar services. But the "reasonable" test allows for some flexibility—a salary may be higher or lower within a reasonable range. *If the business is a…*

•**Regular corporation,** a higher salary may be desired to reduce the double taxation of corporate profits. Salary is deductible by the business and reduces taxable profit.

Profits, on the other hand, are taxed twice—first to the corporation and then when paid out as dividends to shareholders. Moreover, the corporation cannot deduct dividends as it can deduct salary.

Good news: The reduced top tax rate on dividends for individuals—15%—reduces the cost of this double taxation, although it does still exist.

Trap: If an owner/executive of a profitable regular corporation takes a salary that is too large, without taking any dividends, the IRS may recategorize some of the salary as a dividend—costing the company its deduction for the amount.

Safety: Take a salary at the high end of the reasonable range and also a reasonable amount of dividends in light of the business's profitability. A dividend payment record helps protect against any recategorization for taking excessive salary compensation.

•**S corporation,** a lower salary may be desired. This is because salary is subject to payroll tax for Social Security (12.4% on up to $94,200 in 2006) and Medicare (2.9% of all salary).

There is no problem with double taxation of profits with an S corporation because all of its profits are taxed to its owners when earned as regular income—only once.

Danger: If an audit finds that a salary taken is unreasonably low to avoid payroll taxes, the IRS may increase it for tax purposes.

What to do: Check with an expert about the range of reasonable salaries in your industry for the work done. Take a salary within that range.

FAMILY ON PAYROLL

Whenever a business is family-owned, having children and other low-tax-bracket family members on the payroll can reduce the tax rate paid by the family on income earned by the business. The business can deduct the salaries at its own high tax rate, while the salaries are taxed at a lower rate (or the tax is zero) to the child or other family member. *Other considerations…*

● **Salary or earned income of children is not subject to the so-called "kiddie tax"** that applies to investment income of children under age 14.

● **Wages paid by a parent's unincorporated business to children under age 18 are not subject to either Social Security or Medicare tax.**

Example: In 2006, a single person can earn income of up to $5,150 offset by the standard deduction—so it is tax free—and take income up to $7,550 taxed at only 10%. And, additional income of up to $30,650 is taxed at only 15%.

Moreover, earned income enables a person to fund a Roth IRA, which can provide totally tax-free returns for decades into the future. Just a few years of these contributions can provide your child a great head start on financial security. In 2006, a person can place up to $4,000 in a Roth IRA if he/she has earned income equal to or greater than $4,000.

So by paying salary to your child, income that might have been taxed at 30% or more to the business or its owner can be turned into tax-free or low-tax-rate income and—if used to fund a Roth IRA—generate a stream of tax-free investment gains into the future.

However, the amount of your child's salary must be reasonable for work he actually does. So be sure that the amount and the nature of the work is documented to support the salary.

RETIREMENT PLANS

Qualified retirement plans are legal tax shelters that can enable business owners to deduct a significant part of their income (subject to certain limitations) and receive tax-favored investment returns on it.

Contribution limits are increased in 2006—for instance, 401(k)s can receive elective deferrals of as much as $15,000 (up from $14,000 in 2005 and subject to certain limitations) plus an additional $5,000 for persons age 50 or over.

Permitted contributions for the other kinds of plans are higher as well. New plan options are available—such as the "solo" 401(k) for sole proprietors. The deduction limits of the solo 401(k) are the same as regular qualified plans at both the individual and entity levels.

The entity level deduction limit for the solo 401(k) is effectively 20% of net earnings from self-employment.

Rules and options are complex, so consult with an expert about setting up the best plan for your situation.

REIMBURSEMENTS

Small-business owners frequently are careless with their paperwork and bookkeeping for expenses—with the result that they needlessly leave money on the table. *Common mistakes…*

● **Owner/employees of corporations pay expenses for their corporations out-of-pocket,** only to discover that they can't personally deduct expenses that should have been paid by the company.

● **Owner/employees take a general expense allowance.**

Snag: An unaccountable allowance is taxable income subject to employment taxes as well as income tax. Expenses paid with it are deductible personally, but only as employee business expenses as miscellaneous itemized deductions. These are permitted only to the extent that they exceed 2% of adjusted gross income—and are not allowed at all if the alternative minimum tax applies. So deductions are reduced or not allowed at all.

● **Owners simply don't pay attention to record keeping,** so deductible expenses aren't recorded and deductions are lost.

What to do: Set up a formal reimbursement program as an "accountable plan" that meets IRS expense documentation rules.

The expense reimbursements received by the business owner then are totally tax free and are fully deductible by the company, maximizing tax savings.

In addition, the system set up to manage reimbursements will ensure that all deductible expenses are identified and none are carelessly thrown away.

FRINGE BENEFITS

Examine with your firm's tax adviser the full range of tax-free and tax-favored fringe benefits that may be available through the business. These benefits will vary with the nature of the business and its form of organization.

Example: The owner/employees of regular corporations can participate in a full range of employee benefits, such as health plans, cafeteria plans, transit checks and employer-provided free parking. In contrast, owners of partnerships, LLCs and sole proprietorships are not employees, so their benefits are subject to more restrictions. Owners of more than 2% of the stock of an S corporation are subject to benefit limitations as well.

Consult a tax professional about the details of your situation.

Useful: IRS Publication 15-B, *Employer's Tax Guide to Fringe Benefits,* which lists a large number of fringe benefits as well as the rules that apply to them.

Partnership and LLC Loopholes

Edward Mendlowitz, CPA, shareholder in the CPA firm, WithumSmith+Brown, 120 Albany St., New Brunswick, NJ 08901. He is also the author of *Introducing Tax Clients to Additional Services* (American Institute of CPAs).

If your business is organized as a partnership or as a limited liability company (LLC), the tax rules are different than those for a corporation.

Partnerships and LLCs are treated the same for tax purposes even though their legal aspects are different. Both report their activities using Form 1065, *US Return of Partnership Income,* except for one-person LLCs, which use Schedule C of the proprietor's individual tax return if their owner is an individual. Owners of a partnership are called partners while owners of LLCs are called members. *Tax preparation loopholes you should know about...*

Loophole: Partnerships and LLCs pay no income tax. This is true even though they are required to file federal and state income tax returns reporting their business income. So they avoid the double tax that regular corporations face when income is first taxed to the corporation, and then again to shareholders when distributed to them.

Income or loss from a partnership or an LLC is reported on its partners' or members' individual returns, combined with their other income. In general, the owners are taxed in proportion to their ownership interests, receiving annual profit and loss information on Schedule K-1 (Form 1065), *Partner's Share of Income, Credits, Deductions, etc.*

Loophole: Guaranteed payments, analogous to salary, to partners or members are treated as an expense and are thus deductible from the gross income of the entity. These type of payments are also subject to the self-employment tax, even though the activity, such as owning rental property, might not be.

Loophole: There is no withholding on income received from the business. Partners and members must file estimated taxes to cover the income passing through to them.

Also, even though the K-1 is issued as of the last day of the year, income is considered to have been earned ratably during the entire year, requiring proper quarterly payments. Only if the income is bunched up at the end of the partnership's or LLC's year can the annualization exception be used.

Loophole: Allocation of partnership and LLC profits and losses among owners can easily be changed. Once the initial allocation is set up in the agreement, it can then simply be changed year to year—in light of the changing circumstances of the business and its owners—by reflecting so on the tax return and modifying the partnership or LLC agreement as applicable.

Loophole: Members of partnerships and LLCs can deduct business losses exceeding their own investment in the entity. Certain partnership and LLC recourse debt (debt for which you are personally liable) can be considered part of a partner's or member's tax basis, thus permitting deductions for losses that exceed the cash investments.

Loophole: Unreimbursable partnership and LLC expenses paid by a partner or a member can be aggregated and deducted on the partnership section of Schedule E for Form

1040—*Supplemental Income and Loss (from rental real estate, royalties, partnerships, S corporations, estates, trusts, REMICs, etc.).* This provides a total deduction of the expenses, not limited to only the excess of the amounts exceeding 2% of adjusted gross income.

***Loophole:* State operations are segregated.** Where separate partnerships or LLCs have been set up in each state in which a parent entity is doing business, only that state's transactions need be reported to the state tax agency—not the entire business's activities.

Caution: Some states tax LLCs differently from partnerships. Because each state has its own rules governing taxation of LLCs, work with an adviser familiar with your state's rules.

***Loophole:* Joint ventures can file as partnerships after the fact.** If there is no formal organizational agreement to the contrary, and the venture actually acted like a partnership, the decision to file as one can be made after the end of the year when filing the return.

Caution: LLCs cannot be set up retroactively since they must first be registered with the state they are organized in.

***Loophole:* Purchased or inherited partnership or LLC interests can have the basis stepped up.** Increased depreciation deductions can be taken when basis is stepped up to purchase price or value at inheritance.

This can significantly reduce taxable income reported from the entity. In such a case, the entity makes a special election under Section 754 of the Tax Code. The entity will report the extra deductions for that partner or member on the owner's K-1.

Note: Foreign partners or members will have recourse debt figured differently than nonrecourse debt (and in a more costly way tax-wise) for US estate tax purposes.

Twelve Easy High-Tech Ways to Simplify Business Tax Chores

Barbara Weltman, an attorney based in Millwood, NY, *www.barbaraweltman.com.* She is author of *J.K. Lasser's 1001 Deductions and Tax Breaks* (Wiley).

Time is money to small-business owners, so tax-related time-savers put money in your pocket and boost your bottom line. *Some tech-based processes you can use to operate more efficiently and save money...*

ACCOUNTING

***Chore:* Keeping payroll records.** Use Web-based systems to upload employee time records to your accountant or a payroll company (such as ADP or PayChex). The accountant or payroll company processes all the information—then checks can be printed in the accountant/payroll company's office or the small business's office. This process relieves the small business of the in-house expense for payroll processing, which saves money even with the outsourcing cost.

***Chore:* Distributing payroll checks.** Set up direct deposit with your bank or with your employees' banks. This eliminates the time and cost of generating paper checks, and employees appreciate the convenience of not having to make a trip to the bank. And you may save bank fees—ask your bank about incentives for employees who set up accounts with them.

Caution: You cannot require an employee to accept direct deposit and must make paper checks available to those who prefer them.

***Chore:* General ledger.** Like payroll, company data on income and expenses can be transmitted to your accountant, who can maintain general-ledger account information. You save on the cost of an in-house bookkeeper—you only need someone to input income and expenses in your accounting software.

RECORD KEEPING

***Chore:* Substantiating travel and entertainment expenses.** Employees usually are required to document their travel and entertainment (T&E) costs to the company. Doing so is mandatory if the company maintains an accountable plan so that employees are not taxed on company advances or reimbursements of T&E costs. Substantiation can be simplified if employees are issued company credit cards that can be used only for company-related T&E. The statements generated by the credit card company act as substantiation for the T&E expenses.

Chore: **Administering HRA/FSA disbursements.** If the business has a health reimbursement arrangement (HRA) or flexible spending arrangement (FSA) for medical costs, employees must substantiate their medical payments to the company to obtain reimbursement. Substantiation and reimbursement can be collapsed into one step if a company issues employees credit or debit cards that can only be used to pay medical expenses. The employees do not have to seek reimbursement—they're automatically covered for their expenses because the credit or debit card has a spending limit equal to the HRA/FSA reimbursement limit. The statements generated by the credit card company act as substantiation for the medical expenses.

Important: Businesses that rely on these cards for these expenses must review monthly statements from the credit card company to make sure there is no employee abuse (e.g., charging nonmedical expenses).

COMMUNICATION

Chore: **Getting your information to the accountant.** Income and expense information can be easily sent on-line. This will enable the accountant not only to prepare returns, but also to monitor activities throughout the year and advise accordingly. The accountant does not have to travel to the business as often, saving you money.

Example: In viewing information on-line, your accountant notices that the expenses for inventory are growing at an alarming rate compared with sales and can recommend cutting back on inventory.

Receipts and other paper documents can be scanned and sent on-line to the accountant.

An accountant can more easily e-mail prepared documents to the business if the documents are required by a third party (e.g., a bank, if the business is applying for a loan).

Chore: **Getting information from the IRS.** The IRS's new Transcript Delivery System (TDS) enables practitioners to obtain tax return transcripts and account information of their clients in minutes over a secure line, saving clients the time of finding the information in their files.

Note: Only tax practitioners who have e-filed 100 or more returns can use TDS.

TAX PAYMENTS

Chore: **Paying taxes.** Businesses can pay their federal taxes electronically using the Electronic Federal Tax Payment System (EFTPS) online. Payments can be scheduled up to 120 days in advance, one convenience that is especially appreciated by business owners who travel a lot and may not be at the office when a tax payment is due.

Note: Tax payments can be charged to any major credit card, but this is a more costly alternative. While the IRS does not assess a fee for credit card payments, credit card companies charge a convenience fee of 2.5% of the tax charged on the card.

ELECTRONIC FORMS

Chore: **Furnishing W-2 forms to every employee.** Instead of creating paper forms, generate electronic forms that can be e-mailed to employees. Payroll information already in a business's computer system can be easily accessed to create W-2 forms.

Chore: **Preparing 1099-MISC forms for each independent contractor.** Computer accounting systems enable sorting of disbursement information to make the preparation of these forms much easier.

Note: If a business wants to issue electronic 1099s, it needs permission from the contractors.

Bonus: If you file 1099s electronically, you receive an additional month to file them with the IRS (e.g., a deadline of March 31, 2007, instead of February 28, 2007).

Chore: **Receiving the 1099s from investments.** You can access Form 1099 information on-line from your brokerage firm and transmit the information to your tax preparer. Contact your broker for instructions.

Bonus: If corrected 1099s are issued, as happened dramatically in 2003 because of errors made by investment firms, the information is available more quickly to preparers.

FILING RETURNS

Chore: Filing quarterly and annual returns. *E-filing is an easy way for businesses to meet their many filing obligations...*

● **Income tax returns**—all types of business returns (including corporate returns) can now be filed electronically with the IRS.

● **Payroll tax returns**—Form 941, *Employer's Quarterly Federal Tax Return,* as well as Form 940, *Employer's Annual Federal Unemployment (FUTA) Tax Return,* can be filed electronically with the IRS. W-2 information can be filed electronically with the Social Security Administration (for information about W-2 on-line, visit *www.ssa.gov/bso/bsowelcome.htm*).

● **The employee benefit plan return**—the annual information return for qualified retirement plans and certain other employee benefit plans—can be e-filed with the Department of Labor's Employee Benefits Security Administration. For information about EFAST, the ERISA filing acceptance system, visit *www.efast.dol.gov.*

Note: Check on state opportunities to file electronically for sales tax returns and other state forms.

How to Turn Your Company's Operating Loss into a Big Windfall

Dennis R. Kroner, a financial adviser at UBS Financial Services, Inc., 1 N. Wacker Dr., Chicago 60606. He teaches financial planning as an adjunct faculty member at DePaul University. Mr. Kroner chaired the AICPA committee that was responsible for drafting as well as administering the PFS (personal finance specialist) exam.

Net operating losses (NOLs) and Roth IRAs—you wouldn't think they would go together, but they do. Here's how the combination can work for you.

Business may not always be great. Some years, your company might report a loss—and you might be able to take that loss on your personal tax return (if your business is other than a C corporation).

Trap: Such a loss may cause you to lose valuable tax deductions (see below).

Strategy: Make lemonade from lemon years. Convert all or part of a traditional IRA into a Roth IRA. The conversion will create enough income to absorb the NOL for the current year.

GAINING FROM LOSS

In some situations, you may report a net operating loss on your personal tax return.

Most common: Your loss from your business in a given year may exceed your other income. If you run your company as a sole proprietorship, S corporation, partnership or limited liability company, a business loss may flow through to your personal tax return and create an NOL.

Example: You are a 50% owner of an S corporation that reports a $300,000 loss this year. Your share of this loss is $150,000.

To take the entire $150,000 deduction, you need to have at least $150,000 worth of basis in the corporation. Generally, you can get basis from equity investment in and personal loans to the corporate entity.

If you can deduct the loss, and the loss exceeds your other income, you have an NOL.

Example: Your income from wages, investments, rents, etc., adds up to $90,000. With a $150,000 loss from your S corporation, you have a $60,000 NOL.

An NOL generally can be carried back two years or carried forward for 20 years, offsetting taxable income.

ROTH IRA REVELATIONS

A traditional IRA may be converted to a Roth IRA, in whole or in part. Such a conversion will trigger tax on the income that was tax deferred in the traditional IRA.

Example: You have $125,000 in your traditional IRA, all of which resulted from deductible contributions. If you convert, say, $80,000 of this IRA to a Roth IRA, you'll pick up an extra $80,000 in taxable income that year.

Why would you accelerate taxable income? Because, in the NOL situation described above, the income created will be taxed at low rates or be tax free, rather than at higher tax rates in future years.

Example: Converting $80,000 worth of IRA money to a Roth IRA will offset a $60,000 NOL, leaving only $20,000 in taxable income. This form of income will be taxed at only 10% and 15%.

Long-term benefit: Five years after a conversion, as long as you're at least 59½ years old, all withdrawals from your Roth IRA will be tax free.

LOOPHOLES

Roth IRA conversions are not permitted in the years when your modified adjusted gross income (MAGI), exclusive of the amount being converted and any required minimum distributions, exceeds $100,000. This limit keeps many people from converting a traditional IRA to a Roth IRA.

However, if you have an NOL for the year, your MAGI may very well be under the limit of $100,000. Therefore, you can convert a traditional IRA to a Roth IRA.

Loophole: A low MAGI likely will mean you're in a low tax bracket. Thus, you may have a relatively low tax bill when you execute a Roth IRA conversion.

Alternatively, an NOL that you're carrying forward from a prior year may reduce your MAGI below the $100,000 mark and permit a Roth IRA conversion.

Loophole: Consider tapping a home-equity line of credit to pay any tax on your Roth IRA conversion. On such debt up to $100,000, the interest will be deductible.

The Tax Code has no prohibition against deducting the home-equity loan interest on debt used to fund a Roth IRA conversion. Having a Roth can result in tax-free income.

DISAPPEARING DEDUCTIONS

A Roth IRA conversion, moreover, may help to keep you from wasting deductions in an NOL year.

Trap: When calculating your NOL for a carryback or carryforward, an excess of "nonbusiness" deductions over "nonbusiness" income can't be counted.

Therefore, if nonbusiness deductions exceed your nonbusiness income, those deductions may be permanently lost.

Example: Your income from wages this year is $80,000, plus $10,000 in investment income, for a total of $90,000.

You have a deductible S corporation loss of $150,000 as well as $50,000 worth of expenses for mortgage interest and real estate taxes, for a total of $200,000.

With $200,000 worth of deductions and $90,000 in income, you might think your NOL would be $110,000.

However, the excess of nonbusiness deductions ($50,000) above the nonbusiness income ($10,000) can't be counted toward your NOL.

Thus, your NOL is reduced by $40,000, to $70,000, and you wind up permanently losing $40,000 worth of deductible outlays.

ROTH IRA TO THE RESCUE

The above problem may be alleviated by converting some money held in a traditional IRA to a Roth IRA.

Example: The facts are the same as above, except that you convert $40,000 worth of your traditional IRA to a Roth IRA.

Although the Tax Code is not clear on this issue, it seems apparent that a Roth IRA conversion would generate nonbusiness income.

The Roth IRA conversion adds $40,000 to your nonbusiness income so that your gross income becomes $130,000, not $90,000. Your $200,000 in deductions remains the same, so you still have a $70,000 NOL—$200,000 minus $130,000.

Your nonbusiness deductions ($50,000 in this example) now do not exceed your nonbusiness income ($50,000, counting the Roth IRA conversion and your investment income).

Therefore, no adjustment to your NOL is required.

You've converted $40,000 worth of your traditional IRA to a Roth IRA yet you have incurred no additional tax and you have not reduced your NOL. So, this conversion is tax free.

You've taken the $40,000 in itemized deductions you would not have been able to use and managed to use it to offset the tax you would otherwise owe on a conversion to a Roth IRA.

FINAL THOUGHTS

As the above example indicates, implementing a Roth IRA conversion can be a savvy tax move if you have a current NOL or one that you have carried forward from previous years.

Second chance: What's more, the Tax Code permits you to "recharacterize" (reverse) a Roth IRA conversion until October 15 of the succeeding tax year.

Therefore, you have time to look back and undo the conversion if subsequent events indicate that you didn't make the best choice.

Caution: As is the case with many sophisticated tax-planning maneuvers, the alternative minimum tax (AMT) needs to be considered. Check with your tax adviser before you decide to convert a traditional IRA to a Roth IRA.

Big Tax Saving Ideas for Small-Business Owners

Martin S. Kaplan, CPA, 11 Penn Plaza in New York City, *www.irsmaven.com.* He is a frequent speaker at insurance, banking and financial planning seminars and is the author of *What the IRS Doesn't Want You to Know* (Wiley).

Small-business owners can't afford to miss out on any tax-minimizing planning or filing strategies. *Here are some of the very best of them...*

●**Get the IRS audit technique guide for your kind of business.** This way you can learn what an IRS auditor would be looking for in an audit and use the information to make your tax return audit-proof. Log on to *www.irs.gov,* then click on "Businesses" and then on "Market Segment Understandings."

●**Maximize all business retirement plan contributions.** One of the best benefits of having your own business is that you can shelter much of your income from it in a tax-favored retirement plan. You can do this even if your business is only a sideline and you also participate in an employer's plan.

Deductible contributions to your own retirement plan can be made as late as the extended due date of your tax return even if you file your return earlier.

Tactic: Extend your return to October 15, then file it immediately—deducting your plan contribution to increase your tax refund. Then, when you receive the refund (before the extension expires), use it to help fund the retirement plan contribution.

If you don't have a business retirement plan yet, you can open a simplified employee pension (SEP) plan anytime before the due date of your 2006 tax return to get a deduction for contributions made for 2006. Consult a retirement plan specialist for details.

●**Deduct up to $108,000 of any business equipment acquired during 2006.** The cost can be deducted immediately, rather than over a period of years through depreciation, by using a "Section 179 election."

If your business acquired more than the specified limit of equipment during the year, select the items for which the election will provide the most benefit and apply it to them.

Note: If you bought a sport-utility vehicle (SUV) weighing more than 6,000 pounds for business use, its price can be deducted using the election, but the election write-off is limited to $25,000 of the SUV's cost.

●**Maximize Schedule C deductions.** Business owners can claim a 100% deduction for expenses that are subject to limitations elsewhere on the return.

Examples: Legal fees, tax planning fees and job hunting expenses normally are claimed among miscellaneous deductions, the total of which is deductible only to the extent it exceeds 2% of adjusted gross income.

But, to the extent they are legitimately related to your own business, even if it is only a sideline, they are 100% deductible on Schedule C.

Other deductions that can escape limitations that otherwise apply include those for use of computers, phones and electronic equipment, and travel, work-related publications and auto expenses.

● **Deduct business start-up costs incurred after October 22, 2004.** Business start-up expenses—those incurred before a new business actually starts operating—before this date had to be deducted over 60 months. But now up to $5,000 of start-up costs incurred after October 22, 2004, are currently deductible, with the balance deducted over 180 months.

● **Document profit motive if your business runs at a loss.** Business losses can be deducted against ordinary income, such as salary and investment income. This means that a business can effectively be a legal tax shelter if it runs at a loss, as many do, during a start-up or growth stage.

But if a business incurs sustained losses, the IRS may suspect it is being run without a profit motive just for the tax benefits—especially if the business is a sideline or run from one's home. Then the IRS will challenge the loss deductions.

Important: Document your business's profit motive. Create a business plan that explains current losses. Also consult with experts, change operations to improve results, keep full business records—and keep a diary or other record that illustrates how you have taken all these steps. As long as you can document a real profit motive, your loss deductions will be safe.

Two-edged tactic: You can file IRS Form 5213, *Election to Postpone Determination as to Whether the Presumption Applies That an Activity Is Engaged in for Profit,* to save a new business's profit motive from being challenged by the IRS for five years. In the meantime, loss deductions are safe.

Downside: This puts the IRS on notice that you are running a loss-making business and it increases the odds that it will draw IRS attention after the five years are up. If it's then still running at a loss, you could lose five years' worth of back deductions and get a big back tax bill.

In contrast, if you don't file the form, the IRS may never look at your business at all, in light of today's low audit rates.

So unless you are sure your business will have a profitable record in five years, it's probably smart to not file the form and just document its profit motive by standard means.

● **Check inventory calculations.** If your business has inventory, look over your ending inventory schedule and inventory valuations with an expert. Rules are complex, and this is an audit target area.

● **Report all the 1099s.** If you are a self-employed business proprietor providing services as an independent contractor, you may well have received 1099s reporting payments to you from clients and customers.

Double-check them all and report them all on your return—even if there is a mistake. IRS computers will be looking for these figures and will flag your return for an extra look if not found. If a 1099 is erroneous, report it on your return, but make a correcting adjustment with a note of explanation to minimize audit risk.

More from Martin Kaplan, CPA...

Protect Small-Business Deductions That the IRS Looks At Every Time

Those tax deductions that straddle the border between business and personal pose the greatest audit risk for small-business owners.

Examples: Travel, meals and entertainment, driving, home offices, insurance, phone expenses.

These are all examined by the IRS on *every audit,* since it always suspects that business owners are deducting personal costs.

TURNABOUT

The key to protecting these deductions is to look at special record-keeping requirements as an opportunity for making your return audit-proof—even for items well into the gray area between business and personal.

When the Tax Code or IRS rules set specific paperwork requirements for a deduction and you meet them, an IRS auditor normally has little incentive to inquire any further—and a real incentive not to, since auditors are under increasing pressure to close cases.

Example: If your records for meal deductions show, as required, who you entertained, when, where, the business purpose and the amount, an auditor is very unlikely to insist on verification that you really discussed business at the meal. It would not be cost-effective to do so and would add to the backlog of cases, so you can expect the deduction to be allowed —virtually audit-proof.

Moreover, there's a carryover benefit when the auditor moves on to items that are less well documented. If an auditor starts by examining records that are full and complete, then moves on to records for another item that are less than perfect but still professionally presented, he/she is likely to view the latter in a manner that still leads to a satisfactory audit result. *Reasons...*

●**The overall quality of the records** indicates that you aren't trying to "get away with something," so suspicions are not aroused.

●**High-quality records** will increase your chance of winning at IRS Appeals or in the small case division of Tax Court, should you go there. The auditor knows it and so has a practical reason to give enough to avoid an appeal.

●**When you present tax records in good order,** you are being considerate, helping the auditor do his job—and it is human nature for consideration to be returned.

Strategy: If called for an audit, try to direct the auditor to your best-documented deductions first.

PITFALLS

Two easy ways to lose the audit-proofing benefit that good records can give to gray area deductions…

●**The "pig rule."** The courts know that they often approve business deductions for items that are really of a personal nature when all of the required legal forms are followed—but the courts also warn what happens when people try to push these rules too far. *As one Court of Appeals has stated…*

"Perhaps in recognition of human nature, the courts have been liberal in the cases of shareholder[s]…channeling particular types of personal transactions through corporations. They have even approved payment of personal living expenses…but there is a principle of too much; phrased colloquially, when a pig becomes a

hog it is slaughtered." [*Dolese,* CA-10, 605 F.2d 1146, 1154.]

Real-life examples of the "pig rule"…

●A professional deducted six personal telephone lines. That piqued the IRS auditor's interest, so he looked up the phone numbers—and found that most were those of the professional's relatives. The professional not only lost a deduction for one or two business lines he could easily have had, but had his entire return scrutinized.

●One consultant took deductions for multiple trips to distant cities that offset almost all her income. She had records for the trips—but the auditor asked why the trips hadn't produced any consulting income. She said she had been seeking jobs that she didn't get—but couldn't produce any evidence, such as "turndown" letters from prospective clients, to support her claim.

The auditor might have believed she took one such trip—but not that she had spent all her income on such trips. She lost her deductions.

●In other cases, people have deducted three meals a day, business driving costs for seven days a week and work expenses for 52 weeks a year.

But no matter how "complete" records are, an IRS auditor is going to have a hard time believing such deductions. They only invite questions about your honesty that good records are meant to prevent.

●**False records.** Another way to have "excellent" records become worthless is to show the IRS they are false.

Example: One client called me after giving the IRS meticulous records for his meal expenses in town for a period during which his travel records showed he was out of town.

Automobile records also often snag those who exaggerate driving deductions. The simplest way to deduct business driving expenses is the cents-per-mile method (44.5 cents during 2006), which I recommend because it is nearly audit proof with an adequate driving log.

But larger deductions may be available using the "actual cost" method that entails recording all costs of car ownership and allocating a portion to business driving.

Trap: People who produce driving diaries that exaggerate deductions claimed under this method often are tripped up by inconsistencies between their diaries and their auto maintenance records, which the IRS can examine if this method of deduction is used.

PROTECTING BIG DEDUCTIONS

You may be entitled to deductions that look very large to the IRS and serve as an audit red flag. In that case, you should still take them—but be prepared to show that your records are honest and that you are not an example of the "pig rule" in action.

Example: The standard home-office tax deduction is not by itself much of an audit red flag these days. Technical rules do apply to the deduction—such as that the office must be used exclusively for business—but auditors do not actually visit homes to see that they are being followed. Thus, if you genuinely use a home office as the principal place of conducting a business, you can expect reasonable deductions for it to pass without much problem.

One client of mine deducts 80% of his home as a home office—legitimately, as the home space holds his business inventory. But such a large deduction is asking for an audit—so it should be backed up with floor plans for the home and photographs that show how it is used, to stand up to an audit that may arise.

Prepare similar records in advance to prove the honesty of any other apparently "extraordinary" deduction that may be an audit red flag.

Good News for Small Businesses

It is becoming easier to get a business loan. Banks are in better financial shape than they were when the technology bubble burst in 2001. They will boost business loans now that mortgage refinancing has slowed and interest rates are rising. Consider community banks. They are more likely than large banks to have funds available to small businesses.

John Rutledge, PhD, chairman of Rutledge Institute for Capital & Growth and Rutledge Capital, both in Cos Cob, CT, www.rutledgecapital.com.

Audit-Proof Your Small-Business Tax Return

Stuart I. Nathanson, CPA, a partner specializing in small-business matters with ERE LLP, an accounting and advisory firm that provides financial statement assurance and tax and business consulting services to clients that range from closely held businesses to multinational companies, high-net-worth families and tax-exempt organizations, 440 Park Ave. S., New York City 10016.

There is no way to guarantee that your tax return will escape IRS scrutiny. But whether you operate your business as a sole proprietorship, limited liability company, or S or C corporation, there are steps you can take to sharply cut the risk of an audit.

RED FLAGS

The IRS definitely has identifiable audit targets. It will look more closely at certain issues than others and considers various positions that taxpayers take on their returns as invitations to an audit.

Best defense: Know all these audit targets well. And, take steps to cement your tax return position so that if you're questioned, you have nothing to fear. *Examples...*

●**Compensation.** Owners of S corporations who perform services for the business should be sure to take a reasonable salary. Owners often skip salary so they can avoid paying FICA taxes. This is something the IRS always looks for when it audits an S corporation return. A reasonable salary is based on the relevant facts and circumstances involved in a given situation. One consideration is to compare compensation paid to the amount the individual would have been paid by an unrelated company.

Owners of C corporations should not take more compensation than what they can justify as reasonable based on the nature and extent of the services they performed. C corporation owners often inflate their salaries to increase the corporate deductions for them. In an audit, the IRS will disallow compensation that is not reasonable.

There's no one rule for determining what's reasonable. Factors that can be used include what the organization would have to pay an outsider to perform the same work and what a hypothetical investor would permit as compensation so that he/she can obtain a return on his investment.

●**Worker classification.** The IRS is always on the lookout for misclassification of workers as independent contractors rather than employees. If the workers are independent contractors, the company avoids paying employment taxes. But you must treat workers as employees rather than independent contractors if you exercise control over how, when and where they perform their duties.

Important: Treat all workers doing the same job in the same manner, as either employees or contractors. If you treat some as employees and others as contractors, the IRS can say they're all employees and assess employment taxes.

●**Travel and entertainment (T&E) expenses.** Even though you can now deduct only half of your meals and entertainment costs, the IRS still looks closely at these deductions. The auditor wants to know if you've written off personal expenditures as business expenses.

To convince an auditor that your T&E deductions are legitimate, have all necessary substantiation. For details on required substantiation of these expenses, review IRS Publication 463, *Travel, Entertainment, Gift, and Car Expenses,* at *www.irs.gov* or call 800-829-3676.

What's not a red flag: Over the years, some steps that taxpayers take have become known as red flags when, in fact, there is little evidence to support this view.

Example: Don't hesitate to request a filing extension if you want one. It's not likely to increase the chances that your tax return will be audited.

You can obtain an automatic extension without giving any reason for needing added time to file the return.

MISTAKES TO AVOID

Each year, the IRS identifies a number of common errors found on taxpayer returns. *If you avoid these mistakes, you'll minimize IRS attention to your return...*

●**Not completing the return.** Failure to answer questions or provide information on the return can lead to further IRS inquiry and delay the processing of a refund.

Example: Take care to include the correct business code number, using the North American Industry Classification System, on the return. In one recent case, the IRS determined that a business was in fact a personal service corporation because the wrong code number was put on the return and, as such, assessed an additional tax.

●**Failing to report income.** The IRS is always on the hunt for unreported income. There are numerous audit manuals for agents to use in determining whether income has been omitted. The audit manuals under the IRS Market Segment Specialization Program are geared toward specific industries. For details, go to *www.irs.gov/ businesses/small/article/0,,id=108149,00.html.*

●**Taking positions that don't make sense.** Be sure to keep expenses in line with your type of business. A company may deduct the cost of four cars, for instance. If there are several salespeople, this may be reasonable. But for a retail establishment that does not make deliveries, the deduction may be excessive and the return may be flagged for audit. Similarly, what may be reasonable meal expenses for someone in sales would not be reasonable for a tradesperson.

●**Failing to capitalize certain costs.** Businesses want to deduct payments up-front, but the tax law requires certain expenses to be capitalized and written off over time. Claiming deductions for items that should be capitalized is a common problem and can lead to an audit.

Suggestion: Explore with your adviser the special options to write off costs up-front that might otherwise have to be capitalized.

Example: Costs relating to environmental remediation.

●**Creating problems on state tax returns.** Many states have tax rules that differ from federal law, and the failure to observe these differences may lead to an audit on the state level. Be sure that state tax returns account for differences in state tax rules.

WORK WITH ACCOUNTANTS

Understand the limits of what accountants can and cannot do for you. Some business owners may want to be aggressive in their filing positions, but accountants have a professional responsibility to follow the tax rules. They risk preparer penalties if they flout these rules.

Do not ignore any IRS inquiries regarding a return, however trivial they may seem. Inform your accountant immediately of the IRS notice and be sure to respond promptly.

Caution: Some accounting firms advertise themselves as providing "audit-proof" services. They may indeed pay the IRS penalties that result from positions taken on a tax return, but they can't protect you from being selected by the IRS for a tax audit, nor will they cover the tax or any interest you may owe as a result of the audit.

How to Fight Age Discrimination

Alan L. Sklover, partner at Sklover & Associates, LLC, a New York City firm that specializes in employment law for executives, *www.executivelaw.com*. He's also the author of *Fired, Downsized, or Laid Off: What Your Employer Doesn't Want You to Know About How to Fight Back* (Henry Holt).

While the country has made a lot of progress in combating discrimination, the careers of numerous workers still are hurt by age bias.

The federal *Age Discrimination in Employment Act* (ADEA) defines age discrimination as putting an employee or job seeker at a disadvantage because he/she is over age 40.

In practice, vulnerability to age discrimination increases when an employee reaches the age of 50 and peaks between ages 56 and 60. This is primarily because older employees are expensive to keep on the payroll due to their higher salaries, medical costs and pension benefits.

Regardless of the motive, refusing to hire or promote someone based on his age is illegal except in the very few instances in which the jobs are legitimately age-related.

Example: A movie role that requires an actor in his 20s.

ARE YOU A VICTIM?

Watch for signs of age discrimination...

●**Your boss asks when you're planning to retire.** This may arise out of a benign interest, but it also could be a discriminatory effort to encourage you to retire.

●**A supervisor questions your comfort with technology.** This inquiry could be the result of problems you had with technology...or it could be a reflection of the stereotypical view that older employees are not comfortable with computers.

●**You are not invited to participate in the company sporting events,** such as a weekend football game. This could be a consequence of your past reluctance to play. It also could be a subtle sign of bias—that you're considered too old for sports.

●**The organization passes you over for opportunities that are professionally challenging or long-term in nature,** such as a transfer to a start-up branch.

●**Colleagues make wisecracks regarding your age.** Don't be paranoid about an isolated remark. After the second slight, however, it's wise to inform your boss or someone in the human resources department.

●**Performance reviews suddenly become negative.** Be especially wary if this happens just as you're about to become vested in the company pension plan or eligible for lifetime medical coverage.

TAKING ACTION

Whenever possible, give your company an opportunity to rectify the discrimination. Legal action is a last resort. It's expensive and time-consuming—and there's no guarantee that you will win.

Steps to take...

●**Keep a record of incidents that indicate discrimination.** If a colleague questions your ability to adapt to new technology, for example, write down what he said...when he said it... and who else was present at the time. If possible, get him to write his comments in a memo or an e-mail to you, your boss or a human resources representative.

●**Write a letter to the CEO of the company.** Don't threaten legal action at this point or even mention the word "law" or "lawyer." Instead, say that you believe you have been denied opportunities or other job benefits because of your age.

The CEO usually will refer the matter to the head of the human resources or legal department. When he gets a communication from the CEO, he usually responds much faster than if you had contacted him on your own.

Example: Margaret, a securities analyst, was age 56 when she lost a promotion to a 36-year-old colleague. When Margaret asked for an explanation, the company responded that it wanted a "fresh" face who was familiar with "newer" methods of analysis.

Result: When Margaret sent a memo to the CEO challenging that assessment and citing age discrimination, the company compromised by creating a "codirectorship" for the two analysts.

●**Write a second letter if the company does not answer you within one month.** Respectfully state that you would like to work out the problem without a lawyer. But, at this point, it makes sense to consult an attorney who is knowledgeable about age-discrimination law. (Check with your local bar association.) He can guide you in your discussions.

If you're in a major city, expect to pay about $350 for a legal consultation. Elsewhere, the fee is about $150.

●**Have your attorney contact the company.** If after two letters your firm still fails to correct the bias, ask your attorney to write to the CEO on your behalf.

Example: Steve, 62, was the only software salesman in his company over age 30. His colleagues called him "Grandpa" and kidded him about Viagra. And, when the economy turned down three years ago, Steve was laid off despite having the second-highest sales performance. He tried to negotiate with the firm on his own. When that did not work, he had his attorney write a letter.

Result: The firm added a three-year credit to his pension calculation.

In the unusual event that you take legal action against an employer, most attorneys will agree to a contingency fee, a portion of the monetary damages that you collect. While every case is different, you could receive up to two years of compensation, sometimes even more, and possibly be reinstated in your job.

Job Hunting Advice For Seniors

Jerry Weinger, chairman and chief executive officer of Bernard Haldane Associates located in New York City, the nation's oldest and largest career-management firm, *www.job-hunting.com.* Founded in 1947, the company operates more than 100 offices in the US, Canada, Australia and the United Kingdom.

Job seekers who are age 55 and older face an array of special challenges to landing a job, from negative attitudes toward older workers to blatant discrimination.

You can overcome these challenges and find satisfying employment if you take the right approach. *What to do…*

FIRST STEPS
●**Take responsibility for advancing your own career.** This is empowering and will give you strong motivation to keep searching for a new job.

●**Update your résumé.** Use current business language and style. Limit the résumé to two pages, omitting entry-level jobs that date back from the beginning of your career. Be sure to include key dates. And, don't try to conceal the length of your career—look at it as depth and experience.

●**Keep regular business hours.** View your search as a full-time job. Start every morning with a purpose to keep your search for employment on course.

●**Dress for success.** Dress professionally so that you'll feel more confident. Try for a contemporary look.

STRUCTURE YOUR SEARCH
●**Learn how to network.** Allocate your job-search time so that the majority is spent networking with potential hiring decision makers. Building your contact network is essential to

generating interviews—61% of jobs are acquired this way.

Strategy: Don't ask someone for a position. Instead, ask for help with your search. Ask for advice about your approach and goals, as well as help critiquing your résumé and checking salary ranges. Use your family, social and professional connections. *Other strategies...*

•When at networking events, wear a name tag that also displays your interests and expertise.

•Be assertive. Introduce yourself and help others make contacts. Limit talk time so you can work the room effectively to meet as many people as possible.

•Use social events as a networking opportunity. Introduce yourself to new people.

•Tell colleagues what you do and exchange contact information. Hand out business cards that list your name and contact information.

•Use notes, e-mail and phone calls to follow up with your new contacts. Don't lose the contact—stay in touch even if there are no immediate opportunities.

•**Use the Internet.** The Web is overstated as a job finder—relatively few people actually do get a job this way. But using the Internet effectively as part of a job search is vital. *Use it to...*

•Research companies and industry trends—information that you can use during a job interview. *Note:* Some companies post job openings on their Web site, although information may not be up to date.

•Find networking contacts on-line. Look for people you would like to meet at company Web sites, as well as through industry and trade associations. Then use networking to make a connection.

•Apply on-line. Make sure that your résumé is in a format that can be opened up and read by employers, such as *Microsoft Word* or ASCII. *Caution:* When using a résumé template, proofread and modify your words to best represent you. For example, delete unused portions of the template so that it does not look like you used a cookie-cutter résumé.

•Send a cover letter with your e-mailed résumé. Continue an e-mail dialogue with a potential employer—before and after an interview. *Examples:* Confirm the time and date of an interview...thank the interviewer for his/her time...

and follow up to find out if he would like to see you again.

•Visit Web sites that could be useful in your job hunt, such as *www.seniors4hire.org...www.seniorjobbank.org...www.fortyplus.org...*and *www.experienceworks.org.*

•**Update your technical skills.** Virtually every job now requires some computer skills. Become proficient in the basic computer and Internet skills. Include an e-mail address on your résumé to demonstrate that you are Internet savvy.

•**Brush up on your interviewing skills.** Turn your age into a positive by emphasizing your range and depth of experience and your ability to handle tough situations. Show your flexible attitude—you may have to report to a younger boss and your office may be a cubicle.

KEEP YOUR SPIRITS UP

•**Don't get frustrated.** Bolster your hope and optimism during job searches. Frustration becomes a downward spiral, blocking many unwary job hunters. Don't blame uncontrollable factors, such as your age. If you do, it's time to stop and reevaluate your approach. Don't focus on the reasons you can't get a job. Implement strategies that will get you a job.

•**Put a positive spin on your situation.** *Stay away from these negatives...*

•Don't say that you will do anything—this sounds desperate and the lack of focus makes employers wary.

•Don't tell interviewers that you're returning to work to recoup your stock market losses—your intentions sound temporary.

•Don't bad-mouth a former employer if you were laid off due to downsizing—the company you are interviewing with identifies with the former employer and not with you.

•**Seek professional help.** If you find yourself repeating unsuccessful tactics, meet with a professional career adviser who can provide objective input.

Always remember the immortal words of Winston Churchill: "Never give up. Never, never give up. Never, never, never give up!"

Make Sure Your Résumé Is Read

To get your résumé past spam filters, send it in plain text in the body of an e-mail, not as an attachment. Also, send it to one company at a time, and avoid words that spam filters search for, such as *free* and *cash*. Don't use colored backgrounds. And, don't use an e-mail address containing a lot of numbers—spam typically contains numbers in the subject line.

Recommendations from Job-Hunt.org, reported in The Wall Street Journal.

Job Interviewers' Sneaky Tricks

John McDorman, managing partner at Transition Consulting, a search and outplacement firm in Dallas.

Job hunters beware. Some questions that just seem like friendly small talk during or immediately after an interview might be part of the screening process.

If the interviewer notes your previous places of employment and says, "I can understand why you left. I've heard complaints about the upper management there," don't take the bait. Be either positive or neutral when asked about your relationship with previous employers, co-workers, neighbors, family or anyone else.

If an interviewer asks, "What do you do for fun?" avoid answers that center entirely on you. Rather than say, "I like to golf and watch baseball on television," say, "I like to golf with good friends and watch baseball games with my children."

The interviewer may be trying to determine if you enjoy socializing. The appropriate answers indicate that you are more likely to work well with others.

What to Reveal About A Health Problem at a Job Interview

Job hunters do not have to tell prospective employers about their health problems—and employers legally cannot ask about candidates' health. If you will need some accommodation, such as special computer equipment or time off during the work week for treatment, consider disclosing this or you risk not getting what you need. If you tell a prospective employer that you need an accommodation for a medical condition, he/she then can legally ask more about the condition to determine what modifications or services you might need. If you decide not to mention an illness and the employer later finds out about it and fires you because of it, you may have a legal claim against the employer.

Debra L. Raskin, an attorney specializing in employment and labor law on behalf of employees, and a partner in the firm of Vladeck, Waldman, Elias & Engelhard, PC, New York City.

Are You Being Paid a Fair Salary?

Find the value of your job by visiting free salary sites on the Web. Read job descriptions carefully—titles vary widely by company and industry, and not all sites use the same ones. Salary.com is fast and easy to use, with a large database. You can receive the free basic salary report or get more detailed personalized information starting at $29.95.* America's Career InfoNet (*www.acinet.org*) has salary ranges for over 500 occupations and can perform free detailed searches. The US Department of Labor/Bureau of Labor Statistics (*www.bls.gov/oco*) has detailed job descriptions and links to industry-specific organizations.

Money, Time-Life Bldg., Rockefeller Center, New York City 10020.

*Price subject to change.

20

Ultimate Security

How to Prevent Crime... Against Yourself, Your Home and Your Car

According to the FBI, one property crime occurs in the US every three seconds...and one robbery every 1.2 minutes.

However, you don't have to spend lots of money on security products to decrease the chance of being a crime victim. There's no need to turn your home into a fortress or to turn your automobile into a tank.

AT HOME

Make your house less of a target in the eyes of burglars...

•**Doors.** If given a choice, most criminals avoid a house with heavy doors and conspicuous dead bolt locks. The back door is especially important because it's the preferred entry point for many burglars.

Often overlooked: An open garage door gives crooks an opportunity to steal its contents and also, if there's no car, it signals that the house may be unoccupied. The heavier the garage door, the more effective it is as a crime deterrent.

Important: Never open a door unless you recognize the person on the other side. Make sure all doors have peepholes. Don't rely on an inside chain lock. They can easily be broken.

•**Lights.** When you go out at night, leave lights switched on in a way that makes burglars believe that someone is home. It's not enough, for instance, to just turn on the back porch light every time you leave the house. If you do, burglars can easily spot the pattern and realize that you're not at home.

Instead, vary the pattern, leaving the lights on in different rooms on different occasions— or consider using a timer.

Captain Robert L. Snow, commander of the homicide branch of the Indianapolis Police Department. He is also the author of *The Complete Guide to Personal and Home Safety: What You Need to Know* (Perseus).

Even better, leave the television on and put a bowl of snacks on the coffee table. If the TV isn't visible from a window, place a radio near the front door instead and turn it up just loud enough to lead someone outside the door to believe there are people in the house. Tune the radio to a talk station.

Leaving home before sunset and forgetting to turn on lights or the television can be an invitation to burglars, who often drive through neighborhoods to spot easy targets. When they see a dark house at 2 am, crooks have no idea if the occupants are inside because few people are awake at that hour. But when a residence is unlit at 7 pm, they see it as a possible target.

●**Mail.** If you receive mail that contains your Social Security number, install a mailbox with a lock or rent a post office box.

Reason: Social Security numbers are gold to identity thieves.

If you regularly receive checks by mail, ask the sender to deposit these electronically in your bank account instead. Many organizations, including the Social Security Administration, offer this service.

●**Neighborhood watch.** Join or organize a neighborhood watch program in which volunteer residents are trained to patrol their areas. Almost every police department believes that neighborhood watch programs are the single most effective deterrents to crime.

Most local police and sheriffs' departments and some state attorneys general offices can help set up watch programs.

Helpful: The Neighborhood Watch Program of the National Sheriffs' Association (703-836-7827, *www.usaonwatch.org*).

●**Item ID.** Engrave your initials on valuable items in your home, such as TVs and cameras, to help with recovery if they are stolen. Many police departments and neighborhood watch organizations will assist with engraving.

Bottom line: If your house is burglarized…

●Don't go inside. If you already are inside, leave immediately.

●Call 911.

●Resist the temptation to straighten up the house before police arrive. You don't want to destroy evidence.

ON FOOT

The most effective way to prevent getting robbed or mugged is also the most overlooked —being observant. In today's fast-paced world, many people are too preoccupied to even notice their surroundings.

Examples: Two men are just sitting in an idling car near an ATM, or a person you don't know is walking unusually close behind you. In both cases, the people may have innocent and legitimate reasons for their actions. On the other hand, they could be looking for a victim to rob. By noticing suspicious actions, you can reduce the chance that you'll be that victim.

Increase your awareness by thinking like a policeman. Just as a cop might do, take a close look at passersby as you walk along. Try to spot people whose actions seem unusual, like the person who walks close behind you.

When you spot a suspicious person or situation, move away.

For more protection…

●**Appear to be alert by looking oncoming pedestrians in the eye.** (Do not stare, however.) This simple measure will often work because purse snatchers and muggers look for unobservant victims. Looking people briefly in the eye gives you the appearance of awareness.

●**Carry your wallet in an inside pocket.** If you have a purse, keep it close to your body. Most people know this, but will let their guard down if they are in a "safe" area, such as an upscale shopping mall. But that is the type of area where crooks are likely to prey.

●**Consider carrying a whistle or other noisemaker.** It can be useful if you're physically unable to move very fast or if you walk in areas where a shout or scream is unlikely to be heard.

If you are a victim…

●**Shout as loudly you can.** Screaming or using a noisemaker is frequently effective because most crooks fear drawing attention to themselves.

●**Fight back.** Resist physically only if you are in imminent danger of serious injury. It's better to make lots of noise before things even progress to that point. Criminals know that they haven't done anything really criminal yet and will usually just flee before the noise you make brings a passerby or the police.

Myth: A course in self-defense will help you fight off an attacker.

Reality: Judo, karate and other techniques can bolster self-confidence, and that's important in helping you not look like a victim. But training in self-defense will rarely help an individual who is in a confrontation with a toughened streetwise attacker. Moreover, against an assailant with a weapon, it's often best not to offer any resistance.

BEHIND THE WHEEL

Just because your car hasn't been looted or stolen in, say, 30 years, don't assume it's safe. Criminals are more sophisticated and constantly searching for unsuspecting drivers and fresh areas in which to operate.

To protect yourself and your vehicle…

●**Stay in your car if you're rear-ended on the road.** Bumping the car ahead of him/her is often a crook's ploy to rob the driver of his money and car.

Instead of getting out, drive to the nearest gas station and signal to the other driver to follow you. Crooks will nearly always head in the other direction.

●**Don't rely solely on club-type devices to lock the steering wheel.** Clubs are effective against most small-time crooks, but sophisticated auto thieves can easily thwart them. For additional protection, install a reinforced steering collar.

Typical cost: Less than $25, available at specialty auto stores.

●**Use parking garages as a last resort.** Most of these are not nearly as safe as generally believed. Instead, park only in open lots or park on the street in well-lit and well-traveled areas. Those are the places criminals are less likely to be lurking.

Most Effective Deterrents To Home Burglars

Simon Hakim, PhD, economics professor, and George F. Rengert, PhD, professor of criminal justice, both at Temple University, Philadelphia, and Yochanan Shachmurove, PhD, professor of economics, The City College of The City University of New York and The University of Pennsylvania, Philadelphia.

In a recent study, the following factors were found to be most effective against risk of home burglary…

●**A burglar alarm is the factor that reduces risk of burglary the most.** It cuts the risk by about 12%.

●**Having neighbors pick up the mail and newspapers when you're not at home** is next most important, reducing risk by about 8%.

●**An automatic time switch and/or motion detector** to turn exterior lights on and off reduces risk about 7%.

●**Having a car in the driveway** when no one is home reduces risk about 4%.

●**Having a dog in the household,** installing deadbolt locks and having a radio or television timer to turn them on and off when nobody is home, each reduce risk by less than 3%.

Altogether, taking these steps can reduce risk of burglary by about one-third.

Wise Ways To Protect Yourself From Muggers, Carjackers, Pickpockets and More

Roger Shenkle, president of Survival Solutions, a security consulting firm, Box 476, Gambill, MD 21054. He is a former US Army counterintelligence agent.

There are more than a half million robberies in the US each year—and that figure doesn't include the 150,000 stolen purses and wallets…30,000 carjackings…and nearly 250,000 rapes, attempted rapes and sexual assaults. The numbers add up to almost one million victims.

How to protect yourself...

MUGGERS AND RAPISTS

Maintaining "situational awareness"—that is military-speak for paying careful attention to what's going on around you—is the best way to avoid street crime. People get so caught up in their own lives that they don't spot danger until it is too late.

Situational awareness is especially important in places *between* the places where you spend time—the deserted parking lot you traverse to get from the mall to your car...or the empty stairwell you descend to get from your office to the street.

When you leave a building and enter a parking lot or garage, look for lingerers. If you see anyone suspicious, go back and ask someone to walk you to your car. If no one is available, call the police and ask them to send a cruiser. It's usually a mistake to try to rush to your car because there often is not time to unlock the door, start the engine and drive away.

When you're in a potentially dangerous area, walk with a quick, confident gait. This makes you less appealing to criminals.

Caution: If the choice is between, say, walking confidently through a dangerous-looking group of teens or reversing course—it's best to reverse course.

Other high-risk situations...

• **Jogging.** Don't wear headphones unless you're certain your jogging route is safe. Headphones will reduce your ability to hear danger. When jogging on a sidewalk, go against the flow of traffic so a vehicle can't follow behind you. On city sidewalks, stay close to the road, not near buildings, to make it harder for a predator to jump you from a doorway. Always avoid secluded areas.

• **ATMs.** After dark or in crime-prone areas, go to an ATM that is located inside a store—not one that is visible from the street. Don't assume that an ATM is safe just because it is in a locked bank vestibule accessible only with an ATM card. Muggers carry stolen cards so that they can buzz themselves in and corner victims.

• **Unfamiliar locations.** If you don't know whether a certain part of town is safe, call the local police department's non-emergency number. They will tell you what neighborhoods you should avoid.

Important: If you're mugged, hand over your money immediately. Try to escape only if your instincts inform you that you might be attacked even if you do turn over your cash. If you do decide to flee, try a diversionary tactic. Throw some cash so that the mugger has to choose between pursuing you or retrieving the money. If your assailant tries to force you into a car in a public place, you're usually better off resisting right there rather than being driven to a more deserted site.

CARJACKERS

Most carjackings happen when vehicles are stopped at red lights or stop signs. If you're driving in a neighborhood that makes you uncomfortable, lock all your doors and roll up your windows. Also, turn off the radio to cut down on any distractions. When you come to a stop, leave enough room between your car and the one ahead so that you can maneuver quickly. Choose the lane farthest from the curb—you'll have more warning if someone on the sidewalk heads toward your car.

If you think you're about to be carjacked and no other cars are around, run the red light, blast your horn and flash your lights. If a carjacker is beside your vehicle with a gun drawn, let him/her have the car—aside from the engine block, no part of a car is likely to stop a bullet.

If confronted when you're unlocking your car, throw your keys to the side and run so that the pursuer must choose between following you and taking your car.

Carjacking gangs sometimes use a "bump-and-rob" technique—they cause a minor car accident, then steal the victim's car when he gets out to exchange insurance information.

Self-defense: If you're involved in a minor accident in a solitary area, stay in your car, keep the engine running and yell through the closed window for the other driver to follow you. Drive to the nearest police station or a well-lit, crowded area—an open gas station is a good option.

If possible, write down the other vehicle's license plate number and call the police on your cell phone to report the accident and where you're heading.

PICKPOCKETS AND PURSE SNATCHERS

A wallet is best kept in a front pants pocket. If you wrap a thick rubber band around it, you're more likely to feel friction if someone tries to slide it out. A purse should be held firmly against the body, not allowed to dangle freely. A fanny pack should be worn in front, with the zipper closed and secured with a safety pin.

Backpacks are the least secure and should be held against the chest when in high-crime areas.

The most secure spot to keep credit cards, passports or other light valuables is in a flat pouch worn under your shirt and attached to a chain or string around your neck.

The most common place to get pickpocketed is on a train or subway car while it is stopped at a station. The thief takes the wallet and makes a quick escape before the train departs. The victim usually is miles away before he notices his wallet missing.

From the time that you board a train or subway until the doors close, keep a hand in the pocket that contains your wallet.

Diversions are another common pickpocket technique.

Example: Someone bumps into you—or stops short in front of you so that you bump into him—while a partner picks your pocket.

Whenever you're jostled, always check for your wallet.

Child Abduction Prevention

A 30-minute DVD program called KidSmartz examines techniques used by child predators and tells parents how to effectively discuss abduction prevention with children. Half of the profits are donated to National Center for Missing and Exploited Children.

Cost: About $15.

Available at Borders, Amazon.com, Wal-Mart and other major retailers.

Should You Install a Fire Sprinkler in Your Home?

A home fire-sprinkler system can give your family extra time to escape and limit fire damage. It is activated by a fire's high temperature, and only the sprinklers closest to the fire open. Because the sprinklers react while a fire still is small, water damage is minimized. Sprinklers do not respond to minor kitchen mishaps, such as burned toast.

Cost: About $1.50 to $2 per square foot for new home construction and $3 to $5 per square foot for an existing home.

Information: Home Fire Sprinkler Coalition, 888-635-7222, *www.homefiresprinkler.org.*

Meri-K Appy, president, Home Safety Council, Washington, DC, *www.homesafetycouncil.org.*

How to Be Financially Prepared for Any Disaster

Nigel B. Taylor, a CFP in Santa Monica, CA. His wealth-management firm, Taylor & Associates, serves individuals, families and businesses. He is former president of the Los Angeles Society of the Institute of Certified Financial Planners. His Web site is *www.protectassets.com.*

If you had just 10 minutes to evacuate your home during a natural disaster, what would you take with you? Where would you get cash if ATM and credit card networks were down? Would your insurance be adequate to rebuild your home?

Obviously, the safety of you and your family is your first concern—but ensuring your financial security is second. *As a certified financial planner based in disaster-prone Southern California, here's what I tell my clients...*

323

●**Keep enough cash in the house for a weekend away.** It can take that long after a disaster for merchants to be able to accept cred-' it or bank cards.

Also keep $300 in one-dollar bills on hand.

Reason: Stores may not be able to make change. After the last earthquake in this area, some people had to hand over $20 bills to pay for a carton of milk or a bottle of water.

●**Keep important items in a secure, fire-safe box near the front door**—perhaps in a coat closet. (Keep all original documents in a safe-deposit box or a fireproof safe.) The box should be lightweight so that you can easily carry it to your vehicle in an emergency. *The box should contain…*

●Legal papers. Copies of titles to your home and vehicles, marriage and birth certificates, passports, insurance policies, military and medical records, Social Security cards, driver's license numbers, wills and powers of attorney.

●Extra supplies of medications if your doctor will prescribe them. Rotate them monthly so that the newest medication always is available. Also keep lists of medications, doctors' phone numbers, etc. People who have extreme allergies should include Epi-Pen injectors.

●Financial records. Copies of credit card and employee benefit statements, household budget, tax returns for the last three years, contact and account numbers for financial accounts.

●Key to your safe-deposit box, if you have a box.

●Extra checks.

●Inventory of your household possessions, including professional appraisals for valuables, such as jewelry and antiques, and receipts for the cost of major home improvements, like kitchen remodeling or a new deck.

Helpful: Use a digital camera or camcorder to record your home's contents for insurance purposes. Go room by room, giving an audio or written description of the approximate cost, condition and age of each piece of furniture, appliance and decorative element—even towels and clothing. Send a copy on DVD or CD to your insurance agent, as well as copies of receipts for big-ticket items, to expedite future insurance claims.

While many documents may also be stored in a bank safe-deposit box, keep in mind that your local bank could be closed for several days or weeks after a disaster.

Backup plan: Scan documents into a single electronic file, and save it on your computer hard drive. Also, regularly back up the file to a removable flash storage device that you can take with you in the event of a disaster. These portable storage devices are the size of a cigarette lighter and plug into your computer's USB port. They are available for about $50 in electronics or office-supply stores. You can buy a scanner for under $50, or have your documents scanned at the office-supply store.

●**Maintain an emergency fund.** Keep three months' to a year's worth of basic living expenses—rent/mortgage, food, insurance, etc.—in safe, liquid investments, such as short-term CDs and short-term municipal bonds. This will protect you from a disaster as well as a loss of income—if your place of work is damaged, you may be without a paycheck for some time.

Also: Recent laws have forced all of the financial institutions to implement disaster-continuity plans. Obtain copies of these plans to learn how to access your money after a disaster.

●**Make sure your homeowner's insurance includes appropriate coverage for disaster.** Depending on where you live, you might need flood insurance through the US government's National Flood Insurance Program (annual premiums of $300* and up) and riders for hurricanes and/or earthquakes if you can purchase them ($2,500 per year and up for a $200,000 home with a $10,000 deductible). Such riders are expensive, but losing everything because you're not covered is more expensive.

Smart: Increase your deductible to $3,500. Premiums drop at that level, making riders more affordable. For more information, contact FEMA at *www.fema.gov.*

Make sure that you have "replacement value" coverage that pays you the amount necessary to replace articles with ones of similar quality at current prices. Also, check that you will be reimbursed for living expenses if your home is damaged and uninhabitable.

*All rates subject to change.

Cost: Less than $100* in annual premiums for $10,000 of coverage.

If you have a home office, you will need a commercial policy to cover damage to business-related equipment. (Homeowners' policies do not cover home-based businesses.) Many homeowners' policies limit replacement of computer equipment to $2,500. You can double this coverage for $20 to $30 per year.

Helpful resources: *Disaster Recovery: A Guide to Financial Issues* free from the Red Cross, *www.redcross.org/services/disaster/bepre pared/finrecovery*. FEMA also provides a free guide *Are You Ready?*, which has helpful information on disaster preparation.

*All rates subject to change.

More Tips on Disaster Preparation

The Department of Homeland Security has developed a Web site explaining steps that families and businesses should take to be prepared for disasters—terrorist attacks (explosive, biological, chemical, nuclear, radiation), as well as natural disasters, such as earthquakes and storms. The site details supplies to have, how to make a "family disaster plan" and what to do in different locations (home, vehicle, tall building) if a disaster occurs. Visit *www.ready.gov*.

Home Generator Smarts

To keep a portable home generator running reliably…

●**Add a stabilizer,** available at all auto parts stores, to gasoline to extend the generator's life by up to a year. The cost is about $5 to treat 25 gallons of gas.

●**Check the oil level** every time you fill the gas tank.

●**Test run the generator** at least once every season.

●**Never connect a generator to home wiring**—use properly rated extension cords.

●**Protect against carbon monoxide** by running the generator outside.

Consumer Reports, 101 Truman Ave., Yonkers, NY.

Terror Alert: Our Food Is in Danger

Marion Nestle, PhD, MPH, Paulette Goddard Professor of nutrition, food studies and public health at New York University in New York City. She is also the author of *Safe Food: Bacteria, Biotechnology and Bioterrorism* (University of California).

Virtually all Americans feel threatened by terrorism. But there's relatively little discussion of one of the most frightening scenarios—deliberate food poisoning by our enemies. How safe is our food supply? What can we do to protect ourselves?

Marion Nestle, PhD, MPH, a leading expert in food safety, gives some answers below…

●**Is our food actually vulnerable to terrorism?** Our food is vulnerable, period. According to the Centers for Disease Control and Prevention, there are an estimated 76 million cases of food poisoning yearly in the US, which cause 325,000 hospitalizations and 5,000 deaths.

These are presumably the result of accidental contamination. And if our food-safety system can't prevent them, it certainly can't protect us against intentional food-borne illness.

No one can say for sure just how serious the threat of food terrorism is. Uncertainty is one of the things that makes terrorism so frightening—by nature, it's unpredictable.

●**What are the possible scenarios?** The one known case of politically motivated food terrorism in the US happened in 1984 and involved a domestic group. The members of a religious cult had established a commune in a small town in Oregon, and a dispute arose with their neighbors over use of land. To disrupt a county election, members of the cult sprinkled toxic Salmonella bacterium on salad bars and in cream pitchers in 10 restaurants—750 people got sick, 45 severely enough to be hospitalized.

Other instances of deliberate food contamination both here and abroad include the case of an angry employee at a large medical center in Dallas who gave his coworkers doughnuts and muffins tainted with *Shigella* bacterium, causing severe gastrointestinal illness...citrus fruits harvested in Israel that were laced with mercury...and grapes from Chile that were poisoned with cyanide.

Cases of accidental food poisoning demonstrate the wider vulnerability of our food supply. One outbreak of Salmonella poisoning in 1994 affected more than 220,000 people in 41 states. The source was discovered to be a premixed ice cream base (a mixture of eggs and cream). It was shipped to a processing plant in a tanker truck that had previously carried unpasteurized liquid eggs and hadn't been properly cleaned.

A terrorist who wanted to make hundreds of thousands of people sick could introduce a handful of *Salmonella* or *Listeria* bacterium into a truck, and if no one is checking, it could have far-reaching consequences.

●**Isn't our government checking?** If people assume that everything they eat has passed some sort of government inspection, they're wrong. The current system is riddled with holes.

For one thing, oversight is fragmented. The US Department of Agriculture is responsible for the safety of meat, eggs and poultry, while fruits, vegetables and most other foods fall under the jurisdiction of the Food and Drug Administration.

Other agencies—the US Department of Commerce, which has a hand in seafood inspection, the Environmental Protection Agency and the Customs Department, among others—play lesser roles. However, their efforts are not coordinated with one another.

Big problem: Government inspections aren't routine. Measures to prevent contamination through proper food handling and bacteria control rely on voluntary compliance by food companies and random sampling. Full-scale inspections don't happen unless people start getting sick.

Imported food—an obvious concern when terrorism is the issue—is a case in point. We bring in approximately $50 billion worth of fresh and processed foods yearly, and food imports have been involved in a number of food-poisoning outbreaks.

A few years ago, more than 550 people were unintentionally infected with hepatitis A from green onions that were imported from Mexico. Three of the victims ended up dying.

●**How can we protect ourselves?** By following the same basic household safety procedures that we all should be taking to minimize the risk for accidental contamination. These steps offer some protection against food terrorism by killing bacteria that may be intentionally added to food.

To make sure that meat, poultry, egg dishes, casseroles and other types of foods are fully cooked, always use a clean food thermometer to determine the internal temperature of the food you are cooking.

Cook ground beef, pork roasts and chops to at least 160°F, beef roasts and steaks to 145°F for medium rare, or to 160°F for medium. Cook whole poultry to 180°F and chicken breasts to 170°F. Cook eggs until the yolks and whites are firm. Don't use recipes in which eggs remain raw or only partially cooked.

When reheating leftovers, heat them thoroughly to at least 165°F. When cooking in a microwave oven, make sure there are no cold spots in food where bacteria can survive. Cover food and stir for even cooking. Rotate the dish once or twice during cooking if your microwave does not have a turntable.

Cold foods should be kept at 40°F or colder. Defrost food in the refrigerator. Never thaw food on the counter. Refrigerate or freeze perishables, prepared foods and leftovers within two hours or less.

●**How effective are these practices?** The most effective way to prevent food contamination—either accidental or deliberate—is a coordinated program that's called Hazard Analysis and Critical Control Point (HACCP). This means identifying all the places where contamination can occur and having procedures in place to make sure it doesn't happen.

There are HACCP programs in various food industries, including meat and poultry, eggs and fruit juices, but, by and large, these aren't as effective as they could be because of flaws in design and sloppiness in carrying them out. If we want to prevent intentional contamination, more careful monitoring is essential.

For more information on keeping food free from bacteria, go to the Partnership for Food Safety Education's Web site, *www.fightbac.org* or call the FDA's Food Safety Information Hotline at 888-723-3366.

Dangerous Things That Don't Seem Dangerous at All

Laura Lee, a researcher located in Rochester, MI, and the author of eight books, including *100 Most Dangerous Things in Everyday Life and What You Can Do About Them* (Broadway).

Most of us tend to worry about the wrong things. We worry about safety each time we board an airplane, though we are far more likely to die in a car accident. We worry about a terrorist attack, though the household chemicals we keep under our sinks are more likely to cause us harm.

Some seemingly harmless products pose significant risks that most Americans have never considered. *Here, six of the surprising dangers that most of us encounter regularly...*

DISHWASHERS

Each year, an average of about 7,500 Americans suffer dishwasher-related injuries. Most of these are cuts or punctures caused by upturned knives or forks. In the past 10 years, at least two people were killed when they slipped and fell onto open dishwasher drawers and landed on sharp knives.

Steam burns from opening up the door and leaning over the dishwasher—or reaching in immediately after the cycle is finished—also are common dishwasher injuries.

Young children and pets can be poisoned if they ingest the soap residue in the dispensing compartment. According to research by the Royal Children's Hospital of Australia, far more children are poisoned this way than by eating dishwashing detergent out of the box.

Self-defense: Always load knives and forks into your dishwasher with their pointy ends down. And, stand clear when opening the door immediately after the cycle ends. If children or pets are around, remove any residue from the compartment as soon as the door is opened.

PAPER MONEY

Researchers working at the Medical Center of Wright-Patterson Air Force Base in Ohio found that 87% of dollar bills in circulation carry bacteria, including strains that cause sore throats, urinary tract infections and food poisoning. There's no way to tell how many people get sick from handling money—people rarely know where they picked up a germ when they become ill—but this new evidence suggests that money is an often-overlooked culprit.

Self-defense: Wash your hands frequently when you handle cash. To be ultrasafe, adopt a strategy used by a Chinese bank during the SARS epidemic. When you receive money, put it in a safe place, wash your hands, and don't touch it again for at least 24 hours. That should be long enough for most germs to die.

BAGELS

Their hard crusts require a sharp knife and significant force. The result can be a serious hand injury. How great is the danger? No definitive statistics are available, but American emergency rooms report that palms sliced open by kitchen knives, often with serious ligament or tendon damage, are among the most common accidents they treat. Emergency medics even have a phrase for this type of injury—they call it "bagel hand."

A bagel's hard crust also can damage the esophagus if too large a piece is swallowed. *Environmental Nutrition* once referred to the bagel as an "esophageal terrorist."

Self-defense: Buy a bagel slicer. For $10 to $20, your hands will be safe. If you use a cutting board, slice the bagel away from your body with a good-quality serrated bread knife. If no cutting board is available, use your palm to hold the bagel flat on a counter, being careful not to curl your fingers around it. Slice parallel to the counter and away from your body.

Also: Never try to slice a frozen bagel, thaw it first.

BOOKS

Each year, more than 10,000 Americans suffer book-related injuries, according to the US Consumer Product Safety Commission. Some people fall while reaching for them on high shelves, and others hurt their backs moving boxes of books or wearing overloaded backpacks.

Researchers in Bogotá, Columbia, also have discovered that book dust causes allergic reactions in 12% of librarians. If you have shelves of old books in your home, you could be creating an unhealthy respiratory environment.

Self-defense: A typical hardcover book can weigh three to four pounds, so don't fill a box with them and then try to lift it. If you have respiratory problems, removing old books from your home may help.

COTTON SWABS

Cotton swabs carry warnings on their packaging that caution against putting them in ears —yet that is exactly how most people use them. In 1999 alone, 6,500 people in Britain went to the hospital for cotton-swab accidents —more than twice the number that hurt themselves with razors, the seemingly more dangerous grooming item.

Figures on total injuries aren't kept in the US, but there were at least 100 documented cases of "serious" eardrum injuries caused by cotton swabs in this country between 1992 and 1997.

Self-defense: Never insert a cotton swab in your ear. Even if you don't pierce your eardrum, you may push earwax further in, which can do serious damage to the lining of your ear canal and eardrum. Earwax generally will work its way out on its own through the actions of the jawbone. If it doesn't, consult your doctor, who can remove it safely.

CRUTCHES AND WHEELCHAIRS

These devices, designed to help us cope with injuries, can lead to new ones. Crutches are involved in some 74,000 injuries in the US each year and wheelchairs account for about 95,000. Many of these injuries occur when the crutches or wheelchairs are used on slick or uneven surfaces. Stairs are particularly challenging.

Self-defense: Learn to handle these rehabilitation aids properly before you use them in challenging conditions. Using crutches can be tiring, so rest often. Even if you don't feel tired, prolonged crutch use can cause nerve damage in the armpits and numbness in the hands, leading to falls. Crutches become even more hazardous when set to the incorrect height—the proper height is two inches below your armpit while standing.

Don't let anyone carry your wheelchair up or down a flight of stairs while you are in it unless there are no other options and you trust the carriers' strength and coordination.

The Latest Scams And Rip-Offs: Self-Defense Strategies

Kelly Rote, national spokesperson for Money Management International, provider of nationwide consumer credit counseling located in Houston, TX. Her site on the Web is *www.moneymanagement.org.*

Dan Brecher, Esq., a New York City attorney specializing in claims against brokerage firms.

Matt Brisch, communications specialist at the National Association of Insurance Commissioners (NAIC) in Kansas City, MI.

Michael Brown, president, CardCops, an on-line watchdog based in Malibu, CA, that helps make selling and shopping on-line safer, *www.cardcops.com.*

Overzealous debt collectors, phony insurance salespeople and greedy stockbrokers urging customers to put their homes at risk are among the latest rip-offs to watch out for…

"ZOMBIE" DEBT
Kelly Rote, Money Management International

●**Beware of collection agencies trying to collect on "zombie" debt**—unpaid consumer bills that creditors already have written off as losses. Debt collectors will buy this charged-off debt for just pennies on the dollar and then aggressively squeeze consumers to pay it.

Self-defense: If a debt collector contacts you about a debt that you do not recognize, don't provide any information. Insist on proof of the debt—the original credit agreement and billing statements.

If you are convinced that you do owe the money and your state's statute of limitations on the debt has not expired, consider settling with the agency for a percentage of the amount that is owed. State statutes of limitations are listed at *www.creditinfocenter.com* (at the Web site click on "Rebuild/Repair").

Also review your credit reports from Experian (888-397-3742, *www.experian.com*), Equifax (800-685-1111, *www.equifax.com*) and Trans-Union (800-916-8800, *www.tuc.com*). If a zombie collector has reported the debt delinquency to the credit bureaus after it has ignored your request for proof, it is in violation of the *Fair Debt Collection Practices Act*. File a complaint with the Federal Trade Commission, and notify each credit bureau.

BROKER MISDEEDS
Dan Brecher, Esq.

•**More stockbrokers are urging their customers to tap home equity to buy securities.** In many cases, they're pitching the chance to borrow at today's relatively low mortgage rates to fund the purchase of high-yielding junk bonds. While junk bonds do sport hefty yields, junk bonds and stocks are risky by nature— and not something you would want to pledge a good chunk of your home against.

Self-defense: Don't refinance your mortgage or use home equity to buy stocks or bonds. If you have done so on the advice of your broker and think this advice was inappropriate, you might have reason to seek restitution.

Reason: All brokers have a fiduciary duty to keep customers' interests and financial strength in mind when recommending investments.

•**Brokerages also are not reporting customer complaints,** regulatory actions and criminal convictions in a timely fashion. They are supposed to inform the National Association of Securities Dealers (NASD) of broker wrongdoings and complaints against them within a month of their occurrence—but this often does not happen. This has prompted the NASD to censure and fine 29 securities firms for making late disclosure.

Investors now will be able to find more up-to-date information on complaints and action against brokers on the NASD's Web site, *www.nasd.com.*

Self-defense: If your brokerage has consistently failed to disclose problems in a timely fashion and you believe that you lost money as a result, you might be able to bring a claim against it. The NASD's monthly disciplinary actions are reported in major newspapers and on its Web site.

FAKE INSURANCE
Matt Brisch, NAIC

•**Unlicensed insurance companies**—those that do not have a state's insurance department's approval—take your money and issue "policies," but then don't pay when you file a claim. Fake health insurance was sold to more than 200,000 people between 2000 and 2002, according to the most recent data available.

Fake insurance looks attractive because it is less expensive than the legitimate policies. The main targets of these fake policies are older adults and small businesses looking to reduce health insurance costs. Scams also are common in life and property/casualty insurance.

Self-defense: Be on the lookout for signs that an insurance policy is fake—high-pressure sales tactics, premiums that are at least 15% lower than those from familiar carriers and/or very liberal coverage rules.

Before you purchase any policy, contact your state insurance department to confirm that the company is licensed in your state. Web sites for all state insurance departments are available at *www.naic.org/state_web_map.htm.* This site also maintains a database of complaints and financial information about insurers nationwide. Go to *www.naic.org* and click on "Consumer Information Source."

BUSINESS ID THEFT
Michael Brown, CardCops

•**Credit card thieves are ripping off small-business owners** by using a combination of fake Web sites and stolen credit card numbers.

The victims are businesses that *don't* accept credit cards. The crooks pose as the business and set up a bogus Web site. They establish an account in the business's name with a merchant processing provider—also commonly called an independent sales organization (ISO)—which transfers funds between the retailers and the credit card companies. The crooks then use the stolen credit card numbers to ring up "sales."

When the owners of the stolen credit cards see bogus charges on their bills, they complain to the credit card issuers, which will reimburse them. The card issuers then demand reimbursement from the real merchants, who actually are the victims.

If your business becomes a target of this version of identity theft, it should not be held liable for phony sales.

Self-defense: Contact the ISO that approved the establishment of the bogus account. It is an ISO's responsibility to verify a merchant's identity, and the ISO should be liable for the fraudulent charges.

Also: Sign your business up for the *SelfMonitor* credit-reporting service, available from Dun & Bradstreet (877-753-1444 or *www.dnb.com*). The service will alert you if a merchant account is opened in the name of your business.

Newest Scams That Catch Seniors

Hal Morris, veteran Las Vegas–based consumer affairs journalist who writes widely about scams, schemes and other rip-offs.

Seniors are prime targets for slick characters with sticky fingers. *The latest and recycled rip-offs making the rounds...*

WORK-AT-HOME LURES

Seniors seeking to supplement income are easy prey for work-at-home schemes. These are now the top consumer inquiry category at Better Business Bureaus (BBBs).

With unrealistic promises of earning $550 or more a week, envelope-stuffing may sound like lucrative sideline work. But it requires paying a fee—starting at $40—before learning there is no employment, only instructions on how to send the same envelope-stuffing pitch to others.

At-home craft assembly work projects usually require an investment of hundreds of dollars in equipment, such as sign making or sewing machines, or materials to produce things such as aprons or baby shoes. After producing the items, shady operators refuse to pay because the work is below "quality standards."

Self-defense: Ignore all such pitches.

OUTSOURCING RISKS

The mushrooming trend of US companies outsourcing back-office and customer-assistance services to foreign lands adds a new element to the mounting threat of identity theft. Some tax returns and mortgage documents, for example, are now being processed overseas, mainly in India and the Philippines, where English is the second language for many.

The big fear is that distant shady eyes pose potential risks to the privacy and security of records containing highly personal and financial information. These foreign employees do work on behalf of US banks, insurance companies, brokerage operations, hospitals and medical offices, and billings and transcriptions services, among others.

With most work handled by foreign outside contractors (rather than employees on US companies' payrolls), sensitive information is exposed, including Social Security number, birth date, mother's maiden name, financial account numbers, passwords, PINs, personal income, etc. —all essential information for paving the way to ID theft. As a brand new ID theft element, and with foreign countries involved, it will take a while before wrongdoing statistics roll in.

Identity theft topped the Federal Trade Commission's 2004 listing of consumer complaints for a fifth straight year. Unlike in the US, data-protection laws are not on the books in most countries where personal information is transmitted, processed and stored, points out the Privacy Rights Clearinghouse in San Diego.

Note: You still have the same US credit card and banking protection even if the theft occurs overseas.

Self-defense: Avoid possible improper use of your personal information by asking your service provider for the location of assistance, processing and call centers. If activity is handled via an overseas point and you are worried about a leak in personal data, consider shifting to another provider—after asking the same question.

REJECTED REBATES

Sending an original universal product code (UPC) from packaging, the sales receipt and the rebate forms may not yield the promised refund from a fulfillment house that processes rebate requests. Complaints are flooding in to BBBs from purchasers who often cite no reason for a denied rebate. The Aberdeen Group, a market research firm, says only about 20% of buyers get the rebates they apply for.

Among the excuses for rejecting rebates, even when all details and documentation requirements are adhered to, are—paperwork incomplete...the promotion date expired...photocopy was used...rules weren't followed...submission (along with original documents) was lost.

Self-defense: Make copies of everything you send to rebate centers. Filing a grievance with the Better Business Bureau (*www.bbb.org*) or the Federal Trade Commission (*www.ftc.gov*) often spurs action.

Other steps: Contact the sponsoring manufacturer or retail store involved.

DANGEROUS DRUGS

The Food and Drug Administration (FDA) warns about the risks associated with any drugs you might be tempted to purchase from foreign countries. In some cases, adds the FDA, drugs exported from Canada are actually manufactured in Mexico, Costa Rica, Taiwan, Pakistan, India or Thailand, among other nations.

Many drugs do not bear adequate labeling—sometimes it's in dual languages or there are no labels or instructions for safe use. In some cases, drugs are loose in plastic bags or simply wrapped in tissue paper. In addition, some of the foreign-source drugs have been found to be contaminated or lacking medicine entirely.

Self-defense: Scrutinize drug labels. Verify potential foreign sources for drugs with your pharmacist.

WHEELER DEALERS

Have you been offered a free power wheelchair or other mobility product lately? Beware! The Centers for Medicare & Medicaid Services, which administers Medicare, is encountering scammers now exploiting the Medicare power wheelchair benefit by offering free equipment to those who don't need it or never received it.

Their tempting offer: "We'll give you a free power wheelchair or other mobility product if you promise to use our physicians and agree to waive coinsurance or Medicare Part B deductibles."

Scammers get money by inflating billings to Medicare, charging for equipment and supplies not delivered and falsifying documents to qualify beneficiaries for wheelchairs and other types of equipment that they often do not need. Some do receive power wheelchairs.

Self-defense: Review any supplier's recommendations with your personal doctor, who can best determine your needs. With questions, call the Medicare hotline at 800-633-4227 or visit the Web site at *www.medicare.gov*.

BATTLING THE BULGE

As the nation's average midriff swells, so do weight-loss schemes. Much touted are pills or capsules that can lead to losing weight without exercising or improving your diet. Key buzzwords linked to eliminating fat from the system include "secret," "breakthrough," "guaranteed" and "miraculous."

Self-defense: Giving in to these claims only lightens your wallet. The true weight-loss programs do require slicing calories and increasing exercise.

Always consult your doctor before entering a weight-loss program.

AUTO REPAIR RIP-OFFS

Steer clear of advertised too-good-to-be-true super-low-price specials for routine auto repairs. These scams are constantly being repackaged. Some shops reel in customers with enticing offers, then target their cars for additional work because a mechanic "finds" other problems. Their work is often inferior while the "other problems" inflate the bill.

Early warning signs include a growing list of "must fix" items with no estimates in writing and a sloppy, disorganized service area.

Self-defense: Find a repair shop with technicians who are certified by the National Institute for Automotive Service Excellence (ASE) and that also bears the AAA-Approved Auto Repair sign. Check out shops through your local Better Business Bureau. Ask about complaints made against the company.

VACATION PROMOTIONS

A phone call or piece of mail proclaims you have been "specially selected" or "have won" a fabulous cruise or vacation at a very reasonable price. The scam artist uses some new twist to make the offer appear legitimate. But it is the same old ruse.

Be wary: The "cruise ship" may be a ferry. And lodgings are likely to be shabby. Some deals involve a time-share pitch.

After paying for the "bargain" travel package, other costs pop up. They are often linked to reservations, preferred dates, port charges, hotel taxes and service fees.

Self-defense: Ask for brochures. Read the fine print. Run the offering company's name through your Better Business Bureau.

New Identity Theft Scam

If you have friends or relatives abroad who have invested in the US, warn them about a new scam they may face.

In it, a form that resembles the IRS W-8BEN "tax withholding" form is sent to nonresident aliens who have invested in the US and have US income.

The form is accompanied by a letter supposedly from the IRS saying that the recipient will be taxed at a top rate unless personal and financial data are entered on the form and faxed to a given phone number.

Of course, information provided is used by the wrongdoers to commit fraud or theft.

Truth: The real Form W-8BEN does not ask for such personal information—and is not sent by the IRS, but by the individual's own financial institution.

The scam is now most prevalent in the Caribbean, but it has appeared in South America and Europe as well.

IRS News Release IR-2004-104.

Identity Theft Update: New and Better Ways to Protect Yourself

Linda Foley, executive director of the nonprofit Identity Theft Resource Center in San Diego, which provides information and counseling to victims of identity theft, *www.id theftcenter.org*. Ms. Foley, a victim herself, has provided resources and guidance to law enforcement as well as hundreds of victims throughout the country. She has testified before the Federal Trade Commission, the Social Security Administration and the US House and Senate.

Identity theft is the number-one concern of US consumers. In just the past year, it has cost shoppers and merchants about $300 billion and hit almost 10 million new victims.

What does it mean to your personal and financial security? *National expert Linda Foley answers this question and more below...*

● **How do victims discover that their identity has been stolen?** You might get a call from a debt collector...a bill for merchandise that you never bought...or have your credit card blocked because it has been charged to the limit. Victims often find out when they are denied credit or a loan or when money disappears from their checking or savings accounts. In all cases, someone has obtained your personal financial information and is stealing from you...or stealing in your name.

Seventy percent of identity thieves are unknown to their victims. Many cases occur after your information is stolen from a database that has your personal information on file.

● **Why is identity theft so common?** It is a high-profit, low-risk crime. An average thief can bring in from several hundred to several thousand dollars with a stolen identity. For instance, he/she might open up a new credit card account illegally, buy several laptop computers and then pawn them. Or he could get a second mortgage in another person's name and walk away with cash.

Less than 5% of these thieves are convicted, according to law-enforcement records. Cases cross multiple jurisdictions and are too time-consuming to devote many resources to. Credit card companies are reluctant to report fraud to authorities, fearing negative publicity.

●**How can I protect myself?** *There are four key safeguards...*

●Guard your Social Security number (SSN). It is the most widely accepted piece of identification for obtaining new credit cards, credit reports, federal benefits, etc. Don't carry your Social Security card or any other card that uses that number, such as an employee or student ID. For vital items that you need to carry, such as your health insurance card, make a photocopy and cut off the last four digits of your SSN. Hospitals will accept this if you come in with a life-threatening emergency.

Never allow a merchant to put your SSN on any check that you write. Legally, merchants are not allowed to ask for it. If one insists, threaten to complain to the Better Business Bureau.

●Don't give personal information to anyone unless you initiate the inquiry. Identity thieves routinely trick people into giving them confidential information by claiming to represent legitimate companies or government agencies.

●Pay attention to bank-account statements and credit card bills. If there is a discrepancy on a bill or a bill doesn't arrive, contact the financial institution immediately. Federal and state laws limit your losses to $50 per card if you're victimized, but you must prove that you didn't make the charges.

In addition, don't carry a bank debit card that doubles as a credit card. Money is removed from your account immediately, and you have no legal protection if a thief uses the card.

●Review your credit reports at least once a year. Make sure that no unauthorized accounts have been opened and that no changes have been made to existing accounts. You can obtain one free credit report per year from each of the agencies.

The three reporting agencies are Equifax, 800-685-1111, *www.equifax.com*; Experian, 888-397-3742, *www.experian.com*; and TransUnion, 800-916-8800, *www.tuc.com*.

Helpful: Evaluate your risk of identity theft at my organization's Web site, *www.idtheftcenter. org/idtheftest.shtml*.

●**What should I do if I become a victim of identity theft?**

●Close accounts that you believe have been tampered with or opened fraudulently. You may have to provide affidavits to the companies saying you didn't open the accounts. A generic ID theft affidavit is available from the Federal Trade Commission (FTC) at 877-ID-THEFT, *www.consumer. gov/idtheft*.

●Contact the fraud departments at the three major credit bureaus, and place a "fraud alert" on your name. A fraud alert requests that the credit issuers contact you by telephone before allowing a new account to be opened or an existing account to be altered. Although some credit issuers ignore these alerts, it is the best defense against fraud at this time.

●File a criminal report with local police if you have evidence of fraud—such as a suspicious charge on your credit card bill. Many creditors do require a police report before they will resolve a dispute. If the local authorities will not handle this crime, contact the county or state police.

●Call the FTC at 877-ID-THEFT. A counselor will take your complaint and advise you on how to deal with any resulting credit-related problems.

●Review *Identity Crisis: What to Do If Your Identity Is Stolen,* available from the FTC (877-ID-THEFT, *www.consumer.gov/idtheft*).

●**What is the government doing to protect me?** In December of 2003, *The Fair and Accurate Credit Transactions Act* was signed into law. It enables consumers to obtain a free copy of their credit report every year from each credit-reporting agency...forces the agencies to share consumer calls on identity theft with one another so that victims have "one-call-for-all" protection...and also prohibits companies from printing more than the last five digits of a credit card number on electronic receipts. However, in practical terms, it may take the government a long time to implement these reforms.

● **If my SSN is stolen, will the government provide me with a new one?** The Social Security Administration will assign new numbers to victims of ID theft only under extreme circumstances, such as someone stalking you or threatening your life.

● **Do I need identity theft insurance?** Some insurance and credit card companies are charging from $25 to $100 for ID theft insurance. Most people don't need it, but if you would like the extra protection, make sure the policy will cover time that's lost from work, out-of-pocket expenses and legal fees.

More from Linda Foley...

Security Freeze Protects Against Identity Theft

Strong defense against identity theft is available on a limited basis in several states. A *security freeze* lets an individual block access to his/her credit reports until he personally unlocks the files by contacting the credit bureaus and providing a personal identification number. The process slows credit approval and may delay mortgage applications and various transactions with banks, insurance companies and stores. But it prevents a thief from using your Social Security number to get credit.

To find out which states have security freeze laws, go to *www.pirg.org/consumer/credit/statelaws. htm.*

Beware of Identity Theft In the Workplace

Identity theft crime occurs in the workplace to a surprisingly high degree. The wrongdoers obtain confidential files or personal information (such as Social Security and credit card numbers) that are often needlessly attached to business records and documents. Such numbers shouldn't appear on paychecks, expense statements, time sheets or other documents unless

absolutely necessary. If you find that they do, talk to your boss.

Mark Durham, communications director, Identity Theft 911, 550 15 St., San Francisco 94103. His Web site is *www. identitytheft911.com.*

Be Your Own Private Eye

Steven K. Brown, a former FBI agent and current owner of Millennial Investigative Agency, a private investigation company in St. Augustine, FL, *www.stevenkbrown.com.* He is author of *The Complete Idiot's Guide to Private Investigating* (Alpha).

Looking for an old love or maybe a long-lost friend? Suspicious about a potential employee? Want to check up on your doctor or lawyer?

I have been tracking down people for 31 years—first as an FBI agent and then as a private investigator. *Here are the most effective ways to find people, largely using the Internet...*

CHASE DOWN CLASSMATES

● **Classmates.com** compiles contact information on graduates. Its database currently contains information on about 60 million people from more than 200,000 elementary schools, high schools and colleges. Their database goes back more than 50 years.

Cost: Free to browse names...$39* annually if you want to contact classmates directly.

Alternative: Locate your school's Web site to get the alumni relations officer's e-mail address or phone number. He/she usually will forward messages to former classmates at your request. Or you can use the site's link to your school's alumni magazine, which lists contact information for your class's secretary, who can often help.

FIND A LOST FRIEND

● **Internet search engines offer tremendous power to locate people.** Conduct an advanced search on several search engines using the person's full name and any unique details. For example, try including a middle initial...city of residence...or occupation. The engines will

*All prices subject to change.

search through millions of sites for any references to that person.

Important: For best results, use more than one search engine. *Below I've listed some of my favorites...*

- *www.google.com*
- *www.looksmart.com*
- *www.lycos.com*
- *www.webcrawler.com*

●**National white-page phone directories** help you locate a person's name, address and phone number. *My favorite free sites...*

- *http://directory.superpages.com/people.jsp*
- *www.whitepages.com*
- *www.canada411.com* (for Canadian directories only)
- *www.freeality.com/findet.htm*

Information on free sites tends to be a year old. If you think the person has moved, try a paid site—they are updated more frequently.

My favorite: *http://555-1212.com.*

Cost: $22.99* for 100 searches.

Unpublished versus unlisted numbers: An *unpublished* number is not printed in phone directories, but it is available from an operator if you request it. If a number is *unlisted,* operators don't have access to it. However, most operators will verify the address of a person who has an unlisted telephone number, so that you can write to him.

●**Dig up someone's e-mail address.** *My favorite free sites...*

- *www.theultimates.com/email*
- *www.iaf.net/frames/freeresources.htm*

●**Search publications.** *www.findarticles. com,* owned by the search engine Look Smart, allows you to search 3.5 million articles in 700 newspapers and magazines. Type the person's name into the search box, and click "Look."

●**Verify a death.** The Social Security Administration's Master Death Index contains more than 75 million names and records on the deceased. *http://ssdi.genealogy.rootsweb.com.*

CHECK UP ON YOUR DOCTOR

Disciplinary records often are available by calling your state's department of health and asking for the division that deals with medical disciplinary proceedings. Generally, you will be given a list of the actions and malpractice claims against the doctor. If you want more details, you have to request them in writing.

All the state licensing boards usually can be located through the American Medical Association (AMA) at *www.ama-assn.org/ama/pub/ category/2645.html.* However, the AMA's main Web site, *www.ama-assn.org,* also provides a wealth of information about individual doctors, including their training and specialties.

●**Federation of State Medical Boards** is a convenient nonprofit clearinghouse that allows you to find out about disciplinary actions taken against a doctor by medical boards. *www.doc info.org.* Just go to "Order Options," and click on "Get Immediate Results" or "Mail in Request."

Cost: $9.95* per report.

EXAMINE YOUR LAWYER

Backgrounds of as well as disciplinary actions against lawyers are available from...

●**American Bar Association (ABA),** which publishes a Web link to the disciplinary agency in each state. Here you also can verify that your attorney has been appropriately licensed. Some state ABA Web sites will list disciplinary actions taken against lawyers. Others do not list these actions on their Web sites, but they will make the information available when you request it in writing. *www.abanet.org/cpr/regulation/scpd/ disciplinary.html.* Free.

●**Martindale-Hubbell,** a service providing biographies of practicing lawyers. They include explanations of their experience, specialties, education and major clients. Each attorney is rated by his peers for legal ability and ethics. *www.martindale.com.* Click on "Lawyer Locator." Free.

RUN A CRIMINAL-RECORDS CHECK

There is no single comprehensive government database of criminals that is accessible to the public. *However, you still can investigate prospective employees, business partners and household help...*

*All prices subject to change.

*All prices subject to change.

● **The Federal Bureau of Prisons** provides information on all current and former federal prisoners since 1982. *www.bop.gov.* Click on "Inmate Locator" to search. Free.

● **The Federal Bureau of Investigation** provides links to databases with the names and addresses of convicted sex offenders in each state. *www.fbi.gov/hq/cid/cac/states.htm.* Free.

● **Criminal information.** Most states will provide you with some criminal records, but you must request them in writing. They usually cost less than $20. The amount and detail of information vary by state. For example, Florida offers a database of any current and past criminal on-line. And, Utah discloses only information about sex offenders. Even when a state does not make information available on-line, you often can get Web access to county courthouse records to learn about convictions. Do a search for the county government.

● **Background Check Gateway.** This company provides telephone numbers and Web sites, where you can learn each state's policy for making information available. *www.back groundcheckgateway.com.* Click on "Step 3: Start Your Investigation," then "Criminal History: Does He Have a Criminal Record?" Free.

CATCH UP WITH VETERANS

● **The US Department of Veterans Affairs** will forward a letter to any veteran registered with them. Contact your local office. Free.

● **The US Department of Defense** will supply the mailing addresses for servicemen and -women on active duty in the US Armed Forces. Free to immediate family members and government officials. For all others, $3.50* per inquiry. At *www.defenselink.mil/faq,* type in "Locating Service Members" in the "Search Text" box.

● **VetFriends.com**—a national military membership organization—helps both past and present servicemen and -women find one another. Enroll on its Web site, and receive e-mail when someone from your unit becomes a member. Click on "Start Here." Free. For an annual fee of $39,* you can search the organization's registry and contact others.

● **The National Archives and Records Administration** provides much information, like dates of service…decorations…date and location of death…place of burial, on deceased servicemen and -women. This information generally is free but may incur a charge depending on the search. *www.archives.gov/veterans.*

LEARN ABOUT YOUR NEIGHBORS

Public records kept by your town and county can tell you how much your neighbor paid for his home. And, thanks to the Internet, you can search those records confidentially.

Available: Date and amount of the last sale …who sold it…address where the property tax bill is sent. In some states, you also can get tax and property assessment information.

● **Links to county tax assessors records** from around the country are available at *www. netronline.com/public_records.htm.* Just click on your state, then your county. They also are available at *http://searchenginez.com/real_estate_usa. html* (scroll down to "Real Estate/Property Ownership Records")…and *www.crimetime.com/ online.htm* (click on "State Records," then your state, then "Real Estate Records"). Costs vary.

*All prices subject to change.

*All prices subject to change.

Index